IMPORTS, EXPORTS, AND THE AMERICAN WORKER

IMPORTS, EXPORTS, AND THE AMERICAN WORKER

Susan M. Collins

Editor

BROOKINGS INSTITUTION PRESS

Washington, D.C.

Copyright © 1998 by the Brookings Institution
1775 Massachusetts Avenue, N.W., Washington, D.C. 20036

Library of Congress Cataloging-in-Publication data

Imports, exports, and the American worker / Susan M. Collins, editor.
p. cm.
Includes bibliographical references and index.
ISBN 0-8157-1520-X (alk. paper). — ISBN 0-8157-1519-6 (pbk. : alk. paper)
1. Foreign trade and employment—United States—Congresses.
2. Labor market—United States—Congresses.   3. Wages—United
States—Congresses.   4. Unemployment—United States—Congresses.
5. Emigration and immigration—Government policy—United States—
Congresses.   6. Free trade—United States—Congresses.
I. Collins, Susan Margaret.
HD5710.75.U6I45   1998
331.12′0973—dc21   97-45315
                                                                     CIP

9 8 7 6 5 4 3 2 1

The paper used in this publication meets the minimum requirements of the American
National Standard for Information Sciences—Permanence of Paper for Printed
Library Materials, ANSI Z39-48-1984.

Typeset in Times Roman

Composition by Princeton Editorial Associates
Scottsdale, Arizona, and Roosevelt, New Jersey

Printed by R. R. Donnelley and Sons Co.
Harrisonburg, Virginia

ⓑ THE BROOKINGS INSTITUTION

The Brookings Institution is an independent organization devoted to nonpartisan research, education, and publication in economics, government, foreign policy, and the social sciences generally. Its principal purposes are to aid in the development of sound public policies and to promote public understanding of issues of national importance.

The Institution was founded on December 8, 1927, to merge the activities of the Institute for Government Research, founded in 1916, the Institute of Economics, founded in 1922, and the Robert Brookings Graduate School of Economics and Government, founded in 1924.

The Board of Trustees is responsible for the general administration of the Institution, while the immediate direction of the policies, program, and staff is vested in the President, assisted by an advisory committee of the officers and staff. The by-laws of the Institution state: "It is the function of the Trustees to make possible the conduct of scientific research, and publication, under the most favorable conditions, and to safeguard the independence of the research staff in the pursuit of their studies and in the publication of the results of such studies. It is not a part of their function to determine, control, or influence the conduct of particular investigations or the conclusions reached."

The President bears final responsibility for the decision to publish a manuscript as a Brookings book. In reaching his judgment on the competence, accuracy, and objectivity of each study, the President is advised by the director of the appropriate research program and weighs the views of a panel of expert outside readers who report to him in confidence on the quality of the work. Publication of a work signifies that it is deemed a competent treatment worthy of public consideration but does not imply endorsement of conclusions or recommendations.

The Institution maintains its position of neutrality on issues of public policy in order to safeguard the intellectual freedom of the staff. Hence interpretations or conclusions in Brookings publications should be understood to be solely those of the authors and should not be attributed to the Institution, to its trustees, officers, or other staff members, or to the organizations that support its research.

Foreword

DESPITE RAPID job creation, low rates of unemployment, and the continued overall strength of the U.S. economy, many American workers continue to do poorly. The long stagnation in the purchasing power of wages for the average worker, coupled with an increasing inequality in wages and income, has taken a significant toll. Although recent data suggest that average wages and inequality have begun to improve, real earnings for many low-wage Americans, particularly those with low skills, are lower now than they were in the late 1970s.

Increased economic integration with the rest of the world—especially with developing countries—is frequently seen as a primary cause of these worrisome labor market developments. Indeed, cross-border flows of goods, services, capital, and people have all increased sharply in the past two decades. Furthermore, the idea that increased competition with low-skilled (and low-wage) workers abroad is to blame for the labor market problems of less skilled workers at home has considerable intuitive appeal. However, similar trends and a plausible story are not enough to establish causality. Other factors have also been at work, and something else, such as technological change, may have been the root cause of difficulties faced by many American workers.

Economists have debated intensively the extent to which adverse U.S. labor market trends can be attributed to trade or, more generally, to globalization. At one level, the debate focuses on somewhat technical issues of methodology—

how should available information be used to assess the linkages? On another level, disagreement centers on the bottom line—what conclusions should be drawn from these analyses? Despite the growing literature, analysts continue to reach a range of conclusions, some arguing that globalization is the key to understanding the decline in wages of less-skilled Americans and others arguing that it has played an insignificant role. Unfortunately, disagreements among economists over methodology and the "bottom line" appear to have overshadowed the widespread agreement that policies to restrict international trade are the wrong policy responses.

These are the issues that motivated the Brookings project on Imports, Exports, and the American Worker. The project brought together ten sets of authors with a range of perspectives, advocating different methodological approaches and reaching different conclusions. At a conference held in February 1995, ten papers were presented and then discussed. The presenters and discussants were chosen in part for the diversity of their views. This book contains revised versions of the ten contributed papers, the twenty formal comments, and summaries of the general discussions generated by each paper. It also contains an introductory chapter prepared by the project organizer.

Four papers provide alternative assessments of the extent to which globalization can explain recent U.S. labor market developments. Most of the analyses focus on a narrower question: the impact of trade (and immigration) on the decline in the relative wage of less-educated American workers since the late 1970s. The papers spell out the strengths and weaknesses of the two main empirical approaches to assessing the evidence—the Heckscher-Ohlin approach, which focuses on prices, and the factor-content approach, which uses data on quantities of trade. Although authors disagree about which approach is more informative, there is broad agreement that these frameworks incorporate only some of the channels through which globalization might affect domestic labor markets. Contributors thus begin to explore new ways to look at available data.

The issue of the "bottom line" is just how large a role trade and immigration have played in pushing down the relative wages of the less skilled. Most of the contributors conclude that trade and immigration account for a small to moderate share of the relative wage change, with other factors such as technical change playing a more important role. However, this conclusion is far from unanimous. A few contributors advance the view that international factors have played an insignificant role. A few others find a substantial role for trade, with one arguing the extreme position that trade and immigration are essentially the whole story. Interestingly, many of the contributors stress problems with existing analyses, which imply that the jury is still out.

Despite the diversity of views on the bottom line, contributors to the volume reach a common policy conclusion: trade policies that protect domestic industries are the wrong way to address labor market problems such as rising income inequality, stagnating average real wage growth, and declining opportunities for less-skilled American workers.

Two papers focus on workers who are displaced from their jobs. They document substantial losses incurred by displaced workers. However, contrary to popular opinion, displacements are not predominantly related to trade. There are two separate policy concerns: problems faced by workers displaced from their jobs and hardships associated with the declining real earnings of many Americans, particularly those with less skill. How policy should respond is largely independent of the extent to which globalization is perceived to be the underlying culprit. Instead, attention should focus on improving U.S. policies to assist displaced workers directly.

Four chapters provide a broader perspective on the link between trade and U.S. labor markets. One advances an institutionalist framework for thinking about how international integration might affect American workers. A second studies what happened to Mexican workers as Mexico opened its borders over the past decade. A third offers a historical assessment of U.S. trade policy. The fourth gives a political scientist's analysis of recent U.S. trade liberalizations.

Susan M. Collins, the project organizer, is a senior fellow in the Economic Studies program at the Brookings Institution. She is also associate professor of economics at Georgetown University. The manuscript was edited by Steph Selice and Deborah Styles. Gabi Loeb, Kathleen McDill, and Elaine Zimmerman provided research assistance, and Cynthia Iglesias, Lin Lin, and Gerard Trimarco checked for factual accuracy. The index was prepared by Princeton Editorial Associates. Evelyn Taylor provided administrative assistance. Funding for the project from the Ford Foundation is gratefully acknowledged.

The views expressed in this book are those of the individual authors and should not be attributed to any of the persons or organizations mentioned above or to the trustees, officers, or other staff members of the Brookings Institution.

MICHAEL H. ARMACOST
President

February 1998
Washington, D.C.

Contents

     International Trade and Lower Wages   141
     Edward E. Leamer

     Comment by *Steven J. Davis*   203
     Comment by *Gene M. Grossman*   206
     General Discussion   211

5.   International Trade and Wage Inequality in the
     United States: Some New Results   215
     Jeffrey D. Sachs and Howard J. Shatz

     Comment by *Robert C. Feenstra*   241
     Comment by *Robert Z. Lawrence*   245
     General Discussion   251

PART III. BROADER PERSPECTIVES

Part One

INTRODUCTION

ONE

Economic Integration and the American Worker: An Overview

Susan M. Collins

HEADLINES ANNOUNCING the end of the American dream have appeared in newspapers nationwide. The articles beneath these headlines paint a picture of deteriorating experiences and prospects for many American workers, with stagnant (or falling) wages and growing job insecurity. The same articles often highlight growing U.S. international linkages—in particular, U.S. interactions with countries whose workers earn considerably less than American workers—as a principal cause of these difficulties.

Are American workers doing poorly? If so, is growing internationalization of the U.S. economy a primary cause? Which policy interventions, if any, are desirable? Does the importance of international factors matter when assessing policy options?

The author benefited from discussions with project contributors. Special thanks are due to Jagdish Bhagwati, Barry Bosworth, Gary Burtless, Ed Leamer, and Robert Litan. Research assistance by Lin Lin, Kathleen McDill, Elaine Zimmerman, and especially Gabi Loeb is gratefully acknowledged. The views expressed here are those of the author and should not be ascribed to the institutions or individuals named here.

These questions are at the heart of an expanding literature that has helped to clarify some of the key issues involved.[1] There is growing consensus that many American workers are indeed doing poorly. Real wages have fallen for some groups of workers, and income inequality has increased. These trends are persistent and significant, and as such, they warrant national attention. It is also clear that the U.S. economy has become more integrated with the global economy. Imports and exports have risen relative to domestic production. An increasing share of U.S. trade is with developing countries, and more and more of that trade is in manufactures. In addition, immigration to the United States has surged, while international capital flows have expanded greatly.

However, this literature has also spotlighted areas of disagreement. Most notably, an active and at times heated debate has emerged over how much of the worrisome U.S. labor market trends can be linked to globalization. This debate has proceeded on at least two levels, and the fact that one of them can be quite technical may have obscured the lessons to be learned. At one level, disagreement centers on methodology—*how* one should use available information to assess the linkages between these two sets of developments. Which frameworks are appropriate? Which data are informative? How should the questions of interest be posed to construct testable hypotheses?[2] At a second level, the disagreement centers on the "bottom line"—*what conclusions* should be drawn from the data analysis? There is a range—from those who believe that trade (or more broadly, globalization) is the key to explaining developments such as the decline in wages of less-skilled American workers, to those who argue that globalization plays an insignificant role. Most analysts have settled on intermediate positions. It is interesting that there is no obvious correlation between choice of methodology and the conclusions drawn.

1. The significant literature on trade and U.S. labor markets includes Bhagwati (1991); Bhagwati and Dehejia (1994); Borjas and Ramey (1994); Borjas, Freeman, and Katz (1996); Bound and Johnson (1995); Feenstra and Hanson (1996a, 1996b); Freeman and Katz (1995); Katz and Murphy (1992); Krugman and Lawrence (1994); Lawrence (1996); Lawrence and Slaughter (1993); Leamer (1994); Sachs and Shatz (1994, 1996); Wood (1994, 1995). Useful reviews include Belman and Lee (1996); Burtless (1995); Richardson (1995); and the detailed survey in Cline (1997).

2. Initially, the disagreement about methodology was strongly correlated with the field of the analyst, with labor economists tending to advocate one approach while international trade economists tended to advocate another. As the debate has evolved, this correlation has become much less relevant, as the chapters in this book illustrate.

Despite the wide range of views about how globalization has affected American workers, most contributors to this literature reach a common policy conclusion: the use of trade policies to protect domestic industries will do little to address problems such as rising income inequality, stagnating wages, and declining job opportunities for workers who are less skilled. Indeed, protection often does not even safeguard existing jobs, because firms respond by restructuring or relocating production. If policies are to address these problems, they should be targeted directly on those individuals and families who are doing poorly or are at risk. Issues that arise in this context include how to assess the effectiveness of alternative labor market policies, whether to provide special assistance to workers adversely affected by trade, and how to finance any interventions. It is unfortunate that the disagreements over methodology and the bottom-line importance of globalization appear to have overshadowed the extent of agreement in this regard.

These are the issues that motivated the Brookings project on *Imports, Exports, and the American Worker*. The project brought together ten sets of authors with different perspectives, advocating different methodological approaches and reaching different conclusions. Each chapter is discussed by two individuals, chosen in part for the diversity of their views. This book presents the ten chapters and the formal comments and summaries of the general discussion about each presentation.

The four chapters in part II (by Jagdish Bhagwati, Richard Freeman, Edward Leamer, and Jeffrey Sachs and Howard Shatz) provide alternative assessments of the extent to which globalization can explain recent U.S. labor market developments. Among other issues, these authors discuss evidence based on the two main competing methodologies: the factor content of trade and the Heckscher-Ohlin trade model.

The four chapters in part III provide a broader take on the link between trade and income inequality. Michael Piore presents an institutionalist perspective. Ana Revenga and Claudio Montenegro study the experience of Mexican workers as Mexico opened its borders over the past decade. J. Bradford De Long gives an historical assessment of causes and consequences of U.S. trade policy during the nineteenth century. I. M. Destler reviews recent U.S. trade liberalizations, focusing on the influence of labor.

Both Lori Kletzer and Louis Jacobson provide information about how displaced workers fare in the U.S. labor market. Kletzer asks whether this experience is worse if it is related to trade, and Jacobson assesses alternative interventions for mitigating the costs of displacement.

The main purpose of this introductory chapter is to assess what we know about the link between the internationalization of the U.S. economy and increasing U.S. wage inequality. In addition to an overview of both the debate over methodology and the disagreement over the bottom line, I discuss the ten remaining chapters in this book. I also summarize the major U.S. labor market and international developments at the heart of the debate.

The Issues in a Nutshell

An overview of key issues to be explored provides a useful road map for this book.

The Problem

Despite rapid overall job creation, the wages earned by well-educated Americans relative to those who are less educated rose sharply after 1980. Typically referred to as a rise in the skill premium, this shift coincided with a more general increase in wage and family income inequality. Furthermore, slow growth in average wages has implied that American workers who are less skilled (or workers who at the bottom of the pay scale overall) have seen significant declines in the purchasing power of their earnings.

The Suspects

Because changes in the supply of less-skilled U.S. workers relative to other U.S. workers cannot account for the increased skill premium, analysts point to one or more of the following possible suspects to account for the increased skill premium.[3]

GLOBALIZATION. This is defined as a change in goods, services, labor, or capital available from the rest of the world. Such shocks might occur because of developments in trade policy (in the United States or abroad), in the productive capacity of U.S. trading partners, in immigration, or in cross-border capital flows. However, neither actual trade flows nor prices of tradables are ideal measures of globalization, because both trade quantities and prices are also determined by factors such as technology and domestic demand.

---

3. Indeed, the relative price of skilled labor has been rising in the face of an increasing relative supply of more-skilled workers. However, there has been a slowdown in the growth of the fraction of the work force with high levels of education. For further discussion of the role of changes in domestic labor supply, see Bound and Johnson (1995); Cline (1997).

There are at least two reasons for the popularity and tenacity of the view that the primary culprit is increased U.S. interaction with the global economy—and especially with less-developed countries (LDCs) that have relatively low wages. First, the rising skill premium coincides with an increase in trade with LDCs, as well as in immigration and capital flows. However, similarity in trends is not enough to establish causality. Another factor (such as technical change) could have caused changes in relative wages as well as in trade flows or in the prices of traded goods.

In addition, the connection between trade and wages is highly intuitive. Simple supply and demand suggests that American workers who are less educated will have to settle for lower wages if they must now compete with a vast pool of "similar" workers in other countries. However, this connection says nothing about magnitudes. Trade with low-wage countries is a relatively small component of U.S. economic activity, while the skill premium increase has been large. Furthermore, models of how wages are determined in a global economy show that this simple framework can be misleading—trade with LDCs could (but need not) hurt American workers who are less skilled.

TECHNOLOGICAL CHANGE. New methods of production might increase the demand for skilled workers relative to those who are less skilled. Technical change concentrated in particular economic sectors could cause a disproportionate expansion of industries using highly skilled labor. Technical change could also be "factor biased," leading firms to substitute away from workers who are less skilled toward capital and highly skilled labor. However, productivity changes are treated as the "residual" in many empirical studies, and those that do try to measure it directly have focused on the "sector-biased" component.

OTHER DOMESTIC DEVELOPMENTS. Other developments in the United States could have influenced wages and employment opportunities for workers who are less skilled. These include institutional factors, such as the declining importance of unions or changes in the implicit contract between workers and firms. Such factors are even more difficult to incorporate in quantitative analyses.

How to Assess the Causes

Establishing what has actually caused the rise in the U.S. skill premium requires three things: a clearly specified question, measures of relevant variables such as globalization and technical change, and a model of the determinants of the wage of skilled workers relative to those who are less skilled. However, various analyses pose somewhat different questions, and the "exogenous" components of both trade and technical change are difficult to measure. Most existing analyses have used one of two frameworks.

—The *"factor content of trade"* approach is based on a simple labor supply and demand framework in which imports raise the effective supply of domestic factors of production while exports raise the effective demand. The framework's appeal comes from its intuitive nature and ease of empirical implementation. One key drawback is that this approach treats trade flows as "exogenous" measures of globalization; however, trade flows reflect many factors, including technology.

—The *"Heckscher-Ohlin"* approach is based on the workhorse model of international trade. In this framework, wages of those workers who are less skilled and of other factors of production are shown to be related to the prices of goods and services that they produce. Thus, empirical implementation has focused on testing for a decline in the relative prices of products using disproportionate amounts of labor by workers who are less skilled. One key drawback is that this approach treats prices of goods the United States trades as "exogenous" measures of globalization, but it is difficult to adjust for the effects of technical change on relative prices.

Both models rely on simplifying assumptions. Although analysts disagree about which stylized view is more appropriate, there is broad agreement that these frameworks incorporate only some of the potential channels through which globalization might matter. These problems help to explain the range of conclusions among economists.

The Bottom Line

Taking the results from both types of empirical analyses at face value, the weight of evidence supports the view that other factors have been significantly more important than globalization in explaining the rise of the skill premium. Factor content analyses find that trade and immigration together account for up to 2 percentage points of an 18 percentage-point rise in the wage of college-educated versus high school–educated workers. (They also find that trade, and especially immigration, had a greater impact on relative wages of Americans who are least skilled—those with less than twelve years of schooling.) Similarly, there has been no significant drop in relative prices of goods requiring intensive labor by workers who are less skilled—at least in the key decade of the 1980s. However, limitations of existing empirical analyses imply that the jury is still out. It is possible that globalization played a somewhat larger role in the decline in relative wages of American workers who are less skilled. Indeed, contributors to this project reach a range of conclusions.

Policy Implications

Two policy concerns are apparent: problems faced by workers displaced from their jobs; and hardships associated with declining real earnings of many Americans, particularly those who are less skilled. How policy should respond is largely independent of the extent to which globalization is perceived to be the underlying culprit. In particular, even analysts who conclude that globalization is to blame emphasize that trade policies are poor tools to use in assisting American workers. Instead, attention should focus on improving U.S. policies to assist displaced workers directly. In this context, new approaches to provide insurance against major income losses warrant further examination.

What Has Happened to American Workers?

An analysis of recent U.S. labor market performance finds that for American workers, there is both good news and bad news. The good news relates to rapid overall job creation. Average annual employment growth was 1.7 percent from 1973 to 1996, slightly faster than the growth rate from 1950 to 1973. By 1997, the civilian unemployment rate had fallen below 5 percent. Furthermore, a number of studies document that recent employment expansion has been concentrated among higher-paying job categories.[4] The bad news for American workers is associated with three worrisome trends: poor average wage growth, a significant decline in the relative wages of workers with fewer skills, and growing inequality of wages and income.

Stagnant Wage Growth

As shown in table 1-1, growth in average compensation fell precipitously from 2.67 percent per year in 1960–73 to 0.96 percent per year in 1973–83 and just 0.38 percent per year in 1983–95. These figures refer to "real" compensation—which includes wages as well as fringe benefits—and ad-

4. Civilian employment data are from U.S. Council of Economic Advisers (1997, table B-34). Pages 140–44 summarize studies of the characteristics of recent employment growth.

Table 1-1. *Annualized Percentage Growth Rates of Productivity and Average Compensation, 1960–95*[a]

Years	Real compensation	Real earnings	Productivity	Labor's share of GDP
1960–73	2.67	2.04	3.01	64.75
1973–83	0.96	−0.29	1.09	65.29
1983–95	0.38	−0.57	0.96	64.51
1973–95	0.64	−0.44	1.02	64.88
Changes in percentage growth rates				
1960–73 vs. 1973–95	−2.03	−2.48	−1.99	

Sources: Author's calculations from U.S. Bureau of Labor Statistics, Basic Industry Data and Industry Analytical Ratios for the Nonfarm Business Sector; and U.S. Council for Economic Advisers (1997, table B-45).

a. Earnings are average hourly earnings in private nonagricultural industries. Compensation includes wages and salaries of employees plus other benefits. Earnings and compensation are deflated by the Personal Consumption Expenditures deflator. Productivity refers to the nonfarm business sector. Data on labor's share of GDP are annual averages.

just for changes in prices of consumption goods to provide a measure of purchasing power. Table 1-1 also shows that a much bleaker (though misleading) picture could be painted using real hourly earnings, which have *fallen* by 0.44 percent per year since 1973. However, this series overstates the earnings decline, because it excludes rising health and other benefits.[5]

Nearly all of the slowdown in real compensation growth can be accounted for by a slowdown in U.S. productivity growth.[6] Table 1-1 shows that both series grew roughly 2 percent per year more slowly after 1973. Unfortunately, the causes of this drop in productivity growth are not fully understood. Recent analyses point to domestic developments playing a role, including demographic factors, a deterioration in educational skills, and persistently low rates of investment.[7] The fact that the slowdown was experienced in virtually all other industrial countries suggests that global factors may be at work. But increased competitive pressure from a global marketplace seems more likely to spur innovation than to impede it. It is not obvious that globalization per se should have reduced U.S. productivity and therefore wage growth.

5. A second problem with the hourly earnings data is that they have not been benchmarked recently. See Bosworth and Perry (1994) for a discussion.

6. Lawrence (1996), Lawrence and Slaughter (1993), and Bosworth and Perry (1994) contain additional analyses of the slowdown in average compensation and a discussion of alternate indicators.

7. For a discussion of the U.S. productivity slowdown, and additional references, see Baily, Burtless, and Litan (1993, pp. 15–47).

The sluggish performance of average real compensation has not been the focus of the debate over whether internationalization is harming American workers. However, it is surely at the heart of the growing concerns about the problems these workers face.

Rising Skill Premium

There has been a sharp rise in the gap between wages of highly educated workers and those with less schooling. Because years of education are often used as an indicator of "skill," this gap is typically called the "skill premium."[8] Education-based indicators are preferable to the alternative of focusing on the wage of production versus nonproduction workers, under the assumption that production workers are relatively less skilled. As Leamer documents, these categories are highly heterogeneous.[9] Indeed, the rise in the premium paid to nonproduction workers relative to those in production was less than half of the rise in the premium paid to college-educated versus high school–educated workers.[10]

After falling or remaining roughly constant in the 1970s, skill premia rose sharply during the 1980s and early 1990s. Although the precise amount of increase depends on the series chosen, the general trends are clear. Figure 1-1 documents the timing of the increase in earnings of male college graduates relative to high school graduates. The discussion of evidence below highlights a study by Borjas, Freeman, and Katz that analyzes an 18 percent rise in the premium for college-educated versus high school–educated workers from 1980 to 1990.[11] This 18 percent rise in the college

8. Educational attainment may actually be a poor measure of underlying skill. In particular, many American workers with high school diplomas may be quite skilled in relevant activities. Although their share of the total is falling, high school graduates continue to make up the majority of the U.S. labor force and it seems misleading to label this group "unskilled" as has been common in this literature. Although the convention of identifying skill level with years of schooling is followed, the discussion distinguishes between the labor of high-skilled workers (H) and of those who are less skilled (L).

9. Leamer (chapter 4, table 4-2). See also Mishel and Bernstein (1994).

10. Lawrence (1996, table 3.3, p. 60).

11. Borjas, Freeman, and Katz (1996, p. 250). The 18 percent increase in the college relative to high school earnings premium is based on a regression which controls for age and sex. Other studies find similar increases in skill premia. For example, Burtless (1996a, table 4) provides educational premia in selected years for a broad sample of workers that includes both women and men, and adjusts for industry of employment. From 1979 to 1993, the premium for completing high school jumps from 13 percent to 32 percent while the premium for completing

Figure 1-1. *Ratio of Median Earnings for College-Educated versus High School–Educated Male Workers Employed Full Time, Full Year, 1967–95*

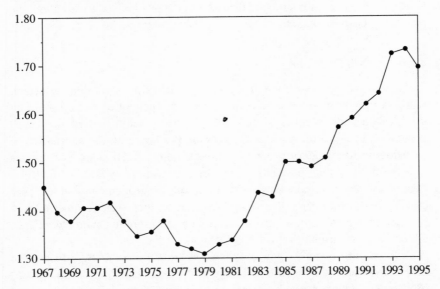

Source: U.S. Council of Economic Advisers tabulations of the March Current Population Survey, various years.

skill premium has been the focus of the debate about whether globalization is to blame for the problems facing American workers.

Growing Inequality

The rise in the skill premium is only part of a much broader increase in income inequality in the United States. In particular, inequality in labor earnings has grown sharply.[12] Table 1-2 shows that between 1973 and 1993, both male and female low-wage workers experienced significantly slower earnings growth than higher-wage workers. Men in the bottom of the ten-decile distribution saw their real earnings fall by a striking 21.5 percent. However, women saw considerably greater earnings growth throughout the earnings distribution. This is presumably because of a variety of develop-

---

college jumps from 38 percent to 63 percent. Both premia are roughly constant during the 1970s.

12. The rise in earnings inequality has been documented by a large and growing literature. For example, see Katz and Murphy (1992); Levy and Murnane (1992); Bound and Johnson (1992, 1995); Kosters (1994); Burtless (1990, 1996a); Blackburn, Bloom, and Freeman (1990); Murphy and Welch (1991).

Table 1-2. *Percentage Changes in Real Earnings for Full-Time, Full-Year Civilian Workers, 1973–93*

Percentile	Males	Females
5	−21.4	2.1
10	−21.5	−3.0
25	−18.5	2.1
50	−7.5	11.1
75	1.3	19.8
90	7.6	28.9
95	13.9	30.7

Source: Gary Burtless's calculations from Current Population Survey data, 1974, 1994.

ments, including their penetration of a broader range of occupations and industries as well as reduced discrimination.[13]

The growing earnings inequality is part of a more general rise in U.S. family income inequality that began during the early 1970s and accelerated after the 1980s. This pattern is evident in figure 1-2, which shows the evolution of the Gini coefficient for the income of U.S. families since 1947. (This measure of inequality ranges from zero, if all families had equal incomes, to one, if all income were earned by a single family.)

Concerns about recent experiences of American workers probably stem from the broader rise in income inequality among American families, not just from the increased gap between earnings of workers with different levels of education. But only about *one-third* of the increase in earnings inequality is attributable to identifiable differences among workers, including differences in education. Fully two-thirds of the increase is among workers who share the same education, work experience, gender, and other characteristics.[14] Further, less than half of the rise in overall income inequality can be attributed to the increase in labor income inequality.[15] Even

13. See Burtless (1996a, 1996b).

14. For example, see Burtless (1996a) and the discussion in U.S. Council of Economic Advisers (1997, chapter 5). Note that part of the increased inequality within groups could be due to a combination of skill differences that are not reflected in observable characteristics such as education, and a rise in the underlying skill premium. Note also that recent discussions of a "winner-take-all" society focus on the big wage increases for those at the top, not the wage declines for those at the bottom relative to those in the middle of earnings distributions. See also Gottschalk and Moffitt (1994) for a decomposition of increased earnings inequality into permanent versus transitory components.

15. See Burtless (1996a). Other factors that account for the increased inequality include declining male labor force participation, an increased correlation between

14   SUSAN M. COLLINS

Figure 1-2. *Family Income Inequality: Gini Ratios for Families, 1947–95*

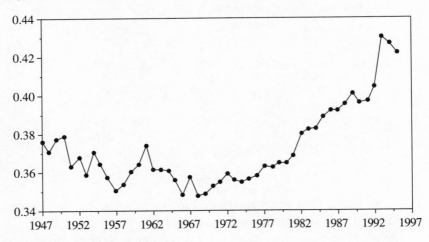

Source: U.S. Bureau of the Census data.

if globalization were to "explain" fully 100 percent of the rise in the skill premium, it likely explains a much smaller share of the overall rise in family income inequality.[16] Explanations of the rising skill premium should not be interpreted as explanations of growing overall inequality. Indeed, it is much more difficult to tell a story in which globalization is at the heart of these broader domestic trends. To date, there has been little attempt to do so.

International Comparisons

The employment trends in figure 1-3 highlight that the United States has been better at creating jobs than Japan and especially the European Union. Indeed, Europe has experienced large, sustained increases in unemployment rates. As shown in figure 1-4, however, the United States also stands out for its lack of growth in real wages. As noted above, relatively slow

the earnings of spouses, and increased concentration of nonlabor earnings. Dividend payments, which are concentrated among wealthy families, have increased; government transfer payments, which are concentrated among poorer families, have declined.

16. For example, suppose that the higher skill premium were to explain 25 percent of the increased earnings inequality and that increased earnings inequality were to explain 50 percent of the rise in family income inequality. Then globalization might explain only one-eighth of the increased overall inequality. Of course, a complete decomposition would incorporate correlations between the increased skill premium and and other factors.

Figure 1-3. *Change in Employment in the United States, Japan, and the European Union,*[a] *1970–95*

Employment index (1970 = 100)

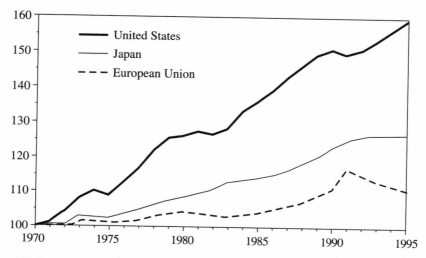

Source: OECD databank, 1996.

a. European Union data do not include data for Ireland, Greece, Finland, or Luxembourg.

Figure 1-4. *Change in Real Wages in the United States, Japan, and the European Union,*[a] *1970–95*

Real-wage index (1970 = 100)

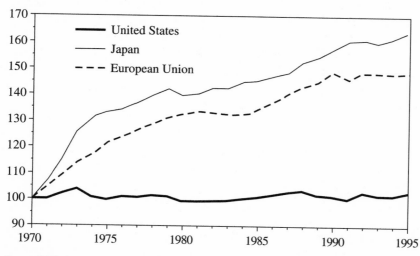

Source: OECD databank, 1996.

a. European Union data do not include data for Ireland, Greece, Finland, or Luxembourg.

growth in U.S. real wages is largely a story about relatively slow growth in U.S. productivity. Aggregate labor productivity growth in 1970–95 was about 0.9 percent in the United States, compared with 2.2 percent and 2.6 percent in Germany and Japan, respectively.[17]

The United States is also somewhat unusual in its extent of increasing inequality since the 1970s.[18] Freeman and Katz conclude that, while wage inequality also rose significantly in the United Kingdom, only the United States experienced sharp declines in the real wages of its poorest workers, increases in family income inequality, and rising poverty rates among families with working head(s) of household.[19] But all of the Organization for Economic Cooperation and Development (OECD) countries studied experienced some *combination* of stagnant or falling real wages, growing income inequality, slow employment growth, or persistent unemployment. This suggests that common forces may be at work, with differences across countries explaining the alternative ways in which these forces are manifested. One such major difference is in labor market and wage-setting institutions. The United States and the United Kingdom are characterized by relatively decentralized labor markets and little government intervention—an environment less likely to prevent declines in wages or rising income disparities.

International Integration

The U.S. economy has become more integrated with the global economy. Trade flows provide one indicator of integration.[20] In 1960, the United States exported only about 4.8 percent of goods and services produced domestically, while imports from other countries accounted for 4.3 percent of gross domestic product (GDP). By 1995, exports and imports had jumped to 11.1 percent and 12.4 percent of GDP, respectively, with most of the increase in the 1970s. There also was an increase in the

17. Organization for Economic Cooperation and Development (1996).

18. Recent cross-country comparisons of inequality include Gottschalk and Smeeding (1997) and the papers in Freeman and Katz (1995).

19. Freeman and Katz (1995).

20. Another indicator of growing international integration is the surge in cross-border capital flows. However, key features of the rise in direct foreign investment (DFI) and the growth of multinational corporations suggest that these trends are not at the heart of adverse U.S. labor market trends. See Lawrence and Slaughter (1993); Lawrence (1996); Brainard and Riker (1997).

extent of *outsourcing*—the shift abroad of the production of intermediate inputs.[21]

Cross-border flows of people provide a second indicator. Immigrants rose from just 4.7 percent of the U.S. population in 1970 to 8.2 percent by 1992.[22] During the 1950s, some two-thirds came from Europe or Canada; by the early 1990s, this figure had fallen to 21 percent. Over this same period, immigrants from LDCs in Asia and Latin America increased from just 30 percent to 75 percent of the U.S. immigrant total. Because immigrants are less educated, on average, than native-born Americans, immigration has increased the relative supply of less-skilled workers in the American labor force.[23]

Nonetheless, the United States remains considerably less dependent on the global economy than many of its trading partners.[24] Recent emphasis on globalization may partly reflect a qualitative change in perceptions of America's place in the world economy. As Leamer documents in chapter 4, the United States is no longer the world's unchallenged productive and technological leader. In the 1960s, the United States stood out relative to its trading partners as being well endowed with both capital and skilled labor. In comparison, even the other industrial economies were relatively more abundant in less-skilled labor (and at considerably lower wages). By the

21. Feenstra and Hanson (1996a, pp. 241–42) estimate that imported inputs jumped from 5.7 percent of total U.S. manufactured imports in 1972 to 11.6 percent in 1990, with most of the rise occurring between 1979 and 1987. Outsourcing is concentrated in sectors such as footwear, electrical machinery, and toys, where production stages range from presumably high-skill-intensive product design to relatively low-skill-intensive product assembly. See also Feenstra and Hanson (1996b).

22. For further discussion, see Friedberg and Hunt (1995); Borjas (1995). Available data suggest that the inflow of illegal immigrants would add perhaps one-third to the legal inflow, that inclusion of illegals raises the share of immigrants from 8.2 to 9.5 percent of the 1992 U.S. population and that roughly 40 percent of the illegal immigrants have come from Mexico. Friedberg and Hunt (1995).

23. For example, Borjas, Freeman, and Katz (1996, pp. 249–50) estimate that immigration raised the supply of high school graduates relative to college graduates by about 1 percent during 1980–90, partially offsetting the domestic shift towards more-educated workers.

24. This point is emphasized in Krugman (1995a). To illustrate, the World Bank, *World Development Report 1997* lists U.S. trade (exports plus imports) as 24 percent of GDP in 1995, compared with 46 percent for Germany and 71 percent for Canada. The only high-income country with a lower trade share is Japan (17 percent). Of course, the low U.S. trade share is due in large part to the size of the U.S. economy. The World Bank (1997, table 3, pp. 218–19).

Table 1-3. *Direction of U.S. Imports and Exports, 1970, 1980, and 1995*[a]
Percent of total, unless otherwise specified

Countries	Imports			Exports		
	1970	1980	1995	1970	1980	1995
Total trade (millions of U.S.$)	42,452	256,959	770,947	43,231	220,781	582,526
			Percent of total trade			
Total trade	100.0	100.0	100.0	100.0	100.0	100.0
OECD countries	72.1	49.4	55.6	66.7	57.6	57.4
Japan	14.7	12.8	16.5	10.8	9.4	11.0
Canada	27.7	16.3	19.2	21.0	16.0	21.6
Europe	27.6	18.8	19.2	32.4	30.0	22.5
Oil-exporting countries	3.9	22.2	4.7	4.4	7.7	3.4
Non-oil developing countries	23.9	28.1	39.6	28.8	34.4	39.2
Mexico	3.1	5.0	8.1	3.9	6.9	7.8
China[b]	...	0.5	6.3	...	1.7	2.0
Four Asian NIEs	4.9	7.1	11.0	4.2	6.8	12.7
Country/area not specified	0.1	0.0	0.0	...	0.5	0.1

Sources: 1970 data are taken from 1977 International Monetary Fund (IMF) *Direction of Trade Annual 1970–76*, pp. 254–55, 291; 1980 data are taken from 1987 IMF *Direction of Trade Statistics Yearbook*, pp. 404–06; 1995 data are taken from 1996 IMF *Direction of Trade Statistics Yearbook*, pp. 445–47; and 1980 trade data for the United States and Taiwan are taken from *Taiwan Statistical Data Book* (1992, p. 196).

a. Newly industrialized economies (NIEs) include Hong Kong, Korea, Singapore, and Taiwan. European countries include Austria, Belgium-Luxembourg, Denmark, Finland, France, Western Germany (eastern Germany in 1995), Greece, Iceland, Ireland, Italy, Netherlands, Norway, Portugal, Spain, Sweden, Switzerland, and the United Kingdom. OECD countries include Canada, Japan, Australia, New Zealand, and European countries as defined above (Mexico and Turkey are excluded from this definition). Using the trade data taken from *Taiwan Statistical Data Book*, U.S. imports from the four Asian NIEs in 1970 were 4.8 percent of its total imports, and U.S. exports to the four Asian NIEs in 1970 were 3.8 percent of its total exports.

b. Data for China were unavailable in 1970.

1980s, however, U.S. factor endowments were no longer so unique. Many other industrial countries had similar stocks of capital and skilled labor (relative to their supplies of less-skilled labor).

Trade with Less-Developed Economies

Concerns over the link between trade and problems of less-skilled American workers focus on the recent increase in trade with nonindustrial countries. Table 1-3 shows the main sources of U.S. imports and the main destination of U.S. exports. In 1970, nonoil-developing countries accounted for roughly one-quarter of U.S. imports and exports. Between 1980 and 1995, their import share jumped to nearly 40 percent, largely due to growth in trade with the dynamic Asian economies. By 1995, almost 40 percent of U.S. exports also went to developing economies, though this rise was more gradual.

Table 1-4. *Shares in U.S. Imports of Manufactures, 1973, 1980, 1989, and 1995*[a]

Percent, unless otherwise specified

Countries	1973	1980	1989	1995
Total U.S. imports of manufactures (billions of U.S.$)	45.00	124.23	366.48	607.82
	Percent of total U.S. imports of manufactures			
Total U.S. imports of manufactures	100.0	100.0	100.0	100.0
Selected OECD countries	80.2	72.8	65.4	57.7
Canada	24.8	18.3	16.1	16.6
Western Europe	34.9	29.0	23.4	20.7
Japan	20.5	25.5	25.9	20.4
Developing countries	17.9	23.7	30.8	33.6
Four Asian NIEs	. . .	14.6	19.9	18.4
China	. . .	0.6	3.1	7.6
Mexico	. . .	2.9	4.8	7.8
Other countries	2.0	3.5	3.8	8.8

Sources: General Agreement on Tariffs and Trade (GATT) International Trade 1976–77, vol. 2: 1989–90, 1990–91, appendix tables; and World Trade Organization *Annual Report 1996,*, vol. 2.

a. Selected OECD countries do not include Australia or New Zealand. Data for individual developing countries were unavailable for 1973; only an aggregate was provided.

The composition of U.S. trade with LDCs has shifted from primary products to manufactures. Table 1-4 shows that, in 1973, 80 percent of U.S. manufactured imports came from Canada, Western Europe, or Japan, and only 18 percent from LDCs. By 1995, the share from these industrial countries was less than 60 percent, while the LDC share had grown to about 34 percent.

Increases in U.S. trade with developing countries primarily reflect a combination of trade policy changes and expanded productive capacity in key developing countries. In these countries, the inward-looking development strategy of import substitution has largely given way to one with an outward orientation, often strongly promoting manufactured exports. This so-called rush to reform is largely a phenomenon of the late 1980s and 1990s.[25] Given the timing of these developments, one would expect the

25. Sachs and Warner (1995) and Rodrik (1994) provide discussions of the evolution of trade policies in LDCs. The World Bank, *World Development Report 1987* classifies forty-one developing countries in terms of their outward orientation, finding little change overall between 1963–73 versus 1973–83. The IMF has studied trade policies of thirty-six major developing countries since the mid-1980s. Of these, twenty-eight were initially classified as having significant or tight trade

increased availability of manufactures from nonindustrial countries to have more pronounced implications for the United States after 1980 than during the 1970s.

Still, U.S. imports of manufactures from LDCs are small compared with U.S. economic activity. These imports accounted for just 3 percent of U.S. GDP in 1995 (up from less than 0.5 percent in 1973). In 1995, they were 16 percent of value-added U.S. manufacturing and about 33 percent of total U.S. manufactures imports. Part of the debate over the role of international trade focuses on these magnitudes, which seem modest relative to the dramatic deterioration in wages of less-skilled Americans.[26]

Wages of the "Average" U.S. Trading Partner

This discussion has documented the rise in U.S. trade with nonindustrial countries. On average, these countries have lower wages than industrial countries, suggesting that the wage of the "average" U.S. trading partner might have fallen. However, this assumption turns out to be incorrect, as shown by table 1-5. The average wage paid to manufacturing workers among America's trade partners has risen steadily, from 38 percent of the U.S. wage in 1960 to 66 percent in 1975 and to 85 percent in 1992. The 1960 figure reflects the fact that wages in industrial countries remained quite low relative to those in the United States for decades after World War II. Wages for workers in America's developed-country and developing-country trading partners have risen significantly over the past thirty years. The increases are more than enough to offset the rise in the share of U.S. trade from LDCs.[27] Similarly, the broader U.S. Bureau of Labor Statistics measure of the compensation of manufacturing production workers in

controls. By 1991, seventeen had initiated "comprehensive" reforms, whereas eleven had initiated "partial" reforms. The other eight countries, initially classified as open or relatively open, either maintained their status or liberalized further. IMF (1992, p. 45).

26. These data come from table 1-4 and U.S. Council of Economic Advisers (1997, pp. 300–01); table B-1 GDP data used in calculation.

27. Some might argue that the real issue is not the average wages of U.S. trading partners overall, but what has happened to the average wage of the countries relevant for trade in manufactured goods. However, this wage has not fallen either. Suppose that the U.S. manufactures trade was exclusively with other industrial countries in 1975 (an extreme assumption) and had shrunk to 63 percent by 1992 (the actual figures for the data used in table 1-5). Then the average wage of U.S. trading partners in manufacturing would have stayed roughly constant—at about 84.7 percent of the U.S. level.

Table 1-5. *Wages of U.S. Trading Partners as a Percentage of U.S. Manufacturing Wages, 1960, 1975, and 1992*[a]

	1960	1975	1992
U.S. wages in nominal dollars	388.49	820.58	2,032.72
U.S. wage			
Overall	38.1	65.8	84.7
Industrial countries	48.6	83.8	116.4
Other countries	13.5	22.2	28.1
Share of U.S. trade			
Industrial countries	70.1	70.8	64.1 (63.2)[b]
Other countries	29.9	29.2	35.9 (36.8)[b]

Source: Author's calculations from International Labour Organization, *Yearbook of Labour Statistics;* IMF *Direction of Trade Statistics Yearbook;* and IMF *International Financial Statistics,* various years.

a. Wages are monthly wages in manufacturing. Trade weights were based on total U.S. trade with its thirty-five largest trading partners (IMF *International Financial Statistic*), fifteen of which are classified as industrial and twenty of which as nonindustrial. The industrial countries are those classified as such according to IMF resources. Foreign-country wages were converted to U.S. dollars using a nominal exchange rate (IMF *International Financial Statistic*) and then indexed to the U.S. wage of that year. Trade weights were used to construct average wages for U.S. trading partners overall, as well as industrial and nonindustrial-country partners.

b. Trade weights are based on manufactured trade and were available for 1992 only.

twenty-five countries that are major U.S. trading partners has risen from 60 percent of the U.S. level in 1975 to 95 percent in 1995.[28]

These numbers make it possible to rebut the claim that the United States now tends to trade with countries with relatively lower wages than it did in the past.[29] However, they are not the appropriate numbers for evaluating the competetive position of American workers, because they ignore productivity. Available data do not paint a complete picture, because there are problems in obtaining comparable manufacturing productivity series for developing countries. But the key point is that low wages tend to be associated with low labor productivity. For instance, recent studies find that although compensation in India, the Philippines, and Malaysia was just 5 to 10 percent of the level in the United States, low productivity implied that labor costs per unit of output were similar to or higher than in the United States.[30]

28. U.S. Bureau of Labor Statistics (1996, table 1).
29. Note that a cross-country comparison of workers' living standards requires adjusting for national differences in prices of goods and services, using purchasing power instead of nominal exchange rates.
30. Golub (1997a, 1997b).

Methodological Issues

In evaluating the relationship between globalization and income inequality, the key question can be stated as: *How much of the rise in the U.S.
skill premium can be attributed to globalization as opposed to technological change or developments originating at home?*[31]

I have documented that the rise in the U.S. skill premium coincided with
increases in manufactures trade and immigration from developing
countries. But a correlation is not enough to establish causality, much less
to answer the question posed here. This requires a model linking shocks
from abroad to labor market developments at home, as well as measures of
the "globalization shock" and other variables in question.

The two most popular frameworks for making sense out of the data are
the Hecksher-Ohlin (HO) approach and the factor content approach.[32] The
discussion that follows provides an overview of each, including advantages
and shortcomings. It takes the view that, despite limitations, both approaches provide useful information but neither is definitive. In this regard,
project contributors expressed a range of views. Bhagwati and Leamer
strongly advocated the HO framework; Sachs and Shatz used both approaches in their work. Freeman also saw value in both, but on balance,
found factor content studies more informative. Related empirical findings
are discussed in the next section.

The Heckscher-Ohlin Model

The HO model is the workhorse of international trade theory. The
simplest version shows how production, employment, wages, and other key
variables are determined in an economy that produces two goods using two
factors of production. Suppose that the two factors are less-skilled labor (L)
and highly skilled labor (H) and the two goods are apparel (A) and
machinery (M). Apparel production is relatively intensive in its usage of L,
whereas machinery production is relatively intensive in H. Wages are fully
flexible, ensuring full employment. The domestic economy is assumed to
be small and open. In other words, it trades freely with the rest of the world,

---

31. Deardorff and Hakura (1994) stress that it matters how the underlying
question is formulated. They discuss a range of alternative questions that have
been—or could be—posed. The point has since been emphasized by many others
including Bhagwati and Grossman in this volume.

32. See Cline (1997) for a detailed, comprehensive review of the literature.

taking as given the world prices of both goods. Domestic products and those produced abroad are assumed to be perfect substitutes. It should be noted that this model, in which L and H can move between sectors, is meant to describe the long run—perhaps ten or more years. It also assumes that markets are competitive, and it is not well equipped to handle issues such as how rents are distributed between workers and owners.

A key relationship follows from these assumptions: *A decrease in the price of apparel relative to machine tools will, all else being equal, be associated with a decrease in the wage of less-skilled relative to highly skilled workers.*[33] This result, called the Stolper-Samuelson theorem, has been the basis for various empirical studies. If prices are determined in world markets, then changes in goods prices can be used as measures of "globalization shocks." Indeed, developments abroad affect the domestic economy through changes in relative goods prices, so failure to find evidence of a relative price change constitutes proof that globalization could not have caused an observed change in the skill premium—something else must have happened.[34] If the presumed globalization shock is the increased availability of apparel (L-intensive goods) in world markets due to liberalization and expanded productive capabilities in developing countries, then the world relative price of apparel should have fallen.

The model generates a second testable implication about the effects of a globalization shock. If the decline in the relative price of less-skilled labor were due to lower relative apparel prices induced by an increased availability of apparel produced in LDCs, then production of both apparel and machinery should become more L intensive. This is because all sectors should substitute away from more expensive factors of production toward relatively cheap labor that is less skilled.

33. Note that the relationship between relative prices and wages is a very general one, not specific to trade. It will also hold in a closed economy.

In the simple version of the model, the change in relative wages can be shown to be a multiple of the change in relative prices—the magnification effect. However, in more complex versions of the model, with many goods and many factors, the relationship between goods prices and factor prices is weaker than the Stolper-Samuelson relationship. In general, there is a correlation between changes in the prices of factors and changes in the prices of goods (weighted by factor intensity), but there need be no magnification effect. All that can be said is that declines in the prices of less-skill-intensive goods will tend to be associated with declines in the wages of less-skilled workers. See the excellent discussion in Deardorff (1994).

34. This point is emphasized in Grossman (1987) and more recently in Lawrence and Slaughter (1993).

Empirical Implementation

Empirical analyses based on the HO model typically explore whether prices of goods that intensively use less-skilled labor have fallen relative to prices of other goods. For example, changes in goods prices can be regressed on a measure of each industry's skill intensity. This work has tended to attribute to technical change any relative wage changes not associated with changes in goods prices. Leamer innovatively takes the opposite tack by trying to account for developments in relative wages implied by (sectoral) productivity changes and attributing any residual to globalization.[35]

The fact that observed price changes can only be interpreted as globalization shocks after they are adjusted for productivity changes raises a difficult issue for empirical implementation. Suppose that technological improvements in the *M* sector make it possible to produce machinery using fewer workers. Producers of machinery could now pay workers more and still charge the same price for their output. In this model, the *M* sector would expand (hire more of both types of workers). Because *M* production is intensive in *H* workers, increased demand would raise their relative wage. Thus, sector-biased technical change could explain a rise in the skill premium.[36] However, productivity changes could also cause changes in relative goods prices without changing relative wages. Technical innovation in *M* could simply be passed on to consumers as lower prices.

Analysts taking this approach disagree about the conclusions for two main reasons: studies focus on different time periods, and they use different price measures.[37] In terms of prices, three considerations arise. One is whether to use U.S. domestic prices (available for many market sectors and over a long period) or prices of U.S. imports and exports, which are probably better measures of global shocks. Another is whether to give

---

35. More formally, Leamer computes the wage changes necessary for maintaining zero profits given observed product price changes, factor shares, and productivity growth for 450 manufacturing industries. Implementation requires assumptions about how much sectoral productivity growth is passed through to product prices. See Leamer for details and Grossman for a critique in chapter 4.

36. In the simple version of the HO model, it is primarily the sector bias of technical change that matters. Leamer and Jones (chapter 4 and a comment to chapter 2, respectively, in this volume) and Krugman (1995b) provide additional discussion of the roles of sector-biased versus factor-biased technical change.

37. Studies also use different measures of an industry's skill intensity. Those using the production/nonproduction worker distinction to measure low skill versus high skill include Sachs and Shatz (1994; chapter 5 in this volume) and Lawrence and Slaughter (1993). Leamer (chapter 4 in this volume) constructs a skill measure based on industry wage differentials. Lawrence (1996) uses years of schooling.

special treatment to particular industries, such as computers, because of measurement problems associated with major productivity and quality changes. The third issue is whether, and if so how, to adjust for (sectoral) productivity growth as well as for any changes in intermediate-goods prices. The resulting "effective, value-added" prices are arguably better measures of any globalization shock but are still not direct indicators of external developments.[38]

Theoretical Considerations—Strengths and Weaknesses

There are many attractive features of the simple HO framework. It is based on a general equilibrium model, which means that it simultaneously and consistently accounts for what happens in the markets for each good and each type of labor. Its results are based on explicit assumptions. The framework is powerful in that it can be used to analyze a wide range of issues, though various versions are arguably appropriate in different contexts.

The model implies relationships between other variables of interest—with some surprising implications. For example, there is no necessary link between changes in quantities and relative wages. An increase in the relative supply of less-skilled labor could be absorbed without a rise in the skill premium, through an expansion of the clothing sector. This result challenges proponents of the factor content approach to spell out the assumptions under which it makes sense to assume a simple relationship between relative quantities of labor and wages. But the result is also troubling, because wages of American workers do seem sensitive to changes in domestic labor supply.

Trade theorists have stressed that this simple version of the HO model may be misleading. In more complex (and realistic) versions, reducing barriers to trade with countries that are abundant in low-skilled labor may lower relative prices of apparel but actually raise the real wages of Americans who are less skilled.[39] This is more likely the case if the United States imports different types of apparel than it produces domestically. Then a reduction in world prices of imports need not injure the domestic apparel industry and can make *all* Americans better off. Versions of the HO

38. Both Sachs and Shatz and Leamer (in this volume) attempt to extract industry-specific productivity growth from price changes. Sachs and Shatz also adjust for intermediate-goods prices. See Grossman (1987) and Revenga (1992) for empirical analyses that address the potential endogeneity of traded-goods prices.

39. See the contributions to this volume by Bhagwati, Leamer, and Jones.

model that include nontraded goods also seem more appropriate, given the importance of services (many of which are not traded) in the U.S. economy. Finally, Krugman has argued that the simple, small-country version of the HO model is the wrong framework to use in trying to make sense of recent developments in the United States.[40] In particular, the United States influences prices in world markets. As a result, changes in traded-goods prices may be poor measures of developments abroad.

Factor Content or Quantities Approach

The factor content approach is based on a simple framework of relative supply and demand. The idea is that globalization implies shifts in relative labor supply that are relevant for determination of wages in the United States. Imports can be thought of as embodying the foreign workers and capital used to produce them. An increase in U.S. imports of apparel produced in a developing country using relatively large amounts of less-skilled labor effectively increases the relative supply of less-skilled workers in the United States. The same is true of an increase in less-skilled immigrants to the United States. Similarly, exports can be thought of as embodying the domestic workers and capital used to produce them. Because U.S. exports are shipped abroad, an increase in exports of machinery produced using large amounts of highly skilled labor effectively reduces the domestic supply of such workers.

Empirical Implementation

Empirical implementation requires two steps. The first is to estimate the shift in the effective relative supply of labor. Most studies use information about usage of highly skilled and less-skilled labor in U.S. manufacturing industries to calculate the amounts of each labor type embodied in the trade of goods. This implies a change in the number of domestic jobs for each skill type by industry and for the economy overall, assuming wages stay the same. Immigrant flows directly reduce the number of jobs economywide for U.S. residents in each skill group.

The second step is to estimate the implied effect on the skill premium. This requires a measure of the sensitivity of wages to changes in labor supply—their elasticity. The more difficult it is to substitute workers who are less skilled for those who are more highly skilled (or the lower the

40. Krugman (1995b).

elasticity of substitution), the more relative wages of less-skilled workers must fall to maintain full employment in response to an increase in their relative supply. Thus, the relative wage change implied by trade (and immigration) can be constructed by dividing the relative supply shift by an estimate of this elasticity.

The range of results in the literature comes from different assumptions for both steps. In chapter 5 of this volume, Sachs and Shatz find a large trade effect primarily because they use an unusually low elasticity of substitution. Adrian Wood concludes that trade can explain *all* of the skill premium rise, both because he assumes a low elasticity and because his methodology generates a huge relative supply shift.[41] He correctly points out that U.S. production techniques understate the less-skilled labor embodied in manufactured imports from developing countries. Compared with the United States, LDCs are likely to produce a less-skill-intensive mix of goods in each industrial category and to produce each good using relatively more less-skilled labor. However, his analysis goes much too far in the other direction by using production information from LDCs. Further, his estimates are scaled upward by large but ad hoc factors to reflect hypothesized effects on nontraded sectors.[42]

Theoretical Considerations

The initial formulations of this approach used what economists call partial equilibrium. They looked at the market in the United States for less-skilled workers relative to those who are more skilled, without explicitly taking into account what was happening in other markets, such as markets for the goods being produced by these workers. But partial equilibrium models can be misleading, because they do not incorporate the interactions among markets. Contributions by Deardorff and Staiger and by Krugman have set out general equilibrium models in which the factor content approach is the correct way to infer the effects of globalization on domestic relative wages.[43] These models treat the United States as initially

41. Wood (1994; see especially pp. 132–37, 149, and 165).
42. Critiques of Wood's (1994) estimates include Freeman (chapter 3 in this volume), Sachs and Shatz (1994), and Lawrence (1996). Wood's assumption that LDC production information is relevant for the United States is highly unrealistic, as illustrated by the implication that LDCs could produce machinery (the U.S. export) at half the U.S. production cost. Sachs and Shatz find at best weak evidence to support the view that employment displaced by trade with LDCs is more *L* intensive than suggested by industry averages. Sachs and Shatz (1994, pp. 32–33).
43. Deardorff and Staiger (1988); Krugman (1995b).

closed and ask what the availability of manufactured imports from LDCs (a move from no trade to a little trade) would have done to relative wages. They explicitly assume there are no other changes—the United States acquires the same technology, experiences the same (domestic) shifts in relative supply of less-skilled labor, and so on. Thus, the factor content approach may provide an appropriate way to examine the effects of trade with LDCs in the absence of any other developments. In practice, we do not know whether changes in other factors, such as technology, have *caused* the observed changes in trade flows—and this approach makes no attempt to sort this out. Another difficulty is that the appropriate elasticity (the one which would exist in the absence of trade) is not directly observable.[44]

Other Channels and Perspectives

Globalization may affect U.S. labor markets through channels that are not captured in either the simple HO model or the model underlying the factor content approach. Some of the discussion in this volume explores alternative frameworks.[45]

In chapter 2, Bhagwati postulates that increased integration in a global marketplace may have narrowed the margin of comparative advantage many industries in the United States and other industrial economies enjoy.[46] Industries are now more footloose, and there is greater volatility in those industries in which a given country enjoys a comparative advantage. Bhagwati notes that this volatility could raise labor turnover, reduce skill acquisition, and lead to a rise in the skill premium. However, William Dickens, in his comments on chapter 2, concludes there is little evidence of such a rise in labor turnover.

Sachs and Shatz develop three simple models in chapter 5 to illustrate that globalization could depress the wages of workers who are less skilled without changing the price of less-skill-intensive goods. However, the

---

44. For a detailed critique of the factor content approach, see Leamer (1996). See also the chapters by Bhagwati, Freeman, and Leamer in this volume.

45. In addition to the channels discussed here, some analysts have examined the possibility that globalization has adversely affected American workers because it has expanded competition and reduced the wage premia (or rents) earned in some sectors. For an assessment of this channel, and additional references, see Lawrence (1996, chapter 4).

Rodrik (1997) argues that an important part of the problem for Americans who are less skilled may be trade with other industrial countries, since this should make domestic labor demand more elastic. However, there appears to be little evidence that the elasticity of demand for American workers has increased.

46. See Bhagwati and Dehejia (1994) for a more formal treatment.

empirical evidence they present relies on the standard factor content and relative price approaches discussed above. In one model, liberalization abroad causes U.S. firms to outsource less-skill-intensive production. Workers displaced from the import-competing sector push down wages of less-skilled workers in the nontraded-goods sector. An alternative, fuller model of outsourcing has been developed by Feenstra and Hanson.[47] This model could explain the observed rise in skill intensity of production within U.S. industries. Sachs and Shatz's second (partial equilibrium) model focuses on the effects of import competition if the domestic industry is monopolistic. In their third model, globalization increases the market for U.S. products, inducing skill-biased technical change that reduces U.S. relative demand for less-skilled workers.

Finally, in chapter 6, Michael Piore suggests an institutionalist framework for thinking about how international integration might affect American workers. He identifies the 1970s as a period in which the economic environment experienced major strains, with increased instability of oil and other prices. Piore sees adjustment to change as involving a series of stages, each influenced by the international environment. As a result, business strategies are characterized not by a continuum of clearly specified alternatives, but by discrete options that will evolve in different directions over time. Piore focuses on two options. The "high road" adjusts through raising skill levels and increasing the extent of cooperation among workers, thus facilitating social cohesion; the "low road" takes advantage of labor market deregulation in a way that widens disparities in earnings and job security of workers. In this scenario, labor market problems of the 1980s and 1990s could have grown from adjustments to global developments of the 1970s.

The Evidence

Is the rise in the U.S. skill premium largely attributable to globalization— that is, increased availability of manufactured goods made by less-skilled workers from relatively low-wage, developing countries? In this section I assess the evidence, focusing on the two popular approaches discussed above.

Evidence Based on HO Models

The HO model implies that globalization would influence the skill premium through its effect on relative goods prices. Most of the work in this

47. Feenstra and Hanson (1996a, 1996b). See also Feenstra's comment on chapter 5.

category examines whether prices of less-skill-intensive goods have fallen relative to prices of other goods.[48] Sachs and Shatz (chapter 5) and Leamer (chapter 4) conclude that price changes are consistent, with globalization having played an important role. Other authors in this volume (including Bhagwati, Freeman, Robert Lawrence, and myself) disagree. Relative prices of less-skill-intensive goods did not fall during the critical decade of the 1980s, but they may have during the 1970s and 1990s.

A careful reading of evidence presented by Sachs and Shatz (chapter 5) suggests that *any decline in the relative price of less-skill-intensive goods during the 1980s reflected productivity and input cost developments, not globalization.* Their analysis regresses domestic price measures on an indicator of skill intensity for 450 manufacturing industries, excluding computers. A strength of their work is that, for 1978–89, they try to adjust prices for changes in input costs and for (sectoral) productivity changes. They then compare results for alternative price measures. As has been discussed, these adjustments are appropriate if price changes are to be interpreted as globalization shocks. A weakness is that they use production/nonproduction worker ratios to measure differences in skill across industries. The estimated coefficient on their skill measure has the expected sign: less-skill-intensive industries experienced relative price declines. The coefficient is statistically significant using final output prices; significant (but much less so) using value-added prices that adjust for changes in intermediates prices; and insignificant using effective, value-added prices that also adjust for productivity changes.[49] Surprisingly, Sachs and Shatz focus on the results based on value-added prices (with no productivity adjustment) and the period 1978–95, for which the estimated skill coefficient is the largest. Lawrence's analysis for 1980–90 finds even less support for the globalization hypothesis. Many of his estimates are the wrong sign, implying that low-skill-intensive industries had relatively large price increases.[50]

48. Krugman (1995a) follows a somewhat different approach. He empirically implements a stylized version of the classical trade model. He shows that the same exogenous shock consistent with large employment changes in countries with rigid wages (his characterization of Europe) would be consistent with quite small changes in relative wages in a country where wages are flexible and trade is a small share of the economy (his characterizations of the United States).

49. In particular, the coefficients on the skill ratio (with t-statistics given in parentheses) are -0.26 (3.95) for output prices, -0.34 (1.99) for value-added prices, and -0.12 (1.29) for effective value-added prices. These estimates refer to the period 1978–89, the only period for which regressions results are given for all three price definitions. Sachs and Shatz go on to use the estimates for value-added prices during the period 1978–95: -0.81 (3.32) (see table 5-6 in this volume).

50. Lawrence (1996, p. 62) uses an education-based measure of the skill premium. However, he uses prices of final goods, not value-added or effective

The result for the 1970s comes from Leamer's careful data analysis to compute the earnings changes associated with sectoral productivity growth in manufacturing. He concludes that it is not productivity but other factors (interpreted as globalization) that explain most of the real wage reductions of less-skilled American workers during the 1970s. However, his analysis implies that globalization *raised* real wages of those who were less skilled during the 1980s—the period in which most of the increase in U.S. manufactures imports from LDCs occurred. In this context, Leamer points out that the prices of textiles and apparel relative to overall producer prices (a metric of what has happened to prices of less-skill-intensive manufactures) fell much more rapidly during 1973–81 than during 1953–73. However, as Leamer acknowledges, the fact that this metric has been stable since 1981 is a problem for the globalization story, in light of the timing of increased manufactures trade with LDCs. Another difficulty with Leamer's findings is that they are based on an unusual measure of the wage gap, which grew during the 1970s and contracted during the 1980s.[51]

Analysts have explored other developments. In particular, the HO model implies that if globalization were the driving force, the decline in the relative wage of less-skilled Americans should cause U.S. producers to use these workers more intensively. Instead, there appears to have been a shift toward using more skilled labor throughout the U.S. economy.[52] This shift is evident across different manufacturing industries and market sectors, including those market sectors that primarily produce goods and services that are not traded. It is also evident in subsidiaries of U.S. multinational corporations located in countries whose workers earn low wages.

Evidence from Factor Content Studies

As was discussed earlier, estimates of the implications of globalization for relative wages involve two key steps. The first is to estimate the effects on the supply of less-skilled workers relative to those who are more highly skilled. In addition, the effect on relative wages from changes in relative

prices. When computers are excluded, he fails to find a statistically significant relationship between changes in goods prices and skill intensity. When computers are included, his coefficient estimate has the wrong sign, suggesting that low-skill-intensive industries had larger price increases than other industries. The estimates are statistically insignificant for his sample of 143 domestic (wholesale) prices but strongly significant for his smaller samples of import prices (thirty industries) and export prices (twenty industries).

51. See Grossman comment on chapter 4 in this volume for a discussion of additional difficulties with this analysis.

52. See Berman, Bound, and Griliches (1994); Burtless (1996a); Lawrence (1996).

Table 1-6. *Factor Content Results: Effects of Trade and Immigration, 1980–90*

	Effects from		
	Trade	Immigration and trade	Memo
Relative labor supply			Elasticity[a]
Dropouts vs. all other	0.023	0.120	(–0.322)
High school vs. college educated	0.017	0.023	(–0.709)
Relative wages			Total change[b]
Dropouts vs. all other	–0.004	–0.039	(–0.08)
High school vs. college educated	–0.012	–0.016	(–0.18)

Source: Borjas, Freeman, and Katz (1996, table 3, pp. 249–50). See Katz and Murphy (1992) for definitions of high school and college equivalents.

a. Elasticities of relative wages to relative labor supplies were assumed to be –0.322 for dropouts relative to other workers and –0.709 for high school equivalents relative to college equivalents.

b. Total changes of relative wages from 1980 to 1990.

labor supplies can be calculated given an estimate of the elasticity that measures the responsiveness of relative wages to changes in such supplies. Factor content analyses can only provide an estimate of the effects of developments abroad under the assumption that technology and other determinants of trade flows remain unchanged. With this significant caveat in mind, results from these studies point to a modest role for trade and immigration, given reasonable assumptions about elasticities and the skill usage of manufacturing production.

This discussion focuses on the analysis by Borjas, Freeman, and Katz—hereafter referred to as BFK—summarized in Freeman (chapter 3 in this volume), because it includes effects from both trade and immigration for 1980–90.[53] As reported in table 1-6, BFK consider two definitions of less-skilled versus highly skilled workers: high school dropouts (DO) relative to all others (AO) and high school–educated workers (HS) relative to college-educated workers (CO).[54] First consider the implications of trade alone. BFK estimate that the factor content of net trade increased the relative supply of DO/AO and of HS/CO by roughly 2 percent. Although the results depend on particulars such as time period and definition of skill groups, other recent studies (including Sachs and Shatz in chapter 5) obtain a similar estimate of the effect of trade in manufacturing on the relative

53. Note that the calculations presented are actually reported in logarithms that are approximately equal to percentage changes.

54. These groups are defined in Katz and Murphy (1992).

supply of less-skilled workers.[55] An important exception is Wood.[56] As discussed above, his adjustments significantly increase the relative numbers of less-skilled workers embodied in U.S. trade flows but are unreasonably large.

Even though the effects of trade on relative labor supplies have been modest for the aggregate economy, they have been large in some sectors. For instance, in chapter 5, Sachs and Shatz find that while trade with LDCs reduced manufacturing employment by 5.7 percent overall between 1978 and 1990, it reduced manufacturing employment by 23.5 percent in the industries with the greatest usage of less-skilled workers relative to those who are highly skilled.[57]

The bottom panel of table 1-6 gives BFK's findings for wages. During 1980–90, relative wages of DO/AO and HS/CO fell by about 8 percent and 18 percent, respectively. Trade accounts for little of the declines in relative wages—only 0.4 and 1.2 percentage points of the total changes for high school dropouts and for workers with a high school diploma, respectively.

Estimates of the importance of trade are sensitive to which labor demand elasticity is used and to how the implied relative supply shift is measured. Despite similar estimates of the relative labor supply shift, Sachs and Shatz suggest that the effects from trade might have accounted for as much as 5 percentage points of the decline in relative wages for high school–educatedworkers. The difference comes primarily from their assumption that it is quite difficult to substitute between high- and low-skilled workers. The implied sensitivity of relative wages to changes in labor supply is thus unusually large.[58] Wood concludes that trade could explain all of the decline in the skill premium, because he compounds his huge estimate of the relative supply shift with a similarly large assumed sensitivity of relative wages.

Finally, as shown in table 1-6, BFK conclude that immigrants have increased the relative supply of less-skilled workers and that the shift was

55. Sachs and Shatz focus on the implications of trade for the relative supply of less-skilled workers in the nonmanufacturing sector.

56. Wood (1994, 1995, and comment on chapter 3 in this volume).

57. This breakdown is based on production and nonproduction workers as measures of less- and highly skilled workers. See also Lawrence, who uses the same trade data but defines skill categories based on education. Lawrence (1996, table 2.2).

58. Sachs and Shatz assume the elasticity of substitution between workers with a high school versus a college education is $1/3$ to $1/2$, implying an elasticity of relative wages to relative labor supply of 2–3. More standard among labor economists is an elasticity of substitution of about 1.5 and a wage elasticity of 0.7. See Katz and Murphy (1992, pp. 68–69).

dramatic for high school dropouts relative to other workers. The estimates imply that immigration and trade combined account for 1.6 percentage points of the 18 percentage point fall in relative wages of high school–educated workers. However, the heavy concentration of less-educated workers among recent immigrants implies that immigration and trade together explain roughly half of the 8 percentage point fall in relative wages of high school dropouts.

Other Evidence

Much of the discussion about the implications of increased U.S. interaction with developing-country trading partners suggests that initially high-wage American workers will experience wage declines, whereas initially low-wage, foreign workers will enjoy wage increases. In chapter 7, Revenga and Montenegro examine the experience of Mexican workers since the major Mexican trade liberalization of the mid-1980s.[59] One of their main findings is that after 1987, wages of nonproduction workers in Mexico rose much more rapidly than wages of production workers. Taking nonproduction workers as the more-skilled group, there appears to have been significantly more convergence between skilled U.S. and Mexican workers than between less-skilled workers in the two countries. They also argue that the convergence reflects rising Mexican wages, not falling American wages. Just as in the United States, Mexico has seen a sharp rise in the skill premium. Although there has been no decrease in the share of skilled workers within Mexican industries, this share has not increased, as it has in the United States. However, industries that are skill intensive have grown relatively rapidly in Mexico, so that there has been a shift toward more-skilled workers throughout the economy.

The "Bottom Line"

In sum, available evidence suggests that globalization (including trade and immigration) may explain 1 to 2 percentage points of the 18 percentage point overall change in wages for high school–educated workers relative to those who are college educated. Trade, and especially immigration, may account for much larger changes in the relative wages of the least-educated

59. To organize the data, they chose a Ricardian framework. Appropriately, this focuses on productivity differences across countries. It also allows for shifts in the ranges of goods produced and traded, but is less well suited to explaining wage differences among skill groups or industries.

Americans—those who did not complete high school. But the many problems with existing analyses imply that the jury is still out. In particular, existing evidence does not fully distinguish the effects of technical change from globalization and is based on highly restrictive assumptions about the channels through which increased international integration might influence U.S. labor markets. Once all of the pieces to the puzzle have been assembled, the role of globalization may turn out to have been more substantial.

What Role for Policy?

Concerns about the potential effects of increased global integration on American workers raise two sets of issues for policymakers. The first set of concerns relates to difficulties associated with adjusting to structural change. Evolution in economic opportunities—whether from technical innovations, international competition, or other factors—will cause some firms (and sectors) to thrive while others do poorly. Jobs are created as employers expand or companies are created, whereas jobs are eliminated as employers contract their labor force or go out of business. Although this churning of the economy is beneficial overall, those involuntarily displaced from their jobs shoulder a disproportionate share of the costs from adjustment. One important issue for policy is how to assist such displaced workers.

The second set of issues relates to the decline in relative earnings of less-skilled workers. Real wages have grown slowly overall and have actually fallen for many at the bottom of the earnings distribution. This has exacerbated labor market difficulties for displaced workers and reduced earnings prospects for many who are not displaced. Despite active debate over the extent to which international integration is to blame, there is considerable agreement about appropriate policy responses to address both sets of concerns.[60]

Rationales for Policy Intervention

The large wage premium earned by more-educated workers has prompted a significant rise in the share of Americans who complete high

60. Wood (1994) contains an excellent discussion of policy options in the context of globalization. See also Baily, Burtless, and Litan (1993); Lawrence (1996); Lawrence and Litan (1986).

school and go on to college. Over time, this labor supply response should go a long way to alleviating the apparent mismatch between the high demand for skilled workers relative to the available supply. But this adjustment mechanism primarily affects new entrants into the labor force. Moreover, not every worker can become highly skilled. Of particular concern are those with weak basic skills. There are four distinct rationales for intervention.

EFFICIENCY. Policymakers might seek to improve the efficiency with which productive resources, including workers, are used. Assistance programs can be designed to address market failures that slow reemployment or limit education and training opportunities. However, intervention should avoid reducing overall efficiency by prolonging periods of joblessness.

EQUITY. Displaced workers bear the costs from structural adjustments that benefit the economy overall. When displacements can be attributed to government trade or other policy, some argue that fairness dictates compensation. However, the affected groups are difficult to identify, and it is not obvious that they deserve special treatment. An alternative and perhaps more defensible position calls for assisting all workers unlucky enough to lose their jobs involuntarily, regardless of the cause. Broader equity considerations arise from growing earnings and family income inequality. Here again, views of fairness are varied and complex.

POLITICAL CONSIDERATIONS. Maintaining an open international trading system is both in the direct economic interest of the United States and an important means to promote healthy economies abroad. Government programs to assist those injured by trade may help to maintain the requisite political support—particularly if expense precludes more general assistance programs.

SOCIAL TENSIONS.[61] Poor earnings prospects for workers who are less skilled appear to have exacerbated the serious problems of crime, racial tension, and urban decay. To the extent that globalization has or is perceived to have contributed to adverse labor market conditions, trade and other international interactions can increase social strains. These issues raise the urgency of addressing such problems as declining earnings opportunities for many Americans who are less skilled.

Trade Policies

Economists remain divided in their assessment of precisely how much of the plight of less-skilled workers can be attributed to international

---

61. Concerns about social cohesion are emphasized in Wood (1994) and Rodrik (1997).

economic integration. What has received much less attention is the considerable agreement (illustrated among contributors to this volume) that protectionist trade policy would be a poor response. Analysts such as Leamer and Wood—who argue that globalization has been a major force in reducing the relative wage of less-skilled Americans—explicitly reject protection. Even Rodrik's provocative monograph, "Has Globalization Gone Too Far?", concludes that protection is not a solution.[62] This message is strongly echoed by those such as Freeman, Grossman, Sachs, and myself who conclude that trade has (or may have) had a "moderate" impact, and by those such as Bhagwati and Lawrence who conclude that trade has not been a significant factor.

The lack of support for trade policy responses should not be interpreted as a lack of concern about the difficulties faced by many American workers. This position grows out of an understanding that protecting domestic markets is a poor way to help workers who fear losing their jobs, or to raise the earnings of those who are less skilled.

There are many problems with trade protection as a means of assisting workers. First, it is expensive. Tariff and nontariff barriers (NTBs) work by reducing the supply of imports of particular goods, thereby typically raising domestic prices and production relative to what they would be in the absence of protection. Workers and capital owners in protected market sectors gain, at the expense of consumers who pay higher prices (and perhaps see less product diversity). A study estimating the effects of U.S. protection in twenty-one market sectors in 1990 concludes that "the consumer surplus loss per job saved is an astounding $170,000 per year. In other words, consumers pay over six times the average annual compensation of manufacturing workers to preserve jobs through import restraints."[63]

In addition, protection need not maintain overall industry employment. For example, trade barriers may encourage firms to undertake investments that improve competiveness and that shift production to more capital-intensive techniques. Even if industrywide employment is maintained, there is no presumption that *existing* jobs will be saved. Plant relocations and restructuring may result in the displacement of substantial numbers of those currently employed. Furthermore, many jobs saved in the protected industry are often offset by associated job losses in related industries. For

62. Rodrik argues that globalization contributes to social disintegration by exacerbating tensions among groups. He does not see protection as a solution because, in addition to its costs in terms of poor economic efficiency, it would generate its own set of social conflicts. Rodrik (1997, p. 72).

63. Hufbauer and Elliott (1994, p. 11).

example, trade protection that raises domestic steel prices reduces the competitiveness of industries, such as automobiles, that use steel. Similarly, higher apparel prices will tend to slow retail growth.[64]

For those unhappy about the extent of existing programs to assist displaced workers (or poor people), trade barriers may seem attractive. The associated costs are hidden and widely dispersed (through higher prices). No budget outlays are required. But lack of transparency is a poor justification for a policy choice that is both expensive and of limited effectiveness.

Assisting Displaced Workers

Individuals displaced from their jobs suffer substantial losses.[65] Income often declines in the months before actual job loss. Once permanently displaced, workers need significant amounts of time to find new jobs. A new job tends to pay lower wages—and this "earnings gap" (relative to earnings at the previous job) is persistent. Jacobson (chapter 11 in this volume) estimates the present value of the total earnings loss for the average displaced worker at $80,000, of which about $60,000 is due to lower earnings on the new job over the remaining years of work.[66]

Overall, the probability of becoming displaced appears to have been about the same in the early 1980s and the early 1990s (table 1-7). However, the composition of the displaced worker population has changed. Displacement probabilities have declined for blue-collar workers and for those under age thirty-five but have increased for white-collar workers and those who are older.

Displacement is not predominantly an international trade–related phenomenon. In chapter 10, Kletzer concludes that industries facing significant import competition do not have higher displacement rates on average. Nor do most displaced workers come from such industries. Overall, workers in industries with high import penetration are no more likely to be displaced than workers in other industries, although a few high-impact sectors such as apparel do have high rates of displacement.[67]

However, the evidence on whether workers displaced from import-competingindustries face greater hardships is mixed. Such workers take

64. Lawrence and Litan (1986) provide further discussion and examples.
65. For further discussion of the experiences of displaced workers, see Jacobson (chapter 11 in this volume); Kletzer (chapter 10 in this volume); U.S. Council of Economic Advisers (1997, esp. pp. 144–62); Farber (1993); Haveman (1993, 1994); Jacobson, LaLonde, and Sullivan (1993); Leigh (1995).
66. The material in this paragraph is drawn from Jacobson (see chapter 11).
67. Similarly, Haveman (1994) concludes that trade actually served to reduce the volume of job displacements in three of the nine years studied. His work uses a general equilibrium framework.

Table 1-7. *Changing Incidence of Displacement,*
1981–82, 1991–92

	Displacement rates[a]	
	1981–82	*1991–92*
Total	3.9	3.8
Occupations		
White collar	2.6	3.6
Blue collar	7.3	5.2
Age		
25–34	5.0	3.8
35–44	3.8	3.9
45–54	3.0	3.8
55+	3.6	4.3

Source: U.S. Council of Economic Advisers database (1996).

a. Displaced workers as a percentage of total workers. The sample includes only workers with three or more years of tenure in their current jobs.

longer to become reemployed and may have somewhat greater earnings losses.[68] In particular, Kletzer finds that workers displaced from import-sensitive industries do appear to have more difficulty in finding new jobs, but this result can be attributed to differences in worker characteristics. Workers displaced from import-sensitive industries are more likely to be female, younger, and less educated.

Like most other industrial-country governments, the United States maintains a variety of programs to assist displaced workers.[69] These include many types of "active" assistance, such as job search assistance (JSA), retraining, and career development programs to help displaced workers find new jobs and maintain their earnings. The programs also include forms of "passive" assistance such as unemployment insurance (UI), welfare, and earned income tax credits (EITCs), which make up America's social safety net.[70]

The focus of most policy interventions has been on the period between permanent displacement and reemployment—trying to both shorten the

68. Kletzer (chapter 10 in this volume) finds that "trade-displaced" workers do not have greater earnings losses, whereas Haveman (1993) finds that they do. Both authors conclude that this group has longer unemployment spells following displacement.

69. Compared with many other industrial countries, the United States devotes few government resources to either passive or active labor market interventions. For example, in terms of national incomes, Canada and Germany devote more than three times the amount the United States does. Japan devotes somewhat less than the United States. However, Japan has an extensive and well-developed training system that is integrated into the general educational system and actively involves private employers. Leigh (1995).

70. Leigh (1995) provides a useful summary and assessment of active and passive policies in the United States and other industrial economies.

spell of joblessness and increase earnings on the new job. Although the conventional wisdom once favored classroom training as a means to obtain these objectives, a main point of Jacobson's discussion in chapter 11 is that such training is expensive but offers little additional benefit compared with JSA.[71] Though the net payoffs from JSA are small, he concludes that they are cost effective. Similarly, Leigh concludes that the training programs that seem to work best are those delivered on the job or in worklike settings.[72] Employer involvement is also important in making sure that the skills being taught to workers in the training programs are marketable. However, it is difficult (and expensive) to design a program that helps *all* displaced workers, particularly those with weak basic skills.

Jacobson also argues that insurance schemes could be designed so as to better insure workers against the potentially large income losses associated with displacement. For instance, UI could be reoriented to provide greater support to those unemployed for long spells, but (perhaps) less support during the initial weeks of unemployment. Such changes appear to be unpopular, however.

A system of "earnings insurance" may be preferable as a means of mitigating income losses from displacement.[73] Unlike UI, this scheme would encourage displaced workers to become reemployed quickly by providing earnings supplements (a percentage of the earnings gap between the old and new jobs) for a fixed period following the date of displacement.[74] Similarly, an advantage to the EITC (an important part of the U.S. antipoverty effort) is that it appears to produce relatively little distortion of work incentives.[75]

Any of these programs could be general (available to all displaced workers) or targeted specifically at those injured by trade (or, more broadly, international integration). In fact, the United States has maintained a program of Trade Adjustment Assistance (TAA) since 1962 that provides supplementary assistance to those whose job loss is trade related. (See

---

71. JSA might include basic workshops on how to search for a job and a clearinghouse of information to help match job seekers with openings. One way to strengthen such a program would be to improve the current Employment Service (the U.S. government's primary job placement service for unemployed people). See Baily, Burtless, and Litan (1993); Leigh (1995).

72. Leigh (1995).

73. Baily, Burtless, and Litan (1993, pp. 194–97).

74. Lawrence and Litan suggest another innovative insurance scheme, designed to insure *communities* against significant declines in tax revenues that are not related to changes in tax policy. Lawrence and Litan (1986, pp. 119–22).

75. Eissa and Liebman (1995).

Destler and Jacobson in chapters 9 and 11, respectively, for descriptions and further discussion.) It is difficult to justify TAA in terms of efficiency or equity. Identifying which displacements are trade related is difficult, and it is not obvious that this group deserves special assistance. In addition, the increased benefits may slow reemployment.[76]

However, there may be an argument for TAA as a means of fostering support for an open trading system. Destler argues that although the program was too restrictive to play a significant role in the 1960s, it proved useful during the 1970s by helping to form a coalition that supported liberalization. Growing costs and questions about TAA's equity and efficiency led to significant cutbacks, and he concludes that the program played little role in recent trade debates.

Addressing Broader Concerns: Productivity and Equity

Though a full consideration of options is beyond the scope of this chapter, it is appropriate to conclude by outlining two ingredients of a promising policy response.[77] First, faster productivity growth is the key to raising average wages and living standards. Increasing U.S. investment rates will likely help boost productivity growth. Ideally, additional investments should be financed from domestic saving. In addition, improving the skills of workers at the bottom of the wage distribution would augment their earnings potential. It is particularly important to increase the occupational skills of workers without college degrees. Such an endeavor would be most effective if it involved a cooperative effort by the public sector (to ensure that schools adequately prepare youths for the workplace) and the private sector (to offer appropriate on-the-job training [OJT] opportunities).

References

Baily, Martin N., Gary Burtless, and Robert E. Litan, eds. 1993. *Growth with Equity: Economic Policymaking for the Next Century.* Brookings.
Belman, Dale, and Thea M. Lee. 1996. "International Trade and the Performance of U.S. Labor Markets." In *U.S. Trade Policy and Global Growth: New Directions in the International Economy,* edited by Robert A. Blecker, 61–104. Armonk, N.Y.: M. E. Sharpe for Economic Policy Institute.

---

76. For further discussion of the TAA Program, see Destler and Jacobson (chapters 9 and 11 in this volume); see also Lawrence and Litan (1986); Richardson (1982).

77. This discussion draws on Baily, Burtless, and Litan (1993), which provides additional details as well as policy options.

Berman, Eli, John Bound, and Zvi Griliches. 1994. "Changes in the Demand for Skilled Labor within U.S. Manufacturing: Evidence from the Annual Survey of Manufactures." *Quarterly Journal of Economics* 109 (May): 367–98.

Bhagwati, Jagdish N. 1991. "Free Traders and Free Immigrationists: Strangers or Friends?" Working Paper 20. New York: Russell Sage Foundation.

Bhagwati, Jagdish, and Vivek H. Dehejia. 1994. "Freer Trade and Wages of the Unskilled—Is Marx Striking Again?" In *Trade and Wages: Leveling Wages Down?* edited by Jagdish Bhagwati and Marvin H. Kosters, 36–75. Washington: American Enterprise Institute.

Blackburn, McKinley L., David E. Bloom, and Richard B. Freeman. 1990. "The Declining Economic Position of Less Skilled American Men." In *A Future of Lousy Jobs?* edited by Gary Burtless, 31–76. Brookings.

Borjas, George J. 1995. "The Economic Benefits from Immigration." *Journal of Economic Perspectives* 9 (2): 3–22.

Borjas, George J., and Valerie Ramey. 1994. "Time Series Evidence on the Sources of Trends in Wage Inequality." *American Economic Review* 84 (May): 10–16.

Borjas, George J., Richard B. Freeman, and Lawrence F. Katz. 1996. "Searching for the Effect of Immigration on the Labor Market." *American Economic Review* 86 (May): 246–51.

Bosworth, Barry, and George L. Perry. 1994. "Productivity and Real Wages: Is There a Puzzle?" *Brookings Papers on Economic Activity 1:* 317–35.

Bound, John, and George Johnson. 1992. "Changes in the Structure of Wages in the 1980s: An Evaluation of Alternative Explanations." *American Economic Review* 82 (June): 371–92.

———. 1995. "What Are the Causes of Rising Wage Inequality in the United States?" *Federal Reserve Bank of New York Economic Policy Review* 1 (January): 9–17.

Brainard, S. Lael, and David A. Riker. 1997. "Are U.S. Multinationals Exporting U.S. Jobs?" Working Paper 5958. Cambridge, Mass.: National Bureau of Economic Research.

Burtless, Gary. 1990. "Earnings Inequality over the Business and Demographic Cycles." In *A Future of Lousy Jobs? The Changing Structure of U.S. Wages,* edited by Gary Burtless, 77–117. Brookings.

———. 1995. "International Trade and the Rise in Earnings Inequality." *Journal of Economic Literature* 33 (June): 800–16.

———. 1996a. "Widening U.S. Income Inequality and the Growth in World Trade." *Tokyo Club Papers* 9: 129–60.

———. 1996b. "The Progress and Distribution of U.S. Living Standards, 1959–1995." Unpublished paper. The Brookings Institution.

Cline, William R. 1997. *Trade, Jobs, and Income Distribution.* Washington: Institute for International Economics.

Council for Economic Planning and Development. 1992. "Taiwan Statistical Data Book." Taiwan, Province of China.

Deardorff, Alan V. 1994. "Overview of the Stolper-Samuelson Theorem." In *The Stolper-Samuelson Theorem: A Golden Jubilee,* edited by Alan V. Deardorff, and Robert M. Stern, 7–34. University of Michigan Press.

Deardorff, Alan V., and Dalia S. Hakura. 1994. "Trade and Wages—What Are the Questions?" In *Trade and Wages: Leveling Wages Down?* edited by Jagdish Bhagwati and Marvin H. Kosters, 76–107. Washington: American Enterprise Institute.

Deardorff, Alan V., and Robert W. Staiger. 1988. "An Interpretation of the Factor Content of Trade." *Journal of International Economics* 24 (February): 93–107.

Eissa, Nada, and Jeffrey B. Liebman. 1995. "Labor Supply Response to the Earned Income Tax Credit." Working Paper 5158. Cambridge, Mass.: National Bureau of Economic Research.

Farber, Henry S. 1993. "The Incidence and Costs of Job Loss: 1982–91." *Brookings Papers on Economic Activity: Microeconomics* 1: 73–119.

———. 1996. "The Changing Face of Job Loss in the United States, 1981–1993." Working Paper 5596. Cambridge, Mass.: National Bureau of Economic Research.

———. 1995. "Are Your Wages Set in Beijing?" *Journal of Economic Perspectives* 9 (Summer): 15–32.

Feenstra, Robert C., and Gordon H. Hanson. 1996a. "Globalization, Outsourcing, and Wage Inequality." *American Economic Review* 86 (May): 240–45.

———. 1996b. "Foreign Investment, Outsourcing and Relative Wages." In *Political Economy of Trade Policy: Essays in Honor of Jagdish Bhagwati,* edited by Robert C. Feenstra, Gene M. Grossman, and Douglas A. Irwin, 89–127. MIT Press.

Freeman, Richard B., and Lawrence F. Katz. 1995. "Introduction and Summary." In *Differences and Changes in Wage Structures,* 1–22. National Bureau of Economic Research and University of Chicago Press.

Friedberg, Rachel M., and Jennifer Hunt. 1995. "The Impact of Immigrants on Host Country Wages, Employment, and Growth." *Journal of Economic Perspectives* 9 (2): 23–44.

GATT. Various years. *International Trade.* Geneva.

Golub, Stephen S. 1997a. "International Labor Standards and International Trade." IMF Working Paper WP/97/37. Washington: International Monetary Fund (April).

———. 1997b. "Globalization, Technological Change, and the Welfare State: The Political Economy of International Labor Standards." Paper prepared for Third Annual Conference of the Economic Studies Program, American Institute for Contemporary German Studies. Johns Hopkins University, Washington, D.C.

Gottschalk, Peter, and Robert Moffitt. 1994. "The Growth of Earnings Instability in the U.S. Labor Market." *Brookings Papers on Economic Activity 2:* 217–54.

Gottschalk, Peter, and Timothy M. Smeeding. 1997. "Cross-National Comparisons of Earnings and Income Inequality." *Journal of Economic Literature* 35 (June): 633–87.

Grossman, Gene M. 1987. "The Employment and Wage Effects of Import Competition in the United States." *Journal of International Economic Integration* 2: 1–23.

Haveman, Jon D. 1993. "The Effect of Trade-Induced Displacement on Unemployment and Wages." CIBER Working Paper 93-108. Lafayette, Ind.: Purdue University.

———. 1994. "The Influence of Changing Trade Patterns on Displacements of Labor." CIBER Working Paper 94-012. Lafayette, Ind.: Purdue University.

Hufbauer, Gary Clyde, and Kimberly Ann Elliott. 1994. *Measuring the Costs of Protection in the United States.* Washington: Institute for International Economics.

International Labour Organization. 1960–95. *Yearbook of Labour Statistics.* Geneva.

International Monetary Fund. 1977. *Direction of Trade Statistics Yearbook.*
———. 1987. *Direction of Trade Statistics Yearbook.*
———. 1992. "Issues and Developments in International Trade Policy." *World Economic and Financial Surveys,* 40–49.
———. 1996. *Direction of Trade Statistics Yearbook.*
———. Various years. *International Financial Statistics.*
Jacobson, Louis, Robert LaLonde, and Daniel Sullivan. 1993. *The Costs of Worker Dislocation.* Kalamazoo, Mich.: Upjohn Institute for Employment Research.
Katz, Lawrence F., and Kevin Murphy. 1992. "Changes in Relative Wages 1963–87: Supply and Demand Factors." *Quarterly Journal of Economics* 107 (February): 35–78.
Kosters, Marvin H. 1994. "An Overview of Changing Wage Patterns in the Labor Market." In *Trade and Wages: Leveling Wages Down?* edited by Jagdish Bhagwati, and Marvin H. Kosters, 1–35. Washington: American Enterprise Institute.
Krugman, Paul. 1995a. "Growing World Trade: Causes and Consequences." *Brookings Papers on Economic Activity 1:* 327–77.
———. 1995b. "Technology, Trade, and Factor Prices." Working Paper 5355. Cambridge, Mass.: National Bureau of Economic Research.
Krugman, Paul, and Robert Z. Lawrence. 1994. "Trade, Jobs, and Wages." *Scientific American* 270: 22–27.
Lawrence, Robert Z. 1996. *Single World, Divided Nations? International Trade and OECD Labor Markets.* Brookings.
Lawrence, Robert Z., and Robert E. Litan. 1986. *Saving Free Trade: A Pragmatic Approach.* Brookings.
Lawrence, Robert Z., and Matthew J. Slaughter. 1993. "International Trade and American Wages in the 1980s: Giant Sucking Sound or Small Hiccup?" *Brookings Papers on Economic Activity: Microeconomics* 2: 161–210.
Leamer, Edward E. 1994. "Trade, Wages, and Revolving-Door Ideas." Working Paper 4716. Cambridge, Mass.: National Bureau of Economic Research.
———. 1996. "What's the Use of Factor Contents?" Working Paper 5448. Cambridge, Mass.: National Bureau of Economic Research.
Leigh, Duane. 1995. *Assisting Workers Displaced by Structural Change.* Kalamazoo, Mich.: Upjohn Institute for Employment Research.
Levy, Frank, and Richard J. Murnane. 1992. "U.S. Earnings Levels and Earnings Inequality: A Review of Recent Trends and Proposed Explanations." *Journal of Economic Literature* 30 (September): 1333–81.
Mishel, Lawrence, and Jared Bernstein. 1994. "Is the Technology Black Box Empty? An Empirical Examination of the Impact of Technology on Wage Inequality and Employment Structure." Washington: Economic Policy Institute.
Murphy, Kevin M., and Finis Welch. 1991. "The Role of International Trade in Wage Differentials." In *Workers and Their Wages: Changing Patterns in the United States,* edited by Marvin H. Kosters, 38–69. Washington: American Enterprise Institute.
Organization for Economic Cooperation and Development. 1977. OECD data bank. Paris.
Revenga, Ana L. 1992. "Exporting Jobs: The Impact of Import Competition on Employment and Wages in U.S. Manufacturing." *Quarterly Journal of Economics* 107 (February): 255–84.
Richardson, J. David. 1982. "Trade Adjustment Assistance under the United States Trade Act of 1974: An Analytical Examination and Worker Survey." In *Import*

Competition and Response, edited by Jagdish N. Bhagwati, 321–57. National Bureau of Economic Research Conference Report. University of Chicago Press.

———. 1995. "Income Inequality and Trade: How to Think, What to Conclude." *Journal of Economic Perspectives* 9 (Summer): 33–55.

Rodrik, Dani. 1994. "The Rush to Free Trade in the Developing World: Why So Late? Why Now? Will It Last?" In *Voting for Reform: Democracy, Political Liberalization, and Economic Adjustment,* edited by Stephen Haggard and Steven B. Webb. Oxford University Press.

———. 1997. *Has Globalization Gone Too Far?* Washington: Institute for International Economics.

Sachs, Jeffrey D., and Howard J. Shatz. 1994. "Trade and Jobs in U.S. Manufacturing." *Brookings Papers on Economic Activity 1:* 1–84.

———. 1996. "U.S. Trade with Developing Countries and Wage Inequality." *American Economic Review* 86 (May): 234–39.

Sachs, Jeffrey D., and Andrew Warner. 1995. "Economic Reform and the Process of Global Integration." *Brookings Papers on Economic Activity 1:* 1–118.

U.S. Bureau of Labor Statistics. 1996. *International Comparisons of Hourly Compensation Costs for Production Workers in Manufacturing, 1995.* Report 909 (September).

U.S. Council of Economic Advisers. 1996. *Job Creation and Employment Opportunities: The United States Labor Market, 1993–1996.* Report by the Council of Economic Advisers with the U.S. Department of Labor, Office of the Chief Economist (April).

———. 1997. *Economic Report of the President.*

U.S. Department of Labor. 1996. "International Comparison of Hourly Compensation Costs for Production Workers in Manufacturing, 1995." Bureau of Labor Statistics, Report 909, September.

Wood, Adrian. 1994. *North-South Trade, Employment, and Inequality.* New York: Oxford University Press.

———. 1995. "How Trade Hurt Unskilled Workers." *Journal of Economic Perspectives* 9 (Summer): 57–80.

The World Bank. 1987. *World Development Report 1987.* Oxford University Press for the World Bank.

———. 1997. *World Development Report 1997.* Oxford University Press for the World Bank.

———. *World Development Indicators.* Washington, D.C.: World Bank.

World Trade Organization. 1996. *Annual Report 1996.* Vol. 2. Geneva.

Part Two

METHODOLOGY AND EVIDENCE

TWO

Trade and Wages:
A Malign Relationship?

Jagdish Bhagwati

THE DECLINE in real wages of unskilled workers in the United States during the 1980s, and the increase instead in the unemployment of such workers in Europe (due to the comparative inflexibility of European labor markets vis-à-vis those of the United States), has prompted a search for possible explanations.[1] This search has become more acute in light of evidence that the adverse trend for unskilled workers has not yet been mitigated in the 1990s.

I thank Manmohan Agarwal, Don Davis, Vivek Dehejia, Bill Dickens, Robert Feenstra, Marvin Kosters, Robert Lawrence, Edward Leamer, Jacob Mincer, Arvind Panagariya, T. N. Srinivasan, and Martin Wolf for their helpful comments. Susan Collins deserves special thanks for many careful and constructive suggestions. A first draft of this paper was completed in February 1995 and revisions finalized in October 1995.

1. Note that this contrast between the United States and Europe is just that. It is supposed to explain only the differential impact of technical change, trade, and the like on wages in one country and on unemployment in the other. This labor market explanation is almost a cliché by now, having been propounded by virtually every economist who has spoken on the issue in the last several years. Among the more recent writings on the subject are popular pieces by Paul Krugman, me, and many others. Inflexible and hence distortion-characterized labor markets can be modeled in alternative ways, either as Brecher (1974a, 1974b) economies with a uniform, across-all-sectors, minimum-real-wage floor, or as relevant only to the modern sector in a dualistic economy. In the latter case, we can model the modern sector as

49

The political leadership in both the the United States and the European Union (EU) has also become more alert to the potential explosiveness of this issue. President Clinton, at a White House ceremony to gather support for the Uruguay Round ratification by Congress, focused solely on it. He emphatically stated that although Americans were worried about the effects of trade on their wages and jobs, trade was "not the cause but rather the solution" (indeed, "the only solution") to their problems. This was great politics, of course, but—as the disagreements among economists in this book suggest—not necessarily great economics as well.

Of course, the president, like Jacques Delors and others in Europe who fear competition from the so-called Asian ants (alluding to Aesop's fable of the grasshopper and the ant), was speaking to the preferred explanation (or the haunting fear) of the unions and of many policymakers that international trade is a principal source of the pressures that translate into declining wages and unemployment of unskilled workers. As a colleague and I have written elsewhere, "Is Marx striking again?" Perhaps we should have added, "with the aid of Samuelson." The principal reason why many think that trade may be harming real wages of unskilled workers is the early postwar work of Paul Samuelson on factor price equalization (FPE) and, more directly, on the Stolper-Samuelson theorem that bears immediately on the issue at hand (though, as I argue here, one can develop an altogether new argument as to why trade may be exercising a downward pressure on real wages because of increased volatility of what I call the "kaleidoscopic comparative advantage" that has now emerged in the world economy).[2]

I have earlier examined the question of alternative trade explanations, and then again at great length.[3] My conclusion was that the Samuelson-type trade explanation is exceptionally weak for the 1980s and that there are good theoretical and empirical reasons why this is so.

---

subject to trade union–set rigidities or government-set minimum wages, with the former in turn being modeled in alternative ways and, in turn, combined with different equilibrating intersectoral labor market mechanisms such as in the Harris-Todaro (1970) model. In Bhagwati and Dehejia (1994) and Bhagwati (1995a), the effect of unions has already been formally discussed. Davis (1995) has more recently used the Brecher-economy model instead in an ingenious way.

2. Samuelson (1948, 1949); Stolper and Samuelson (1941). Strictly speaking, the Stolper-Samuelson argument relates the decline in real wages of unskilled workers to decline in the relative price of products producted by unskilled-labor-intensive work. The FPE argument, centrally related to the Heckscher-Ohlin (HO) theory, links the decline in the relative price of unskilled-labor-intensive goods to free trade with countries with abundant unskilled labor.

3. Bhagwati (1991b); Bhagwati and Dehejia (1994). Additional insights may be found in Bhagwati (1994, 1995a, and 1995b).

In this chapter, I recapitulate, elaborate, and evaluate the main linkages that have been advanced between trade and real wages, extending the argument well beyond that presented in our longer paper, in light of further empirical research and theoretical reflections that have emerged since.[4] The two chapters are therefore best read together and in the sequence in which they were written.

Clarifications and Caveats

At the outset, let me clarify a few things and state a few caveats.

First, as Deardorff and Hakura have pointed out, it is necessary to be clear about the theoretical question one is asking.[5] In particular, let me note two different questions, the first of which I address in this chapter.

Question 1: Will the freeing of trade, or an exogenous change abroad, adversely affect the real wages of unskilled workers?[6] The empirical counterpart of this question, of course, is whether this happened during the 1980s and since.

Question 2: If domestic technical change is driving down the real wages of unskilled workers, would the adverse effect on real wages be dampened or amplified if the economy were characterized by free trade rather than by protection?

It is clear that the former is the policy question that we are asking today. Thus, the question during the North American Free Trade Agreement (NAFTA) debate was whether freer trade with Mexico would adversely affect wages of unskilled workers in the United States. When we look at the 1980s, we want to know whether the emergence of developing countries in world trade (with or without rich-country liberalization) has done damage to the real wages of unskilled workers in these rich countries.

A second key point is that if we are to assert that the emergence of the poor countries in world trade is the cause of the declining real wages of unskilled workers in the rich countries, then the intermediating mechanism in conventional general equilibrium price theory models has to be (as argued in the analysis in the next section of this chapter) a decline in the relative prices of the unskilled-labor-intensive importables. If the goods prices

4. Bhagwati and Dehejia (1994).
5. Deardorff and Hakura (1994).
6. Such an exogenous change abroad would, generally speaking, shift the foreign offer curve facing us, and hence the equilibrium terms of trade and the factor rewards that are to be explained.

Figure 2-1

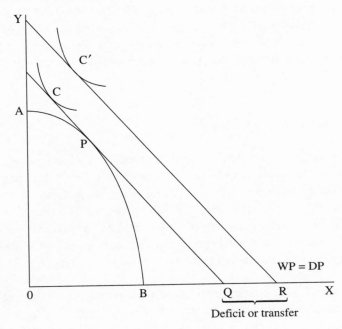

Deficit or transfer

have not changed as required, then it is impossible to logically sustain the argument that trade with poor countries is the cause of the phenomenon we seek to explain.

Keeping in mind what I discuss in the next section, this appears to me to be the case. This is especially so in the face of arguments in the United States such as the one stating that the *trade deficit* in the 1980s must have had an impact on real wages because we have a good correlation between its size and the real-wage decline and because imports are unskilled labor intensive. But the explanation is not compelling, unless it is simultaneously shown that the transfer has been attended by a decline in the (relative) prices of the unskilled-labor-intensive goods: an intermediate step in formal analysis, without which we cannot get from the alleged cause to the observed effect. The required decline in the relevant goods prices cannot simply be assumed, implicitly or explicitly, as having happened!

As demonstrated in figure 2-1, it is perfectly possible for an inward or outward transfer (that is, a trade deficit or surplus) to have no impact at all on the terms of trade, and hence no impact on real wages.[7] In the figure, AB is the production possibility curve defined over traded goods X and Y. The given world prices, equal to domestic prices under assumed free trade, are given by QR, which determines domestic production at P and national income, measured in good X, at OQ. Consumption then is at C. Assume now an inward transfer, equal to the trade deficit, of QR. Added to the national income OQ, the transfer implies that the national expenditure has now increased from OQ to OR. At the given goods prices, it then leads to consumption at C'. Note that the absorption of the transfer QR has led (by assumption, of course) to no change in the goods price ratio QR. Hence, there is no change in factor prices either (because, as I argue here, the two are related—given technology, as shown by Paul Samuelson). Neither the trade deficit, nor increase therein, nor the associated increase in imports (whether unskilled labor intensive or not) has any impact whatsoever on the real wages of productive factors in this construct.

Indeed, as Deardorff and Hakura point out, the problem with many of the empirical studies of the relationship between trade and wages, including the ones cited most often, is that the relationships estimated between alleged causes and effects have not been grounded in well-specified models whose validity is then tested as it should be.[8] As I argue here, the factor content calculations for the United States that were held to show the adverse impact were not undertaken in the context of a clear model. This would have enabled the investigators to see immediately that they should also test whether the goods prices behaved in the manner required by their inference. I therefore agree with these authors that many of the current empirical studies are often tantalizing, but leave one with no plausible conclusions.[9]

Alternative Theoretical Approaches

I now distinguish among several theoretical approaches that can be taken to the problem, several to be found in the literature to date, probing them in

7. Of course, there are numerous ways in which transfers *can* affect goods prices (that is, the terms of trade); see any graduate-level textbook, such as Bhagwati and Srinivasan (1983, chapter 12). The point in the text is that they need not. Any analysis that assumes that they must have (and that too in a particular direction), just because real wages of unskilled workers fell and imports are unskilled labor intensive, is not acceptable.

8. Deardorff and Hakura (1994).

9. My critique of the Borjas-Ramey (1994) paper in the next section is similar in spirit.

some depth both from the analytical viewpoint and also in regard to their consonance with the facts as I see them.

Economywide, North-South (Stolper-Samuelson) Explanation

Prices of unskilled-labor-intensive goods have fallen and caused the real wages of such labor to fall, in turn. Most economists' favorite explanation has been that increased trade with the South (that is, poor countries) has led to the fall in the real wages of unskilled workers (L_u) in the North (that is, rich countries).

In essence, the argument proceeds as follows, though it is only implicit in many of the writings on the problem. Take two polar cases. First, consider the case where the primary change comes from the South liberalizing trade or experiencing trade-expanding growth. Next, consider the case where the primary change comes instead from the North liberalizing its trade. (In reality, the North also experiences growth due to "fundamentals" such as technical change.) Thus, observed trade of the North with the South can increase for reasons other than growth or trade liberalization in the South (the first-case scenario) and trade liberalization in the North (the second-case scenario). I consider the case of technical change in the North in depth in the context of the critique of writings by Adrian Wood, George Borjas, and Valerie Ramey.[10]

Figure 2-2 considers the first case, where the change comes from the South. The initial offer curve of the South, offering L_u-intensive exports, is S. It intersects with the offer curve of the North, which exports skilled-labor (L_s)-intensive goods. OF would then be the world terms of trade (and hence the domestic goods prices in the North and the South as well if they had free trade). Now, assume that the South's offer curve expands to S' and the world terms of trade shift to OF'. This means that the world price of L_u-intensive goods has fallen. This, in turn, means that in the "passive" North the domestic prices of these goods would have fallen too.

Figure 2-3 shows the other polar case where the removal or reduction of the North's own tariffs is the initiating change. Here, the offer curve of the North shifts from N to N'. The world terms of trade increase in favor of the L_u-intensive goods from OF to OF', instead of falling. But because tariffs in the North have fallen, their domestic prices will fall (except in the paradoxical "Metzler" case, where the terms of trade worsen more than the tariffs fall).

In both cases, the effect would be to reduce the domestic prices of the L_u-intensive goods in the North. From there, the argument proceeds by deducing (with Stolper and Samuelson, as discussed later in this chapter)

10. Wood (1994); Borjas and Ramey (1994).

Figure 2-2

Unskilled
labor-intensive
goods
(south—exports
north—imports)

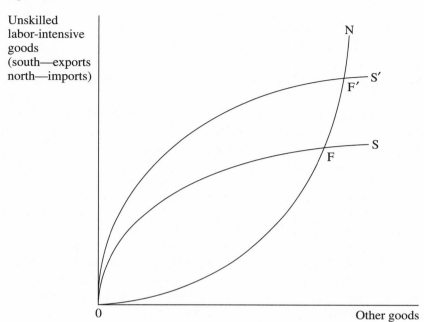

0   Other goods

Figure 2-3

Unskilled
labor-intensive
goods
(south—exports
north—imports)

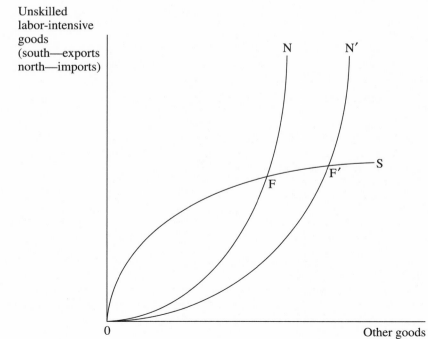

0   Other goods

that the real wages of L_u must therefore fall. The critical element then is that the domestic prices of L_u-intensive goods fall in the North, not that their world prices do. Also, as in the first case, this can be a consequence not of liberalization by the North, but of trade liberalization by the South or (even more tellingly) of simple trade-expanding growth by the South.[11] Hence, the concern that trade with the poor countries drives down the real wages of unskilled workers in the rich countries is one that can arise, not only in the context of liberalizing trade with the South (as in the case of NAFTA), but also in the context of the expansion of such trade at any given level of trade barriers.

GOODS PRICES AND FACTOR PRICES. A critical intermediating step for both cases leading to a fall in the real wages of unskilled workers in the North is that the domestic prices of the goods using unskilled labor should have fallen, as I first noted in 1990 when reviewing a paper in draft by Borjas and others.[12] The authors argued that trade was the cause of the decline in real wages, but they had not examined the behavior of goods prices.[13]

Thus, in general equilibrium in figure 2-4 there is the familiar Samuelson relationship between goods prices (P_x/P_y) and factor prices or the "wage differential" (W_u/W_s) in the right quadrant, and the Stolper-Samuelson relationship between the goods prices and the real wage of unskilled labor in the left quadrant (assuming, as explained later in this chapter, that the economy is incompletely specialized in production). Each half of figure 2-4, while familiar to students of trade theory, can be intuitively explained.

The Samuelson half of the diagram follows from the convexity of X and Y isoquants, cost minimization, and the assumption that, at every factor price ratio imaginable, X is L_s intensive and Y is L_u intensive.[14] Then, it is quite intuitive that, if unskilled labor (L_u) becomes more expensive (that is,

11. As we know from the massive trade and growth literature inspired by Harry Johnson in the 1960s, growth can also be trade reducing, at constant goods prices. My own assumptions are that this is unlikely.

12. Borjas and others (1992). Richard Freeman and I were both spending a year at the Russell Sage Foundation in New York. The Borjas-Freeman-Katz paper was mentioned to me by Eric Wanner, president of the foundation, over lunch in November 1990, and then a draft was given to me by Freeman. I had been working on a long essay on the relationship between free trade and free immigration in theory and in history (which became Bhagwati [1991a]).

13. See the detailed critique in Bhagwati (1991a, 1991b), and subsequently in Bhagwati and Dehejia (1994).

14. That is, the factor-intensity ranking of the two goods is invariant to changes in the factor price ratio. When it is not, the curve in the Samuelson half of the

Figure 2-4

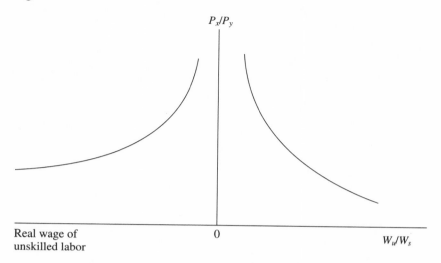

it goes further down the horizontal axis marked W_u/W_s), the price of the good using L_u intensively (that is, good Y) will rise, so that P_x/P_y will fall, pushing the curve down the vertical axis. Hence the curve tracing the relationship between P_x/P_y and W_u/W_s is monotonically falling from left to right.

The Stolper-Samuelson half of the diagram is better understood in light of the discussion of figures 2-5 and 2-6. But its essence can be understood by noting that the real wage of a productive factor in terms of a good, in competitive equilibrium, is nothing other than the marginal physical product of that factor in producing that good. When Wu/Ws falls, the factor proportions U/S rise in each good's production. Therefore, the marginal physical product of unskilled labor (U) falls in terms of every good, and unambiguously, regardless of what the factor consumes.[15] This means that, as the left-hand-side, Stolper-Samuelson half of figure 2-4 shows, the real

---

diagram will curl back on itself. This is the case where factor-intensity rankings are "reversible" and the unique relationship between goods and factor prices breaks down.

15. Note that I use the phrase "in every good." This presupposes that every good is being produced in equilibrium. When the economy is completely specialized, the argument breaks down. Instead of the real wage of one factor falling and the other correspondingly rising, both factors can improve their real wages, as I argue later in this chapter.

Figure 2-5

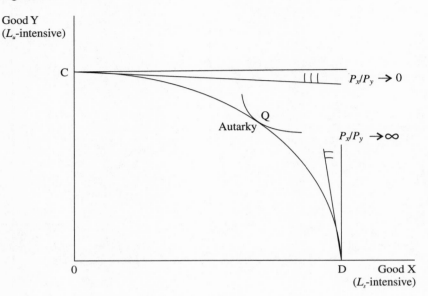

Figure 2-6

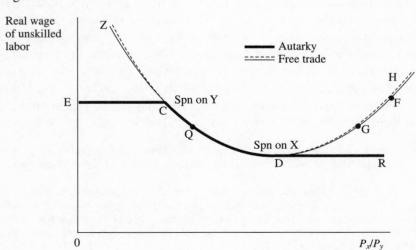

wage of unskilled labor also falls unambiguously as W_u/W_s falls (and P_x/P_y rises in the Samuelson half of figure 2-4).

Evidently, then, the real wage of unskilled workers cannot fall unless the relative price of the good that is intensively using unskilled labor has fallen. Note that, as I argue here, this analytical necessity has nothing to do with what happens to quantities (of imports, production, consumption, and the like).

Having then examined the terms of trade data for U.S. exports and imports of manufactures and finding that they showed a slight rise in the relative prices of imports, I conjectured that the domestic goods prices of the unskilled-labor-intensive goods may have actually risen rather than fallen, as required by their conclusion.[16] If so, the influential Borjas-Freeman-Katz study was flawed, not merely in its analytical methodology (which failed to note the key role of change in goods prices in the argumentation), but, I also feared, in its empirical conclusion linking real wage decline to trade (in the Stolper-Samuelson fashion).

The detailed and careful empirical investigation by Lawrence and Slaughter that followed my papers did confirm my conjecture for the United States.[17] The subsequent article by Sachs and Shatz appears to overturn the Lawrence-Slaughter findings.[18] However, it does not do anything of the kind. At the outset, it relies on removing from the data set the prices of computers, a procedure that is inadequately defended by the authors. And, even then, the new data set yields a coefficient of the required sign that is both quite small and statistically insignificant.[19] Some accounts by well-known journalists in the *Financial Times* and the *Economist,* misled no doubt by hasty reading, have reported this finding without realizing (if I may be permitted some levity) that, although Noam Chomsky correctly argues that two negatives make a positive in every human language (whereas two positives do not make a negative in any), the two

16. Bhagwati (1991a).

17. Lawrence and Slaughter (1993); Bhagwati (1991a, 1991b).

18. Sachs and Shatz (1994).

19. Thus, Sachs and Shatz estimate the following equation, dummying out for computers (p. 38):

The change in price =
$$0.04 - 0.02 \text{ low-skill intensity} - 0.02 \text{ computer dummy}, \quad R^2 = -0.03$$
$$(1.47) \qquad (-0.62) \qquad\qquad\qquad (-1.04)$$

The parentheses under the coefficients represent *t*-statistics. Note that none of the variables are significant. The authors note that these results are "less than robust" (p. 36) while arguing that they are in the "right" direction.

negatives of a small coefficient (and a statistically insignificant one to boot) do not add up to a positive support for this contention.[20]

Lawrence notes this and also reports that the goods price behavior in Germany and Japan, with and without computers, does not support the trade explanation either.[21] Besides, the shifts in factor ratios also do not support the explanation for the U.S. data, according to Lawrence and others.

In short, the necessary empirical evidence on price behavior during the 1980s for the absolutely critical element in *this* particular trade explanation—though I must qualify the argument for the distinction that I draw here between "gross" and "net" goods price change when more than one parametric or policy change is at work—is currently nonexistent, whereas the price evidence in the contrary direction seems to be quite robust indeed.[22] Perhaps this Lawrence-Slaughter conclusion will be overturned by further work; as of now, it has survived scrutiny. Even the further empirical work on estimating goods prices for the United States, by Leamer in chapter 4 of this book, confirms that the 1980s are *not* characterized by the behavior required to get the Stolper-Samuelson argument off the ground.[23] This evidence, carefully marshalled by scholars respected for their careful empirical work, is then the crux of the scientific skepticism that meets the Samuelson-type argument linking the decline in real wages in the North to their trade with the South.[24]

20. The latest victims were the excellent *Financial Times* journalists Stephanie Flanders and Martin Wolf, prompting me to write a letter to the editor arguing that nothing of the sort claimed by the cited authors had been demonstrated.

21. Lawrence (1994).

22. On the other hand, I find it difficult to accept the wholly different argument leveled against the trade-and-wages pessimists, advanced by even eminent authors, that trade from developing countries is such a small proportion of total trade, or that the import ratio is so small, that we cannot have the tail wagging the dog. In economics, however, the tail *does* wag the dog; prices are determined at the margin. The volume of transactions has no intrinsic meaning in itself. Indeed, the mere threat of a transaction in an integrated market, without any transactions occurring, can change a price.

23. Leamer finds that the prices did behave as required *before* the 1980s. Could we then have a delayed impact on the real wage of unskilled labor during the 1980s, even though 1980s prices behaved perversely? The trouble is that, if this idea is formalized, there is still no obvious relief. Suppose we argue that it takes time for labor to move out of the adversely affected import-competing industries. Then its real wage will decline even more precipitously in these industries right away, with the impact *reducing* as labor moves out of them into other industries. The impact on average real wages for the entire economy could then well have been to fall before the 1980s and then to rise during the 1980s.

24. As this book goes to press, Sachs and Shatz, whose earlier results published by Brookings were noted above, have produced new results presented in chapter 5

GOODS PRICES AND REAL WAGES. Besides, even if the goods prices were behaving as required, the conclusion that the result would be a decline in the *real* wage of unskilled labor requires *added* assumptions familiar to the students of the Stolper-Samuelsontheorem, many of which can be violated in the real world.[25] I recount some of the main arguments pertinent here. We should recall that the "core" Stolper-Samuelson theorem, in its simplest 2 × 2 version, says simply that the real wage of the factor employed intensively in the good whose price has fallen will also fall unequivocally, whereas (by the same logic) the other factor's real wage will rise unequivocally.

This core proposition (as also the FPE theorem, of course, which requires a unique relationship between goods and factor prices to deduce FPE from goods price equalization) fails as soon as one gets complete specialization (that is, nondiversification) in production. *Both* factors will improve their real wages as goods prices change further, lifting both boats rather than sinking one as the other symmetrically rises. The goods prices may change sufficiently to have the *lifting-all-boats* effect outweigh the *redistributive* effect embodied in the Stolper-Samuelson argument, leaving both factors better off than before. Even when the price of unskilled-labor-intensive imports has declined (as it does not appear to have done during the 1980s), the real wage of unskilled labor could have improved, if the goods price change was substantial enough to produce the nondiversification (that is, specialization in production on one of the two goods, and a sufficiently large lifting-all-boats effect).

To see this, consider figures 2-5 and 2-6. The real wage of unskilled labor (in terms of a mix of both goods, X and Y), is mapped out in these matching figures for different goods price ratios P_x/P_y, given the supply of unskilled and skilled labor, assuming that good X is L_s intensive while good Y is L_u intensive. Two cases are distinguished: one is autarky, the other is free trade.

---

of this book. Lawrence, in his comment on chapter 5, argues convincingly that the authors have not overturned the Lawrence-Salughter-Leamer results for the 1980s, the critical period. I would add that the proposed shift to and measurement of value-added prices is also a theoretically tricky one and must be carefully handled, as trade theorists know from the extensive theoretical literature on effective rates of protection. Finally, the authors' argument that it is possible for factor prices to change without goods prices changing (if factor supplies change, for instance) is true but obvious. From Paul Samuelson's work we know that complete specialization, for example, kills the unique relationship between goods and factor prices.

25. Bhagwati and Dehejia (1994).

First, in figure 2-5, assume autarky and lower Px/Py continuously, taking equilibrium production from D to C. Because good X is assumed to be intensive in the use of skilled labor, *Ls,* the (relative) factor price of unskilled labor (that is, W_u/W_s) rises, and that of skilled labor falls, as P_x/P_y falls successively and takes the economy's production from D to C; this is seen readily from the Samuelson half of figure 2-4. As discussed by reference to figure 2-4, then the real wage of unskilled labor rises unambiguously from D to C as P_x/P_y falls, implying that the real wage of unskilled labor rises with the rise of the price of the good Y that uses unskilled labor intensively.

Under autarky, production must equal consumption; the range DC thus defines all the real-wage variations that are possible under autarky. As depicted in figure 2-6, ECQDR is the thick-lined curve linking the real wage of unskilled labor to alternative goods price ratios under autarky. The real wage does not change, once complete specialization is reached at C and at D; further variations in Px/Py leave production specialized at these points, at maximum levels feasible.

Next, under free trade, production is no longer equal to consumption. Therefore it is now possible to specialize in production at D and at C and to trade from there at P_x/P_y higher than DS and below CV, respectively.[26] Correspondingly, the real wage will now improve for *both* factors, and unskilled labor at both D and C as P_x/P_y therefore varies further. The free-trade curve in figure 2-6 is therefore ZCDH.

It follows that:

—CD is the range over which the conventional Stolper-Samuelson redistributive effect, leading to a fall in the real wage of one factor and a rise in that of the other factor, operates;

—The real wage of unskilled labor will fall (in figure 2-6) from equilibrium production in autarky at Q when free trade reduces the relative price of good Y that uses unskilled labor intensively (that is, P_x/P_y rises). This fall in real wage will continue as P_x/P_y rises to when specialization in L_s-intensive good X emerges at D; but

—For P_x/P_y improving *beyond* that, the real wage of unskilled labor will bounce back, improving up to G(=Q) and then beyond to *improvement over autarky* and even to F(=C) and even beyond to levels that exceed the best real wage achievable under autarky.

26. DS is the goods price ratio tangent to the production possibility curve CD at D, and hence the minimum price ratio P_x/P_y at which the economy reaches specialization on good X. Similarly, CV is the maximum price ratio Px/Py at which the economy specializes on good Y.

If we are indeed in this ballpark, in ranges of real wages along DGFH in figure 2-6 that obtain when complete specialization on Y, and away from X, has been reached, then of course it becomes critical to know what the consumption patterns are. That is, as terms of trade continue to improve beyond what brings about specialization in production in the 2×2 model, both factors will benefit. However, their benefit will depend on how much of the other good they consume (with no benefit for a factor in the extreme case where none of the other good is consumed by that factor). In this regard, several studies such as William Cline's on textiles show that the lower-income groups are fairly intensive in their consumption of imported, unskilled-labor-intensive goods.[27] The adverse Stolper-Samuelson effect is therefore that much more likely to be swamped by the lifting-all-boats effect at issue.

—Equally, scale economies can overturn the redistributive effect, improving the real wages of both factors. Panagariya demonstrated this first, using the conventional model where perfect competition is allowed to continue.[28] Helpman and Krugman then demonstrated the result when scale economies lead to imperfect competition.[29] Then, Brown and others noted that the Helpman-Krugman result was under the special case where the output per firm did not change with trade and extended the analysis to the more general case where this is not so.[30]

I am known for my skepticism about the empirical importance of scale economies and could be properly chided if I show warmth toward them when they produce results I would like to see! But the Panagariya-Helpman-Krugman reminders are important in the present context for those who think that scale economies are truly significant in thinking about the real world.

—Then again, there could be lifting-all-boats effects from more competition and discipline resulting from the freeing of trade, causing X-efficiency effects that may be formally modeled as Hicks-neutral technical change. If we do this, and if we assume that the effect operates throughout

27. Cline (1990).
28. Panagariya (1980).
29. Helpman and Krugman (1985).
30. Brown, Deardorff, and Stern (1993). These authors have a fuller analysis of the effects of scale economies on factor rewards than the single point I have highlighted. They have also used the Michigan CGE model, as applied to U.S.-Mexican trade, incorporating the scale effects. They have argued that the real wages in the United States will, in fact, rise, not fall, as a result of freeing trade with Mexico.

the economy, in both traded sectors in a 2 × 2 model, then clearly both factors get their real wages improving from this cause, countervailing and possibly reversing the fall in the real wage of the Stolper-Samuelson-effect-impacted factor. Evidently, the argument can be extended to the case where the Hicks-neutral technical change is differentially greater in the import-competing sector and, with suitable assumptions, to biased technical change as well.

The empirical evidence on this hypothesis is hard to find. However, Levinsohn's ingenious work on the imports-as-competition hypothesis, though not quite in the form suggested here, is successful in testing that hypothesis using Turkish industry data under ideal, near-controlled-experiment conditions.[31] More work needs to be done to make this argument empirically more compelling.

Five further comments should be made, however.

1. Though the observed goods prices do not conform to the Stolper-Samuelson thesis, the *quantity*-of-imports studies, such as Wood's much-cited work, suggest otherwise; imports of unskilled-labor-intensive goods have certainly increased, and such increases have been associated with the fall in real wages.[32] However, the intermediation via price fall cannot be avoided. This is readily seen through figure 2-7 where apparel imports, increasing with increased domestic demand, leave both the price and domestic production unchanged and hence could not affect the wages of unskilled workers in apparel manufacture.

This argument also becomes critical in entertaining skepticism concerning, if not rejecting, the Borjas-Ramey argument that the growth of imports has led to the decline in the wages of unskilled workers.[33] They show that there is a tight time-series relationship between imports as a share of gross domestic product (GDP) and the skilled-wage differential (rather than the real wage of unskilled workers); note that there are no data here on relative goods prices. But in general equilibrium analysis, it is easy to show that *both* the correlated phenomena may be a result of technical change, for example (the explanation that seems much more likely to many).[34]

To see this, consider figure 2-8. If Hicks-neutral technical change (that is, isoquants uniformly renumbered upward) is in the skilled-labor-

31. Levinsohn (1993).
32. Wood (1994).
33. Borjas and Ramey (1994).
34. Indeed, for the specific configuration of technical change and factor-intensity conditions modeled later in this chapter, such correlation is inevitable, not just a possibility.

Figure 2-7

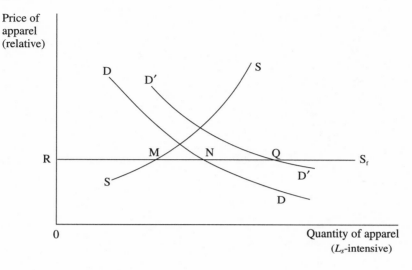

Figure 2-8

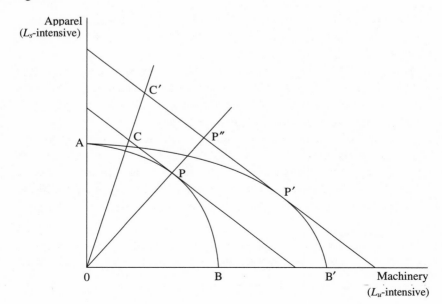

Figure 2-9

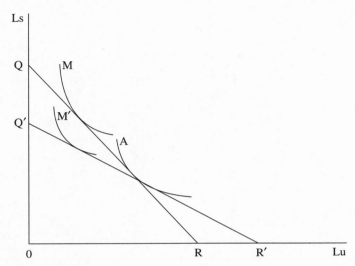

intensive good, machinery, it will lead to a disproportionate increase in the output of machinery—indeed, even in a decline in output of the other unskilled-labor-intensive good, apparel (this being the well-known Rybczynski effect);[35] in figure 2-8, then, the output will shift from P to P′, not P″. If there is no reason to expect the income elasticity of demand for the two goods to be significantly different from unity (that is, for consumption to shift from C to a point substantially different from C′ along C′P′), then the net effect will surely be to increase imports (and trade) as a proportion of GNP as the economy grows due to the technical change.[36]

One can also show that the Hicks-neutral technical change in machinery will increase the relative wage of skilled labor, because it will disproportionately increase the demand for such labor in which it is intensive. Figure 2-9 shows this, using the well-known Findlay-Grubert diagram.[37] Given the goods price ratio exchanging A for M, we can take the tangent QR to these two isoquants and that yields the associated factor price ratio. When Hicks-neutral technical change occurs in machinery, the same M can be produced by less factors, shifting M down to M′. The new factor price

35. Rybczynski (1955).
36. Note that the increased demand is not being arbitrarily introduced into the analysis; it is intrinsic to the analysis of technical change as such change increases income.
37. Findlay and Grubert (1959).

ratio Q'R', consistent with the same goods price ratio A/M, is then yielded by the tangent to A and M'. Q'R' relative to QR then shows a rise in the relative wage for skilled labor. Thus both the variables—the skilled-wage differential and imports as a share of GNP—will move up with (relatively greater) technical change in the skilled-labor-intensive industries, and this will happen at unchanging relative goods prices.

The technical-change explanation also better fits the observed changes in factor proportions in the United States, as noted by Lawrence and Slaughter.[38] Nearly everywhere, the proportion of skilled to unskilled labor has risen, not fallen. However, that is exactly the opposite of what we would expect if the driving force in the real-wage decline had been a trade-induced decline in the price of unskilled-labor-intensive importables, and what we would expect if technical change in the skilled-labor-using industries (as well as skilled-labor-using technical change)[39] were the source of the change.[40]

Thus I find it difficult to accept the argument, often advanced by Adrian Wood, that almost all "quantity" data point towards trade as the source of the problem and that it is only "prices" that do not conform. To say that is akin to arguing that, in a production of *Hamlet,* if only the prince were missing, everything else would go along just fine! And, as I have just explained, even the nonprice "quantities" such as import ratios are consistent with a nontrade explanation, whereas "quantities" such as factor proportion changes are more consonant with the technical-change explanation.[41]

38. Lawrence and Slaughter (1993).

39. This is consistent with the altogether different proposition that, despite technical change using skilled labor in both sectors, the real wage of unskilled labor can rise and the wage differential of skilled labor to unskilled labor can fall.

40. Indeed, the claim that a dramatic onrush of unskilled-labor-saving technical change is behind the disturbing phenomenon of declining unskilled wages is backed by other evidence and analyses reviewed in Bhagwati and Dehejia (1994). This cited chapter also considers the "gloom-and-doom" argument: underlying production functions in different industries may be characterized by capital-skills complementarity, as originally investigated by Zvi Griliches, and even capital accumulation may then lead to falling real wages of those without skills. If technical change accentuates that kind of complementarity, as it seems to do, the prospects of either technical change or capital accumulation offering significant improvement to unskilled workers also begins to dim greatly.

41. I should add the observation that, if we are looking at technical change, this will generally affect the quality of goods as well. It is then most likely that the unadjusted price data will understate the price fall in goods characterized by more rapid quality change. But ever since Irving Kravis's (1956) pathbreaking work, the exports of the United States are well known to be from Schumpeterian innovative industries. A quality adjustment, leading to hedonic price estimates, is therefore likely to show an even greater rise in the relative price of unskilled-labor-intensive importable goods.

2. Let me then turn to the question: Why did domestic goods prices of labor-intensive goods not fall during the 1980s? I offer two alternative explanations and then draw relevant implications from them.

Explanation 1: One major explanation is that, even though the domestic prices of unskilled-labor-intensive goods would have fallen as the pessimists fear, the voluntary export restraints (VERs) on textiles, shoes, and the like, and the antidumping actions against several other products that broke out in the early 1980s, would have implied export restraints that would translate into an effective (countervailing) rise in cost, insurance, and freight-landed prices and hence in U.S. domestic prices as well.

Textile trade experts note that the Asian competition in textiles and apparel broke out seriously during the latter half of the 1970s. However, its effects on domestic adjustment were substantially mitigated by the swift response of the industry in tightening the Multi-Fiber Agreement's (MFA's) restrictiveness. Indeed, it is well known that administered protection (consisting of antidumping actions, VERs, and a variety of export-restraining arrangements between governments) broke out for certain in the first half of the 1980s in the United States and Europe. The restrictiveness of trade barriers may therefore have generally increased, offsetting the Stolper-Samuelson effect by selectively moderating the goods price effect, as necessary, in the first place (as the price data of Lawrence and others indicate). Such elasticity and also selectivity are, in fact, a characteristic of the "administered" protection embodied in antidumping actions, VERs, and the like, and make them both a preferred instrument of protection by industry and also a more serious hazard to free trade than conventional protection.[42]

Explanation 2: An alternative explanation, of course, is that the downward effect of trade resulting from trade-augmenting changes in the South (whether growth or trade liberalization there), as typified by the outward shift of the South's offer curve in figure 2-2, on the world prices of labor-intensive goods has been *more than offset* by the simultaneous upward effect on them due to technical change in the North, the latter resulting in an outward shift of the North's offer curve, as in figure 2-3. This latter is, in fact, the hypothesis that I have developed in depth in my analysis of why the findings of Wood and colleagues are unpersuasive.

In short, one could then argue, in the former case, that the trade-induced pressure on domestic, labor-intensive goods prices in the United States (and

---

42. The fact that world and not just domestic prices of unskilled-labor-intensive goods have increased instead of fallen suggests that the VER explanation may be relevant: VERs may be expected to raise the export prices by the amount of the rents.

possibly in other Organization for Economic Cooperation and Development [OECD] countries) was offset by countervailing administered protection; and, in the latter case, that it was overwhelmed by the effect on goods prices of technical change. The domestic goods price change that one observes is the *gross* price change, a result of several factors; but what is truly needed is the *net* price change attributable to the alleged trade factor. Estimating the latter in a properly specified model that can net out the effects of the other factors is what is required, but not currently available. What we do know now is that the observed, gross price change is not supportive of the fears of the trade-and-wages pessimists. That does cripple the case advanced by these pessimists for now.

3. What does all this say about prospects? The typical worry often voiced is: when "big," poor countries such as China and India come on board with their trade expansion from domestic growth and/or their trade liberalization, all hell will break loose, pushing the prices of labor-intensive goods down to low levels and crushing the real wages of unskilled workers as a result.

If the reason why the domestic prices of unskilled-labor-intensive goods here did not fall during the 1980s was the compensating growth of administered protection—a possibility I suggested for investigation—this would not be reassuring. It would mean that trade did not hurt real wages, because protection prevented it from doing so by offsetting the fall in goods prices that trade would have induced. That is surely no argument for being free from worry on the income distributional effects of trade if protectionist responses are to be ruled out!

But we can easily exaggerate the pressure on the prices of unskilled-labor-intensive goods from trade liberalization in poor countries, or from the expansion of their trade at any given level of their trade barriers, and the adverse effect on real wages of unskilled workers in rich countries.

Thus, regarding effects on goods prices, the focus on the expansion (in formal terms, as in figures 2-2 and 2-3) of the offer curve from the poor countries is misleading. It forgets that the offer curve of the rich countries will also be expanding. Given the fact that the poor countries' national incomes add up to only a small fraction of the national incomes of the rich countries, and that the averages of the trade-to-GNP ratios between the two groups are not far apart, the net demand for the unskilled-labor-intensive exports of the poor countries may well rise rather than fall.[43]

43. Of course, one could argue that, if the offer curve of the developing countries had *not* shifted outward, our own net growth of demand for imports

But even if prices were to fall for imported unskilled-labor-intensive goods in the next decade, recall that it is by no means inevitable that this will translate into a fall, rather than a rise, in the real wages of unskilled workers in the OECD countries. I have already recounted several reasons, implicit and explicit in the Stolper and Samuelson paper, why *all* factors of production can gain from the fall in import prices, and the associated trade expansion that trade with the South may bring. These reasons are not at all unrealistic. It is then simply a fallacy to think that the hand of the Stolper-Samuelson theorem is an iron fist aimed at the real wages of unskilled workers.

4. It is also worth noting that the adverse effect on the real wages of unskilled workers, if any, will increase with the decline in the prices of unskilled-labor-intensive goods. But so will the gains from trade increase as the improvement in the terms of trade becomes greater. The latter would increase our income further still and thus, other things being equal, lead to more revenue at any given tax rates. This should correspondingly ease the constraints on spending to relieve the increased trade-determined distress to unskilled workers. We therefore have a built-in stabilizer in terms of reduced revenue constraints as the impact on real wages of unskilled workers rises (if at all) if trade with the South drives down the real wages of unskilled workers.

5. But whether one is a pessimist or an optimist (as I am) on the issue at hand, agreement on one policy option seems possible. Both could unite in support of policy programs to *limit the growth of population* (and hence of unskilled workers) *in the large, poor countries.* The optimists will support such programs simply because they are desirable for large and poor countries such as India and China, and this is also the considered view of these countries' policymakers, as evident from the Cairo Conference on Population in 1995.

But the pessimists should support population control programs, in our own interest. It is easy to see why. Immigration, which *directly* brings unskilled aliens from the poor countries into our midst, cannot be totally controlled by us. Borders often tend to get beyond control (as at the Rio

---

would have resulted in a *greater* rise in the price of the unskilled-labor-intensive importables, and hence in the real wages of unskilled labor over the 1980s. This may be the only real kernel of valid argument for those who contend that trade has hurt our workers, other things being equal.

Grande) because our political traditions prevent us from shooting at illegal immigrants coming across borders. If trade is also feared by the pessimists as simply an *indirect* way of letting in such alien labor, both phenomena amounting to pressure on the real wages of unskilled workers, then the situation is fairly grim—especially if the decline of the political ability to redistribute prevents us from compensating for the decline in real wages of unskilled workers.[44] In that case, the pessimists can only hope for lower pressures from unskilled workers abroad. On the one hand, this implies our assistance in acceleration of their capital accumulation, and on the other hand, in effective control of their population growth.

The shift from the Bush administration's more complacent attitudes toward population control, prompted largely by the religious Right, to the Clinton administration's energetic support of effective population policies at Cairo, prompted partly by liberal views concerning women's rights, can then also be explained as one response (among several) to the fears of the adverse effect of trade with the South on the real wages of unskilled workers.

"Kaleidoscopic" Comparative Advantage and Higher Labor Turnover: An Alternative Trade Explanation

My view of the Stolper-Samuelson, North-South trade explanation of the decline in the real wage of our unskilled workers during and since the 1980s is profoundly skeptical, based on current evidence. It is so on theoretical grounds as well.[45]

But that is not all that one can say about the possible effect of trade on real wages. I have suggested, and Dehejia has explored analytically, an alternative trade explanation for real wage decline.[46] The explanation, which has nothing to do with the Stolper-Samuelson analytical framework

---

44. The parallel between trade and immigration as indirect and direct ways of affecting real wages in the same direction was at the heart of the political debate on the first national immigration legislation ever enacted anywhere, in the United Kingdom in 1905. At the time, free traders were free immigrationists, whereas the protectionists were anti-immigrationists. Free immigration was described as "free trade in paupers." See Bhagwati (1991a) for details and an analysis.

45. I have concentrated here on several reasons why the Stolper-Samuelson theorem may not prevail. These would generally undermine the FPE theorem as well. Of course, the Stolper-Samuelson effect could obtain in the rich countries even if the FPE theorem did not prevail.

46. Bhagwati (1991b); Bhagwati and Dehejia (1994); Dehejia (1992a, 1992b).

and looks at trade more generally than in a North-South framework, has essentially four parts.

1. Greater internationalization of markets (that is, rising trade-to-GNP ratios, greater role of transnational corporations in globalizing production), the diffusion of production know-how within OECD countries (as documented by Baumol and colleagues), and the increased integration of world capital markets (as discussed by Frankel) have narrowed the margin of comparative advantage enjoyed by many industries in any major OECD country.[47] There are now, therefore, more industries free to move about than ever, leading to greater volatility in comparative advantage—that is, more "knife-edge" and hence kaleidoscopic comparative advantage, between countries.

2. This will lead to higher labor turnover between industries and hence to more frictional unemployment.

3. Increased labor turnover could flatten the growth profile of earnings due to less skill accumulation.

4. These three factors could also explain an increasing wage differential, all else being equal, if skilled workers have greater transferability of workplace-acquired skills than do unskilled workers.[48] This theory has yet to be investigated. In particular, whether comparative advantage has indeed become "thin," resulting in the kaleidoscope effect (element 1), has not been documented empirically.[49] I might add that there is some suggestive evidence on elements 3 and 4 of the explanation above in labor studies and also in Lynch's work.[50]

The evidence on element 2, concerning higher labor turnover, has undergone a flip-flop. But fortunately for the Bhagwati-Dehejia argument, it is presently in favor of their hypothesis that labor turnover rates increased in the 1980s. Whereas the early thinking was that such turnover had indeed increased, later studies suggested otherwise.[51] Thus, as Bill Dickens notes in

47. Baumol and others (1989); Frankel (1994).

48. As for increased differential in favor of skilled workers, increased turnover could explain that if we were also to argue that skilled workers are more likely to use the search period between jobs to add to their skills through study than unskilled workers. Once one has been trained and "socialized" to train, it is easier to find the motivation to retool and retrain; if a person has never been socialized to train in the first place, he or she may more readily do nothing during fallow periods.

49. My former Columbia student, Don Davis, now at Harvard, tells me that he plans to explore this question, using some of the existing literature on changes in "product-line" specialization of firms. The theoretical exploration of the concept of "knife-edge," kaleidoscopic comparative advantage, especially the conditions under which it is accentuated by globalization, is also necessary.

50. Bhagwati and Dehejia (1994); Lynch (1995).

51. See, in particular, Economics Focus Column (1993) and OECD (1994).

his comment on this chapter, recent U.S. data from the Current Population Survey (CPS) show that the percentage of men who have worked at their current employer for less than a year did not fall in the 1980s. Similarly, Dickens argues that the U.S. Department of Labor data on the reallocation of employment between industries seem to show no upward trend (though the Bhagwati-Dehejia thesis would survive if there were also increased turnover within industries). Similar conclusions have been drawn by others.[52]

On the other hand, Rose's findings, and the related findings of the National Commission for Employment Policy (an independent commission set up under the Job Training Partnership Act [JTPA] as an independent advisory body reporting to both the president and Congress), have used more pertinent longitudinal data to argue the opposite.[53] In short, the Bhagwati-Dehejia thesis is back in the picture for now, as far as the turnover hypothesis is concerned.

Rents, Unionization, and the Like

These arguments are economywide trade explanations. But there are industry-specific trade explanations, of course, on what happens to industries affected by import competition.

Where these are competitive industries, clearly the earnings of the productive factors within them will be reduced at the outset. When the industry is wiped out, these earnings will, naturally, fall to zero. However, the *overall, final* effect on real wages of these factors, including unskilled workers, cannot be determined without finding out the general equilibrium implications of the parametric change. This will take into account, for instance, the absorption of the displaced factors elsewhere in the economy, which means going back to the economywide explanation.

What does the presence of unions, and hence of rents to unskilled workers in the unionized sectors, do for the argument? There are indeed models of several kinds of imperfect competition in factor markets in the general equilibrium analysis of international trade that could be extended to address the question of the overall impact of changing goods prices on real wages. But the answers can be quite unexpected. For example, if unions maintain a wage differential between homogeneous insiders and outsiders, the conventional inferences such as that a fall in the relative price of the unionized sector's good will lead to a fall in its relative production and therefore presumably a fall in the unionized factor intensively used in it,

52. Diebold and others (1994); Farber (1995).
53. Rose (1993, 1994, and 1995).

will not necessarily hold. This undermines the Stolper-Samuelson type argument (inferring factor reward changes from goods price changes). To my knowledge, there is no analysis of the effects of price declines in unionized industries (such as autos) that satisfactorily addresses these deeper analytical issues arising when the effects of unions are considered in an analytically appropriate fashion.

Then again, we know that during the 1980s the "big" unionized sectors in the U.S. economy, especially autos and steel, were politically powerful enough to significantly shield themselves through antidumping actions and VERs, OMAs, and the like from the effects of foreign competition (which, incidentally, was overwhelmingly from the North, not the South). Given both the small percentage of the U.S. unskilled labor force in unionized manufacturing sectors even then, and the substantial cushioning of competition through trade restraints, it is highly unlikely that the analysts can demonstrate (through this route) a significant overall role for trade in affecting real wages in the United States during the 1980s.[54]

The Question of International Capital Mobility: Globalization and Real Wages

So far, I have considered only the question of a direct link between trade and real wages. But there are fears of an adverse impact on real wages of unskilled workers that follow from fears arising from international capital mobility.

—Thus a major worry of the unions is that the outflow of capital drives down real wages of unskilled labor. However, during the 1980s in the United States, more direct foreign investment (DFI) came in than went out, both during the period and relative to the 1950s and 1960s. Moreover, the United States ran a current account deficit so that foreign savings came in, if that is the measure one wants to work with instead. The facts are therefore against that hypothesis.

—But again, if one uses a bargaining-type framework, the bargaining power of employers has it might be said to have increased vis-à-vis that of employees. Employers can increasingly say in a global economy that they will pack their bags and leave. Therefore, for any given output, its distribution between L_u income and other income including profits may have shifted against L_u.

54. For a complementary discussion of rents, citing the broader literature on the subject that includes efficiency-wage arguments, see Bhagwati and Dehejia (1994).

To my knowledge, systematic empirical evidence for such a bargaining model as a determinant of relative rewards between factors within any U.S. industry is not available. Nor do we know whether, for any of these industries, there is evidence of an international relocation elsewhere of part of its local production having altered distribution against L_u income.[55]

At a time when total union membership is down to roughly 12 percent of U.S. private sector employment, however, I doubt if this explanation is likely to be important. The exception, of course, is if the decline in unionism is itself significantly attributed (as it probably cannot be) to the loss of bargaining power due to the threat of firms leaving for other countries.

Static versus Dynamic Effects

My analysis of different approaches to the question of the link between trade and wages would not be complete without reference to the growth or dynamic effects that trade can have on wages, affecting several different "fundamentals" such as the rate of accumulation and technical change.

If indeed technical change or accumulation is agreeably affected, even as the initial static effect on real wages is adverse, the overall effect in the long run could swamp the static effect. The effect of trade on X-efficiency via competition (as discussed previously in reference to Levinsohn's work) suggests, for example, that if this effect operates continuously and is not a onetime effect, it would certainly help to improve growth rates and hence to pull up real wages over time.

This is a matter of importance, because we will have to make up our minds as to how trade, in specific parametric cases, interacts with growth; and how this in turn affects real wages of unskilled workers. Evidently, the East Asian countries, whose rapid growth rates of capital and income since the 1950s cannot be separated from their outward orientation in trade, did fairly well in real wages. This outweighs any static, adverse effect that the importation of unskilled-labor-saving technology may have had on real wages in the short run.[56]

55. The threat of exit may exist, of course, even if no exit has actually occurred in the industry.

56. In considering trade to have been a significant engine of the East Asian miracle, I find myself in disagreement with Krugman (1994). Krugman denies that there was a miracle by noting that much of the exceptionally high growth is attributable simply to high rates of capital accumulation. But those high rates of accumulation themselves need to be explained. This is where (contrary to Rodrik's recent arguments) I consider the outward orientation of their trade policy and its

Our problem today may then well be that, with our growth rates being low (whether exogenously or endogenously to trade), we are unable to outweigh the drag on real wages being provided by either trade (which I doubt) or by technology (which I suspect is the true and overwhelming cause of the problem).

Conclusions

I conclude somewhat optimistically about the effect of freer trade on the real wages of unskilled workers in the rich countries.

The North-South (Stolper-Samuelson) argument, even theoretically, is not as much of an iron fist aimed at workers as is commonly assumed. Besides, the price evidence for the argument is missing; though sophisticated econometric analysis may, as I have argued, tease out more on the issue, such analysis has yet to be undertaken.

The evidence for the alternative North-North (Bhagwati-Dehejia) hypothesis, while elements in the chain of arguments sustaining it are now in hand, is still incomplete.

The capital-mobility-cum-bargaining model still awaits a proper general equilibrium test; in any event, the unionized sector to which it applies is only a small fraction (less than 12 percent) of the U.S. labor force.

The big-ticket weapons in the war chest of the pessimists are, therefore, without much firepower, at least for now.

Yet the issue remains politically salient, just because the linkage seems overwhelmingly intuitive. It will continue to affect policy in several areas, and not to our advantage.

Thus, to cite one compelling example, it certainly fuels the push for including labor standards in the World Trade Organization (WTO). The objective of the unions to provide the main political force for such inclusion in a social clause is precisely to raise the cost of production of their rivals in the poor countries in any way they can.This issue is dividing the rich and the poor countries. It is also an issue where I fear that the current U.S. position lacks probity and statesmanship and appears instead to be a prisoner of lobby-led, special-interest politics.[57]

---

role in creating and sustaining high incentives to invest to have been critical. Besides, the tremendously high private rates of accumulation are indeed, by conventional standards, a "miracle"—that is, hugely off the curve. See my letter to the editor in the *Financial Times* (Bhagwati [1996]).

57. I have discussed the nuanced objections to a social clause in the WTO, and outlined a set of alternative and better ways to promote one's ideas about labor standards, in several writings and in TV, radio, and other debates with the protagonists of a social clause. In particular, I would urge the reader to consult Bhagwati (1995c).

In turn, I have no doubt that it is a principal reason for the infatuation of the United States with preferential trading arrangements (PTAs) such as Free Trade Areas, even though the WTO has been jump-started and we would expect the United States to return to multilateralism. These PTAs between a hegemon and nonhegemons enable the hegemon (and its lobbies pushing for trade-*un*related issues such as intellectual property protection, environmental demands, labor standards demands, and the like) to extract significant concessions from nonhegemons when the latter are bargained with one-on-one, rather than in their greater numbers and strength in Geneva. The concessions that President Salinas made on these nontrade issues to the United States were far greater than those available from the poor countries en bloc at Geneva. And now Chile will have to accept them to get into NAFTA.

The *sequential bargaining* with nonhegemons—made possible by choosing the PTA route selectively with economically and politically vulnerable nonhegemons rather than exclusively the multilateral mode of trade negotiations with all nonhegemons—enables the hegemon to extract much more on nontrade issues (what John Whalley has called "side payments") than what the hegemon can extract in the multilateral context directly. The desire to raise the poor countries' costs of production to "manageable" levels by imposing expensive environmental and labor standards on them is then more readily fulfilled if the PTAs are embraced as a *strategic* bargaining strategy alongside the multilateral negotiations.[58] This desire has political salience precisely because of the fear that free trade imperils our real wages (and jobs).

Comment by William Dickens

Jagdish Bhagwati is to be complimented for his early and frequent reminders to those doing empirical work on trade and wages: Think carefully about what exactly you are asking, and do your measurement in a theoretical context. Bhagwati and others have forced a useful reconsideration of the data linking changes in trade patterns to changes in employment, and changes in employment to changes in relative wages. Bhagwati's criticism of the treatment of trade deficits in this literature is particularly compelling. However, I am surprised that Bhagwati and others are so quick

58. I have developed the idea of sequential bargaining, and the associated idea of a "selfish hegemon" that pursues an agenda serving its national interest (defined with or without lobbies), in several writings. See, in particular, Bhagwati (1994).

to dismiss studies of the factor content embodied in trade as having no value. There are some important questions for which quantity studies provide answers at least as compelling as the studies of import prices that Bhagwati and other trade economists seem to prefer.

We are here because the U.S. income distribution has undergone a major change. The popular question "Did trade cause the change?" is not well formed; the volume and nature of trade are not exogenous events but depend on other foreign and domestic factors. I can think of two reasonable ways to translate the question so that it might make sense from the perspective of an economist. First, during the period in which the growth in earnings inequality has occurred, there has been an expansion in the volume of U.S. trade commonly attributed to falling transportation and communications costs, and to some extent to the liberalization of international capital markets. We might ask whether the increased volume of trade due to these exogenous technical and political changes has played a major role in the decline of wages at the lower end of the distribution, or alternatively, if the changes in our income distribution would have happened in autarky. It is true that factor content studies might give misleading answers if we care about the first question. But I will argue that factor content studies allow us to draw some conclusions about the difference between actual experience and what would have happened in autarky. However, if we ignored factor content studies and based our analysis only on price studies, we might be misled into believing that changes abroad had caused changes in income distribution that were actually due to changes in the domestic economy, which would have shifted our income distribution in the absence of trade.

Consider first the simplest HO model with two goods and two factors—skilled and unskilled labor—and the assumption that the United States is a small country. In that case, an increase in the international price of the skill-intensive good relative to the other will certainly produce an increase in the relative price of skilled labor. However, making the usual assumption of factor content studies that all other factors are unchanged, it must also be that the amount of low-skilled labor embodied in U.S. imports has increased. Imports must crowd out production in the unskilled-labor-intensive sector to produce the increase in effective supply that leads to lower wages for unskilled workers.

Is it reasonable to assume that all other factors are unchanged? Most certainly not. Nearly all the factor content studies suggest that an alternative hypothesis that might explain the change in relative wages is a shift in technology lowering the demand for unskilled workers. Most factor content studies suggest that there has been little if any change in the factor content of U.S. trade. However, because the United States is relatively rich in skilled labor, such a shift in domestic demand for skilled labor caused by technical change could reduce the need for imports and mask the effects of a change in import prices. A change in domestic demand of the right magnitude could leave the factor content of U.S. trade unchanged. Factor content studies could, therefore, give us a misleading answer to our first question. However, if a shift in domestic demand is masking the international effects, then the changes in income distribution would have occurred in autarky. To a first-order approximation, a shift in domestic demand large enough to offset a change in international goods prices would also be enough to produce the same observed change in the income distribution in autarky. I can think of several reasons why quantity studies might overstate the extent to which income distribution may have grown more unequal with trade than under autarky, but it is unlikely that they will understate it.

If we stick with the simplest small-country, HO theory, the trade economists' preference for import price studies as the way to divine the role of trade in changing our distribution of income is understandable. It will always tell us what the effects of exogenous changes that affect trade volume are and how our circumstances between trade and autarky would differ. However, if we assume that theory we also assume our answer. A small country that trades with the rest of the world and is incompletely specialized cannot experience a change in factor prices that is not caused by trade because of the FPE theorem. Domestic changes in factor prices can only be due to changes in world factor prices or changes in transportation costs. But, both in levels and in changes, the FPE theorem is wildly at odds with the facts for the United States, as Bhagwati has noted. We have much higher wages than much of the rest of the world, and we seem to experience changes in the prices of factors and goods that result from changes in domestic supply and demand.

Simply assuming that the United States is a large country does not solve the problem. The United States should then influence world factor prices; but U.S. prices should still move one for one with foreign prices, which still does not seem to be the case. One alternative would be to assume that foreign and domestic goods are not perfect substitutes and that there is imperfect competition in product markets. If we do this, then there is an immediate and obvious problem with import price studies: changes in the domestic factor supply and demand (such as those that might be caused by technical change) will affect import prices. In particular, a decline in the demand for unskilled labor in the United States will lead to a fall in domestic prices of goods produced with unskilled labor, which may lead to a fall in the landed price of imports competing with those goods. If we tried to infer from such a price change that increasing trade was responsible for our shifting income distribution, we would be dead wrong. The price studies have been equivocal on whether prices of low-skilled goods have declined. However, even if we were satisfied that these prices had fallen, similar or even worse changes in our distribution of income might have occurred with no trade at all.

The endogenous nature of foreign prices is not the only problem with price studies. Though landed prices probably reflect any declines in transportation costs, they may not reflect the changes in importer, wholesaler, and retailer costs due to cheaper and faster communications. Relative price measures are further plagued by the problems of measuring quality. Such problems could be severe. Several years ago Jonathan Leonard, John Abowd, and I began a project to see if imports induced improvements in productivity. Just to see what the data might hold, we ran the naive regression of the change in productivity on the change in import penetration ratio by industry and found a negative coefficient. One interpretation of this result would be that slow domestic productivity growth allowed foreign competition to take over a market. But our examination of the industries showing low measured productivity growth and substantial increases in imports suggested an alternative interpretation. The industries with large increases in the share of imports were often industries in which U.S. producers had been completely eliminated from the low end of the market and were left only in high-quality or specialty goods. This suggested to us that the price indices for the domestic producers were overstating the quality-adjusted changes in domestic prices. True productivity growth was understated. It is easy to imagine that the mirror-image problem would be an understatement of the quality-adjusted prices of imports—particularly those from low-wage countries. It may appear that the price of these goods is falling more than the true quality-adjusted price has.

I therefore believe we learn more when we consider quantity studies and price studies together than we could learn from either group by itself. In particular, we can now say with some certainty that if exogenous changes in world factor prices or transportation costs are behind our widening distribution of income, the effect has either been quite small, or it has not come through HO channels, or much the same changes would have occurred in the absence of trade.

Wood has argued that existing quantity studies understate the extent to which trade has affected the demand for labor because they measure the skill content of imports using current skill ratios in developed countries in too highly aggregated data.[59] He argues that the amount of low-skilled labor embodied in an import into a developed country is understated by looking at how much unskilled labor would be used to produce goods in the same industrial category in the developed country. One reason is because the product is probably one that takes more low-skilled labor than the average for the industry. Another is that the phases of production requiring the least skill are the ones that have been shifted overseas.

The problem with this argument is that it suggests we should have been seeing a rapid decline in the use of unskilled labor in traded-good industries in the United States. We have, but a second question is "rapid compared with what?" We have also seen rapid declines in the use of unskilled labor to produce nontraded goods. Gary Burtless suggests that as the gap between rich and poor has been growing, the use of unskilled labor has declined as rapidly in both the traded- and nontraded-goods sectors. The shipping of jobs overseas could, naturally, explain the decline in manufacturing, and some other phenomenon the change in services, but it seems more plausible that the same factor explains the change in both sectors.[60]

Of course, changes in quantities traded are not necessary to affect factor prices if such prices are not set competitively. If wages are explicitly or implicitly bargained over, then the threat of competition from abroad or the relocation of production could be enough to lower the wages of less-skilled workers. From what I have heard over and over from union leaders, such effects are being felt by their constituents. Bhagwati dismisses the likely importance of these effects by noting how small a fraction of the U.S. labor force is organized in unions, but that is not entirely fair. There are many firms that pay careful attention to the wages offered by union competitors when setting their own. However, even this cannot be the main explanation of the changes in our income distribution. If it were, we would expect to see all firms hiring more rather than less unskilled labor as prices for it are driven down. At the very least, we would expect firms that produce non-traded goods to snap up this cheap labor.

Finally, there is Bhagwati's alternative explanation for the declining wages of low-skilled workers—that increased openness has led to declining job tenure and consequently declining amounts of specific human capital, and thus lower wages for less-skilled workers. There are a number of problems with this analysis. First, there is little evidence of declining tenure. The CPS regularly asks workers how long they have been with their

59. Wood (1994).
60. Burtless (1996).

current employer. Since 1983 the median job tenure has remained fairly constant—about 4.5 years. If anything, it has been increasing. Those who have worked for their employer for less than a year have declined from 27.3 percent of the labor force to 27 percent of the labor force, whereas those working for the same employer for more than twenty years have increased from 9.9 to 10.2 percent.[61] However, these results are based on people's recollection of how long they have been with their current employers, and there may be reason to believe that the extent of this recall bias has been changing over time. The analysis of the Panel Study of Income Dynamics (PSID) done by Steve Rose and others gets around the problem of recall bias by using longitudinal analysis of data on people's employers.[62] However, the PSID is not a random sample of the labor force. Only "household heads" and "spouses" are surveyed; other earners in a household are missed. From the CPS data we know that older workers are changing jobs more frequently and younger workers less frequently. Younger workers are underrepresented in the PSID, and it may therefore overstate any decline in job stability.

Considering the PSID and the CPS together, we have an unclear picture of what is going on. Adding other data sources helps clarify the picture a little. The Displaced Worker Survey (DWS)—a regular addition to the CPS—shows that, controlling for business-cycle conditions, an increasing fraction of people report that they have recently lost their jobs. The CPS also shows an increasing fraction of unemployed people reporting that they have been permanently rather than temporarily laid off. However, the temporary-permanent distinction is a judgment call. The increased reporting of job loss and downsizing may be influencing workers' perceptions of the likelihood of recall. No study has demonstrated that the true recall rate has declined or that the actual rate of job loss has increased.

We can also look at the rate of change of industry composition and firm size. If rapid shifts in comparative advantage are causing more job instability, we would expect it to show up in such measures. Data from the Census of Manufacturers showed no increase in the variability of firm size over time between the 1970s and 1980s. No data are available for the rest of the economy, but if trade is having an effect on employment stability, we would certainly expect it to show up in manufacturing data. Similarly, there is no evidence of a secular trend in the rate of allocation of employment between industries. Therefore, if there has been an increase in turnover, it

---

61. Horvath (1982); Sehgal (1984); U.S. Department of Labor, U.S. Bureau of Labor Statistics (1987); U.S. Department of Labor (1992).

62. Rose (1995).

seems unlikely that it is due to increased instability of product demand resulting from lowered barriers to trade.[63]

In the end, then, I agree with Bhagwati that the weight of evidence suggest little or no role for trade in changing our distribution of income, or at least the same changes would likely have happened in the absence of trade. However, unlike Bhagwati, I do think that studies of the changing factor composition of imports contributes to my understanding of these issues.

Comment by Ronald W. Jones

It is frequently the case that issues arise in economics that attract the attention of more than one subdiscipline of our profession. So it is with the recent behavior of wage rates, both of skilled and unskilled workers in the United States, and possible explanations that are rooted either in the character of technical progress and education on the one hand, or changing events in international markets on the other. There is, of course, the task of sorting out precisely what has happened to wage rates, as well as identifying what changes in technology and traded-goods markets have taken place, and this I leave to others possessing both absolute and comparative advantages. What can theory, especially trade theory, tell us to expect about the links between wage rates and these potentially causal influences? Not surprisingly, theory does not speak with a unique voice. Here I shall attempt to lay out various theoretical scenarios, basing my remarks on the chapter by Bhagwati and, as well, on those remarks by Ed Leamer at this conference that bear on the theoretical possibilities.

The FPE Theorem

As a preliminary step I should like to make explicit my views as to the relevance of the FPE theorem to this topic. This has long been a centerpiece of theoretical discussions of the possible consequence of international commodity trade, and has even made the pages of the *Economist* in its remarks on the expected outcomes of NAFTA. Two qualifications to the theorem are frequently, and correctly, made. If countries do not share the

63. U.S. Council of Economic Advisers (1994).

same technology, there is no basis for factor prices being equated between countries in the absence of direct international mobility of those factors. Also, if the number of productive factors exceeds the number of international markets in goods, factor prices need not be equalized. However, the great popularity of the two-commodity version of HO theory tends to disguise yet a third caveat of the theorem that arises when many commodities can be produced, namely, that countries produce at least as many goods *in common* as there are factors. Admittedly, the two-commodity case qualifies the theorem in the case in which one or more countries are completely specialized. However, in my view the many-commodity version of HO theory serves to bring to the fore one of the most basic characteristics of trade: a country need not produce many of the goods it consumes, and therefore countries may produce different subsets of goods, with or without overlaps. Trade theorists are well versed in the proposition that a country need not produce for international markets as many goods as it has factors. In the two-commodity case this observation leads naturally to the possibility of a country's being completely specialized. Bhagwati makes good use of this possibility in suggesting that a price change can "lift all boats"—that is, raise both wages and returns to human (or physical) capital. In the many-commodity case there emerges the possibility that countries may be incompletely specialized, but to different commodities. With a large menu of production possibilities available, countries will produce the same array of commodities only if their factor endowments are quite close together. Thus even if countries share the same technology and employ no more factors than the number of commodities produced for trade, factor prices need not be equalized with trade.

The Stolper-Samuelson Theorem

Of far more relevance to the issue of the effect of trade on wage rates or the pattern of wage rates is the Stolper-Samuelson theorem. In the 2×2 version this links a change in (relative) commodity prices to changes in factor prices. This is a setting in which the adverse consequences for unskilled American labor of a price fall in world markets for the commodity in which unskilled labor is intensively used is perhaps the most strong. The technology available in America need not be the same as that used abroad; all that is required is that the relative prices change as stated. In the scenario in which (1) the only factors are skilled and unskilled labor, (2) there is a global increase in output of the commodity that uses unskilled labor at home intensively, and (3) this translates into a decrease domestically in the relative price of that good. Not only does the real return to unskilled labor fall, the gap between skilled and unskilled returns widens since skilled wages rise by a magnified amount of the price change. The interests of unskilled labor could be served by a policy of protection. However, a tariff at a given rate would still pass on the drop in world price to domestic markets. By contrast, suppose there is a quota, say of the type embodied in the MFA. If America imports this good, which has fallen in price in world markets, and the quota is binding, the price of the good on domestic markets will not fall—it may actually rise. That is, income effects of the terms of trade change encourage even greater demand for the quotaed good at home, serving to drive up the price and thus the real return to unskilled labor.[64] Even in this most simple setting, alterations in the basic Stolper-Samuelson scenario may result in increases in the world output of the commodity produced at home with unskilled-labor-intensive techniques, and yet real wages of unskilled workers in America may rise. Bhagwati is careful to stress that a Stolper-Samuelson type of depressing effect on unskilled wages of lower world prices of these goods can be blunted by protection. He sees little evidence of important domestic price changes in the 1980s.

Further variations in the simple scenario reveal how, in a multi-commodity setting, the standard Stolper-Samuelson conclusions may be reversed. For ease of exposition, suppose all labor is of the same skill level, and that capital is the single other factor of production. In figure 2-10, three positively sloped curves labeled 1, 2, and 3 reveal, for a given technology, how capital/labor ratios on the horizontal axis would be increased in each commodity if the wage/rental ratio is increased. As drawn, commodity 3 is the most capital intensive, followed by 2 and 1 in that order; no factor-intensity reversals are assumed. Assume that all three goods are traded on world markets at given prices. These prices support the heavy, broken line: a country with an extremely low capital/labor endowment ratio would produce only the first commodity, but in the range in which * and ** appear the country would be incompletely specialized to commodities 1 and 2. Further increases in the capital/labor endowment ratio would lead to complete specialization in the second commodity, whereas a country with endowment ratio H would produce both commodities 2 and 3. Let H represent home endowments and * the initial foreign endowment. Then

---

64. The effect of alterations in the terms of trade causing domestic prices of goods subject to quota to move in the opposite direction has been noted by Chipman (1987) and by Greenwood and Kimbrough (1987).

JAGDISH BHAGWATI

Figure 2-10

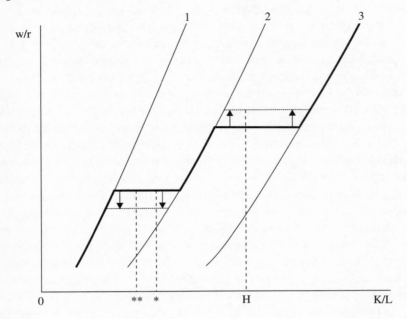

commodity 2 is produced both at home and abroad, but in each country a different commodity is also produced. Suppose this scenario is altered because the foreign country's labor force expands. (This is a proxy for new, labor-abundant countries joining the world trading nexus.) If the new endowment abroad changes to **, world prices change. Let commodity 3 serve as numeraire. The growth in the labor force abroad causes the price of commodity 1 to fall since more is produced, and of commodity 2 to rise since foreign labor is taken out of its production (the Rybczynski effect). Such a rise in p_2 widens the range of K/L ratios at which only commodity 2 is produced. The upshot: in the foreign country the increase in the labor force indeed causes the wage rate to fall. However, in the home country, commodity 2 is the labor-intensive good and as a consequence of its price rise the wage increases by a magnified amount. Thus home labor has benefited from the entry of new workers into the labor force abroad.

Note the similarity to the phenomenon of factor-intensity reversal in the two-commodity case, allowing two countries to share the same technology but have a different ranking of factor intensities.[65] In one country commodity 2 is capitalintensive; in the other it is labor intensive. But in the two-commodity version of reversal, the comparison is with a single other commodity, implying that curves such as 1 and 2 in figure 2-10 intersect. Here countries do not produce the same pair of commodities. Rather, at home, commodity 2 is the labor-intensive commodity because the other commodity also produced is commodity 3, further up the capital-intensity scale. In general, countries produce different commodities in a free-trade equilibrium, but there may be some overlap. In such a case, the commonly produced commodity must be at the high end of the ranking for one country and the low end for the other. Furthermore, note that although figure 2-10 has been drawn to suggest both countries share identical technologies, this is not at all required. All that is necessary is that commodity 2 be the capital-intensive commodity abroad and the labor-intensive commodity at home.

One possible objection to this story is that it does not seem to capture the possibility that the type of good that has proliferated in world markets along with the increase in the world labor supply is also produced at home. (Above, the home country did not produce the first commodity.) Figure 2-11 is drawn to illustrate the case in which some commodity, such as textiles, is really a differentiated product. In the international trade literature differentiated products were introduced in the development of theories to explain intraindustry trade, and it was convenient to assume that techniques of production were identical over all varieties.[66] Instead, suppose the capital-abundant home country produces a higher-quality type of textiles, T, than is produced abroad (T*). However, in demand these two varieties are highly substitutable, so that when the labor force expands abroad, the supply of textiles T* rises, reducing both its price and that of T. In figure 2-11 these price changes are shown by reductions in the range in which only T and T* are produced. Given the assumed factor endowments at home and abroad, home real wages rise since textiles in that country are capital intensive. Once again, the multicommodity HO model is consistent with a rising real wage at home in response to the rest of the world's expansion in labor supply.

As pointed out by Bhagwati and Leamer, if a country imports a commodity and does not produce it—in other words, if the range of goods

65. The popularity of the CES type of production function has perhaps made factor-intensity reversals seem more common. The CES function was chosen because of analytical convenience. One property is that except in the Cobb-Douglas case, intensity reversals are built into the functions.

66. For example, see Helpman and Krugman (1985).

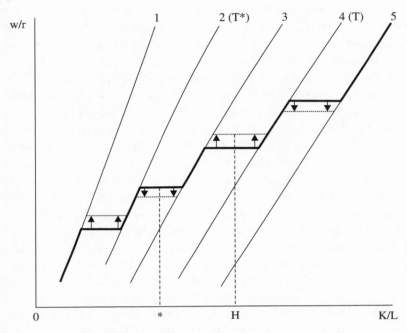

Figure 2-11

produced at home and abroad have no overlaps—a decrease in the import price serves to raise real incomes of all factors at home via the reduced cost of living. In this sense the real wage would rise.

Deficits and Nontraded Goods

If a country runs a deficit and is importing a commodity that is produced at home with labor-intensive techniques, what can be said about the effect on real wages? One line of reasoning suggests that the effect on the local economy would be like having more labor, with a consequent fall in wages. Trade theory suggests a different outcome if the model is now extended to include a nontradables sector as well. Bhagwati illustrates, correctly, that if commodity prices are held constant as the country runs a deficit and both tradables are produced, wages are also constant and that is the end of the story. However, there is no necessity that a country produce two traded goods—it may be concentrated in exportables and the nontradable. In that event, focus shifts away from a comparison of factor intensities between exportables and importables and toward a comparison of tradables and nontradables. Suppose nontradables are labor intensive (a popular assumption). Then if the country runs a deficit, spending rises relative to production, and this drives up the price of nontradables. As a consequence, the real wage is raised, counter to the earlier argument.[67]

A more classical kind of setting can be described, which links the deficit to the literature on the transfer problem. Suppose the home country is large, so that a deficit, which represents a shift of spending from the rest of the world to the home country, can alter world prices. The direction of the price change then depends on a comparison of taste patterns at home and abroad. The home country is assumed to be importing labor-intensive products. If the trade pattern is reflective of a taste pattern favoring the labor-intensive product, and if tastes are homothetic (so that marginal taste patterns also favor the labor-intensive product), a shift of world spending toward home consumers will serve to raise the relative price of labor-intensive importables, and thus the real wage. (This is the so-called antiorthodox result in the transfer literature.)

Three-Factor Models

An expansion of the model on the factor side allows for a more explicit analysis of the separate returns to skilled and unskilled labor. Thus suppose commodities are produced using these two types of labor as well as capital. If all three factors are substitutes, in the sense that an increase in the supply of any one will serve to raise the marginal products of the other two, general remarks can be made that are similar to those in the two-factor, many-commodity case. In particular, this is a good setting in which to emphasize a point stressed by Ed Leamer, namely that investment in capital and/or in developing human skills can help to improve the wage level of the unskilled workers—even if they are not the ones developing their skills. If the country produces three tradables and world prices are fixed and the endowment change (of capital or human skills) is small, admittedly factor prices will also remain unchanged. But the many-commodity case yields richer

67. In the framework of Sanyal and Jones (1982), all tradables are middle products—the output of the input tier of the economy, where goods are produced with specific factors and labor, and the input to the output tier of the economy, where tradables are combined with labor to produce a variety of nontraded consumer goods. In such a setting, a country that chooses to run a trade deficit must release labor to the output tier, and this must serve to increase the real wage.

results when investment is larger in scale; even without any changes in world prices, the country may move up the scale of production in the sense of changing the group of traded goods produced to encompass those with higher intensities in human or physical capital and thus improve the level of real wages.

There are several simplified versions of three-factor models:

—The specific-factors 3×2 model. This is a tractable model, whose properties have been well laid out.[68] The income-distribution fallout of a fall in the price of import-competing goods depends on which factor is mobile, and in which industries the specific factors are employed. The case most conducive to the result that American wages for unskilled workers fall when the domestic price of importables falls, has unskilled workers used only in import-competing industries. If skilled workers are mobile, such a price change may not improve their real returns, but they will fare well relative to unskilled workers. If, instead, physical capital is mobile between sectors and skilled labor is employed only in exportables, the relative ranking is as above, except now the positive gap between wage rates for unskilled and skilled workers widens even further.

—A broader interpretation of the 3×2 model has both exportables and importables using all three factors, but in different proportions. Now the possibility of complementarity between two of the factors is suggested. Suppose importables are the most unskilled labor-intensive sector, and exportables use skilled labor especially heavily (as in the later case in the first scenario above). If the price of importables falls (as foreigners produce more) and if human and physical capital are particularly strong complements, capital may be the big loser with the real wage of unskilled workers not changing much, and skilled labor the big winner.[69]

—A 3×3 model. If three goods are produced with the help of three distinctive inputs, factor intensities alone once again link commodity prices with factor prices. One possibility is that all three goods are traded with two importables (one of them strongly intensive in its use of unskilled labor, the other in capital) and one exportable (strongly intensive in the use of skilled labor). With strong enough intensity assumptions (for example, satisfying the Kemp and Wegge conditions), a fall in the price of unskilled-labor-intensive importables would lower wage rates for the unskilled, and unambiguously benefit capital and skilled labor.[70] By an ingenious use of the

68. In particular, see Jones (1971) and Samuelson (1971).
69. For this and other possibilities in the general 3×2 case, see Jones and Easton (1983).
70. Kemp and Wegge (1969).

Gruen and Corden model, Ronald Findlay has tradable goods using only capital and unskilled labor, with importables being labor intensive, and a third, nontradable service sector using unskilled labor in conjunction with skilled labor.[71] If the price of labor-intensive importables falls, the unskilled wage rate is depressed in Stolper-Samuelson fashion for the 2 × 2 tradable "nugget." This wage fall encourages an expansion in the service sector, drawing unskilled labor out of the traded-goods sector, which serves to contract the output of importables and expand that of exportables in typical Rybczynski fashion.[72] The "hit" that is taken in the form of output reductions in the import-competing sector is thus accentuated by the loss of labor from the tradable sector.

Technical Progress

The plight of American workers in recent years is sometimes linked to the nature of technological progress, or the lack of it. In concluding his chapter, Bhagwati seems to favor technical change as a cause of the fall in real wages over a trade explanation. Two characteristics of changes in technology have been distinguished: in which sector does technical progress take place (and by how much), and is technical progress labor saving or capital saving? The point is often stressed (for example, by Leamer in chapter 4) that the bias in technical progress is not the key issue in determining the fate of real wages. Rather, regardless of the bias, if technical progress takes place only in the capital-intensive sector of the economy (in a 2 × 2 model), the return to capital rises and the wage rate must fall. For small changes in technology it is certainly correct that at constant commodity prices it is only the differences in Hicksian measures of technical progress, and not the bias, that matters for factor prices. If the country is large enough that commodity prices are not constant, bias would come into its own since this affects the relative amounts of goods produced. Here I wish to illustrate a different way in which bias may prove important, if shifts in production functions are finite.

Figure 2-12 illustrates the point. Initially two goods are produced, X using techniques shown at A, and Y produced with the bundle of capital and

71. Gruen and Corden (1970); Findlay (1993).

72. A generalized production structure has many kinds of industry-specific capital. With trade, such a model reduces either to an $(n + 1) \times n$ version of the specific-factors model or to an $n \times n$ model with one "nugget" like that in Gruen and Corden (1970). For details, see Jones and Marjit (1992).

Figure 2-12

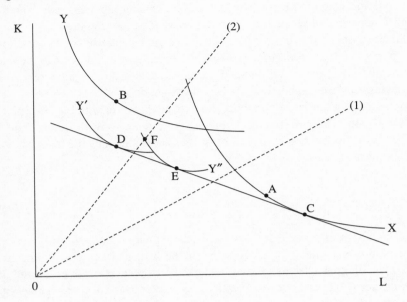

labor shown by B. Suppose that technical progress is limited to the capital-intensive Y sector, leading to a reduction of the wage rate if both goods are produced. X would be produced at point C. Two alternative types of technical progress in the Y industry are illustrated. In one the unit-value isoquant shifts to Y′, with technique D selected—a fairly unbiased shift. In the alternative case the shift is to unit-value isoquant Y″. If both goods are produced, the new technique would be shown by E, a strong capital-saving bias. If the composition of endowments is such that both commodities are produced after the change, the bias has not affected the amount of the wage rate reduction. This is exemplified in the case of a country with endowment proportions shown by ray (1). However, for a more capital-abundant country, illustrated by ray (2), biased technical progress of the kind shown by Y″ might serve to *increase* the wage/rental ratio as shown by point F. The point is that any change in technology alters the position and shape of the Hicksian composite unit-value isoquant for the economy. Factor prices are indicated by the slope of such an isoquant where it is intersected by the factor endowment ray. It is quite possible, with finite changes, that technical progress can serve to alter the composition of a nation's traded goods if it is factor biased in a particular direction, even if the composition would remain the same with neutral progress of the same Hicksian amount.

Technical progress can sometimes cause prices to change. Suppose that technical change is concentrated on the skilled-labor-intensive sector of a two-sector economy. This would tend to increase skilled wages and lower unskilled wages if commodity prices are constant. But it may also lead to a softening of the relative price of skill-intensive commodities. If so, the effect on creating wage dispersion could be dampened but not obliterated. However, note that the relationship between relative wage rates and relative commodity prices would seem to run counter to factor-intensity rankings if the source of the disturbance, technological progress, were not identified.

Other Remarks

In discussing various routes through which wage patterns are affected, Bhagwati remarks on the possibility that greater volatility in the terms of trade would lead to higher labor turnover. One possible consequence, which he stresses, is that skill acquisition would be dampened in such a case, and this could lead to slower growth of earnings. Furthermore, unskilled workers are less apt to use idle time (between jobs) to increase their skills. This line of argument may well have some validity, but so also might an "Avis" model, in which less security in employment makes workers try harder, especially if their skills are of a lower order. In my view this argument is related to another one put forward by Bhagwati, whereby a major consequence of international trade is that by creating more competition it serves to "lift all boats" in that greater efficiency is encouraged in all traded sectors and this could improve overall levels of productivity. If greater competition implies less security and more uncertainty, the competition argument might run counter to the original thesis that volatility leads to slower rate of skill improvement. Following up on the argument concerning the benefits of competition, a strong case *against* protection could be mounted by those concerned with improving wage levels for unskilled workers if they are intensively used in the import-competing sector: allowing freer trade encourages technical progress in the labor-intensive, import-competing sector, and this serves to raise real wages.

Finally, consider the changing nature of trade. Not only has trade increased as a fraction of GDP, but the fraction of trade that is reflected in intermediate goods, goods in process, and raw materials has itself risen. As Jones and Kierzkowski argue, this reflects a greater fragmentation of production processes in world markets, aided by scale gains in greater division of labor and lowered relative costs of services that facilitate fragmentation at the international level.[73] Lower transport costs, speedier and more reliable means of communication, and more information generally about conditions in other countries have encouraged formerly integrated production processes to be split up, with some parts produced in some countries and others elsewhere. Whereas previously an advanced country's unskilled labor might be used as part of an integrated production process in which that country possessed a comparative advantage, with fragmentation it becomes possible to separate out more unskilled-labor-intensive parts of the process and have them undertaken in countries with cheap labor. This may not be good news for unskilled American labor. It is an argument that seems to go hand in hand with one that asserts that labor skills are now easier to identify and classify, with the result that unskilled labor will no longer get an "average" wage for labor of indeterminate abilities, but a lower wage appropriate to lower skill levels.

International trade theory supplies a set of models of use in explaining the functional distribution of income. These models do not lead to a unique result concerning wage rates in advanced countries. Instead, they point to the importance of key ingredients: the factor-intensity composition of trade, the nature of technical progress, changes in the commodity terms of trade, and development of human and physical capital. Although a general presumption may emerge that increases in world production of and falling prices for commodities produced with unskilled-labor-intensive techniques abroad spells trouble for unskilled workers in the United States, alternative outcomes are possible. As Bhagwati has continually stressed, freer trade need not prove to be a curse for the American worker.

General Discussion

Gene Grossman opened the discussion by reiterating that factor content studies may either under- or overstate the effects of trade on labor markets. He stressed that the key point is that imports are not a measure of foreign competition, but instead will respond to domestic as well as to foreign conditions. William Dickens continued to argue that, given the range of domestic and foreign developments he believed to be plausible, factor content studies were unlikely to overstate the effects of trade, thus providing an upper bound.

73. Jones and Kierzkowski (1990).

Dani Rodrik took issue with the role that many trade economists have taken in the debate over trade and wages. He argued that, while it is certainly possible to construct models that suggest other conclusions, a core proposition from trade theory is that foreign competition in less-skilled, labor-intensive products will tend to depress real wages of less-skilled labor. Further, the effects are likely to be stronger in the short run, when labor is a quasi-fixed factor, than in the long run. In his view, many trade economists have downplayed this proposition, perhaps in the interests of promoting free trade. He argued that those who take this approach risk losing credibility. Instead, he advocated the approach of acknowledging that trade with labor-abundant countries was likely to adversely affect less-skilled domestic workers, while emphasizing the gains to other groups as a means of promoting freer trade.

William Cline took issue with the claim that trade can have no effect unless relative prices change. To make his point, he observed that there was a large increase in the real volume of U.S. apparel imports in the 1980s, which significantly outpaced growth in domestic demand for apparel. Declines in domestic production are too small to account for the discrepancy. If we were sure that apparel quality had remained constant, these developments would strongly suggest that apparel prices had indeed fallen. However, in his view the resolution to the puzzle was to recognize that apparel is not a homogeneous good and that it is very likely that domestic firms responded to competitive pressures by some combination of quality upgrading and reduced production. He agreed with a recent assessment by Richard Cooper that, in these circumstances, observed domestic prices of apparel may not decline even though output falls, and labor is released into the general economy, putting downward pressure on wages.

Adrian Wood also raised concerns about sectoral aggregation. He agreed strongly with Ronald Jones that the rising share of trade in intermediates and the splitting up of production processes into separate products are very important trends that are poorly captured in available statistics. He argued that even finely disaggregated industries are extremely diverse—and many of the changes are occurring within these industries. He wondered whether these measurement difficulties might explain why the data do not show some of the developments that many have expected to observe.

Gregory Woodhead noted that the discussion Bhagwati presents missed some aspects of the situation for American workers by focusing on the manufacturing sector. In particular, the big losers are often those who are displaced from jobs in one manufacturing industry and are forced to find jobs in other sectors of the economy.

James Albrecht suggested that the dichotomy between theoretical trade economists and empirical labor economists had been overblown by some. He saw potential insights from more work that merged trade theory with relevant theory in labor economics, such as the efficiency wage and the equilibrium search theories that have been developed to help explain persistence of unemployment.

References

Baumol, William, Sue Blackman, and Edward Wolff. 1989. *Productivity and American Leadership: The Long View.* MIT Press.
Bhagwati, Jagdish. 1991a. "Free Traders and Free Immigrationists: Strangers or Friends?" Working Paper 20. New York: Russell Sage Foundation.
———. 1991b. "Trade and Income Distribution." Paper presented at the Columbia University Conference on Deindustrialization, November 15–16.
———. 1994. "Free Trade: Old and New Challenges." *Economic Journal* 104 (March): 231–46.
———. 1995a. "Trade and Wages: Choosing among Alternative Explanations." *Federal Reserve Bank of New York Economic Policy Review* 1 (January): 42–47.
———. 1995b. "Free Trade, 'Fairness,' and the New Protectionism: Reflection on an Agenda for the World Trade Organization." 1994 Harold Wincott Lecture, Institute for Economic Affairs, London.
———. 1995c. "Trade Liberalisation and 'Fair Trade' Demands: Addressing the Environmental and Labour Standards Issue." *World Economy* 18 (November): 745–59.
———. 1996. "Private Investment and the East Asian 'Miracle' [Letter to the editor]." *Financial Times,* January 15, p. 14.
Bhagwati, Jagdish, and Vivek H. Dehejia. 1994. "Freer Trade and Wages of the Unskilled—Is Marx Striking Again?" In *Trade & Wages,* edited by Jagdish Bhagwati and Marvin H. Kosters, 36–75. Washington: American Enterprise Institute.
Bhagwati, Jagdish, and Marvin H. Kosters, eds. 1994. *Trade & Wages.* Washington: American Enterprise Institute.
Bhagwati, Jagdish N., and T. N. Srinivasan. 1983. *Lectures on International Trade.* MIT Press.
Borjas, George J., Richard B. Freeman, and Lawrence F. Katz. 1992. "On the Labor Market Effects of Immigration and Trade." In *Immigration and the Work Force: Economic Consequences for the United States and Source Areas,* edited by George J. Borjas and Richard B. Freeman, 213–44. University of Chicago Press.
Borjas, George J., and Valerie A. Ramey. 1994. "Time-Series Evidence on the Sources of Trends in Wage Inequality." *American Economic Review* 84 (May): 10–16.
Brecher, Richard A. 1974a. "Minimum Wage Rates and the Pure Theory of International Trade." *Quarterly Journal of Economics* 88 (February): 98–116.
———. 1974b. "Optimal Commercial Policy for a Minimum-Wage Economy." *Journal of International Economics* 4 (May): 139–49.

Brown, Drusilla, Alan Deardorff, and Robert Stern. 1993. "Protection and Real Wages: Old and New Trade Theories and their Empirical Counterparts." Paper prepared for conference at Bocconi University, Milan, Italy, May 27–28.

Burtless, Gary. 1996. "Widening U.S. Income Inequality and the Growth in World Trade." *Tokyo Club Papers* 9. Tokyo Club Foundation for Global Studies.

Chipman, John S. 1987. "International Trade." In *The New Palgrave: A Dictionary of Economics,* vol. 2, 922–55.

Cline, William. 1990. *The Future of World Trade in Textiles and Apparel.* Washington: Institute for International Economics.

Davis, Donald. 1995. "Does European Unemployment Prop Up American Wages?" Harvard University, Department of Economics.

Deardorff, Alan V., and Dalia S. Hakura. 1994. "Trade and Wages—What Are the Questions?" In *Trade & Wages,* edited by Jagdish Bhagwati and Marvin Kosters. Washington: American Enterprise Institute.

Dehejia, Vivek. 1992a. "Capital-Skill Complementarity and Endogenous Wage Structure." Columbia University, Department of Economics.

———. 1992b. "Kaleidoscopic Comparative Advantage and the Rising Skill Differential." Columbia University, Department of Economics.

Diebold, Francis X., David Neumark, and Daniel Polsky. 1994. "Job Stability in the United States." Working Paper 4859. Cambridge, Mass.: National Bureau of Economic Research.

Economics Focus Column. 1993. "Musical Chairs." *Economist,* July 17, p. 67.

Farber, Henry. 1995. "Are Lifetime Jobs Disappearing? Job Duration in the United States: 1973–1993." Princeton University, Department of Economics.

Findlay, Ronald. 1993. "Wage Dispersion, International Trade and the Services Sector." In *Trade, Growth and Development: The Role of Politics and Institutions,* edited by Göte Hansson, 28–40. Routledge.

Findlay, Ronald, and Harry Grubert. 1959. "Factor Intensities, Technological Progress, and the Terms of Trade." *Oxford Economic Papers* 11 (February): 111–21.

Frankel, Jeffrey, ed. 1994. *The Internationalization of Equity Markets.* University of Chicago Press.

Greenwood, Jeremy, and Kent P. Kimbrough. 1987. "An Investigation in the Theory of Foreign Exchange Controls." *Canadian Journal of Economics* 20 (May): 271–88.

Gruen, F. H., and W. M. Corden. 1970. "A Tariff that Worsens the Terms of Trade." In *Studies in International Economics,* edited by J. A. McDougall and R. H. Snape, 55–58. Amsterdam: North-Holland.

Harris, John R., and Michael P. Todaro. 1970. "Migration, Unemployment and Development: A Two-Sector Analysis." *American Economic Review* 60 (March): 126–42.

Helpman, Elhanan, and Paul R. Krugman. 1985. *Market Structure and Foreign Trade: Increasing Returns, Imperfect Competition, and the International Economy.* MIT Press.

Horvath, Francis W. 1982. "Job Tenure of Workers in January 1981." *Monthly Labor Review* 105 (September): 34–36.

Jones, Ronald W. 1971. "A Three-Factor Model in Theory, Trade and History." In *Trade, Balance of Payments and Growth: Papers in International Economics in Honor of Charles P. Kindleberger,* edited by Jagdish Bhagwati and others. Amsterdam: North-Holland.

Jones, Ronald W., and Stephen T. Easton. 1983. "Factor Intensities and Factor Substitution in General Equilibrium." *Journal of International Economics* 15 (August): 65–99.

Jones, Ronald W., and Henryk Kierzkowski. 1990. "The Role of Services in Production and International Trade: A Theoretical Framework." In *The Political Economy of International Trade,* edited by Ronald W. Jones and Anne O. Krueger, 31–48. Basil Blackwell.

Jones, Ronald W., and Sugata Marjit. 1992. "International Trade and Endogenous Production Structures." In *Economic Theory and International Trade: Essays in Memoriam—J. Trout Rader,* edited by Wilhelm Neuefeind and Raymond Riezman, 173–96. Springer-Verlag.

Kemp, Murray C., and Leon L. Wegge. 1969. "On the Relation between Commodity Prices and Factor Rewards." *International Economic Review* 1 (October): 407–13.

Kravis, Irving B. 1956. "'Availability' and Other Influences on the Commodity Composition of Trade." *Journal of Political Economy* 64 (April): 143–55.

Krugman, Paul. 1994. "The Myth of Asia's Miracle." *Foreign Affairs* 73 (November/December): 62–78.

Lawrence, Robert Z. 1994. "Trade, Multinationals, and Labor." Working Paper 4836. Cambridge, Mass.: National Bureau of Economic Research (August).

Lawrence, Robert Z., and Matthew J. Slaughter. 1993. "International Trade and American Wages in the 1980s: Giant Sucking Sound or Small Hiccup?" *Brookings Papers on Economic Activity: Microeconomics* 2: 161–226.

Levinsohn, James. 1993. "Testing the Imports-as-Market-Discipline Hypothesis." *Journal of International Economics* 35 (August): 1–22.

Lynch, Lisa. 1995. "Growing Wage Gap: Is Training the Answer?" *Economic Policy Review, Federal Reserve Bank of New York* 1 (January): 54–58.

Office of the President. 1994. *Economic Report of the President.* Government Printing Office.

Organization for Economic Cooperation and Development. 1994. *The OECD Jobs Study: Facts, Analysis, Strategies.* Paris.

Panagariya, Arvind. 1980. "Variable Returns to Scale in General Equilibrium Theory Once Again." *Journal of International Economics* 10 (November): 499–526.

Rose, Stephen J. 1993. "Declining Family Incomes in the 1980s: New Evidence from Longitudinal Data." *Challenge* 36 (November–December): 29–35.

————. 1994. "On Shaky Ground: Rising Fears about Incomes and Earnings." Research Report 94-02. Washington: National Commission for Employment Policy (October).

————. 1995. "Declining Job Security and the Professionalization of Opportunity." Research Report 95-04. Washington: National Commission for Employment Policy (May).

Rybczynski, Tad M. 1955. "Factor Endowments and Relative Commodity Prices." *Economica* 22 (November): 336–41.

Sachs, Jeffrey D., and Howard J. Shatz. 1994. "Trade and Jobs in U.S. Manufacturing." *Brookings Papers on Economic Activity 1:* 1–84.

Samuelson, Paul A. 1948. "International Trade and the Equalization of Factor Prices." *Economic Journal* 58 (June): 163–84.

————. 1949. "International Factor Price Equalisation Once Again." *Economic Journal* 59 (June): 181–97.

―――. 1971. "Ohlin Was Right." *Swedish Journal of Economics* 73 (December): 365–84.

Sanyal, Kalyan K., and Ronald W. Jones. 1982. "The Theory of Trade in Middle Products." *American Economic Review* 72 (March): 16–31.

Sehgal, Ellen. 1984. "Occupational Mobility and Job Tenure in 1983." *Monthly Labor Review* 107 (October): 18–23.

Stolper, Wolfgang F., and Paul A. Samuelson. 1941. "Protection and Real Wages." *Review of Economic Studies* 9: 58–73.

Wood, Adrian. 1994. *North-South Trade, Employment and Inequality: Changing Fortunes in a Skill-Driven World*. Oxford, England: Clarendon Press.

U.S. Department of Labor, Bureau of Labor Statistics. 1987. *Job Tenure*. Mimeo (January).

U.S. Department of Labor. 1992. "Employee Tenure and Occupational Mobility in the Early 1990s." *BLS News*. USDL 92-386 (June 26).

THREE

Will Globalization Dominate U.S. Labor Market Outcomes?

Richard B. Freeman

THE ROUGH concordance in the 1980s and 1990s between the falling real wages of less-skilled men in the United States and rising joblessness in Europe, and increased imports of manufacturing goods and sizeable immigration from less, developed countries (LDCs) has directed attention to how economic relations between economies with vastly different wages and factor endowments affect labor market outcomes. Relying on factor price equalization (FPE) arguments, some economists and others argue that trade is the cause of the falling wages of low-skill workers in the United States and of unemployment in Europe. I will call this the "globalization explains everything" claim. Other economists reject the notion that trade has had *any* deleterious effects. I will call this the "globalization explains nothing" claim. Regardless of its effects in the past, many analysts fear that globalization will have a devastating effect on the living standards of low-skill Westerners, as China, India, Indonesia, and other countries with large populations enter the world economy with massive exports of low-skill-intensive manufacturing goods—and people.

In this chapter I argue that our current state of knowledge suggests that both the "everything" and "nothing" polar claims are incorrect. As best I

I have benefited from the comments of Adrian Wood and Dani Rodrik and thank them for their help.

can tell from a diverse set of studies, globalization is not *the* cause of the problems of less-skilled Westerners, though it has contributed to the falling relative demand for their services. My current assessment—based on extant factor content studies and studies of changes in prices in sectors likely to be most affected by globalization, and the changes in wages of workers likely to be most affected by trade—is that globalization has a moderate effect on labor demand. I also reject the notion that globalization is likely to dominate U.S. or other labor market outcomes in advanced countries in the forseeable future. I offer this answer with trepidation. Economists do not have a good track record as soothsayers, and neither trade nor labor economists are an exception. Recall the great dollar shortage; the conventional wisdom that the Common Market would cure Europe's ills; the belief that a good U.S. recovery would help poor people in the 1980s; the 1930s consensus that unions were dead; and so on. This could be one of those issues where Ross Perot and Jimmie Goldsmith understand better what will happen than academics do; their wealth came in part from great foresight about economic events.

Rejecting the "globalization explains everything" hypothesis in the recent past or in the future does not mean that I accept the view that technological change nor any other single cause explains most of the observed decline in relative earnings. There is evidence for some globalization effect, and legitimate arguments that the "true effect" is larger than most studies find. The case for "technology is everything" is based more on treating residuals as technological change than on hard evidence, and it is far from consistent with all the data.[1] Much as I might prefer to have a more dramatic message—trade makes the sky fall or it cures all ills—I believe that this is a case in which conventional wisdom has got it more or less right, albeit with a wide margin of uncertainty.

Some Basic Facts

The natural place to begin is with the three trends of concern: the immiserization of low-skill workers in the United States, increased joblessness in Europe, and the increase in trade with LDCs.

Impoverishment of Low-Skill American Men

That an economic disaster has befallen low-skill Americans, especially young men, is firmly established. Researchers using several data sources,

1. The one exception is Krueger (1993); see also Mishel and Bernstein (1994).

including household survey data from the Current Population Survey (CPS), other household surveys, and establishment surveys, have documented that wage inequality and skill differentials in earnings and employment increased sharply in the United States from the mid-1970s through the 1980s and into the 1990s.[2] The drop in the relative position of less-skilled workers shows up in various ways:

—greater educational earnings differentials;

—greater age earnings differentials for those who did not graduate from college;

—greater occupational wage differentials;

—a widened earnings distribution overall and within detailed groups;

—reduced time worked by low-skill workers;

—smaller gender differentials; and

—falling real earnings for a large proportion of the work force.

Rather than review this terrain, which has been so highly worked over, I draw attention to aspects of the changes that are particularly relevant to the globalization–labor market issue.

First, in the United States the real wages of low-skill workers fell in absolute as well as relative terms. Had increased earnings inequality coincided with rapidly growing real earnings, so that the living standards of low-skill workers increased or held steady, no one would be sounding the alarm. But in the past decade or two, real earnings grew sluggishly, reducing the economic position of low-skill men (especially younger men) by staggering amounts.[3] For instance, the real hourly wages of young males with twelve or fewer years of schooling dropped by 20 percent from 1979 to 1989.[4] The real hourly earnings of all men in the bottom decile of the earnings distribution also fell by about 20 percent since the early or mid-1970s.

If the increase in earnings inequality took the form solely of changes in wages among identifiable skill groups, or if changes in within-group differentials occurred contemporaneously with changes in across-group differentials, explaining the rise of inequality would be easier. But all extant data sets show an increase in within-group earnings inequality. One major data set, the March files of the CPS, indicates that this increase began earlier than the rise in differentials among observable skill groups. (Another data set, the Annual Demographic Files of the CPS, shows a different timing

2. See Katz and Murphy (1992).

3. Whether real earnings fell, held steady, or rose modestly depends on the years covered, the deflator used, and how fringe benefits are treated.

4. Freeman and Katz (1994, p. 33).

in the increase in within-group inequality.)[5] A "full explanation" of the increase in inequality has to explain why pay inequality among carpenters, accountants, and sales clerks outside the traded-goods sector has risen, as well as why differentials between college and high school graduates or between nonproduction and production workers in manufacturing have risen.

Had the annual hours worked by different skill groups been stable, the problem would also be easier, for we could then use changes in hourly earnings as our sole measure of the twist in the labor market against less-skilled workers. But despite huge drops in relative pay for some groups of workers, the relative employment of those who are less skilled deteriorated, their relative unemployment rate failed to improve, and the proportion of low-skill men who were incarcerated rose. The implication is that changes in relative earnings *understate* the fall in relative demand for those groups; the twist in the job market exceeds the huge increase in hourly earnings inequality.

Further complicating the problem of explanation, one low-wage group, women, improved their standing. The gender differential declined even among low-skill workers, because the real wages of less-educated women have been roughly constant, while those of their male compatriots fell.[6] Because it is in the highly female-labor-intensive industries such as clothing manufacturing that LDC import penetration (imports/domestic consumption) is greatest and increased most in percentage points, the fact that the real wages of less-skilled women rose relative to those of less-skilled men creates a major problem for any standard trade model that makes the traded-goods sector the key determinant of changes in wages.[7] The key prediction for wages in a Heckscher-Ohlin (HO) model is that the group most intensively employed in the sectors that compete with cheap imports should have the greatest loss of wages. But in no advanced countries has the pay or employment of low-skill women fallen as much as that of men. Evidently, factors beyond trade have affected the labor market for women. Presumably these include the growth of service sector jobs and the possible movement of women into non-import-competing manufacturing.

5. Freeman and Katz (1994, p. 36).

6. At the upper end of the skill distribution, women have moved into many high wage professional and managerial jobs, such as law, medicine, and the like, where they have enjoyed more rapid wage increases than their male compatriots (though there still remains a gender gap).

7. See Organization for Economic Cooperation and Development (OECD) (1995, table 3.5), p. 65.

Unemployment in Europe

Although my focus in this chapter is on the United States, I also refer to European developments at various points. There are two facts to note about European labor market experience. First, the rate of unemployment in Europe, after having been lower throughout the post–World War II period than the rate in the United States, grew to exceed the U.S. level after 1983.[8] The ratio of employment to the population of working age and hours worked per employee in Europe relative to the United States has shown a downward trend since the 1970s, creating an even greater U.S.-European gap in the percentage of the adult population employed and in person-hours worked by that population. In addition, in the OECD–Europe, nearly half of unemployed workers are out of work for more than a year compared with about 10 percent of unemployed workers in the United States.[9]

If wage inequality had risen in Europe as much as in the United States or was near U.S. levels, or if the real wages of low-skill Europeans had fallen, high joblessness would be a devastating indictment of European reliance on institutional forces to determine labor market outcomes. But the second important aspect of European developments is that (save for the United Kingdom) Europe avoided U.S.-level inequality or changes in inequality; wages at the bottom of the distribution rose rather than fell (increasing slightly in the United Kingdom).[10] By the early 1990s, workers in the bottom tiers of the wage distribution in Europe had higher compensation than workers in the bottom tiers in the United States.[11] Moreover, despite this, employment versus population rates for men who did not complete high school were higher in Europe than in the United States.[12] In any case, the likely effect of trade on the job market in Europe is on employment. This has implications for interpreting factor content studies in the United States as well as in Europe.

Globalization

Spurred by debates over trade barriers, much analysis has concentrated on the effects of trade with LDCs. But the concept of globalization properly goes beyond reduced trade barriers and increased trade with LDCs. It

8. Freeman (1994, figure 1.2, pp. 3–4).
9. Freeman (1994, figure 1.3, p. 6).
10. Freeman and Katz (1994).
11. Freeman (1994).
12. OECD (1994).

includes immigration, international capital mobility, and the transmission of technology across national lines. We must consider them all if we are to give the "globalization explains everything" hypothesis full opportunity to explain the troubles of low-skill Western workers.

TRADE AND TRADE BARRIERS. The most commonly used indicator of the trade component of globalization is the ratio of exports plus imports to gross domestic product (GDP). In the United States this ratio more than doubled. Trade in Europe has increased less dramatically but has also gone up relative to GDP. More important for current purposes, however, is that imports of manufactures from LDCs increased greatly. By 1990, 35 percent of U.S. imports were from LDCs, compared with 14 percent in 1970. In the European Economic Community (EEC) 12 percent of imports were from LDCs (a lower figure due largely to high levels of intra-European trade) compared with 5 percent in 1970. In 1992, 58 percent of LDC exports to the advanced Western countries consisted of light-manufacturing goods compared with 5 percent in 1955.[13]

Trade barriers in advanced countries have fallen, which presumably contributed to the rise in LDC imports. Panel A of table 3-1 shows the average size of tariffs in 1950 and 1990. But panel B of this table reveals a continued role of several nontariff measures in a number of sectors in which LDCs have or may gain comparative advantage. These range from voluntary restraints under the Multi-Fiber Agreement (MFA) to antidumping and countervailing duty actions to various licensing requirements. Panel C in the table shows that there has been relatively little decline in nontariff measures in the United States and none in the EEC.

The increase in manufacturing imports from LDCs presumably reflects several forces, some emanating from developed countries (such as the reduction in trade barriers) and some from the move of LDCs to free trade.[14] The shift in LDC development strategies from import substitution to export promotion, under World Bank and International Monetary Fund (IMF) pressures, has been substantial. Table 3-2 shows a massive increase in the trade share of the GDP of major LDC countries.

Developments in LDC labor markets also contributed to the increased role of those countries in world markets. The LDC share of the world work force increased from 69 percent in 1965 to 75 percent in 1990; mean years of schooling in the LDC world rose from 2.4 years in 1960 to 5.3 years in

---

13. OECD (1994a) for 1992 data; Wood (1994) for 1955 data.
14. Rodrik (1992).

Table 3-1. *Changes in Tariffs and Nontariff Measures in the United States and the European Community, 1950, 1990*

A. Average tariff rates on manufactured products

	1950	1990
United States	14	5
United Kingdom	23	6
Germany	26	6
France	18	6
Italy	25	6

B. Import coverage ratios of nontariff measures[a]

	All measures	Volume-restraining measures
All items	18	11
Food	38	26
Clothing	63	58
Textile	38	34
Footwear	22	8
Leather	14	1
Iron and steel	54	34
Vehicles	55	28

C. Trends in trade coverage ratios

	1981	1990
All sectors, all nontariff measures		
United States	100	80
European Community	100	113
Nonfuel trade, core measures		
United States	100	106
European Community	100	109

Sources: United Nations Committee on Trade and Development (UNCTAD) (1994, p. 123); and OECD (1994a, tables 3.8, 3.9).

a. For selected OECD countries, including the United States.

Table 3-2. *Ratios of Exports and Imports as a Percentage of GDP in Selected Low-Wage Countries That Have Increased Their Presence in the World Trading System, Selected Years, 1970–92*[a]

	1970–72	1980–82	1990–92
Chile	25.6	44.5	67.2
China	5.5	15.3	36.1
Egypt	32.7	74.8	68.3
Greece	29.7	47.3	54.9
India	8.5	15.8	19.4
Indonesia	30.5	51.3	52.7
Korea	41.2	75.0	63.0
Malaysia	75.4	111.3	161.1
Mexico	14.9	24.2	32.5
Pakistan	21.6	34.9	40.0
Philippines	40.9	49.8	62.0
Portugal	57.2	73.4	81.3
Thailand	35.5	52.5	79.4
Turkey	16.8	26.4	43.4

Source: OECD (1994a, table 2.1).

a. Countries excluded are Algeria, Bangladesh, and Brazil, which did not substantially increase their trade ratios; Hong Kong, Singapore, and Spain, as relatively high-wage countries; and the oil-producing countries.

1986.[15] The LDC share of world manufacturing employment grew more rapidly than its share of the work force—from 40 percent in 1960 to 53 percent in 1986. This suggests that these countries attained the skills and wherewithal to play a larger role in world trade in manufacturing goods.

Although Western imports of manufacturing goods produced in LDCs increased greatly, analysts have tended to ignore a second fact about LDC-advanced country trade: *the LDC import share of overall commodity consumption in the advanced countries did not rise.* Changes in oil and other primary-product prices kept the LDC import share of consumption roughly constant in North America (5.1 percent of commodity consumption from

15. My tabulations are based on World Bank data for individual countries given in the Bank's publicly available diskettes on social indicators. The LDC share of world manufacturing employment grew more rapidly than its share of the work force—from 40 percent in 1960 to 53 percent in 1986. This suggests that these countries attained the skills and wherewithal to play a larger role in world trade in manufacturing goods.

Table 3-3. *Increased Foreign-Born in the United States and Western Europe, Selected Years, 1950–90*
Percent

	1950	1960	1970	1980	1990
United States					
Foreign-born population	6.9	5.4	4.7	6.2	7.9
Immigrant flows per decade born in LDCs[a]	n.a.	51	79	88	n.a.
Foreign-born population from LDCs	n.a.	n.a.	n.a.	n.a.	74.4
Western Europe					
Foreign-born population	1.3	n.a.	2.2	3.1	4.5

Sources: U.S. Department of Commerce (1993, tables 54, 55); and OECD (1995, table 6.1).
n.a. Not available.
a. Data are the decadal flows in the respective years shown. Data are estimated as the total, minus Europe, Japan, and Canada, plus the Soviet Union (treated as an LDC).

LDCs in 1980–81 and 5.2 percent in 1989–90) and reduced it in the European Union ([EU] 7.6 percent of consumption from LDCs in 1980–81 and 4.9 percent in 1989–90). Although increased energy prices were at the heart of discussions of the real wage problems of Westerners in the 1970s, the potential effect of reduced energy prices on OECD job markets has received little attention in the globalization–labor market debate. If the rise in energy prices was a major cause for the slowdown or decline in real wages in the United States and for the growth of unemployment in western Europe, why did the fall in relative energy prices not lead to a rebound in real earnings?

IMMIGRATION. In the period of rising inequality, the United States increased its immigrant population (see table 3-3). In the 1970 census, 4.8 percent of the population was born overseas; in the 1990 census, 7.9 percent were born overseas.[16] The latter figure understates the proportion in the population, because the census undercounts Hispanics in general and illegal immigrants in particular. From the 1950s to the mid-1960s most immigrants to the United States were from advanced countries; in the 1970s and 1980s most were from LDCs. With changes in the nation's immigration law, special allowances for refugees, and admittance of many immigrants on family reunification grounds, about three-quarters of the foreign-born in 1990 were from LDCs.

16. U.S. Bureau of the Census.

Simply because an immigrant comes from an LDC does not mean that he or she adds to the supply of less-skilled labor in the United States. Indian medical doctors or Ph.D.s and Filipina nurses are proof that the United States (and other advanced countries) can "import" highly educated workers from LDCs—shades of the old brain-drain debate. Still, nearly all of the less-skilled immigrants to the United States are from LDCs, largely from Mexico and Latin America. Borjas has shown that, on average, the education and earnings capacity of immigrants has fallen further behind that of natives in the 1970s and 1980s.[17] The skill structure of the immigrant stream is in fact bimodal. A disproportionate number of U.S. immigrants have less than a high school education, and a disproportionate number are highly skilled. On average, the latter group dominates the flow.

The magnitude of immigration flows to the United States has been large relative to increased trade with LDCs. Immigration represents a long-term change in the nation's labor endowment. In the period of rising wage inequality, immigration raised the supply of high school dropouts by roughly 25 percent, which far exceeds the increase in the "implicit labor supply" of these workers due to trade.[18] These calculations show that *the stock of immigrants had a much larger effect on factor endowments than net trade.* Adjustments in skill coefficients à la Wood would raise the relative effect of trade, but this would not gainsay that immigration substantially affected the nation's factor endowments. To the extent that adherents to "globalization explains everything" base their assessments solely on trade, they are implicitly assuming that immigration (and anything else that might affect demand and supply) has zero effect on the job market. Otherwise, we will be in the unbelievable situation of explaining more than 100 percent of the deterioration in the job market of less-skilled workers, whereas we normally are dealing with large, unexplained residuals. Because immigrants tend to work in import-competing activities, I interpret immigration and trade as substitute means of moving the U.S. factor endowment toward the world factor endowment of unskilled workers.[19] The sum of the immigrant and trade flows would be the proper measure of the globalization effect on national labor endowments.

There is moreover an important difference between the potential effects of immigration and trade that suggests that immigration may pose a greater

17. Borjas (1995).

18. According to factor content calculations by Borjas, Freeman, and Katz (1996).

19. Abowd and Freeman (1991).

long-term challenge to less-skilled workers. Whereas unskilled Americans can find "refuge" from competition with unskilled, low-wage foreign workers through employment in nontraded goods or in skill-intensive export sectors, these workers have no such locational advantage in competition with immigrants. Trade exports the services of low-skill workers from LDCs in goods that the U.S. imports and affects low-skill U.S. workers to the extent that the United States produces those goods. Immigration exports the services of low-skill workers from LDCs to *all* domestic employers. Specialization in tradables that use high-skill workers "protects" low-skill Westerners from competition with low-wage workers in LDC countries, but not from low-wage immigrants from those countries.

Diffusion of Technology

Diffusion of modern technology to LDCs has arguably eroded the advantage that low-wage Americans had over LDC workers in access to advanced technology. Some erosion of technology occurred because of the expansion of multinational companies, or transnational companies (TNCs), as UNCTAD calls them. UNCTAD estimates that one-third of world output is "under the common governance of TNCs and hence potentially part of an integrated international production system," with access to similar to technology.[20] In terms of direct employment, however, the figures on TNCs are less impressive. UNCTAD estimates that 73 million people were directly employed in TNCs or their affiliates in 1992, with 25 million employed by U.S. TNCs in 1990.[21] Of the total, an estimated 12 million worked in LDCs—"less than 2 percent of the economically active population in most of those countries."[22] These statistics suggest that direct access to modern technologies at the workplace through TNC employment is relatively modest. If technological transfer through TNCs is a major factor bringing LDC labor to the technology frontier, it must be occurring through indirect means: linking workers in local firms that supply the TNC to TNC technology.[23] Such outsourcing may be important, but at present, we lack credible estimates that show that it has massive effects.

20. UNCTAD (1994, p. xxii).
21. UNCTAD (1994, p. 175).
22. UNCTAD (1994, p. 185).
23. The UNCTAD (1994) report does show convincingly that the vast bulk of technology receipts to American and other Western firms come from affiliated enterprises in developing countries (p. 142).

Another potentially important mode of technology transfer is through the education of LDC students in Western universities—a topic I ignore here, although it surely deserves attention.

Finally, capital flows may also have made employees in LDCs more competitive with less-skilled workers in the United States and other developed countries. At one time, I would have stressed direct foreign investment (DFI) and capital flows rather than the flow of technology as central to globalization. But the rapid change in the direction of capital flows that turned the United States from creditor to debtor and that brought considerable LDC capital into the country makes it hard to argue that international investment has adversely affected the wages of low-skill Americans. Still, UNCTAD stresses DFIs in its analysis of TNCs, and investments in Mexico were a key issue in the North American Free Trade Agreement (NAFTA) debate. I do not explore capital flows in this chapter.

In sum, various changes—in immigration, in trade resulting from reduced trade barriers, in the increased number of LDC workers with sufficient skills to produce manufactured goods for world markets, in the potential transfer of technology and integration of work across international borders by multinationals, and in capital flows—increased the linkages between the United States and LDCs in ways that placed greater pressure on the economic position of less-skilled Americans than in the past. The question is not whether these factors operate, but the magnitude of their effects.

Evidence and Its Interpretation

"As the billions of people who live in East Asia and Latin America qualify for good, modern jobs, the half billion Europeans and North Americans who used to tower over the rest of the world will find their upward progress in living standards encountering tough resistance."[24]

Efforts to estimate whether globalization contributed to the growing immiserization of Western workers has taken four forms:

—studies that exploit quantity data on the "factor content" of import and export industries and of immigration to estimate the implicit change in factor endowments in advanced countries due to trade;

—studies that exploit price data to see if the world economy has induced sizeable drops in the prices of goods produced by low-skilled Westerners, which would then translate into lower wages;

24. Paul Samuelson, quoted in Bhagwati and Dehejia (1994, p. 41).

—studies that exploit regional variation in immigrant flows—for example, between states such as California, New York, Florida, and Texas, and mid-American states—to infer the effects of immigration on native wages and employment; and

—studies that exploit differences across countries and over time in trade flows to assess the effects of trade on wages or employment.

Factor Content Analyses

Let us consider first factor content studies, in which labor input coefficients are used to weight observed changes in trade flows to determine how those changes alter "effective" labor endowments. The *change* in endowments due to a *change* in trade is estimated as the multiplicand of a matrix of sectoral labor skill inputs (a_{ij}, where i = labor skill and j = industry) and a vector of changes in sectoral imports (M_j) minus exports (X_j).[25] If tomorrow the United States imported ten additional children's toys produced with an unskilled labor input coefficient of 0.5, this technique would estimate that the nation's effective endowment of unskilled workers had increased by five (or alternatively, that demand for those workers would fall by five) compared with the alternative in which those ten toys were produced domestically. Any trade-balancing flow of exports in skill-intensive sectors would, contrarily, reduce the effective endowment of skilled workers (raise their demand) and increase their pay. Deardorff and Staiger show that changes in the factor content of trade can be used to indicate the effects of trade on relative factor prices in one version of the trade model. The basic idea is that factor content calculations produce "autarky-equivalent" factor endowments that map into relative factor prices.[26] However, to turn the estimates of increases in factor endowments into changes in wages requires one additional parameter: an estimate of how relative wages respond to a change in the relative supply of labor skills. These estimates have come from time series analyses for the entire economy.[27]

25. Alternatively, multiplying the matrix of skill coefficients by the vector of exports minus imports gives the estimated change in labor demand for skill i at existing wages due to actual trade flows.

26. Deardorff and Staiger (1988).

27. Leamer has usefully pointed out that estimates of the response of relative wages to changes in supply may differ depending on trade. But there is no evidence that elasticities have changed dramatically over time as the U.S. economy has become more open, nor that they differ across countries with different degrees of openness.

What do factor content of trade studies find? Given that the United States imports goods that require intensive low-skill labor to produce and exports goods that require intensive high-skill labor to produce, they necessarily show a change in relative endowments toward the scarce factor—unskilled labor—which in turn implies some loss of relative pay. But studies that use observed skill coefficients for industries yield modest estimated impacts. As an example, consider the analysis by Borjas, Freeman, and Katz, which updates and modifies their 1989 paper by making an adjustment for the trade deficit to focus on the factor content of trade with a trade balance.[28] This study estimates that the change in trade across industries from 1980 to 1990 increased the supply of workers with less than twelve years of schooling by 2.3 percentage points, while reducing the implicit number of college graduates by 1.3 percentage points.[29] The net shift in the implicit endowment of less-educated to more-educated workers due to trade from 1980 to 1990 was roughly a 4 percent increase in the number of workers who had not graduated from high school relative to college graduates (1.023/0.987). By contrast, the change in immigration over the period had a much larger effect on the number of workers with less than twelve years of schooling. In 1990 immigrants added 26.2 percent more workers with less than twelve years of schooling to the nation's endowment of those workers. This compares to an additional 12.2 percent increase in the nation's endowment of workers with less than twelve years of schooling in 1980, due to an influx of immigrants. Thus, the 1980–90 immigration raised the implicit supply of less-educated workers by considerably more than did the growth of trade over the same period.

Other studies that examine the effect of the volume of trade on employment give similar magnitudes of effects. Sachs and Shatz report that increased import penetration from LDCs from 1978 to 1990 reduced manufacturing employment modestly.[30] Cooper showed that the number of less-skilled workers displaced by imports in low-wage industries was small relative to the supply of less-skilled workers in the rest of the economy.[31] OECD estimates of the loss of employment due to trade also show modest effects.[32] In a study of European data, Cortes and Pisani-Ferry use factor content analysis to assess the effects of French trade with non-OECD countries from 1977 to 1993, finding that it "resulted in a job loss of about 350,000,

28. Borjas, Freeman, and Katz (1996).
29. Borjas, Freeman, and Katz (1996, table 3, p. 248).
30. See chapter 5.
31. Cooper (1994).
32. OECD (1995).

almost entirely among low-skill workers."[33] Because there was no fall in the relative earnings of less-skilled French workers, this statistic tells their entire story. They conclude that trade had at most a modest effect on the implicit labor supply of workers by skill.

The insight these studies bring is that *by itself* the observed *volume* of trade flows has not displaced enough workers to support the "globalization explains everything" hypothesis. The analysis must be "augmented" in various ways to obtain a large quantitative effect.[34]

Why do factor content and related job displacement studies show only a modest effect of trade on the job market for less-skilled male workers? There are three reasons.

First, the relatively modest proportion of American workers employed in the major traded-goods sector, manufacturing, and thus directly "at risk" of being displaced due to imports of LDC goods. In 1995, 18.5 million Americans worked in manufacturing; this was just 14.8 percent of employed people. Despite the trade deficit, approximately 33 percent of these workers were employed in exporting industries, and an (overlapping) 38 percent employed in high-technology industries. Only 2 percent of the work force was in the manufacturing sectors that faced substantial LDC import competition (apparel, leather, furniture). Taking these figures back to 1980, before LDC imports rose rapidly to the United States, raises the number of Americans employed in manufacturing to 20.3 million, or 21 percent of the total, but does not greatly increase the number employed in industries subject to substantial LDC import competition. Bringing tradable services into the picture would increase the proportion "at risk." Still, the number of U.S. employees directly competing with LDC workers is modest compared with, for example, the influx of women workers into the economy and the overall growth of employment over these periods.[35]

Second, even within manufacturing, the less-skilled workers whose fall in wages are in question are not exclusively employed in import-intensive sectors. A sizable number work in export industries. The more modest the difference in skill coefficients between the sectors, the smaller the potential loss of unskilled jobs due to trade. In 1993 the United States had positive net exports in six industries; 62 percent of employees in those industries were production workers, compared with 71 percent of employees in

33. Cortes and Pisani-Ferry (1995, p. 24). They further note that this is due largely to a trade deficit rather than differing factor contents of imports and exports.
34. See Wood (1994).
35. U.S. Bureau of the Census (1996, table 654, with export and import industries from table 1308).

Table 3-4. *Average Characteristics of the 1980 U.S. Labor Force*[a]
Percent

	Age 16–24	African American	Female	Some college education or higher
Top twenty export industries	18	8	30	26
Top twenty import industries	20	11	45	15
Nontraded goods and services	25	10	51	31

Source: Abowd and Freeman (1991, table 8).
a. Industry averages weighted by employment in each industry.

industries with trade deficits.[36] The differences in skill mixes between export and import sectors are in the "right direction" for an explanation of trade flows based on relative factor endowments, but these differences are more modest than many might expect. Table 3-4 shows that even in 1980 the average characteristics of workers in industries that were import intensive and export intensive were not that different, though they clearly differ in the direction that would be expected from comparative advantage. The smaller the differences in skill mixes between export and import industries, the smaller the effect of changes in their relative size on the two groups of workers.

Finally, despite wages one-tenth of those in the United States, LDC imports have not wiped out employment in broadly defined, import-intensive sectors. Presumably this reflects differences in U.S.-produced and imported products in broad industry aggregates. LDC competition notwithstanding, employment in apparel manufacturing in the United States was 0.9 million in 1995.[37]

Given these facts, it is hard to see how pressures on wages emanating from trade volumes could determine wages economywide. Consider two economies, A and B. In A, 75 percent of the nation's unskilled workers are in import-competing industries, and increased trade with LDCs potentially displaces one in ten of those workers through increased imports. In B, 15 percent of unskilled workers are in import-competing industries, and trade potentially displaces one in ten of them through increased imports. To argue that trade affects the wages of unskilled workers in B to the same extent it does in A seems farfetched (although given appropriate assumptions, this is an implication of FPE). If this does not seem farfetched, change the numbers. What if 2 percent of unskilled workers are employed in the

36. U.S. Bureau of the Census (1994, tables 656 and 1332).
37. U.S. Bureau of the Census (1996, table 654).

import-competing industries in economy B . . . or 0.2 percent? Quantities do not matter if the demand for unskilled labor is infinitely elastic, which seems contrary to statistical evidence; otherwise they do matter. If trade is going to have a huge effect on unskilled Americans, though actual flows potentially displace relatively few workers and have only modest effects on the nation's relative endowments of labor skills, then trade will have to work (and quite powerfully) in other ways. This may be through Wood's augmented factor content calculations, or through the price changes that some trade economists believe are the sole legitimate piece of evidence on the effects of globalization on the labor market.

Augmented Factor Content

Wood's factor content study differs from the conventional ones in a number of ways that leads him to endorse the "globalization explains everything" hypothesis.[38] His result comes first by increasing the unskilled-labor input ratios used in these calculations, and then by augmenting the factor content calculations with other mechanisms, such as induced technical change and spillovers to nonmanufacturing. Wood argues that estimated changes in effective labor endowments based on existing labor input coefficients in advanced countries *understate* the impact of trade. Existing input coefficients are biased against finding a big disemployment effect, because they fail to take into account the labor-intensive goods that would be produced in sectors absent trade. LDCs export different and noncompeting goods within sectors than the goods produced by advanced countries (for example, we make high-tech toys, the Chinese make low-tech toys). The "right" labor skill coefficients to determine how imports alter relative factor endowments are those for the imported products. Wood uses the coefficients in developing countries adjusted for labor demand responses to higher wages in advanced countries as the right ones. With his coefficients, the decline in labor demand for unskilled workers due to imports of manufactures is estimated to be "ten times" as large as conventional ones.[39] This is no trivial adjustment, though by itself it does not bring the estimated effect of trade close to "everything."

Is it right? The problem of differing mixes of products within industries is real. Ideally, we should estimate trade effects using the labor input coefficients associated with the actual goods displaced by the imports than

38. Wood (1994).
39. Wood (1994, p. 10).

by input coefficients for an entire sector in some pretrade period. Wood's adjustment is presumably in the right direction, though my guess is that it is excessive.[40]

Second, Wood asserts that trade with LDCs induced substantial labor-saving innovation in the traded-goods sector. This further reduces demand for unskilled labor. The problem of induced technical change is a real one, and the adjustment may be in the right direction but evidence on its magnitude is weak. Sachs and Shatz find little difference in the rate of change of total factor productivity by skill intensity of labor in manufacturing in the 1980s, though they note that the link between low-skill intensity and the rate of change in total factor productivity in the 1980s was more negative than in the 1970s (when it was positive).[41] More evidence is needed to establish the magnitude of the effect, if any, of trade pressures on technological change.

Even if one accepts Wood's adjusted factor content analysis for traded goods and his estimate of induced technological change, the problem remains that most unskilled workers are employed outside the traded-goods sector. His adjustment in input coefficients and estimated induced change in input coefficients raise the proportion of the fall in demand for unskilled labor due to trade from the 10 percent or so found in standard factor content calculations to about 50 percent. To reach a higher estimate, it is necessary to attribute some of the economywide change in demand for less-skilled workers to trade. Wood analyzes the extent to which trade-induced technological changes might spill over to nontraded sectors. The evidence is far from conclusive.

The Wood analysis lays out the path one must follow in the factor content approach to attribute immiserization of less-skilled workers in the West to globalization. Some of the steps along the way are problematic (as Wood is fully aware). Shift-share analyses (of which the factor content calculations are an example) rarely explain large economic changes. Something more must be added in, which Wood does.

Assessing Factor Content Studies

Some trade economists have criticized factor content studies because they concentrate on the quantity side of the economy.[42] Others support this model.[43]

---

40. It is normal in factor content studies to use base-period input ratios and ensuing changes in imports. Thus, the labor-intensive goods that presumably make up the increased imports are included in the base-period inputs. What is really needed to deal with this problem are "marginal" input coefficients rather than average coefficients for an entire sector.

41. See chapter 5.

42. Bhagwati and Dehejia (1994); Leamer (1994); Deardorff and Hakura (1994).

43. Sachs and Shatz (1994), and chapter 5 in this book; Cooper (1994); Krugman (1995).

The first criticism of the factor content calculations is that they "do not necessarily capture the effect of price pressures that operate through trade."[44] "It is the *absence of trade barriers,* and not any measure of the volume or terms of trade, that affects factor prices."[45] Consider the following scenario. Manufacturer X tells his workers that he and his competitors are going to import toys currently produced in his U.S. factory, or move his plant to an LDC to produce the toys at far lower cost than in the United States. The workers accept a cut in pay to keep their jobs. In this situation we would observe lower pay due to the possibility of trade, but no trade. The invisible hand would have done its job, with proper invisibility. Factor content analyses, which measure the globalization effect on the basis of *observed trade,* would tell us that trade did not affect pay, when in fact it was the determining factor. One can have FPE without trade or with relatively little trade.

How plausible is this scenario? I do not doubt that manufacturers' threats to move overseas have some effect on wage setting. Certainly, the message is there. In early 1995, the head of the U.K. Confederation of Business Industry declared that Western workers would have to lower their wage expectations to compete in the global market with low-wage workers from developing countries.[46] The problem with factor content calculations is that like other fixed-coefficient analyses, they treat changes in production (due to imports) as output shocks that affect employment at *existing* wages. If wages adjusted rapidly to the threat of imports, limiting import flows, factor content estimates of trade pressures will be biased downward. Deardorff and Hakura stress that "the volume of trade and the level of wages are simultaneously determined," implying that the trade-wage link is not a meaningful one to explore without additional specification of why one or the other shifted the equilibrium.[47] An empirical response might be to instrument the volume of trade on its potential determinants, such as exchange rates, as Revenga has done with respect to the effect of trade on employment by industry (without greatly changing the magnitudes of results obtained from analyses that assume trade flows are exogenous).[48]

In the United States, where the wages of less-skilled workers have fallen sharply, factor content calculations will understate the trade pressure. If the pay of low-skill Americans had not fallen in the 1980s, I would expect to

44. Lawrence (1994, p. 16).
45. Deardorff and Hakura (1994, p. 78).
46. *Financial Times,* January 13, 1995.
47. Deardorff and Hakura (1994, pp. 77–78).
48. Revenga (1992).

see greater imports and loss of jobs, producing a greater estimated trade-induceddisemployment than in the factor content calculation. But the situation is different in western Europe, where labor market institutions maintain the wages of less-skilled workers. With roughly fixed relative wages, factor content studies should give a more accurate picture of trade effects in Europe, because the "threat effect" and simultaneity in wage and import determination is basically ruled out.[49] In such a situation, one would expect to see greater LDC import flows into Europe and greater estimated employment displacement effects than in the United States. In fact, LDC import flows are lower into Europe and displacement effects in Europe are, if anything, lower than estimates of those effects in the United States (as in the study of France conducted by Cortes and Pisani-Ferry).[50] The working assumption in U.S. studies, that increased imports index the magnitude of the exogenous shock to the job market resulting from reduced trade barriers and the increased competence of LDC workers, may not be all that wrong.

A second problem is that the conventional factor content studies ignore responses of demand for output to potential changes in prices (Wood makes adjustments for this).[51] Assume that the United States did not import more low-tech children's toys during the 1980s but produced them domestically. They would do so at higher prices. Presumably this would result in fewer low-tech toys being produced than were imported, as demand shifted to other products. By assuming that consumers would buy the same amount of higher-priced, domestically produced goods as they actually bought of imports, the factor content calculations *overstate* the potential effect of imports on the employment of unskilled labor. What is needed to assess the possible magnitude of this effect are elasticities and cross elasticities of product demand, which are not readily available.

The third criticism with factor content studies is that they often have not adequately laid out the counterfactual underlying the calculations.[52] The thrust of the critique directs attention to the question of why imports from LDCs increased so much in the 1980s and 1990s? Imports to the West could have risen for any and all of the reasons given earlier: reductions of trade barriers, increased skills of workers in LDCs, spread of technology, or changes in

49. This is what motivates the factor content analysis by Cortes and Pisani-Ferry (1995) regarding the French situation: "The French labor market is far from flexible [in its wage-setting behavior]. We therefore consider it unlikely that factor prices have adjusted in the absence of changes in trade flows" (p. 13).
50. Cortes and Pisani-Ferry (1995).
51. Wood (1994).
52. See Collins (1991).

development policies in LDCs. Or they could have risen because the United States (or other advanced economies) were stretched to the limit, so that import-competing sectors could not have have increased their production and hired more workers. In this case, the causality runs from labor (that is, other) shortages to imports. Given the levels of joblessness of unskilled workers in OECD countries in the 1980s and 1990s (including the United States) and the seemingly sizeable supply elasticity of women workers, this is an implausible assumption. As long as the volume of imports increased as a result of reduced trade barriers, increased competence of LDC workers, the spread of technology, and LDC policies and was not overly affected by reductions in wages in the United States, the increase in imports from LDCs is a reasonable proxy for the shift in production induced by these exogenous changes.

But problems with a mode of analysis do not mean that it is useless, nor that the volume of trade (which underlies the calculations) is irrelevant to assessing the trade-labor market linkage, as some trade economists have claimed. Indeed, in response to criticisms, in chapter 5 Sachs and Shatz argue that the capital flows that may underlie increased LDC exports can yield trade-induced declines in the wages of unskilled labor, with no change in relative prices, and that monopolistic competition can also reduce employment without showing up in goods prices. Krugman makes an even more forceful defense of the factor content studies, stressing that the basic equation linking relative wages to the increment in relative labor supplies due to the factor content of trade can, in fact, be derived from a simple general equilibrium model that exploits the insights in Deardorff and Staiger.[53] The counterfactual for this model is, "What would wages have been absent the 'exogenous' increase in the possibility of importing LDC goods?" To empirical economists, this is the natural way of posing the issue and goes a long way toward clarifying the thought experiment involved in factor content studies.

This is not to deny the problems with factor analyses of quantities. Analyses of quantities do not provide "the" answer to the question of how trade affects labor. Recognizing the imperfections in these calculations, an empiricist wants to see other evidence as well. What does other evidence show?

Price Studies

Some trade theorists favor analyses of the prices of the goods produced by low-skill labor. Price declines due to imports should lower the relative

53. Krugman (1995); Deardorff and Staiger (1988).

wages of the unskilled labor used in import-competing activities, so that changes in relative prices vary inversely with the proportion of unskilled workers in the sectors' work force. Moreover, because less-skilled labor constitutes only a proportion of the cost of production, a given percentage change in the price of output due to foreign competition requires an even greater proportionate decrease in the wages of workers. This approach is viewed as "testing" the proposition that changes in the price of goods due to imports leads to changes in the prices of the factor used intensively in import-competing activities. In fact, it is a *consistency check,* not a test of causality.

If the *sole* reason for the proportion of unskilled labor among economic sectors to be correlated with price changes was the possibility of trade, this correlation would be a causal test of the globalization effect. But virtually any price determination model implies that decreases in the wages of an input should reduce the price of output.[54] The test therefore probes a more general relation: the extent to which reductions in the wages of low-skill workers (because of anything, including trade) have been passed on to consumers through reductions in prices. In autarky one would expect an inverse correlation between changes in the prices of an economic sector and the proportion of low-skill workers if their wages were falling because of a drop in the minimum wage or in union strength, or because of biased technological change. One would also expect such a correlation in a world where trade reduced goods prices in sectors that intensively use low-skill labor. Regressions of prices on factor intensities can yield evidence *consistent* with globalization, but they cannot demonstrate the trade is a cause (much less the sole one) of the relation. It is simply erroneous to take product price changes as solely determined by trade and then assert that the presence or absence of a correlation with factor intensity proves anything.

Empirical work on the relation between the proportion of unskilled workers in an economic sector and changes in prices has moved from the claim that there is virtually no relation and therefore no trade effect on the labor market to the claim that there is some relation and thus some trade effect on the labor market.

Bhagwati and Dehejia as well as Krugman and Lawrence looked at aggregate price data, found little evidence of relative price declines, and

54. For instance, assume that the wages of low-skill workers fall because the minimum wage falls or because unions become weaker. As long as industry price setting is reasonably competitive, fulfilling a no-profits condition, one would observe a negative correlation between changes in output prices and the share of employment performed by unskilled workers (more properly, their share of costs). The economy could have no trade at all.

concluded that trade had no effect on the labor market.[55] Lawrence and Slaughter examined how changes in import prices and export prices are related to the share of production labor across industries (adjusted in some calculations for changes in industry productivity by multiplying prices by an index of total factor productivity), and do not find much.[56] These studies were taken to support the "globalization explains nothing" view. But they could just as easily be taken to support the view that trade does us no good whatsoever. If trade does not gain lower-priced goods for the United States, what is the benefit from trade? What is the value in importing Mexican goods if they cost as much as the same goods would cost in autarky? The claim that trade has no effect on relative prices is as much an indictment of our ability to measure the benefits of trade with LDCs as it is of our ability to measure the costs of such trade on less-skilled workers, at least in the context of the HO model.

Ensuing studies have found evidence for some price effects. In one paper Sachs and Shatz regress changes in output prices for industries in manufacturing and find a weakly determined negative effect on the production-worker share of employment.[57] They further note that before the 1980s low-skill-intensive sectors did not exhibit any tendency for relative price declines, and interpret this evidence as suggesting that relative prices exerted some pressure on less-skilled wages. Their chapter in this book shows stronger negative relations between the production-worker share of employment and changes in various price variables for 1978–95. This is consistent with some (possibly large) trade effects, though, as noted, these relations cannot prove that trade is the cause of the change in relative prices.

Freeman and Revenga report significant negative correlations between the growth of imports and changes in value-added prices by industry across OECD countries, and a weak negative relation between the proportion of production workers by industry and changes in those prices.[58] But they also report no relation between the share of women workers by industry (the group most intensively employed in import-competing sectors) and changes in relative prices, presumably because demand for labor in non-traded-goods activities placed upward pressure on women's wages.

I regard the relative or absolute improvement in the economic position of low-skill women—who are the factor of production most intensively

55. Bhagwati and Dehejia (1994); Krugman and Lawrence (1994).
56. Lawrence and Slaughter (1993).
57. They also include a dummy variable for computers (due to the likely inaccuracy of prices for this good). They get a larger negative coefficient without adjusting for changes in total factor productivity than after making such an adjustment.
58. Freeman and Revenga (1995).

employed in apparel manufacturing and other sectors where LDC imports have increased greatly, and who suffer the greatest displacement as a result—as powerful evidence against the "globalization explains everything" view.[59] In contrast with these studies, in chapter 4 Leamer reports that relative producer prices in labor-intensive industries fell in the 1970s and then *rose* in the 1980s. He concludes that producer price changes implied a 4 percent mandated reduction per year in wages of low-wage workers in the 1970s, offset by 2 percent per year gains in the 1980s. This gives the paradoxical result that in the period when skill differentials were falling (the 1970s) prices worked in the opposite direction, whereas when those differentials were rising (the 1980s), trade was operating to reduce them.[60]

Without gainsaying the value of examining price data, the data have problems. Import prices exist for relatively few industries and cover only some goods in those industries. Output prices suffer from aggregation problems, because the sectors with imports presumably include domestic goods that differ in important dimensions from the imports. Value-added prices and changes thereof differ from output prices and changes thereof.[61] Unmeasured changes in the quality of products, which I would expect to be more severe in high-skill-intensive sectors, may upwardly bias the estimated coefficients on the proportion of unskilled workers. The measures of labor skills used in the price studies are also crude. The proportion of production workers fails to recognize the difference between such workers across sectors, nor readily translates into indicators of human capital such as education or age. The ratio of the pay of nonproduction to production workers is not the same as the ratio of the pay of college graduates to high school graduates, much less the ratio of pay of workers in high deciles of the earnings distribution relative to that of workers in low deciles. The rise in non-production-worker pay to production-worker pay has been far more modest: on the order of one-third the rise in differentials by education group.[62]

But the biggest problem in studies is the absence of a full-blown, price-determining model, one that incorporates industrial organization factors that might affect durable-goods industries in particular (Borjas and Ramey

59. See Kletzer, chapter 10.
60. See chapter 4.
61. Sachs and Shatz, chapter 5; Freeman and Revenga (1995).
62. The U.S. Department of Labor Report on the American Workforce (1994, table 2-6) shows increases in the college to high-school earnings differential on the order of 25 percent and between college and high-school dropouts on the order of 30 percent between 1979 and 1993. By contrast, data in *U.S. Statistical Abstract 1996* (table 1210) on the payroll for all workers and for production workers, and on the production workers' share of the workforce, suggest increases in the earnings of nonproduction to production workers of about 11 percent.

stress the reduction in rents in those sectors in their analysis), or of shifts in consumer demand that might affect prices.[63] Although some might respond that the prices are set on world markets and are thus not affected by other factors, this claim has not been tested and surely cannot hold at the aggregate level, given differences in the particular goods imported and produced domestically. Finally, none of the studies includes prices for the service sector, where the bulk of unskilled workers are employed.

All of these problems imply that though price studies provide a clue to trade effects on relative wages, they are far from the final word some thought they would be in the globalization debate. When an economy moves toward free trade, there should be information on trade effects in both price data and quantity data.

Additional Evidence

Three additional pieces of evidence merit attention in assessing the effect of globalization on labor market outcomes.

First is evidence on immigration. Most studies of the effect of immigration on the job market exploit the geographic concentration of immigrants and find that employment and wages of native-born, low-skill workers is not that different in immigrant gateways such as New York or Houston or Miami or (until the recent California depression) in Los Angeles than in Midwestern or southern cities with little immigrant flow.[64] It is difficult to accept the globalization story for the entire economy without explaining this seemingly contrary cross-area evidence. The largest estimated effects of immigration come not from area studies but from analyses that assert that by changing relative labor supplies, immigration must have changed relative earnings by an elasticity obtained from time series analysis.[65] A paper by Borjas, Freeman, and Katz suggests that the failure to find sizeable immigration effects in area studies is due to migration of natives from areas of high immigration, exogenous shifts in regional economic conditions, and possibly the response of capital to influxes of immigrant labor (such as in the apparel industry in New York or Los Angeles).[66]

Second is evidence on the ratios of unskilled to skilled employment within industries. Those who argue that trade is not the prime cause of the decline in demand for less-skilled workers stress that the ratio of unskilled workers fell in all sectors over this period, whereas the contraction of

63. Borjas and Ramey (1994).
64. Altonji and Card (1991); LaLonde and Topel (1991); Card (1990).
65. Borjas, Freeeman, and Katz (1992).
66. Borjas, Freeman, and Katz (1996).

low-skill-intensive industries due to trade should have "freed" unskilled workers to move to other sectors, which will have a wage incentive to hire them.[67] The decrease in ratios of unskilled to skilled employment throughout the economy does not prove that trade is not a major cause of the immiserization of less-skilled workers, but it indicates that trade cannot be the full story of reduced demand for these workers.

Third, some analysts have brought aggregate cross-country or time series evidence, not directly related to the trade models, to bear on the globalization issue. Wood points out that a composite indicator of changes in demand for skills—based on changes in wage and unemployment differentials—across fourteen countries is strongly correlated with changes in LDC import penetration ratios.[68] Borjas and Ramey have found a strong correlation in time series data between educational differentials and durable-goods imports as a share of GDP. They argue that these imports account for most of the change in the differentials by squeezing economic rents in relatively union-intensive and concentrated sectors.[69] When many things are happening, there is value to these sorts of comparisons, but they are hardly a smoking gun.

In sum, the empirical studies leave a wide band of uncertainty. The fact that neither factor content nor price analyses show huge trade effects, the big stretch needed to make the content calculations consistent with substantial effects, the fall in demand for less-skilled workers in non-traded-goods sectors, the absence of evidence that trade contributed to rises in earnings differentials within groups, and the failure of the wages of female unskilled workers to fall as much as those of unskilled male workers all lead me to conclude that the weight of the evidence favors the moderate (but possibly dull) claim that trade matters some, but that it is far from all that matters.

And in the Future?

Many people might argue: "Maybe trade with Singapore, Korea, Taiwan, Mexico, and Malaysia is not enough to dominate the U.S. job market. But just wait till China, India, and Indonesia really arrive. Then globalization will truly have a severe impact on low-skill Westerners."

It is commonplace in the trade–labor market debate for those who reject trade as *the* explanation of the past decline in the relative demand for

67. Berman, Bound, and Griliches (1993).
68. Wood (1994).
69. Borjas and Ramey (1994).

less-skilled workers to hedge their conclusion by noting that there is a chance that in the future, pressures for FPE will grow. As China, India, Indonesia, and the former Soviet Union come full scale into the world economy, the argument goes, they will export goods made by low-skill workers in magnitudes that are sure to devastate low-skill Westerners.

At the heart of this argument is the strength of forces for FPE. In a world where trade operates in an HO manner (trade flows determined by factor endowments), where producers have the same technology, where trade establishes a single world price for a good, and where advanced countries compete with LDCs in the same tradable-goods sectors, the wages of factors used in traded goods should be equated across countries.

The question is whether the logic of FPE captures economic reality enough to base prognostications largely on this force. For years many trade economists rejected FPE as a description of the world. The wide and in some cases increasing variation in pay levels among countries seemed to reduce it to a textbook proposition of little relevance.[70] Reflecting this view, Bhagwati and Dehejia have enumerated some of the theoretical stretches needed to establish FPE.[71] Leamer, by contrast, takes it as our best guide to what is and what will happen in the world.[72]

Complete FPE implies that in an economy fully integrated in the world trading system (and which fulfills the relevant assumptions of the model), *nothing* domestic affects wages. Relative wages are set by world factor endowments even if trade is only a small part (no part) of the economy. Whether 5 percent or 95 percent of less-skilled workers are employed in import-competing activities, the pay of all of those workers is determined in the global market, independent of changes in domestic market conditions. Transportation costs, immediacy of delivery, and the like are assumed to be irrelevant in differentiating the location of production. Free trade establishes a single, global, labor market that sets the wages for inputs involved in traded activities. Only when the country specializes in the production of skill-intensive tradables and produces *no* unskilled-intensive tradables does the domestic labor market set wages for unskilled labor.

These strong predictions run counter to diverse evidence on the effects of domestic developments on pay. These include the effect of baby booms

---

70. For an exception see Krueger (1968).
71. Bhagwati and Dehejia (1994).
72. Leamer (1994).

on the pay of young workers, of the relative number of college graduates on educational premium, of sectoral developments on industrial pay, of local labor market conditions on wages, and so on. In the United States, wage differences among states persisted for decades despite free trade, migration, and capital flows. Around the world, wage differences between workers with seemingly similar skills have also persisted for decades, albeit exaggerated by the divergence between purchasing-power parities and exchange rates, and by differences in labor skills not accounted for in many wage comparisons. Norman and Venables stress that in an HO model in which costs of trade are taken seriously, goods trade alone does not equalize factor prices.[73]

I believe that the effect of globalization on the future of low-skill Westerners is less dire than those who expect the wages of those workers to fall toward the rates of similarly skilled workers in LDCs. There are several reasons why I reject the view that globalization will devastate the economic position of low-skill Westerners.

As more and more low-skill Western workers find employment in non-traded-goods activities, the potential for imports from LDCs to reduce their employment or wages should lessen. As I have noted, in the standard trade model, when a country no longer produces less-skill-intensive goods (so that its unskilled workers are either employed in nontraded goods and thus "sheltered" from low-wage foreign competition, or are employed as cooperating factors in traded skill-intensive exports), those workers are in a separate labor market from comparably skilled, low-wage foreigners. The closer Western economies get to the situation in which less, skilled workers do not work in low-wage import-competing activities, the smaller the trade-induced pressures on low-skilled workers. As the proportion of un-skilled workers in manufacturing is already modest, I expect that we will move quickly (albeit not painlessly) to a world in which unskilled workers in the West do not compete directly with unskilled workers in LDCs through trade. If an increasing proportion of services produced by low-wage workers become tradable, then this expectation will prove incorrect.

I also believe that in societies like the United States where workers and firms make substantial investments in labor skills, the supply of workers by skill will change in response to trade pressures against less-skilled workers. If half of today's unskilled workers become skilled tomorrow, analyses that stress the adverse effect of trade on "the" less-skilled workers will at the

73. Norman and Venables (1993).

minimum exaggerate those effects. Half of the less-skilled workers will in fact benefit from the increase in pay for the skilled workers.

The issue hinges on how easy is it for people with limited education and blue-collar job skills to transform themselves into workers with largely white-collar (perhaps computer-oriented) skills. If unskilled labor is highly malleable, the "globalization causes immiserization" argument has got it all wrong. If, on the other hand, unskilled labor is not readily malleable—if a large proportion of our population does not have the capacity to obtain the white-collar, college-type skills that seem necessary for good jobs—the supply-side solution will not work. Elasticities of supply to college and specific occupations tend to be high among young people (my stylized elasticity is two), suggesting that this argument has merit over the long run. But among older workers, the record of training the displaced labor force for better jobs is poor. Surely there is a substantial proportion of the unskilled population that will not find it easy to invest in skills. Despite rising skill differentials, a sizeable number of American students still drop out of high school.

There is another possible benefit of globalization to low-skill workers ignored in the analysis: the reduced price of commodities and higher quality or variety of goods available from an open economy. The FPE argument holds that the real pay of the scarce factor (unskilled labor in the United States) falls as a result of trade, assuming no difference in consumption patterns between the scarce and plentiful factors. Whatever benefits reduced prices due to trade bring to unskilled labor are more than offset by reductions in pay. But if low-skill workers are more likely to buy "cheap imports" than high-skill workers (which income classes are most likely to buy cheap Chinese products?), perhaps those gains are larger than we recognize and the adverse effects of trade on the real wages of less-skilled workers are exaggerated.

Finally, I believe that the positive and negative effects of trade have been oversold in recent years, in part because they have been at the center of the political debate. Wildly heralded trade agreements such as the U.S.-Canadian agreement, the Common Market, and NAFTA have not dominated our economies in the ways their advocates or opponents predicted. Other factors—technological changes that occur independent of trade, unexpected political developments (such as German reunification and instability in various regions of the world), policies to educate and train workers, union activities, firm compensation policies, and welfare-state and related social policies—have also influenced the well-being of less-skilled workers. I would expect them to continue to do so.

Summary

I have argued for using both quantity and price data to assess the effects of globalization on the labor market. I am leery of analyses or models that throw away seemingly relevant evidence (be it the volume of trade or prices). Those data do not fit some theoretical structure, particularly given the impressive skills of trade theorists in building models that can accomodate various patterns, evidence, and assumptions (albeit with some problems beyond the two-country, two-goods case). In particular, I defend the factor content calculations and cite Deardorff and Staiger as well as Krugman for providing theoretical structures that show that this tool does, more or less, what labor economists and others who have used it have intended it to do.[74]

With respect to the substance of the trade-labor debate, I contrasted two polar opposite views of the globalization–labor market relation: the "globalization explains everything" view—which attributes the immiserization of low-wage workers in advanced countries to globalization and more specifically to trade with LDCs; and the "globalization explains nothing" view—which claims that globalization, and trade in particular, has had no effect on the wages or employ of low-skill workers in advanced countries. I reject the "nothing" view but believe that the current state of evidence falls short of the "everything" view. Factor content studies suggest only a modest trade effect, unless one follows Wood in augmenting the standard model.[75] Several studies of the relation between changes in relative prices and the skill content of employment are consistent with a trade effect. But they are also consistent with changes in the wages of unskilled workers falling for other reasons and being passed on in lower relative prices. That workers who face the most severe LDC competition—less-skilled women (in apparel manufacturing and related sectors)—have increased their pay relative to less-skilled men makes it difficult to believe the "everything" view.

I also highlight the importance of immigration of less-skilled workers on the job market as a major part of any analysis of globalization. Even with the addition of immigration, however, my assessment is a moderate one. To paraphrase a famous economist criticizing the views of another eminent colleague, trade matters, but it is not all that matters. In taking this moderate view of how globalization has affected low-skill workers, I could, of

74. Deardorff and Staiger (1988); Krugman (1995).
75. Wood (1994).

course, be utterly wrong. But I am willing to to bet with Edward Leamer or Jagdish Bhagwati or Adrian Wood, and (given some limit on the stakes) to take on Ross Perot and Jimmie Goldsmith, as well. Better yet, maybe I can arbitrage between the "everything" adherents and the "nothing" adherents and make a riskless profit, which would prove that even labor economists can make some money from trade.

Comment by Dani Rodrik

This is a useful chapter that does a thorough job of summarizing and evaluating the literature on trade and wages. It integrates theory and evidence admirably, never departing too far from common sense. The conclusion—that the truth lies somewhere between the two extreme views of "trade explains everything" and "trade explains nothing"—is perhaps not a shocker. But it is a useful reminder at a time when tempers are running high and slogans are taking over.

What I found particularly helpful in this chapter is the attention that immigration receives along with trade. Trade economists tend to have a blind spot on immigration, perhaps because they work with models in which goods are mobile but factors of production are not. As Richard Freeman reminds us, however, in all likelihood the labor market impact of immigration in the United States has been more significant than that of trade with low-income countries.

There is little for me to disagree with here. To fulfill my discussant's obligations, however, let me play the role of the devil's advocate. Let me claim that perhaps Freeman underestimates the role played by international economic integration in labor market outcomes.

The first step in my argument is to suggest that we may be asking the wrong question. Freeman, along with almost everyone else, focuses on the question, "How much have trade and migration reduced the demand for unskilled labor in the developed countries?" Because the relevant volumes of trade and migration are small relative to the domestic stocks of unskilled labor, the answer is almost a foregone conclusion: some but not a whole lot. But suppose we ask the question, "How much has international economic integration affected the *elasticity of demand* for unskilled labor?" Because an elasticity concerns changes at the margin, this question cannot be simply answered by looking at volumes of trade and immigration.

To appreciate the point, consider what would happen if the rest of the world consisted of economies identical to that of the United States, in terms of their relative factor endowments and levels of wealth. Because there would be no comparative advantage, economic integration would result in little trade (save of course for trade based on scale economies). But the services of U.S. workers would now become more easily substitutable thanks to the possibilities of trade, migration, and capital outflows. Hence, although U.S. labor would not face a reduction in demand (because the rest of the world is assumed to be no more labor abundant than the United States), it would certainly be confronted with a demand that is more elastic.

I would argue that this alone, even absent a simultaneous inward shift in the demand schedule, has a profound and adverse impact on U.S.-based workers. Stated in grandiose terms, a large increase in the elasticity of demand for unskilled workers is likely to undermine the traditional implicit understanding—social contract—between business and employees. In more concrete terms familiar to economists, such an increase implies the following:

—The costs of increased benefits and improved working conditions can no longer be passed on (or shared with) employers. The larger the elasticity of demand for labor, the higher the share of any such costs that must be borne by the workers themselves. Hence globalization makes it difficult to sustain the postwar bargain under which workers would receive continued improvements in pay and benefits in return for labor peace and loyalty.

—Shocks to labor demand (caused, say, by shocks in labor productivity) now result in much greater volatility in both earnings and hours worked (assuming that there is some positive elasticity to labor supply). This is important insofar as it can account directly for the widening wage inequality since the late 1970s, as well as for the increase in within-group inequality; Gottschalk and Moffitt report that between one-third and one-half of the widening wage distribution from the 1970s to the 1980s can be attributed to the increase in the short-term variance in earnings.[76] The increase in volatility is greatest in the least-skilled groups, these being the ones for which demand has presumably become most elastic.

—Third, to the extent that wages are determined in bargaining between workers and employers, an increase in the elasticity of demand for labor

76. Gottschalk and Moffitt (1994, pp. 217–54).

would result in a lower share of the enterprise surplus ending up with workers. The more readily substituted workers in Akron would be with those in Monterrey or Bombay, the less bargaining power they have and the lower the wages they will receive. Although this argument is valid only in industries where there are economic rents to be shared between employers and workers, it is not difficult to believe that the presence of a few such important industries could set norms for others as well.

From this perspective, the main story about globalization is the change in the (actual or perceived) elasticity of demand for unskilled workers, and not the reduction in the demand per se. The focus on trade with (and immigration from) low-wage countries ignores the fact that unskilled workers in Germany or France are also in competition with similar workers in the United Kingdom or the United States, markets with which the former countries are considerably more tightly integrated than with India and China. And although North-North trade may have little perceptible impact on the demand for unskilled labor, it certainly makes this demand more elastic in all countries involved.

Freeman touches on the issues I have raised here when he discusses the possibility that the key difference nowadays is business's ability to make threats about moving overseas. I think he is perhaps too quick in dismissing the significance of this. He suggests that if such threats were important in practice, we would have observed a much greater import penetration in continental Europe than we have, in view of the constancy of relative wages there. However, one way in which Europe has avoided higher import penetration is by being more inclined to impose import protection against low-income countries. In any case the appropriate counterfactual is not quite clear. Perhaps the relative wages of unskilled workers in Europe would have risen in the absence of the implicit threat from employers.

We could debate endlessly whether enough occurred in terms of actual trade, immigration, and capital flows during the 1980s to trigger fundamental changes in the operation of labor markets in the advanced industrial countries. But the fact that "globalization" has now become a refrain for both employers and workers surely counts as evidence in itself. The perception of high elasticity/high substitutability matters as much as the reality. It is therefore not too farfetched to believe that the traditional behavioral patterns in the labor market have either collapsed or are under severe strain. If we have indeed experienced a regime switch in business-labor relations, the prospects for unskilled labor may be considerably bleaker than is supposed in this chapter.

Comment by Adrian Wood

I agree with much of what Richard Freeman says in this characteristically lucid, stimulating, informative, and readable chapter, but to keep my comments brief, I focus on the area of disagreement between us. Specifically, I review his five reasons for doubting that "globalization explains everything" and try to explain why I find none of them particularly persuasive.

The phrase "globalization explains everything" is designed to prejudice the reader against the underlying hypothesis. But if one reads the small print, Freeman defines this phrase in such a way as to correspond closely with my own views. In particular, I believe that the position of unskilled workers in developed countries would not have deteriorated over the past couple of decades if these countries had remained industrially self-sufficient, with developing countries as suppliers merely of a few primary products. What happened instead (globalization) was caused mainly, I think, by reductions in various sorts of barriers to trade, with flows of capital and technology largely as a response to these barrier reductions. But I also accept that in the United States, and perhaps in other developed countries, unskilled immigration compounded the misfortunes of unskilled, native workers.

On to Freeman's five reasons for doubting that globalization accounts for all or most of the deterioration in the position of unskilled workers. One of them concerns the evidence on product price movements. By the end of his chapter, given the larger price changes found by Sachs and Shatz (chapter 5) and the magnification effect (relative wage changes are bound to be much larger than relative price changes), Freeman's position seems to be that, yes, the price evidence is consistent with the trade explanation but is consistent with other explanations too. True enough, but this does not make it evidence *against* the trade explanation—merely neutral.

A second reason is the *absence of evidence that trade contributed to rises in wage differentials within skill groups* (categorized by schooling, years of experience, and occupation). But again, I see this as a neutral point, in the absence of evidence that trade did *not* raise intragroup inequality. Moreover, I find it plausible that trade did have such an effect (and in chapter 5 Sachs and Shatz spell out such a theory). Most economists believe that intragroup wage inequality arises largely from unmeasured differences in skill. So if trade boosts the returns to the skills that we can measure, why should it not do so also for the skills that we cannot measure?

A third reason is the *failure of female unskilled wages to fall as much as male unskilled wages,* given the concentration of manufactured imports from developing countries on female-intensive sectors. However, these imports are not so concentrated on female-intensive sectors as Freeman believes. Of OECD imports of manufactures from developing countries in 1993, 44 percent were in two such sectors (textiles and clothing, and electrical machinery), but 56 percent were not; for low-income countries only, the non-female-intensive share was 53 percent.[77] Moreover, as Freeman's own table 3-4 confirms, manufacturing is and always has been male intensive, relative to the nontraded sectors. Contraction of manufacturing employment should thus have tended to hurt males more than females, as indeed it has.

A fourth reason is that the *relative demand for unskilled labor has fallen also in nontraded sectors.* This is true, but is just the continuation of a secular trend in all sectors, which for most of the past century has been associated with *narrowing* wage differentials, because the relative supply of unskilled labor has tended to fall slightly faster. Something happened to upset the long-term tendency for unskilled workers in developed countries to win this race (as Tinbergen once called it) between demand and supply. That something, in my opinion, was a rather sudden exposure to the developing world's vast pool of much-lower-paid unskilled labor.

Freeman's fifth reason for doubt is the *big stretch needed to make factor content calculations consistent with huge effects.* I simply have a different view of the facts on this point. The effects on unskilled workers seem to me to be not huge but moderate (up to about 25 percentage points, depending on what indicator is considered, spread over a couple of decades). The standard approach to factor content calculations is indisputably biased downward, by ignoring differences in skill intensity between imports and domestic output in the "same" manufacturing sectors and by leaving out the service sectors. And even properly done factor content calculations omit two ways in which low-wage foreign competition can depress the demand for unskilled labor without increasing imports, namely through relative price changes and defensive innovation. The methods that I use in making estimates of the impact of trade large enough to explain the current plight of unskilled workers are approximate, but do not appear to me to involve any stretch, let alone a big one.[78]

---

77. World Bank (1995, indicators table 16).
78. Wood (1994, chapter 4); Wood (1995, pp. 64–72).

General Discussion

Edward Leamer disagreed with Richard Freeman's assessment of the usefulness of factor content studies. He identified three problems with these studies. First, the factor content of trade is a symptom not a cause of underlying changes of interest. For example, an increase in the low-skill-labor content of U.S. trade might reflect changes in technology, and thus does not provide a means of distinguishing among globalization, technical change, or other possible exogenous developments. Second, to translate factor content shifts into wage changes, the labor demand elasticities that would exist in autarky are needed—which are not observable. Third, Leamer cautioned that international trade may not be equivalent to shifts in domestic labor supply. In particular, some international trade equilibria (such as those involving some degree of specialization) cannot be replicated in a closed economy.

Susan Collins also expressed concerns about the factor content methodology. She stressed that this approach encourages people to think about all changes in trade flows as exogenous shocks, to assume that such shocks are identical to shifts in effective labor supply, and to conclude that the wage implications of all labor supply shifts can be computed using a single estimate of labor elasticity. Two of the lessons from the general equilibrium models favored by international trade economists are that the underlying source of change may be important and that the relationship between changes in factor supplies and factor prices may be much more complex than a simple partial equilibrium, supply and demand structure suggests.

A number of participants commented on the international dimensions of recent labor market developments. William Cline argued that the more evidence that increasing wage inequality is a common development across many countries, the more persuasive an explanation based on international trade. Steven Davis elaborated on his reading of the evidence. He believed that there had been significant increases in wage inequality outside of the United States, in particular for the United Kingdom, and to some extent for both Canada and France as well. Freeman, however, saw the evidence from Canada and France as less conclusive. He agreed that the top half of the wage distribution in France has enjoyed increases but noted that the bottom half has not seen declines. Many of the European countries have seen pressures emerging through rising unemployment, not increasing wage dispersion.

Davis also summarized some other patterns in advanced economies. In eight of the nine he has studied, returns to experience have increased since the late 1970s. Recent developments in the returns to education are more puzzling. Although the fall in the returns to schooling during the 1970s was widespread, the United States is an outlier in experiencing large increases in the returns to schooling more recently. Japan, at the other end of the spectrum, has seem little change. Overall, Davis concludes that the evidence suggests that other developed countries have experienced milder forms of the dramatic changes seen in the United States.

Henry Aaron raised the issue of union rents and asked how the empirical analysis discussed in Freeman's paper incorporates their role. He noted that unions have directly and indirectly supported wage premiums. As unionization has declined (perhaps accelerated by increased exposure to international trade), "cover" for these wage premiums has declined as well. Freeman responded that wage premiums do not appear to have declined along with the significant decline in unionization. He explained that wages tend to be much more compressed inside the unionized sector. Thus, as unionization declines, workers move into the wider wage distribution that characterizes the nonunion sector. This shift explains roughly 20 percent of the overall rise in U.S. wage inequality. In this context, Marina Whitman noted that there has been no fall in the wage premium paid to workers in the automobile sector relative to workers in manufacturing overall. Instead, there has been a fall in the employment of unionized workers, related to outsourcing and other developments.

Whitman also raised a puzzle about movements in the U.S. terms of trade. She noted that though the terms of trade deteriorated sharply after the oil price rise in 1973, they have not returned to the pre-1973 level despite the fact that, in real terms, oil prices are lower than they were in the early 1970s. She suggested that a better understanding of the evolution of the terms of trade would shed light on the other puzzling developments that have occurred over the past fifteen years.

Gary Burtless cautioned against use of production versus nonproduction workers to distinguish between less-skilled and highly skilled labor. He noted that the wage gap between production and nonproduction workers has risen by just 4 percent since the late 1970s, while the relative wage of college graduates has risen by 20 percent to 100 percent, depending on the group considered. In his view, the production/nonproduction worker data is not informative for examining the key issues of interest.

Finally, William Cline agreed with Freeman that immigration may have played a more important role than increases in trade in explaining the poor

138   RICHARD B. FREEMAN

wage performance of less-skilled Americans. He and other participants advocated greater attention to the role of immigration in future analyses of this issue.

References

Abowd, John M., and Richard B. Freeman. 1991. *Immigration, Trade and the Labor Market.* University of Chicago Press for National Bureau of Economic Research.
Altonji, Joseph G., and David Card. 1991. "The Effects of Immigration on the Labor Market Outcomes of Less-Skilled Natives." In *Immigration, Trade and the Labor Market,* edited by John M. Abowd, and Richard B. Freeman, 201–34. University of Chicago Press for National Bureau of Economic Research.
Berman, Eli, John Bound, and Zvi Griliches. 1993. "Changes in the Demand for Skilled Labor within U.S. Manufacturing Industries: Evidence from the Annual Survey of Manufacturing." Working Paper 4255. Cambridge, Mass.: National Bureau of Economic Research (January).
Bhagwati, Jagdish, and Vivek Dehejia. 1994. "Freer Trade and Wages of the Unskilled: Is Marx Striking Again?" In *Trade and Wages: Leveling Wages Down?* edited by Jagdish Bhagwati and Marvin H. Kosters, 36–75. Washington: American Enterprise Institute.
Borjas, George J. 1992. "National Origin and the Skills of Immigrants in the Postwar Period." In *Immigration and the Work Force: Economic Consequences for the United States and Source Areas,* edited by George J. Borjas and Richard B. Freeman, 17–48. University of Chicago Press for National Bureau of Economic Research.
———. 1995. "The Economic Benefits from Immigration." *Journal of Economic Perspectives* 9 (Spring): 3–22.
Borjas, George J., Richard B. Freeman, and Lawrence F. Katz. 1992. "On the Labor Market Effects of Immigration and Trade." In *Immigration and the Work Force: Economic Consequences for the United States and Source Areas,* edited by George J. Borjas and Richard B. Freeman, 213–44. University of Chicago Press for National Bureau of Economic Research.
———. 1996. "Searching for the Effect of Immigration on the Labor Market." *American Economic Review* 86 (May, *Papers and Proceedings, 1995*): 246–51.
Borjas, George J., and Valerie A. Ramey. 1994. "Time Series Evidence on the Sources of Trends in Wage Inequality." *American Economic Review* 84 (May, *Papers and Proceedings, 1994*): 10–16.
Card, David. 1990. "The Impact of the Mariel Boatlift on the Miami Labor Market." *Industrial and Labor Relations Review* 43 (January): 245–57.
Collins, Susan M. 1991. "Immigrants, Labor Market Pressures, and the Composition of the Aggregate Demand." In *Immigration, Trade, and the Labor Market,* edited by John M. Abowd and Richard B. Freeman, 305–18. University of Chicago Press for National Bureau of Economic Research.
Cooper, Richard. 1994. "Foreign Trade, Wages, and Unemployment." Discussion Paper 1701. Cambridge, Mass.: Harvard Institute for Economic Research (November).

Cortes, O. S. Jean, and J. Pisani-Ferry. 1995. "Trade with Emerging Countries and the Labour Market: The French Case." Paper presented at CEPII-ECARE Conference on International Trade and Employment: The European Experience, Paris, September 25.

Deardorff, Alan V., and Dalia S. Hakura. 1994. "Trade and Wages—What Are the Questions?" In *Trade and Wages: Leveling Wages Down?* edited by Jagdish Bhagwati and Marvin H. Kosters, 76–107. Washington: American Enterprise Institute.

Deardorff, Alan V., and Robert W. Staiger. 1988. "An Interpretation of the Factor Content of Trade." *Journal of International Economics* 24: 93–107.

Freeman, Richard. 1994. "How Labor Fares in Advanced Economies." In *Working under Different Rules,* edited by Richard Freeman. New York: Russell Sage Foundation.

Freeman, Richard, and Lawrence Katz. 1994. "Rising Wage Inequality: The United States vs. Other Advanced Countries." In *Working under Different Rules,* edited by Richard B. Freeman. New York: Russell Sage Foundation.

Freeman, Richard B., and Ana Revenga. 1995. "How Much Has LDC Trade Affected Western Job Markets?" Paper presented at CEPII-ECARE Conference on International Trade and Employment: The European Experience Paris, September 24.

Gottschalk, Peter, and Robert Moffitt. 1994. "The Growth of Earnings Instability in the U.S. Labor Market." *Brookings Papers on Economic Activity 2:* 217–54.

Katz, Lawrence F., and Kevin M. Murphy. 1992. "Changes in Relative Wages, 1963–1987: Supply and Demand Factors." *Quarterly Journal of Economics* 107 (February): 35–78.

Krueger, Alan B. 1993. "How Computers Have Changed the Wage Structure: Evidence from Microdata, 1984–1989." *Quarterly Journal of Economics* 108 (February): 33–60.

Krueger, Anne O. 1968. "Factor Endowments and Per Capita Income Differences among Countries." *Economic Journal* (September): 641–59.

Krugman, Paul R. 1995. "Technology, Trade, and Factor Prices." Working Paper 5355. Cambridge, Mass.: National Bureau of Economic Research (November).

Krugman, Paul R., and Robert Z. Lawrence. 1994. "Trade, Jobs, and Wages." *Scientific American* 270 (April): 44–49.

LaLonde, Robert J., and Robert H. Topel. 1991. "Labor Market Adjustments to Increased Immigration." In *Immigration, Trade, and the Labor Market,* edited by John M. Abowd and Richard B. Freeman, 167–200. University of Chicago Press for National Bureau of Economic Research.

Lawrence, Robert Z. 1994. "The Impact of Trade on OECD Labor Markets." Occasional Paper 45. Washington: Group of Thirty.

Lawrence, Robert Z., and Matthew J. Slaughter. 1993. "International American Trade and American Wages in the 1980s: Giant Sucking Sound or Small Hiccup?" *Brookings Papers on Economic Activity: Microeconomics* 2: 161–210.

Leamer, Edward E. 1984. *Sources of International Comparative Advantage: Theory and Practice.* MIT Press.

———. 1994. "Trade, Wages, and Revolving Door Ideas." Working Paper 4716. Cambridge, Mass.: National Bureau of Economic Research (April).

Mishel, Lawrence, and Jared Bernstein. 1994. "Is the Technology Black Box Empty? An Empirical Examination of the Impact of Technology on Wage Inequality and the Employment Structure." Technical Working Paper. Washington: Economic Policy Institute.

Murphy, Kevin M., and Finis Welch. 1991. "The Role of International Trade in Wage Differentials." In *Workers and Their Wages: Changing Patterns in the United States,* edited by Marvin H. Kosters, 39–69. Washington: American Enterprise Institute Press.

Norman, Victor D., and Anthony J. Venables. 1993. "International Trade, Factor Mobility, and Trade Costs." Discussion Paper 766. London: Centre for Economic Policy Research (February).

Organization for Economic Cooperation and Development. 1994a. *Background Document for a Study on Economic and Other Linkages with Major Developing Economies.* Paris (August).

———. 1994b. *The OECD Jobs Study: Facts, Analysis, Strategies.* Paris.

———. 1995. *Linkages: OECD and Major Developing Economies.* Paris.

Revenga, Ana L. 1992. "Exporting Jobs? The Impact of Import Competition on Employment and Wages in U.S. Manufacturing." *Quarterly Journal of Economics* 107 (February): 255–84.

Rodrik, Dani. 1992. "The Rush to Free Trade in the Developing World: Why So Late? Why Now? Will It Last?" Working Paper 3947. Cambridge, Mass.: National Bureau of Economic Research (January).

United Nations Committee on Trade and Development. 1994. *World Investment Report 1994: Transnational Corporations, Employment, and the Workplace.* New York.

U.S. Bureau of the Census. Various years. *Statistical Abstract of the United States.*

U.S. Department of Labor. 1994. "Report on the American Workforce."

Wood, Adrian. 1994. *North-South Trade, Employment and Inequality: Changing Fortunes in a Skill-Driven World.* Oxford, England: Clarendon Press.

———. 1995. "How Trade Hurt Unskilled Workers." *Journal of Economic Perspectives* 9 (Summer): 57–80.

World Bank. 1995. *World Development Report 1995.* Oxford University Press for the World Bank.

FOUR

In Search of Stolper-Samuelson Linkages between International Trade and Lower Wages

Edward E. Leamer

WITH THE widening of the gap between wages of unskilled and skilled workers has come an intense effort by economists on both sides of the Atlantic to identify the cause. The top three suspects are education, technology, and international trade. Most casual observers hold the opinion that all three of these suspects are guilty. The public schools in the United States seem to be doing a poorer job preparing their graduates for the job market and have been adding to the supply of unskilled, ill-prepared workers. On the demand side, technological change is altering the nature of work. Many functions are being technologically transferred from unskilled to skilled workers (for example, typing this manuscript), while others are being downgraded to require the most minimal level of education (for example, clerking at McDonald's). Last of the three suspects is international trade.

The work presented in this chapter was partially supported by NSF Grant SBR-9409011. The assistance of Christopher Thornberg, Robert Murdock, and Nadia Soboleva is gratefully acknowledged. I have benefited much from the comments of the discussants (Gene Grossman and Steve Davis) and the editor (Susan Collins), and from comments of participants at seminars at Dartmouth and Columbia, particularly Ronald Findlay.

Figure 4-1. *Gross Hourly Earnings of Manufacturing Production and Nonsupervisory Workers and Trade Dependence, 1960–92*

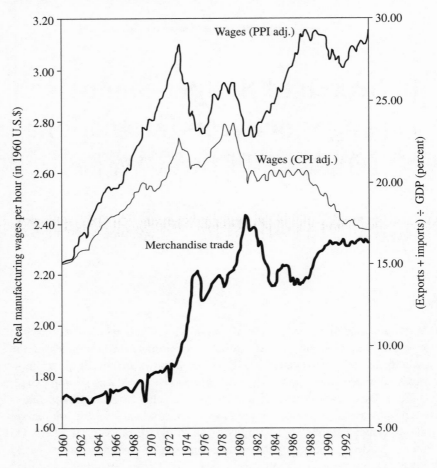

Source: Citibase (Citibank Economic Database), New York: Citibank N.A.

Unlike the eyewitness accounts of the "damage" being done by a deteriorating educational system and the information revolution, the evidence against international trade is mostly circumstantial and largely captured in figures 4-1 and 4-2. Figure 4-1 compares over the last several decades the levels of real wages in manufacturing (using both the Consumer Price Index [CPI] deflator and the Producer Price Index [PPI] deflator) and the U.S. trade dependence ratio, the ratio of exports plus imports divided by gross

Figure 4-2. *Industrial Wages and Population, 1989*

Wages per hour (1985 U.S.$)

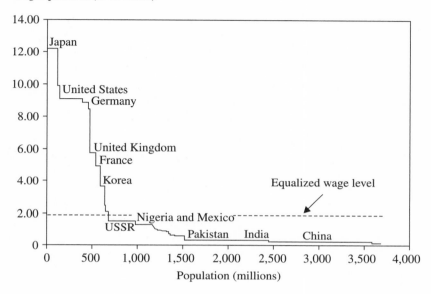

Source: Song (1993).

domestic product (GDP). Figure 4-2 illustrates the vast differences between wages earned by U.S. manufacturing workers and wages earned in much of the rest of the world.

Figure 4-1 reveals that the abrupt halt in the early 1970s to the previously steady rise in real wages came suspiciously at a time when the United States was experiencing a rapid increase in trade dependence. The reason why increasing trade dependence might hold down U.S. wages is suggested by figure 4-2, in which each country is represented by a line segment with height equal to 1989 wages and width equal to population, and countries are sorted by wage levels. If this is the global labor pool, it is a strange one indeed, with the liquid deep at one end and barely there at the other. What could possibly be holding up the high end? Barriers is one answer. The arbitrage opportunities suggested by figure 4-2 have not genuinely been present, because of the real and threatened interventions by governments that isolate workers in the high-wage countries from competition with workers in the low-wage third world. Now, according to this line of think-ing, with the liberalizations that are sweeping the globe, U.S. workers are suddenly in direct competition with a huge mass of workers around the globe who are receiving wages that are a tiny fraction of U.S. ones. If the work forces in China and India and Mexico and South America are integrated through the exchange of products with the U.S. work force, how could the United States resist at least some decrease in wages of unskilled workers?

Although public opinion holds all three suspects guilty of wage suppression, the jury of academics seems to be rendering a quite different verdict. Education and globalization have been found innocent and technological change guilty. Labor economists have not found evidence of much change in the relative supply of unskilled workers as a result of educational failures. They also do not find evidence of much change in the demand for labor coming from international trade. Like Sherlock Holmes who counseled, "Eliminate the impossible, and all that is left is the truth," once these economists found education and globalization innocent, they have chosen to convict technology. Never mind that there is little organized evidence against this culprit.

My view is different. First of all, I object, Your Honor; the evidence that has been presented in support of the innocence of globalization is "incompetent, irrelevant, and immaterial." I move for a mistrial. ("Overruled; sit down, Mr. Scheck.")

Second, this is a crime that most likely could not have been committed by any one of the culprits, but requires that all three be working together. If, for example, the educational system had created a work force in the United States that had few unskilled workers, then economic integration of the goods markets with Mexico could benefit all U.S. workers, even the lowest skilled. Our fear of the North American Free Trade Agreement (NAFTA) speaks volumes regarding our confidence in our educational system.

Third, I would argue, the question is not: Which is the guilty force? The real question is: What are we going to do about it? If we find education and globalization innocent and technology guilty, we seem to me to be edging toward a passive response: There is nothing that we can do. The continuing and persistent belief that globalization is guilty (never mind the academic argument to the contrary) probably comes from the fact that globalization has an apparent remedy: economic isolation. A guilty verdict against education also points to a remedy. But educational investments have a long gestation period, and we cannot expect to have much fast impact on the income inequality trends by pulling the education lever.

Though free trade remains a target of political rhetoric, with both NAFTA and the World Trade Organization (WTO) now passed, the option of economic isolation may be gone. This leaves us with a question: What private educational investments and public investments in immobile knowledge or infrastructure assets are most appropriate for the twenty-first century—when products can be shipped around the globe with little risk of government intervention, when liquid pools of physical and knowledge capital can freely seek out workers with the lowest wages relative to productivity, and when computers are prepared to do many mundane tasks with great accuracy and efficiency?

This chapter will not move us much closer to an answer to this important question. It has the more modest goal of establishing the role that *one form* of globalization plays in the income inequality drama, namely relative price reductions for labor-intensive tradables. The view I offer is that at the end of World War II, countries sorted themselves into two different groups. Europe and Japan and the Asian newly industrialized countries (NICs) chose economic integration with the United States. But most of the rest of the world opted for inward-looking isolationist policies. Those that chose integration experienced a period of technological backwardness, but the technological lead that the United States enjoyed in the 1960s vis-à-vis the integrated economies dissipated rapidly in the 1970s, even as the gap increased vis-à-vis the isolated countries. Economic isolationism eventually collapsed as this technological gap became more and more intolerable. Now the global economy faces the wrenching task of integrating the enormous number of low-skilled workers living in countries that formerly chose isolation. This integration may or may not mean lower wages for unskilled workers in the advanced, high-wage countries.

One possibility is that high rates of investment in immobile assets, particularly human capital and infrastructure, will assure that these advanced countries will continue to attract more than their share of mobile physical and knowledge assets and will continue to have work forces that command comfortably high wages. Another possibility is that a combination of trade and capital flows will eliminate entirely the economic separation of workers at different points on the globe, and that wage levels will be determined only by skills and effort and not at all by geography. This would surely mean greatly reduced levels of wages of unskilled workers in the advanced, high-wage countries, because the liberalizations of the last two decades have added enormously to the supply of unskilled workers with no commensurate increase in human or physical capital.

Before I proceed I should emphasize that the forces that might be affecting income inequality in the United States are diverse and interactive. A list of possibilities is provided in the display below. Included are U.S. investment rates, U.S. labor supply changes, technological change, increased international factor mobility, and increased trade in goods and services. On this list are many forms of "globalization" including the increased international mobility of intangible knowledge assets, reduced market power for unions, delocalization of assembly operations, and so on. In this chapter only one globalization effect is considered: lower prices for labor-intensive tradables. The economic liberalizations that have increased the supply of labor-intensive tradables in the longer run will doubtless divert physical capital from the high-wage, developed countries to the low-wage, developing countries, which of course can work against labor in the high-wage countries. This and other forms of "globalization" are not considered here, not because they are unimportant or less important, but only because it is hard enough to try to get one piece of the puzzle to fit, let alone two or more! (Think about that metaphor.)

Forces Lowering Wages of Unskilled U.S. Workers

Inadequate investment
  Education failures
  Low savings rate
Labor-force changes
  Female labor-force participation
Aging
Technological change
  Factor-biased productivity improvements in manufacturing
  Sectoral-biased productivity improvements in manufacturing
  Productivity gains in services
International factor mobility
  Immigration
  Capital flows

Technology transfers
Globalization of the markets for goods and services
  Lower prices for labor-intensive tradables (for example, apparel)
  Foreign demand for local services from an external deficit
  Reduced market power (for example, autos and steel)
  Delocalization (for example, assembly in Mexico)
  Internationalization of the service sector (for example, computer programming in India)

The first step in the argument is to get clear the circumstances in which price reductions for labor-intensive tradables will drive down wages in high-wage markets. The Heckscher-Ohlin (HO) model is a particularly rich conceptual setting for thinking about this issue. This is a model that ought to remind us that *prices are set on the margin*. It does not matter that trade in manufactures is a small proportion of GDP. It does not matter that employment in apparel is only 1 percent of the work force. What matters is whether or not the marginal unskilled worker is employed in the apparel sector, sewing the same garments as a Chinese worker whose wages are one-twentieth of the U.S. level. Then lower prices for apparel as a consequence of increased Chinese apparel supply causes lower wages for all unskilled workers in the same regional labor pool as the U.S. garment worker.

Wage determination in an HO model is described by the Stolper-Samuelson theorem, which links product prices with wages. This theorem reminds us that what matters is not the level of imports of apparel but rather their price. The quantity-oriented tradition of computing the labor embodied in trade and comparing it with the size of the U.S. labor force suffers from several defects that are more fully discussed by me elsewhere.[1] First and foremost is the fact that the factor contents are the *net* external factor supplies. The net external labor supply can change if the external price of labor changes, but it can also change if there are changes in either the internal labor demand or the internal labor supply. For example, technological change that lowers the internal demand for unskilled labor may offset the increase in imports of the services of unskilled workers that might otherwise have come from a fall in the external price. This can keep the imports of labor services low, even as the external marketplace is selecting a lower price for labor.

The first section is designed to present the HO model in as transparent a way as possible. An intellectual bridge between trade theory and labor economics is formed in this section by concentrating completely on the labor demand curve. What does the HO model imply about the labor demand curve? There are many surprising results. Indeed, the most important message of the HO model is that trade in commodities transforms a local labor demand curve into a global labor demand, even though there is not direct arbitrage through labor migration. Another important idea that comes from an HO framework is that the effects on wages of both globaliation and technological change should be studied by cross-industry, not within-industry, comparisons. In this general equilibrium framework, with product prices held fixed and to a first order of approximation, it does not matter that the technological change reduces the inputs of unskilled workers in every sector; what matters is whether the technological improvement is concentrated in sectors that are intensive in unskilled workers, intensive in skilled workers, or intensive in capital. *Factor bias does not matter; sector bias does.*[2]

1. Leamer (1995b).
2. Factor bias can matter if the change is large enough to allow second-order effects, or if the factor-biased technological change precipitates sectoral-biased price adjustments, for example, reduction of prices of labor-intensive tradables as a

The second section is a discussion of various data displays suggested by the HO framework. From this section arises one important conclusion. The three decades under examination had quite different outcomes. The 1960s had relative price stability, growth in all sectors of the economy, and wage gains at every level of skill. The 1970s was the Stolper-Samuelson decade, with price, trade, and employment data consistent with the presence of Stolper-Samuelson effects on wage inequality. The 1980s on the other hand have no evidence of Stolper-Samuelson effects, but globalization nonetheless may be operative through, for example, declines in market power in metals and autos, or through the external deficit that makes the marginal demand for workers come from the local nontraded sector.

When the HO framework is only a loose guide for the examination of the data, it is impossible to infer how much effect relative price variability is having on wage rates. Therefore, in the final section of this chapter, I present a formal data analysis using a specific HO model that attempts to separate the technology effects and the Stolper-Samuelson effects on wage levels and wage inequality. Data on price changes, factor shares, and technological change are used to estimate the "mandated" wage changes required to maintain zero profits across sectors. In this exercise the separation of technology from globalization effects depends on how the observed product price variability is split between technological change and globalization. Ideally, one would have a global supply and demand model that could help to determine what impact technological change is having on product prices. Here a common "pass-through" rate is assumed for all sectors, meaning that a given percent of the technological improvement is passed on to consumers in the form of lower prices. The remaining variability in product prices is attributed to "globalization," thus acting as if product prices were completely determined by the external marketplace.

The analysis is done with the labor force sliced by wage levels and by the usual production/nonproduction distinction. Two conclusions emerge: the residual "globalization" effects on income inequality generally dominate the technological effects; and the 1970s was the Stolper-Samuelson decade with product price changes causing increases in inequality. Product price variability in the 1980s actually worked in the opposite direction. The numbers that emerge from this analysis are very large: 4 percent mandated reduction per year in wages of low-wage workers in the 1970s offset by

---

consequence of labor-saving technological changes. However, if the demand for nontradables is highly elastic, the released factors can be absorbed in nontradables with little or no change in tradables prices.

2 percent per year gains in the 1980s. Accumulated over the two decades, these numbers are big enough to account for most of the increase in income inequality in the United States.

The major shortcomings of the estimates of the relative impact of globalization and technological change reported in the third section of this chapter are the following:

—The estimates are based on one special HO model, which presumes first, that the demand for labor is infinitely elastic, and second, that the globalization "shock" is a product price change which stimulates a factor price response. In this framework, education cannot matter at all because changes in the supply of unskilled or skilled workers have no effect on wages.

—The separation of the observed changes of product prices into globalization and technological components is questionable. In particular, a constant pass-through rate is a doubtful assumption.

—The data on prices, factor shares, and total factor productivity (TFP) are all measured with error.

—There is no consideration whatsoever to the adjustment process by which the labor markets might absorb the news of product price changes. The mandated wage changes apply only over a time frame long enough to allow complete separation of worker and capital from the sectors in which they were originally deployed.

In other words, much is left to be done. We need to compute the "globalization" effects allowing for product-mix changes and/or allowing for the possibility that the marginal demand for labor comes internally from the non-traded-goods sector. We need to be more careful about the demand side to determine how technological change alters product prices. We need to link product price changes more clearly to globalization. We need to explore other ways of measuring the factor shares and TFP. We need to adjust econometrically for measurement errors including outlier problems. We need to consider empirically other forms of globalization including the effect of the external deficit on the demand for nontradables, the increased mobility of knowledge and physical assets, and reduced market power especially in metals and transportation equipment. Finally, we need to explore the implications of other conceptual frameworks, namely the Ricardo-Viner framework that has sector-specific, labor-related assets, as well as the Chamberlainian framework, with increasing returns to scale and imperfect competition.

Nonetheless, I believe that this chapter supports the view that increased competition from low-wage, developing countries during the 1970s had an important impact on the U.S. labor market either in that decade or sub-sequently. This was the Heckscher-Ohlin, Stolper-Samuelson decade during which there were substantial relative price declines for labor-inten-sive products made in the United States. The 1980s experienced no continu-ing price declines for labor-intensive goods, presumably because the U.S. economy had isolated itself from low-wage competition by product upgrad-ing or by trade restrictions, particularly the Multi-Fiber Agreement (MFA). If it is the MFA, then we can expect another round of price reductions of labor-intensive products made in the United States as the MFA is phased out according to plan or as Mexico is able to access the U.S. marketplace relatively free of MFA restrictions. If it is product upgrading, then the United States may have positioned itself so that most categories of labor will benefit from cheaper imports coming from low-wage, developing countries. Research is under way to separate these two possibilities.

A Heckscher-Ohlin Theory of Labor Demand

We make two important mistakes when we analyze data: taking the theory too seriously, and not taking the theory seriously enough. In practice we always make some of both kinds of errors; it is a judgment call as to which is the more severe. Probably because of my extensive training in general equilibrium, international trade economics, I am disturbed that there is so little of international trade theory evident in the measurement methods that are now commonplace in the empirical literature connecting globalization to local labor markets. Indeed there seem to be some major misconceptions about this theory about which I have complained elsewhere.[3]

The goal of this section is to add a dash of trade theory to the debate by laying out the essential aspects of the traditional HO general equilibrium model as clearly as possible. Toward that end, I focus exclusively on the demand for labor and ask the simple question: How might "globalization" and "technological change" alter the U.S. demand for labor? It should be repeated again for emphasis that "globalization" and "technological change" have many potential routes by which they can affect the local labor markets. The globalization "shock" that is emphasized here is an increase in the foreign supply of unskilled workers associated with the economic liberalizations that are sweeping the globe. The technology shock is ex-ogenous, sectoral-biased productivity improvements. Two basic questions

3. Leamer (1994). Also see the review by Deardorff and Hakura (1994).

are posed: What might keep the wages of unskilled workers in the United States high as the global labor market absorbs huge increases in the supply of unskilled workers from formerly isolated regions? And what kind of technological change tends to lower wages of unskilled workers and increase income inequality? These questions are answered indirectly by a series of labor demand curves depicted in figures 4-3 to 4-9. Details of the derivations of these labor demand curves can be found in appendix B to this chapter.

Two standard results in an HO framework describe the demand for labor. The factor price equalization (FPE) theorem identifies conditions under which the demand for labor is infinitely elastic.[4] The Stolper-Samuelson theorem explains how changes in product prices shift the demand for labor up and down. These results have two important implications for a study of the impact of "globalization" on the U.S. labor market. First, with the reduction of the U.S. share of world GDP should come an increase in the elasticity of the labor demand. Second, unless the U.S. marketplace is so large that it completely controls product prices, the news of the foreign liberalizations is communicated to the U.S. labor market through changes in product prices that shift the labor demand up or down. In other words, price shocks cause price reactions. This conflicts with many studies by labor economists who measure the global shock with quantity measures (levels of imports or the factor content of trade) and who sometimes measure the reaction with quantity measures (employment levels).

The content of these two theorems is communicated in figures 4-3 and 4-4, which are built on the following assumptions:

—two goods (machinery and apparel) and two factors of production (capital and labor);

—constant returns-to-scale production functions;

—factors costlessly mobile between sectors but completely immobile internationally; and

—a country that is too small to affect world prices.

Figure 4-3 contrasts the relatively inelastic labor demand of a closed economy with the infinitely elastic labor demand of a small, open economy that faces fixed world product prices. The shifting up or down of the labor demand in response to a reduction in the price of the labor-intensive good is illustrated in figure 4-4. The horizontal axis in both these figures is the

---

4. Incidentally, in my Graham Lecture (Leamer [1995a]), I have argued that it would be better to call this the "factor price insensitivity theorem," meaning that wages do not change with labor supplies.

Figure 4-3. *Labor Demand in Two-Good, Two-Factor HO Model*

Wage/apparel price

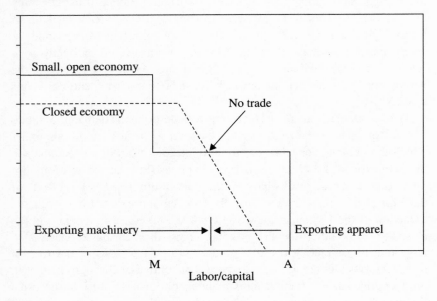

Figure 4-4. *Globalization Effect and Labor Demand: Reduced Relative Price of Apparel*

Wage/apparel price

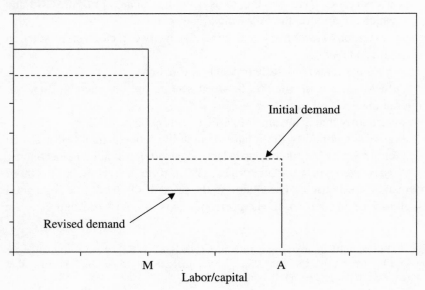

ratio of labor to capital; the vertical axis is the real wage in buying power over apparel, the labor-intensive good. The labels M and A on the horizontal axes refer to the labor intensities of the two products, machinery and apparel, which are assumed technologically fixed without materially affecting the discussion. The horizontal scale in figure 4-3 is separated into a region in which the country exports apparel and a region in which the country exports machinery. The no-trade point occurs when the pretrade and post-trade product prices are identical, thus where the labor demand functions for the closed and open economies cross.

The extreme elasticity of a labor demand curve for a small, open economy comes from an ultrasensitive response of product mix to changes in labor or capital supply.[5] More generally, both wages and output mix will respond to labor supply increases. In a Ricardo-Viner unit of time, the output mix is relatively unresponsive to labor supply changes, and it is wages that do the adjusting.[6] In an HO unit of time with product prices given and factors mobile between sectors, outputs are ultrasensitive to labor supply changes and wages can stay fixed even as labor supply changes. Ultrasensitive output responses can occur only over a time long enough to allow substantial reshuffling of capital between sectors. The HO clock surely does not click year by year. Decade by decade is a better estimate of the speed. It may well be that the HO forces work so slowly that by the time they might become operative, other changes in the economy have made them irrelevant.

Notice in figure 4-3 that the labor demand function of the open economy is infinitely elastic only for labor-to-capital ratios between M and A. The input intensities in the two sectors are assumed to be fixed; and if the labor-to-capital, factor supply ratio is outside the interval between M and A, the open economy specializes completely in one product and has one factor that is redundant and that commands a zero return. The closed economy has zero returns for one factor over a broader set of labor-to-capital ratios because demand has to be satisfied internally, and complete specialization of a closed economy is inconsistent with utility functions that place value on product diversity.

An important feature of these labor demand curves is that relatively high wages are provided by the open economy in comparison with the closed economy when labor is very abundant, but also when labor is very scarce.

5. The Jones magnification result is $\hat{M} < 0 < \hat{L} < \hat{A}$, meaning that the percentage change in outputs magnifies the percentage change in labor (here assumed to be positive).

6. A Ricardo-Viner model has sector-specific assets.

Trade theory has tended to concentrate attention on the segment of the labor demand curve between M and A, within which openness raises wages for labor-abundant countries but lowers wages for labor scarce countries. But in the labor-scarce segment between zero and M, openness also raises real wages. This extremely important and often overlooked feature of an HO model is worth repeating in a somewhat different way. If two regions are economically integrated and if they are sufficiently similar in factor abundance, then economic integration will lower the return to capital and raise the wage rate in the labor-abundant country, and will have the opposite effect on earnings in the capital-abundant country. In other words, there are winners and losers. But *if the countries are sufficiently dissimilar in their factor supply ratios and if the integrated equilibrium has one or both countries fully specialized, then both factors in both regions can be made better off from economic integration of the product markets.* Keep in mind here the huge differences in labor abundance of the United States compared with low-wage Asia. Absent capital mobility, this raises the possibility that labor on both sides of the Pacific can gain from increased cross-Pacific trade.

The impact of a fall in the price of apparel on the labor demand schedule, as described by the Stolper-Samuelson theorem, is illustrated in figure 4-4. A reduction in the price of the labor-intensive good lowers the real wage of labor regardless of the numeraire. Thus in the segment between M and A, the labor demand curve is shifted downward. For the economy that is fully specialized in machinery (labor-to-capital abundance ratios less than M), the fall in the relative price of apparel means that labor commands a higher wage in terms of apparel (though the same in terms of machinery). Thus for highly capital-abundant countries, increased supply of apparel from Asia increases the earnings of both capital and labor. (More on this possibility in figure 4-5.)

The labor demand schedule in figure 4-3 can be easily amended to allow more sectors simply by adding more horizontal segments as in figure 4-5, each segment selecting a different pair of products. This figure reminds us that the increased competition from labor-abundant countries shifts downward only the right tail of the labor demand curve applicable to labor-abundant countries, but shifts upward the demand for labor at lower levels of labor supply. Higher real wages accrue to capital-abundant countries from cheaper imports of noncompeting goods. Thus "globalization" of this form is a problem only for those countries or regions that are forced because of inadequate supplies of capital to compete with low-wage Asia. For more capital-abundant countries, the rising tide of Asian trade lifts all boats. This establishes one method of escape from the forces of

Figure 4-5. *Labor Demand with Various Products: Small, Open Economy*

Wage/apparel price

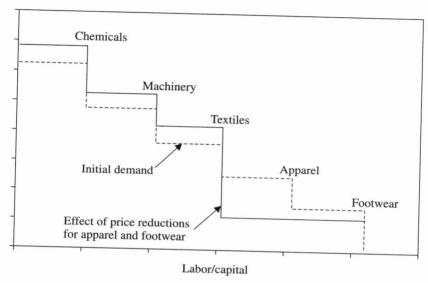

Labor/capital

global wage equalization: capital investments that support product upgrading. A question can summarize this discussion: what is the source of the marginal demand for unskilled workers in your community? If it is apparel or footwear manufacturing because your community lacks the skills and capital to support an upgraded product mix, then the twenty-first century promises to be a difficult time.

If the model allows another factor of production, say human capital, then there are more complex choices of product mix and a variety of demand functions for unskilled labor depending on the supply of human capital. Figure 4-6 illustrates the demand for unskilled labor of two hypothetical countries with different ratios of skilled to unskilled workers. The horizontal axis for this demand curve is, as before, the ratio of unskilled labor to physical capital. Figure 4-6 offers a more complicated version of the message of figure 4-5: "Protection" from competition with low-wage countries can come from high rates of investment. *The problem is not trade by itself, but a combination of trade and the deplorably low U.S. rates of investment in all kinds of capital.*[7]

7. Parenthetically, this model suggests two methods for fighting income inequality caused by globalization: broadening the ownership of human capital or

Figure 4-6. *Demand for Unskilled Workers: Three-Factor Model*

Wage/apparel price

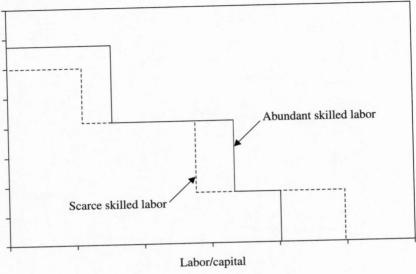

Labor/capital

The next topic is the trade deficit and the "overvaluation" of the dollar. To think about the possible effects of a trade deficit, this simple model needs nontraded goods whose prices can be influenced by local demand. The labor demand function for a country with two tradables and one labor-intensive nontradable is illustrated in figure 4-7. This demand curve has an interval of infinite elasticity which occurs when the country produces

---

raising the wage of unskilled workers by increasing the total amount of human capital. Broadened ownership of human capital could be achieved, for example, by dispersing public funds for general education. But increased total human capital stock could be achieved most efficiently with educational tax incentives that would encourage especially the most able to invest in more education. The solution that broadens the ownership of human capital is economically inefficient, because investments are undertaken that offer relatively low rates of return. This lowers the total human capital stock created by a given investment level. The apparently elitist policy that concentrates educational investments on the most able is the preferred method of fighting income inequality for a country that has a product mix that is almost the same as the high-wage countries—that is, one with relatively low output levels of labor-intensive manufactures. For this kind of country, a small stimulus for the most able to increase educational attainment can reduce inequality by raising the wage level of unskilled workers. Among Organization for Economic Cooperation and Development (OECD) countries, the United States has an unusually large apparel sector and may be the country that is least able to fight income inequality with elitist educational policy.

Figure 4-7. *Labor Demand with Labor-Intensive Nontradeables*

Wage/apparel price

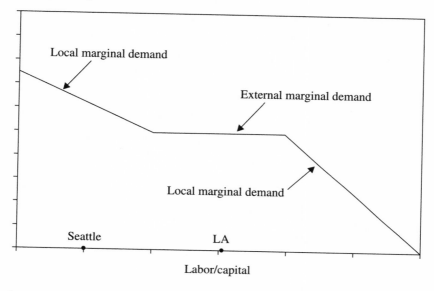

both tradables. In this interval the two zero-profit conditions for tradables can be used to solve for the two internal factor prices as a function of the two external product prices. These internal factor prices determine the price of nontraded goods from the nontraded-goods-zero-profit condition. In this

---

We can also use a three-factor model to make some remarks about *increased capital mobility*. Suppose that globalization means not just integration of the goods markets and equalization of goods prices, but also freedom for capital to find locations on the globe with the highest rates of return. Then capital will flow out of the high-wage countries. The flow will stop when the return is equalized. If the supply of skilled workers in the high-wage country is relatively small compared with unskilled workers, equalization of the return to capital can only occur with equalization of the other two factor costs, including low wages for unskilled workers. But if the supply of skilled workers is great enough, the capital outflow can be terminated by a decline in the rental price of human capital, not wages of unskilled workers. Thus, at least in this model, *the assault on income equality represented by capital mobility toward the low-wage, developing regions can be completely met by educational investments that attract capital by lowering the cost of complementary skilled inputs.* Of course, this lower private return to skills reduces the attractiveness of investments in skills. In the longer run, human capital in a skill-abundant country can be turned into more productive investments in physical assets in the emerging regions, thus creating new pressure for low wages. Public subsidies to education are then the natural means of maintaining reasonably low levels of income inequality.

Figure 4-8. *Labor Demand: Effect of a Trade Deficit on Labor-Intensive Nontradables*

Wage/apparel price

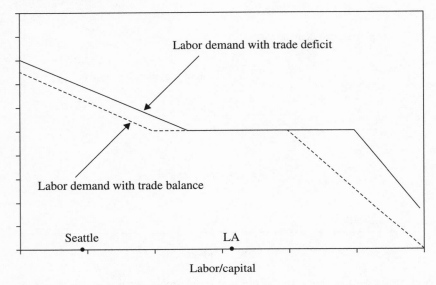

Labor/capital

interval the marginal demand for labor is external, because the international exchange of products is creating implicitly an infinitely elastic external demand for labor services. But if labor is very scarce or quite abundant, the economy will fully specialize on one traded good and will produce also the nontraded good. In that event the marginal demand for labor can be said to be internal in the nontradables sector.

An external deficit raises the demand for nontradables and may or may not affect wages. If the marginal demand for labor is internal, then the increase in demand for nontradables must be contained by higher prices for nontradables and therefore higher wages. But if the marginal demand for labor is external, the increased demand for nontradables can be met simply by shifting resources from the tradables sector. Because the opportunity cost of these productive resources in tradables is fixed, there is no change in the price of nontradables and no change in wages. These possibilities are depicted in figure 4-8, which shows how an external deficit affects the demand for labor if the nontradable is labor intensive.[8]

8. Although this figure can be used to think about the impact of the U.S. trade deficit in the mid-1980s on U.S. wages, it needs to be applied with care. Any

Figures 4-7 and 4-8 can also allow us to contrast "globalization" of the product market from "globalization" of the factor market. Into each figure I have inserted two labor/capital ratios that are provocatively labeled "Seattle" and "LA." Seattle is rich in capital and opts for a mix of tradables that is concentrated on capital-intensive goods like aerospace and software design. The city of Los Angeles has a higher ratio of workers to capital because of an earlier migrant inflow. In LA, wages are lower and the mix of manufactures is more diverse, including an active garment district. Each of these communities is exposed to one form of globalization and isolated from the other. Immigrants into Seattle would have to be absorbed into the non-traded-goods sectors and would drive down wages, but further immigration into LA can be absorbed in the tradables sector with no effect on wages. On the other hand, workers in LA are exposed to competition with Chinese apparel manufacturers, whereas no sector in Seattle competes with China. Thus Seattle is exposed to migrant shocks but isolated from product price shocks; LA is isolated from further migrant shocks but exposed to product price shocks.[9]

Another important isolating force that can support high wages in the face of increased competition from low-wage countries is technological superiority. The United States enjoyed a substantial technological and organizational advantage in the 1960s, and part of the globalization story surely has to do with the increased fluidity of technology and the mostly uncompensated transfer of U.S. knowledge assets to other countries. This transfer may or may not drive down wages of U.S. unskilled workers depending on its impact on international relative prices of products. In any case, it seems unlikely that technological superiority can be used anymore to support high wages in the United States, because international commerce by itself carries

---

question regarding the effects of a deficit suffers terrible vagueness, because there are many different ways that government policy might affect the external deficit and these different policies are unlikely to have the same impact on the economy. For example, the external deficit might be reduced by increased personal income taxes or by reduced defense expenditure; the deficit might be reduced by increased private savings encouraged by favorable tax treatment for IRAs; the external deficit might be reduced by a NAFTA agreement that creates new external investment opportunities; and so on and so on. It is completely inconceivable that all these policies and all the other possibilities would have the same impact on the demand for labor. In the models presented here with the capital stock given, an external deficit could have an effect on labor demand in one of two ways. A deficit can cause or be accompanied by changes in relative prices of tradables or a deficit can cause or be accompanied by changes in the demand for nontradables.

9. Borjas and Ramey (1993) report the following data, which do show much lower skill premia in Seattle than in Los Angeles, but also an increase over time in

Figure 4-9. *Labor Demand: Effect of Technological Change in the Capital-Intensive Sector*

Wage/apparel price

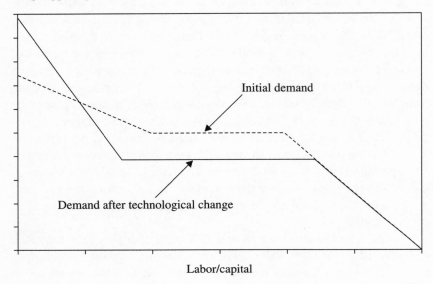

Labor/capital

stowaway knowledge assets, and other knowledge assets are sold or deployed abroad by multinational firms.

The effect of technological superiority on the demand for labor depends on whether the superiority is concentrated in labor-intensive or capital-intensivesectors. The simplest case of neutral technological differences refers to a country using a superior technology that affects labor and capital productivities proportionately in both sectors. Then the demand curve in

---

both locations. The former finding conforms with the theory just presented; the latter tends to contradict it.

Returns to Skills in Metropolitan Areas

| | Year | Log wage ratio of college graduates to | |
		High school dropouts	High school graduates
Los Angeles	1976	0.578	0.311
	1990	0.841	0.471
Seattle	1976	0.220	0.196
	1990	0.532	0.293

figure 4-3 is just shifted proportionately upward. If this hypothetical second country uses the same technology in apparel but a superior one in machinery, the labor demand curve shifts in a more interesting way depicted in figure 4-9.[10]

Figure 4-9 can also be interpreted as a depiction of the effect of proprietary and local technological improvement in the capital-intensive sector, a kind of change that improves productivity but does not force down world product prices. Although one cannot see it in figure 4-9, the shift down or up in the labor demand schedule depends on whether the technological change is concentrated in the capital-intensive or the labor-intensive sector, not on whether the change is labor saving or capital saving. It is the sector bias that matters, not the factor bias. This is made completely transparent in the algebra presented in the third section of this chapter. Figure 4-9 is a first step toward understanding the impact of the computer revolution, although this technological change is neither proprietary nor local and needs to be studied with a model that allows relative price variability. One possibility is that the technological improvement is fully passed on to consumers in lower prices. In that event the nominal wage level stays the same and real wages rise depending on the numeraire good.[11]

Evidence

A data analysis based on a specialized HO *model,* such as the one-cone, "even" model, allows a close link between theory and data, but does so only by an uncomfortable commitment to a highly specialized version of the general theory. The general HO framework can drive the data analysis, but only if we are willing to tolerate an uncomfortably fuzzy link between theory and data. The best treatment to these two kinds of discomfort is: some of each. In this section, the empirical facts are presented with only a "light" touch of the HO framework. In the next section, a formal data analysis is presented based explicitly on the one-cone, HO model.

The key plot elements of the HO fable are relative product prices and product mix. According to the theory, a decline in the relative price of

10. This labor demand curve is derived on the assumption that the superior technology in machinery is more capital intensive than the inferior technology, and thus the region of incomplete specialization is broadened.

11. Another possibility is that labor-saving technological change shifts the comparative advantage of all countries toward the labor-intensive goods. The consequent increased supply induces offsetting price reductions and then Stolper-Samuelson amplifications. More on this later in the chapter.

Figure 4-10. *Apparel Sector: Prices, Trade, and Employment, 1960–93*

Sources: Bartelsman and Gray (1996); and author's calculations.

labor-intensive manufactures is met in some communities by product upgrading. Other communities too abundant in unskilled workers to allow product upgrading experience declines in wages of unskilled workers and increases in returns to skills and/or capital.

From this section arises one important conclusion. The three decades under examination had very different outcomes. The 1960s had relative price stability, growth in all sectors of the economy, and wage gains at every level of skill. The 1970s was the Stolper-Samuelson decade with price, trade, and employment data consistent with the presence of Stolper-Samuelson effects on wage inequality. The 1980s on the other hand have no evidence of Stolper-Samuelson effects, but globalization may nonetheless be operating either through declines in market power in metals and autos or through the external deficit that makes the marginal demand for workers come from the local nontraded sector, or through delocalization, or through. . . .

Figure 4-10, which depicts prices, trade, and employment in apparel, tells the story. The price of apparel relative to the overall PPI remained constant from 1960 to 1970, then fell by 30 percent over the next decade, at which point apparel prices stabilized. Employment in apparel increased during the 1960s from 1.2 million to 1.4 million, but began a decline in

1973 that has seen employment drop to under 1.0 million with no end in sight. Meanwhile, the employment loss is matched almost exactly by increases in imports as a share of domestic output, beginning at about zero and reaching 35 percent by 1985.[12] But, you may object, this is too small a share of total U.S. employment to matter. Does the tail wag the dog? Yes, indeed, the tail does wag the dog, if you believe in economics. Prices are set on the margin. Then what about the timing? Did not most of the increase in inequality come in the 1980s, not the 1970s? This is a difficult question. First of all, I am not yet willing to accept this timing of the increase in income inequality as a fact. On the contrary, I will show below that the *sectoral* wage inequality increased most in the 1970s and was relatively constant in the 1980s. But even if the increase in *worker* wage inequality is concentrated in the 1980s, this may be due to delayed Stolper-Samuelson effects. These effects are operative only over periods that are long enough to allow complete mobility of factors of production among sectors. The initial redistribution induced by price changes accrue mostly to sector-specific factors—say skilled workers in apparel—and only over time will this spill over to unskilled workers throughout the economy.

There is one more question that needs addressing: Why did the price declines for apparel not continue into the 1980s? This question needs answering if we are to form a clear vision of the future. One possibility is that the MFA that controls trade in apparel and textiles had more bite in the 1980s than the 1970s. With the scheduled phaseout of the MFA (again!) and with Mexican apparel exports to the United States soon to be free of the MFA, this portends another burst of inequality caused by cheaper imports of apparel and textiles. Another possibility is that through product upgrading, U.S. apparel producers by 1980 no longer were in competition with low-wage Asian sources of supply. T-shirts and jeans are imported; women's high-fashion clothing was made locally. This upgrading allows import prices of apparel to fall even as prices paid to U.S. producers do not. This upgrading interpretation is much more optimistic since it suggests that the U.S. economy is positioned to allow gains from increased trade with low-wage countries to accrue to all factors of production.

Other figures discussed in this section depict additional supportive evidence. It is shown that the United States has become increasingly dependent on imports of most manufactures but especially of labor-intensive manufactures, apparel and footwear. There are many more countries that

12. Sorry, but that is where my data on production levels terminate.

were exporters of labor-intensive products in 1990 than there were in 1960. The United States, which once had a distinctive pattern of factor supplies with abundance of land, human capital, and physical capital, is now surrounded by other competitors with equal or superior capital/worker and skill ratios. Product prices of apparel and also textiles fell substantially during the 1970s. Employment levels in these labor-intensive sectors have declined substantially from their peak levels in 1970. Wage levels in these unskilled sectors have declined, and the gap between wages paid in the most labor-intensive sectors and other sectors has increased.

What Happened in 1972–73?

One of the most surprising features of many of the graphs now to be discussed is the abrupt change in the series in the early 1970s. Take a look again at the real wage data in figure 4-1. Before 1972, real hourly earnings of production workers in manufacturing climbed virtually along a straight line at about 2.5 percent per year. The dip in real wages in 1973 that came from a burst in inflation in producer prices was offset by relatively rapid wage increases until 1978, when again the series on real wages dips. Thereafter real wages never got close to the trend line of the 1960s. This sharp break in the behavior of this series in 1972–73 is a highly unusual feature that cries out for explanation. This same kind of break occurs in many of the series now to be discussed, and no explanation of the changes in wages is going to be very satisfying if it cannot offer some interpretation of this remarkable transition.

Real Wages of Production Workers by Two-Digit Sectors: Three Subperiods

The transition year 1972 is also evident in the disaggregated wage data depicted in figure 4-11. Until that year wages in every two-digit sector grew at a similar rate. The burst of product price inflation of 1973 reduced wages in all sectors uniformly. In the subsequent decade, real wages fluctuated substantially but by 1985 had regained or slightly exceeded their 1972 levels in all sectors except apparel. Thereafter, slow growth in real wages in many sectors resumed.

This figure has two vertical lines that separate what seem to be three distinct subperiods: first the pleasant 1960s with substantial and general wage increases; next the turbulent 1970s with real wages regaining their initial levels only at the end of the decade; and finally in the 1980s, a

Figure 4-11. *Wages Deflated by Overall PPI: Various Industries, 1960–93*

Real wages per hour (1960 U.S.$)

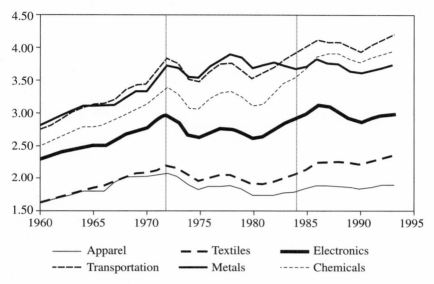

Sources: Bartelsman and Gray (1996); and author's calculations.

mixture of the first two subperiods, with some real wage growth and some turbulence. The Stolper-Samuelson effects seem clearly present in the 1970s, but the 1980s will remain a mystery as far as this discussion is concerned.[13] It is quite possible that product upgrading during the 1970s isolated the U.S. labor market from low-wage Asian competition. Another form of globalization may be operative in the 1980s, perhaps the diminished-market-power hypothesis explored by Borjas and Ramey, or perhaps related to the external deficit.[14] The sharp rise in wages in chemicals and the decline in metals wages in the 1980s may be important parts of the puzzle.

Skill Premiums: Sectoral Wages Divided by Wages in Apparel

As Bell and Freeman have observed, wages can differ across sectors for a variety of reasons, including economic rents to immobile workers and

13. The divergence of apparel and textile wages in the 1970s may be evidence of product upgrading in the textile sector aimed at escaping foreign, low-wage, low-skill competition.

14. Borjas and Ramey (1993).

Figure 4-12. *Skill Premiums: Wages Divided by Apparel Wages, 1960–93*

Relative wages per hour

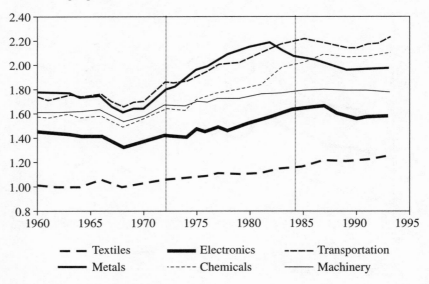

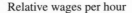

Sources: Bartelsman and Gray (1996); and author's calculations.

compensation for undesirable features of the work, such as effort levels (efficiency wages), safety, and high local costs of living.[15] But within the framework of the HO model, the only reason that wages differ across manufacturing sectors is differences in the skill mixes. To keep the story brief enough for a single sitting, we adopt the HO framework and interpret the wage differences evident in figure 4-11 as indicators of skills. With this as a given, the changes over time of the sectoral distribution of wages can come either from changes in the compensation for skills or from changes of the sectoral skill intensities. In the next section, both are explicitly allowed. For the moment, we abstract from changes in the skill intensities and take changes in wage differences across sectors to be indicators only of changes in the compensation for skills.

Figure 4-12 depicts the average wages in a sector relative to apparel wages and is (boldly) labeled a skill premium. Here again we see the three subperiods. In the first, except for a dip in the late 1960s, there was little change in these skill premiums. In the second subperiod, there was a

15. Bell and Freeman (1991).

substantial increase in the skill premiums. Then in the third period, the skill premiums stayed relatively constant. Although this figure suggests that most of the increase in income inequality came between 1970 and 1982, the consensus view is that the 1980s actually experienced the greatest increase in inequality. For example, Borjas and Ramey's estimate based on annual demographic files from the Current Population Survey (CPS) of the premium for a college education relative to high school dropouts is relatively constant until 1981, after which it increases dramatically.[16] This conflict between individual data and industry aggregates will not be resolved here, but here is one conjecture. High school dropouts may have become increasingly unemployable in manufacturing, and the skill premiums in figure 4-12 implicitly compare college graduates with high school graduates.

Cumulative Four-Digit Sectoral Wages

The cumulative distribution of wages depicted in figure 4-13 is perhaps the most dramatic way of summarizing the three-decades story. The horizontal axis in this figure is the level of sectoral real hourly earnings of production workers using the PPI as the deflator. On the vertical axis is the percent of production workers employed in sectors that pay on average no more than the indicated real wage. In this figure the growth in real wages in all sectors of the economy from 1961 to 1971 is indicated by the shift rightward of this cumulative distribution. There is some slight tendency for the higher-paid sectors to award relatively large wage increases. This can be seen in the numerical details of this cumulative that are reported in table 4-1. Indeed, it is the case that the 10th percentile and the median wage grew at the rate of 2.5 percent from 1961 to 1971, whereas the 90th percentile grew at the rate of 3.0 percent.

In the next decade, from 1971 to 1981, real wages generally fell, more at the lower levels of initial wages than at the higher ones. The exception is that wages continued to rise for those above the 95th percentile. Then from 1981 to 1991, the experience of the previous decade was largely reversed, bringing the cumulative for 1991 back to its 1971 position for wages lower than the 70th percentile. Above the 70th percentile, wages in 1991 exceeded their 1971 levels.

Relative Prices: Two-Digit Data

The relevance of the HO model for studying the impact of globalization on wages and the skill premium depends fundamentally on reductions in

16. Borjas and Ramey (1993).

Figure 4-13. *Cumulative Sectoral Distribution of Real Wages of Production Workers*[a]

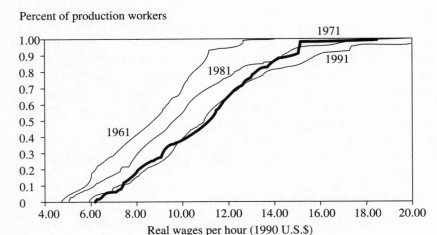

Percent of production workers

Sources: Bartelsman and Gray (1996); and author's calculations.

a. PPI deflator.

prices of labor-intensive tradables, a change that can be associated with increased foreign competition and that can be mapped into the kind of wage changes that have occurred over the last several decades. Lawrence and Slaughter have argued that there is no association between price changes and labor intensities, which would seem to be a decisive finding against the HO model.[17] This finding is echoed by Bhagwati and Dehejia and by Krugman and Lawrence.[18] Even Sachs and Shatz, who are overall sympathetic to the idea that increased competition with low-wage, developing countries is lowering wages of unskilled workers, nevertheless have a hard time finding supporting evidence in the price data.[19] The conclusions of these authors seem based primarily on the subperiods over which they have measured relative prices. In fact, the two-digit relative price data in figure 4-14 evidence three distinct subperiods. Most of the relative price reductions of labor-intensive products occurred in the turbulent middle period from 1972 to 1983. In the first period, from 1960 to 1972, the price of the labor-intensive products (apparel and textiles) relative to the overall PPI fell modestly by about 4 percent and 8 percent, respectively. In the second

17. Lawrence and Slaughter (1993).
18. Bhagwati and Dehejia (1994); Krugman and Lawrence (1993).
19. Sachs and Shatz (1994).

Table 4-1. *Employment Percentiles of Distribution of Production Hourly Wages across Sectors, Selected Years, 1961–91, Deflated by PPI*[a]

	1961	1971	1981	1991	Annualized rate of growth				Growth			
					1961–71	1971–81	1981–91	1961–91	1961–72	1971–82	1981–92	1961–92
PPI	0.27	0.34	0.81	1.00								
10th Percentile	5.79	7.42	6.17	7.32	2.52	−1.83	1.72	0.79	28.26	−16.90	18.63	26.44
Median	8.66	11.04	9.64	11.03	2.46	−1.34	1.35	0.81	27.51	−12.66	14.32	27.31
90th Percentile	11.13	14.98	14.46	16.10	3.02	−0.35	1.08	1.24	34.62	−3.46	11.33	44.68

Source: Bartelsman and Gray (1996).

a. In 1961, 10 percent of workers were employed in sectors that paid $5.79 per hour or less.

Figure 4-14. *Relative Produce Prices, 1960–92*

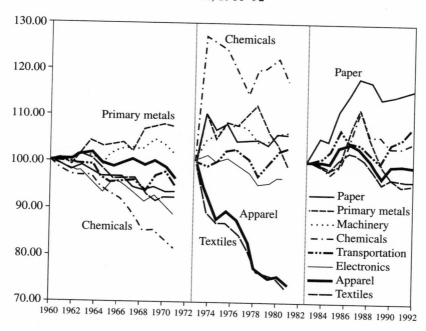

Sources: Bartelsman and Gray (1996); and author's calculations.

period, from 1972 to 1983, prices of these labor-intensive products fell by another 30 percent. Then in the third period, there was little change in the relative price of apparel and textiles.[20]

20. The middle decade experienced a huge increase in the price of petroleum that, however, cannot account for the relative price decline of apparel and textiles, because energy inputs are a small share of costs in manufacturing.

Figure 4-15. *World Factor Supplies, 1965*

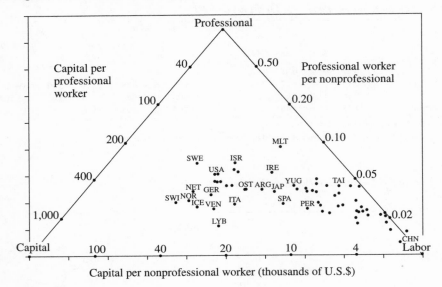

Capital per nonprofessional worker (thousands of U.S.$)

Source: Song (1993).

World Factor Supplies

The price variability that is displayed in figure 4-14 could be due strictly to internal factors such as shifts in demand, technological change, or U.S. factor supply changes. To argue that globalization is a driving force behind the price reductions for labor-intensive products in the 1970s, we need to show first the increase in world supply and second the increase in U.S. imports that would be associated with lower global prices. The increase in world supply in an HO framework comes from relatively rapid capital accumulation in labor-abundant countries. This did indeed occur. Figures 4-15 and 4-16 illustrate the differences in factor supplies of capital, professional workers, and nonprofessional workers for a large number of countries in 1965 and 1988, respectively. Straight lines coming from one of the vertices in these triangles vary one factor and hold the other two fixed. Thus the three factor ratios can be read from the scales on the edges of these triangles.

Roughly speaking, countries that are clustered around the U.S. point are the ones that are most likely to be U.S. competitors. Interpreted in that way, these figures suggest why the United States might be getting itself into difficulties internationally. The 1965 figure has the United States on the

Figure 4-16. *World Factor Supplies, 1988*

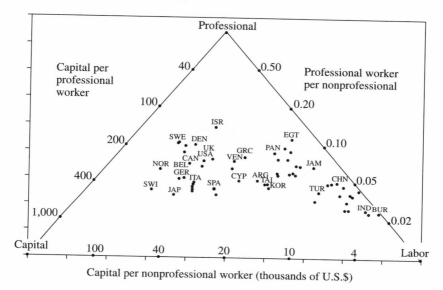

Source: Song (1993).

edge of the advanced countries with abundance of both professional workers and also capital. From this uniqueness presumably came relatively great gains from trade and also insulation from competition with the most labor-abundant countries. But by 1988 the United States is only one of many. The United States is exceeded in both physical capital and human capital per worker by a collection of OECD countries. More alarming, on the other side are a group of low-wage countries with ratios of human and physical capital that are high enough to turn these countries into U.S. competitors, especially as the "high-end" marketplaces are taken over by the advanced OECD countries with higher investment rates than the United States.

World Trade in Labor-Intensive Manufactures

The increase in global supply of labor-intensive tradables is suggested by figures 4-17 and 4-18, which report the net export data, comparing 1965 with 1988. These data apply to my labor-intensive aggregate composed of nonmetallic mineral manufactures, furniture, travel goods, apparel, and footwear.[21] A full view and a zoomed view are provided. If there were no

21. Leamer (1984).

Figure 4-17. *Labor-Intensive Net Exports per Worker, 1965 and 1988*

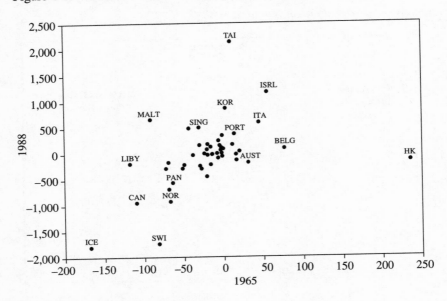

Source: Song (1993).

Figure 4-18. *Labor-Intensive Net Exports per Worker, 1965 and 1988: Zoomed View*

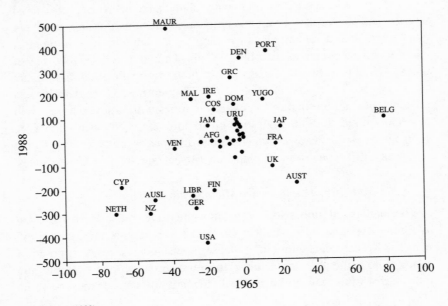

Source: Song (1993).

Figure 4-19. *U.S. Net Exports/Production: Largest Surpluses, 1958–85*

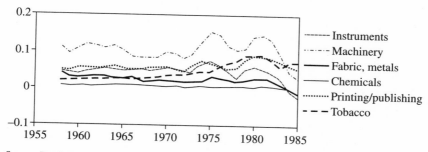

Sources: Bartelsman and Gray (1996); and author's calculations.

Figure 4-20. *U.S. Net Exports/Production: Largest Deficits, 1958–85*

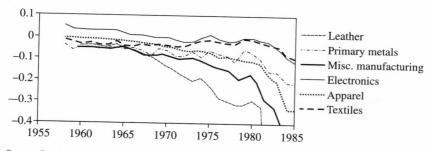

Sources: Bartelsman and Gray (1996); and author's calculations.

change in comparative advantage from 1965 to 1988, these data would all lie on a straight line. For most of my other aggregates, the patterns of trade are highly stable. But comparative advantage in labor-intensive manufactures displayed in these figures is in turmoil, with a large number of countries shifting from being net importers to being net exporters, a feature particularly apparent in the zoomed view. In response, France, the United Kingdom, Austria, and even Hong Kong switch in the opposite direction. Japan and Belgium, although still having positive net exports of this category, are substantially reducing their export dependence on this product, falling from the list of top ten net exporters to well back in the pack. Moving in the same direction, net imports per worker by the United States increased by a factor of twenty-five over this period.

Net Exports

Next in the story we need to link these increases in world output levels to U.S. trade. Figures 4-19 and 4-20 depict the U.S. sectoral net export-dependence ratios, first the surplus sectors and then the deficit sectors. This OECD database extends only to 1985, and the three-decades story is necessarily incomplete. The first two decades are apparent in these figures. Figure 4-19 shows that the United States has enjoyed a long-standing comparative *ad*vantage in *industrial machinery, chemicals, tobacco products, instruments, and fabricated metals.* These trade balances generally floated downward until 1972 when the trade dependence of the United States began to increase. But these net export ratios took a nosedive in 1981–85, with the exception of tobacco. Figure 4-20 shows that the United States has had a long-standing comparative *dis*advantage in *leather products, miscellaneous manufactures, apparel, primary metals, and textiles.* Electronics was once a source of foreign exchange but switched to being a net import item in the 1970s. These trade deficits generally increase gradually until 1972 when imports of leather, miscellaneous manufactures, apparel, and primary metals began to increase dramatically.

Employment

Employment levels in manufacturing sectors are depicted in figures 4-21 and 4-22, first for the sectors that had early peak employment levels and then for the late-peaking sectors. These figures also tell the three-decades story. Employment in most sectors of the economy was growing in the first period up to the early 1970s. The 1970s brought substantial declines in employment in apparel, textiles, and metals. Apparel employment levels continued to decline in the 1980s. The 1980s also brought declines in employment in machinery, electronics, and instruments. Peak employment in transportation was also in 1970, but high variability disguises any clear trend.

The employment reductions in apparel and textiles are a natural feature of the HO framework, and these data support the idea that the Stolper-Samuelson effects were probably present during the 1970s. Metals prices did not decline in the face of increased international competition, and the reduction in employment in metals does not seem to be an HO outcome but is more likely connected to market-power considerations. Likewise, the decline in employment in machinery and electronics in the 1980s is not associated with any dramatic relative price movements in manufacturing, and these events may more likely be connected to the external deficit to which we now turn.

Figure 4-21. *U.S. Manufacturing Employment: Sectors with Early Peaks, 1960–93*

Employment (in thousands)

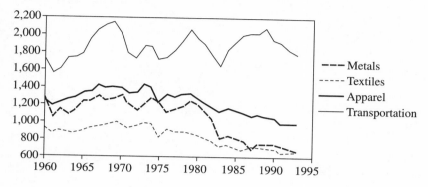

Sources: Bartelsman and Gray (1996); and author's calculations.

Figure 4-22. *U.S. Manufacturing Employment: Sectors with Late Peaks, 1960–93*

Employment (in thousands)

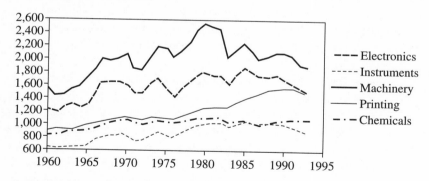

Sources: Bartelsman and Gray (1996); and author's calculations.

The Exchange Rate and the External Deficit

The decade of the 1970s appears to be a period in which the Stolper-Samuelson effects were present, but the 1980s were quite different, with no substantial further reduction of the prices of labor-intensive products. An appealing interpretation of these facts is that the U.S. economy isolated

Figure 4-23. *U.S. Trade Surplus, 1960–93*

(Exports – imports)/GDP (percent)

Sources: Citibase (Citibank Economic Database), New York: Citibank N.A.; and author's calculations.

itself in the late 1970s from low-wage Asian competition by product upgrading. Jeans and T-shirts were sewn in Asia; women's high-fashion clothing was sewn in the United States. This segmentation of the market allowed import prices to continue to fall with no further reduction in U.S. producer prices.

Although Stolper-Samuelson price reductions were not evident in the 1980s, most data sets indicate that the income inequality trends were especially evident. Within the HO framework adopted in this chapter, there is another route by which "globalization" can affect U.S. wages: demand for nontradables associated with the external deficit. Mostly as a teaser, I now display the data on the exchange rate and the external deficit. The U.S. trade surplus, illustrated in figure 4-23, has a negative trend beginning in the 1960s and reaching a low point of –3 percent of GDP in 1986. Figure 4-24 shows the increased volatility of the exchange rate that came from the breaking down of the Bretton Woods fixed exchange rate system. The dollar devalued by about 30 percent from 1970 to 1981, at which point it more than recovered, reaching a dramatic peak in 1985, only to come crashing down to its 1980 level by 1988. The period of increased volatility of the dollar conforms suspiciously well with the period of stagnant and volatile real wages depicted in figure 4-1.

Figure 4-24. *Weighted Average Exchange Rate for U.S. Dollar, 1967–93*

Index (March 1973 = 100)

Sources: Citibase (Citibank Economic Database), New York: Citibank N.A.; and author's calculations.

Formal Decomposition of Technological and Stolper-Samuelson Effects

This section reports a formal statistical analysis of a National Bureau of Economic Research (NBER) database on four-digit Standard Industrial Classification (SIC) products compiled by Bartelsman and Gray.[22] The goal is to estimate the impacts of both technological change and globalization on U.S. wages. This analysis uses the one-cone, HO model as a straitjacket. It is assumed that within each decade the mix of tradables produced is constant and sufficient to determine factor prices uniquely. The mix is allowed to vary from decade to decade. This data analysis is thus built on the (unlikely) assumption that the only way that globalization can affect the U.S. labor market is via relative price changes that induce Stolper-Samuelson wage responses. The external deficit is not a consideration, except as it may affect relative prices of tradables. Market power in autos and steel is also not considered.

A crucial step in this attempt to separate the effects of "globalization" from "technological change" is the division of the observed product price changes into components separately associated with these two forces. This

22. Bartelsman and Gray (1996).

calls for an elaborate consideration of both supply and demand sides of a general equilibrium model. Here we use a simple "pass-through" assumption that a selected proportion of the productivity increase is passed on to consumers in the form of lower prices. The residual price variability is attributed to "globalization" on the assumption that tradable-goods prices are determined in the international marketplace. Of course, in markets in which the United States is a major supplier or demander, these product price changes can come from events strictly internal to the United States. Thus we may be putting the "globalization" label onto something strictly internal to the United States. I would defend the analysis against this criticism in two ways. First, this is the methodological mirror image of the usual procedure, which extracts first the globalization effect and attributes everything else to technology.[23] It seems interesting, at least, to go in the opposite direction, first extracting the technological effect and then attributing everything else to globalization. Second and more important, even if the United States has market power, internal prices of tradables can be affected by tariffs and/or nontariff barriers (NTBs). Thus we are getting an answer to the policy question, whether or not the shock is internal or external. For example, when we conclude that relative price declines for apparel and textiles have led to increased income inequality, we are elliptically saying that things would have been different if the United States had used barriers aggressively to maintain relative prices. It does not matter whether the relative price decline came from internal or external events. To remind the reader of this point, the g—for general—replaces globalization in the narrative below.

Methodology for Estimating the Separate Effects of Globalization and Technological Change on Factor Prices

The foundation of the Stolper-Samuelson theorem is the set of zero-profit conditions $p = A'w$, where p is the vector of product prices, w is the vector of factor costs and A is the matrix of input intensities, inputs per unit of output. Differentiating one of these zero-profit conditions produces

$$dp_i = \sum_k (A_{ik}dw_k + dA_{ik}w_k).$$

Using the usual notation $\hat{x} = dx/x$ this can be written as

$$\hat{p}_i = dp_i/p_1 = \sum_k [(A_{ik}w_k/p_i)(dw_k/w_k) + dA_{ik}w_k/p_i] = \sum_k \theta_{ik}\hat{w}_k + \sum_k \theta_{ik}\hat{A}_{ik}.$$

23. See Mishel and Bernstein (1994) for criticism of this procedure.

Then the input intensity $A_{ik} = v_{ik}/Q_i$, can be differentiated to obtain

$$\hat{A}_{ik} = \hat{v}_{ik} - \hat{Q}_i.$$

Using this and the standard measurement in the growth of total factor productivity implies

$$\hat{TFP}_i = \hat{Q}_i - \sum_k \theta_{ik}\hat{v}_{ik} = -\sum_k \theta_{ik}\hat{A}_{ik},$$

from which we obtain the fundamental condition linking product price changes, factor costs changes, and technology changes

$$\hat{p}_i = \sum_k \theta_{ik}\hat{w}_k - \hat{TFP}_i = \theta_i\hat{w} - \hat{TFP}_i. \tag{4-1}$$

This is the equation that will serve as a foundation for separating the impacts of globalization and technology on factor prices. From data on a cross section of 450 four-digit SIC industries describing price changes $\hat{p}$, TFP growth $\hat{TFP}$, and beginning-period factor shares θ, we may estimate this equation and interpret the coefficients on the factor shares as the *"mandated"* changes in factor costs, $\hat{w}$.[24] These are the changes in factor costs that are needed to keep the zero-profits condition operative in the face of changes in technology and product prices. These mandated wage changes can then be compared with actual wage changes. If the two conform adequately, we will argue that we have provided an accurate explanation of the trends in wages. Incidentally, the mandated changes in factor costs may induce actual factor costs in a later decade. The model and the data analysis is entirely silent on issues of timing.

An important apparent implication of equation 4-1 is that the factor bias of technological change is entirely irrelevant. What matters is only the sectoral distribution of TFP growth, because only TFP growth by sector enters the equation. This conclusion applies only to small changes and only if the technological change does not induce sector-biased price changes.[25] For discrete changes, we need to include the second-order effects

24. See Leamer (1993, 1994) and Baldwin and Cain (1994) for regressions of this type, and Hilton (1984) for a related analysis.

25. The startling conclusion that only sector bias matters was stated unequivocally in the original version of this chapter. A graph produced by Ronald Findlay and some words from Paul Krugman suggested otherwise. What follows is a mapping of the graph and the words into the algebra. In particular, Ronald Findlay's graph forced me to realize the potential importance of second-order effects; Paul Krugman's words made me realize the possibility that factor-biased technological change could induce sectoral-biased price changes.

$$dp_i = \sum_k (A_{ik}dw_k + dA_{ik}w_k + dw_k dA_{ik}).$$

Dividing this by the initial price level produces the equation

$$\hat{p}_i = dp_i / p_1 = \sum_k \theta_{ik}\hat{w}_k + \sum_k \theta_{ik}\hat{A}_{ik} + \sum_k [(A_{ik}w_k / p_i)(dA_{ik}/A_{ik})(dw_k / w_k)].$$

Thus, including the second-order effects, we have

$$\hat{p}_i = \theta_i \hat{w} - T\hat{F}P_i + \hat{A}_i diag(\theta_i)\hat{w}.$$

This does allow factor bias to matter in the general equilibrium through second-order effects involving the product of percentage changes in inputs and percentage changes in wages. This makes life even more complicated since a data analysis that properly deals with these second-order effects must allow for the endogeneity of the factor intensities A.

A second problem with equation 4-1 is that it is an equilibrium condition entirely silent on the relationship between price changes and TFP growth. Without knowledge of the price changes induced by TFP growth, it is impossible to disentangle the effects of technological change from the effects of globalization and other sources of product price variability. To make the underidentification problem clear, we can separate this equation into two, one part that is due to technology (t) and another that is due to other factors (g) (g standing for globalization but also encompassing demand shifts)

$$\hat{p}_i(t) + \hat{p}_i(g) = \theta_i \hat{w}(t) + \theta_i \hat{w}(g) - T\hat{F}P_i ,$$

where

$$\hat{p}_i(t) = \theta_i \hat{w}(t) - T\hat{F}P_i$$

$$\hat{p}_i(g) = \theta_i \hat{w}(g)$$

$$\hat{p}_i = \hat{p}_i(t) + \hat{p}_i(g) .$$

Obviously there are many values of the g-effect on wages that are compatible with this set of equations, given data on TFP growth and product price changes. To make any headway in disentangling the globalization effects from the technological effects, we need to get a handle on that portion of the product price change that is due to technological change. To do this in a completely convincing manner, we need to model worldwide demand and supply conditions. This would require a very large modeling effort. An *expedient* alternative is to assume that all sectors have the same "rate of technological pass-through" to product prices, namely $\hat{p}_i(t) = -\lambda \ T\hat{F}P_i$ where λ is the pass-through rate that is common across sectors.

A zero pass-through rate applies if technological change is specific to a small, open economy that takes product prices as given from the rest of the world. It may be that there are other conditions in which sectors would experience a common pass-through rate, but this would require a special kind of model. Generally, the effect of technological change on product prices is not even confined to the sector experiencing the change. For example, labor-saving technological change regardless of the sectors in which it occurs may induce product price reductions in labor-intensive tradables, thereby shifting demand to labor-intensive products and thus absorbing the workers released by the technological change. In other words, factor-biased technological change may induce sectoral-biased price changes. Then the factor bias of the technological change would matter. But the need for compensating sectoral-biased price changes is less, or possibly not present at all, if the demand for nontradables is highly elastic and if the nontradables sector can absorb the released factors without necessitating changes in the price of tradables.

Intermediate inputs raise yet another difficulty with the pass-through assumption. Including intermediate inputs in equation 4-1 is no great problem. We simply need to include in the equation the inner product of the materials inputs shares γ and the product prices

Zero-profit identity: $\quad \hat{p}_i = \theta_i \hat{w} + \gamma_i \hat{p} - T\hat{F}P_i$. $\qquad\qquad$ (4-2)

The product prices on the right-hand side of this equation can be moved to the left to create a Stolper-Samuelson system of equations implicitly defining a mapping of "value-added prices" into factor prices

$$\hat{p}_i - \gamma_i \hat{p} = \theta_i \hat{w} - T\hat{F}P_i .$$

This looks good, because it is exactly as before, with value-added prices in place of final goods prices. But the next step is where the danger lurks, namely appropriately treating TFP effects on prices. The assumption that will be used in the calculations below is that TFP improvements affect only value-added prices

Pass-through assumption: $\quad \hat{p}_i(t) - \gamma_i \hat{p}(t) = -\lambda \ T\hat{F}P.$ $\qquad$ (4-3)

In fact, productivity improvements in one sector are likely to have both forward and backward linkages to other sectors. These affect the demand for inputs in the sector experiencing the improvement and also alter the prices of materials in sectors that use the product as an input. An alternative would be to apply the pass-through to final goods prices and to allow for the indirect effect of technological improvements on materials prices. If only the first-round effect on input prices is considered this produces the equation

$$\hat{p}_i(t) - \gamma_i'\{-\lambda \ \hat{TFP}_i\} = -\lambda \ \hat{TFP}_i \,,$$

which basically says that technologically induced price reductions are especially great in sectors that use as inputs the products experiencing technological improvements. Unfortunately, the data set we will be analyzing has materials inputs and materials input prices by sector but not the full set of input-output linkages. Anyway, if one went that route, allowing only for first-round effects would be uncomfortable.

Thus to do the job right, we really need a complete worldwide, general equilibrium, input-output model. We need this to deal with second-order effects, to select pass-through rates, and also to determine sectoral-biased price changes induced by factor-biased technological change. For now we can plow ahead, remembering that we are implicitly assuming that the second-order effects are small, that pass-through rates are similar and apply to value-added prices, and that the factor biases in technological change have not been enough to cause sectoral-biased price changes for tradable goods, possibly because of the absorptive capacity of the nontraded sectors.

Given the pass-through assumption 4-3, we can find the mandated changes in factor prices that accompany the technological change, namely factor prices satisfying

$$-\lambda \ \hat{TFP}_i = \theta_i \hat{w}(t) - \hat{TFP}_i \,, \text{ or equivalently}$$

Technological effect on wages: $(1 - \lambda)\hat{TFP}_i = \theta_i \hat{w}(t) \,.$ (4-4)

After allowing for some effect of technological change on product prices, what is left over is the globalization effect

$$\hat{p}_i(g) - \gamma_i \hat{p}(g) = (\hat{p}_i - \gamma_i \hat{p}) - [\hat{p}_i(t) - \gamma_i \hat{p}(t)] = \hat{p}_i - \gamma_i \hat{p} + \lambda \ \hat{TFP}_i \,.$$

Inserting this into 4-2 produces the equation linking g-price changes to mandated earnings.

Globalization effect on wages: $\hat{p}_i + \lambda \ \hat{TFP}_i = \theta_i \hat{w}(g) + \gamma_i \hat{p} \,.$ (4-5)

The data analysis I discuss next thus involves two kinds of equations, both with factor shares as explanatory variables. In one set of equations, suggested by 4-4, the dependent variable is the sectoral growth in TFP. The estimated coefficients from this regression are multiplied by $(1 - \lambda)$ to find the technological effect on mandated earnings. In the other set of equations, suggested by equation 4-5, the dependent variable is the sectoral-inflation rate adjusted for TFP-induced changes. On the right hand side of equation 4-5 is the inner product of materials shares and product price changes. The data set does not contain detailed information on the material input shares, but it does contain the overall materials share and the corresponding price level, sector by sector. This is all that we need; we can replace the inner product of materials shares and price inflation rates with the overall materials share times the price inflation rate of materials inputs, sector by sector.

Descriptive Statistics

Descriptive statistics of the Bartelsman and Gray NBER data on the *hourly earnings* of production workers and the average *annual earnings* of production and nonproduction workers are reported in table 4-2.[26] The HO theory used here to explore quantitatively the impact of technological change and globalization on wages assumes that workers and other factors are mobile across sectors. At any point in time, the average wage in an industrial sector would then be determined exclusively by the skill mix in the sector, and not by historical sector-specific investments by workers in human or locational capital. With the additional assumption that skill proportions in each sector are (roughly) constant over time, changes in the distribution of wages across sectors would be driven by changes in wages at different levels of skills. Then the intersectoral dispersion of wages would be an indicator of income inequality. The first purpose of the displays in table 4-2 and the cumulative distributions in figure 4-13 is to support mildly this interpretation of the intersectoral distribution of earnings.

A way to measure wage inequality that does not rely on an assumption of fixed factor ratios would be to find subcategories of workers with skill levels that are fairly uniform within groups and substantially different across groups—perhaps scientists in one group and delivery workers in another. Then differences in the average wage levels of these categories could be used to measure income inequality. Unfortunately, data on employment and earnings for subcategories of workers are difficult to find. Data categorized into production and nonproduction workers are readily available and have been used by Lawrence and Slaughter to study the

26. Defined as PRODW/PRODH, PRODW/PRODE, (PAY – PRODW)/(EMP – PRODE).

Table 4-2. *Earnings Data, 1961, 1971, 1981, and 1991*[a]

| | Hourly wages of production workers | | | | Average annual earnings (thousands of U.S.$) | | | | | | | | |
| | | | | | Production workers | | | | Nonproduction workers | | | | |
	1961	1971	1981	1991	1961	1971	1981	1991	1961	1961[b]	1971	1981	1991
Mean	2.27	3.53	7.61	11.11	4.53	6.98	14.94	22.53	7.33	7.17	10.89	22.99	35.98
Median	2.28	3.55	7.46	10.82	4.63	7.05	14.60	21.87	7.33	7.29	10.99	22.95	35.55
Maximum	3.89	6.20	15.06	27.67	8.13	11.86	29.06	83.00	20.29	9.86	15.25	38.80	54.47
Minimum	1.19	2.00	3.42	4.00	2.20	3.66	5.88	4.00	2.87	2.87	4.93	12.25	17.50
Standard deviation	0.52	0.77	2.21	3.30	1.11	1.63	4.58	7.53	1.54	1.01	1.49	4.06	6.52
Coefficient of variation[c]	**0.23**	**0.22**	**0.29**	**0.30**	**0.24**	**0.23**	0.31	0.33	0.21	0.14	0.14	0.18	0.18
Range/median	**1.18**	**1.18**	**1.56**	**2.19**	**1.28**	**1.16**	1.59	3.61	2.38	0.96	0.94	1.16	1.04
Range/minimum	**2.28**	**2.10**	**3.40**	**5.92**	**2.69**	**2.24**	3.94	19.75	6.07	2.44	2.09	2.17	2.11
N	450	450	450	450	450	450	449	448	449	438	450	450	450

Ratio of nonproduction/production earnings					
	1961	1961[b]	1971	1981	1991
Mean	**1.62**	**1.58**	**1.56**	**1.54**	1.60
Median	**1.58**	**1.57**	**1.56**	1.57	**1.63**

Source: Bartelsman and Gray (1996).

a. Data not weighted by employment levels.

b. Vetted sample.

c. Income inequality measures in bold.

relationship between wages and globalization.[27] But some colleagues and I have argued that these categories are actually rather broad and suspiciously heterogeneous.[28] The second function of the displays in table 4-2 is to cast a bit more doubt on the usefulness of the production/nonproduction categorization for studying wage inequality across skill groups.

Table 4-2 has a variety of statistics concerning earnings and has several measures of income inequality highlighted in boldface. (These statistics are not weighted by sector size and can be influenced by relatively unimportant sectors.) Uncorrected for inflation, average hourly *earnings* of production workers rose from $2.27 to $11.11 per hour from 1961 to 1991. Over the same period, average *annual earnings* of production workers rose from $4,530 to $22,530 and nonproduction workers from $7,330 ($7,170) to $35,980. If one thought that the categories of production and nonproduction sorted workers by skill, then the ratio of nonproduction to production earnings would be the measure of income inequality. These ratios for the median earnings in the four periods were 1.58, 1.56, 1.57, and 1.63, thus suggesting that most of the increase in income inequality came after 1980, which is fairly similar with other measures of wage inequality.[29] However, there is a substantial amount of wage inequality across sectors *within* the production and nonproduction categories. In 1971, for example, there was a sector that had average production workers of $3,660 and another with $11,860. In the same period, average earnings of nonproduction workers varied across sectors from a low of $4,930 to a high of $15,250. The substantial overlap of the ranges of these earnings numbers casts doubt on the usefulness of the production/nonproduction categories.

Other measures of wage inequality of the economy are the coefficient of variation, the range relative to the median and the range relative to the minimum (*across sectors*), all of which are reported in table 4-2. Most of these suggest an increase in inequality in 1971–81 and some further increase in 1981–91. The coefficient of variation of hourly wages of production workers remained almost unchanged from 1961 to 1971, but then grew by about one-third by 1981, with little change thereafter. The coefficient of variation of the average annual earnings of production workers is similar, as is the coefficient of variation of annual earnings of nonproduction workers, after vetting some extreme sectors in 1961.

Descriptive statistics for TFP growth are reported in table 4-3. Note that the middle period, 1971–81, was a period of little TFP growth on average

27. Lawrence and Slaughter (1993).
28. Leamer (1994); Mishel and Bernstein (1994).
29. For example, see Borjas and Ramey (1993).

Table 4-3. *TFP Annualized Compound Growth Rate, 1961–91*

	1961–71	1971–81	1981–91
Mean	0.78	0.00	0.33
Value-added weighted mean	0.79	0.17	0.46
Median	0.66	−0.08	0.36
Maximum	10.78	18.33	11.88
Minimum	−4.46	−10.56	−11.66
Standard deviation	1.72	2.18	11.78
Coefficient of variation	2.19	1,831.41	5.43
N	450	450	449

Sources: Bartelsman and Gray (1996); and author's calculations.

but a great deal of dispersion across sectors. The first decade, 1961–1971, had TFP growth of about 8 percent annually. The third decade, 1981–91, had TFP growth of about 4 percent annually. Both had standard errors of about 1.7 percent. Incidentally, the increased dispersion of the TFP growth figures during the turbulent 1970s is a worrisome reminder that measurement errors may be important.

Discussion of Estimates

Finally, we turn to estimates of equations 4-4 and 4-5 for pass-through rates equal to one and zero. Because the calculation of factor shares is somewhat suspect, it makes sense first just to look at the correlations between price inflation rates and various beginning-of-period sectoral indicators in table 4-4. Notice in this table that the price changes are hardly correlated with any of the sectoral indicators in the first decade, 1961–71. In the second decade, 1971–81, price increases were especially high in capital intensive, high-production-wage sectors. In the third decade, 1981–91, price changes were negatively correlated with capital intensity and with material costs. Thus at a first glance, the three-decade story seems to apply. Relative price changes mattered little for determining relative wages in the 1960s; product price changes worked to lower wages in the 1970s, particularly for low-wage production workers; then in the 1980s it was capital that suffered with, possibly, all forms of labor gaining.

Although the simple correlations in table 4-4 are highly suggestive, an implication of equations 4-4 and 4-5 is that simple correlations of price changes with arbitrarily scaled industry indicators cannot tell the story. Multiple regressions on factor shares are needed. The final set of tables report attempts to find regressions of this type that make sense. Table 4-5

Table 4-4. *Cross-Section Correlations of Price Inflation Rates with Various Series, 1961–91*[a]

	Unweighted			Weighted by employment[b]		
	1961–71	1971–81	1981–91	1961–71	1971–81	1981–91
Capital per worker	–0.17	0.36	–0.33	–0.14	0.42	–0.24
Capital per earnings	–0.19	0.31	–0.34	–0.15	0.41	–0.23
Average wages	0.07	0.30	–0.13	0.06	0.16	–0.13
Nonproduction wages (average)	–0.03	0.14	–0.12	–0.06	0.09	–0.18
Production wages (average)	0.10	0.35	–0.12	0.09	0.37	–0.09
Ratio of nonproduction to production workers	0.07	0.01	0.08	0.08	–0.13	0.10
Materials costs as a share of value of shipments	–0.14	0.12	–0.38	–0.08	0.15	–0.27

Sources: Bartelsman and Gray (1996); and author's calculations.

a. 450 four-digit SIC manufacturing sectors.

b. Weighted correlations are estimated as the square root of the R^2 from the weighted OLS regressions where the dependent variable is the price inflation and the independent variable is the seria of interest. Sign is determined by the sign of the corresponding coefficient. Weights are defined as the average employment for each sector over the 1961–91 period.

reports data on earnings shares and the corresponding definitions of earnings in terms of the Bartlesman and Gray data series. These earnings shares have two important features that need to be mentioned. First, in the absence of direct data on capital rental costs, the capital earnings are simply set to 10 percent of book values of plants, equipment, and inventories. The best approach would be to multiply the sum of the real rate of interest plus depreciation times the capital current market value. The 10 percent real rate of interest is arbitrary but probably not very important, because it affects mostly the capital coefficients in the subsequent regressions and not much the labor coefficients. More important is the implicit assumption that depreciation rates do not vary across sectors. A second observation about the calculations reported in table 4-5 is that the earnings of each factor are divided by total earnings, not the value of shipments. Included in the value of shipments are rents to sector-specific assets that come from unexpected price variability. These are explicitly excluded from consideration by the HO conceptual framework that we are using.

To determine earnings of "high-wage" and "low-wage" workers, the wage differences across sectors are interpreted as coming entirely from differences in the mixes of skilled and unskilled workers with the lowest wage sector having entirely low-wage workers and the highest wage sector

Table 4-5. *Average Factor Shares of 450 SIC Industries, 1961, 1971, 1981, and 1991*

	1961	1971	1981	1991	Formula for earnings[a]
Labor	0.32	0.32	0.27	0.26	PAY
Total					
High wage	0.25	0.21	0.17	0.17	$wH \times [PAY - (wL) \times EMP] \div (wH - wL)$
Low wage	0.07	0.11	0.09	0.09	$wL \times [-PAY + (wH) \times EMP] \div (wH - wL)$
Production	0.22	0.21	0.17	0.16	PRODW
High wage	0.14	0.13	0.12	0.13	$wH \times [PRODW - (wL) \times PRODE] \div (wH - wL)$
Low wage	0.08	0.08	0.05	0.03	$wL \times [-PRODW + (wH) \times PRODE] \div (wH - wL)$
Nonproduction	0.10	0.11	0.09	0.10	$(PAY - PRODW) = NPRODW$
High wage	0.07	0.09	0.06	0.07	$wH \times [NPRODW - (wL) \times NPRODE] \div (wH - wL)$
Low wage	0.03	0.02	0.03	0.03	$wL \times [-NPRODW + (wH) \times NPRODE] \div (wH - wL)$
Capital	0.07	0.08	0.08	0.09	$0.1 \times [(PLANT + EQUIP) \times PIINV + INVENT]$
Plant and equipment	0.05	0.06	0.06	0.07	$0.1 \times (PLANT + EQUIP) \times PIINV$
Plant	0.03	0.03	0.03	0.03	$0.1 \times (PLANT) \times PIINV$
Equipment	0.02	0.03	0.03	0.04	$0.1 \times EQUIP \times PIINV$
Inventories	0.02	0.02	0.02	0.02	$0.1 \times INVENT$
Materials	0.61	0.60	0.65	0.65	MATCOST
Energy	0.02	0.02	0.04	0.03	ENERGY
Other	0.59	0.58	0.61	0.62	MATCOST − ENERGY
Production					
wH	8.13	11.86	29.06	83.00	$Max(PRODW \div PRODE)$
wL	2.20	3.66	5.88	4.00	$Min(PRODW \div PRODE)$
Nonproduction					
wH	14.93	15.25	38.80	54.47	$Max[(PAY - PRODW) \div (EMP - PRODE)]$
wL	2.87	4.93	12.25	17.50	$Min[(PAY - PRODW) \div (EMP - PRODE)]$
Total					
wH	9.00	13.39	36.13	46.81	$Max(PAY \div EMP)$
wL	1.92	4.03	7.32	12.01	$Min(PAY \div EMP)$

Excluded observations and their SIC codes[b]

	Nonproduction wage	SIC code	Code interpretation
1961	0.93	2519	Household furniture, not classified elsewhere
	20.28	3942	Dolls and stuffed toys
	20.25	2647	Paper products
	16.40	3519	Internal combustion engines, not classified elsewhere
1981	65.66	3339	Primary nonferrous metals, not classified elsewhere
1991	205	2384	Robes and dressing gowns
	2	2794	Printing

Sources: Bartelsman and Gray (1996); and author's calculations.

a. Total earnings = PAY + 0.1 × [(PLANT + EQUIP) × PIINV + INVENT] + MATCOST. wH and wL refer to the highest and lowest earnings per worker across the 450 sectors in the given year. Labor shares have been calculated on vetted samples.

b. Nonproduction wage estimates for 1961, 1981, and 1991 include observations that greatly deviate from the rest of the sample. These observations were excluded from the calculation of all labor shares for the corresponding year and subsequently are excluded from the later regressions (tables 4-6–4-8). For total wages only one observation in 1991 (SIC 2794) was excluded.

having entirely high-wage workers. The proportion of high-wage and low-wage workers in other sectors is linearly extrapolated from the level of the wage. In the middle of table 4-5 are the wage levels that are used to separate workers into high-wage and low-wage categories. At the bottom are sectors that have been excluded because of extreme values of the nonproduction wage. Note, by the way, that the high-wage production workers are paid considerably more than the low-wage nonproduction workers, thus the apparent overlapping of skills of the two groups.

According to the numbers reported in table 4-5, materials constitute the largest share of total earnings, beginning at 61 percent and rising to 65 percent. This increase occurred exclusively in the 1971–81 decade. The capital share also grew, but only slightly, from 7 percent to 9 percent. The gain to materials and capital is almost exactly matched by a reduction in the share of production workers, which fell from 22 percent to 16 percent. This shift away from production workers is the focus of much of Lawrence and Slaughter's discussion.[30] The separation of workers into high-wage and low-wage subcategories has left a larger share of high-wage than low-wage workers. This means that in every case the mean wage level across sectors is lower than the median; the distributions are skewed to the right.

Table 4-6 contains estimates of equations 4-4 and 4-5 for three decades, 1961–71, 1971–81, and 1981–91, using only labor, capital, and materials as inputs. The dependent variables are the compound annualized rate of increase in product prices over the decade and also the annualized growth of TFP. Explanatory variables are beginning-of-period factor shares θ for labor, capital, and materials. The top part of the table contains regressions of price inflation rates and TFP growth rates over three decades on the beginning-of-the-decade capital and labor shares. These regressions are used to form estimates of "mandated" earnings growth reported in the bottom part of the table. The set of regressions in the middle panel at the top of this table use the sum of inflation plus TFP growth as the dependent variable, implicitly assuming that technological change is passed on completely to consumers through lower prices. Notice that these numbers are just the sum of counterparts on the left and right. All these are weighted regression estimates with employment levels averaged over the three initial periods as weights.[31]

---

30. Lawrence and Slaughter (1993).

31. Weights are kept constant to avoid changes in the results coming from changing weights. Weights in econometric terms are the inverses of the variances (not standard errors). Employment weights and value-added weights give similar results. Unweighted regressions are entirely different.

Table 4-6. *Regressions of Inflation and TFP Growth on Beginning-of-Period Earnings Shares: Capital and Labor, 1961–91*[a]

	Annualized price inflation			Annualized price inflation plus annualized TFP growth			Annualized TFP growth		
	1961– 71	1971– 81	1981– 91	1961– 71	1971– 81	1981– 91	1961– 71	1971– 81	1981– 91
Estimates									
Labor share	3.27	5.73	5.31	3.19	6.50	2.51	–0.07	0.78	–2.80
Capital share	–5.32	7.27	–4.07	7.93	9.24	9.30	13.25	1.98	13.37
Materials share	b	b	b	b	b	b	c	c	c
Standard errors									
Labor share	0.32	0.73	0.66	0.23	0.31	0.39	0.39	0.78	0.68
Capital share	1.49	2.88	2.34	1.05	1.24	1.38	1.80	3.08	2.39
Mean of dependent variable	1.91	8.01	2.38	2.74	8.18	2.70	0.83	0.17	0.32
S.D. of dependent variable	2.10	5.78	2.88	2.15	5.18	2.17	1.91	3.12	2.24
S.E. of regression	1.44	2.89	2.14	1.02	1.24	1.26	1.74	3.09	2.18

	0 Percent pass-through			100 Percent pass-through		
MAEG[d] due to price changes unrelated to technology[e]						
Labor	1.35	–2.29	2.93	1.28	–1.51	0.13
Capital	–7.24	–0.75	–6.45	6.02	1.23	6.92
MAREG[f] due to technological change						
Labor	–0.07	0.78	–2.80	0.83	0.17	0.32
Capital	13.25	1.98	13.37	0.83	0.17	0.32
Total MAEG						
Labor	1.28	–1.51	0.13	2.11	–1.34	0.45
Capital	6.02	1.23	6.92	6.85	1.40	7.25
Percent "share" due to "globalization"[g]						
Labor	95	75	51	61	90	29
Capital	35	27	33	88	88	96

Sources: Bartelsman and Gray (1996); and author's calculations.

a. 450 four-digit SIC manufacturing sectors.

b. The materials share coefficient is set equal to the sector-specific materials inflation rate.

c. Materials input shares are excluded because the pass-through is assumed to apply to value-added prices.

d. MAEG = mandated annualized earnings growth.

e. Estimates minus inflation.

f. MAREG = mandated annualized real earnings growth.

g. Absolute effect ÷ sum of absolute effects.

The coefficients for the 1961–71 price-inflation equation reported in the first column of table 4-6 suggest that a 3.27 percent rate of increase in wage rates and a –5.32 percent rate of increase in capital rental rates would have been consistent with the least change in profits in the economy. With overall inflation equal to 1.91 percent, this means a net annualized real increase in earnings of these factors equal to 1.35 percent and –7.24 percent, which are numbers reported under the heading "Mandated annualized earnings growth due to price changes unrelated to technology." Below those numbers are the effects of sectoral bias in technological change that are not accompanied by any price changes. These are just the regressions of TFP growth on factor shares. In this 1961–71 period, technological change worked slightly against labor and very much in favor of capital. The sum of these two sets of numbers are reported next in the same column. Thus the total mandated change in labor earnings is 1.28 percent per year, mostly due to the positive g-effect. Capital had a much higher mandated earnings growth of 6.02 percent per year, with a huge technological effect offsetting a large g-effect. If, on the other hand, the pass-through rate is 100 percent and any technological improvement also lowers prices by 100 percent of the TFP growth, then the TFP effect on earnings is neutral across factors and equal to the average TFP improvement in that decade of 0.83 percent. After adjusting for the TFP effect on prices, the mandated growth in wages due to the g-effect is reduced to 1.28 percent. Thus, although the choice of pass-through rate does not much affect the total mandated earnings in 1961–71, it does affect the separation into t-effects and g-effects.

The three-decades story is quite evident in this table.

THE 1960S. Capital-intensive sectors experienced rapid technological improvement but also relative price reductions. These offsetting effects left both labor and capital with improving conditions.

THE 1970S. Wage levels were under downward pressure in the 1970s, entirely because of product price changes that strongly worked against labor.

THE 1980S. Technological change worked strongly against labor. Whether the pass-through rate is low or high, the total mandated wage increases were modest; positive if high and negative if low.

Table 4-7 has the same analysis, with labor categories divided into high-wage and low-wage subcategories. The mandated wage changes from this table are depicted in figure 4-25. Here again the three-decades story emerges clearly. The decade of the 1970s is when the g-effect (non-TFP) worked strongly against low-wage workers. This was offset by favorable conditions in the 1980s. This conclusion is not at all affected by the

Table 4-7. *Regressions of Inflation and TFP Growth on Beginning-of-Period Earnings Shares: Capital and High-Wage and Low-Wage Labor, 1961–91*[a]

	Annualized price inflation			Annualized price inflation plus annualized TFP growth			Annualized TFP growth		
	1961– 71	1971– 81	1981– 91	1961– 71	1971– 81	1981– 91	1961– 71	1971– 81	1981– 91
Estimates									
Labor									
High wage	3.47	6.34	5.36	2.81	8.30	0.47	–0.65	1.96	–4.89
Low wage	2.58	4.79	5.26	4.38	3.75	5.13	1.80	–1.04	–0.14
Capital Share	–5.46	6.56	–4.14	8.30	7.17	11.54	13.75	0.61	15.68
Materials share	b	b	b	b	b	b	c	c	c
Standard errors									
Labor									
High wage	0.45	1.03	0.98	0.32	0.43	0.56	0.54	1.10	0.99
Low wage	1.08	1.34	1.13	0.76	0.55	0.65	1.30	1.43	1.15
Capital share	1.51	3.00	2.47	1.07	1.24	1.41	1.82	3.20	2.50
Mean of dependent variable	1.91	8.01	2.38	2.74	8.18	2.70	0.83	0.17	0.32
S.D. of dependent variable	2.10	5.78	2.88	2.15	5.18	2.17	1.91	3.12	2.24
S.E. of regression	1.44	2.89	2.14	1.01	1.20	1.22	1.73	3.09	2.16

	0 Percent pass-through			100 Percent pass-through		
MAEG[d] *due to price changes unrelated to technology*[e]						
Labor						
High wage	1.56	–1.67	2.98	0.90	0.29	1.91
Low wage	0.67	–3.23	2.89	2.46	–4.27	2.75
Capital	–7.37	–1.46	–6.52	6.39	–0.85	9.16
MAREG[f] *due to technological change*						
Labor						
High wage	–0.65	1.96	–4.89	0.83	0.17	0.32
Low wage	1.80	–1.04	–0.14	0.83	0.17	0.32
Capital	13.75	0.61	15.68	0.83	0.17	0.32
Total MAEG						
Labor						
High wage	0.90	0.29	–1.91	1.73	0.46	–1.59
Low wage	2.46	–4.27	2.75	3.29	–4.10	3.07
Capital	6.39	–0.85	9.16	7.21	–0.68	9.48
Percent "share" due to "globalization"[g]						
Labor						
High wage	70	46	38	52	63	86
Low wage	27	76	95	75	96	90
Capital	35	70	29	89	83	97

Sources: Bartelsman and Gray (1996); and author's calculations.

a. 450 four-digit SIC manufacturing sectors.

b. The materials share coefficient is set equal to the sector-specific materials inflation rate.

c. Materials input shares are excluded because the pass-through is assumed to apply to value-added prices.

d. MAEG = mandated annualized earnings growth.

e. Estimates minus inflation.

f. MAREG = mandated annualized real earnings growth.

g. Absolute effect ÷ sum of absolute effects.

Figure 4-25. *Mandated Wage Changes: Low-Wage and High-Wage Workers,*
1960s–80s

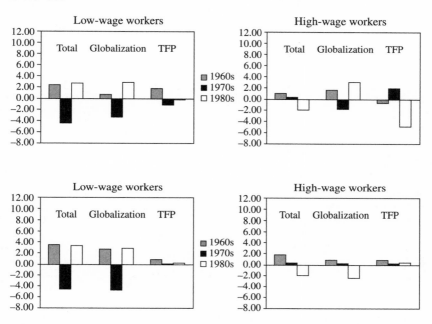

Sources: Citibase (Citibank Economic Database), New York: Citibank N.A.; and author's calculations.

pass-through rate. High-wage workers had smaller mandated wage changes
with gains in the 1960s offset by losses in the 1980s. The division of the
total losses in the 1980s depends critically on the pass-through rate, with the
g-effect dominating for high pass-through rates and the t-effect dominating
for low pass-through rates.

Finally, table 4-8 and figure 4-26 report the same analysis for produc-
tion/nonproduction subcategories of labor. The conclusions suggested by
this table are somewhat different. The pattern of the total effects for production workers is similar to the pattern for low-wage workers, but the nonproduction workers have positive mandated wage increases in all three
decades, unlike high-wage workers, who had negative values for the 1980s.
For the zero pass-through rate, much more of the action is on the technology side. In particular, the loss suffered by production workers in the 1970s
is attributable to technology, not globalization. The reverse conclusion
applies if the pass-through is 100 percent, where the action is all due to
globalization. With zero pass-through, technological change is working

Table 4-8. *Regressions of Inflation and TFP Growth on Beginning-of-Period Earnings Shares: Capital and Production and Nonproduction Labor, 1961–91[a]*

	Annualized price inflation			Annualized price inflation plus annualized TFP growth			Annualized TFP growth		
	1961–71	1971–81	1981–91	1961–71	1971–81	1981–91	1961–71	1971–81	1981–91
Estimates									
Labor									
Nonproduction	0.68	0.06	5.82	3.62	10.70	3.71	2.94	10.64	–2.11
Production	4.90	9.34	4.89	2.92	3.83	1.52	–1.98	–5.50	–3.37
Capital share	–5.95	6.71	–3.86	8.04	9.66	9.79	13.99	2.95	13.65
Materials share	b	b	b	b	b	b	c	c	c
Standard errors									
Labor									
Nonproduction	0.81	1.59	1.26	0.58	0.66	0.74	0.98	1.65	1.28
Production	0.57	1.15	1.10	0.41	0.48	0.64	0.69	1.20	1.12
Capital share	1.48	2.83	2.38	1.06	1.17	1.39	1.79	2.94	2.43
Mean of dependent variable	1.91	8.01	2.38	2.74	8.18	2.70	0.83	0.17	0.32
S.D. of dependent variable	2.10	5.78	2.88	2.15	5.18	2.17	1.91	3.12	2.24
S.E. of regression	1.42	2.84	2.14	1.02	1.18	1.25	1.72	2.95	2.18

	0 Percent pass-through			*100 Percent pass-through*		
MAEG[d] *due to price changes unrelated to technology*[e]						
Labor						
Nonproduction	–1.23	–7.95	3.45	1.71	2.68	1.33
Production	2.99	1.32	2.51	1.01	–4.18	–0.86
Capital	–7.87	–1.31	–6.24	6.12	1.65	7.41
MAREG[f] *due to technological change*						
Labor						
Nonproduction	2.94	10.64	–2.11	0.83	0.17	0.32
Production	–1.98	–5.50	–3.37	0.83	0.17	0.32
Capital	13.99	2.95	13.65	0.83	0.17	0.32
Total MAEG						
Labor						
Nonproduction	1.71	2.68	1.33	2.54	2.85	1.65
Production	1.01	–4.18	–0.86	1.83	–4.01	–0.54
Capital	6.12	1.65	7.41	6.95	1.82	7.73
Percent "share" due to "globalization"[g]						
Labor						
Nonproduction	29	43	62	67	94	81
Production	60	19	43	55	96	73
Capital	36	31	31	88	91	96

Sources: Bartelsman and Gray (1996); and author's calculations.

a. 450 four-digit SIC manufacturing sectors.

b. The materials share coefficient is set equal to the sector-specific materials inflation rate.

c. Materials input shares are excluded because the pass-through is assumed to apply to value-added prices.

d. MAEG = mandated annualized earnings growth.

e. Estimates minus inflation.

f. MAREG = mandated annualized real earnings growth.

g. Absolute effect ÷ sum of absolute effects.

Figure 4-26. *Mandated Wage Changes: Production and Nonproduction Workers, 1960s–80s*

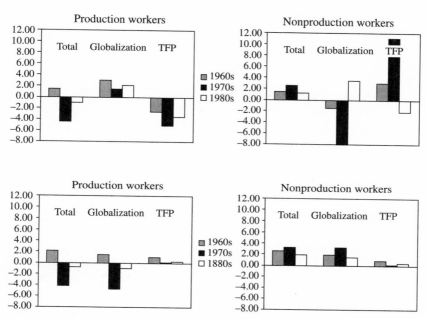

Sources: Citibase (Citibank Economic Database), New York: Citibank N.A.; and author's calculations.

against production workers and in favor of nonproduction workers, except in the 1980s, when both kinds of labor suffered from sectoral bias in technological change. (Is that corporate downsizing?)

Thus the conclusions that g-effects dominate t-effects and that the 1970s was the Stolper-Samuelson decade, with product price changes causing increases in inequality, are found in three of the four cases—the exception being the estimates applicable to production/nonproduction workers using a zero pass-through. In that case it is the t-effects that dominate, the globalization effect worked to the advantage of production workers in the 1970s.

Appendix A: Documentation of Database Used in Section 3

See documentation in Bartelsman and Gray (1996). This database contains annual information on 450 manufacturing industries from 1958 to 1991. The industries are those defined in the 1972 Standard Industrial

Classification, and cover the entire manufacturing sector. Much of the data is taken from the Annual Surveys of Manufactures and Censuses of Manufactures, with the remainder created based on information from various government agencies.

Variable Descriptions and Comments

SIC, YEAR—identify each observation in the dataset (SIC ranges from 2011 to 3999 and YEAR ranges from 58 to 91)

EMP—number of employees (in thousands)—does not include employees in auxiliary (administrative) units

PAY—total payroll (millions of dollars)—does not include Social Security or other legally mandated payments, or employer payments for some fringe benefits

PRODE—number of production workers (in thousands)

PRODH—number of production worker hours (in millions of hours)

PRODW—production worker wages (millions of dollars)

VADD—value added by manufacture (millions of dollars; equals shipments – materials + inventory change)

MATCOST—cost of materials (millions of dollars)—includes energy spending, so to calculate spending on nonenergy materials one must use (MATCOST – ENERGY)

ENERGY—expenditures on purchased fuels and electrical energy (millions of dollars)

VSHIP—value of industry shipments (millions of dollars; not adjusted for inventory changes)

INVENT—end-of-year inventories (millions of dollars; pre-1982 based on any generally accepted accounting method; post-1982 based either at cost or at market, with LIFO users asked to report preadjustment values)

INVEST—new capital spending (millions of dollars; combines spending on structures and equipment)

CAP—real capital stock (millions of 1987 dollars, equals EQUIP + PLANT)

EQUIP—real equipment capital stock (millions of 1987 dollars)

PLANT—real structures capital stock (millions of 1987 dollars)

PISHIP—price deflator for value of shipments (equals 1 in 1987)

PIMAT—price deflator for materials (1 in 1987; all materials, not just nonenergy materials)

PIEN—price deflator for energy (1 in 1987)

PIINV—price deflator for new investment (1 in 1987; combines deflators for structures and equipment)

TFP—five-factor total factor productivity growth (calculated from other variables; expressed as annual growth rate)

Appendix B: Derivation of the Labor Demand Curves

The key building block of the HO model is the Lerner-Pearce diagram, figure 4-27, which illustrates the relationship between goods prices and factor prices. In this diagram there are unit-value isoquants for two hypothetical products, a labor-intensive good labelled apparel and a capital-intensive good labelled machinery. These unit-value isoquants indicate combinations of capital and labor that are required to produce a unit value of the good. "Tangent" to these two unit-value isoquants is a straight line which is the only unit-isocost line satisfying a zero-profit condition in both goods. The equation for this unit isocost is $1 = wL + rK$ where L and K are labor and capital inputs and w and r are the corresponding factor prices. From this equation one can solve for the intersections with the axes of this

Figure 4-27. *Lerner-Pearce Diagram for Fixed-Input Technologies*

Capital

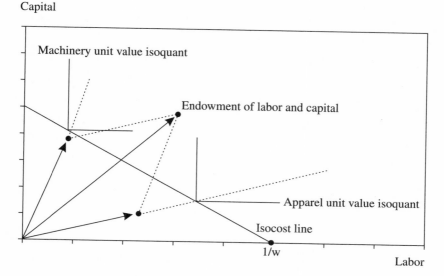

unit isoquant. On the horizontal axis is the inverse of the wage rate ($1/w$) and on the vertical axis is the inverse of the rental rate on capital ($1/r$). Perhaps without the reader's full awareness, this has established the FPE theorem, which I prefer to call the factor price insensitivity (FPI) theorem: factor prices depend on product prices but not on factor supplies. In other words, the long-run demand for labor in a small, open economy is infinitely elastic.

Also in this diagram is the parallelogram indicating the allocation of capital and labor between the two industries, with input ratios conforming to the technologically fixed input ratios in each industries. (Nothing of substance hinges on substitutability of inputs at the level of the industry.) From straightforward manipulation of this parallelogram, one can derive the Rybczynski theorem: An increase in labor supply increases output of the labor-intensive good and decreases output of the capital-intensive good. Thus even as the economy is growing, one output is declining. It is this extreme shift in output mix that allows the labor demand of the economy to be infinitely elastic.

It is also easy to see from figure 4-27 that a reduction of the price of apparel causes a decline in the wage rate. A reduction of the apparel price makes the apparel unit-value isoquant shift outward—it takes more capital and labor to produce a unit value of apparel. This shifting outward of the apparel unit-value isoquant shifts the intersection of the unit-cost line to the right, and thus selects a lower wage rate. This is the familiar Stolper-Samuelson theorem.

Figure 4-28 allows a third factor and more goods into the model. I have used triangular displays of this kind to discuss alternative paths of development.[32] Here each vertex represents one of the three factors (unskilled workers, skilled workers, and physical capital). A movement in the triangle directly toward one of the vertices corresponds to an increase in that factor, holding fixed the other two. In the diagram are three products that use no skilled workers and that use an increasing amount of physical capital: apparel, textiles, and steel. One product uses all three inputs (chemicals/aircraft) and one uses only physical capital and skilled workers (software). The message of the model is not hurt by the fact that these characterizations are suggestive but far from accurate.

32. Leamer (1987).

Figure 4-28. *Factor Endowment Triangle*

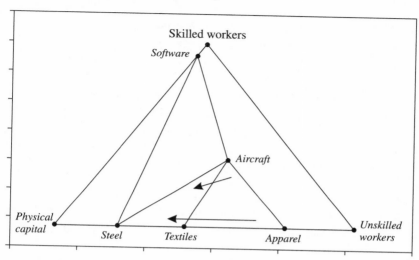

Figure 4-28 is completed by connecting the product points with straight lines to form "cones of diversification."[33] These cones select countries with sufficiently similar factor supply ratios that they have the same factor prices and output mix. In this diagram, movement toward a vertex corresponds to an increase in the supply of the factor, which cannot raise the return to that factor. In other words, the demand for a factor is not upwardly sloping. This implies that the triangle of diversification formed by the apparel, textiles, and aircraft points has the lowest wages. The product mix with steel, textiles, and aircraft has higher wages for the unskilled; and the product mix of software, steel, and aircraft has the highest wages. Thus the labelling of three cones of diversification as "low," "medium," and "high," refering to the level of wages of unskilled workers.

With this as the model, figure 4-6 illustrates the demand for unskilled labor of two hypothetical countries with different ratios of skilled to unskilled workers. The horizontal axis for this demand curve is, as before, the

33. The way that the diagram is divided depends on product prices. Implicitly it has been assumed that aircraft have a high enough price that it is advantageous to produce them everywhere in the world, and therefore all the other product points are connected with lines to the aircraft point.

ratio of unskilled labor to physical capital. These two demand curves correspond with the two arrows pointing toward the physical-capital vertex in figure 4-28. The skill-abundant country with the arrow closer to the skilled-worker vertex in figure 4-28 exits the low-wage cone at a relatively low ratio of unskilled workers to physical capital. It also enters the highest-wage cone at a relatively low ratio of unskilled to skilled workers.

We can also use figure 4-28 to make some remarks about increased capital mobility. The cone that has the highest wages for unskilled workers also has the lowest return to physical capital. Suppose that globalization means not just integration of the goods markets and equalization of goods prices, but also freedom for capital to find locations on the globe with the highest rates of return. Then capital will flow out of the high-wage countries located in the software-steel-chemicals/aircraft cone and into countries located in the cones with higher returns to physical capital. As capital leaves the high-wage cones, the factor supply is dragged away from the physical-capital vertex in figure 4-28.

Now there are two possibilities. If the supply of skilled workers is relatively small compared with unskilled workers, this loss of capital drags the factor endowment point through the moderate-wage, steel-textiles-chemicals/aircraft cone and into the very-low-wage, textiles-apparel-chemicals/aircraft cone. But if the supply of skilled workers is great enough, loss of capital can drag the country away from the physical-capital vertex along the path depicted in figure 4-28. This country *does not* get dragged into cones with lower wages. Instead, it loses the steel sector and specializes in the skill-intensive sectors, software and chemicals/aircraft. This country competes in chemicals/aircraft against the low-wage countries but does so by offsetting its cost disadvantage at low skills with cost advantages at high skills. In other words, it opts for high wages for low-skilled workers and a low premium for skills. Thus, at least in this model, the assault on income equality represented by capital mobility toward the low-wage, developing regions can be completely met by educational investments that attract capital by lowering the cost of complementary skilled inputs. This lower private return to skills reduces the attractiveness of investments in skills. In the longer run, human capital in a skill-abundant country can be turned into more productive investments in physical assets in the emerging regions, thus dragging the country round the bend into the low-wage cone.

The next topic is the trade deficit and the "overvaluation" of the dollar. In order to think about the possible effects of a trade deficit and also issues of product choice this simple model needs *nontraded goods* whose prices

Figure 4-29. *Lerner-Pearce Diagram for Specialization Choice: Moderate Wages*

Capital

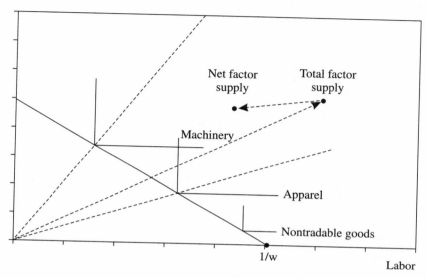

can be influenced by local demand. Figures 4-29 and 4-30 are Lerner-Pearce diagrams with a labor-intensive nontradable. In figure 4-29 wages and the return to capital are determined externally, and these factor prices select the price of nontradables from the nontradables zero profit condition. In figure 4-30, the demand for nontradables is too great at that externally determined price to leave enough labor for the tradables sector to allow the production of both apparel and machinery. The economy accordingly fully specializes in machinery production, and chokes off demand for the non-tradable with relatively high nontradable prices. This selects a high-wage equilibrium with a concentrated mix of tradables. There is also a low-wage equilibrium in which the economy produces only apparel and the non-tradable.

These ideas are summarized in the labor demand function with non-traded goods illustrated in figure 4-8. This demand curve has an interval of infinite elasticity selected when the country produces both goods. In this interval the two zero-profit conditions can be used to solve for the two internal factor prices as a function of the two external product prices. These internal factor prices determine the price of nontraded goods from the

Figure 4-30. *Lerner-Pearce Diagram for Specialization Choice: High Wages*

Capital

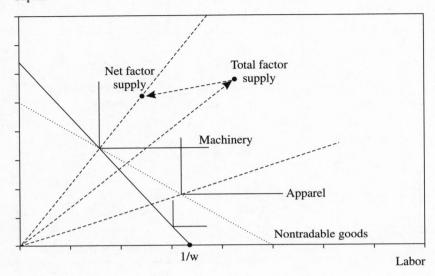

Figure 4-31. *Lerner-Pearce Diagram: Effect of Technological Change on Wages*

Capital

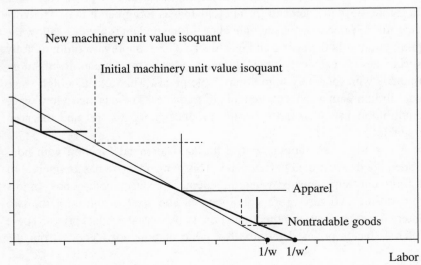

nontraded-goods, zero-profit condition. But if labor is very scarce or very abundant, the economy will fully specialize on one traded good and produce also the nontraded good.

Finally, figure 4-31 shows the effect of labor-saving technological change in the capital-intensive sector, which at constant product prices causes a reduction in wages from w to w'. If the supply of factors to the tradables sector is held fixed, relatively more capital and labor must be allocated to the apparel sector, because the input mix in the machinery sector has become less like the factor supply vector. (Use figure 4-27 to check this assertion.) The economy thus produces more machinery because of the technological improvement and more apparel because of the reallocation of the factors. Depending on which force dominates and also on the elasticities of demand, relative prices can go either way. If relative prices do vary, there will be technologically induced Stolper-Samuelson effects.

Comment by Steven J. Davis

Since I have been teamed with Gene Grossman to discuss Ed Leamer's chapter 4, I have taken my job to be presenting a labor economist's perspective on the way that Leamer advocates for looking at the linkages between international trade and relative wage movements. Leamer covers a lot of ground, and my comments do not attempt to address all of the many issues included. Instead, my aim is to identify several reasons for skepticism about the approach that Leamer advocates.

First is the notion of an infinitely elastic labor demand curve. Leamer qualified this assumption somewhat in his oral remarks and in parts of his chapter, but much of the framework that is the basis for his analysis takes it seriously. To a labor economist, the concept of an infinitely elastic labor demand schedule is nonsensical. Our view is grounded in a substantial body of evidence. There are many successful empirical studies by labor economists that relate relative wage movements to relative supply shifts. For example, numerous studies for the United States show that relative shifts in the proportions of more-educated versus less-educated workers influence the skill premium. Other studies focus on implications of changes in the age distribution of the work force for the U.S. wage structure.

There are also studies for other countries. In particular, some for countries like Canada that are small relative to the size of the world

This comment was prepared from the conference transcript.

economy also find evidence that relative supply shifts affect relative wages. These results support the view that the findings for the United States are not simply attributable to the fact that the United States is large relative to the rest of the world. Perhaps even more striking are studies that account for region-specific relative wage movements within the United States in terms of region-specific relative supply movements in the labor market. Even when there is clearly the potential for labor mobility to arbitrage away region-specific relative wage movements, those movements persist for several years and are closely tied to relative supply movements.

On the basis of these empirical findings, an infinitely elastic labor demand schedule seems to be a strange place to begin to think about wages. That does not mean that I wish to discard the insights of the HO model. On the contrary, I believe that the HO model is quite useful, particularly because it pushes us to think about factor proportions and when they matter. What I would like to see is a model that welds some of the insights from the HO framework into a model with differentiated products so that both the external sector and the local sector matter on the margin. In the model Leamer focuses on, we are either on a margin where the external sector matters, in which case labor demand is infinitely elastic, or we are on a margin where the local economy matters, in which case labor demand is downwardly sloping. I would find more interesting and relevant a model in which various domestic shifts and international shocks lead us to slide along both margins at the same time.

Second, in Leamer's framework it is product price changes not output-quantity shifts that matter. I recognize the theoretical arguments behind this structure, and agree that they should be given some weight. However, in the labor literature, I can think of few studies that relate product price changes to relative wage movements. Labor economists, while in my view often rightly criticized for being atheoretical, are good at sniffing out significant covariances in the data. If there were lots of significant covariances between relative wage movements and product price movements, I would have expected to see lots of labor economists running regressions to figure out what the relationships look like under various conditions. Therefore, I am skeptical that significant covariances exist among these variables. The labor literature thus suggests taking an alternative tack.

In this context, it is worth emphasizing that the Stolper-Samuelson linkage between product prices and relative wage movements stressed by trade theorists is not inherently international. It is simply a relationship between product prices and wage movements that ought to hold in any setting where prices are set competitively and returns to scale are not important.

My third point concerns Leamer's emphasis that it is the sectoral bias of technical change that matters, not the factor bias. Although Leamer acknowledges in a footnote that factor bias might play a role through "second-order" effects or if it results in sectoral price changes, the thrust of his argument is that these channels are relatively unimportant. However, this claim is based on his reliance on a linear approximation in which factor cost shares are held constant. It is straightforward to show, for example using a CES production function, that if technical change influences cost shares in one or both sectors, relative factor prices are affected even if product prices remain constant. This can occur with technical change that is either neutral or factor biased.

The issue then is whether factor cost shares have remained relatively constant, as Leamer's approach assumes. Available data suggest that they have not. In recent work with John Haltiwanger, I constructed the labor cost share in manufacturing of nonproduction (relative to production) workers. We found that this share rose from 43 percent in 1977 to 50 percent in 1986, a moderate increase. It would be preferable to look at labor cost shares based on different educational groupings, instead of the more difficult to interpret production/nonproduction breakdown. Although I do not have those figures, I am quite confident that they would show an even larger increase in the cost share of more-skilled workers, since there has been both a substantial educational upgrading of the manufacturing work force and a dramatic rise in the relative wage of more-educated workers during the 1980s. These trends lead me to doubt the relevance of the linear approximation that underlies Leamer's analysis.

The final issue I would like to raise is the source of wage variation that Leamer focuses on in his chapter. In particular, his empirical analysis is associated with changes in the structure of mean production-worker wages across industries. But this component actually accounts for a relatively small proportion of the overall increase in hourly wage inequality. I refer here to a decomposition from some of my work with John Haltiwanger.[34] Our decomposition is based on only 22 industries, compared with Leamer's much larger number—450 industries. Nonetheless, our data suggest that an upper bound for what Leamer's measure could account for is only about 20 percent of the total increase in inequality. This comes from the sum of

34. See, for example, Davis and Haltiwanger (1991, 1995).

between-plant wage inequality within industries plus between-industry wage inequality. Though this sum behaves similarly to overall wage-inequality trends in some periods, there are other periods in which it behaves quite differently. Furthermore, the largest component of increased wage inequality is the increase in the variance of wages among nonproduction workers within plants. That particular component is completely missing from Leamer's empirical analysis. It also strikes me as difficult, if not impossible, to understand this component—and thus most of the increase in wage inequality—in terms of the simple HO approach that Leamer advocates.

For all of these reasons, I remain unconvinced that the framework Leamer advocates for analyzing whether relative wage changes have been linked to international trade is the appropriate framework.

Comment by Gene M. Grossman

How much of the widening of the wage gap between skilled and unskilled workers in the United States has been caused by the increasing integration of the world economy? Not much, say a host of labor economists and such trade economists as Paul Krugman and Robert Lawrence. Wrong, says Ed Leamer: "The 1970s was a Stolper-Samuelson decade with price, trade, and employment data consistent with the presence of Stolper-Samuelson effects on wage inequality." Moreover, "the residual 'globalization' effects on income inequality dominate the technological effects" for this decade.

Part of the reason that economists cannot agree on the answer to the question is that they cannot agree on what the question means. What is meant by "increasing integration"? Are we talking about reduced trade barriers and lower transportation and communication costs? Or are we talking about lower prices of tradable goods in the United States, perhaps due to capital accumulation and technological learning abroad? Or are we talking about increased trade flows, arising for whatever reason? And what is meant by "caused"? Are we speaking loosely, as in "associated with," or do we really mean that some exogenous events outside the United States were directly responsible for the income inequality trends?

Some economists have taken changes in trade flows as indicative of the increased integration of the United States and world economies. Leamer points out, and rightly so, that one cannot treat trade quantities as exogenous.[35] The volume of trade conducted by the United States surely

35. Krugman (1995) identifies conditions under which the volume of trade and the associated factor content of trade *can* be used to identify the effects of certain

reflects events taking place both within and outside its borders. So I applauded when I read that "the globalization 'shock' that is emphasized in this chapter is an increase in the foreign supply of unskilled workers *associated with the economic liberalizations that are sweeping the globe*" (emphasis added). But I was disappointed to find that Leamer does not, in fact, attempt to identify the effects of these liberalizations directly. Rather, he constructs an analytical framework in which *all* declines in the U.S. prices of traded manufactured goods are treated as being the result of increasing integration, except (perhaps) those that can be linked to domestic, sectoral productivity improvements. Moreover, his empirical analysis neglects nontraded sectors, including services. Leamer's approach replaces the unappealing assumption of exogenous quantities with the equally unappealing assumption of exogenous prices.

In my view, we should attribute to "increasing integration" only those events in the U.S. economy that can be linked to exogenous movements in the net export-supply and import-demand curves of our trading partners. These movements could be due to improvements in transportation technology, or the tearing down of trade barriers in the developing countries, or the accumulation of capital and production capabilities there, or whatever. But we cannot take either quantity movements or price changes as a primitive cause; if one wants to answer the question seriously, there is no avoiding the need to identify shifts in foreign offer curves.

Another (but related) reason that different economists provide different answers to the question posed at the outset is that they have different views of the world economy. In this chapter, Leamer presents evidence that he derives from taking the United States to be a reasonably close approximation to a small, open economy producing costlessly tradable manufactured goods that are perfect substitutes for goods produced abroad. Moreover, it is an economy that produces, or at least produced in the past, exactly as many of these goods as there are intersectorally distinct—mobile factors of production. In this setting, there can be only two potential causes of factor

aspects of "globalization" on wages in the United States. He examines a hypothetical world where skills-enhancing technological progress is common to the United States and its OECD trade partners, and he attributes the labor market response to these technical gains to the effects of technology, not trade. For the effects of globalization, he limits his attention to the growth of U.S. trade with non-OECD trade partners. These countries, he assumes, are too small to affect world prices. Then their *total* volume of trade with the United States is an upper bound on the change in trade flows that could be due to increased integration, and the associated factor content of that trade can be used to calculate an upper bound for the effects on the U.S. labor market.

price movements: total factor productivity changes in tradables sectors, and the exogenous forces of globalization. By contrast, (for example) Krugman views the United States as a large country and he sees technological progress as an OECD-wide phenomenon.[36] Because he interprets "increasing integration" to mean increasing trade with the non-OECD countries, he regards this phenomenon as having almost no effect on traded-goods prices.

Leamer's analysis in this chapter has two distinct parts. In the second section, he weaves a "story" spiced by bits of evidence. In the third section, he attempts a more formal exploration of the data. I will discuss each in turn.

The story of the second section is that, due to anemic investment rates and an inadequate educational system, the U.S. factor endowment bundle became less different from the average world endowment through the late 1960s and 1970s, at the same time that the NICs were ending their economic isolationism. As a result, U.S. trade and production patterns shifted, with the marginal unskilled worker still working in the labor-intensive footwear and apparel industries but finding less demand for his or her services there. Thus, the declining real wage and the rising skill premium were caused by external forces, in the light of the unfortunate change in U.S. relative factor endowments. In the 1980s, events were different, either because protection of the apparel and textile sectors prevented further erosion of competitive advantage there, or because the marginal worker was no longer involved in activities directly in competition with workers in less-developed countries (LDCs). The evidence Leamer presents that is consistent with this story is that:

—Real wages indeed fell during the 1970s, while recovering in the 1980s.

—The "skill premium" (measured as the relative wage of an average worker in a more-skill-intensive sector to the wage of an average worker in the apparel sector) rose during the 1970s but leveled off during the 1980s.[37]

—The relative price of apparel and textiles (compared with other traded manufactures) fell during the 1970s but showed no noticeable trend during the 1980s.

—Employment in unskilled-labor-intensive manufacturing sectors fell consistently through the 1970s, whereas net imports of these goods were rising sharply.

36. Krugman (1995).
37. This is an unorthodox notion of the skill premium, as Leamer concedes. For movements in this measure to mimic movements in the earnings of a skilled individual relative to an unskilled individual, Leamer needs zero substitutability between skilled and unskilled labor.

The trade and employment patterns of the 1980s are more difficult to interpret, because they reflect to a great extent the large exchange rate swings of the decade, which caused a growing then shrinking overall trade deficit.

By and large, Leamer tells a *consistent* story. But is it also *convincing*? I am disturbed by his decision to downplay several aspects of the history. First, the 1970s was a decade dominated by two oil-price shocks and the adjustments thereto, by a large recession, and by an unprecedented rise in inflation. Is it not possible that the fall in real wages was at least partly due to the high unemployment rates and to higher than expected price hikes? Is it not possible that the relative fate of different sectors had something to do with their relative reliance on energy and their ability to adjust to the increased oil prices? Is it not possible that the reversals of the 1980s were at least partly due to a catch-up in wages and to the return of relative oil prices to historical levels?

Second, Leamer's story ignores nontraded goods, except when he wants to talk about the real appreciation of the dollar and the trade deficit of the mid-1980s. As is well known, only 15 percent of American jobs are in the manufacturing sectors. Most unskilled workers are employed in the service sector. And though it is indeed theoretically possible (as Leamer notes) that the marginal unskilled worker is employed in the textile or apparel sector and that unskilled wages are fully determined there, it seems at least as plausible that events in the construction industry and in retail trade and in the fast-food sector had something to do with the determination of unskilled wages. Leamer suggests that the demand for labor might be highly elastic in these sectors or that prices in these sectors might have had to adjust to factor costs that were fully determined by exogenous traded-goods prices. But because the United States is a large country, and because countries seem to trade much less than would be expected if one believed in costless mobility of goods, and because the nontraded sector looms large in the U.S. economy, it would appear that the burden of proof lies with Leamer if he wants to argue this way.

In his second section, Leamer does not give the alternative story—which blames technology for most of the wage trends of the last two decades— much of a chance. Mightn't the relative productivity slowdown in labor-intensive service sectors as compared with the manufacturing sector as a whole have played a part in the relative wage movements? Not if the world is viewed through a lens where factor prices are fully determined by exogenously given prices of traded goods. But why should we suspect that this is the case? Mightn't the oft-claimed factor bias in the technological progress of the last two decades (that is, skill using and labor saving) have played a role, and couldn't this also account for some of the changes in employment and trade patterns? Not if the United States is a small, fully open economy producing perfect substitutes for trade goods. But why should we suspect that events at home have no effect on domestic prices? In short, the second section gives us a story that is consistent with some facts, but does not tell us how much we need to rely on the story to explain the facts. These are the purported objectives of the third section.

In the third section, Leamer computes total factor productivity growth in each manufacturing sector for each of three decades. He regresses these on factor shares, looking for evidence that TFP growth was much slower in labor-intensive and especially low-wage industries in the 1970s, when average real wages were falling, especially in low-wage sectors. When he fails to find much evidence of this, he concludes that globalization must have been the cause.

But there are several problems here of which Leamer himself is well aware.

—Total factor productivity is undoubtedly measured with error. Moreover, because the computation of TFP makes direct use of the factor shares, the measurement error is bound to be correlated with the included right-hand side variables.

—Leamer uses domestic prices in his regressions for the total mandated wage changes. But these can be taken to represent the effects of globalization only if the United States is small in relation to world markets. When Baldwin and Cain regress *international* prices (instead of U.S. prices) on factor shares, they find little evidence that foreign prices have been falling, especially in unskilled-labor-intensive sectors.[38]

—The data set includes only manufacturing sectors, thereby excluding the possibility that wage trends were driven by slow TFP growth in non-traded services.

—The regressions allow no avenue for factor-biased technological progress to affect product prices and thus factor prices, removing by assumption the main competing hypothesis put forward by the "trade-can't-be-that-important" school.

—The fact that TFP growth was strongly positively correlated with capital share in the 1960s and 1980s but not the 1970s, and that domestic price movements were negatively correlated with capital share in the 1960s and 1980s but positively so in the 1970s, suggests that the oil-price shock

38. Baldwin and Cain (1994).

may have been the culprit here. It fell most heavily on industries using capital, and as cost increases were passed on to domestic consumers. But the small-country assumption precludes this interpretation of the regression results.

—Different domestic goods may substitute more or less imperfectly for imports, but Leamer neglects this by imposing identical "pass-through" rates in all sectors.

In short, the analysis imposes such a straitjacket on the data that I think skeptics could never be convinced.

I wonder whether it really matters whether and to what extent "globalization" contributed to the growing income inequality in the United States. Many trade economists are keen to find trade innocent, because they fear that if trade contributed to the problem, then protection might be part of the "solution." Leamer believes that trade did contribute to the problem, but he is no more keen to see protection implemented than any of his trade-economist brethren. This should not be as surprising as it first seems; after all, economic theory tells us that the appropriate tools for improving the distribution of income do not depend on what forces gave rise to the inequality in the first place.

As Leamer puts it, "the question is not: 'Which is the guilty force?' The real question is: 'What are we going to do about it?'" Though I question the specific arguments he gives for endorsing government promotion of education, savings, and investments in infrastructure—he sees physical and human capital accumulation as a way to give the United States a more distinctive factor endowment, thus making it more immune to further declines in the price of labor-intensive manufactures; I see the case for these investments as resting on the existence of externalities—I couldn't agree more with his bottom line.

General Discussion

J. David Richardson began the discussion by asking whether available evidence concludes that labor demand has become more elastic due to increased globalization, as our trade models imply should have happened. Richard Freeman responded that studies never find large labor demand elasticities. Furthermore, he did not believe that our measures are precise enough to detect whether there have been any changes in these modest elasticities. Edward Leamer reiterated the point that the HO model does not imply that globalization should make labor demand infinitely elastic, but simply that the elasticity should increase. However, these trade models are relevant for long time horizons of a decade or more. His presumption was that most labor demand estimates are based on short-term concepts of a month or a year and may tell us little about whether there has been a trend rise in the elasticity over the long run.

Robert Lawrence found the chapter's longer-run perspective useful and interesting for two reasons. This perspective reminds us that there was considerable globalization during the 1960s and early 1970s. In addition, the timing of relative price changes does not coincide with the timing of the labor market developments of concern, which confirms his view that globalization was not the "culprit." In particular, the chapter concludes that relative prices of textiles and apparel declined during the 1970s, not during the 1980s when skill premia rose. Both of these comments generated additional discussion.

Edward Leamer contended that, using his measure of wage premia, the timing of relative price changes is consistent with globalization as a "culprit." His measure, based on industry-level data, takes the lowest-wage industry—apparel—as a measure of wages to low-skill workers, and industry wage premia relative to apparel as indicators of skill premia. Using these indicators, there were significant increases in wage premia during 1970–82, but not later in the 1980s.

Catherine Mann argued that the chapter uncovers another timing mismatch that does not support the view that globalization has caused adverse labor market developments. Although it finds that relative goods prices changed primarily during the 1970s, she noted that measures of increased international linkage, such as trade imbalances and exchange rate variation, point to the 1980s as the period of major developments.

Steven Davis also took issue with the view that increased globalization was concentrated in the 1960s and 1970s. He provided two pieces of evidence that suggest the biggest changes occurred in the 1980s. Sharp cost reductions and significant technical improvements in telecommunications led to rapid expansions in trade in services during the 1980s. Further, there appears to have been a large and steady decline in transport costs (freight plus insurance divided by import value) for manufactured goods. This measure fell from about 5.3 percent in 1978 to just 3.8 percent in 1992.

J. Bradford Jensen introduced some of the results from his work with Andrew Bernard using plant-level data. This work concludes that much of the changes in wage structure and employment of different worker groups is driven by shifts between plants within the same detailed industry sector.

Michael Piore followed up on this comment by arguing that these plant-level findings suggest that technical change and trade expansion may not be separable. Trade may in fact be driving (or intertwined with the forces that are driving) technical change. Lewis Alexander agreed that technical change and globalization may not be separable. He referred to additional plant-level studies that conclude that for many industries, changes in wage structure occur across plants. He expressed concern that focusing on industry-level data may cause analysts to miss key developments. Leamer defended industries as the appropriate unit of analysis if one is using trade models as the conceptual framework.

Various participants noted that existing discussions have underemphasized some of the changes that may play important roles. Mann pointed out that, although relative prices of labor-intensive goods may not have changed during the 1980s, there have been significant changes in prices of traded relative to nontraded goods. Lawrence Mishel noted that energy prices rose substantially during the 1970s, increasing the price of capital-intensive relative to labor-intensive products. This trend was reversed in the 1980s. Mishel also stressed that most studies focus on whether import competition might put downward pressure on domestic wages, while ignoring the export sector. He cited the recent strike at Caterpillar to make the point that even successful exporting firms can feel pressure to lower wages of domestic employees. Piore suggested that the role of the United States in the international marketplace may also be relevant. Thus, trade expansion may have a qualitatively different impact domestically when the United States is the acknowledged technical leader, as was true during the 1960s, than it would today, when the U.S. position has changed.

References

Baldwin, Robert E., and Glen G. Cain. 1994. "Trade and U.S. Relative Wages: Preliminary Results." University of Wisconsin, Department of Economics.

Bartlesman, Eric, and Wayne B. Gray. 1996. "The NBER Manufacturing Productivity Database." Working Paper 205. Cambridge, Mass.: National Bureau of Economic Research.

Bell, Linda A., and Richard B. Freeman. 1991. "The Causes of Increasing Interindustry Wage Dispersion in the United States." *Industrial and Labor Relations Review* 44 (January): 275–87.

Bhagwati, Jagdish, and Vivek H. Dehejia. 1994. "Freer Trade and Wages of the Unskilled—Is Marx Striking Again?" In *Trade and Wages: Leveling Wages Down?* edited by Jagdish Bhagwati and Marvin H. Kosters, 36–75. Washington: American Enterprise Institute.

Bhagwati, Jagdish, and Marvin H. Kosters. 1994. *Trade and Wages: Leveling Wages Down?* Washington: American Enterprise Institute.

Borjas, George J., and Valerie A. Ramey. 1993. "Foreign Competition, Market Power, and Wage Inequality: Theory and Evidence." Working Paper 4556. Cambridge, Mass.: National Bureau of Economic Research.

Davis, Steven J., and John C. Haltiwanger. 1991. "Wage Dispersion between and within U.S. Manufacturing Plants, 1963–86." *Brookings Papers on Economic Activity: Microeconomics:* 115–200.

———. 1995. "Employer Size and Wage Distribution in U.S. Manufacturing." Working Paper 5393. Cambridge, Mass.: National Bureau of Economic Research (December).

Deardorff, Alan V., and Dalia S. Hakura. 1994. "Trade and Wages: What Are the Questions?" In *Trade and Wages: Leveling Wages Down?* edited by Jadgish Bhagwati and Marvin H. Kosters, 76–107. Washington: American Enterprise Institute.

Hilton, R. Spence. 1984. "Commodity Trade and Relative Returns to Factors of Production." *Journal of International Economics* 16 (May): 259–70.

Krugman, Paul R. 1995. "Technology, Trade, and Factor Prices." Working Paper 5355. Cambridge, Mass.: National Bureau of Economic Research (November).

Krugman, Paul, and Robert Z. Lawrence. 1993. "Trade, Jobs and Wages." Working Paper 4478. Cambridge, Mass.: National Bureau of Economic Research.

Lawrence, Robert Z., and Matthew J. Slaughter. 1993. "International Trade and American Wages in the 1980s: Giant Sucking Sound or Small Hiccup?" *Brookings Papers on Economic Activity 2: Microeconomics:* 161–226.

Leamer, Edward E. 1984. *Sources of International Comparative Advantage: Theory and Evidence.* MIT Press.

———. 1987. "Paths of Development in the Three-Factor *n*-Good General Equilibrium Model." *Journal of Political Economy* 95 (October): 961–99.

———. 1993. "Wage Effects of a U.S.-Mexican Free Trade Agreement." In *The Mexico-U.S. Free Trade Agreement,* edited by Peter M. Garber, 57–125. MIT Press.

———. 1994. "Trade, Wages and Revolving Door Ideas." Working Paper 4716. Cambridge, Mass.: National Bureau of Economic Research (April).

———. 1995a. "The Heckscher-Ohlin Model in Theory and Practice." *Princeton Studies in International Finance* 77 (February).

———. 1995b. "What's the Use of Factor Contents?" Working Paper 5448. Cambridge, Mass.: National Bureau of Economic Research.

Mishel, Lawrence, and Jared Bernstein. 1994. "Is the Technology Black Box Empty? An Empirical Examination of the Impact of Technology on Wage Inequality and the Employment Structure." Washington: Economic Policy Institute.

Sachs, Jeffrey D., and Howard J. Shatz. 1994. "Trade and Jobs in U.S. Manufacturing." *Brookings Papers on Economic Activity 1:* 1–84.

Song, Ligang. 1993. "Sources of International Comparative Advantage: Further Evidence." Ph.D. dissertation, Australian National University.

FIVE

International Trade and Wage Inequality in the United States: Some New Results

Jeffrey D. Sachs and Howard J. Shatz

THE EFFECTS of U.S. trade with developing countries on U.S. wage inequality and employment patterns continue to be a subject of enormous contention. The charge that trade between the United States and developing countries lowers the wages of unskilled U.S. workers, or perhaps all U.S. workers, has entered the American political debate with considerable force, and the debate among economists has heated up as well. The range of opinion is enormous, sometimes even within the writings of the same author. Paul Krugman, for example, dismissed fears of low-wage trade competition as nothing more than the confusion of the nineteenth century "pauper labor argument" revisited.[1] A few months later, Krugman acknowledged that growing North-South trade could account for some, but not most, of the widening inequality.[2] More recently, Krugman and coauthor Anthony Venables presented a theoretical model in which the falling cost of

We thank Steven S. Saeger, Robert Z. Lawrence, Susan Collins, Donald Davis, Alan Krueger, and Wayne Gray for helpful comments and suggestions and for use of their data. All remaining errors are our own.

1. Krugman (1995a).
2. Krugman (1995b).

international transport, and therefore rising international trade between the "North" (developed countries) and the "South" (developing countries), can eventually lead to an *absolute* decline in the wage levels of the North, as a result of deindustrialization and convergence of income with the South.[3] This model suggests that the "pauper labor argument" is not simply confusion but rather an unresolved empirical question.

In fact, a wide range of theories suggests that increased trade with developing countries, whether the result of falling transport costs, falling protectionist barriers, or increased capacity of developing countries to produce goods for world markets, can lead to downward pressures on low-skilled wages. Theory also suggests circumstances in which increased trade will not produce such downward pressures. Most important, if the developing countries are producing and exporting goods to the United States that are not produced in the U.S. economy, then low-wage workers will not in general feel the brunt of increased trade flows.

The Heckscher-Ohlin-Samuelson (HOS) model, with its Stolper-Samuelson corollary, is the benchmark theoretical treatment of North-South trade —that is, trade between high-wage and low-wage economies.[4] The baseline model in recent debates rests on the following assumptions. There are two kinds of factor inputs, skilled labor, L_s, and unskilled labor, L_u. There are two output sectors as well. To economize on subscripts and superscripts, we denote the skilled-labor-intensive sector as S, and the unskilled-intensive sector as U. Let L_{ij} be the input of L_i in sector j. Then, we assume $L_{uu}/L_{su} > L_{us}/L_{ss}$ at all factor prices. There are constant returns to scale in production, perfect competition, full employment, and identical technologies in both countries. The skilled-labor-intensive good is numeraire ($P_s = 1$), and P_u denotes the relative price of U. The wage (in units of the numeraire, of course) is W_u for L_u, and W_s for L_s.

Now, assume a rise in trade between the skilled-labor-intensive economy (the North) and the unskilled-labor-intensive economy (the South), due to the elimination of protectionist barriers. Comparing the free-trade equilibrium with autarky, the HOS theory predicts (1) a rise in the production and export of S in the North, and in the production and export of U in the South; (2) a fall in P_u, the relative price of U, in the North; (3) a fall in the relative wage of unskilled workers in the North, W_u/W_s (and in the relative

3. Krugman and Venables (1995).
4. For discussions revolving around the HOS model see, for example, Lawrence and Slaughter (1993); Wood (1994); Sachs and Shatz (1994); Leamer (1995).

wage of skilled workers in the South); and (4) a rise in the ratio of unskilled to skilled workers in each sector in the North, as firms economize on skilled workers after the rise in their relative wage. Thus, L_{ui}/L_{si} rises in each sector i ($i = U,S$).

If we consider the period of the 1980s as one of falling trade barriers in the developing countries, how do the various predictions of the HOS model fare in empirical terms?[5] Predictions 1 and 3 seem to be consistent with the data. U.S. production and net exports of unskilled-labor-intensive goods have declined in the past two decades, while net imports of these goods from developing countries have risen. At the same time, the relative wage of low-skilled workers has fallen significantly in the United States. This basic correlation of increased U.S. trade with developing countries and U.S. relative wage trends is, of course, the starting point of the controversy. Prediction 4 seems to be contrary to the facts, since virtually all manufacturing sectors in the United States have experienced a reduction in L_u/L_s, rather than an increase, despite the fall in W_u/W_s. This pattern suggests that technological shifts ("unskilled-labor-saving technical change") are at work, perhaps in addition to the effects of trade.

A significant controversy has arisen around prediction 2. There is no conclusive agreement among researchers on the trends of relative prices of low-skilled goods (for example, apparel, footwear, and assembly operations). The absence of clear evidence on relative price trends has led some observers to conclude that trade must have played a small or insignificant role in the widening of U.S. wage inequality.[6] Bhagwati argues that increased trade with developing countries can be the culprit in rising wage inequality only if the relative prices of U goods have declined; because they have not, trade must not be the cause of widening wage inequalities. (Krugman and Lawrence also point to the price data, and to the circumstantial evidence in favor of L_u-saving technical change, to suggest that it is technology rather than trade that accounts for the observed wage trends.)[7]

In our view, the conclusion that trade has played a small or even insignificant role in widening U.S. wage inequality is premature, and perhaps simply incorrect, for two reasons. First, the HOS model is not the only theoretical basis for a link between trade and relative wages. There are, in fact, many channels by which increased trade with low-wage countries could lead to a fall in the relative or absolute wages of unskilled workers.

5. See Sachs and Warner (1995) for a demonstration of falling trade barriers in the 1980s.
6. See in particular Bhagwati and Dehejia (1994); Bhagwati (1995).
7. Krugman and Lawrence (1994).

For example, the Krugman and Venables study is based on agglomeration economies arising from transport costs and increasing returns to scale, rather than from HOS assumptions, yet it still delivers the prediction of factor price equalization (FPE) between North and South as transport costs fall to low levels.[8] In the first part of this chapter we demonstrate several additional channels through which an expansion of North-South trade causes a fall in the relative wage of unskilled workers in the North, *even when there are no changes in relative output prices.*

Second, the evidence on relative prices is much more supportive of HOS predictions than Bhagwati or some others have suggested. Because of the so-called magnification effect, according to which relative price changes lead to more-than-proportionate changes in relative wages, even very small changes in relative prices—hard to detect in the data—would be consistent with large relative wage movements. Krugman makes an illustrative calculation in which the magnification effect is roughly three—a 1 percent reduction in the relative price of unskilled-labor-intensive goods leads to a 3 percent reduction in the relative wage of unskilled workers.[9] In fact, there are reasons to believe that the relative price of unskilled-labor-intensive goods has declined during the past fifteen years, by an economically meaningful margin.

It is our purpose in this chapter to show that theory and evidence are more supportive of the trade-wage link than recent criticisms have led many to believe. The first half of the chapter emphasizes the theoretical robustness of the trade-wage linkage, even beyond the assumptions of the HOS model. The second half revisits the empirical evidence, especially the price data, and shows that in fact the weight of the evidence points to economically significant relative price movements of the sort predicted by the HOS model.

Theoretical Issues

Increased trade between the U.S. and low-wage, developing countries could put downward pressure on U.S. unskilled wages for many reasons. The HOS model emphasizes one: the fall in the relative price of U goods, which is then passed through to the wages of unskilled workers. There are, in fact, a variety of ways that the same outcome may apply even when P_u does not change.

8. Krugman and Venables (1995).
9. Krugman (1995b).

Capital Mobility

The first, and potentially important, channel in addition to HOS is capital mobility. If the capital stock of L_u-intensive sectors can move from the United States to developing countries, then W_u/W_s can decline even if there is no change in P_u. Consider the following simple model to illustrate this point. We assume that there are two tradeable sectors, S and U, as well as a nontradeable sector N. The S sector is a final good, while U is an intermediate good used in the production of S. The price of S is taken as numeraire, and P_u is the relative price of the U and P_n is the relative price of N. The unskilled good U is produced either domestically, with output D_u, or in the partner country, with output F_u. K_u is the capital stock used in U production, and is divided between U.S.-based enterprises (K_d) and foreign-based enterprises (K_f), with $K_u = K_d + K_f$. Capital is sector specific, so that K_u cannot be used in N production and K_n cannot be used in U production.

The full model is as follows:

$S = S(L_s, U)$ production function of S, (5-1)

$D_u = \min(L_{uu}, K_d)$ production function of D_u, (5-2)

$F_u = K_f$ production of F_u, (5-3)

$L^*_{uu} = Kf$ foreign labor employed in F_u, (5-4)

$U = D_u + F_u$ total production of U, (5-5)

$K_d = K_u - K_f$ domestic capital stock in U, (5-6)

$N = N(L_{un}, K_n)$ production function of N, (5-7)

$L_u = L_{uu} + L_{un}$ total unskilled labor, (5-8)

$W_s = \partial S/\partial L_s$ labor demand for L_s in S, (5-9)

$W_u = P_n(\partial N/\partial L_{un})$ labor demand for Lu in N, (5-10)

$P_u = \partial S/\partial U$ demand for U in S, (5-11)

$\pi_f = P_u F_u - W^*_u L^*_{uu}$ quasi rents (profits) on Kf, (5-12)

$Y = S - P_u F_u + P_n N + \pi_f$ definition of national income, (5-13)

$N = f(Y, P_n)$ final demand for nontradeables. (5-14)

The production functions for S and N are standard, neoclassical, constant-returns-to-scale production functions. The skilled labor force is fixed at L_s, and is fully employed in the S sector. The unskilled labor force is fixed at L_u, and is divided between the domestic U sector (L_{uu}) and the nontradeable sector (L_{un}). The amount of K_u allocated to the foreign country, K_f, is taken to be exogenous, and is presumed to be determined by the regulations governing direct foreign investment (DFI) in the South (as well as by country risk, relative factor prices, tax policies, and other considerations). Foreign output and labor input in the production of F_u are determined by the amount of K_f, according to equations 5-3 and 5-4. The home country takes the foreign wage in the U sector as given. Presumably, $W^*_u << W_u$. Therefore, the quasi rents earned by K_u are higher when employed abroad than at home. Full capital mobility would lead to $K_f = K_u$, $K_d = 0$.

Notice that the supply of U is fixed, because $U = D_u + F_u = K_d + K_f = K$. Thus, U may be produced at home or abroad, but the total amount of U is unchanging. Because both L_s and U are fixed, the supply of S is also fixed. Moreover, the marginal product of L_s is also fixed, so that W_s is fixed, according to equation 5-9. The marginal product of U in the production of S is also fixed. Therefore, P_u is fixed, according to equation 5-11, since $\partial S/\partial U$ is a function of U/L_s, which is fixed.

Now, suppose that the developing country liberalizes its foreign-investment regime, so that it becomes possible to shift more of K_u to the foreign country. Because W_u^* is less than W_u, entrepreneurs will want to shift capital to K_f, in order to earn higher quasi rents. We assume that the permitted shift in K_f is exogenous, and look at the comparative static effects of $\partial K_f > 0$. As K_d falls, L_{uu} declines by an equal amount, and L_{un} rises by the same amount. Low-skilled workers lose their jobs in tradables and are forced to find jobs in nontradables. The production of nontradeables goods increases. The wage of low-skilled workers will be determined by equation 5-10, with W_u equal to the marginal value product of labor in N. Because the employment in N is rising, with an unchanged capital stock, the physical marginal product $\partial N/\partial L_{un}$ will decrease.

P_n may rise or fall. P_n will tend to fall because of the increased production of N; it may rise, however, because of a positive income effect—that is, a rise in Y in equation 13. This is due to the increased quasi rents enjoyed by the owners of K_f. As long as the income effect is relatively small (either $\partial f/\partial Y$ is small, or W^*_u is close to W_u), then P_n will fall. In this case, W_u surely declines, because $W_u = P_n(\partial N/\partial L_{un})$. Note, therefore, that W_u can fall even though P_u remains completely unchanged.

This mechanism, whether or not it is empirically important, is certainly in the minds of those who argue that increased trade with developing countries is "eliminating jobs" in the U sectors within manufacturing. As capital moves to the low-wage, foreign country, overall manufacturing employment is reduced, and unskilled workers are pushed into the nontradeables sector. Note that the shift of capital abroad does not have to show up in the data as DFI or outsourcing, because the physical capital could actually be sold outright to a foreign producer. For example, the machinery in a U.S. footwear firm could be sold on the secondary market to a Chinese producer, so that the imports of Chinese footwear would not show up as outsourcing by a U.S. firm, nor as DFI.[10]

In case K_f is the result of DFI, it is worthwhile noting the balance-of-payments accounting of a rise in K_f. From the production side, $Y = (S - P_u F_u) + P_n N + \pi_f$, and from the final-demand side, $Y = C_s + P_n N$, where C_s is the final domestic demand for S. The trade deficit is equal to the net imports of S plus the net imports of U, or $TD = (C_s - S) + P_u F_u$, so that $TD = \pi_f$. Thus, the trade deficit is equal to the earnings on DFI. The United States becomes a rentier country, running a trade deficit financed by profits on overseas investment. This clears up the confusion raised by Krugman, in which he erroneously argued that "large-scale deindustrialization can take place only if low-wage nations are major exporters of capital to high-wage nations."[11] The low-wage countries run export surpluses, which pay for the repatriation of profits on DFI from the North.

With a small amendment to the technological assumptions, we can get a simple and interesting expression for the change in wage inequality. Suppose now that production of S requires sector-specific capital K_s, as well as L_s and U, according to

$$S = S[\min(L_{ss}, K_s], U) \qquad (5\text{-}1')$$

Suppose also that the production of D_u and N use skilled labor as well as unskilled labor, so that

$$D_u = \min(L_{uu}, L_{us}/\alpha, K_d) \qquad (5\text{-}2')$$

$$N = N(L_{un}, L_{sn}, K_n) \qquad (5\text{-}7').$$

In the short term, K_s and K_n are fixed and sector specific. L_{ss} is therefore also fixed, according to the fixed-coefficients technology in equation 5-1'. As before, P_u will be unchanged when K_u is shifted abroad, since $P_u = \partial S/\partial U$, which will be unaffected by the rise in K_f.

---

10. Feenstra and Hanson (1996) also consider the effects of capital mobility on relative wages. They develop a theoretical model in which an increase in the capital stock of developing countries relative to that of advanced countries decreases the relative wage of unskilled workers in both regions and increases the prices of the more-skilled activities. They also examine empirical evidence and find these patterns in U.S.-Mexican economic relations.

11. Krugman (1994, p. A15 national edition, p. A17 local edition).

The fall in K_d, by contrast, releases *both* L_u and L_s from the D_u sector, forcing their reemployment in the nontradeables sector. Specifically, $\partial L_{un} = -\partial K_d > 0$ and $\partial L_{us} = -\alpha(\partial K_d) > 0$. According to equation 5-7', the relative wage of skilled and unskilled workers is governed by the relative supplies of L_{un} and L_{sn}. Letting σ_{su} be the Hicks elasticity of substitution between L_{un} and L_{us} in the production of N, we can write:

$$w_u - w_s = -(l_u - l_s)/\sigma_{su} \tag{5-15}$$

where the lower-case variable signifies the proportionate change of the upper-case variable (that is, $w_u = \partial W_u/W_u$). According to equation 5-15, the proportionate widening of the gap between low-skilled and high-skilled workers is *determined in the nontradeables market,* according to the changing ratio of unskilled to skilled workers in the N sector. As long as the ratio of unskilled to skilled labor released from D_u is greater than the preexisting ratio of unskilled to skilled labor in nontradeables, the nontradeables sector must become more intensive in unskilled labor than it was previously. To absorb this higher proportion of unskilled labor, the relative wage of unskilled labor must decline.

Import Competition with Monopolistic, Import-Competing Sector

Consider now a slightly different mechanism, depending on imperfect competition, that leads to the same shift of unskilled labor from tradeables to nontradeables. Return to the orginal model, equations 5-1–5-14. Suppose, however, that K_d is fixed, with no mobility of capital abroad ($K_f = 0$) or profits from foreign investment. Foreign production is now limited by the size of the *foreign-owned* capital stock, so that equation 5-3 becomes

$$F_u = K^*_f \tag{5-3'}$$

Suppose also that the domestic U industry is monopolized, while the foreign industry is made up of competitive firms with a total output Fu. Thus, the foreign imports represent a *competitive fringe* of the domestic monopolist. We introduce one more key assumption. Suppose now that the production technology $D_u = \min(L_{ud}, K_d)$ represents the low-marginal-cost method of production of U, but there exists another method potentially available at world price P^* (this could represent an alternative imported input, for which the United States is a price taker). Assuming that $W_u < P^*$, it pays to use the technology in equation 5-2, because marginal costs are lower. Even in this case, however, the domestic monopolist will be unable to charge a price higher than P^*, because a price of P^* would elicit an infinitely elastic supply of the high-cost alternative to U.

The demand curve for the domestic monopolist is easily found. The derived demand for U is determined in equation 5-1 such that $\partial S/\partial U = P_u$, for the price range $0 \leq P_u \leq P^*$. This implicitly determines a market-demand equation $U = U(L_s, P_u)$. Because $U = D_u + F_u$, the derived demand for the domestic producer is $D_u = U(L_s, P_u) - F_u$. For the monopolist, L_s and F_u are given, and P_u is the choice variable. For an inelastic derived demand for U, the domestic monopolist should set the domestic price at the limit price P^*—that is, at the maximum level such that the input at price P^* will not be used. Then, domestic production is equal to $U(L_s, P^*) - F_u$. Note that the foreign competitive firms also sell into the U.S. market at the price P^*, earning pure quasi rents on K^*_f. These quasi rents are earned because of the fixed, short-run supply of foreign capacity in the production of U.

Notice, then, what happens when the foreign firms increase their production and export capacity as the result of an increase in K^*_f. The U.S. monopolist keeps the U.S. market price unchanged at P^*, and absorbs the increased foreign competition by a one-for-one reduction of domestic production. Therefore, as F_u increases by one unit, D_u falls by one unit. This prompts an equivalent reduction in employment of L_{uu}, and the laid-off, unskilled worker must find work in the nontradables sector. The increased nontradable-sector employment results in a fall in the marginal physical product of labor in the nontradeables sector—that is, $\partial N/\partial L_{un}$ falls. Also, P_n falls as the result of a rising supply of N combined with a negative-income effect on the demand for N (monopoly profits are diminished by the increased competition from abroad). Thus, the wage of unskilled workers will fall, because $W_u = P_n(\partial N/\partial L_{un})$, and both P_n and $\partial N/\partial L_{un}$ decline.

Note that in this model, the trade balance must be zero, so that the imports of F_u are paid for by the exports of S. Higher F_u (caused by a rise in K^*_f) prompts a negative-income effect, which causes a decline in domestic consumption of the tradeable final good S. This leads to a larger trade surplus of S, which pays for the imports of F_u.

We can easily extend the model to include employment of skilled labor in D_u and N, as we did before. Once again, the rise in K^*_f will elicit a shift of *both* unskilled and skilled labor to the nontradeables sector. As long as the ratio of unskilled to skilled workers rises in the nontradeables sector as a result of this influx of labor, the relative wage of unskilled workers will decline.

Increasing Division of Labor and the Scope of the Market

A third possibility for a fall in W_u/W_s emerges from the classical idea that the division of labor in the economy is limited by the scope of the market.

Frank and Cook have argued that the rising inequality in U.S. labor markets results partly from the fact that global markets extend the ability of the top-quality producers to reach an international marketplace.[12] We use the framework of Murphy and colleagues (hereafter the MSV study) to construct a simple example of how internationalization can widen wage inequalities.[13] Once again, to highlight the differences with the HOS model, we study a case in which relative output market prices are unchanging.

Suppose that there are a number of goods that may all be produced by a standardized technology

$$Q_i = L_i, \tag{5-16}$$

$$L_i = L_{ui} + L_{si}. \tag{5-17}$$

Output of sector i is equal to total labor input, and labor input is equal to the simple sum of unskilled and skilled labor. According to this technology, there is no market advantage to have labor skills. Now, suppose that for each sector, there is an alternative advanced technology that requires a fixed cost F of skilled labor and then allows production at a lower marginal cost.

$$Q_i = \theta \, (L_{iu} + L_{si}), \text{ with } \theta > 1 \text{ and fixed cost } L_{si} = F. \tag{5-18}$$

Now suppose that there are N sectors in total, but that $NF > L_s$. There is a shortage of skilled workers, so that only a fraction of sectors will be able to engage in high-technology production. For simplicity, we will assume that $F = L_s$, that is, *there is just enough skilled labor in the economy to support high-tech production in a single sector.* (This assumption could easily be relaxed; we take the simplest case for purposes of illustration.) The scarcity of skilled labor will allow it to earn a premium once high-technology production is introduced.

We also assume that the high technology is proprietary, monopolized by a single firm in each sector; high-tech production, if carried out at all, will be carried out by a monopolist. Finally, we assume that market demand is governed by a standard CES utility function over the N goods, of the form

$$U(C_1, C_2, C_3, \ldots, C_N) = [(1/N)\Sigma \, C_i\text{-}\rho]^{-1/\rho}.$$

Of course, this leads to a market demand for output of sector i given by

$$Ci = (1/N)(Pi/P)^{-\sigma}Y \text{ with } \sigma = 1/(1 + \rho), \tag{5-20}$$

where P is the true price index corresponding to equation 5-19. We assume that $\rho > 0$, so that $\sigma < 1$—that is, market demand for each output is price inelastic.

12. Frank and Cook (1995).
13. Murphy, Shleifer, and Vishny (1989).

Consider first a closed-economy variant of the model. We start by analyzing the equilibrium in which all sectors use low-technology production. Labor is divided equally among the N sectors. Setting the wage of unskilled workers as numeraire, it is clear that $W_s = P_i = W_u = 1$ for all goods i. Production is simply $Q_i = (L_u + L_s)/N$.

Now we ask whether any single monopolist will choose to engage in high-tech production, assuming that the other $N - 1$ sectors are engaged in low-tech production. Notice that the monopolist's pricing strategy is straightforward. Because the elasticity of demand for sector i is $\sigma < 1$ and is therefore always inelastic, the monopolist will raise the price as high as possible without provoking entry by the low-technology competitive fringe. In other words, the monopolist will set the price of sector i at 1 (or just infinitesimally below 1). Market demand will therefore be Y/N. Total marginal production costs are $(Y/N)/\theta$; fixed costs are $W_s F$, and profits π_i will be

$$\pi_i = (Y/N) - (Y/N)/\theta - W_s F \tag{5-21}$$

Notice that W_s must be greater than or equal to 1, because skilled workers can always earn a wage equal to 1 by working in low-tech production. Initially, with no high-tech production in the economy, $W_s = 1$. Because $Y = L_u + L_s$, the conditions for positive profits in the introduction of high-tech production is

$$\pi_i \geq 0 \text{ iff } F \leq [(\theta - 1)/\theta](L_u + L_s)/N. \tag{5-22}$$

Clearly, if θ is close to 1 and $(L_u + L_s)/N$ is small, then profits would be negative and the high technology will not be adopted. Market demand, measured as average employment per sector, is too small to cover the fixed cost F.[14]

When the economy is opened to trade, all sectors are subject to the aggregate demand given by

$$C_i = (1/N)(P_i/P)-\sigma(Y + Y^*). \tag{5-23}$$

Notice that world demand has now replaced domestic demand in each sector's demand function. A potential high-tech monopolist would now be

14. As MSV point out, it may be possible that high-tech production is feasible if a *group* of high-tech monopolists simultaneously choose the high-tech production strategy, because the increased output of each one could spill over to raise the market demand of the others. We have ruled out this particular possibility for simplicity, by assuming that there is only enough skilled labor to supply one high-tech sector.

able to export to world markets. Once again, the monopolist would set a market price of 1. The opening of world trade would therefore not change the relative prices of goods, but it would expand the market, thereby allowing a change in production technology. It is easy to check the new zero profit condition, under the initial condition that $W_s = 1$. We find

$$\pi_i \geq 0 \text{ iff } F \leq [(\theta - 1)/\theta](L_u + L_s + Y^*)/N. \tag{5-22'}$$

Clearly, for a large enough value of Y^*, it is possible for high-technology production to be profitable in the open economy, when it is not in the closed economy.

Assuming that high-technology production is profitable, all potential monopolists will bid for the skilled labor. The skilled wage will rise until the point where the pure profits of high-tech production are exhausted; that is, the profits are converted entirely into quasi rents earned by the scarce factor, skilled labor. From equation 5-22', and the zero-profit condition $\pi_i = 0$, we find that

$$W_s = [(\theta - 1)/\theta](L_u + L_s + D^*)/(F^*N) > 1. \tag{5-24}$$

The conclusion is that trade liberalization raises the real wage of high-skilled workers, even though it does not affect relative output prices or the real wage of low-skilled workrs. The larger world market allows for a change in technology to the benefit of high-skilled workers. Note that low-skilled workers do not suffer, because they face the same wages and output prices as in the closed economy. The skilled workers, by contrast, enjoy an absolute gain in utility.

Multiple Channels of Influence

We have identified several channels through which increased U.S. trade with developing countries can lower the relative wages of unskilled labor: the HOS effect, operating through a fall in P_u; capital flows from the United States to developing countries, reducing the capital stock and thereby the employment of unskilled workers in manufacturing; increased import competition facing a domestic monopolist, thereby prompting a loss of manufacturing-sector jobs of unskilled labor; and an increased division of labor (proxied by a technology with higher fixed costs, but lower variable costs), made possible by an expansion of the market.

No theoretical, simulation, or econometric model yet exists that integrates these various forces, but there is no reason why they cannot all operate simultaneously. Labor markets tend to be segmented in the short term, so that workers in different sectors might be subjected to different kinds of influences. In some sectors, the physical capital is easily transported to low-wage countries; in other sectors, increased import competition causes job losses of domestic monopolists. In still other sectors, a fall in the relative price of unskilled-intensive goods delivers HOS-type effects, even though they apply to just a subset of the labor market.

For this reason alone, the search for trade effects should not be limited to a specific phenomenon, such as the fall in P_u. It is not correct to conclude that trade has had little effect on W_u/W_s because P_u has not declined, even putting aside the question of the empirical evidence on the trend in P_u. Economists will have to look over the range of evidence—trade flows, employment changes, shifts in technology, and price changes—to reach an appropriate assessment of the effects of trade on wage inequality.

Empirical Implications

Earlier studies have uncovered several important facts concerning trends in U.S. trade, wages, and employment:

—U.S. trade with low-wage countries tends to conform broadly to the expected HOS pattern. On average, the U.S. exports skilled-labor-intensive goods and imports unskilled-labor-intensive goods from the developing countries.

—U.S. trade with low-wage countries increased significantly during the 1980s, with trade measured as a percentage of manufacturing value-added and economywide gross domestic product (GDP).

—The timing of the widening of wage inequality is similar to the timing of increased U.S. trade with low-wage countries (increasing throughout the 1980s), though the timing of both shifts is imprecise, with the dating of turning points depending on the particular measures that are examined.

The linkages of changing trade patterns to changing employment patterns have been studied in many works.[15] The first two of these studies examine the employment content of changing net trade vectors. As predicted by HOS, the rise of net imports from developing countries is unskilled-labor-intensive relative to the rest of the manufacturing sector.

This can be seen in table 5-1, which shows the factor content of the changing net trade with developing and developed countries.[16] One hundred thirty-one manufacturing sectors are ranked by decile, in order of decreasing

15. Borjas, Freeman, and Katz (1992); Sachs and Shatz (1994); Saeger (1995).
16. Reproduced from Sachs and Shatz (1994, table 13, p. 29).

Table 5-1. *Accounting for Trade Effects on U.S. Employment*[a]
Percent

| | Change in total employment | | |
| | Developing-country trade | Developed-country trade | All trade |
Skill decile			
1	0.2	12.2	12.3
2	–0.9	0.9	0.0
3	–2.8	–1.7	–4.4
4	–2.3	2.9	0.5
5	–2.0	–1.6	–3.6
6	–5.5	–2.4	–7.9
7	–5.2	–1.4	–6.6
8	–2.6	–2.1	–4.7
9	–3.4	–6.7	–10.1
10	–23.5	–3.6	–27.1
All manufacturing[b]	–5.7	–0.2	–5.9
Production workers[b]	–6.2	–1.0	–7.2
Nonproduction workers[b]	–3.3	2.2	–2.1

Sources: Authors' calculations described in the text; and from Sachs and Shatz (1994), based on National Bureau of Economic Research Manufacturing Productivity Database; U.S. Department of Commerce Trade statistics; and U.S. Dept. of Commerce, Bureau of Economic Analysis 1987 annual input-output tables.

a. Import figures, originally reported on a customs-value basis, have been increased by factors for c.i.f. value (cost, insurance, and freight), tariffs, and tariff equivalents of quotas.

skill intensity. (In this study, skilled labor is equated with nonproduction workers and unskilled labor is equated with production workers.) For each decile and for all manufacturing, we measure the implicit decline in employment of skilled (nonproduction), unskilled (production), and all workers due to the rise of net imports from developing countries, developed countries, and all countries between 1978 and 1990, compared with a counterfactual in which net trade relative to final demand in each sector is assumed to remain at its 1978 level. By this definition of the counterfactual, increased trade with low-wage countries reduced the employment of low-skilled workers by 6.2 percent and that of high-skilled workers by 3.3 percent between 1978 and 1990. Trade with all countries reduced low-skilled employment by 7.2 percent and high-skilled employment by 2.1 percent. In the lowest-skilled decile, 27.1 percent of all jobs in 1978 were eliminated by trade. Trade with low-wage countries caused 23.5 percentage points of the change, whereas trade with advanced countries caused only 3.6 percentage points of it.

Perhaps equally important, the net import vector is unskilled-labor-intensive relative to the *rest of the economy* as well. This suggests that labor shed from the manufacturing sector would require a rise in the ratio L_u/L_s in the nontradables sector. We make this argument in two steps. First, Saeger shows that increased net imports from developing countries are indeed associated with overall "deindustrialization," defined in this case as a declining share of the labor force in manufacturing.[17] *Controlling for per capita income and other structural characteristics of the economy (for example, changes in natural resource production as a percent of GDP), increased net imports of manufactures from developing countries are associated with decreases in overall employment in manufacturing, measured as a percent of total employment.* On average, within the Organization for Economic Cooperation and Development (OECD) economies, the rising net imports from developing countries in the 1970s and 1980s can be associated with a decline in the share of manufacturing employment in overall employment of 2 to 3 percentage points. For the United States, Saeger estimates the effect to be a decline of 2.7 percentage points, about one-third of the total decrease in the manufacturing share of employment.

The labor released from U.S. manufacturing as a result of increased net imports from developing countries must be absorbed by the nontradeables sector (mainly services), or by unemployment, as is more typically the case in the European context of downwardly rigid wages. It is therefore necessary to compare the skill intensity of the labor released from import-competing sectors and the skill intensity of the nontradeables sectors. For this purpose, we equate unskilled workers with a high school education or less, and skilled workers with more than a high school education. (We measure L_u and L_s in this way, rather than as production versus nonproduction workers, because the education-based measure is a more appropriate yardstick than the production-based measure for the nonmanufacturing sector.)

One categorization is shown in table 5-2, where we compare the (education-based) ratio L_u/L_s for various manufacturing sectors. We first rank the sectors into deciles, from lowest L_u/L_s to highest, grouping the industries so that each decile has approximately the same level of 1979 employment. We also take two weighted sums of L_u/L_s over 131 manufacturing sectors. First, we weight by each sector's share in U.S. manufacturing exports to developing countries, w_i^x, and then by each sector's share in manufacturing imports from developing countries, $w_i m$.[18] We see that U.S. exports to developing countries are more

17. Saeger (1995).

18. The weights $w_i x$ is defined as $X_i/\Sigma X_j$, where X_i is U.S. exports to low-wage countries from sector i, and ΣX_j is total U.S. manufacturing exports to low-wage countries (the sum over all sectors). The weights $w_i m$ is defined as $M_i/\Sigma M_j$, where M_i is U.S. imports from low-wage countries in sector i, and ΣM_j is total U.S. manufacturing imports from low-wage countries.

Table 5-2. *Skill Level of Manufacturing, 1979 and 1990*

	1979	1990
A. High school to college employment ratio by decile[a]		
Education decile[b]		
1	0.89	0.47
2	1.28	0.81
3	1.72	1.05
4	2.08	1.33
5	2.47	1.79
6	2.63	1.78
7	3.09	2.21
8	3.54	2.46
9	4.59	3.84
10	6.98	4.42
B. Trade-weighted averages of high school to college employment ratio, all manufacturing		
Weights[c]		
Import	4.05	2.87
Export	2.22	1.61

Source: National Bureau of Economic Research, Current Population Survey (CPS), annual earnings file extracts and U.S. Department of Commerce trade statistics.

a. High school workers are those with a high school education or less. College workers are those with at least some college education. In both cases, only those workers with a full-time job during the week before the CPS was taken were included.

b. Industries are ranked from high skill to low skill, according to the ratio of high school workers to college workers and then grouped so that each decile has approximately equal levels of 1979 employment.

c. Weights are sector shares of exports or imports to or from the top nine less-developed country (LDC) trade partners (see text).

skilled labor intensive than U.S. imports from developing countries and that the relationship holds through the 1980s.

In table 5-3, we show the same ratios, L_u/L_s, for manufacturing as a whole, the nontraded sector (including government), and the private, non-traded sector. It is clear that manufacturing is far less skilled than the

---

Rather than using trade with all developing countries, we use trade with only the top nine developing-country trade partners: Brazil, China, Hong Kong, Korea, Mexico, Malaysia, Singapore, Taiwan, and Thailand. These nine countries accounted for 79 percent of the growth in trade from LDCs between 1978 and 1990. In 1978 they accounted for 16.2 percent of all imports to the United States and 13.6 percent of all exports from the United States. By 1990, they accounted for 26.8 percent of all U.S. imports and 21.9 percent of all U.S. exports. In addition, in 1978 they accounted for 55.6 percent of all developing-country imports to the United States and 37.2 percent of all developing-country exports from the United States. By 1990, these figures were 73.6 percent and 62.1 percent, respectively.

Table 5-3. *High School and College Employment in Manufacturing and the Nontraded Sector, 1979*[a,b]

In thousands

	High school	College	L_u/L_s
Manufacturing	14,378.4	5,991.0	2.40
Nontraded[c]	26,198.0	22,278.2	1.18
Private nontraded[d]	23,925.7	19,825.1	1.21

Source: National Bureau of Economic Research, CPS, annual earnings file

a. High school workers are those with a high school education or less. College workers are those with at least some college education. In both cases, only those workers with a full-time job during the week before the CPS was taken were included.

b. The mining sector and the agriculture, forestry, and fishing sector were omitted from all calculations.

c. The nontraded sector includes construction; transport, communication, and public utilities; wholesale and retail trade; finance, insurance, and real estate; services; and public administration.

d. The private nontraded sector includes all of the above except public administration.

nontraded sector, whether the latter includes government or not. Comparing table 5-2 with table 5-3, it is also clear that both the import-competing and export-competing sectors of manufacturing are less skill intensive than the nontraded sector, though the import-competing industries are far less so. A cutback in manufacturing employment (and especially import-competing manufacturing employment) will therefore release *relatively unskilled* workers into the service sector. This will lead to a fall in the relative wage of unskilled workers, with the effect being larger should those employees come from the import-competing sector of manufacturing.

The precise magnitude of this effect is of course much harder to determine. As a crude estimate, we examine the following counterfactual. How much lower would L_{sn} and L_{un} have been if the net trade vector with developing countries had remained unchanged after 1978, so that labor would not have been "released" from the manufacturing sector? (As before, we define "unchanged" in the counterfactual as an unchanging ratio of net trade to final demand in each manufacturing sector.) Panel A of table 5-4 shows the results of the counterfactual when workers are categorized as low skilled if they have a high school education or less, and high skilled if they have some college. We estimate that due to changes in net trade, manufacturing lost 5.5 percent of its 1979 low-skilled workers and 4.9 percent of its high-skilled workers.

Because the ratio L_u/L_s is much higher in manufacturing than nontradeables, this translates into a far higher ratio of L_u/L_s "released" into the nontraded sector than is initially present in nontradeables, as shown in Panel B of table 5-4. That panel also shows that these extra employees

Table 5-4. *Effects of Trade on Manufacturing Employment, 1979–90*

A. Change in employment by country group and education group (percent)[a,b,c]

	LDC trade	Developed-country trade	All trade
All employees	–3.7	–1.6	–5.3
High school employees	–4.0	–1.5	–5.5
College employees	–3.0	–2.0	–4.9

B. Employees released from manufacturing due to trade (in thousands)

		New nontraded Lu/Ls	
High school	College	All nontraded[d]	Private nontraded[e]
790.8	293.6	1.20	1.23

Sources: Authors' calculations from the National Bureau of Economic Research CPS annual earnings file extracts; and U.S. Department of Commerce (1993, annual input-output tables); National Bureau of Economic Research Manufacturing Productivity Database; and U.S. Department of Commerce trade statistics.

a. High school workers are those with a high school education or less. College workers are those with at least some college education. Only those workers with a full-time job during the week before the CPS was taken were included.

b. The change in net imports for the computer sector has been constrained to equal zero. In addition, eight industries were treated as pure intermediate-goods industries, so that they were considered as producing no output for final demand. Therefore, changes in imports or exports would not have had the multiplier effects seen in other industries. The eight industries and their U.S. Bureau of Economic Analysis (BFA) codes are:

16 Broad, narrow fabrics, mills   37 Primary iron and steel
25 Paperboard containers   38 Primary nonferrous metals
28 Plastics and synthetics   39 Metal containers
33 Leather tanning and finishing   57 Electronic components

BEA codes were used, rather than Standard Industrial Classification (SIC), because the input-output tables used in the calculations are in BEA codes. Also, the calculations use 1979 employment data and 1978 trade data. Also, LDC trade for the calculations includes all developing countries, not just the top nine, as used elsewhere.

c. The mining sector and the agriculture, forestry, and fishing sector were omitted from all calculations.

d. The nontraded sector includes construction; transport, communication, and public utilities; wholesale and retail trade; finance, insurance, and real estate; services; and public administration.

e. The private nontraded sector includes all of the above except public administration.

would have increased L_u/L_s to 1.20 (from 1.18) for the whole nontraded sector, and to 1.23 (from 1.21) for the private, nontraded sector, assuming that the private sector rather than the government absorbed them.

Table 5-5 then shows the effect on wages. For the whole nontraded sector, with the counterfactual as a baseline, we see that L_{un}/L_{sn} is estimated to have risen by 1.68 percent as a result of the shifts in net trade. We can therefore calculate the decline in W_u/W_s associated with the rise in L_{un}/L_{sn}. Assuming an elasticity of substitution of 1/3 between L_u and L_s, the relative wage W_u/W_s would have declined by 5.04 percent. For an elasticity of substitution of 1/2, W_u/W_s would have declined by 3.36 percent. For the private, nontraded sector, had government not absorbed any workers, L_{un}/L_{sn}

Table 5-5. *Change in Nontraded Skill Levels and Wages due to Trade*[a,b]
Rise in Lu/Ls, and Change in Wu/Ws, in the Nontraded Sector

	Public and private nontraded[c]	Private nontraded[d]
Percent change in L_u/L_s	1.68	1.80
Percent change in W_u/W_s		
Elasticity of substitution = 1/3	5.04	5.39
Elasticity of substitution = 1/2	3.36	3.40

Sources: Authors' counterfactual calculations from the National Bureau of Economic Research, CPS, annual earnings file extracts; and U.S. Department of Commerce (1987 annual input-output tables).

a. High school workers are those with a high school education or less. College workers are those with at least some college education. In both cases, only those workers with a full-time job in the week before the CPS was taken are included.

b. The mining sector and the agriculture, forestry, and fishing sector were omitted from all calculations.

c. The nontraded sector includes construction; transport, communication, and public utilities; wholesale and retail trade; finance, insurance, and real estate; services; and public administration.

d. The private nontraded sector includes all of the above except public administration.

is estimated to have risen by 1.80 percent as a result of the shifts in net trade. With an elasticity of substitution of 1/3 between L_u and L_s, the relative wage W_u/W_s would have declined by 5.39 percent. For an elasticity of substitution of 1/2, W_u/W_s would have declined by 3.40 percent. Unfortunately, we lack appropriate econometric estimates of the short-run and long-run elasticities of substitution between L_{un} and L_{sn} to judge which of these estimates in more appropriate.

In addition to "deindustrialization" due to increased trade with developing countries, W_u/W_s can fall simply as the result of a decline in P_u, even without a decline in manufacturing employment, as we know from the HOS model. Much of the empirical debate over the past two years has revolved around the question of whether P_u has in fact declined, with Bhagwati in particular asserting that there is no evidence of a decline in P_u, and therefore no evidence for an effect of trade on wages. Even though the "therefore" is theoretically unjustified, the evidence on P_u is empirically important, if not definitive.

In fact, the quality of data on international trade prices leaves much to be desired. First, recall the basis of the HOS theory. (In the discussion that follows, we drop the convention that $P_s = 1$, and therefore carry a term equal to the nominal change in P_s.) In a model of two goods and two factors and with no specialization, there is a one-to-one relationship between the percentage change in P_u/P_s and the percentage change in W_u/W_s. Specifically, with technology given by $S = S(L_{ss}, L_{us})$ and $U = U(L_{us}, L_{uu})$, where each function is constant returns to scale, we know

$$p_s = \beta_{ss} w_s + (1 - \beta_{ss}) w_u, \tag{5-25}$$
$$p_u = \beta_{su} w_s + (1 - \beta_{su}) w_u,$$

where β_{ss} is the share of skilled labor in total output of sector S, and β_{su} is the share of skilled labor in total output of sector U. By assumption, $\beta_{ss} > \beta_{su}$. The lower-case variables p_s, p_u, w_s, and w_u, represent the log changes of the respective upper-case variables. It is immediate that $(w_s - w_u) = \gamma (p_s - p_u)$, where $\gamma = [1/(\beta_{ss} - \beta_{su})] > 1$. This is an implication of the famous "magnification effect": the proportionate change in relative wages is greater than the proportionate change in relative prices.

The simple relationship between $(w_s - w_u)$ and $(p_s - p_u)$ becomes more complicated if we take into account the distinction between value-added and gross output, and the role of technical change. In particular, suppose that the gross output functions can be written:

$$Q_s = Q_s[S(L_{ss}, L_{us}), M_s] T_s, \text{ and}$$
$$Q_u = Q_u(U(L_{us}, L_{uu}), M_u) T_u. \tag{5-26}$$

Here Q represents gross output. T_s and T_u are the pure levels of technical progress in gross output in the S and the U sectors, respectively. S and U are now defined as the *value-added* functions of the two sectors. M_s and M_u are the intermediate inputs that are combined with value-added to produce gross output.

Now, P_s and P_u are generally measured as gross output prices. Note, however, that there is no simple relationship between these gross output changes and relative wage changes, because of the intervening effects of intermediate input prices and technological change. The relationshp between output prices and input prices is given as follows

$$p_s = \{\beta_{vs}[\beta_{ss} w_s + (1 - \beta_{ss}) w_u] + (1 - \beta_{vs}) p_m\} - \tau_s, \tag{5-27}$$
$$p_u = \{\beta_{vu}[\beta_{su} w_s + (1 - \beta_{su}) w_u] + (1 - \beta_{vu}) p_m\} - \tau_u.$$

In this expression, β_{vs} is the share of value added in gross output in sector S. Now, β_{ss} is defined as the share of skilled labor in value added in S (rather than as the share of skilled labor in gross output). τ_s is the proportionate change in TFP, and p_m is the proportionate change in materials prices. Other variables are defined analogously. We see that before relating relative price changes to relative wage changes, we must adjust the relative price changes to account for technology and intermediate inputs. In particular, the revised expression is:

$$(w_s - w_u) = \Gamma (p_s' - p_u') \tag{5-28}$$
$$| \quad p_s' = [(p_s + \tau_s) - (1 - \beta_{vs}) p_m]/\beta_{vs},$$
$$| \quad p_u' = [(p_u + \tau_u) - (1 - \beta_{vu}) p_m]/\beta_{vu}.$$

Price changes should be adjusted for changes in total factor productivity, and for movements of intermediate-goods prices. In some contexts, p_s' and p_u' are referred to as changes in "effective" prices.

Consider one relevant example. If the price of skilled-labor-intensive goods declines, but the reason is a *rise* in TFP in the S sector, there is no reason to expect a decline in W_s/W_u. For example, the sharp decline in computer prices in the past decade is *not* a cause for the decline of the relative wage of skilled engineers employed intensively in computer production, because (quality-adjusted) computer prices are falling as a result of technological progress.

With the backdrop of equation 5-28, consider just how flimsy Bhagwati's rejection is of the trade-wage linkage based on the ostensible evidence of relative price movements. The data on trade prices to which Bhagwati refers, from the study by Lawrence and Slaughter, are subject to at least five serious problems.[19] First, out of 143 three-digit manufacturing sectors, the import price data cover only fifty-one sectors, and only thirty start in 1980 and run through the whole decade. Likewise, the export price data cover only forty-six sectors, and only nineteen start in 1980. Second, the trade data do not adjust for intermediate input prices. Third, the trade data do not adjust for productivity changes. Fourth, the trade data (like many kinds of price data) do not adequately control for quality changes, so that the price increases are overstated for commodities with important quality improvements, such as computers. Fifth, trade data often do not reflect actual transactions costs, because an important proportion of manufacturing trade is actually within affiliates of the same firm. Enterprises use internal transfer prices for tax and other purposes that may be very different from prices that apply in arms-length transactions. We should then add the important theoretical point that *even small movements in relative prices could be associated with rather large movements in relative wages.*

If we compare domestic U.S. prices with the prices of U.S. imports and exports, we discover that the office-machinery sector (that is, computers) presents a special problem. There is a vast discrepancy between computer prices measured using the domestic prices, constructed by the U.S. Bureau of Economic Analysis, and the international trade prices, constructed by the U.S. Bureau of Labor Statistics. In particular, the domestic prices fall sharply, while the trade prices do not. This is probably because the trade prices do not adequately reflect the improving quality of the computers in international trade (so that the measured prices vastly understate the decline

19. Lawrence and Slaughter (1993).

of quality-adjusted prices). When we formally test the discrepancy between trade prices and domestic output prices for thirty overlapping
sectors, we can reject the hypothesis that the discrepancy in computer
prices is due merely to sampling error.[20] For this reason, we always add
a dummy variable for the computer sector in cross-sectoral price
equations.

The empirical question is whether the relative price of unskilled-intensive goods actually fell in the 1980s, as would be a necessary condition for
HOS effects to operate. To answer this question, we rely on two data sets.
For 1978–89, we use domestic output prices for 450 four-digit manufacturing sectors based on the 1972 Standard Industrial Classification (rather than
the 50 or so sectors used by Lawrence and Slaughter for which trade price
data are available for at least some time during the period 1980–90).[21] For
1989–95, we use domestic output prices for 410 four-digit manufacturing
sectors based on the 1987 SIC. These data were developed and kindly
provided by Alan Krueger, whose 1995 study reaches similar conclusions to
those reported here. Using a concordance between the 1972 and 1987 SIC
classifications, kindly provided by Wayne Gray, we also merge the two data
sets to construct a single time series over the entire interval 1978–95. For
both data sets, we can construct value-added prices as well as gross output
prices. For the earlier data set, we can also try to adjust for productivity,
using an estimate of sectoral TFP developed by Gray.[22] Although these TFP
estimates are carefully made given the data, they are no doubt subject to
enormous error themselves, so that we can not rely heavily on the TFP-
adjusted estimates.

Letting p_i be the proportionate change in output prices of sector i, we ask
whether p_i rises less (or falls more) for unskilled-labor-intensive sectors. Of
course, the theoretically correct measure is not output prices per se, but

---

20. Let P_{ti} be the trade price index for sector i, and P_{di} be the domestic price
index for sector i, both measured in 1990 with a base $P_{ti} = P_{di} = 1$ in 1978. We
assume that discrepancies in the two prices are due to random errors, plus a fixed
effect for the computer sector, so that:

$$\ln(P_{ti}/P_{di}) = \beta_0 + \beta_1 \theta_i + \varepsilon_i$$

where $\theta_i = 1$ for i = computers, and qi = 0 otherwise. We test the null hypothesis that
$\beta_1 = 0$, which we reject at $p = .0001$. Only one other industry dummy variable is
found to be significant, that for sugar and confectionary products, which reflects
the discrepancy between the U.S. domestic and international trade prices caused by
the highly protectionist U.S. trade regime for sugar.

21. Lawrence and Slaughter (1993).

22. Gray (1989, 1992).

rather output prices adjusted for intermediate input prices and technical change. As a basic regression model, we use the following:

$$dp_i = \beta_0 + \beta_{1[L_u/(L_u + L_s)]_i} + \beta_{2Z_i} + \varepsilon_i. \tag{5-29}$$

The change in prices over a particular time period is regressed on the sectoral share of unskilled labor in total employment, and in principle, on industry characteristics, Z_i. In fact, the only variable that we include for Z_i is a dummy variable for the four-digit SIC computer sectors, which we include for reasons just explained. The HOS hypothesis is that $\beta_1 < 0$, that is, unskilled-labor-intensive sectors experienced smaller increases in prices than skilled-labor-intensive sectors. We use several variants for the time period and for measuring prices, including gross output prices, value-added prices, and value-added prices adjusted for TFP. As in Krueger, we run the regression with weighted least squares, with weights equal to the value of shipments of the sector at the start of the sample period.[23] Our proxy for L_u is the number of production workers, and for L_s the number of nonproduction workers. Thus, $L_u/(L_u + L_s)$ is the share of production workers in total employment.

The main result, shown in table 5-6, is that *there is consistent evidence that the price increases in L_u-intensive sectors were considerably below those of L_s-intensive sectors during 1978–95.* According to the estimate in column 3, based on valued-added prices and the entire time period, an industry with unskilled workers as 30 percent of its total work force (that is, $L_u/(L_u + L_s) = 0.3$) would have experienced a 40 percent rise in its value-added price from 1978 to 1995 relative to an industry with a skill ratio of 90 percent. The ratios of 30 percent and 90 percent are approximately the bounds of the highest-skilled and lowest-skilled industries in manufacturing.

Table 5-7 shows some examples of price changes from industries within the top two and bottom two skill deciles.[24] The table also shows weighted averages of price changes for the deciles indicated. The weights are each industry's share of its decile's 1978 value of shipments. The computer industries, SIC 357, were not included in the weighted averages because of the data problems mentioned earlier. Weighted average prices rose in all deciles for all time periods, but the increases for the top deciles are well above those for the bottom deciles.

23. Krueger (1995).
24. The deciles, please note, were formed from 131 three-digit industries grouped from highest skilled (Decile 1) to lowest skilled (Decile 10). We then labelled each four-digit industry with the decile of its three-digit group. For example, 2086, soft drinks, is within 208, beverages, which is in Decile 1.

Table 5-6. *Regressions of Change in Price on Skill Level, 1978–95*

	Dependent price variable[a]							
	Value added			Effective value added:	Output			Effective output:
	1978–89	1989–95	1978–95	1978–89	1978–89	1989–95	1978–95	1978–89
Independent variables								
Skill ratio[b]	−0.34[c]	−0.36[c]	−0.81[d]	−0.12	−0.26[d]	−0.15[d]	−0.45[d]	−0.18[d]
	(1.99)	(2.44)	(3.32)	(1.29)	(3.95)	(4.23)	(5.32)	(2.42)
Computer dummy[e]	−2.78d	−0.14	−0.62	−0.23[c]	−1.66[d]	−0.13	−0.53[d]	−1.61[d]
	(14.83)	(0.38)	(1.18)	(2.21)	(22.84)	(1.40)	(2.92)	(19.70)
Constant	0.63[d]	0.41[d]	1.12[d]	0.65[d]	0.66[d]	0.23[d]	0.92[d]	0.59[d]
	(4.95)	(3.79)	(6.12)	(8.97)	(13.31)	(8.80)	(14.49)	(10.65)
Adjusted R^2	0.33	0.01	0.02	0.01	0.54	0.04	0.07	0.47
N	450	410	410	450	450	410	410	449
Year of shipments value weight	1978	1989	1978	1978	1978	1989	1978	1978

Source: National Bureau of Economic Research Manufacturing Productivity Database and Krueger (1995). *t*-statistics are shown in parentheses.

a. The dependent variable is the log change of price during the indicated time period. Four price variables were used: value-added price; effective value-added price, which takes account of (TFP); output price; and effective output price, which is the annual change in output price plus the annual change in TFP.

b. The skill ratio is the 1978 ratio of production workers to total workers for each sector, so that a low skill-ratio number indicates a high-skill sector.

c. Significant at .05 level.

d. Significant at .01 level.

e. The computer dummy equals one for all four-digit industries within three-digit Sector 357 under the 1972 SIC.

Table 5-7. *Price Changes for Representative Industries, 1978–95*
Percent

	Value-added price			Output price		
	1978–89	1989–95	1978–95	1978–89	1989–95	1978–95
Decile 1[a]						
2711 Newspapers	86.5	37.3	123.8	79.0	31.1	110.1
2086 Soft drinks	69.8	20.3	90.1	57.6	12.8	70.4
Decile average[b]	53.3	14.0	67.3	57.3	17.9	75.2
Decile 2						
3724 Aircraft engines	56.2	30.8	87.0	54.6	21.3	75.9
Decile average	50.1	19.7	69.8	53.1	15.0	68.1
Decile 9						
3221 Glass containers	46.0	9.9	55.9	51.2	13.5	64.7
Decile average	44.5	13.7	58.2	43.4	14.3	57.7
Decile 10						
2211 Cotton weaving mills	17.2	7.9	25.1	30.5	7.5	38.0
2281 Yarn mills	5.1	−12.1	−7.0	28.2	1.8	30.0
Decile average	21.0	22.0	43.0	32.9	20.3	53.2

Source: National Bureau of Economic Research Manufacturing Productivity Database and Krueger (1995).

a. Deciles were formed by ranking 131, three-digit industries by proportion of unskilled to total employees and grouping the industries into ten equal groups, such that Decile 1 is the most skilled and Decile 10 is the least skilled. Production workers were used as a proxy for unskilled workers. Each four-digit industry was then deemed to be in the decile indicated by its three-digit group.

b. Decile averages are weighted averages, with the weights formed by 1978 industry shipments divided by 1978 decile shipments within each decile.

To provide an additional summary of the changes in relative prices, we calculate the percentage change in U.S. valued-added prices and effective prices weighted by the share of each sector's trade with developing countries.[25] An import price index is constructed by weighting value-added prices by weights w_i^m, the share of sector i in total U.S. manufacturing imports from developing countries. Similarly, an export price index is constructed using the weights w_i^x, the share of sector i in total U.S. manufacturing exports to developing countries. We see in figure 5-1 that the import-weighted price index falls steadily relative to the export price index, by 21.9 percentage points between 1978 and 1989, and by an additional 8.3 percentage points between 1989 and 1995.

Conclusions

In this chapter we have reviewed and extended the theoretical and empirical debate on the linkages of U.S.–developing country trade and U.S. wage inequality between skilled and unskilled workers. On a theoretical level, a wide range of models deliver the prediction that increased trade with low-wage countries will increase the wage inequality between high-skilled and low-skilled workers. It is misleading to pin all of our attention on the baseline HOS model, though that baseline model is indeed enormously important and the appropriate starting point of analysis. On the empirical front, a considerable range of evidence also points in the direction of at least some relative wage effects from trade. This evidence includes observed shifts in employment and their relationship to observed shifts in trade, the relative skill intensity of the manufacturing versus service sectors, and the trends of relative prices. Another look at the trade data, including measures of value-added prices rather than gross output prices, and an extension of the data to 1995, point in the direction of falling relative prices of commodities intensive in low-skilled labor, the kind of price effect that we expect from increased U.S.–developing country trade, and the kind that can contribute to a widening of wage inequalities between skilled and unskilled workers. Further work is now required to refine both the theoretical framework (for example, by integrating the range of HOS

25. Again, only the top nine developing-country trade partners are used.

Figure 5-1. *Growth in Trade-Weighted, Value-Added Manufacturing Prices, 1978–95*[a]

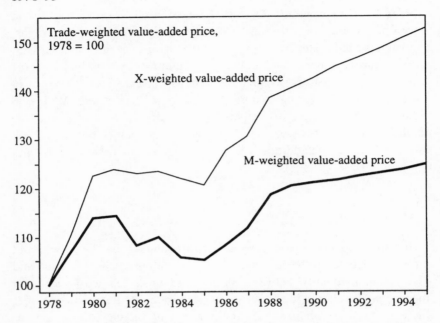

Sources: National Bureau of Economic Research Manufacturing Productivity Database and Krueger (1995).

a. Each observation is the weighted average of the value-added price for 105 three-digit manufacturing sectors. The weights are each sector's share of exports or imports to or from the U.S.'s top nine LDC trade partners: Brazil, China, Hong Kong, Korea, Malaysia, Mexico, Singapore, Taiwan, and Thailand.

Specifically, each observation is:

$\Sigma W_i P_i$, where W_i is the weight for sector i, and P_i is the value-added price for sector i.

Weights are computed as:

$T_i / \Sigma T_i$, where T_i is the trade flow, either exports or imports, for sector i to or from the nine LDCs.

The value-added price for each sector is computed based on the annual log change from the following equation:

$$p_o = \beta_v p_v + \beta_m p_m + \beta_e p_e,$$

where p is the log change in price from year t to $t + 1$, β is the share in total output, o is output, v is value added, m is materials, and e is energy. Share of value added in output is computed as one minus the share of materials in output.

Figures for 1990 to 1994 are a linear extrapolation of the 1989 to 1995 price change, as there were no data available for this period. For the change from 1989 to 1995, there were no separate cost and price figures for materials and energy. Rather, cost and price figures were available only for intermediates.

and non-HOS models into a more comprehensive model) and the empirical work (for example, by improving the estimates of effective prices, and by placing the data into a large-scale econometric or simulation framework to study general equilibrium implications of the observed trade, employment, and price changes).

Comment by Robert C. Feenstra

This chapter by Jeffrey Sachs and Howard Shatz is subtitled "Some New Results," which is apt, because it revisits a number of questions that have arisen in the controversy over trade and wages and also attempts to add some new information to the debate. I would say that it is not as successful as the authors' earlier paper in offering an overall perspective on the extent to which trade accounts for the decline in relative wages of blue-collar workers, but it does still offer some useful insights on specific questions.[26] Indeed, each issue analyzed by the authors should really be viewed as a *response* to those who believe that trade *does not* account for the decline in relative wages to any significant extent. In my comments, I attempt to explain exactly how the responses of Sachs and Shatz should be interpreted in light of existing literature, and how this chapter therefore fits into the ongoing debate.

Sachs and Shatz begin by outlining four predictions of the HOS model when trade barriers are reduced between two countries. Although some of these predictions are uncontroversial, others appear to contradict the experience of the United States: namely, that the relative price of unskilled-labor-intensive goods should fall, and that all industries should shift toward employing more unskilled labor. The former prediction contradicts the evidence presented by Lawrence and Slaughter and occupies the second half of the chapter and of my comments.[27] The latter prediction contradicts the relative movement toward skilled labor in many U.S. industries during the 1980s and is addressed by Sachs and Shatz using several theoretical models. The point of these models is that there are plausible circumstances under which increased trade can lead to a shift toward skilled labor in the manufacturing sector, in contrast to the HOS model, but in conformity to the observed facts.

The first of these models assumes that the skilled-labor-intensive good is produced using skilled labor and an intermediate input, which is itself produced with unskilled labor and capital. By introducing the vertical structure of production, this model bears some similarity to work a colleague and I have done concerning the outsourcing of production activities from a Northern to a Southern country.[28] But the similarity between these models is limited by some special assumption made by Sachs and Shatz. In

26. Sachs and Shatz (1994).
27. Lawrence and Slaughter (1993).
28. Feenstra and Hanson (1996).

particular, they assume that the intermediate input can be produced either at home or abroad, but must be produced using home capital. That is, the technology for producing the intermediate is apparently not available to any foreign firm. Home capital prefers to produce the intermediate input abroad, since the foreign wages of unskilled labor are lower (by assumption), but is restricted on the extent of its foreign investment. As these restrictions are relaxed, more capital flows abroad, which leads to less unskilled labor being employed in the production of the intermediate inputs at home. The only place where this unskilled labor can flow is to the nontradables sector, and in so moving, the relative wages of unskilled labor are reduced.

By aggregating the production activity of the intermediate input and the final good, this model predicts a shift in relative employment toward skilled labor, consistent with the U.S. experience. But surprisingly, the relative product prices are *constant*. This follows because home capital uses an identical technology for producing the intermediate input in either country, so that the outflow of this capital has no impact on the total available quantity (domestic plus imports) of the intermediate input. Combining this with the fixed supply of skilled labor at home, the output of the skilled-labor-intensive good is also fixed. Therefore, the marginal product of the intermediate input in the skilled-labor-intensive final good is unchanged, so that the relative price of the skilled-labor-intensive final product and the unskilled-labor-intensive intermediate input are *unchanged* by the capital flow.

Thus, this model predicts a shift in relative employment toward skilled labor, which is consistent with the data, and a change in wages that occurs without any change at all in the relative price of traded goods. The latter result is significant, because there is considerable controversy about whether the prices or quantities of traded goods are the best measure of international competition. Grossman has argued that trade *prices* must be used, because the quantity of imports is determined in part by the performance of the domestic industry, and therefore does not simply measure competition from abroad.[29] The emphasis on prices is maintained and expressed cogently by Richardson, who provides an example where the change in imports of a final good is unrelated to wages, because prices do not change.[30] The model presented by Sachs and Shatz offers a counterexample where increased imports of the intermediate good are directly

29. Grossman (1986, 1987).
30. Richardson (1995).

responsible for the change in wages, though prices again do not change. The critical distinction between the examples of Richardson and that of Sachs and Shatz is the former is dealing with imports of a *final good,* whereas the latter are dealing with imports of an *intermediate input.*

Sachs and Shatz also use the model to clear up the confusion that has arisen in the literature about what represents outsourcing. Although the outward movement of home capital may represent DFI, they stress that there is no *necessary* investment flow, and the outward movement may instead represent the sale of machinery to foreigners. In that case, the outsourcing in not related to trade within a multinational company, but rather, it is an arms-length transaction reflected in the import of the inter-mediate inputs. I fully agree that outsourcing should not be confused with DFI or transactions within multinational companies, and there has been an unfortunate tendency to do so in the literature.[31]

Although several other models are presented that predict a relative shift toward the employment of skilled labor, it is this first model that is the basis for the empirical work that follows.[32] Sachs and Shatz take the structure of their model seriously—one in which labor is released from the traded goods into the nontraded sector—and investigate whether the implications for wages seem to fit the U.S. economy. In their model, the release of labor from the traded goods will lead to an increase in the relative wage of skilled labor if and only if the labor released has a *lower* ratio of skilled labor to unskilled labor than that found initially in the nontraded sector. At first glance, this result seems to contradict the simplest supply and demand story. The literature has apparently taken it for granted that if the ratio of skilled labor to unskilled labor rises in the traded-goods sector (shifting out the relative demand curve), this would automatically imply an increase in the relative wages of skilled workers (moving along the supply curve). In contrast, Sachs and Shatz argue that this link between the demand shift and increase in relative wages will hold if and only if the nontraded sector becomes less skill intensive as it absorbs workers from the traded goods.

On reflection, the result of Sachs and Shatz seems entirely correct. The problem with the simplest supply and demand story comes with the use of

31. Lawrence (1994); Slaughter (1995).
32. One criticism I would have of the third model is that when trade opened, the number of product varieties (N) should rise along with consumer income, and in that case it does not necessarily follow that the skilled-labor-intensive technology will become profitable.

the relative supply curve (where the relative supply of skilled workers to unskilled workers is an increasing function of their relative wage). In fact, the inverse supply curve of workers facing the traded-goods sector can be obtained directly from the production function for nontraded goods in equation 5-7′ of this chapter

$$N = N(L_s-L_{ss},\ L_u-L_{us}-L_{uu},\ K_n),\tag{5-7′}$$

where L_{ss} is the skilled-labor used in the final good, L_{us} (L_{uu}) is the unskilled labor used in the final (intermediate) product, and L_s (L_u) is the endowment of skilled (unskilled) labor. We assume this production function is concave. Then the supply of *each* of these factors is certainly an upward sloping function in its wage (equal to the marginal products). However, it is not possible to express the marginal products of equation 5-7′ as a function of the *relative* supply $L_{ss}/(L_{us} + L_{uu})$; conversely, the relative supply cannot be expressed as a function of the relative wage. As suggested by the arguments appearing in equation 5-7′, the impact of releasing labor from the traded goods sector will depend on how its ratio of skilled labor to unskilled labor compares with that employed in the nontraded sector, and only if the labor released is less skill intensive will the relative wage of unskilled labor fall.

These theoretical observations lead Sachs and Shatz to devote considerable attention to comparing the ratio of skilled labor to unskilled labor in manufacturing and nontraded goods, in table 5-5. I have only two criticisms of this analysis. First, the sector labelled "nontradables" should actually be labelled "services" (with the exception of the construction industry). The point is that many of the industries included within their "nontraded" sectors, (such as finance, insurance, and legal services) are highly traded. This mislabelling does not really affect their analysis, however, because these industries are still the residual sources of labor supply and demand outside the manufacturing sector. The second criticism is that Sachs and Shatz frequently compare the *overall* skill-to-unskilled ratio within manufacturing and services (with the result that the manufacturing sector is less skilled than services). The more appropriate comparison is to contrast the labor *released* from manufacturing due to outsourcing with that employed in services. The former will certainly consist of a high ratio of unskilled workers.

In the final section of their chapter, Sachs and Shatz turn to a discussion of the relative prices of traded goods. This discussion is prompted by the finding in Lawrence and Slaughter that the prices of unskilled-labor-intensive import goods apparently did not fall relative to more-skill-intensive imports during the 1980s.[33] In their earlier paper, Sachs and Shatz reexamined the evidence, paying special attention to the price index for computers.[34] Their exclusion of that product from some regressions was criticized by Lawrence.[35] Sachs and Shatz go to some pains to justify the special treatment of computers in this earlier paper and also use domestic rather than import or export prices. They also attribute the original evidence on prices to Bhagwati,[36] though this seems inappropriate, as he was simply making use of the evidence presented by Lawrence and Slaughter.[37]

In any case, the discussion of prices seems rather out of place in light of the prediction of Sachs and Shatz's (first) theoretical model that the prices of traded goods are *unchanged* due to the capital flow and outsourcing. Even if the simplifying assumptions of that model are relaxed, the prediction for prices *would not* involve comparing the relative prices of traded goods. Rather, the implication would be that the price index for domestically produced components within any industry would rise relative to that of imported components, as shown in a study by a colleague and myself.[38] In that paper, the rising relative wage of skilled labor is reflected in *rising domestic prices relative to import prices,* and this prediction is confirmed in the U.S. data. A somewhat different implication flows from the model of Sachs and Shatz, where the labor flow to the nontraded-goods sector leads to *a falling relative price of nontraded goods.*[39] Here again, the focus should not be on the comparative prices of traded goods, but rather on the movement in their prices relative to those of domestic products. This type of price information would provide a better test of their theoretical model.

Comment by Robert Z. Lawrence

Ed Leamer introduced the metaphor of a trial, and I would like too sustain it. Thus this paper has some of the flavor of the well-known explanation of the man who was accused of murder. Seeking to cover all bases, he

33. Lawrence and Slaughter (1993).
34. Sachs and Shatz (1994).
35. Lawrence (1994).
36. While referencing Bhagwati and Dehejia (1994).
37. Lawrence and Slaughter (1993).
38. Feenstra and Hanson (1996).
39. Given their specification of nontraded demand in equation 5-14, the relative price of nontraded goods will fall only if income effects are weak. However, the falling relative price would be guaranteed if demand for nontraded goods was

informed the judge, "Your Honor, I was not there, I did not have a gun, it went off by accident." In this chapter Jeffrey Sachs and Howard Shatz similarly cover the bases for those who believe that trade has seriously depressed the relative wages of unskilled U.S. workers. In the first half of the chapter, they provide a range of models showing that trade can depress relative wages even if there is no impact on prices. In the second half, they present evidence that the relative prices of traded goods have actually fallen by large amounts. This eclectic approach allows readers who believe that trade has played a major role in reducing wages to take their pick. If they find the empirical price evidence unconvincing, they can invoke one or several of the theoretical models advanced by Sachs and Shatz. If they accept the authors' empirical judgments, they can invoke the traditional HO explanation for wage inequality. The unfortunate feature of this chapter is that, like the accused man I alluded to, you cannot believe both types of explanation simultaneously. The evidence that prices have fallen implies that the models in the first half of the chapter fail to capture reality.

In addition to their own models, which indicate that trade affects wages even without changing relative traded-goods prices, reference is made to the work of Krugman and Venables, who show that with scale economies, average real wages in the North can fall as declining transportation costs lead to more trade.[40] These models, the authors claim, show the "theoretical robustness of the trade-wage linkage" that is present even in models that do not make the HO assumptions.

The introduction of these models indicates a subtle development in the authors' views. The central message of an earlier paper by Sachs and Shatz was astonishment at economists who did not accept the predictions of the HO model.[41] The first half suggests this may not be the best way to model the relationship in any case. I agree with Sachs and Shatz that wages will be influenced by a number of channels other than those captured by the conventional HO model. However, I believe relative unskilled-wage responses could readily be positive as well as negative.

The fact that theorists such as Sachs and Shatz can contrive models that produce a particular result is not definitive proof that the result is "theoretically robust." To be sure, many exogenous shocks are likely to influence both trade flows and wage rates—in most general equilibrium systems,

---

respecified as a function of its price relative to that of the skilled-labor-intensive final good, along with income that enters with an elasticity of unity.

40. Krugman and Venables (1995).

41. Sachs and Shatz (1994).

everything depends on everything else. But we also know there are other models in which growing trade in imported products and declining relative prices of labor-intensive products could lead to higher rather than lower wages. For example, using the same model cited by Sachs and Shatz, Krugman and Venables show that under different conditions, declining transportation costs may actually increase rather than lower wages in the North. Also, Lawrence and Lawrence, for example, show how increased imports can be associated with rising relative union wages.[42] Moreover, even within the context of the HO model itself, complete specialization could lead to the relationship between prices and wages being overturned. In particular, once we allow for specialization, there are well-known models in which a *rising price* of the most labor-intensive, imported products can be associated with a decline in the relative wages of less-skilled workers in the developed country![43]

We also know well that the volume of trade can increase in an open economy due to technical change or changes in factor supplies, and that real wages can simultaneously decline for workers at home at *constant* international and domestic goods prices. When trade theorists such as Bhagwati and Leamer claim that the wages of unskilled workers cannot decline, as per the Stolper-Samuelson model, they mean that unless the domestic prices of labor-intensive commodities fall, changes in trade policy or foreign-trade opportunities in the rest of the world cannot be a source of the change in real wages.

In any case, although they may help make some theoretical points, the models the authors present are unrealistic, particularly when it comes to capturing trade between the North and the South. To be sure, some goods produced in the South are intermediate inputs, but many are final consumer goods. In addition, the markets for most goods in which developing countries compete are competitive and are not well characterized as having dominant price-setting monopolists. Indeed, it is noteworthy that Sachs and Shatz themselves make little effort to use these models in their own empirical work in the second part of the chapter—itself an indication of their relevance.

The authors present an interesting traditional net factor content analysis. Specifically, they estimate that on balance over the 1980s, trade displaced

42. Krugman and Venables (1995); Lawrence and Lawrence (1985).
43. See Leamer (1992). One version of this model is when there are three goods (computers, radios, and textiles) and two factors, with the North specializing in the most capital intensive (computers and radios) and the South in the least capital intensive (radios and textiles). As capital flows into (or is accumulated) in the South, the relative price of the midrange good (radios) falls as the South increases its production of radios and reduces its production of textiles. This drives up the relative price of the least-labor-intensive product (textiles). Meanwhile, the North shifts into the most-capital-intensive good (computers) and the wage rate in the North falls.

791,000 workers who were high school educated and 294,000 who were college educated. The authors go on to claim that this indicates a major role for trade in reducing the relative wages of workers with no more than a high school education. In fact a more reasonable interpretation is that their results actually confirm that the impact of trade on relative wages of those with a high school education has been small. The calculations Sachs and Shatz offer suggest that the displacement would lead to a decline in (economywide) relative wages of less-educated workers of 3.4 to 5 percent. But three questionable aspects of their methodology lead to an overstatement of the relative wage impact.

First, they assume that these workers must all be reemployed in the nontraded sector. This ignores the possibility (which may be absent in their theoretical model, but is certainly likely in reality) that lower relative wages of unskilled workers will raise their employment in manufacturing as well as nontraded goods. Second, they compare the displacement to levels of employment in 1979. However, because they are explaining 1990 relative wages, they should use 1990 employment, which is considerably larger (and the impacts of the displacement correspondingly smaller). Third, and most important, they use elasticities of substitution of 0.5 or less, which are decidedly low, although, as the survey by Hamermesh makes clear, there is considerable uncertainty associated with this parameter.[44] A typical estimate would be that of Katz and Murphy, who obtain an elasticity of 1.4.[45] If one takes their estimates of high school and college worker displacement and corrects for the three questionable procedures, one is led to conclude that trade reduced relative high school wages by about 1.0 percent. This implies that trade accounts for only 10 percent or less of the growing college premium.

It should of course be born in mind that this methdology should be used with great caution. It is quite possible that in an open economy, the trade shifts actually observed occurred not because of a shift in the foreign offer curve but instead because of domestic technical change and other shocks.

Sachs and Shatz attack the work I did with Slaughter on the issue of price evidence. They fault Bhagwati, who is merely a consumer of the data, for what they term his "flimsy rejection of the trade-wage linkage based on 'ostensible evidence.'" They argue that the import price data we used covers only fifty-one sectors. It is true that import price coverage was not complete until 1985. However, after that, the price data cover all imports,

44. Hamermesh (1986).
45. Katz and Murphy (1992).

even though individual series are not published for all subcategories. In any case, many empirical studies rely on data samples, and the relevant question is not coverage but possible bias. As work undertaken for me by Shatz suggests, the import prices available early are not disproportionately biased on the basis of skill. A second complaint they have involves the use of final prices that may by affected by intermediate input prices as well as sectoral value added. This is a relevant point. Moreover, even in this work, Shatz and Sachs ignore the role of factors besides labor (that is, capital) and so their own measure continues to suffer from a weakness they consider serious. In addition, Sachs and Shatz believe we did not consider productivity changes in our paper.[46] But in table 3 of our paper we provided estimates of effective prices, and in table 4 we reported domestic price changes that used data fully covering the manufacturing sector.

Finally, Sachs and Shatz believe that our import price data are deficient because these data do not adequately reflect quality changes. Yet when it comes to using the domestic price data, they dummy out computers from their observations, apparently because they do not like the quality adjustments in these data. They cannot reject the use of import data because there are no productivity adjustments in computer prices and then reject the domestic price data because there are adjustments. I do not understand why computers should be allowed to play no role in this story. Surely in weighted least-squares regressions, these prices should be allowed to enter in in some form or other. Indeed, we already knew from Sachs and Shatz's earlier work that regressions excluding computers show a moderate positive relationship between relative price changes and skill intensity. Moreover, I suspect that more quality adjustment would tend to lower the prices of skilled-labor-intensive products by more than that of unskilled-labor-intensive products, thereby weakening their conclusions.

Sachs and Shatz claim the consistent result from their empirical work is that price increases in unskilled-labor-intensive industries were considerably below those in skilled-labor-intensive sectors. However, the specification they prefer does not have significant explanatory power for the period most relevant for the wage changes we are interested in.

It is important to distinguish between the results for the 1980s and those for the 1990s. Most of the change we are interested in occurred in the 1980s. As measured by the employment cost index, for example, the ratio of compensation of white-collar to blue-collar workers increased by 10 percent

46. Lawrence and Slaughter (1993).

between 1981 and 1989, and just 2 percent between 1989 and 1995. There is actually no evidence of increasing inequality between 1991 and 1995. In my work with Slaughter, we looked only at the 1980s and used export, import, and domestic prices. With computers included in the samples, we found no evidence of relative price declines for unskilled-labor-intensive goods.

In their 1994 paper, Sachs and Shatz dropped computers and obtained a negative coefficient that was not significant for import prices and was significant for domestic prices. Aside from lengthening the observation period, this chapter has three innovations. It uses weighted least squares, considers value-added price measures, and uses data at the four-digit rather than three-digit level. For the 1980s, the value-added equation (excluding computers) gives essentially the same result as in their earlier work for output prices. The example of computer prices does highlight the problem of separating technical changes and pure price changes. This points to the use of effective measures in explaining wages. However, the effective value-added regression, the most important in terms of their formulation, has a negative coefficient, *but it is not significant.* This replicates the lack of significance they obtained for both import and domestic prices in their earlier study of effective prices and calls into question their own characterization of their results.

Actually, we should not be surprised at this finding, because their earlier work showed that once computers are excluded, there was not a significant relationship between TFP and skill intensity during the 1980s. Finally, it does appear that when data from the 1990s are introduced into the sample or when they are used alone, there is evidence that the relative prices of unskilled-labor-intensive goods declined. This we have already learned from Krueger.[47]

All in all, I still believe that as far as the 1980s are concerned, the evidence that trade operated to reduce the relative price of labor-intensive products remains less than compelling. In my own recent work, I have run additional regressions over the 1980s relating relative traded and domestic prices, to estimates of the ratio of high school–educated workers to college-educated workers.[48] Regardless of whether computer prices are included or excluded, they do not show a statistically signficant negative relationship.

In sum, I am much less convinced than the authors that the results in this chapter are new or that I should change my view that the price evidence supporting the HO model in the 1980s is weak. I think the more solid

47. Krueger (1995).
48. Lawrence (1996).

evidence in this chapter is presented by the net factor content estimates. These confirm the estimates made by Krugman and myself that, operating through the HO channel, trade played only a minor role in the growing inequality in U.S. wages.[49]

General Discussion

A number of participants were pleased to see this chapter's emphasis on the nontraded-goods sector and hoped that this work would encourage others to go further in this direction.

There was some discussion of the observation that in the United States, productivity growth has been considerably slower in the services sector than in manufacturing. However, Robert Blecker stressed that our measures of productivity growth are highly uncertain, especially in the service sector. Barry Bluestone wondered whether a significant reallocation of less-skilled labor into the nontraded goods sector, due to globalization, might explain the slower productivity growth. He suggested that cross-country evidence could be used to examine this relationship. He noted the very different example of Sweden, where various institutions had helped to maintain relatively high wages, preventing a reallocation of labor into services. However, the Swedish services sector has experienced productivity gains that parallel those in Swedish manufacturing.

William Cline advocated dividing the nontraded-goods sector into sub-sectors. He noted that there is a high-productivity, high-wage growth segment, including financial services. There is also a low-wage, low-productivity growth segment, including retail services. He would expect most of the less-skilled displaced workers to have been forced into the latter segment, not to have been randomly distributed throughout services. In this context, Sachs said he had been surprised to find that most of the employment increase went to business and repair services and to professional services (which are relatively skill intensive) and not to retailing.

Cline and Robert Blecker suggested that technological changes might be induced by import competition in some sectors. However, Sachs noted that the term "induced technological change" is used too loosely. It is important to distinguish between movements along an isoquant (for instance to a more-capital-intensive process as a result of changes in factor prices) and

49. Krugman (1995); Lawrence (1996).

technical change (resulting from discovery of new processes). He noted that this distinction is difficult to make in practice, however. His analysis finds little evidence of a general relationship between import competition and productivity gains, although a few trade-affected sectors such as textiles do exhibit rapid productivity growth.

Some participants offered explanations for this chapter's finding of a shift toward increased usage of skilled workers throughout the U.S. economy between 1978 and 1990. Hank Farber noted that there has been a significant increase in educational attainment so that the older cohorts are much less educated than the younger ones. He wondered whether the observed shift to greater skill intensity might not simply reflect this cohort effect. Edward Leamer suggested that product upgrading within sectors may have caused a shift in the input mix toward more skilled workers.

Leamer also expressed his concern about the widespread usage of work by Deardorff and Staiger to justify the factor content approach to assessing the impact of trade on domestic labor markets. He stressed that their work is based on three key assumptions. The first is that the product mix is the same in the home and foreign regions (a one-cone, HO model). Second, changing product prices related to globalization is assumed to be the only source of change. In particular, there are no technology or factor supply changes. Third, the elasticity of labor demand that would exist in autarky is known. (This demand elasticity is required to translate quantity changes into relative factor price changes.) However, Leamer argued that the product mixes are actually different, that there have been changes in both technology and factor supplies, and that we do not know the relevant labor demand elasticity.

Gary Burtless argued that the issue of foreign competition potentially depriving workers of large rents warrants more serious consideration than it is given in the chapter. However, Sachs did not find it compelling that foreign competition would influence bargaining in the portion of the labor force not directly exposed to trade (such as teachers). This accounts for most U.S. employment.

References

Bartelsman, Eric J., and Wayne Gray. 1996. "The NBER Manufacturing Productivity Database." Technical Working Paper 205. Cambridge, Mass.: NBER (October).

Bhagwati, Jagdish. 1995. "Paupers' Trade View Has Not Been Proven [Letter to the editor]." *Financial Times,* August 4, p. 18.

Bhagwati, Jagdish, and Vivek H. Dehejia. 1994. "Freer Trade and Wages of the Unskilled—Is Marx Striking Again?" In *Trade and Wages: Leveling Wages*

Down? edited by Jagdish Bhagwati and Marvin H. Kosters, 36–75. Washington: American Enterprise Institute.

Bhagwati, Jagdish, and Marvin H. Kosters. 1994. *Trade and Wages: Leveling Wages Down?* Washington: American Enterprise Institute.

Borjas, George J., Richard B. Freeman, and Lawrence F. Katz. 1992. "On the Labor Market Effects of Immigration and Trade." In *Immigration and the Work Force: Economic Consequences for the United States and Source Areas,* edited by George J. Borjas and Richard B. Freeman, 213–44. University of Chicago Press.

Feenstra, Robert C., and Gordon H. Hanson. 1996. "Foreign Investment, Outsourcing and Relative Wages." In *Political Economy of Trade Policy: Essays in Honor of Jagdish Bhagwati,* edited by Robert C. Feenstra, Gene M. Grossman, and Douglas A. Irwin. MIT Press.

Frank, Robert H., and Philip J. Cook. 1995. *The Winner-Take-All Society: How More and More Americans Compete for Ever Fewer and Bigger Prizes, Encouraging Economic Waste, Income Inequality, and an Impoverished Cultural Life.* Free Press.

Gray, Wayne. 1989. "Productivity Database." Cambridge, Mass.: National Bureau of Economic Research.

———. 1992. "Updating Productivity Data through 1989." Cambridge, Mass.: National Bureau of Economic Research.

Grossman, Gene M. 1986. "Imports as a Cause of Injury: The Case of the U.S. Steel Industry." *Journal of International Economics* 20 (May): 201–23.

———. 1987. "The Employment and Wage Effects of Import Competition in the United States." *Journal of International Economics Integration* 2: 1–23.

Hamermesh, Daniel. 1986. "The Demand for Labor in the Long Run." In *Handbook of Labor Economics,* edited by Orly Ashenfelter and Richard Layard, 429–71. Amsterdam: Elsevier Science Publishers.

Katz, Lawrence F., and Kevin M. Murphy. 1992. "Changes in Relative Wages, 1963–1987: Supply and Demand Factors." *Quarterly Journal of Economics* 107 (February): 35–78.

Krueger, Alan B. 1995. "Labor Market Shifts and the Price Puzzle Revisited." Paper prepared for a conference in honor of Assar Lindbeck, "Unemployment and Wage Dispersion: Is There a Tradeoff?" Princeton University, June 16–18.

Krugman, Paul R. 1994. "Fantasy Economics." *New York Times,* September 26, p. A15 (national) and p. A17 (local).

———. 1995a. "The End Is Not Quite Nigh." *Economist,* April 29, pp. 99–100.

———. 1995b. "Growing World Trade: Causes and Consequences." *Brookings Papers on Economic Activity* 1: 327–62.

Krugman, Paul R., and Robert Z. Lawrence. 1994. "Trade, Jobs, and Wages." *Scientific American* 270 (April): 44–49.

Krugman, Paul, and Anthony J. Venables. 1995. "Globalization and the Inequality of Nations." *Quarterly Journal of Economics* 110 (November): 857–80.

Lawrence, Colin, and Robert Z. Lawrence. 1985. "Manufacturing Wage Dispersion: An End Game Interpretation." *Brookings Papers on Economic Activity* 1: 47–116.

Lawrence, Robert Z. 1994. "Trade, Multinationals, and Labor." Working Paper 4836. Cambridge, Mass.: National Bureau of Economic Research.

———. 1996. *Single World: Divided Nations? International Trade and OECD Labor Markets.* Brookings.

Lawrence, Robert Z., and Matthew J. Slaughter. 1993. "Trade and American Wages in the 1980s: Giant Sucking Sound or Small Hiccup?" *Brookings Papers on Economic Activity Microeconomics 2:* 161–226.

Leamer, Edward. 1992. "Wage Effects of a U.S. Mexico Free Trade Agreement." Working Paper 3991. Cambridge, Mass.: National Bureau of Economic Research.

———. 1995. "The Heckscher-Ohlin Model in Theory and Practice." *Princeton Studies in International Finance* 77 (February).

Murphy, Kevin M., Andrei Shleifer, and Robert Vishny. 1989. "Income Distribution, Market Size, and Industrialization." *Quarterly Journal of Economics* 104 (August): 537–64.

National Bureau of Economic Research. 1994. "Documents for use with the NBER CPS Labor Extracts Annual Earnings File Extracts 1979–1993 CD-ROM." Unpublished paper. Cambridge, Mass. September.

Richardson, J. David. 1995. "Income Inequality and Trade: How to Think, What to Conclude." *Journal of Economic Perspectives* 9 (Summer): 33–55.

Sachs, Jeffrey D., and Howard J. Shatz. 1994. "Trade and Jobs in U.S. Manufacturing." *Brookings Papers on Economic Activity* 1: 1–84.

Sachs, Jeffrey D., and Andrew Warner. 1995. "Economic Reform and the Process of Global Integration." *Brookings Papers on Economic Activity.* 1: 1–118.

Saeger, Steven S. 1995. "Trade and Deindustrialization: Myth and Reality in the OECD." Harvard University, Department of Economics.

Slaughter, Matthew J. 1995. "Multinational Corporations, Outsourcing, and American Wage Divergence." Working Paper 5253. Cambridge, Mass.: National Bureau of Economic Research.

U.S. Department of Commerce, U.S. Bureau of Economic Analysis. 1993. *1987 Annual Input-Output Accounts Diskette* (Data diskette, accession number 51-92-40-001).

Wood, Adrian. 1994. *North-South Trade, Employment, and Inequality: Changing Fortunes in a Skill-Driven World.* Oxford, England: Clarendon Press.

Part Three

BROADER PERSPECTIVES

SIX

Trade and the Social Structure of Economic Activity

Michael J. Piore

IN THE LAST fifteen years, the U.S. labor market has passed through a period of substantial structural adjustment. Very large numbers of people have been permanently displaced from stable, secure jobs and forced into unemployment and/or considerably less-attractive positions in the labor market, jobs inconsistent with their previous social status or accustomed patterns of life. We are emerging from this period with a distribution of wage and salary income not only more unequal than it was in the past but seemingly increasingly so. Given the rate of increase in average income levels, people in the lower part of the wage and salary distribution actually experience declines, not only in their social status, but in their absolute standard of living.[1]

Associated with these structural changes is a substantial increase in the involvement of the United States in the international marketplace, an increased involvement as measured by any number of indicators, but particularly by the weight of imports and exports in our national income. The precise role that trade has played is of course a matter of some dispute, one which this volume was intended to help clarify.[2] Meanwhile, however, in

1. Levy and Murnane (1992).
2. Bound and Johnson (1992); Lawrence and Slaughter (1993); Murphy and Welch (1991); Katz and Murphy (1992); Kruse (1988).

1995 we twice committed ourselves to further trade expansion, first in the North American Free Trade Agreement (NAFTA) and then once again in the renewal of the General Agreement on Tariffs and Trade (GATT). Trade, in fact, is the only one of the several factors promoting structural adjustment that has been openly debated in the public policy arena. If structural adjustment continues at the pace and in the direction in the coming decade that it has in the past, it would seem reasonable for those who are its victims to react against the new trading regime, whatever its precise responsibility for their plight.

In thinking about the period we have recently passed through and contemplating the future, it is difficult not to be reminded of Karl Polanyi's classic work, *The Great Transformation.*[3] That book was written against the backdrop of the Great Depression, the rise of communism and fascism in Europe, and World War II. It saw those events as the product of a century-long struggle between society and the market economy. In the first part of that struggle, the market had gained progressively, removing those laws and customs that embedded land and labor in a dense network of social relations, and turning them into the "factors of production" that moved around freely in response to price fluctuations, as they were conceived in economic theory. But in the second half of the century, society began to reassert itself, and the struggle became more equal. In the aftermath of World War I, the industrial world recommitted itself to free trade and the gold standard. Market fluctuations overwhelmed stable social relations, until in the end, the force of society reasserted itself in, if anything, a more brutal and certainly more commanding way. The fascist and communist regimes of Europe and World War II against which Polanyi wrote were the result.

Unlike other writers who inveighed against the market in this period, Polanyi did not see this struggle so much as an expression of class conflict or narrow economic interests, but rather as a conflict between goals and ideals that all human beings share. One set of goals, dependent on material well-being and the expansion of productive forces, was associated with the market. The other set had to do with the way in which we realize ourselves as human beings in a network of social relations that the uninhibited operation of the market continually threatens and tends to destroy. The debate about economic policy was not a mere veil over the naked clash of interests, but an intellectual and political endeavor to reconcile different conceptions of what we are as human beings and the relationship between

3. Polanyi (1957 [originally published 1944]).

these conceptions and the economic activities in which we are engaged. Particular groups did, however, come to represent one or another of the positions in that debate—sometimes for ideological or intellectual reasons, sometimes to protect their own social or political interests. In the debates about economic policy in the nineteenth century, the economics profession represented the forces of the market, just as we do today.

Indeed, it is amazing how little has changed despite war and depression, despite Polanyi's efforts to draw lessons from those tragedies. Economics as a science has made enormous strides since Polanyi's day; in the last decade standard trade theory has been revolutionized. But the intellectual arguments mustered on behalf of trade in the policy debates are essentially the same today as they were then. They have proved once again to be intellectually and politically commanding. The disruptive effects of a market economy and their ability to produce political chaos and reaction remain as well. We see ominous signs—quite recently in Mexico, but even before that in Warsaw Pact–era Eastern Europe and in the former Soviet Union, and in the neofascist resurgence in the western European democracies—of the continuing ability of the market to disrupt social relations and provoke political reaction. This is perhaps not surprising. Prudence might suggest that the proponents of the market stop short of the kind of victory that historically has produced reaction. But because our intellectual apparatus has continued to abstract from the social forces out of which this reaction grows, we have no way of even thinking about what that point might be. Without intellectual legitimation, the forces arrayed against an expansion of trade appear to us as so many reactionaries and special interests, and in the heat of our righteous battle against them, how would we ever come to think that we had gone too far?

Polanyi himself, for all of his insights into the problem, is not much help in this regard. But he does provide a clue in a secondary argument in his book to where we might begin to look. This is what I want to pursue in this chapter. The clue is the suggestion that the operative dichotomy is not between the society and the *economy,* but between the society and the free market. Productive activity is embedded in a social structure, and economic growth and development, to the extent that they depend on productive relations, are actually dependent on social forces as well. The fluctuations attendant on an unregulated market economy are as disruptive of the development of production relations as they are of social relations in general. Thus the society is not something to be taken into account after the economy has done its work, through, for example, a redistributive system of taxes and transfers. A complete economic theory must understand the society and the economy as of a piece. This chapter is an attempt to move in that direction. It sketches out a view of the relationship between trade and the social relations of production, particularly the social relations of production as they have evolved in the United States in recent years.

To do so, I depart at several critical junctures from the analytical approach conventional in economics (or, at least, from the terms in which the economist's case for trade is conventionally framed). This is perhaps an inevitable part of an attempt to incorporate a perspective that eludes conventional analysis. In my particular case, however, its attraction grows less out of any prior conviction that economic activity has to be understood as socially embedded, than the attempt to find a conceptual framework that will encompass my own research findings. Nonetheless, the approach is not personal or idiosyncratic. Polanyi himself articulated much the same approach in his later writings.[4] The approach is also close to that of the older historical and institutional schools of economics; I shall use the term "institutionalist" as shorthand for it.[5] But the same approach—or at least important elements of it—is developed in the recent writings of a number of analysts who see themselves as very much a part of the economics mainstream and do not link it specifically to the social issues with which we are concerned here.[6]

The remainder of this chapter is organized as follows: The next section outlines the elements of the institutionalist approach that seem most important for conventional economists trying to follow the argument. It is followed by a brief discussion of the "sweatshop" that illustrates the way in which an institutionalist might understand a labor market institution. The sweatshop is a pattern of production that is important historically, and actually of some interest in the current debates about the role of labor standards in trade between industrialized countries and the developing economies of the third world. But it is used here largely to illustrate the way in which institutionalists understand labor market institutions. The production patterns at stake in the current structural transformation involve a rather different story, a story about mass production and its transformation in the 1970s and 1980s. The third section of the chapter tells that story, largely, though not exclusively, as it has emerged through my own research. In the fourth section, I recast that story in analytical terms and try to draw out some of its lessons for how we think about trade and its impact upon labor.

4. Polanyi (1971).
5. Hodgson (1994); Commons (1934); Holmstrom and Milgrom (1994).
6. Arthur (1988); Milgrom and Roberts (1994); North (1990).

The concluding section summarizes the basic argument and draws out its central implications for contemporary public policy debate.

The Institutionalist Perspective

Economics is to a great extent a science concerned with choice among alternatives. A critical dimension of its conceptual apparatus is thus the way in which those alternatives are characterized. The conventional characterization is in terms of a continuum, as if the characteristics that interest us in the world could be had in virtually any combination. Thus, to take one of the classic textbook problems, we think of the business firm as selecting the proportions of capital and labor (or of skilled and unskilled workers) from a choice set in which the same output can be produced with proportions of capital and labor that vary continually along an isoquant from virtually all capital and no labor at one extreme to all labor and no capital at the other. In the institutionalist perspective from which we are working here, choices are by contrast always among an extremely limited number of discrete alternatives. It is as if the isoquant were to collapse into a few widely dispersed points on the capital-labor map. We can talk about those alternatives as business strategies, and *strategic choice* is one of several names associated with the framework in which we are working.

Why choices might present themselves in this particular way is a separate question. It might reflect the structure of the human mind. It might be because of the nature of institutions, which tend to structure the environment in which decisions are made.[7] But one need not necessarily have a specific answer to this question in mind to try and understand the world in these terms. Perhaps the presumption of limited, discrete alternatives is no less natural than the continuum of alternatives that economic analysis generally presumes.

A second point that distinguishes the institutionalist perspective is that the discrete alternatives that the economic agents actually face are not fully worked out in advance. In most cases, the agent is already pursuing a given policy; business as usual means essentially to continue that pursuit, trying

7. Before World War II, for example, when production declined, some industries tended to systematically lay off excess workers, but in other industries standard practice was to shorten the workweek. The unemployment insurance (UI) system created in the 1930s, however, indemnified only full-time unemployment. In the course of the early postwar decades, virtually every industry was induced to abandon work sharing, and the system of layoff and recall became standard.

to do a little better all the time. The process of doing better might be thought of as continuous, but what is being traced out along the continuum is a process of "creation" or "learning," not a choice set. The process is actually captured by economic models of learning by doing and path specificity.[8] The choice an agent makes when he or she picks a different strategy is thus really a choice to embark on a different learning process or process of creation. Lean production, mass production, and sweating, to take specific alternatives I discuss, are not therefore truly alternative production techniques. They are alternative directions in which production techniques might evolve in time, and are best thought of as alternative development paths.

Modern management techniques, such as benchmarking, *kan ban,* and statistical quality control, which have emerged in association with the strategy of lean production, highlight the learning element of the managerial process and serve to underscore and illustrate it, although learning is an integral dimension not simply of lean production but of all production strategies. In benchmarking, the firm identifies the achievements (usually the quantitative achievements) of best-practice producers, and then uses them both to guide and to evaluate the evolution of its own practices as it "learns by doing," so to speak. In *kan ban,* in-process inventories are eliminated in order to highlight the relationship among the various organizations and operations involved in production and force the identification and resolution of problems in coordination among them. In statistical quality control, the traditional practice of repairing defects is, in effect, discarded; defective products within the accepted range of variability are simply scrapped, but when defects exceed that range, production is halted and an attempt is made to identify and correct the process producing the problem.

A third characteristic of the institutionalist perspective is that economic processes are viewed, in an important sense, as *intellectual* (or *cognitive*) and *social.*[9] The alternative strategies considered by the firm emerge through discussion and debate among the economic actors; the firm works out the specific practices associated with those strategies through discussion and debate as well. The participants in these discussions include employees of the firm. But they also include people attached to other social networks to which the firm's employees belong—networks composed of the firm's clients and suppliers and the professional communities from which its employees are drawn, yet (important for the argument that

8. Arthur (1988).
9. Piore (1995); Sabel (1994); Schon (1983); Senge (1990).

follows) that extend into and are influenced by the political and public policymaking communities.

Unlike the discussions of scholarly and scientific communities that often focus on theory, the debates central to progression along a strategic production path tend to center on the *interpretation of practice* in somewhat the same way that debate among literary scholars centers on the interpretation of text. The institutionalist approach thus focuses attention on the question of how this debate is structured. Managerial practices like benchmarking, *kan ban,* and statistical quality control are essentially instruments for doing this. The concern with the emergence of alternatives and their evolution through discussion and debate also affect research strategy.[10] In labor economics in particular, institutionalists have tended to study the economy through open-ended interviews with the economic actors; such interviews are not primarily concerned with gathering information that can be reduced to precise answers to specific questions. Rather, they constitute windows into how the respondents think about the problems that they face and how that thinking evolves over time through debates about practice.[11] One might look at and use the business press in a similar way, not as a source of journalistic accounts of what is happening or of "anecdotes" to illustrate an argument, but as one of the forums in which the debate about practice occurs, and hence a window for the outside observer on the process through which alternative strategies are formulated.

Finally, because the process through which strategies emerge and evolve is cognitive and embedded in social networks, strategies tend to group around a limited number of discrete alternatives, not only on the level of the productive unit but also in the aggregate. In other words, the discontinuity observed in managerial choice is not smoothed out through aggregation but is reflected in the macroeconomic structure. This is partly because productive enterprises borrow strategies from each other and use the experience of others to guide their own learning. But it is more fundamentally because the strategies emerge through discussion and debate among people in different productive units and between practitioners and politicians and policymakers. The emerging conceptions of the strategic alternatives tend therefore to be reflected in law and public policies, which then act to reinforce the tendencies within the productive unit. A clear example of this is the way in which the notion of a job that emerged in mass production, which I discuss below, came to be reflected in labor law. An extensive

10. Piore and others (1994).
11. Piore (1979).

literature traces out another example of this process: the emergence of the conception of unemployment in several different countries.[12] It is this process that I argue is ultimately that key to thinking about the impact of trade on the labor market. An important corollary of this idea is that one can expect the choices made at the firm level about productive strategies to be reflected in indicators such as the growing dispersion of wage and salary income in the national economy.

The Sweatshop

Perhaps the clearest illustration of an institutionalist mode of analysis and its application to the labor process is the continuing effort to regulate the sweatshop.[13]

The U.S. analogues to the reassertion of social standards that Polanyi describes in England in the latter half of the nineteenth century were campaigns for minimal labor standards at the turn of the century. These centered around a panoply of specific legislative proposals—outlawing child labor and regulating minimum wages, maximum hours, health standards, and fire laws and safety. The efforts were of only limited success at the time, but all came to fruition under the New Deal. They constitute the core of the minimal standards that have governed the labor market in the postwar period, at least until recently. The standards themselves reflect the original campaign. They involve a number of different pieces of legislation, and enforcement responsibility is dispersed across a variety of agencies and departments. But violations tend to cluster; shops tend systematically to be involved in multiple violations. It thus appears as if the regulations are of a piece. And, indeed, these shops are characterized in the labor and business press as sweatshops. The press accounts of the original campaigns also make clear that the sweatshop was also what reformers at the turn of the century were attempting to control, despite the way in which that attempt was organized around different legislative campaigns.

When one tries to understand the sweatshop as a single phenomenon, the key seems to be the way in which all costs are made variable—dependent solely on the level of output regardless of the time required for production. Workers are paid by the piece. They tend to own or rent their own equipment

12. Salais, Baverez, and Renaud (1986); Keyssar (1986); Mansfield (1994).
13. Piore (1990).

(for example, a sewing machine) when they use equipment at all. When they work at home, they also pay rent and utilities. In factory production, these become the major components of fixed cost. The attempt to minimize those costs by cramming as many workers and as much inventory as possible into the space available is chiefly responsible for the health and fire hazards associated with this form of production. Children become a part of the story, because with a piece rate and minimal fixed costs, the employer cares little about productivity.

As soon as a binding minimum hourly rate is imposed, the whole structure of incentives shifts. The employer is now concerned about productivity in a way in which he or she did not have to be before. Because they are low-productivity workers, children are excluded from the production process. There is now also an incentive to rationalize the plant layout to facilitate work flow. This itself improves health and safety. It also extends the managerial span of control so that health and safety regulation become a marginal adjustment, rather than (as in the sweatshop) a discontinuous change in the organization of the work process.

Capital equipment has much the same effect as a minimum hourly wage: the fixed costs it entails create an incentive to organize production so as to monitor productivity even at a zero wage. This is no doubt the principal reason why the sweatshop is found in only some industries even in the early stages of industrial development and tends to disappear as industrialization proceeds. In the earliest stages of industrialization, when production was embedded in a household economy and constrained to fit its social structure, of course, that structure also acted to prevent industrial homework from deteriorating into sweatshops. This is what it tends to do when production begins to move into the factory and even work done at home is forced to compete with unregulated factory labor.

The notion of the sweatshop as a distinct form of production, historically intermediate between the household economy and modern, capital-intensive forms, helps to clarify the recent debate about minimal international labor standards. It suggests that it is possible conceptually to distinguish concerns Polanyi raises about the preservation of social forms from a kind of disguised protectionism, even from the kind of imperialism of moral standards that the third world sees in these proposals. But for the current debate about trade in the United States, the relevant production forms have much less to do with the sweatshop than with those that grow out of the strategy of mass production and the alternative strategies that have developed in the last decade.

Mass Production and Industrial Adjustment in the 1970s and 1980s

My basic understanding of these choices has developed in the context of the argument Charles Sabel and I presented more than ten years ago in *The Second Industrial Divide*.[14] Although it has evolved considerably under the impact of subsequent developments, the original argument is still a valid starting point. The central position is that the evolution of the productive structure in the United States and throughout the industrial world has been driven by a pursuit of the division of labor. Managers and engineers understood what they were trying to do in terms originally laid out by Adam Smith in his famous pin factory example, and extended and popularized in the twentieth century by Frederick Taylor and Henry Ford. Economic development was thus conceived as the process through which the master pinmaker evolved into the pin factory in which one worker pulled the wire, a second cut it, a third headed the pin, a fourth pointed it, and so on.[15]

The driving force in this process was *specialization*—first the specialization of the work force and ultimately the specialization of capital equipment. In the extreme, under mass production, both capital equipment and semiskilled labor became dedicated to the specific make and model of a given product. Each time the model was changed, the capital equipment had essentially to be scrapped and the labor force retrained. This rendered productive resources completely inflexible or, more precisely, inelastic.

The tendencies associated with mass production, moreover, were present throughout the system, and even relatively general tasks and functions were defined in the narrowest possible terms. This made the productive structure enormously sensitive to variation in economic conditions, whether it be in consumer taste and fashion or in the supply of basic inputs. Consequently, it placed an exceptionally high premium on the stabilization of the underlying economic environment. Where the environment could not be stabilized, producers were forced to use alternative production techniques, which were generally considered less than optimal.

The institutional development of the American economy throughout the late nineteenth century and for the greater part of the twentieth has been guided by the attempt to create and maintain an environment hospitable to mass production. Most of the characteristic economic institutions—the corporation, mass industrial unions, the Keynesian welfare state—were

14. Piore and Sabel (1984).
15. Smith (1976) [reprint]); Young (1928).

more or less consciously designed to maximize the realm of stability in which mass production could effectively operate. Where institutions were not actually molded to this purpose, they tended, sometimes inadvertently, to presume it. The labor institutions as they emerged in the decades immediately after World War II most certainly have to be understood in this way.

Only a brief description of these institutions is possible here.[16] For blue-collar workers in manufacturing, at least, the fulcrum of the institutional structure was the notion of a well-defined "job" consisting of a series of specific tasks that were the work the incumbent would be called on to perform. The idea that it was possible and meaningful to define work in this way was predicated on the stabilization of the work process associated with mass production. As the system developed, a worker's rights and responsibilities came to be attached to these jobs. The processes of wage setting, career advancement, a system of industrial jurisprudence, and job security were built around them. The system did not emerge whole at the end of the war; its basic logic was then perhaps only dimly perceived. The idea of mass production provided the direction for a process of creation and learning. The practices of the firm interacted with public policy over time. The system emerged gradually as the legal framework in which the economy was housed developed through legislative amendments, court interpretations, and managerial practice in the course of the subsequent postwar decades.[17]

The framework was not exactly the same for managerial and professional workers and lower-level, white-collar workers even within manufacturing, and less so outside it. But the evolution of the work process tended everywhere toward a narrow, functional specialization in which the organization of work under mass production was the extreme manifestation, and which tended to presume the stability and predictability of the underlying economic environment.

The Strains of the 1970s

Because it presumed stable background conditions, this institutional structure was severely strained by economic developments in the 1970s. The period was characterized by wide fluctuations in parameters of business decisions that business had become accustomed to treating as essentially fixed. The most salient of these newly variable parameters was the price of energy—rising suddenly with the Arab oil boycott in 1973, falling

16. See Doeringer and Piore (1971); Piore and Sabel (1984); Katz (1985).
17. See Katz (1985).

as the boycott eased, rising again with the Iranian revolution, and then continuing to fluctuate unpredictably in response to events in the Middle East. In automobile sales, these fluctuations produced an oscillation in demand between large and small cars that that canonical mass production industry found particularly difficult to follow. But the impact of unstable energy prices was not confined to automobiles; it led to variation in the composition of product demand or the structure of production of most manufacturing industries and frequently affected both demand and production. Energy, moveover, was not the only previously stable parameter of the economic environment that began to vary unpredictably in the 1970s and 1980s. The shift in 1971 was from a regime of fixed exchange rates (in which the value of the dollar was pegged to gold) to one of variable rates, and the value of the dollar varied over an increasingly wide range as the decade passed. There were also sudden and unpredictable shifts in interest rates and in composition of international demand. The general climate of instability was further augmented by economic deregulation and by the increased competitive pressure produced by expanding international trade. It clashed with the prevailing business strategy and the institutions and organizational structures that had grown up around it.

The clash was hardly confined to the structure of labor institutions; in the eyes of managers trying to cope with the problems it presented, labor institutions may have in fact been decidedly secondary. But it was certainly present in the domain of labor, and in that domain it came to center around the well-defined jobs that had become the key to the system. When managers were called on to continually reorganize the production process in response to changes in product demand or in the availability or cost of resources, it was difficult to respect the existing job jurisdictions or even to write down meaningful job definitions. Yet the order and structure of everything that went on in the workplace had come to depend so heavily on such jobs that without them the labor process seemed to degenerate into chaos and anarchy. This was certainly so in the eyes of the work force and their unions, but, in a different way, even for those responsible for management.

The reaction to this clash between the rigidity of the institutional structure and the fluidity of the economic environment was the attempt to move toward a more flexible system. In association with developments in computer technology, it led to more-flexible technologies that depended less on narrowly specialized labor and dedicated capital equipment. It also led to the development of similarly flexible organizational models and institutional designs as well. These developments are the subject of an enormous literature, largely a practical-managerial literature, but also (and increasingly) an analytical literature spread over several scholarly disciplines.[18] Again, even that part of this literature narrowly focused on labor adjustments has become so extensive that any effort to summarize it briefly will do violence to its subtlety and complexity. Nonetheless, when one tries to capture it in an analytical framework that presumes a limited number of discrete alternatives, the search for new, flexible approaches to production fall into two broad categories. These may be termed—somewhat rhetorically—the high road and the low road to industrial adjustment.[19]

In the high-road strategy, the emphasis is on the capacity of the organization to rapidly rearrange the components of the production process in response to changes in the composition of demand and/or the availability of alternative inputs. It thus seeks *integration* across components of the production process that under the mass-production strategy were insulated in a way that permitted each to pursue its own specialty. For ideas about how to do this, American companies have drawn heavily on Japanese practice. The paradigmatic reform is the *kan ban* system. The in-process inventories that previously insulated a company from its subcontractors, and by extension the inventories in-house that insulated one operation from another, are removed, and components arrive "just in time" to be used in the production process. This has a simple and direct effect on the flexibility of the system: it is no longer necessary to work off old inventories and build up new ones to change the product. But it also has important indirect effects, forcing close cooperation along the production chain. Moreover, without buffer stocks, trouble anywhere along the line will stop the whole production chain. It therefore leads to careful and continual analysis of the interrelationship among the parts. The new strategy is typically characterized as "lean"[20] but also as "fragile."[21]

In human-resource policy and work organization, the high-road strategy requires a much more broadly trained labor force. It tends to break down the old divisions between labor and management. The practical knowledge of the work force is critical to rapid adjustment. There is more emphasis on teamwork. Pay systems are altered to reflect these changes. Wages in the new strategy tend to be decoupled from the job and linked instead to skill and group performance.

18. The flavor of this literature is suggested by Nohria and Eccles (1992); Allen and Scott Morton (1994); and Best (1990).
19. Applebaum and Batt (1993); Bailey (1992); MacDuffie (1991); Osterman (1994).
20. Abernathy and others (1995); Womack, Jones, and Roos (1990).
21. MacDuffie (1991).

Analysts have paid considerably less attention to the low-road adjustment path. Indeed, I do not know of a single study of this approach comparable to the high-road literature (a point to which I return). The basic thrust of the strategy in the short run is to take advantage of labor market deregulation, the growing weakness of trade unions, and the increasing permissiveness of government policy to make up for any competitive disadvantage of the prevailing work structures themselves.[22] The operation of the postwar system without the original constraints is, however, bound to lead over time to a very different pattern of work organization and labor relations. It is unclear how much the proponents of the low-road strategy really understand that process or where exactly they expect it to lead. The divergence between the high-road and the low-road adjustment paths along these dimensions would seem to be an important factor in the polarization of wage and salary income that we are experiencing. Most of us who have thought about solving the structural-adjustment problems within the productive system itself have thought in terms of tilting the choice that enterprises are making further in favor of the high-road adjustment path.

Tilting the Adjustment Path

From this perspective, there appear to be three basic problems: the inability to gain closure in the debates about alternatives within the managerial community; the unresolved tensions within the high-road strategy; and the basic contradictions between the social requirements of the productive system, at least as understood in the high-performance strategy and the evolution of the social structure outside the workplace. Some understanding of each of these elements is necessary. Even more important, we will argue what the trade policy *debate* is playing into.

The basic problem is that the commitment to one or another of the adjustment strategies is not a commitment to a well-defined organizational blueprint that can be implemented by strict adherence to plan. It is instead a commitment to a general direction of movement, to working out the specific approach through practice. *Kan ban* is again to the point. The removal of in-process inventories forces the participants to work out a series of new relationships with each other. Management need not know what those relationships are; indeed, if it did know, it might not need to remove the inventories. In many companies, however, the continuing attraction of the

22. Harrison and Bluestone (1988).

low-road strategy forestalls this process of "learning by doing." Here too, *kan ban* is illustrative, but in this case *kan ban* in its strict sense of a system of on-time delivery of supplier parts. In the high-road adjustment strategy, this is supposed to produce close collaboration between contractor and supplier. But low-road strategists are also attracted to *kan ban;* they see it as a way of shifting inventory costs to the suppliers. Used in this second way, it tends to embitter supplier relations and produce a more confrontational relationship, one at arm's length. Many companies have managed to get commitment to *kan ban* as a tactic without gaining closure in the debates about the basic adjustment strategy. As a result, purchasing managers administer the policy in different ways, and the low-road managers poison the collaborative relations the high-road managers are trying to foster.

This is easiest to see in the case of *kan ban* but is even more prevalent in labor relations where the conflicts within management play into disputes within the union. Managers who see teams and quality circles as ways of undermining worker loyalties to their union make it almost impossible for managers who see these same reforms as vehicles for a collaborative system of production to gain the trust of union leaders (who must in turn carry along the rank and file) necessary to develop them in this way. Similar conflicts surround worker training. In the low-road faction, flexibility means simply getting the work force that once memorized the production routines for a single product to memorize a wider repertoire. The high-road faction thinks in terms of flexibility through general education and broad conceptual training in which the rank and file could actually participate in working out the sequence of product changes over time.

But there are also problems inherent in the high-road strategy itself. Companies seem to have conceived of this strategy initially in terms of a core-periphery model. The company would bind certain of their employees closely to the firm, making heavy investments in their education and training. It would also invest in a set of social relations to facilitate integration across function specialties and offer permanent employment commitments to safeguard these investments and encourage worker loyalty and commitment. This core labor force would be supplemented by a set of generally unskilled, temporary employees to provide a further buffer of flexibility. As the economy has evolved, however, this distinction has not been easy to maintain. Both the level of demand and the range of skills required to meet it vary too widely and unpredictably to provide stable employment opportunities. Even companies such as IBM and Digital that historically provided such employment security have been forced to lay off not just relatively unskilled workers, but also professional and managerial employees. The new strategy continues to require high skills, worker commitment, and integration across functional specialties, but companies must now obtain these in other ways. In the long run, moveover, the lack of employment security with the firm creates a potential skills problem. Without employment continuity, a firm no longer has the incentive to invest in worker education and training. It is therefore unclear that the market will provide workers with enough incentive and sufficient information to invest in themselves. And if the market does manage to substitute for the firm in this way, it will do so by reinforcing the very occupational and professional identities that constitute the most serious barriers to integration across functional lines.

These problems are reinforced by changes in the social structure outside the firm. This is especially evident in the rise of dual-career households. These limit the ability of workers to move geographically and strengthen the attachment to local labor markets in which employment continuity is dependent on these same professional and occupational identities.

Both the problems of individual companies in providing employment security and the conflicts between company attachment and the emergent social structure suggest that the high-wage strategy may be easier to work out in industrial districts where firms are linked to each other in networks, rather than in the relatively closed and self-contained organizations that arose under mass production. There are models of such networks in older industries such as the garment industry, but paradoxically those industries have tended to adjust by moving abroad. There are a few high-tech networks that have grown up in the new competitive environment—most notably Silicon Valley in California and, to a lesser extent, Route 128 in Boston—but this form of industrial organization is much more prevalent in Europe than in the United States.[23]

To recapitulate: American business became committed in the course of the late nineteenth century to a basic business strategy built around the progressive division of labor into narrow, functional specializations and (wherever possible) the mass production of standardized products using dedicated capital equipment and narrowly trained, semiskilled workers. The labor dimensions of this strategy were extended and perfected in the early postwar debates through a set of institutions and procedures based on clear and explicit lines of authority and responsibility and (for blue-collar, manufacturing employees) stable, well-defined jobs. The viability of these

23. Saxenian (1994).

arrangements and of the basic business strategy with which it was associated, depended on the stability of the business environment. That stability was ruptured by events in the 1970s. The instability and uncertainty generated in the process have continued to mark the environment in which American business operates.

In the face of this, managers have reacted by attempting to develop two basic strategic alternatives. One of these is a set of so-called high performance work practices associated with lean production, mass customization, and flexible specialization. These practices involve collaborative work relations that abrogate and integrate across the boundaries of functional specialties and break down traditional distinctions between labor and management. The other is based on driving down wages and other input costs by taking advantage of the conservative political climate, deregulation, and increased competitive pressure unleashed in part by the harshness of the business environment itself. These strategies, and particularly the high-performance alternative, have been difficult to work out. That process has been confused with continuing debates among managerial factions that agree on basic reforms but interpret them in contradictory and incomparable ways. It has been further disrupted by tensions between the need for greater worker commitment to the firm and for integration across functional specialties, on the one hand, and by economic and social forces pushing the worker back on the local labor market on the other hand, where he or she is dependent on occupational and professional identities reflecting the functional divisions of the old institutions to find new jobs.

The Role of Trade

How does trade become a part of this story? How does the story presented here lead us to think about trade policy?

This story divides conceptually into two distinct components. One is about a change in the economic environment that renders existing business strategy ineffective. The second is about the development and implementation of some strategic alternative. Trade enters each component. It is part of the broader series of changes in the environment that promotes structural adjustment. But it also influences the process through which that adjustment occurs.

The Business Environment and the Trading Regime

Trade policy is obviously complex and multidimensional and, as a result, often contradictory. Nonetheless, it seems possible to identify at least three dimensions of the policies emergent over the last several decades that seem important in understanding firm-level adjustments and business strategies. One of these is the relentless expansion of trade—especially in a country like the United States, whose involvement in and dependence on world markets was hitherto quite circumscribed. It may not be exactly true that the expansion has accelerated in the last decade. But it is probably true that the various institutional developments, such as the growing integration within the European Community, the renegotiation of GATT and, of course, NAFTA, have operated to make the openness of the American economy increasingly salient in managerial consciousness.

A second dimension of the trade environment is its general instability and uncertainty. This was signaled by the movement at the beginning of the 1970s to break the link between the dollar and gold and to move to a regime of fluctuating exchange rates, and reinforced by the wide swing in the value of the dollar during the 1980s. Other factors contributing to the climate surrounding the international trading regime were the radical shifts in demand associated with the recycling of petrodollars and the third-world debt crisis. Third (and closely related but distinct) has been the generally deflationary policies of the major industrial countries and the International Monetary Fund (IMF) and the way in which they have imposed austerity on one other, on third world countries, and lately on eastern Europe and the nations of the former Soviet Union. This means that the expansion of trade and the general uncertainty associated with it, is occurring in a world economy marked by excess capacity, where any imbalance tends to lead to a further decline in demand on the one hand and expansion of supply on the other.

These effects—expansion, instability, uncertainty, and excess capacity—are in an important sense more than mere characteristics of the trading environment. They can be said to constitute the basic characteristics of the trading *regime,* in the sense that they are the outgrowth of a fairly coherent strategy associated with a single policymaking community pursued in a well-defined domain of policymaking activity. Like a business strategy, it is probably good to think of a trade regime as a direction of movement rather than as a fixed institution. My own interviews with business executives suggest that it is indeed viewed in this way.

Nonetheless, it would be extremely difficult to separate the trading regime from the various other aspects of the business environment that have influenced strategic decisions over the last decade. The trading environment encouraged firms to adopt more flexible production strategies and organizational structures, but so did the deregulation of markets and the new computer technologies underlying flexible manufacturing systems, computer-aided design, and the like.[24] It is unclear that these factors are conceptually distinct. To the extent that market regulations are viewed as nontariff barriers (NTBs) to trade, their removal is bound up with the new trading regime. In the 1960s, computers were viewed as a solution to centralized planning and the coordination of large bureaucratic organizations. Their emergence in the 1970s and 1980s as vehicles of flexibility may as well have been a product of the environment in which the technology reached its maturity as an inherent characteristic of the technology itself. Recent analysis suggests that in firm-level data, these factors tend to be associated.[25] This is certainly the impression that emerges in the interviews from which I have abstracted the story presented here. In any case, whether by accident or because they are themselves intertwined, all of the environmental forces appear to have been moving in the same direction.

However, it is worth distinguishing between two dimensions of those forces. One is the sheer competitive pressure they exerted on business enterprises. But the second is the instability and uncertainty they generated. It is this last that seems to have been most critical in terms of the perceived need to abandon mass production and to develop more flexible structures.

The instability and uncertainty are salient characteristics of the new international trading regime as it emerged in the last several decades, but they are not inevitable products of the expansion of trade. They were generated instead by the shift toward a flexible exchange rate regime after 1971; by the way the industrialized world reacted to the oil crisis, the capital flows generated, and the debt crisis of the third world that eventually ensued as a consequence; and, more generally, by the failure of the major trading countries and the international banking agencies to develop a more coherent system for coordinated macroeconomic management.[26]

The nature of the trading environment may have interacted with other forces to make this process irreversible. For example, technologies that permit a firm to shift rapidly among products and/or alternative inputs in response to variations in exchange rates also reduce the cost of developing products responsive to rapid changes in fashion or specialized to the tastes of particular consumer groups. Once these technologies are in place, they become an independent factor, breaking up mass markets and promoting competition among producers, and contribute in this way to the instability of the business environment.

24. Allen and Scott Morton (1994).
25. Bernard and Jensen (1995). An anomalous *negative* collocation between wages and tariff protection that shows up at the industry level is also suggestive of such relationships. See Gaston and Trefler (1994).
26. Kindleberger (1988); Block (1977).

On the other hand, the dichotomy drawn here between the high-road and the low-road adjustment paths obscures important variants within these broad strategies that make the adjustment process even now more sensitive to the stability and uncertainty of the international trading environment than it otherwise appears. There is, for example, an important difference between customized mass production, in which the firm builds in advance of the market the capacity to produce a specified set of products, and true customization, in which the product is tailored to market requirements as they emerge.[27] In the former, equipment is "preprogrammed" and production workers are cross trained. In the latter, however, production workers must be able to "reprogram" the equipment and possibly even redesign the product continually. True customization therefore requires a significantly higher level of education and much more intense interaction between shop floor personnel and what are normally considered professionals and managers. In the long run, mass customization may turn out to be a way station in the transition toward flexible production strategies. But it is likely to prove easier for firms with a tradition of mass production to master. A more stable international environment would probably prolong the period in which such an intermediate strategy is viable.

The Adjustment Process

The second component of the story we have been telling is the adjustment process itself. Conventional analysis would focus here upon decision-making and choice, and the way in which trade influences the relative cost of alternatives. But from an institutionalist perspective, and as it emerges in discussions with the actors themselves, the intellectual, or cognitive, dimension of the process is salient. The process thus lends itself to division into four distinct stages. First, there is the recognition of the need for adjustment, the recognition that the business environment has indeed changed in ways that make existing strategies and the associated organizational structures no longer viable. Second is the formulation of an alternative strategy or a set of strategies among which to choose. Third (to the extent that the problem is formulated in terms of a set of strategies) is the choice among alternatives. The final stage is the working out of the operational implications of that choice through practice. Trade potentially enters the process at each of these stages in distinct and different ways.

27. Pine (1993).

The first stage—the recognition that a new strategy is required—can be understood in terms of the relationship between institutions and environmental conditions. The institutions can be thought of as having been designed to accommodate a limited range of possible variation in environmental conditions, but inconsistent with the tails of the distribution of possibilities, which lie outside that range. When those outlying conditions materialize in practice, the actors are faced with a dilemma. If the conditions are truly outliers, it would be desirable to preserve the institutional structures and make ad hoc adjustments—in other words, to "muddle through." But the outlying conditions might also signify that the distribution had shifted permanently—that those conditions are no longer "outlying" and require basic institutional reform. This was the dilemma faced by American business in the 1970s.

In retrospect, it is clear that the environmental conditions were not outliers but constituted permanent change. It is therefore tempting to attribute the response to entrenched management and recalcitrant union leaders. But given the information available at the time and the nature of this dilemma, it is unclear that the business and labor practitioners took a particularly long time before they began to act, nor that when they finally did so, it was so obviously the right decision. This is especially so when one recognizes the possibility of adjustments in the international trading regime that would have stabilized the system and obviated the need to adopt alternative strategies. And it is unclear—and from the point of view of trade policy this seems a more important implication—that more exposure to trade would have forced business and labor leaders to recognize the need for adjustment sooner or that a lesser degree of exposure would have postponed that realization.

The point can be extended to the other components of the adjustment process as well—to the formulation of alternative strategies and to their implementation. If adjustment is indeed a cognitive process and one moreover that works itself out over time through interaction with practice, it may actually not be sensitive to the degree of market pressure. Such pressure must be enough to set the process in motion. But once in motion, competitive pressure is as likely to destroy businesses that might otherwise have been able to adjust; to force others to lay off workers whom they could have retained; and perhaps worst of all, to promote draconian cost-cutting measures that in effect push firms onto the low-road adjustment path when a path of high-road adjustment might otherwise have been feasible.

Models of Adjustment Strategy

If adjustment is a cognitive process, what besides competitive pressure actually guides it? In terms of the response of American industry in the last two decades, what is most striking is the salience in managerial thinking of the Japanese. American companies have not slavishly copied Japanese institutions or managerial practices. Yet to the extent that a business strategy is basically a vague direction of movement, the operational details of which are worked out through practice, the high-road strategy was borrowed from Japan. The first phase of adjustment was clearly marked by a shift in the way in which Japanese practice was perceived. In the early 1970s, for example, American carmakers were prepared to attribute everything to wage competition. Company and union officials went to Japan to study shop practice and mainly "saw" on the shop floor so many personnel from subcontractors who paid lower wages than the mother company as to render direct cost comparisons between U.S. and Japanese plants meaningless. By the end of the decade, similar observers focused instead on what workers were actually doing and how they did it. These later studies and companion works on contractor relations, inventory management, and the like provided the intellectual inspiration for the Saturn experiment at General Motors and the reform of practice within the Big Three themselves.[28]

In my own research, the transformation in what American industry looked at and learned from Japan is bracketed by Xerox in 1977 responding to the challenge of Canon and Konishiruko, and Motorola in 1984 attempting to meet Japanese competition in cellular telephones. The Xerox case is more complete but perhaps less interesting. It seems there was little alternative to the way in which the company came to see the challenge it faced or in how it constructed its response. Accustomed to complete monopoly in its technology, Xerox suddenly found itself competing with technologically superior, higher-quality products selling at lower prices and coming from a country with a reputation for low wages and inferior goods. Xerox's share of the U.S. market dropped from 80 percent in 1976 to 13 percent in 1982. The company's very existence was challenged, and management had no clue as to how that challenge had been mounted.[29] It had either to look closely at what the Japanese were doing or to give up and go out of business. But why did a diversified company like Motorola—which had throughout the 1970s retreated from virtually all consumer-durable markets in the face of Japanese competition—suddenly decide to use a completely

28. Katz (1985); Womack, Jones, and Roos (1990).
29. Jacobson and Hillkirk (1986); Kearns and Nadler (1992); Morone (1993).

new product like cellular telephones, which was then a trivial part of the company's business, to try and beat Japan at its own game?

Even more interesting than the cases where companies tried to revise their practices in light of what they could learn about Japan are the cases in which they did not. Unfortunately, we have no case studies of the low-road strategy comparable to those that followed the development of the high-road alternative.

But the garment industry can be taken as a case of this kind. Certain segments of the industry—principally the makers of men's suits—have attempted to work out high-performance human resource strategies, and the academic literature focuses mainly on these.[30] Yet the dominant response of the industry to competitive pressure has been to move production to developing countries. It seems to have done so because it believed that it could not compete with the low wages paid in the third world through reforms of domestic practice. However, the extremely long supply chains this entailed posed major organizational problems in an industry where fashion and seasonality place a premium on timing. These organizational problems, moreover, were frequently compounded by standards of quality and product diversity. It is therefore unclear that the challenge of working out an import strategy was any less than that of outlining the high-performance work practices. To this degree, the choice the garment industry made is not nearly as obvious as it at first appears.[31]

In the diagnoses American industry made of its own organizational problems and the strategies of response it chose to pursue, it is also curious that it paid so little attention to European practice. Both the high-performance and the low-performance strategies—at least to the extent that the garment industry can be taken to represent the latter—were inspired by East Asia. In fact, only part of the threat to the domestic garment industry came from this direction. While our markets were being invaded from below by low-wage competitors in Asia, European producers were picking off the

30. Abernathy and others (1995); Bailey (1989); Berg and others (1996).

31. The most obvious hypothesis is that the choice of adjustment strategy is directed by the apparent source of competitive pressure. This directed the attention of the automobile industry (as well as Xerox and Motorola) toward Japan and the garment industry toward East Asia. Gereffi hypothesized that the difference in response reflects the characteristics of the controlling companies in the supply chain. Garments are driven by the retailers, especially department stores and now specialty stores like The Gap. The automobile industry is driven by the producers themselves. It is not clear, however, that this different explanation can be distinguished from one based on relative wage rates given that producer-dominated industries tend to be relatively capital intensive. See Gereffi (1994).

high end of the market. These producers actually paid wages higher than our own and operated in fashion segments that posed even greater logistical problems for distant producers. In these respects, Europe would seem to be a source of an alternative high-road adjustment strategy, but it has evidently never been perceived this way.

But, in many ways, the centrality of Japan as a model for firms that have adopted the high-road strategy is equally hard to explain. The Japanese labor model presents several current problems in the United States. First, it involves permanent employment commitments of a kind that American companies initially thought they could offer but have since decided they cannot. Second, occupational and professional identities are much weaker in Japan than in the United States. The integration across functional boundaries that flexible forms of production seem to require is therefore not problematic in Japan in the way that it is for us. European practice in the form of such institutions as the apprenticeship (in Germany and other German-speaking countries) and the interfirm cooperation in the industrial districts of central Italy offer models that seem to resolve many of these problems. And yet they appear to have exerted no influence at all in the reforms of the last decade at the company level and have actually had a greater influence among academics and policymakers. Indeed, among academics at least, there is now a reaction against the apprenticeship model. Much of the current criticism is, however, basically irrelevant for the adjustment process as we have characterized it since foreign models serve there only to define the starting point in the development of strategies whose actual content is worked out in practice. Thus, in the formulation of its adjustment strategy, there appears to be ample scope to improve the performance of American business. Is there a role for public policy in this regard?

Conclusions: Some Observations about Politics and Policy

The distinction between environmental pressures on the one hand and the process of adjustment on the other provides a convenient framework for organizing a discussion of policy. But, to facilitate that discussion, it is useful to recapitulate the basic argument I have sought to develop here.

The argument has basically been conducted at two levels. At one level, it is an attempt to lay out a particular conceptual framework for thinking about the process of economic growth and development in general, and the impact of trade in particular. At a second level, it is a substantitive argument about the impact of trade on the course of development of the American economy in the last two decades.

The conceptual framework views the process of economic growth and development as preeminently *cognitive* and *social*. It is cognitive in the sense that it is basically a process of creation and learning. It is social in the sense that it involves the interaction of people through discussion and debate about practical affairs and focuses on the understandings and inter-pretations that emerge in that process. It involves purposive behavior and conscious choice, but the choice is not simply a product of the constraints imposed and the opportunities offered, by the environment. It is a product as well, and more important, of the understandings about the constraints and opportunities that emerge as the actors talk to each other. What the actors choose is, as a result, not a particular location within a set of well-defined alternatives but rather a general direction of movement. The specific content that that movement entails is worked out in practice, again through discussion and debate.

The main focus of my analysis in this chapter has been on the business strategies pursued by firms and the associated strategies of production and human resource management. But those strategies emerged as part of a broader set of debates and discussions including debates about macroeconomic policy, about deregulation, and (of particular sig-nificance in the context of this book) about international trade. The adjustment to trade began at a point when most of American business, particularly in manufacturing but in broad segments of the service in-dustry as well, were committed to a strategy of mass production. To "adjust," therefore, business had first to abandon these initial commit-ments and then to move toward the development of alternatives, first by conceptualizing what those alternatives were, then by selecting among them, and finally by working out the chosen alternative in practice over time.

One question of trade policy is whether the expansion of trade in the U.S. economy over the last decade allowed sufficient time for an adjustment process of this kind to work itself out. Given the fact that business had to abandon a set of long-standing beliefs and commitments, and that to do so it had to be convinced that the changes in the environment in which it was operating were not simply transitory perturbations that would soon go away, time was probably as important as the sheer magnitude of the pres-sure exerted by the pressure of competition from abroad, and a more gradual adjustment process might have been equally effective but with a lesser cost in terms of labor displacement.

But the primary thrust of the institutionalist perspective is to focus attention on the way in which public policy plays into debates and discussions among practitioners. The central debate was about what strategy to pursue once the need for adjustment was finally recognized. It centered around a dichotomy between the high-road and the low-road alternatives.

Only the high-road strategy would seem to be compatible with social cohesion and political stability in the United States over the long run. As a strategy of development, it raises the skill requirements of workers at lower levels of the employment hierarchy. By so doing, it reduces the disparities of skill (and hence presumably of income) between them and higher-level employees. Perhaps more important, it demands a kind of cooperation among different parts of the labor force that creates a direct economic interest at the level of the enterprise in social integration. It will not in itself create a labor force capable of meeting its demands. Indeed, relative to mass production, it reduces the direct incentive for the employer to provide training and employment security. But it does create a more general interest in the business community in high levels of education and training and in institutional arrangements that conserve these by promoting employment continuity, and hence fosters a climate of public policy favorable to reducing social barriers.

The low-road strategy, by contrast, is one in which the business community has little direct economic interest in public policies that promote economic opportunity, employment security, or social cohesion and the skill requirements of the productive structure primarily involve advanced education. The strategy, moreover, tends to widen the skill gap and the disparities in income and employment security within the firms that pursue it, and by the same token between workers within those firms and workers within sectors of the economy pursuing other strategies of development. One might imagine a more continuous distribution of income and skill in which the dichotomy between the top and the bottom of the hierarchy in these firms is bridged by the lower-level jobs in firms pursuing the high-wage strategy but the requirements for communication and cooperation differ across skill and occupational lines. As a result, the nature of the skills associated with different positions in the wage distribution are so different in the two approaches to production that it is hard to believe that the continuity in the income distribution would ever translate into opportunities for economic mobility. Thus the low-road strategy would seem to aggravate all of the conflicts and tensions already present in American society. If the viability of an open trading regime is, as Polanyi's reading of history suggests, problematic and dependent on conditions of social stability, a primary goal of any public policy conducive to the expansion of trade over the long run has to be to promote the high-road path of adjustment.

From this point of view, it is hard not to be concerned about the trade policy debate of recent years. It is not so much the specific trade policies that have emerged from that debate—not NAFTA, for example, or GATT. Indeed, it is really not these *policies* at all, but rather the way the case for them has been composed and the arguments, for and against, have been played out in the political arena. The problem at root is that the proponents of trade expansion have made their argument as part of a broader argument about the virtues of an unregulated market economy. Trade expansion has in this way been tied to a series of other policy proposals. In labor policy, these include the elimination of the legal and collective bargaining restraints on the employer's ability to adjust to trade by lowering wages, reducing benefits, and generally increasing the pace and pressure of work— the elimination, in other words, of virtually all obstacles to the low-road strategy. It is not just that the arguments made in behalf of trade lead people to believe that removing the barriers to such a policy is desirable. Each victory for trade policies cast in these terms suggests that the broader argument is gaining appeal and that the measures already taken to under- mine collective bargaining and minimal labor standards are actually secure and likely to be extended. They thus reinforce the presumption that an unregulated market can be sustained over a long period of time—a presump- tion exactly the opposite from that which, following Polanyi, this chapter starts out. It obviously enhances the attraction of the low-road adjustment strategy.

There are also affects on the high-road alternative. The growing attrac- tion of the low-wage strategy, as we have seen, makes it difficult to gain closure in internal managerial debates. It also leads to situations where new practices critical to the high road are sabotaged by managers committed to cost-cutting tactics and who, with this in mind, administer reforms designed to draw people into high-trust, cooperative relations in ways that actually increase distrust and suspicion among them. To the extent, moreover, that problems the high-road strategy has encountered need supplemental public institutions and interfirm cooperative relations to resolve, the formulation of trade policy in terms that disparage governmental policy and public action creates an intellectual climate in which such policies are difficult to even think of. This discourages strategies predicated on supporting public institutions. This must help account for the fact that American business has looked to the Japanese company, which in terms of labor practices, training, and industrial relations is relatively self-contained, and eschewed European models where public institutions play a prominent role.

These effects have been most apparent in North American trade policy, in particular in the debates about NAFTA and most recently in the discussion of guaranteed loans for Mexico. The link between NAFTA and the unregulated market was first created by the Bush administration, which initiated the negotiation process and launched the national debate. But Democratic victory in 1992 and the emergence of President Clinton as the chief advocate of the treaty provided an opportunity to reshape the terms in which it was interpreted and understood. The early rhetoric of the new administration in fact began to do this. It linked the expanding trade with Mexico to a broader argument for a high-wage labor market. The treaty was understood in these terms as part of a long-term economic strategy in which relatively unskilled, low-paying jobs would gradually migrate abroad, and the U.S. economy would focus increasingly on high-wage, skilled production. The geographic proximity of Mexico would enable work to be divided up in this way, even when close geographic proximity between the different types of work was required. High-wage jobs could therefore be preserved that would otherwise be forced to follow the low-wage work that they complemented to more distant locations.

Interpreted in this way, the treaty might have been associated with a number of other measures promoting a high-wage policy that the president had advocated at one time or another in his campaign, such as an increase in minimum wages, renewed protections for the rights of workers to organize and engage in collective bargaining, programs of training to upgrade worker skills, and extended access to higher education for new entrants into the labor market. Together, these programs would have signaled to employers that the low-road strategy was simply not viable over the long run. The administration also had advocated aid to business planning and technology that would actively promote the high-road strategy; some of these were in fact actually implemented in the first two years of the Clinton administration. But none of them were ever linked in the NAFTA debate to the treaty. And in the end, the case the Democratic administration made was essentially the same as the case Republican predecessors had developed, and it did nothing to shift the terms in which adjustment was conceived in the business community.

The opponents in the debate, first about NAFTA and then GATT, ratified these effects. They could have focused on the adjustment process, debated particular adjustment strategies, and raised in the NAFTA debate demands for the kinds of domestic labor policies that would have fostered the high-performance adjustment strategies—policies to which they were committed on other grounds. They focused instead simply on job loss. They thus seemed to be arguing against trade altogether rather than against a particular regime of trade and adjustment.

Developments in U.S.-Mexican trade since the passage of NAFTA can also be used to illustrate the limits of conventional perspectives on trade and the trade policy debate those perspectives have fostered. Trade did not initially evolve in the way in which either the proponents or the opponents of the treaty envisaged. A major imbalance in trade between the two countries quickly emerged, but the imbalances ran in favor of the relatively high-wage American economy and against the Mexicans. An enormous deficit developed in the Mexican balance of trade, clearly not sustainable over the long run. That deficit was at the heart of the financial crisis that broke out in December 1994.

The conventional diagnosis of that crisis attributed it to a misguided government attempt to maintain a fixed exchange rate for the peso relative to the dollar, an attempt that led to a progressively overvalued peso. The cure, which that diagnosis implied, administered under the tutelage of the U.S. government and the IMF, was devaluation and austerity. It was administered, as is well known, under the tutelage of the U.S. government and the IMF, at the cost of a recession of unprecedented magnitude in terms of the level of unemployment and the rate of decline in economic activity.

But there are signs that the problems may lie deeper—in the fundamentals of real economic adjustment that a correction in exchange rates and financial balances will not reach. The most disturbing of these signs is that traditional industries such as garments, shoes, and furniture, where Mexico was thought to have a comparative advantage relative to the United States, have been particularly hard hit by the opening to trade. They have been swamped by imports at the high end of the market from the United States and Europe. They have also been swamped by imports at the low end of the market, largely from Asia but also in the form of used clothes from the United States.

The United States has also been a vehicle for Asian imports, many of which arrive via discount retail stores likened to U.S. chains that have proliferated in Mexico in the wake of NAFTA. Who have been successful in exporting to the United States are the *maquiladores,* basically subcontractors operating under the tutelage of their U.S. clients. The *maquiladores'* exports, however, compete not with jobs at the bottom of the U.S. wage hierarchy but with intermediate-level, semiskilled jobs—precisely the jobs in the heavily unionized sector of American manufacturing that the opposition to NAFTA was most afraid of losing. Moreover, the *maquiladores* have few direct linkages with the rest of the Mexican economy. Although they obviously enhance local purchasing power, they are basically attached to the U.S. economy and are clearly subordinate within U.S. managerial hierarchies, with only limited control over their own internal operations, let alone their own destinies.

The research that might explain these patterns is still in progress, and I cannot present definitive results. But the institutionalist view of economic adjustment as a cognitive and social process suggest what those results might be. That view implies that the key element in the success of the *maquiladores* is precisely the tutorial that their American clients have provided, teaching them in an intense, hands-on way how to efficiently produce quality goods in volume. The traditional firms have not had the benefit of this kind of tutorial. This has not only limited their capacity to export but also their hold on the domestic market, which has been undermined by the transformation of retailing. This has occurred with imported knowledge and/or U.S. tutors, which has imposed new standards of quality and volume that nothing in the experience of traditional Mexican producers prepares them to meet. The Mexican government, which might have provided that kind of tutorial through some kind of industrial policy, has been preoccupied instead by financial concerns and policies of deregulation conceived in terms of a market ideology and framework basically antagonistic to any kind of structural intervention in the economy.

The most optimistic prognosis to which such a diagnosis leads is that domestic producers will learn with time. But before they have a chance to do so, many of the firms who might have survived with the kind of tutelage the *maquiladores* received from the American supplies will have gone out of business. A balance of trade seems more likely to be achieved over time by the expansion of the *maquiladore* sector. It is equally likely, however, that in that time a Polanyi-like reaction to trade will set in on one side or the other of the U.S.-Mexican border as Americans see the emerging pattern of trade eating into the heart of their job structure and Mexicans perceive the increasingly dependent character of the economic relations trade is drawing them into. The irony is that the institutionalist perspective that leads one to foresee these outcomes suggests that they are not in any way preordained by trade itself. They are instead the product of differential learning—not only on the part of producers, but also within the policymaking community—and could have been forestalled by changes in our perception of the way in which the productive economy is embedded in social processes.

Comment by Barry Bluestone

In this wide-ranging chapter, Michael Piore travels from the works of Karl Polanyi and a consideration of the nineteenth-century sweatshop to his own research on late-twentieth-century, flexible specialization in the modern enterprise—all in hope of shedding some light on how international trade affects labor. It is hard to tell how well he accomplishes this task. The expansive sweep of this work leaves one wanting to come up for air. Nonetheless, by suggesting we consider market institutions and managerial strategy as useful elements in the current trade debate, Piore adds a much-needed dimension to the discussion.

Take one little mystery, for example. In empirical attempts to relate the trend in import penetration to increases in earnings inequality, the timing of the relationship seems out of synch. It was during the 1970s that imports as a share of gross domestic product (GDP) nearly doubled, as table 6-1 indicates. In the 1980s and 1990s, imports as a share of GDP continued to rise, but at a much slower rate than in the previous decade. The pattern in earnings inequality is much the reverse: little change during the 1970s, with rapid growth in inequality thereafter. This would seem to suggest that international trade in general could not account for more than a small fraction of increased inequality.

More consistent with the timing is the growth in imports from less-developed countries (LDCs). By 1990, 35 percent of all U.S. imports were from LDCs, compared with only 14 percent in 1970.[32] This has stirred a number of economists (most prominently Adrian Wood) to suggest that it is this portion of total trade that is to blame for stagnant or falling wage rates among low-skilled workers in the United States and overall growing earnings inequality.[33]

But, the problem with this approach, as noted by a range of economists, is that even with its growth, imports from developing countries are simply too small a proportion of total U.S. GDP—less than 3 percent—to account for any more than a fraction of the enormous increase in wage inequality.[34]

What are we to make of all of this? Following Piore's admonition that we pay more attention to institutional factors and explicit managerial strategies may provide one clue. Consider the following scenario as an explanation

32. See Freeman (1995, p. 19).
33. See Wood (1994, 1995).
34. See Burtless (1995).

Table 6-1. *Imports, Real Wages, and Earnings Inequality*

Year	Imports[a]	Average real weekly earnings[b]	var Ln weekly earnings (index 1975 = 100)
1969	5.3	300.81	104
1979	10.3	291.66	100
1989	11.2	264.22	110
Percent change			
1969–79	94.3	–3.0	–3.8
1979–89	8.7	–9.4	10.0

Sources: Council of Economic Advisers and Karoly (1993, figure 2.14, pp. 19–98).
a. As percentage of GOP.
b. In U.S. dollars.

for the nearly decade-long lag in the response of the wage distribution to the initial 1970s import surge.

When imports from developed countries began to rise at the end the 1960s—before the growth in exports from the less-developed world—neither wages nor employment levels were initially affected. Instead, with domestic oligopoly advantage challenged in one trade-sensitive industry after another, as foreign products gained substantial footholds in such sectors as autos, steel, machine tools, and consumer electronics, firm managers in the United States increasingly found they no longer had the luxury of simply raising prices to compensate for weakening rates of return. What had first been seen as a temporary dip in profits in the late 1960s (as monopoly rents declined) was ultimately viewed by the mid-1970s as an alarming long-term trend. The before-tax profit rate of nonfinancial corporations (as measured by the ratio of capital income—interest, rent, and profits—to the capital stock) fell from a peak of 12.6 percent in 1965 to 9.5 percent by the decade's end. It would continue to fall to 6.4 percent through the busines cycle peak in 1979 and to 5.0 percent in the 1982 recession.[35]

Under mounting pressure from stockholders who saw their dividends slipping and their capital gains turning into capital losses—and increasingly anxious in the face of a new breed of corporate raiders—managers set out to develop strategies to reverse the lengthening shadow of falling profitability. By the end of the 1970s and the beginning of the 1980s, what Piore and other analysts call the low road to profitability became the dominant strategy in one industry after another. This was not so much prompted by the 1980s competition from low-wage rivals in LDCs as by

35. See Baker and Mishel (1995).

the earlier competition from highly efficient and innovative producers in Europe and Japan. Instead of focusing on ways to boost revenues and market share, managers adopted a broad array of "lean and mean" cost-control tactics, including wage and benefit reductions, "two-tier" wage structures, the substitution of part-time and contingent labor for full-time employees, an acceleration in subcontracting and outsourcing, increased use of automation, and expanded multinational production. These tactics could not be implemented with the same efficacy for all segments of the labor force. Highly skilled workers in relative short supply were sheltered from this strategy. The least-skilled workers bore the full brunt, as their services could be procured from abroad by U.S. multinationals and foreign producers, or done away with altogether through automation.

Disseminating such an explicit strategy throughout the economy is not instantaneous. The results do not show up immediately in either wages and employment or in profits. But after 1969, manufacturing employment levels stopped growing. Employment growth became concentrated almost exclusively in the service sector where wage rates were generally lower and the variance in earnings substantially higher.[36] By the 1980s, this began to show up in the aggregate data on workers' earnings. The profits bonus that followed from this strategy took nearly a decade to emerge. But by 1989, the before-tax profit rate was back up to 7.5 percent, and it would continue to rise thereafter. By early 1995, the profit rate exceeded 10 percent for the first time since 1968.[37]

Note that this account of falling wages, growing inequality, and rising profits does not rely on massive increases in imports or massive increases in transnational investment. Merely management's credible threat of moving production offshore in response to import competition can induce vulnerable workers or their unions to settle for wage concessions or benefit reductions. Management need only point to a few compelling examples of where labor's wage demands led to job loss to obtain this outcome.

The key divide in the trade-labor debate is whether technology or trade is to blame for growing inequality. But once one admits of the complex

---

36. In 1987, the mean annual earnings of high school dropouts in manufacturing was $13,768 (in 1987 dollars) compared with only $7,798 in services; similarly, college graduates enjoyed an edge of $33,367 to $27,446 in manufacturing over services. Between 1963 and 1987, the earnings gap between college graduates and high school dropouts working in manufacturing increased by about 15 percent, from 2.1 to 2.4. In services, the ratio grew by 60 percent, from 2.2 to 3.5. See Bluestone (1990).

37. Baker and Mishel (1995).

behavioral models inherent in the institutional approach, untangling explanations from one another is nearly impossible despite heroic attempts.[38] Any variance decomposition is only useful to the extent that the covariance terms do not swamp the independent effects of each variable. There is also every reason to believe that managerial strategies are fraught with feedback effects and interdependencies. Import penetration, for example, may be the single most important factor leading firms to adopt new labor-saving technologies. Was the resulting unemployment due to implementation of new technology or to trade? Was the resulting shift from low-skill to high-skill workers trade induced or technology driven? Only by understanding the complex nature of institutions and managerial strategy is it possible to begin to answer such questions. That much of the growth in inequality is found *within* industries—and especially in domestically provided services—does not suggest, from this perspective, that technology is the culprit any more than trade. Trade could play a significant role in generating the supply conditions in the non-traded-services sector responsible for the increased wage dispersion found there. In this case, import penetration was the initial impetus for an entire sequence of strategies that ultimately led to falling real wages for less-skilled workers and rising inequality. De-industrialization, deunionization, and more rapid diffusion of labor-saving technology may be the apparent causes of these wage patterns, But they may have been set in motion by increased trade from developed countries and later reinforced by low-wage trade with developing countries.[39]

Testing such stories about trade and technology can probably only be accomplished by ingenious cliometricians. They would need to estimate what the impact of alternative scenarios might have yielded. If more companies had followed a high-road strategy of attempting to expand market share through improved product quality and innovation rather than concentrating on pure cost reduction, would wage trends have been any different? If import penetration ratios had grown more slowly during the 1970s, would profits have declined less severely and would management have had the opportunity to explore alternative strategies for maintaining their competitiveness? If we believe the answer to these questions is at least a possible yes, Piore's suggestion that studying institutions and managerial behavior is worth a good deal of attention. The problem of disentangling the causes of growing inequality is made even more difficult if we do not seek

38. One of the most comprehensive attempts is found in Blackburn, Bloom, and Freeman (1990). See also Bluestone (1995).

39. See Bluestone (1994).

a single explanation for the evolving wage patterns across the entire employment distribution. The consensus estimates following from an informal poll of economists deeply involved in attempting to parse out the sources of growing inequality indicated that 45 percent of the increase in wage dispersion was due to technological factors and only 11 percent to changes originating in foreign trade. The remaining 44 percent of the rise in inequality was assigned to a variety of factors, including increased immigration, industry deregulation, a falling minimum wage, and declining unionization.[40] What such figures hide is the real possibility that workers in different industries with various skills have been affected by these factors differentially. For some workers, the loss in income is *entirely* due to trade. Their company simply closed up shop and moved their operations to East Asia. Other workers saw their earnings rise as their firms substituted sophisticated technologies requiring higher skills that the workers gained on the job. In this case, high-skilled workers have experienced rising wages due to technological change. Low-skilled workers have seen their wages fall as the result of being displaced by import penetration from manufacturing jobs with higher wages to lower-wage, service industry positions. Accordingly, former General Motors blue-collar workers who have sustained a 25 to 50 percent loss in earnings are perfectly correct in complaining that imports are responsible for the loss in their standard of living. The GM engineer is equally correct in believing that his high-tech skills are responsible for his rising income.

All of this should lead us to probe much deeper into the institutions and strategies of firms if we are to go much further in explaining wage and distribution dynamics. Piore's contribution lies in reminding us of the relevance of this approach.

Comment by Marina Whitman

As he has done so often throughout his career, Michael Piore attempts in this chapter to put some institutional flesh on the theoretical models and econometric estimates that have formed the underlying bones of the discussion here. His goal, furthermore, is to place the relationship between trade and wages in a broader context: that of the changing nature

40. The informal poll was taken during the Colloquium on U.S. Wage Trends sponsored by the Federal Reserve Bank of New York, November 4, 1994. See Burtless (1995).

of the implicit social contract between American firms and American workers.

Piore's discussion stresses a number of useful insights that are too often ignored by economists. One is that the market transactions on which our profession focuses its attention are always embedded in a particular social structure that includes both the explicit legal/regulatory framework and what Charles Schultze has called implicit social norms, and that every society must somehow mediate the inevitable tensions between the individual self-interest that dominates the former and the requirements of social order provided by the latter. Indeed, the complexity of these relationships may help to explain the fact that, as became increasingly clear throughout the conference that generated this book, neither imaginative models nor sophisticated empirical work has laid to rest the disagreements and conundrums with which the trade-wages issue is fraught.

Piore also reminds us forcibly of the importance of path dependence in economic decisions. This irreversibility of choices is one of which poets and novelists have long been aware—from Omar Khayyám's stern, "The moving finger writes and, having writ, moves on," to Robert Frost's melancholy "The road not taken . . . has made all the difference," to Tom Wolfe's simple "You can't go home again." But, again, economists can use this reminder that we do not make choices on a tabula rasa; history inevitably conditions the set of choices available, for firms and industries and countries no less than for individuals.

One of Piore's most useful insights is his highlighting of the dependence of the so-called Taylorist or mass-production form of industrial organization on a reasonable degree of stability, or at least predictability, in the underlying economic environment. This linkage makes clear why the post-1973 forces that undermined this stability—increased economic openness, economic deregulation, and an acceleration of technological change— placed a premium on shifting rapidly to more flexible ways of organizing production processes. He also points out, correctly, that while increased competitive pressures are inherent in greater economic openness—and are, in fact, an important source of the gains from trade—increased instability in the economic environment is not. It arises instead from certain phenomena, such as the disruptions in energy prices and financial flows caused by the Organization of Petroleum Exporting Countries (OPEC) and the end of the Bretton Woods system of pegged exchange rates, particular to this historical episode.

Finally, Piore is correct in castigating both sides of the NAFTA debate for the terms in which they cast their arguments, focusing on trade balances and on job counting rather than on the impact on the quality of jobs and the distribution of income (and, I might add parenthetically, on the benefits to consumers in the form of broadened choices and lower prices, which hardly entered into the heated debate and about which Piore is also silent).

Having noted a number of points on which Piore's chapter provides cogent insights, let me now cite a number of points on which we disagree. First and foremost, I believe that in his endorsement of the current relevance of Polanyi's belief in "the disruptive effects of a market economy and their ability to produce political chaos and reaction," Piore misidentifies the primary source of disruption. It is rapid change of any sort that is inherently disruptive, producing strong political and social pressures to slow or reverse that change—the forces of reaction—rather than the market economy itself. Indeed, the widespread movement among developing nations toward market economics has been characterized by remarkably little disruption and, as far as the countries of central Europe and the former Soviet Union are concerned, it is worth remembering that the most disruptive political explosions were associated with pressures to shift away from a command-and-control economic environment toward a market-mediated one.

Recent evidence suggests, furthermore, that the "high" and "low" roads to industrial adjustment are not the distinct and mutually exclusive options that Piore outlines. As increased pressures from global competition have squeezed out the oligopoly rents previously enjoyed by firms in a number of American industries, one of the continuing surprises has been the ways in which these rents were shared, not only in the form of large pay premiums and generous perks for executives and workers alike, but also in redundant layers of management and inefficient organization of production processes. Thus, a certain amount of downsizing, streamlining, and contracting out (with its inevitable accompaniment of job dislocations and personal disruption) was inevitable, even in firms genuinely committed to implementing a high-performance workplace.

On a closely related point, it is wishful thinking, I believe, to assert as Piore does, that "the notion of the sweatshop as a distinct form of production . . . [makes it] possible conceptually to distinguish concerns which Polanyi raises about the preservation of social norms from a kind of disguised protectionism, even from the kind of imperialism of moral standards which the third world sees in these proposals." Most social norms are conditioned by the priorities, tastes, incomes, and level of development of a particular society. Attempts to universalize them are bound to be fraught with controversy, especially when the threat of trade sanctions underlies such efforts at harmonization.

Piore is correct in asserting that there are problems, some of which I return to, in conceiving of the high-road strategy in terms of a core-periphery model. But to equate the periphery with "a set of generally unskilled, temporary employees" is to ignore one of the more interesting evolutions in American labor markets. That is the growing cadre of contract employees at all levels—from relatively unskilled clerks and janitors to highly skilled doctors, lawyers, accountants and even executives, a trend highlighted in a *New York Times* article from December 17, 1995, headlined "The Temps in the Gray Flannel Suits." Furthermore, the rapid growth of such a contingent work force, generally regarded as part of the problem in widespread labor-market adjustments, can actually be seen as part of the solution. Under some conditions, which I have described in detail elsewhere,[41] such contingent arrangements, by providing more efficient mechanisms for matching demand and supply in labor markets, can actually reduce the costs associated with the occupational and geographic displacement of workers.

Finally, Piore is a bit too uncritical in his assessment of what Americans can learn from Japan about organizational structures, process design, and relations between management and workers. Certainly, American manufacturing has been well served by its ongoing shift from the structures and processes of mass production to those of lean production pioneered by Japanese firms. But important components of the Japanese high-road strategy, including lifetime employment and seniority-based pay structures, are currently under severe pressure, and concerns about the "deindustrialization" of America are increasingly being replaced by fears about the "hollowing out" of Japan.

Indeed, one of the conundrums confronting both academics and policymakers concerned with the functioning of labor markets is the current shift characteristic of both the United States and Japan, as well as other major industrialized countries, toward greater reliance on external (that is, between-firm) as opposed to internal (that is, within-firm) reallocations of labor in response to structural changes on either the demand or the supply side. As I have shown elsewhere, in a simple model of imperfect competition, such a shift can be interpreted as a rational response to several developments, including the deregulation of capital markets and an exogenous increase in import competition.[42] But this trend in adjustment processes inevitably shifts some of the costs of adjustment away from firms and toward workers, thus becoming more visible and politically sensitive in

41. Whitman (1994).
42. Whitman (forthcoming).

the process. This fact, together with the labor market difficulties currently experienced (albeit in varying forms) in most of the major industrialized nations, is increasing the vulnerability to protectionist pressures in these countries—pressures that have been submerged but not eliminated by the signing of the GATT and NAFTA agreements.

A second conundrum, alluded to but not extensively discussed in Piore's chapter, is how to resolve the inevitable tension between the demands of a high-performance workplace and the weakening of the mutual commitment between firms and workers inherent in the changing nature of the implicit social contract. The question raised by Piore regarding who will have the incentive to pay for training in an environment of increased worker mobility is one aspect of the problem. Another is the question of what will motivate the increased flexibility, initiative, and responsibility demanded of workers in a high-performance workplace. The substitution of professional for institutional loyalty—a model widely reflected in the academic world— is one possibility. But, clearly, a high level of personal insecurity, while characteristic of periods of rapid transition, is not compatible with a high-performance workplace in the steady state.

Finally, all forms of adjustment, internal or external, are mediated and made less painful by rapid growth. Indeed, it is the decades of such rapid growth, rather than the particular characteristics of its labor market institutions, that may be the primary factor in the long-running success of the Japanese adjustment model, with its heavy reliance on reallocation of labor within rather than between firms. But today virtually all of the industrialized countries, including Japan, must confront the implications of the chronically lower growth rates associated with aging populations and the still unexplained step-down in productivity increases since 1973. How to maximize the efficiency and minimize the costs of labor market adjustments in the face of reduced growth rates remains one of the major issues confronting the industrialized nations.

The crux of Piore's chapter is his assertion that the focus of our attention should be less on the relationship between trade and wages per se and more on the broader social context within which these interactions occur. In particular, he argues, both the organizational structure of firms and the public policy environment in which they operate should be arranged so as to encourage the high-road rather than the low-road approach to structural adjustment. But what specific characteristics are most likely to move firms in the desired direction? I know of no complete or definitive answers, but I would suggest a few guidelines—some congruent with the views expressed by Piore, others substantially at odds with them.

Regarding guidelines for firms, perhaps the most fundamental one reflects a concern expressed by Piore: that a firm's implementation of the high-performance workplace concept—be it in the form of quality circles, organization into teams, pay for learning, or whatever—be based on a genuine commitment to a more participatory management style. One indicator of such a commitment is an effective linkage between pay and performance at every level in the organization; the frequent severing of this link for top executives in the 1980s did as much as anything to sow mistrust among workers and frustration among stockholders. A corollary is that compensation should increasingly be related to the breadth of a person's skills and willingness to learn new ones rather than to seniority or location on the organizational chart.

Also critical to the high-road approach is a firm's encouragement of upgrading of employee skills. One way to do this, of course, is by directly assisting or rewarding the acquisition of such skills. Perhaps equally important, however, is that the business community as a whole demand well-trained entrants—that is, that it emulate the Japanese commitment to careful screening of potential employees and thus put effective pressure on our country's woefully inadequate system of education for students who are not college bound. In addition to facilitating the development of a high-performance workplace, such measures would help to enhance the "employability security" that is increasingly replacing "job security" as the objective of a well-functioning social contract.

Finally, business firms, as well as the financial community that keeps score on them, need to move beyond a narrow definition of competitiveness and continuous improvement in terms of downsizing and cost cutting to encompass innovation, strategic risk taking, and growth. The fact that the term "corporate anorexia" has entered the vocabulary of the financial press suggests that such a shift in focus may in fact have begun.

Much of what I have recommended so far is consistent with the spirit of Piore's views. Where we part company is on the role of public policy. Where he urges an increase in the minimum wage, greater use of industrial policy, and more regulation of labor markets, I urge avoidance of the temptation to protect and preserve oligopoly power (however widely shared) through trade barriers or regulatory requirements that restrict competition in product or labor markets. And where he urges that international harmonization of labor standards be increasingly incorporated into trade agreements, I suggest that there are several reasons to avoid the use of actual or threatened trade sanctions to force other countries to harmonize their regulatory standards with our own.

One reason is the tensions and mistrust that such pressures inevitably create in relations with developing nations. Another is that putting too much on the plate threatens to overwhelm the still-fragile negotiating and dispute-settlement mechanisms of multinational and regional trade agreements. Most fundamentally, imposing barriers against the products of developing countries could prove counterproductive, by impeding the economic growth that has historically proved to be the strongest positive force for upgrading conditions of work.

Public policies can help to alleviate the costs of adjustment without increasing the rigidity of labor markets by facilitating the portability of health insurance and pensions—the latter by encouraging the ongoing shift from defined-benefit to defined-contribution plans, for example. Government can help to improve the school-to-work transition by encouraging educational experimentation, which may include arrangements such as vouchers or charter schools, and by encouraging public-private partnerships centered on institutions (such as junior colleges) with a strong focus on lifetime learning.

Piore is troubled by the deregulation of American labor markets and cites with approval the more highly regulated markets of Europe and Japan—the former regulated by government laws and regulations, the latter by custom and a body of case law. But Japan's defining labor market institutions, particularly lifetime employment and seniority-based pay, are cracking under the pressures of prolonged recession, financial fragility, and an overvalued yen. And the nations of western Europe, beset by persistently low levels of job growth and high unemployment, are modifying their regulatory environments to reduce labor market rigidities, and reevaluating the scope and costs of their social safety nets. The fact that virtually all of the industrialized nations are floundering in their efforts to cope with the pressures of structural change suggests caution that reregulation, however well intentioned, not be allowed to impede private sector experimentation toward the development of new and more viable labor market arrangements.

Finally, a word on the role of labor unions. Piore is right to deplore the dramatic decline of American labor unions; history offers ample evidence of the positive role these organizations have played in the development of modern industrial democracies. But, although he describes in some detail the organization and behavior of firms consistent with a high-performance workplace, he offers no parallel description of how labor unions must evolve if they are to be relevant and effective in the new labor market paradigm.

The importance of mutual trust, flexibility, and individual initiative in the ideal workplace of the future will make new demands on both managers and unions schooled in the more rigid and confrontational environments of the mass-production world. Union leaders, in particular, will have to modify their traditional insistence on acting as exclusive intermediary between workers and management. What will be even more difficult, I suspect, is a shift in the unions' focus from job security to employability security as a major pillar of their members' economic well-being. Such a shift poses threats to a union's own organizational boundaries, but it is essential, I believe, if unions are to adapt successfully to the evolution of lifetime work patterns.

Whatever our disagreements on particulars, there is no question that Piore focuses appropriately on the issue that, in my view, has cast a shadow over this entire conference. That is that a market economy is perceived to be well functioning and fair when the three major groups essential to the production process—workers, managers, and stockholders—are all experiencing gains (or even, for brief periods, declines) in economic welfare together. In the 1980s, a growing disconnect between executive compensation and returns to stockholders proved increasingly disruptive, and led ultimately to the passage of legislation aimed at correcting what was widely perceived as an abuse.

Today, there is closer linkage between management compensation and the bottom line (although not, in my view, because the aforementioned legislation has been particularly effective), and both senior managers and stockholders are, as a group, doing extremely well. But workers, beset by stagnating compensation and unanticipated levels of economic insecurity, are outside the magic circle. Frustration levels are high and, with them, the need on the part of both politicians and the public to find a scapegoat. At the moment, the global economy is increasingly becoming a convenient candidate for that role. There is a growing danger that if American workers do not soon begin to rejoin the circle of prosperity, the open, world economy developed under American leadership over the past half-century, which offers the best opportunity for sustained growth to all its participants, could become one of the casualties of this failure.

General Discussion

William Dickens was skeptical about the importance of trade policy in the broad framework laid out in this chapter. Of all the things the federal government does that might influence the choice between high- and low-road strategies, trade policy seemed to him to be one of the least important.

Robert Lawrence argued that the discussion of trade policy was too narrow and that direct foreign investment played a central role in recent U.S. experience. He offered the example of the voluntary restraint arrangement on autos during the 1980s, which pushed Japan to invest in the United States. Ironically, this managed-trade agreement may have helped to promote high-road strategies here.

However, Lawrence did not see a necessary connection between adoption of a high-road strategy and what should happen to the return to skill and education. Although not what actually happened, one could conceive of a high-road strategy that incorporated blue-collar workers more fully into the production process, eliminating white-collar managers and narrowing the income distribution. Alternatively, a high-road strategy could mean increasing flexibility, requiring better skills, and hurting less-skilled workers, which is closer to what appears to have happened.

Susan Collins found it difficult to distinguish between the high- and low-road strategies on a national level. It was not clear to her that the description of a firm pursuing a high-road strategy could fully employ a national pool of labor with the wide range of skills of the U.S. labor market. She wondered whether there was a parallel low-road sector implicitly in the background.

Thea Lee focused on the issue of whether U.S. trade policy should be conditioned on performance in other countries. She disagreed with Marina Whitman's view that only domestic strings should be attached, in favor of the view that it is legitimate to condition access to the American market on desired changes in behavior abroad. If there are reasons to try to steer domestic companies toward the high road, she argued that similar goals should apply to the global economy, although perhaps over a long time frame. Other than diplomacy, which is relatively weak, and war, which is exceedingly strong, she did not see obvious alternatives to conditional trade policy for applying international leverage.

Lee also thought that the concern over country sovereignty, often used as a reason not to attach conditions to trade liberalization, has been applied inconsistently. For instance, regarding NAFTA, her view was that sovereignty was not seen as a problem for insisting on changes in Mexico's policies toward intellectual property.

Robert Blecker stressed that trade liberalization is no longer a simple matter of reducing a tariff, but often involves the much more complex redefinition of institutions and social regulations among participating countries. He saw a perception in the general public that agreements such as NAFTA impose a new regulatory regime on behalf of corporate interest while undermining aspects of social regulation. In his view, this helps account for the strength of the anger many Americans vent related to trade, at times treating trade as a scapegoat for broader frustrations. He agreed with Piore that pushing open markets too quickly runs the risk of sparking a strong negative reaction, fueled in part by developments unrelated to trade.

Finally, Peter Temin suggested that Piore's interpretation may provide a way to reconcile the timing problems discussed in relation to Edward Leamer's chapter. Perhaps this approach to the evolution of business strategy explains why relative price changes occurred in the 1970s but relative wages did not change until the 1980s.

References

Abernathy, Frederick H., and others. 1995. "The Information-Integrated Channel: A Study of the U.S. Apparel Industry in Transition." *Brookings Papers on Economic Activity: Microeconomics* 175–231.

Allen, Thomas J., and Michael S. Scott Morton, eds. 1994. *Information Technology and the Corporation of the 1990s.* Oxford University Press.

Applebaum, Eileen, and Rosemary Batt. 1993. *High-Performance Work Systems: American Models of Work Place Transformation.* Economic Policy Institute.

Arthur, Brian. 1988. "Self-Reinforcing Mechanisms in Economics." In *The Economy as an Evolving Complex System,* edited by Philip W. Anderson, Kenneth J. Arrow, and David Pines. Redwood City, Calif.

Bailey, Thomas. 1989. "Technology Skills and Education in the Apparel Industry." Technical Paper 7. Columbia University, Conservation of Human Resources.

———. 1992. "Employee Participation and Work Reform since Hawthorne." Paper prepared for the Sloan Foundation, Teachers College and Conservation of Human Resources, Columbia University (August).

Baker, Dean. 1996. "Trends in Corporate Profitability: Getting More for Less?" Technical Paper. Washington: Economic Policy Institute.

Baker, Dean, and Lawrence Mishel. 1995. "Profits Up, Wages Down. Worker Losses Yield Big Gains for Business" Briefing Paper. Washington: Economic Policy Institute.

Berg, Peter, and others. 1996. "The Performance Effects of Modular Production in the Apparel Industry." *Industrial Relations* 35 (July): 356–373.

Bernard, Andrew B., and J. Bradford Jensen. 1995. "Exporters, Jobs, and Wages in U.S. Manufacturing: 1976–1987." *Brookings Papers on Economic Activity: Microeconomics,* 67–112.

Best, Michael H. 1990. *The New Competition: Institutions of Industrial Restructuring.* Harvard University Press.

Blackburn, McKinley L., David E. Bloom, and Richard B. Freeman. 1990. "The Declining Economic Position of Less Skilled American Men." In *A Future of*

Lousy Jobs? The Changing Structure of U.S. Wages, edited by Gary Burtless, 31–67. Brookings.

Block, Fred L. 1977. *The Origins of International Economic Disorder: A Study of United States International Monetary Policy from World War II to the Present.* University of California Press.

Bluestone, Barry. 1990. "Comment." In *A Future of Lousy Jobs? The Changing Structure of U.S. Wages,* edited by Gary Burtless, 68–76. Brookings.

———. 1994. "Old Theories in New Bottles: Toward an Explanation of Growing World-Wide Income Inequality." In *The Changing Distribution of Income in an Open U.S. Economy,* edited by Jeffrey H. Bergstrand and others, 331–42. Amsterdam: North-Holland.

———. 1995. "The Inequality Express." *American Prospect* (Winter): 81–93.

Bound, John, and George Johnson. 1992. "Changes in the Structure of Wages in the 1980s: An Evaluation of Alternative Explanations." *American Economic Review* 82 (June): 371–92.

Burtless, Gary. 1995. "International Trade and the Rise in Earnings Inequality." *Journal of Economic Literature* 33 (June): 800–16.

Commons, John R. 1934. *Institutional Economics: Its Place in Political Economy.* New York: Macmillan.

Dalton, George, ed. 1971. *Primitive, Archaic and Modern Economies: Essays of Karl Polanyi.* Beacon Press.

Doeringer, Peter B., and Michael J. Piore. 1971. *Internal Labor Markets and Manpower Analysis.* Lexington, Mass.: Heath.

Freeman, Richard B. 1995. "Are Your Wages Set in Beijing?" *Journal of Economic Perspectives* 9 (Summer): 15–32.

Gaston, Noel, and Daniel Trefler. 1994. "Protection, Trade and Wages: Evidence from U.S. Manufacturing." *Industrial and Labor Relations Review* 47 (July): 574–93.

Gereffi, Gary. 1994. "The Organization of Buyer-Driven Global Commodity Chains: How U.S. Retailers Shape Overseas Production Networks." In *Commodity Chains and Global Capitalism,* edited by Gary Gereffi and Miguel Korzeniewicz, 95–122. Westport, Conn.: Praeger.

Harrison, Bennett, and Barry Bluestone. 1988. *The Great U-Turn: Corporate Restructuring and the Polarizing of America.* Basic Books.

Hodgson, Geoffrey M. 1994. "The Return of Institutional Economics." In *The Handbook of Economic Sociology,* edited by Neil J. Smelser and Richard Swedberg, 58–76. Princeton University Press.

Holmstrom, Bergt, and Paul Milgrom. 1994. "The Firm as an Incentive System." *American Economic Review* 84 (September): 972–91.

Jacobson, Gary, and John Hillkirk. 1986. *Xerox: American Samurai.* Macmillan.

Karoly, Lynn A. 1993. "The Trend in Inequality among Families, Individuals, and Workers in the United States: A Twenty-Five Year Perspective." In *Uneven Tides: Rising Inequality in America,* edited by Sheldon Danziger and Peter Gottschalk, 19–98. New York: Russell Sage Foundation.

Katz, Harry C. 1985. *Shifting Gears: Changing Labor Relations in the U.S. Automobile Industry.* MIT Press.

Katz, Lawrence F., and Kevin M. Murphy. 1992. "Changes in Relative Wages, 1963–1987: Supply and Demand Factors." *Quarterly Journal of Economics* 107 (February): 35–78.

Kearns, David T., and David A. Nadler. 1992. *Prophets in the Dark: How Xerox Reinvented Itself and Beat Back the Japanese.* HarperCollins.

Keyssar, Alexander. 1986. *Out of Work: The First Century of Unemployment in Massachusetts.* Cambridge University Press.

Kindleberger, Charles P. 1988. *The International Economic Order: Essays on Financial Crisis and International Public Goods.* MIT Press.

Kruse, Douglas L. 1988. "International Trade and the Labor Market Experience of Displaced Workers." *Industrial and Labor Relations Review* 41 (April): 402–17.

Lawrence, Robert Z., and Matthew J. Slaughter. 1993. "International Trade and American Wages in the 1980's: Giant Sucking Sound or Small Hiccup?" *Brookings Papers on Economic Activity: Microeconomics 2:* 161–210.

Levy, Frank, and Richard J. Murnane. 1992. "U.S. Earnings Level and Earnings Inequality: A Review of Recent Trends and Proposed Explanations." *Journal of Economic Literature* 30 (September): 1333–81.

MacDuffie, John Paul. 1991. "Beyond Mass Production: Flexible Production Systems and Manufacturing Performance in the World Auto Industry." Ph.D. dissertation, Sloan School of Management, Massachusetts Institute of Technology.

Mansfield, Malcolm. 1994. *La construction sociale du chamage: l'Emergence d'une categorie en Grande Bretagna.* Serie du document de travail, No. 8803. Paris: Groupement Scientifique Institutions, Emploi et Politique Economique.

Milgrom, Paul, and John Roberts. 1995. "Complementarities and Fit: Strategy, Structure, and Organizational Change in Manufacturing." *Journal of Accounting and Economics* 19: 179–208.

Morone, Joseph. 1993. *Winning in High Tech Markets: The Role of General Management, How Motorola, Corning, and General Electric Have Built Global Leadership through Technology.* Harvard Business School Press.

Murphy, Kevin M., and Finis Welch. 1991. "The Role of International Trade in Wage Differentials." In *Workers and Their Wages: Changing Patterns in the United States,* edited by Marvin H. Kosters, 39–76. Washington: American Enterprise Institute.

Nohria, Nitin, and Robert G. Eccles, eds. 1992. *Networks and Organizations: Structure, Form, and Action.* Harvard Business School Press.

North, Douglass C. 1990. *Institutions, Institutional Change and Economic Performance.* Cambridge University Press.

Osterman, Paul. 1994. "How Common Is Workplace Transformation and Who Adopts It?" *Industrial and Labor Relations Review* 47 (January): 173–88.

Pine, Joseph B., II. 1993. *Mass Customization: The New Frontier in Business Competition.* Harvard Business School Press.

Piore, Michael J. 1979. "Qualitative Research Techniques in Economics." *Administrative Science Quarterly* 24 (December): 560–69.

———. 1990. "Labor Standards and Business Strategies." In *Labor Standards and Development in the Global Economy,* edited by Stephen Herzenberg and Jorge F. Perez-Lopez, 35–50. U.S. Department of Labor, U.S. Bureau of International Labor Affairs.

———. 1995. *Beyond Individualism.* Harvard University Press.

Piore, Michael J., and Charles F. Sabel. 1984. *The Second Industrial Divide: Possibilities for Prosperity.* Basic Books.

Piore, Michael J., and others. 1994. "The Organization of Product Development." *Industrial and Corporate Change* 3 (2): 5–14.

Polanyi, Karl. 1957. *The Great Transformation: The Political and Economic Origins of Our Time.* Beacon Press.

———. 1971. *Primitive, Archaic, and Modern Economies: Essays of Karl Polanyi,* edited by George Dalton. Boston: Beacon Press.

Sabel, Charles. 1994. "Learning by Monitoring." In *Handbook of Economic Sociology,* edited by Neil J. Smelser and Richard Swedberg, 137–65. Princeton University Press.

Salais, Robert, Nicole Baverez, and Bénédicte Renaud. 1986. *L'invention du chomage: Historie et transformations d'une categorie en France des années 1890 aux années 1980.* Paris: Presses Universitaires de France.

Saxenian, Annalee. 1994. *Regional Advantage: Culture and Competition in Silicon Valley and Route 128.* Harvard University Press.

Schon, Donald A. 1983. *The Reflective Practitioner: How Professionals Think in Action.* Basic Books.

Senge, Peter A. 1990. *The Fifth Discipline: The Art and Practice of the Learning Organization.* Doubleday/Currency.

Smith, Adam. 1976. *The Wealth of Nations.* University of Chicago Press.

Whitman, Marina V. N. 1994. "Flexible Markets, Flexible Firms." *American Enterprise* 5 (May/June): 26–37.

Whitman, Marina V. N. Forthcoming. "Labor Market Adjustment and Trade: Their Interaction in the Triad." In *International Trade and Investment: New Frontiers for Research,* edited by B. J. Cohen.

Womack, James P., Daniel T. Jones, and Daniel Roos. 1990. *The Machine That Changed the World.* New York: Rawson.

Wood, Adrian. 1994. *North-South Trade, Employment and Inequality: Changing Fortunes in a Skill-Driven World.* Oxford, England: Clarendon Press.

———. 1995. "How Trade Hurt Unskilled Workers." *Journal of Economic Perspectives* 9 (Summer): 57–80.

Young, Allyn. 1928. "Increasing Returns and Economic Progress." *Economic Journal* 38 (December): 527–42.

SEVEN

North American Integration and Factor Price Equalization: Is There Evidence of Wage Convergence between Mexico and the United States?

Ana L. Revenga and Claudio E. Montenegro

DURING RECENT debates over the North American Free Trade Agreement (NAFTA), many opponents of the agreement contended that low-skilled U.S. workers would suffer large losses as a result of increased Mexican exports to the United States. Supporters of NAFTA argued that this was unlikely to be the case because the advantages offered by low Mexican wages would be more than offset by the much higher productivity of U.S. workers. Moreover, supporters claimed that because Mexican wages would rise as a result of the increase in demand for Mexican products, any advantage created by having low-cost labor would diminish over time. On the Mexican side, the arguments have followed similar lines, with proponents arguing that NAFTA will lead to an improvement in wages and living standards for the Mexican population and opponents claiming that it will hurt, above all, low-skilled workers and poor people.

We are grateful to Wayne Gray for kindly supplying us with the NBER Productivity Database, to Jim Tybout and William Cline for their thoughtful discussions of the chapter, and to Susan Collins, Dani Rodrik, Richard Freeman, Ed Leamer, and other conference participants for many helpful comments. All remaining errors are our own.

Table 7-1. *Mexico: Trade Protection in Manufacturing, 1985–90*
Percent

	1985:VI	1986:VI	1987:VI	1988:VI	1989:VI	1990:VI
Average tariff[a] (percent ad valorem)	23.5	24.0	22.7	11.0	12.6	12.5
Maximum tariff	100.0	45.0	40.0	20.0	20.0	20.0
Coverage of import licensing[b]	92.2	46.9	35.8	23.2	22.1	19.9
Coverage of reference prices[b]	18.7	19.6	13.4	0.0	0.0	0.0

Source: Hufbauer and Schott (1992).

a. Production weighted. Does not include the uniform 5 percent surcharge abolished in December 1987.

b. Average share of output subject to import licensing or reference prices, as a percentage of total domestic output.

Deciding who is right is largely an empirical question. To some extent, however, we may already have some answers, because Mexico initiated the liberalization of its external sector long before NAFTA was signed. For most of the manufacturing sector, the reforms implemented between 1985 and 1987 were substantially larger than those proposed by NAFTA. Between 1985 and 1988, import-licensing requirements in manufacturing were scaled back to about one-quarter previous levels, reference prices were removed, and tariff rates on most products were substantially reduced (see table 7-1). As a result of this liberalization, trade between Mexico and the United States has surged. Between 1985 and 1993, Mexican exports to the United States increased by 8.6 percent per year in real terms, whereas exports from the United States to Mexico grew by 17.7 percent annually over the same period. The United States is currently Mexico's primary trading partner, accounting for nearly 80 percent of Mexican exports and for 68 percent of its imports in 1993. And though its weight in total U.S. trade is much smaller, Mexico is still the United State's largest trade partner among the developing countries, and one of its most important overall.

In this chapter we examine what has happened to relative Mexican-U.S. wages by skill level and industry as trade between the two countries has grown. We also try to identify what type of Mexican labor has benefited the most, in relative terms, from the trade liberalization of 1985–87. The primary focus is on understanding developments in the wage structure from the Mexican as opposed to the American side. The reason for this is simple: although numerous studies have analyzed the link between trade patterns and the wage structure in developed countries, relatively few have examined wage changes in middle- and low-income countries.[1] The Mexican trade liberalization experience offers a unique chance to do so.

We use firm-level data for a panel of Mexican manufacturing firms over the 1984 to 1990 period. The data are drawn from Mexico's Annual Survey of Industrial Firms (*Encuesta Industrial Anual*). Although we would have preferred to extend the sample period through 1993, it proved impossible to do so. Fortunately, the sample period is long enough to span the complete implementation of the trade reforms, even if it may be too short to fully capture the effects of those reforms on firms.[2] On the U.S. side, we use industry-level data for the corresponding 1984–90 period. These data were obtained from the National Bureau of Economic Research (NBER) Productivity Database and are drawn from the U.S. Annual Survey of Manufacturers. Both data sets are described in detail in the appendix to this chapter.

Several papers have investigated the link between trade liberalization and movements in relative (and absolute) wages in Mexico. For example, Feliciano used household-level data to examine the impact of trade liberalization on the returns to schooling.[3] She found that wage differentials between skilled and unskilled workers increased between 1986 and 1990 following trade reform. Craig and Epelbaum found a similar rise in earnings dispersion during the late 1980s, but they associated it with a rise in the demand for educated workers resulting from the complementarity between skilled labor and investment in capital.[4] In a study with a somewhat different focus, one of us used firm-level data for the manufacturing sector to identify the effects of the removal of trade protection on wages and employment for 1984–90.[5] She found that tariff and quota reductions were associated with small declines in plant-level employment and wages. Finally, Hanson and Harrison used both plant-level data and data from the Mexican

1. Studies of the link between trade and changes in the wage structure in developed countries include Bound and Johnson (1992); Freeman and Katz (1991); Katz and Murphy (1992); Lawrence and Slaughter (1993); Leamer (1994); Revenga (1992); and Sachs and Shatz (1994) for the United States; Neven and Wyplosz (1994) for Europe; and Katz and Revenga (1989) for Japan. Evidence for some middle-income countries is found in Craig and Epelbaum (1994); Currie and Harrison (1994); Davis (1992); Feliciano (1994); Hanson and Harrison (1994); and Robbins (1993).
2. The limited length of the sample period implies that wage developments in our sample are dominated by the effects of the macroeconomic crisis. Nevertheless, there is enough cross-industry variation in wage behavior for us to try to analyze the impact of trade.
3. Feliciano (1994).
4. Craig and Epelbaum (1994).
5. Revenga (1995).

industrial census to assess whether increased wage inequality in Mexico was linked to the liberalization of trade.[6] They found little evidence consistent with Stolper-Samuelson-type effects and concluded that changes in Mexico's wage structure have been driven mostly by developments within industries.

On the U.S. side, there is an extensive literature that examines the relationship between trade and changes in employment and wages. The results are mixed. Some economists such as Wood have argued that increased trade with developing countries has had a large impact on the U.S. labor market.[7] Others conclude that the effects of trade on employment and wages have been small.[8]

A common characteristic of both developed- and developing-country studies is the duality of approaches used to analyze the impact of trade. Most studies fall in one of two camps: those who adopt a "quantity-oriented" approach, focusing primarily on the labor market impact of changes in trade flows; and those who use a "price-based" approach, examining how trade-induced movements in relative prices link to changes in relative wages. The trade-flow approach has been particularly favored by labor economists, accustomed to thinking in terms of "workers displaced by trade." The price approach, on the other hand, has been more common among trade economists, who link it directly to the implications of standard trade models. This study combines elements of both. In looking at the effects of changes in tariffs (and quotas) on relative wages, it implicitly adopts a price-based approach. It also tries to draw directly from trade theory to derive its testable hypothesis. Yet at the same time it estimates a reduced-form wage equation consistent with most standard labor demand–labor supply models.

In the next section, we describe the data used in the analysis. We then discuss the Mexican trade liberalization episode and present some stylized facts on the evolution of trade between Mexico and the United States. This section also examines the characteristics of Mexico's importing and exporting industries. In the next section we discuss the basic principles linking changes in trade patterns to changes in relative wages and provide a simple theoretical framework for the subsequent empirical analysis. We then present some preliminary evidence on the patterns of changes in employment, wages, and trade protection in Mexico and the United States introduce the econometric strategy used to study the relationship between trade and movements in relative wages; and present the results.

6. Hanson and Harrison (1994).

7. Wood (1994).

8. Bound and Johnson (1992); Grossman (1987); Lawrence and Slaughter (1993); Revenga (1992); Sachs and Shatz (1994).

Data Description

The data used in this chapter are drawn from three sources. Data on trade values and prices come from the United Nations Statistical Office (UNSO) Comtrade database. They provide information on exports and imports by trade partner, as reported by individual countries to the UNSO.

Data on wages and employment in Mexican manufacturing come from the Mexican annual industrial survey and were pulled together by the Secretaria de Comercio y Fomento Industrial (SECOFI). These are annual data on 2,413 Mexican manufacturing plants for 1984–90 and cover approximately 80 percent of total manufacturing output.[9] Workers are classified into two categories: *obreros,* equivalent to production workers; and *empleados,* equivalent to nonproduction workers. We follow others in using "production" workers (*obreros*) to proxy for unskilled workers in manufacturing, and "nonproduction" workers (*empleados*) to proxy for higher-skilled employees.[10] Earnings are defined as the average annual salary for each type of worker in a given plant. In addition to wages and employment, the SECOFI data set also includes information on other relevant firm-level variables, such as the stock of fixed capital and the cost of materials used in production. These plant-level data have been merged with industry price data at the four-digit industrial classification level, and with data on tariff levels and quota coverage.

Data on U.S. wages and employment in manufacturing are drawn from the NBER Productivity Data and come from the annual survey of manufacturers. Details on all three data sources and on variable construction are provided in the appendix to this chapter.

Patterns in Mexican-U.S. Trade

Mexico's Trade Liberalization Episode

After decades of pursuing an import-substitution industrialization strategy, in 1985 the Mexican government initiated a radical liberalization of its external sector. The scope and speed of this liberalization episode are apparent from table 7-1. In just three years, import-licensing requirements were scaled back to

9. As reported by Tybout and Westbrook (1994).
10. Berman, Bound, and Griliches (1994); Sachs and Shatz (1994). This may be far from adequate, because many production workers may be highly skilled and many nonproduction workers may be unskilled. However, this is the only breakdown that is available in both the Mexican and the U.S. manufacturing surveys.

Table 7-2. *Average Tariffs and Import-Licensing Requirements by Sector,*
1985, 1989
Percent

Sector	Tariffs[a]		Import licensing[b]	
	June 1985	December 1989	June 1985	December 1989
Food products	22.6	11.9	98.1	20.5
Beverages and tobacco	77.0	19.7	99.5	19.8
Textiles	32.5	14.8	90.7	1.0
Apparel and footware	46.8	18.5	99.1	0.0
Wood products	37.0	16.9	99.9	0.0
Paper and printing	19.6	6.7	74.5	0.3
Petroleum refining	2.2	4.4	94.3	86.4
Chemical products	28.7	13.4	86.8	2.1
Nonmetallic minerals	31.7	14.9	95.6	0.0
Basic metals	15.1	10.6	86.8	0.0
Metal products	35.7	14.6	74.0	1.1
Machinery and equipment	27.4	16.4	90.7	1.6
Transport equipment	39.2	16.0	99.0	41.0
Other manufacturing	50.8	18.0	91.8	0.0
Total	23.5	12.5	92.2	19.8

Source: Ten Kate (1992, tables 3, 4, 5).
a. Production-weighted average tariff rate.
b. Domestic production value covered by import licenses.

about one-quarter previous levels, reference prices were removed, and tariff rates on most products were substantially reduced. In mid-1985, the average tariff rate was 23.5 percent, and import licensing covered 92.2 percent of national production. By mid-1988, the average tariff had been reduced to 11 percent, with a maximum rate of 20 percent (down from 100 percent in 1985), and the coverage of import licensing had fallen to 23.2 percent of production. These liberalization measures were accompanied by a sharp devaluation of the Mexican peso in 1987 and by the lifting of export controls.

The most protected sectors before trade liberalization included relatively labor-intensive industries such as foodstuffs, beverages and tobacco, apparel and footwear, and wood products. Some less labor-intensive sectors such as transport equipment and petroleum refining, however, were also highly protected (see table 7-2). Average tariffs in 1985 ranged from a low of 15.1 percent in basic metals to a high of 77 percent in beverages and tobacco; import licenses were required for more than 74 percent of products in all industries. The liberalization process proceeded in two steps: first, the government replaced import-licensing requirements with tariff equivalents; then it moved to reduce tariffs. By 1989, most sectors had been significantly liberalized. But import-license requirements remained important in both petroleum refining and transport equipment; in addition, in some sectors average tariffs were kept above 15 percent.

Trends in Trade between Mexico and the United States

Between 1985 and 1993, exports from Mexico to the United States grew in real terms by a cumulative 70 percent. Exports from the United States into Mexico increased by a cumulative 142 percent over the same period (see figures 7-1 and 7-2). The strongest increase in both U.S. imports from and exports to Mexico occurred in manufactured goods, especially in chemical products and machinery and transport equipment.

The United States is presently Mexico's largest trading partner. In 1993, it accounted for 80 percent of Mexican exports and nearly 70 percent of its imports. The weight of trade with Mexico in total U.S. trade is much smaller but nevertheless still significant. In 1993, for example, exports to Mexico represented nearly 10 percent of total U.S. exports, while imports from Mexico accounted for about 7 percent of total U.S. imports. Mexico is the largest U.S. trading partner among the developing countries.[11] Moreover, its importance as a trading partner for the United States has been increasing rapidly between 1978 and 1993, Mexico's share in total U.S. imports nearly tripled. With NAFTA, this tendency is bound to intensify.[12]

Characteristics of Exporting Industries

The standard Hecksher-Ohlin-Samuelson (HOS) trade model suggests that U.S. imports from Mexico should be relatively intensive in unskilled labor and that exports from the United States to Mexico should be relatively intensive in both human and physical capital. A quick and rough look at net export data at the three-digit International Standard Industrial Classification (ISIC) industry level suggests that the broad patterns of Mexican-U.S. trade

11. Of course, the bulk of U.S. trade is with other developed countries. In 1990, for example, imports from developed countries accounted for nearly 65 percent of all U.S. imports (authors' calculations from UNSO Comtrade database). Imports from developing countries represented only 35 percent of total U.S. imports, of which imports from Mexico were roughly one-seventh, or 5 percent.

12. The *Economist* (December 1994) reports that in the first nine months of 1994, U.S. trade with Mexico expanded at twice the rate than with non-NAFTA countries (with respect to trade during the same period in 1993).

Figure 7-1. *U.S. Imports from Mexico, 1978–93*

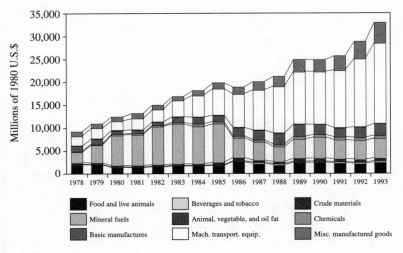

Source: UNSO COMTRADE database.

Figure 7-2. *U.S. Exports to Mexico, 1978–93*

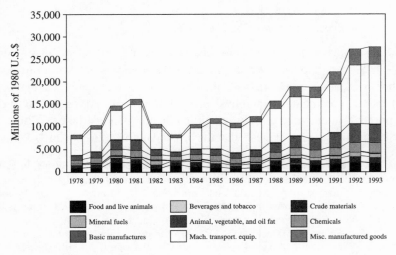

Source: UNSO COMTRADE database.

Table 7-3. *Patterns of U.S.-Mexican Trade by Three-Digit ISIC*

ISIC	Industry	Wage level[a]	Capital intensity
	Mexican manufacturing net exporting industries		
311	Food products	Low	Middle
313	Beverages	Middle	Middle
322	Apparel	Low	Low
324	Footwear	Low	Low
332	Furniture	Low	Low
361	Pottery, china	Low	Middle
362	Glass and glass products	High	High
369	Nonmetallic minerals	Middle	Middle
372	Nonferrous metals	High	High
383	Electrical machinery	Low	Low
384	Transportation equipment	Middle	Middle
	Mexican manufacturing net importing industries		
312	Miscellaneous foods	Middle	Middle
321	Textiles	Low	Middle
331	Wood	Low	High
341	Pulp, paper	Middle	Middle
342	Printing, publishing	Middle	Middle
351	Basic chemicals	High	High
352	Pharmaceuticals	High	High
354	Miscellaneous chemicals	Middle	Low
355	Tires and tubes	Middle	Low
356	Plastics	Low	Low
371	Iron and steel	High	High
381	Metal products	Middle	High
382	Nonelectrical machinery	Middle	Middle

Source: Annual surveys of manufactures.

a. Sectors were classified into low, middle, and high wage by ranking industries by the average wage. The top third was classified as "high wage," the middle third as "middle wage," and the bottom third as "low wage." A similar procedure was used to classify industries by their capital/labor ratios (capital intensity).

are indeed consistent with the predictions of the HOS model. Table 7-3 shows that with regard to the United States, Mexico is a net exporter of primarily labor-intensive goods (apparel, footwear, furniture, pottery, and china) and a net importer of more capital-intensive products (textile fibers, pharmaceuticals, basic chemicals, and nonelectrical machinery). As suggested by HOS trade theory, Mexico's net exports are in sectors with relatively low wages and low capital-labor ratios, whereas its net imports are in higher-wage, higher-capital-intensity sectors. However, there are some indications that the patterns are changing. Since 1985, the largest increases in Mexico's net exports have occurred in fairly capital-intensive industries such as transport equipment and nonelectrical machinery. In

Figure 7-3. *Mexico: Net Exporting Industries by Three-Digit ISIC, 1984–90*

U.S. dollars (thousands)

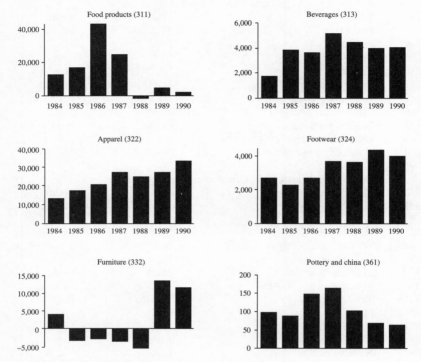

Source: UNSO COMTRADE database.

transport equipment in particular, Mexico went from being a net importer relative to the United States in 1985 to being a net exporter in 1990 (see figure 7-3).

Yet though these industry-level patterns fit the predictions of HOS trade theory, much of U.S-Mexican trade is actually intraindustry. Sectors such as transport equipment, electrical machinery, nonelectrical machinery, or basic chemicals, for example, account for a large (and rising) fraction of both Mexican exports to the United States and of U.S. exports to Mexico (see table 7-4). An analysis of the characteristics of exporting industries based only on net exports tends to miss the importance of this intraindustry trade and can easily mischaracterize Mexico's export sectors.

An alternative way to look at export orientation—one that avoids the problem of leaving out industries in which both imports and exports are high—is to use industry trade dependence ratios—for example, the ratio of

Figure 7-3. (*continued*)

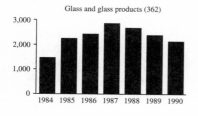

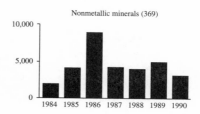

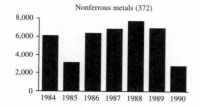

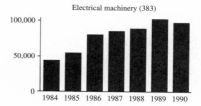

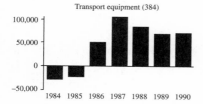

exports to total production. This is the approach favored by many other studies.[13] The drawback of the sectoral trade dependence approach is that it does not link directly to the predictions of simple HOS trade theory.

Table 7-5 ranks Mexican industries by share of exports in total output and presents some basic industry characteristics by export share category. The table shows that when measured in terms of export to production ratios, the higher-export sectors are actually relatively intensive in their use of both capital and skilled labor. High-export sectors pay higher wages on average and also pay their skilled workers relatively more.

Tables 7-3 and 7-5 lead to quite different conclusions regarding the characteristics of Mexico's export industries. The approach followed in table 7-3—which relies on net exports as a measure of comparative advantage—suggests that Mexico's exports come primarily from labor-inten-

13. Freeman and Katz (1991); Currie and Harrison (1994).

Table 7-4. *Trade Shares by Three-Digit ISIC, 1984 and 1990*

ISIC	Industry[a]	Share 1984	Share 1990
	Exports as a share of total exports to the United States		
384	Transportation equipment	0.214	0.347
383	Electrical machinery	0.318	0.273
382	Nonelectrical machinery	0.054	0.096
322	Apparel	0.066	0.064
351	Basic chemicals	0.093	0.037
311	Food products	0.073	0.033
	Imports as a share of total imports from the United States		
384	Transportation equipment	0.240	0.280
383	Electrical machinery	0.193	0.180
382	Nonelectrical machinery	0.139	0.138
351	Basic chemicals	0.166	0.098
356	Plastics	0.020	0.059
381	Metal products	0.029	0.034

Source: UNSO Comtrade database.

a. Data are reported for the top six industries as of 1990.

sive, low-wage sectors. The approach followed in table 7-5—which emphasizes sectoral trade dependence ratios—gives the opposite picture. Relative to other sectors, export-oriented industries in Mexico are skill and capital intensive and pay relatively higher wages.

The contrast between these two sets of results highlights the difficulties of explaining what are fairly complex trade patterns through any single model. HOS trade theory may be appropriate for explaining trade in some goods; new economies-of-scale trade theories may be better suited to explaining others; and Ricardian-type models may provide yet another explanation for particular trade patterns. Which one should be used depends largely on the type of question posed.

A Simple Theoretical Framework

Most analyses of the links between trade and changes in relative wages have relied on the HOS framework. This framework is appealing for several reasons. It fits with a well-accepted fact—that the supply of unskilled labor relative to skilled labor is much larger in the developing countries than in the industrialized world. It also provides a fairly accurate description of the patterns of trade between North and South. Finally, it yields clear predic-

Table 7-5. *Average Wages, Composition of Employment, and K/L Ratios for Mexican Firm Sample by Export Category, Selected Years, 1984–90*

Ranking of sectors by share of exports in total output	Year			
	1984	1986	1988	1990
Top third (high exports)				
Average wage (1987 U.S.$)	4,328.10	3,165.40	3,677.60	4,659.70
	(1,280.3)[a]	(1,355.9)	(1,762.5)	(2,289.6)
Log wage differential	0.685	0.701	0.769	0.914
(skilled-unskilled)	(0.390)	(0.370)	(0.421)	(0.475)
Ratio of unskilled to total employment	0.674	0.662	0.665	0.665
Stock of fixed K per worker	52.3	49.3	44.2	48.6
(millions of 1987 Mexican pesos)	(104.2)	(82.9)	(44.2)	(48.6)
Middle third (medium exports)				
Average wage (1987 U.S.$)	3,651.50	2,618.30	3,009.10	3,669.90
Log wage differential	0.586	0.610	0.647	0.805
(skilled-unskilled)	(0.398)	(0.384)	(0.397)	(0.460)
Ratio of unskilled to total employment	0.713	0.709	0.700	0.699
Stock of fixed K per worker	34.8	34.6	35.6	32.7
(millions of 1987 Mexican pesos)	(85.6)	(84.2)	(122.0)	(125.4)
Bottom third (low exports)				
Average wage (1987 U.S.$)	3,277.10	2,375.50	2,647.40	3,269.10
Log wage differential	0.585	0.592	0.619	0.770
(skilled-unskilled)	(0.372)	(0.348)	(0.373)	(0.448)
Ratio of unskilled to total employment	0.709	0.701	0.693	0.693
Stock of fixed K per worker	28.2	28.3	27.7	23.6
(millions of 1987 Mexican pesos)	(100.2)	(111.1)	(87.7)	(75.7)

Source: Authors' calculations from firm sample.

a. Standard deviations are shown in parentheses.

tions concerning the effects of trade on skill differentials in both North and South. Increased trade between rich and poor countries should yield a narrowing of skill differentials in the developing countries, a widening of skill differentials in the industrial nations, and a narrowing of the gap between unskilled wages in rich and poor countries.

However, the HOS framework is inherently a long-term one, more appropriate for the discussion of changes that occur over decades than for changes that take place within a few years. It does not seem to be the appropriate model for this particular study, where the objective is to understand recent shifts in U.S.-Mexican trade patterns and relative wages (developments that barely span half a decade). We therefore turn to a different framework and use a Ricardian approach, based on the Dornbush-Fischer-Samuelson (DFS) continuum-of-goods model.[14] This approach assumes that each country—Mexico and the United States—has only one factor of production, labor, available in quantities L^* and L, respectively, in each. Both countries can produce a continuum of goods, conveniently indexed on an interval in accordance with diminishing home-country comparative advantage. For parallelism with the DFS exposition, we assume the United States is the home country. A good z is associated with each point in the interval, and for each good there are unit labor requirements in production that differ between the two countries. Following DFS, we let $a(z)$ be the unit labor requirement in the United States and $a^*(z)$ be the corresponding unit labor requirement in Mexico. Then $A(z) \equiv a^*(z)/a(z)$ is the ratio of U.S. to Mexican productivity in good z, where by definition $A'(z) < 0$. In this simple, two-country model, the home country (the United States) will efficiently produce all those goods for which domestic unit labor costs are less than or equal to foreign unit labor costs:

$$a(z)w \le a^*(z)w^*, \tag{7-1}$$

where w and w^* are the average wages of workers in the United States and Mexico, respectively. For a given relative wage $\omega = w/w^*$, the home country will produce the range of goods

$$0 \le z \le \tilde{z}(\omega) \tag{7-2}$$

where you can define a borderline commodity z, for which

$$\tilde{z}(\omega) = A^{-1}(\omega). \tag{7-3}$$

By the same argument, Mexico will produce all goods z^* in the range $\tilde{z}(\omega) \le z^*$.

Now introduce tariffs. For simplicity, assume that the United States imposes no tariffs or trade restrictions on Mexico, but that the latter levies a uniform, ad valorem tariff on all imports from the United States equal to t^*. It then follows that given a relative wage ω, the pattern of specialization is

14. This model is presented in detail in Dornbush, Fischer, and Samuelson (1977). Feenstra and Hanson (1995) have used a similar model to analyze the impact of foreign investment in developing countries on relative wages in both North and South.

Figure 7-4. *A Ricardian Model with Tariffs*

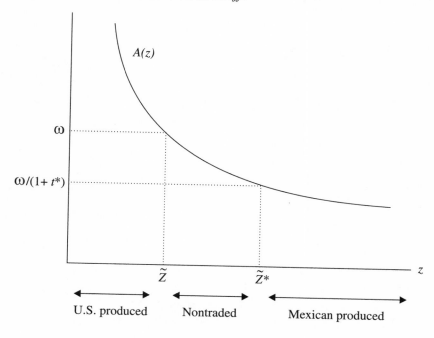

such that the U.S. produces all goods $z \leq \tilde{z}(\omega)$ as before, but Mexico now produces all goods $z \geq \tilde{z}*$ where $\tilde{z}* = A^{-1}\left[\dfrac{w}{w*}(1 + t*)\right]$. Because $\tilde{z} \neq \tilde{z}*$, there is a range of goods z, such that $\tilde{z}* \leq z \leq \tilde{z}$, that are nontraded. This is illustrated in figure 7-4.

Following the DFS model, assume that expenditure shares on each good are constant and that trade is balanced (or alternatively, that there is equilibrium in the market for home goods). It is then easy to derive a unique equilibrium relative wage:

$$\omega = \frac{w}{w*} = \omega\left(\frac{L}{L*}, t*\right) \qquad \text{where } \frac{d\omega}{dt} < 0. \qquad (7\text{-}4)$$

Given this model, it is possible to examine the implications of two events of interest. First, consider what happens if Mexico undergoes trade liberalization and reduces its tariffs with regard to the United States ($\Delta t* < 0$). The effect is a decline in the range of goods produced in Mexico and an incipient trade imbalance. To restore equilibrium in the goods market, the relative wage of Mexican workers must fall relative to that of U.S. workers

Figure 7-5. *Effects of Productivity Growth in Mexico*

(ω must increase). The prices of the previously nontraded Mexican goods will also fall.

Second, consider what happens if Mexico increases its labor productivity—for example, because trade liberalization allows for the import of new capital and technology, or because of an upgrading of skills of the Mexican work force.[15] This effect goes counter to that of the removal of tariffs. Productivity growth in Mexico increases the range of goods it can efficiently produce and decreases the range produced by the United States. This leads to an incipient trade imbalance in the United States and to a decline in the wage of U.S. workers relative to their Mexican counterparts. The prices of all Mexican-produced goods fall after the change, so the wages of both Mexican and U.S. workers go up in real terms. This case is illustrated in figure 7-5.

15. Hanson and Harrison (1994) and Thompson (1994), among others, have documented an increase in foreign investment in new machinery and equipment following trade liberalization. Similarly, there is evidence of a steady increase in the educational attainment of Mexican workers. Enrollments in secondary school, for example, more than doubled in the last two decades, rising from approximately 19 percent in 1970 to 55 percent in 1992.

What does this simple Ricardian framework imply for relative Mexican-U.S. wages? On the one hand, it predicts that trade liberalization would lead to a decline in Mexico's wage relative to the United States. But on the other hand, if trade liberalization were to lead to higher productivity in Mexico, then the outcome could be the complete opposite, with Mexico upgrading its range of products and Mexican wages rising relative to those of U.S. workers. In practice, we probably observe both effects simultaneously. The removal of tariffs may have put downward pressure on wages—especially in those industries that were previously the most protected (see table 7-2). At the same time, higher Mexican productivity—brought about by a combination of increased direct foreign investment (DFI), increased educational attainment in the work force, and especially improvements in efficiency generated by economic reform during the 1980s—may have translated into enhanced ability to export higher value-added goods (such as automobiles).[16] Assuming labor is not perfectly mobile, this in turn would have put upward pressure on wages of labor employed in those sectors, as firms in the expanding industries tried to attract new workers.

Introducing two distinct types of labor into the analysis, skilled and unskilled, adds another twist to the story. Table 7-3 indicates that the "new" export sectors (such as automobile and electrical machinery) are relatively skill intensive, whereas the industries that experienced the largest reductions in trade protection were relatively intensive in the use of unskilled labor. If this is the case, then trade liberalization could easily lead to a widening of skill differentials. It would tend to increase the demand for labor in skill-intensive industries and reduce it in unskilled-intensive ones.[17]

This simple theoretical framework suggest several testable predictions. First, other things held constant, the removal of tariffs (or other trade restrictions) should be associated with a decline in the wages of Mexican workers relative to their U.S. counterparts. Second, sectors undergoing more rapid productivity growth should have experienced an increase in their relative wages with regard to the United States. Third, the productivity effect should be larger for skilled workers, whereas the impact of the removal of tariffs should be felt more by unskilled labor.

16. Oks (1993) documents significant increases in Mexican total factor productivity (TFP) for manufacturing. He finds that much of the increase was brought about by improvements in efficiency within sectors and firms.

17. Interestingly, such a widening of skill differentials has been observed in several other Latin American countries that have undergone rapid trade liberalization, such as Argentina and Chile. See Robbins (1993).

Some Basic Facts and Statistics

Changes in Tariffs and Productivity

The Ricardian model developed here suggests that trade liberalization will affect relative wages mainly through its impact on relative industry demands. The removal of tariffs implies that certain goods previously produced in Mexico will now be more efficiently produced in the United States—trade liberalization should therefore lead to a reduction in the demand for labor in the previously protected industries (mainly those intensive in unskilled labor). On the other hand, productivity growth— whether trade induced or not—should be associated with increases in labor demand and wages in the new export sectors. The net effect is a shift in relative industry demands. Do simple correlations between changes in protection, productivity, employment, and wages support or contradict this argument?

We begin by examining correlations between changes in trade protection and changes in employment and wages. Simple correlations between changes in tariffs and changes in real wages indicate a positive association between the two of .19, whereas the correlation between changes in quota coverages and changes in wages is .14. Reductions in both tariffs and quota coverage would thus appear to be associated with declines in wages. Changes in protection also appear to be weakly correlated with changes in employment although the magnitudes are small, with correlations between changes in industry employment and changes in quotas and tariffs of .05 and .03, respectively. As these correlations indicate, interindustry shifts in employment have not been large but have nevertheless been significant. Between 1986 and 1990, for example, employment in the more export-oriented sectors increased by more than 10 percent, whereas in other industries it increased by only 0.3 percent. At the two-digit ISIC level, the biggest employment increases have come in "new" export sectors such as machinery and equipment, and the biggest declines have been in previously protected sectors such as textiles and apparel. Although not overwhelming, these stylized facts do suggest an impact of trade liberalization on relative industry labor demands.

More evidence along these lines is obtained from regressions of year-to-year changes in wages on initial protection levels and year dummies (where the dummies are meant to capture the effects of all other unmeasured variables). These results reveal that wage growth has been significantly slower in the initially more highly protected industries—by about 7 percent

Table 7-6. *Relative Wages and Employment for Mexican Manufacturing Sample, 1984–90*

Year	Ratio of production to total employment	Ratio of nonproduction wage to production wage[a]
1984	0.694	1.975
1985	0.697	2.164
1986	0.688	2.047
1987	0.685	2.024
1988	0.684	2.121
1989	0.683	2.393
1990	0.684	2.662

Source: Author's calculations from the sample of Mexican manufacturing firms (as detailed in the appendix).

per year (*t*-statistic of 3.407). Similar regressions that include an initial fraction of unskilled workers indicate that wage growth has also been more sluggish in the unskilled-intensive industries. Both of these findings are consistent with our simple Ricardian framework.

How does productivity growth fit into the story? The evidence suggests that, not surprisingly, more protected sectors have lagged behind in productivity performance. The simple cross-industry correlation between value added per worker and tariff protection is –0.28. Regressing productivity growth on initial protection levels and year dummies reveals that productivity growth has been nearly 8 percent slower per year in the highly protected industries. Productivity has also lagged in those sectors that used more unskilled labor. Simple cross-industry correlations also confirm that, as table 7-2 suggests, Mexico tended to protect its labor-intensive industries; the correlation between initial tariff protection and capital per worker is –0.20.

Trends in Relative Wages

Given these facts, what have trade liberalization and the ensuing changes in trade patterns implied for relative wages in Mexico? We begin by presenting some trends in the skilled-unskilled wage gap. Table 7-6 shows the average wage differential for production and nonproduction workers for our sample of Mexican manufacturing firms for 1984–90. The table also presents the average ratio of production to nonproduction employment for the same sample. The trends are clear. Since 1984, there has been a dramatic increase in skill wage differentials among Mexican manufacturing workers.

The ratio of the average hourly nonproduction to production wages increased from 1.975 in 1984 to 2.662 in 1990. However, the increase in the unskilled-skilled wage gap has not been accompanied by a parallel shift in the composition of employment.

Although the skilled-unskilled wage gap has increased for all industries, there is substantial interindustry variation in the trends. Table 7-5 presented average skilled-unskilled wage differentials and the ratio of unskilled to total employment by export category for 1984–90. The table indicates that the skilled-unskilled wage gap has increased more in the high-export sectors than in other industries. However, the ratio of unskilled to total employment has remained relatively stable in all sectors during the period.[18] This last finding suggests that changes in the relative skilled-unskilled wage differential do not reflect a shift in the demand for labor *within* industries toward higher-skilled workers. But it is consistent with a shift in demand *across* industries toward those that demand a higher share of skilled workers (the high-export sectors). It could also reflect a lower labor supply elasticity for skilled workers. If the supply of unskilled workers is more elastic than the supply of skilled workers, comparable shifts in demand for both types of labor would cause skilled wages to increase by more than unskilled wages.

Our next step is to examine movements in relative Mexican-U.S. wages by industry. Figure 7-6 shows real industry wages in 1987 U.S. dollars for production and nonproduction workers in Mexico and the United States, respectively.[19] Figure 7-7 presents the corresponding calculations of relative Mexican-U.S. wages by skill level and export orientation of the sector. These two figures reveal some interesting patterns.

Between 1984 and 1987 the relative Mexican-U.S. wage declined sharply for both production and nonproduction workers. The decline in relative wages was primarily a macroeconomic phenomenon and reflected the steep drop in real wages for all Mexican workers caused by the 1984–86 period of high inflation. However, relative Mexican-U.S. wages rose rapidly following the introduction of a successful stabilization and reform program in 1987, and by 1990 had recovered their 1984 levels. The increase in relative wages was much more pronounced for nonproduction workers than for production workers.[20] Moreover, wages of Mexican nonproduction workers

18. These results are broadly consistent with those reported in Feliciano (1994) and Hanson and Harrison (1994).

19. Relative wages are construed as the average wage in Mexico divided by the average in the U.S. Both wages are expressed in terms of 1987 US$.

20. Note that this is consistent with the general increase in wage disparities between skilled and unskilled workers that has been documented here and in other

Figure 7-6. *Real Wages by Export Orientation, 1984–90*[a]

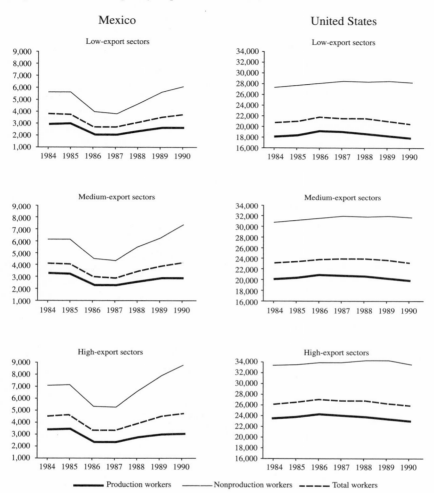

Mexico

United States

Source: Authors' calculations from the sample of Mexican manufacturing firms (as detailed in the appendix).

a. All amounts are shown in 1987 U.S. dollars.

rose relative to those of comparable U.S. workers despite an increase in the levels of wages for the latter. In other words, the wages of skilled Mexican workers converged to U.S. levels; real wages for skilled workers in the United States did not fall in real terms.

studies (Craig and Epelbaum [1994]; Feliciano [1994]; Hanson and Harrison [1994]; and Revenga [1995]).

Figure 7-7. *Relative Mexican-U.S. Wages, 1984–90*[a]

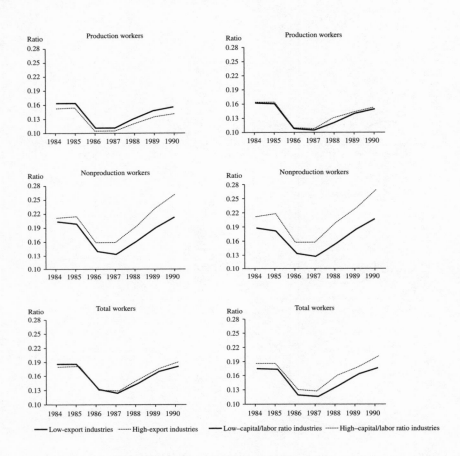

Source: Authors' calculations from the sample of Mexican manufacturing firms (as detailed in the appendix).

a. Relative wages are expressed in 1980 U.S. dollars. To classify industries into high/low exports, the ratio of exports to total output by industry was computed. The top third of the distribution was classified as high exports; the bottom third as low exports. For capital/labor ratios a similar procedure was followed.

U.S.-Mexican Trade and Changes in Relative Wages

The model presented previously suggested three testable hypotheses regarding the impact of trade liberalization on relative Mexican-U.S. wages. A first hypothesis was that, other things being equal, the removal of tariffs and other forms of trade protection should put downward pressure on

Mexican wages with regard to the United States. A second hypothesis was that trade-induced productivity growth would work just in the opposite way. By increasing Mexico's ability to produce more goods efficiently, productivity growth would lead to a rise in Mexico's relative wages. The third hypothesis was that trade liberalization would also have an impact on relative wages within Mexico, because of its effects on the relative demands for skilled and unskilled labor.

At first glance, the stylized facts are consistent with this Ricardian framework. Mexico is moving into new export sectors that employ more skilled labor, are more capital intensive, and have higher value added per worker, whereas the relative importance of its traditional export sectors is declining. At the same time, there is evidence that wages in the sectors that have undergone the biggest reductions in protection levels have lagged behind wages in other industries, and that employment in those sectors has fallen. This has occurred against a backdrop of rising skill differentials within Mexico. Regarding the United States, we have observed a significant increase in the relative wages of workers in the high-export sectors, an increase that is stronger among skilled than among unskilled workers.

In this section, we move beyond these stylized facts and attempt to identify the different channels through which the effects of trade liberalization on wages may operate. In particular, we try to distinguish between the effects of the removal of trade protection per se and the effects of trade-induced productivity growth.

Estimation Strategy

We assume that relative Mexican-U.S. wages in industry j and period t are driven by aggregate factors in Mexico and the United States (such as the growth of gross domestic product (GDP) or nationwide unemployment) and by industry-specific variables (capital intensity of production, changes in productivity linked to the use of new technology, the degree of trade protection to the industry's good, and so forth). We express this relationship in log form as

$$\ln\frac{w_{ij}^M}{w_j^{US}} = \beta_{0j} + \beta_1 \ln TP_j + \beta_2 \ln X_j + \beta_3 \ln Z + \beta_4 \ln F_i + \upsilon_{ij}, \qquad (7\text{-}5)$$

where, for simplicity, we have dropped the period subscript, and where β_{0j} represents an industry fixed effect. Variable w_{ij}^M is the average real wage of a Mexican worker in firm i and industry j; w_j^{US} is the average wage of a U.S. worker in the same industry; TP_j is a vector of trade protection variables for industry j; X_j is a vector of other industry-specific variables that affect wages, including productivity per worker; and Z is a vector of aggregate variables. Because our wage data for Mexico are drawn from a firm-level survey, we also include a vector of firm-specific characteristics (F_i) into our estimation equation.

Despite its simplicity, this model is consistent with a standard static labor demand–labor supply framework in which trade liberalization–induced shifts to industry labor demand are captured by changes in the trade protection variables. Shifts in labor supply are captured by changes in aggregate variables, such as the level of the average real wage (which should proxy for outside opportunities and also for income effects).

Empirical Results for Average Wages

Our empirical results are presented in table 7-7, columns (1)–(4). Columns (1) and (2) correspond to those obtained using ordinary least squares (OLS) and a simple specification with no industry fixed effects. Among the independent variables we include the industry-level import tariff, the coverage of import quotas (in terms of domestic output), a measure of productivity per worker (real value added per worker), the stock of fixed capital per worker, and the ratio of skilled to total employment in the firm. All independent variables (except for the proportion of skilled employees) are expressed in logarithms.[21] We also include year dummies to proxy for the effects of unmeasured changes in the aggregate (Z) variables.[22] Since these two specifications do not include industry dummies, results are mostly driven by the *cross-industry variation* in the data, rather than by changes within industries.

As suggested by the Ricardian model, the results reveal a positive association between Mexican-U.S. relative wages and the trade protection variables; higher tariffs and quotas are strongly associated with higher relative wages. The point estimates are quite large. A 10 percent decrease in the industry tariff is associated with a 3 percent decline in the average wages of Mexican workers relative to U.S. workers employed in the same

21. We also tried estimating the same regressions in first differences and obtained similar results.

22. We estimated similar regressions using a vector of aggregate variables rather than year dummies, but the results we obtained were very similar to those reported in table 7-7. Our vector of aggregate variables included the following (for both Mexico and the U.S.): change in the real average wage for the whole economy; changes in real GDP; change in the nominal $/peso exchange rate; change in real interest rates (proxied by the three-month interest rate minus the rate of inflation); and change in the government deficit as percent of GDP.

Table 7-7. *Regression of Relative Mexican-U.S. Wages on
Trade Protection Variables and Productivity, 1984–90*
Dependent variable = log (relative wage)[a,b]

Independent variables (logs)	Ordinary least squares			
	(1)	(2)	(3)	(4)
Average industry tariff	0.300[c]	0.309[c]	0.081[c]	0.083[c]
	(0.020)	(0.019)	(0.022)	(0.020)
Quota coverage on output	0.375[c]	0.390[c]	0.023[c]	0.012[c]
	(0.012)	(0.011)	(0.006)	(0.005)
Value added per worker	. . .	0.141[c]	. . .	0.153[c]
		(0.015)		(0.007)
Capital per worker	0.055[c]	0.020[c]	0.078[c]	0.045[c]
	(0.008)	(0.009)	(0.004)	(0.004)
Ratio of skilled to total	0.128	0.010	0.751[c]	0.670[c]
employment	(0.065)	(0.066)	(0.033)	(0.031)
Year dummies	Yes	Yes	Yes	Yes
Industry dummies	No	No	Yes	Yes
N	12,150	12,150	12,150	12,150
R^2	0.417	0.428	0.500	0.564

Source: Regressions reflect authors' estimates based on data from sample of Mexican manufacturing firms detailed in the appendix.

a. All variables are expressed in logarithms except for the ratio of skilled to total employment and the dummy variables. Industry dummies are at the four-digit ISIC level. See equation 7-5 in the text and the appendix for details on variables.

b. White-corrected standard errors are shown in parentheses.

c. Significance at the .05 level.

industry. A comparable decrease in the coverage of quotas is associated with an even larger decline in relative wages of nearly 4 percent.

Productivity per worker is also positively associated with relative wages. Wages in industries with higher productivity levels appear to be closer to U.S. levels than wages in industries where productivity has lagged behind. Another way to interpret this result is that as Mexican productivity levels rise towards U.S. levels, so will wages. The capital-per-worker variable picks up a similar effect. It too is positive and significant—suggesting that increases in capital intensity of production can push Mexican wages up toward U.S. levels.

The composition of firm employment appears much less important, especially once productivity is controlled for. Sectors with a higher share of skilled workers pay wages that are significantly closer to U.S. levels (column 1), but this mostly reflects a productivity effect (column 2). This twist suggests an interesting question: are the relative productivities of skilled Mexican and U.S. workers actually more similar than those of unskilled workers? Normally, we would think of unskilled workers in Mexico and the United States as being more substitutable for each other than skilled workers, but it could in fact be just the other way around. We pursue this in the next subsection.

In general, cross-industry movements in relative wages appear to be dominated by the trade protection effects, with productivity-related variables being less important. However, once industry fixed effects are included in the regressions, the results change significantly. With the industry dummies, the regressions primarily pick up variation *within* industries—in other words, how relative wages have evolved over time within a sector in response to changes over time in trade protection and productivity. As columns (3) and (4) show, when industry fixed effects are included in the specification, the magnitude of the trade protection effects diminishes notably, whereas that of the productivity-related measures rises.

Within a sector, changes in both tariffs and quotas are still positively associated with wages, but the coefficient is much smaller. A 10 percent reduction in the import tariff appears to lead to a 0.8 percent decline in the sector's relative wage. The effect of reductions in quotas is even smaller—about one-third the size. Comparing the results with and without industry dummies indicates that the main impact of the reduction in trade protection per se is clearly across industries, and thus on relative industry labor demands. This is broadly consistent with the Ricardian model (and with other standard trade models, including HOS).

The effects of productivity growth, on the other hand, clearly dominate developments within sectors. Two variables—productivity per worker and the ratio of skilled to total employment—explain most of the changes in relative wages that occur within industries. Although the coefficient is much smaller, capital per worker is also significant and works in the same direction. All three coefficients suggest that as production technology converges to U.S. technology (in terms of capital and skilled-labor intensities, and ultimately productivity), so do wages.

To what extent are productivity growth, increased capital and skilled-labor intensities, and trade liberalization independent? Causality clearly runs both ways. Trade liberalization has brought about increased access to new technologies, increased imports of capital goods, and a boom in DFI.[23] At the same time, Mexico's increased productivity has allowed it to move into new export sectors, take greater advantage of the opportunities offered by trade liberalization, and made it a more attractive place for foreign

23. Feenstra and Hanson (1996).

investors. It is therefore difficult, if not impossible, to isolate the effects of trade. At best, one can talk about the effects of the removal of protection as something separable from other indirect effects of trade that work themselves through productivity.

Differences in Relative Wage Changes for Skilled and Unskilled Workers

Can one integrate the findings on the impact of trade liberalization and productivity growth to explain increasing skill differentials in Mexico? As we have discussed, the Ricardian model can easily explain this increase as a combination of two forces at work—on the one hand, an increase in the demand for skills as Mexico upgrades its exports and moves into higher productivity goods; on the other, a reduction in the demand for unskilled labor associated with the removal of protection. What is needed then is to establish two facts: a stronger impact of the removal of trade protection on demand for unskilled labor than on the demand for skilled labor, and a link between productivity growth and the demand for skilled labor.

To explore this, we begin by estimating separate regressions for production and nonproduction workers along the lines suggested by table 7-7. The results obtained from these regressions are shown in table 7-8. Columns (1) and (3) present the specifications without the industry dummies—for example, those driven by the cross-industry variation. These two specifications allow us to identify interindustry demand shifts associated with the removal of trade protection. The estimates indicate that the impact of the removal of protection on wages is somewhat larger for production than for nonproduction workers. Our estimated point elasticity on tariffs is 0.33 for production workers and 0.28 for nonproductions workers, a difference that is statistically significant. Similarly, the point estimates for quotas are 0.41 and 0.36 for production workers and nonproduction workers, respectively.

Columns (2) and (4) in table 7-8 show the results obtained when industry fixed effects are included in the regressions. Within industries, changes in tariffs and quotas have roughly comparable effects on production and nonproduction workers alike. In contrast, the within-sector productivity effect is significantly larger for nonproduction than for production workers. The composition effect is also interesting. An increase in the fraction of skilled labor within an industry appears to be associated with an increase in the relative wage of production workers (and a decrease in the relative wage of nonproduction workers).

As a final exercise, we regress the skill differential directly on the trade protection and productivity variables. Results are shown in table 7-9.

Table 7-8. *Differences in Wage Responsiveness by Skill Level*
Dependent variable = log (relative wage)[a,b]

Independent variables (logs)	Production workers		Nonproduction workers	
	(1)	*(2)*	*(3)*	*(4)*
Average industry tariff	0.326[c]	0.074[c]	0.283[c]	0.085[c]
	(0.021)	(0.021)	(0.019)	(0.026)
Quota coverage on output	0.411[c]	0.015[c]	0.356[c]	0.007
	(0.012)	(0.006)	(0.011)	(0.007)
Value added per worker	0.132[c]	0.128[c]	0.161[c]	0.183[c]
	(0.016)	(0.007)	(0.015)	(0.009)
Capital per worker	−0.008	0.034[c]	0.041[c]	0.055[c]
Ratio of skilled to total	−0.332	0.148[c]	−0.342	−0.179[c]
employment	(0.073)	(0.031)	(0.067)	(0.042)
Year dummies	Yes	Yes	Yes	Yes
Industry dummies	No	Yes	No	Yes
N	12,150	12,150	12,150	12,150
R^2	0.428	0.535	0.409	0.353

Source: Regressions reflect authors' estimates based on data from sample of Mexican manufacturing firms detailed in the appendix.

a. All variables are expressed in logarithms except for the ratio of skilled to total employment and the dummy variables. Industry dummies are at the four-digit ISIC level. See equation 7-5 in the text and the appendix for details on variables.

b. White-corrected standard errors are shown in parentheses.

c. Significance at the .05 level.

Table 7-9. *Explaining the Skill Wage Premium*
Dependent variable = log $[W^s/W^u]^{a,b}$

Independent variables	*(1)*	*(2)*
Average industry tariff	−0.044[c]	0.011
	(0.009)	(0.027)
Quota coverage on output	−0.054[c]	−0.007
	(0.006)	(0.008)
Value added per worker	0.029[c]	0.055[c]
	(0.006)	(0.008)
Capital per worker	0.032[c]	0.021[c]
	(0.003)	(0.004)
Ratio of skilled to total	−0.010	−0.0327[c]
employment	(0.034)	(0.043)
Year dummies	Yes	Yes
Industry dummies	No	Yes
N	12,150	12,150
R^2	0.085	0.289

Source: Regressions reflect authors' estimates based on data from sample of Mexican manufacturing firms detailed in the appendix.

a. All variables are expressed in logarithms except the ratio of skilled to total employment and the dummy variables. Industry dummies are at the four-digit ISIC level.

b. White-corrected standard errors are shown in parentheses.

c. Significance at the .05 level.

Column (1) shows the regressions without industry dummies; column (2) those with industry fixed effects. Overall the estimates confirm the patterns suggested by the separate regressions. A reduction in the industry tariff or in quota coverage increases the skill gap. But this reflects primarily relative shifts in wages across industries. When industry dummies are included in the regression, the effects of tariffs and quotas become insignificant. The coefficients on productivity per worker and on capital per worker, on the other hand, are positive and significant in both specifications. Because these two variables are fairly correlated, they are probably picking up the same thing: capital and technology (or technology-induced productivity growth) are more complementary to skilled labor than to unskilled labor.

Conclusions

In this chapter we have examined recent shifts in relative wages within Mexico and between Mexico and the United States and have attempted to link them, directly and indirectly, to the effects of trade liberalization.

Overall, the results suggest that by itself, the removal of trade protection had a negative impact on the wage of Mexican workers relative to their U.S. counterparts. A 10 percent reduction in tariff and quota protection appears to have been associated with reductions in relative wages of 3 to 4 percent. However, to the extent that trade liberalization allowed for imports of new capital and technology and induced productivity growth, it may have yielded increases in the relative wage. The impact of productivity growth seems particularly important in explaining increases in relative wages over time, within industries.

These two facts combine to provide a plausible explanation for rising skill differentials within Mexico. On the one hand, the reduction of trade barriers seems to have had a larger negative impact on demand for unskilled labor than on demand for skilled workers, pushing unskilled wages down relative to skilled ones. At the same time, productivity growth has been concentrated in more-skill-intensive sectors, raising the relative demand for skilled labor and hence its relative wage. Within industries too, productivity growth appears to have been associated with rising skill differentials.

Appendix

The data used in the chapter come from three different sources:

1. *Data on trade values come from the UNSO Comtrade database.* This data set provides information on imports and exports by commodity and by trade partner, as reported by individual countries to the UNSO.

2. *Data on Mexican manufacturing plants come from SECOFI.* These are annual data, and our sample covers the period 1984 to 1990. In their 1994 study, Westbrook and Tybout report that for a typical industry the SECOFI sample plants represent approximately 80 percent of total output. The sample is biased in the sense that it covers only medium and large firms. Our working sample includes a total of 2,413 firms.

The information provided in the survey permits a breakdown of the workers in two big groups: production workers and nonproduction workers. The first group includes those who perform general, nonskilled activities: machinery-related activities, cleaning, machinery maintenance, stocking, packing, and transport. The nonproduction group includes workers who are in charge of planning, administration, technical supervision, accounting, archives, marketing, selling, advertising, security, and general office activities. The annual wage for each group is calculated as the total payroll to each group divided by the number or workers in each group. This annual wage includes all the cash payments.

3. *Data on American manufacturing industries come from the NBER Productivity database, which includes a total of 450 industries.* The industries are those defined in the 1972 Standard Industrial Classification (SIC), and cover the entire manufacturing sector. Much of the data is taken from the annual surveys of manufactures and censuses of manufactures.

Comment by William R. Cline

Ana Revenga and Claudio Montenegro are to be commended for their painstaking examination of Mexican wages in relation to trade policy. They provide some important stylized facts. However, I am skeptical about their theoretical framework and their interpretation of their results.

An important overall finding in this chapter is that Mexico does not seem to conform with HOS predictions of the impact of liberalization on relative factor prices. In the past several years the ratio of skilled to unskilled wages has risen rather than fallen, as HOS would predict for a country with relatively scarce skilled labor. Feenstra and Hanson find the same thing.[24] In my view, neither Revenga-Monetenegro nor Feenstra-Hanson attribute sufficient weight to a macroeconomic explanation: the impact of Mexico's macroeconomic adjustment program. In the face of high inflation, in December 1987 the government's new Solidarity Pact implemented a heterodox wage price–exchange rate freeze combined with orthodox fiscal adjustment. The wage freeze was a sharp contrast to the quasi indexation based on frequent increases in the minimum wage that had marked policy in the mid-1980s. The result was a sharp decline in the real minimum wage, as inflation fell only with a lag. Even taking account of the relatively small fraction of the labor force employed at wages as low as the minimum wage, it seems likely that this outcome tended to erode low-end wages relative to skilled wages. The authors' table 7-6 shows no change in the nonproduction/production wage ratio during 1984–87, but an increase of almost one-third during 1988–90. Table 7-1 shows that the biggest reduction in nontariff barriers (NTB) occurred in 1985–87. The timing therefore seems to implicate the macrostabilization strategy of 1988 and after, rather than the earlier trade liberalization, as the culprit for rising wage disparities.

Perhaps because the HOS prediction of relative decline in the price of the scarce factor (skilled labor) from liberalization did not seem to fit, the authors invoke a Ricardian trade model as their theoretical framework. Here, it seems to me, they go seriously off track. The Ricardian model does indeed provide a basis for exploring differential productivity in a single-factor world. But the authors' use of this framework seems to me to arrive at decidedly un-Ricardian conclusions. The heart of Ricardian trade theory is that comparative advantage permits nations to gain from trade. Yet Revenga and Montenegro tell us that Mexican wages should be expected to fall when trade is liberalized. But in a one-factor world, there is no other factor to capture the gains from trade. So the authors are standing Ricardo on his head and predicting welfare losses from trade rather than welfare gains. The only conceivable basis for this outcome would be a loss of terms of trade from liberalization. Yet the Mexican economy essentially fits the small-country case relative to the United States, so there should have been no optimal terms of trade story to justify previous protection, nor any net welfare loss from liberalization. My most fundamental problem with this chapter, then, is its claim that on a basis of Ricardian theory, we should expect Mexican wages to fall from liberalization.

24. Feenstra and Hanson (1995).

The authors' linear wage-productivity model does highlight an important point. Unskilled labor costs about seven times as much in the United States as in Mexico (figure 7-6). So U.S. unskilled workers need to be seven times as productive as their Mexican counterparts to be able to compete. In some sectors, cooperating skilled labor and capital, along with superior technology, may make this possible. In others, especially (one would surely expect) sectors where unskilled labor is the main input, U.S. firms would be less likely to overcome the wage differential.

The authors interpret their empirical results in a way that seems to compound the problem of a questionable theoretical framework. They essentially measure cross-section correlations between sectoral protection and sectoral average wage. That is not too surprising, considering that protection is one source of rent, and there tends to be rent sharing with labor. Borjas and Ramey have emphasized such rent sharing in U.S. autos and steel (although because of low wages and high protection in apparel it is possible that for the United States the simple cross-section correlation between protection and wages would be negative).[25] What is surprising is the authors' inference from cross-section correlations that there would be a causal impact whereby reduction of protection would reduce *overall, average* wages. Surely the expectation instead would be that liberalization would reduce the wage rents in the protected sectors, but increase wages in unprotected sectors and especially in export sectors. Otherwise (once again) we would have the non sequitur of a decline rather than increase in aggregate welfare from liberalization (at least in a one-factor world, which the authors specify). So my second problem with this chapter is its use of cross-section correlations of protection and wages to infer that trade liberalization would reduce Mexican wages overall.

The authors do note a countervailing consideration, which is the tendency for wages and productivity to rise when foreign investment enters as a part of the reform package. Revenga and Montenegro thus formulate two opposing forces: Ricardian wage loss and productivity gain from capital flows. I reject the former but agree with the latter. However, the Revenga-Montenegro formulation seems ad hoc when it merely posits, rather than explains, a tendency for the new export sectors to be skill and capital intensive.

The Feenstra-Hanson formulation of a three-factor, single-final-product, multiple-intermediate product model is similar to the Revenga-Montenegro approach but, to my taste, provides a sharper specification of what one

25. Borjas and Ramey (1994).

should suspect from capital inflows. In their world, Mexico has a comparative advantage in unskilled products. Capital inflow shifts the dividing line along the continuum of intermediate products ranked by skilled/unskilled factor proportions. The result is an increase in the relative demand and thus relative wage of skilled labor in Mexico. As formerly marginal U.S. sectors shift to Mexican production, there is a similar rise in relative demand for skilled workers there. The skilled/unskilled wage ratio thus rises in *both* the United States and Mexico. But this is a direct investment phenomenon, not a trade liberalization phenomenon. There is nothing in the Feenstra-Hanson model that would predict a loss of overall average Mexican wages as the result of trade liberalization.

At a more detailed level, it does not seem to me that analysis based on the ratio of exports to output has much meaning; the sectoral trade balance relative to output is a much more meaningful indicator of revealed comparative advantage. Higher export/output ratios unaccompanied by trade surpluses are signs of higher intraindustry trade. What is really being picked up here may be that there is a positive correlation between product differentiation and scale economies (two sources of intraindustry trade), on the one hand, and skills-cum-capital intensity on the other. On the chapter's overall rejection of HOS for Mexican trade, the conclusion may be too hasty. Indeed, the authors first note that the usual measure of comparative advantage (based on sectoral trade balance) does conform with labor intensity (table 7-3). Certainly in the textiles-apparel complex, a core dynamic of NAFTA was that U.S. producers of capital-intensive textile fabric saw a natural alliance with Mexican producers of apparel, who would use U.S. fabric in labor-intensive processing for reexport to the United States. This nexus is prototypically HOS. Because the large U.S. textile firms are more politically organized than small apparel firms, this HOS arrangement also helped NAFTA get past the traditionally powerful opposition of the textile sector to trade liberalization.

Another detail in the estimates concerns comparisons of Mexican and U.S. wages. Most of the variation in this ratio over recent years has surely come from the large swings in the real value of the Mexican peso. The currency was seriously undervalued at the end of 1987, and then became seriously overvalued as the quasi-fixed rate lagged behind inflation (and as finally became clear with the 1994 peso crisis). The authors do not separate out U.S.-Mexican relative wage effects stemming from trade and investment liberalization from those attributable to changes in the real exchange rate, another manifestation of the need to distinguish between macrostabilization and microstructural influences.

The chapter is silent on the main theme of the conference on which this book is based: the impact of North-South trade on wage distribution within the United States and other industrial countries. This issue was a cause célèbre in the run-up to the NAFTA decision. The predominant view among economists was that the Mexican economy was too small to have much impact on U.S. wages. As a caveat to that view, it should be noted that Mexico's unskilled labor force is not small relative to that of the United States. World Bank estimates place 1984 average education of the work force of the United States at 11.3 years, and of Mexico at 5.5 years.[26] Based on estimates by Wood that in 1984, 49.8 percent of the U.S. work force was unskilled, whereas the figure for Korea (average education: 7.1 years) was 86.8 percent unskilled, a reasonable estimate of Mexico's unskilled share of the labor force would be 90 percent unskilled.[27] In absolute terms, this means Mexico has 30 million unskilled workers, compared with about 60 million in the United States. Whereas U.S. GDP is almost 20 times as large as Mexican GDP, the unskilled U.S. work force is only twice as large. Thus, we should not necessarily expect de minimus effects from NAFTA on low-end U.S. wages.

At the same time, the principal effect probably is through immigration. Borjas and colleagues find that overall immigration has been responsible for about one-third of the deterioration in wages of U.S. high school dropouts relative to other workers in the 1980s.[28] So a central underlying notion of NAFTA—that it could relieve long-term pressure on immigration into the United States by providing better opportunities for Mexicans at home—would seem well founded as a way of looking at NAFTA impacts. In this framework, unskilled U.S. workers should gain more from reduced immigration from Mexico (at least over the medium term) than they lose from HOS effects of freer trade.

In sum, Revenga and Montenegro have provided evidence on important trends in Mexico, including a widening of wage differentials and a seeming pattern of rising exports in relatively capital- and skill-intensive sectors (for example, autos) as a part of multinational firm sourcing strategies. However, one should be cautious in accepting their supposedly Ricardian-based theory that we should expect Mexican wages to have fallen from trade liberalization (that theory really would suggest the opposite). Similarly, there could be more HOS evidence (especially in the likely evolution of textiles and apparel) than their analysis suggests.

26. Nehru, Swanson, and Dubey (1995).
27. Wood (1994).
28. Borjas, Freeman, and Katz (1992).

Comment by James R. Tybout

This chapter provides a number of clues to the forces behind North-South relative wage changes and the kinds of things that we might expect on a broader scale as developing countries become a more significant part of the world economy. Although I think it was not the authors' original intention, it demonstrates that other forces are at work besides the traditional Stolper-Samuelson effects, and that those forces can easily dominate, at least in the short run.

Let me begin by elaborating on this last point, since I think it deserved additional emphasis in the chapter. First, on the unimportance of Stolper-Samuelson effects, the authors calculate that the relative price of exportables was 1.03 in 1984 and 1.04 in 1990. Not surprisingly, they also find relative output prices have very little predictive power in wage regressions. Although these findings have been dropped in the second draft of the chapter, I found them important. They convincingly make the case that changes in the terms of trade cannot have not been the main reason that factor prices changed in Mexico vis-à-vis the United States.

What *has* mattered in the short run? Most important, one must remember that major exchange rate shocks accompanied the Mexican trade reforms. During the period 1984–86 the peso rapidly depreciated in real terms; thereafter it climbed steadily in value. Comparison of a Mexican real exchange rate series and any of the series on U.S.-Mexican wage ratios (figure 7-4) reveals a family resemblance.

This pattern is readily explained in the context of the Salter model, which distinguishes tradable from nontradable goods rather than exportables from importables. Given that wages are sticky in the short run, that model predicts that real devaluation immediately increases the price of tradeable goods relative to labor, driving down the real wage. Of course appreciation does the opposite. (Converting peso wages back to U.S. dollars exacerbates the measured fluctuations.) The same logic could be used to explain the inverted-U pattern in U.S. wages: real appreciation of the dollar drives wages up in the mid-1980s, and devaluation pulls them down thereafter.

The Model

Let me now turn to the forces the authors *do* focus on: the effects of commercial policy and, to a lesser extent, productivity growth. To link these variables with wages, the authors appeal to the DFS model. Under the assumption that homogeneous labor is the only input in each sector, they demonstrate several results. First, unilateral trade liberalization reduces the range of goods that Mexico produces domestically, and it drives down Mexican wages relative to U.S. wages. Second, productivity gains—due, perhaps, to improved access to imported capital goods or heightened competitive pressures—increase the range of goods that Mexico can export, and lead to an increase in Mexican wages as trade expands.

Finally, across-the-board productivity gains increase the range of goods that Mexico can profitably produce and export. Presuming that these newly profitable goods are relatively intensive in skilled labor, the authors argue that productivity gains should increase the relative demand for skilled labor and drive up skilled wages.

I found each of these three implications interesting and potentially relevant to the Mexican liberalization experience. But I was troubled by their interpretation as motivations for regressions of relative wages on changes in protection using firm-level panel data (tables 7-7, 7-8, and 7-9).

First, the third implication is really a conjecture, since the authors do not generalize the DFS model to distinguish skilled and unskilled workers. This left me wondering what model the authors had in mind and whether the effect they describe could really be formally demonstrated under plausible assumptions.

More important, if one takes the DFS model literally, there is only one wage per country. (There would have been only two if the extension to skilled workers had been done.) Hence the reaction of the wage in any industry to changes in protection should be the same, regardless of that industry's characteristics and regardless of its particular change in protection. So, while the model provides one interpretation for the aggregate trends in wages depicted by figures 7-6 and 7-7, it provides no basis for explaining cross-industry or cross-firm variation in wages.[29] In fact, when Revenga and Montenegro include time dummies in their models, these control for economywide trends in wages, and the coefficents on variables that proxy for commercial policy are identified exclusively with idiosyncratic variation in the data. In short, if regression parameters are to

29. Leamer (1994) makes a similar point conerning tests for Stolper-Samuelson effects in the Hecksher-Ohlin (HO) model: "Cross-industry comparisons of wages and prices cannot be used to estimate these functions because an explicit assumption of the model is that factors are mobile across sectors and command the same returns."

be identified by industry-specific variation in wages, it is important to explain why factor prices do not equate across industries.

Both of my reservations about the theory could be handled by sacrificing the richness of the DFS continuum of goods and adopting a specific-factors version of the Salter model. One reason to do so is that, as the authors note, it seems to make more sense to distinguish tradeables from nontradeables in Mexico than to distinguish importables from exportables. But more important, because the specific-factors framework treats some inputs as fixed, it generates predictions on the cross-industry pattern of returns to a given factor.

To take a tractable example, suppose that skilled labor and capital are sector specific in the short run, while unskilled labor is mobile.[30] Further, as implied by table 7-5, let tradables be more skill-intensive than nontradables. Then, for instance, relatively rapid productivity growth in the tradable goods industries shifts production toward those sectors, pulling unskilled labor along and driving up the returns to capital and skilled labor in tradable goods relative to nontradable goods. Protection of the tradable-goods industries does the same, as does real devaluation. (What happens to real unskilled wages depends on the relative weights of tradable and nontradable output prices in the output price index.) Subdividing tradables into multiple industries and assuming that some forms of unskilled labor are also industry specific in the short run, this model provides an alternative motivation for the regression models at the end of the chapter.

The Regression Results

Turning to the regression results, I found it interesting that wages are positively associated with protection, both looking across industries and following industries through time. This result is surprisingly robust, although it is strongest in the cross-industry variation. As the authors suggest, this finding probably partly reflects the fact that liberalization depresses demand for labor in the liberalized sectors. Indeed, other studies using the same data have found that reductions in protection are associated with reduced profitability.[31]

30. This assumption is consistent with the finding in table 7-7 that wages among nonproduction workers are more closely related to output prices than wages among production workers.
31. Grether (forthcoming).

But other forces may also be at work. For example, exportable goods have tended to have low protection in Mexico, so the results may simply confirm that exports are concentrated in low-wage industries.[32]

Another source of correlation is the large exchange rate movements I mentioned earlier. The authors are, of course, aware of these movements, and they control for them by including time dummies. This helps a great deal, but it is only a complete solution in the special case where wages equate across sectors at all points in time. If the resource pulls created by exchange rate fluctuations induce temporary cross-industry discrepancies in the return to a given type of worker and these discrepancies depend on tradeability of the product, there remains a spurious source of correlation between protection (which is higher for the less-tradable sectors) and relative wages.

On productivity and wages, I also agree with the authors that sectors with high labor productivity tend to pay their workers more. If nothing else, this is a consequence of high-productivity workers being able to command higher wages. But as with commercial policy variables, there are other reasons why one might expect to find significant coefficients on productivity proxies.

One such reason derives from variable construction. Specifically, wages are imputed as the wage bill divided by number of workers. Hence the dependent variable in table 7-7 is a negative function of employment, and the dependent variable in table 7-9 is a positive function of the ratio of skilled to unskilled employment. Given that productivity is proxied by value added per worker, the ratio of skilled to total employment, and capital per worker, it is unsurprising that significant associations show up between these proxies and wages. This is particularly true when industry dummies are included, which control for permanent technological and worker quality effects, leaving only transitory fluctuations in unit labor costs.

The authors suggest that productivity gains in Mexico have been concentrated in the less-protected (that is, high-import or high-export) industries. It is worth noting that other work with the same database supports that conjecture. First, Thompson finds that between 1985 and 1990, new capital formation took place disproproptionately in the industries exhibiting high trade dependence.[33] This is consistent with the notion that Mexico's unilateral liberalization and assention to the General Agreement on Tariffs and Trade (GATT) signaled a long-term commitment to outward-oriented policies. Second, although Westbrook and I found modest productivity

32. Tybout and Westbrook (1994).
33. Thompson (1994).

growth rates in Mexican manufacturing overall, the tradable-goods producers did better than others.[34] This may have been due to heightened foreign competition, as well as better access to imported capital goods and intermediates.

Conclusion

In this chapter the authors did an excellent job of documenting the trends in Mexican wages since that country's unilerateral trade liberalization in the mid-1980s. It also suggests some interesting interpretations for the forces behind them. I would be interested in seeing a sequel in which the theoretical and empirical linkages between commercial policy, the skilled-unskilled wage gap, and productivity growth are further developed.

General Discussion

Part of the discussion of this chapter focused on trying to explain the finding that Mexican wage inequality grew following liberalization, with relative wages of skilled (nonproduction) workers rising significantly. Michael Piore suggested that it might reflect a process of adjustment to a new regime in which those industries (and firms) with relatively skilled labor may have been better able to take advantage of liberalization and to compete in the U.S. market. He also thought that the finding might reflect longer-term difficulties faced by low-wage industries in Mexico that are competing in the U.S. market with Chinese industries, characterized by both low wages and sophisticated supplier networks.

Robert Blecker emphasized the dualistic nature of the Mexican economy. This received little attention in the chapter but might help to explain the observed combination of an increased Mexican skill premium and more intensive use of nonproduction workers in export industries. He hypothesized that many products sold in Mexico under the import-substitution regime were not of sufficient quality for export to the United States. Therefore, increasing exports requires raising product quality, which will entail shifting to a different organization of work that is likely to involve more nonproduction workers. He also noted that it may be unrealistic to expect liberalization to raise wages of the workers at the bottom of

34. Tybout and Westbrook (1994).

Mexico's distribution, as these workers do not tend to be in the segment of the economy that expands. Gary Burtless noted that he believed production in the informal sector had increased during the 1980s. If such data are available, it would be instructive to examine what happened to wages in the formal relative to the informal sector.

Burtless also thought that institutional developments in Mexico may have been more important than was recognized in this chapter. In particular, he believed that the contribution rate required of firms in the formal sector increased, while the real minimum wage was allowed to decline significantly. However, Revenga disputed Burtless's view that a significant share of Mexican workers were affected by changes in the minimum wage, claiming that it applies to only about 7 percent of the population, including those in the informal sector.

Susan Collins raised the concern that workers considered relatively skilled in the United States may be quite different than those considered relatively skilled in Mexico. She and Richard Freeman stressed that this problem may be compounded by the usage of production versus non-production workers to classify workers as unskilled and skilled, which is problematic for workers in the United States. This makes it somewhat difficult to interpret the trends in the relative wages of U.S. and Mexican skilled workers.

There was also discussion about this chapter's focus on differences in the Mexican-U.S. wage differentials across industries. Ed Leamer noted that in an HO framework, like a Ricardian one, wages of particular types of workers do not differ by industry but are the same economywide. He suggested a version of the Ricardo-Viner model in which skilled workers are industry specific as an attractive alternative for modeling such differentials, because it is based on the assumption that there is a connection between workers and industries. He also postulated that the observed differences in relative wages across industries might reflect a combination of differences in the mix of labor skills used in each industry in Mexico versus the United States and differences in the wage-skill profile in the two countries.

Leamer also argued that the fact that Mexico has both exports and imports in some industries should not be labeled intraindustry trade, which he defined as two-way trade in very similar products. Instead, these two-way flows often reflect the fact that different stages of production—which may use quite different skill mixes—are done in different places. This means that various types of output are aggregated together at the industry level of data used in the analysis. Further, cross-border shipping may imply that much of the value added of an export from Mexico is actually U.S. value added, which would bias the ratio of exports to production, used as a measure of Mexican competitiveness across industries.

Other participants also offered explanations for the finding that Mexican industries that export relatively large shares of production tend to be relatively high wage and intensive in their use of skilled labor and of capital. Adrian Wood wondered whether the data sample might be biased, because it contains primarily large firms. Although these account for 80 percent of manufacturing output, they may account for a much smaller share of employment in Mexican manufacturing. He also emphasized that the export-production ratios should not be interpreted as a measure of comparative advantage. Steven Davis noted that Bernard and Jensen have found a similar result for U.S. plants. He raised the possibility that both of these studies suffer from measurement problems. Larger firms (which tend to be high skill and capital intensive and to pay relatively high wages) are more likely to identify themselves as exporters, whereas small plants are more likely to sell to wholesalers, who may later export.

Finally, Catherine Mann missed an explicit treatment of the role for *maquiladores* and DFI more generally in explaining recent labor market developments in Mexico. She believed that this was an important area for additional study.

References

Berman, Eli, John Bound, and Zvi Griliches. 1994. "Changes in the Demand for Skilled Labor within U.S. Manufacturing: Evidence from the Annual Survey of Manufactures." *Quarterly Journal of Economics* 109 (May): 367–98.

Borjas, George J., Richard B. Freeman, and Lawrence F. Katz. 1992. "On the Labor Market Effects of Immigration and Trade." In *Immigration and the Work Force: Economic Consequences for the United States and Source Areas,* edited by George J. Borjas and Richard B. Freeman, 213–44. University of Chicago Press.

Borjas, George J., and Valerie A. Ramey. 1994. "The Relationship between Wage Inequality and International Trade." In *The Changing Distribution of Income in an Open U.S. Economy,* edited by Jeffrey H. Bergstrand, and others, 217–41. Amsterdam: North-Holland.

Bound, John, and George Johnson. 1992. "Changes in the Structure of Wages in the 1980s: An Evaluation of Alternative Explanations." *American Economic Review* 82 (June): 371–92.

Cragg, Michael, and Mario Epelbaum. 1994. "The Premium for Skills: Evidence from Mexico." Columbia University, Department of Economics.

Currie, Janet, and Ann Harrison. 1994. "Trade Reform and Labor Market Adjustment in Morocco." Paper presented at the World Bank Labor Markets Workshop, July.

Feenstra, Robert C., and Gordon H. Hanson. 1995. "Foreign Investment, Outsourcing and Relative Wages." Working Paper 5121. Cambridge, Mass.: National Bureau of Economic Research (May).

———. 1996. "Foreign Investment, Outsourcing, and Relative Wages." In *Political Economy of Trade Policy: Essays in Honor of Jagdish Bhagwati,* edited by Robert C. Feenstra, Gene M. Grossman, and Douglas A. Irvin. MIT Press.

Feliciano, Zadia M. 1994. "Workers and Trade Liberalization: The Impact of Trade Reforms in Mexico on Wages and Employment." Harvard University, Department of Economics.

Freeman, Richard G., and Lawrence F. Katz. 1991. "Industrial Wage and Employment Determination in an Open Economy." In *Immigration, Trade, and the Labor Market,* edited by John M. Abowd and Richard B. Freeman, 235–60. University of Chicago Press.

Grether, Jean-Marie. 1996. "Trade Liberalization, Market Structure and Performance in Mexican Manufacturing: 1985–1990." In *Industrial Evolution in Developing Countries: Micro Patterns of Turnover, Productivity, and Market Structure,* edited by Mark J. Roberts and James R. Tybout. Oxford University Press.

Grossman, Gene M. 1987. "The Employment and Wage Effects of Import Competition in the United States." *Journal of International Economic Integration* 2 (Spring): 1–23.

Hanson, G., and A. Harrison. 1994. "Trade, Technology and Wage Inequality: Evidence from Mexico." University of Texas, Department of Economics.

Hufbauer, Gary C., and Jeffrey J. Schott. 1992. *North American Free Trade: Issues and Recommendations.* Washington: Institute for International Economics.

Katz, Lawrence F., and Kevin M. Murphy. 1992. "Changes in Relative Wages, 1963–1987: Supply and Demand Factors." *Quarterly Journal of Economics* 107 (February): 35–78.

Katz, Lawrence F., and Ana L. Revenga. 1989. "Changes in the Structure of Wages: The United States vs. Japan." *Journal of the Japanese and International Economies* 3: 522–53.

Lawrence, Robert Z., and Matthew J. Slaughter. 1993. "International Trade and American Wages in the 1980s: Giant Sucking Sound or Small Hiccup?" *Brookings Papers on Economic Activity: Microeconomics* 2: 161–210.

Leamer, Edward W. 1993. "Wage Effects of a U.S.-Mexican Free Trade Agreement" in *The Mexican-U.S. Free Trade Agreement,* edited by Peter N. Garber. MIT Press.

———. 1994. "Trade, Wages, and Revolving Door Ideas." Working Paper 4716. Cambridge, Mass.: National Bureau of Economic Research.

Nehru, Vikram, Eric Swanson, and Ashutosh Dubey. 1995. "A New Database on Human Capital in Developing and Industrial Countries: Sources, Methodology, and Results." *Journal of Development Economics* 46 (April): 379–401.

Oks, Daniel Fernando. 1993. "Mexico: Reform and Productivity Growth." Report 12605-ME. World Bank.

Revenga, Ana L. 1992. "Exporting Jobs? The Impact of Import Competition on Employment and Wages in U.S. Manufacturing." *Quarterly Journal of Economics* 107 (February): 255–84.

———. 1995. "Employment and Wage Effects of Trade Liberalization: The Case of Mexican Manufacturing." Policy Research Working Paper 1524. The World Bank.

Robbins, D. 1993. "Relative Wage Structure in Chile: The Effects of Liberalization." HIID.

Sachs, Jeffrey D., and Howard J. Shatz. 1994. "Trade and Jobs in U.S. Manufacturing." *Brookings Papers on Economic Activity* 1: 1–69.

Ten Kate, Adriaan. 1992. "Trade Liberalization Economic Stabilization in Mexico: Lessons of Experiences." *World Development* 20 (May): 659–72.

Thompson, Aileen J. 1994. "Resource Allocation and Trade Policy in Mexico." Carlton University, Department of Economics.

Tybout, James R., and M. Daniel Westbrook. 1994. "Trade Liberalization and the Dynamics of Efficiency Change in Mexican Manufacturing Industries." *Journal of International Economics* 39: 53–78.

Wood, Adrian. 1994. *North-South Trade, Employment, and Inequality: Changing Fortunes in a Skill-Driven World.* Oxford, England: Clarendon Press.

EIGHT

Trade Policy and America's Standard of Living: A Historical Perspective

J. Bradford De Long

THE UNITED STATES has not always been a free trade–loving country. Since World War II the establishment core of both political parties has had a free (or at least freer)-trade orientation. Relatively broad, bipartisan coalitions have enacted repeated moves toward trade liberalization, supported by broad agreement that the United States has more to gain than to lose from closer integration into an international division of labor.

Before World War II things were different. For a century and a half after the founding of the United States, free trade tended to be the exception, and protectionism the rule. Tariff rates did oscillate. They went up with the Smoot-Hawley tariff at the beginning of the Great Depression, and up to raise revenues to fight the Civil War; they went down in the 1830s as

This chapter has been partially supported by an Alfred P. Sloan Foundation research fellowship. Work on it was begun while I was deputy assistant secretary of the U.S. Department of the Treasury for economic policy. I want to thank Bill Bareeda, Susan Collins, Barry Eichengreen, Jeffrey Frankel, Richard Freeman, Louis Johnston, Ian McLean, Marty Olney, Sherman Robinson, Christina Romer, David Romer, Paul Romer, Andrei Shleifer, Larry Summers, Richard Sutch, Peter Temin, Robert Waldmann, and David Walters for helpful discussions. The views set forward here are solely my own.

southern importers of manufactured goods from Britain made rollback of high tariffs a key sectional issue. But by and large the U.S. policy was explicitly one of moderate to high protection.

The United States before World War II tended toward protectionism for two reasons. First, customs duties were the source of a significant share of federal revenues. As Colbert is reported to have said, taxation is like plucking a goose: the object is to get the most feathers with the least hissing. Tariffs are taxes explicitly levied on foreigners. The tariff leads to a higher price for imported goods, but no American voter writes a check to the government. Economists may argue that tariffs often impose extremely high excess burdens and are an inefficient form of taxation. But from a bureaucrat's point of view tariffs use foreign producers as your tax collectors, and that makes them attractive.

Thus those interested in an expanded role for the federal government, whether in building national roads, a battle fleet, or paying post–Civil War pensions, tended to approve of higher tariffs that raised government resources. They joined political forces with the second group of potential strong supporters of a tariff: those who sought protection for their manufactured goods against foreign competition, especially from the mature, industrial economy of England.

The outcome was a revenue-raising, manufacturing-protecting tariff, enacted and maintained by a coalition of Northeastern (and later Midwestern) manufacturing interests fearing British competition, and of Western (and later Eastern) interests seeking an expanded role for the federal government.

Only after World War I did American manufacturers and workers begin to see foreign industrial countries as potential markets to as great a degree as they saw them potential competitors. As the United States shifted from a manufactures-importing, agricultural goods–exporting economy to a manufactures- and capital-exporting economy, and after the passage of the income tax amendment that made the federal government much less concerned with tariffs as a source of revenue, the pro-protectionist coalition that held sway for most of the first century and a half the United States existed broke down.[1]

By the end of World War II, the dominant political constellation in both political parties was close to what we see today. The dominance of

---

1. For more on the political economy of America's pre–World War II tariff, see Taussig (1931). See also Baack and Ray (1973, 1983). Also useful are Hansen (1990); Kaplan and Ryley (1994); Edwards (1970); and Goldstein (1993).

protectionist pressures in the United States was gone. Pressures for increased protection have, for the most part, remained relatively dormant for nearly half a century. Opposition to free trade has usually focused on preventing further liberalization—and not on rolling back liberalization that had previously taken place.

How did the protectionism from 1800 to 1940 affect America's standard of living? Economists' standard tools suggest that the tariff reduced the living standard of Americans—and the real wages of American workers—by about 0.7 percent of national product in the short run. Suppose that the elasticity of demand for imports was one. Then a 30 percent tariff (a little lower than the average value over the period 1800–1940) would reduce the import share of national demand from a counterfactual level of 9 percent to the actual level of about 7 percent of national product, with the consumer and producer surplus foregone on a discouraged import amounting on average to 15 percent of its value. The net result? A reduction in real incomes of 0.3 percent of national product, with little reason to think that this reduction in real incomes fell disproportionately on capital rather than on labor.

In the long run, standard tools suggest that the costs of the tariff were considerably greater. The tariff made imported capital goods more expensive and presumably raised the price of domestic capital goods that were substitutes for imports as well. A high-tariff economy is a lower-investment economy, a lower–capital stock economy, and a lower-wage economy. The wedge driven between the amount of savings and the amount of investment by the tariff would, in the steady state of a growth model, reduce national product and real wages by about one-twentieth.

For the pre–Civil War period, this simple calculation may be seriously off. The American South was a huge supplier in the world cotton market. Tariffs on manufactured imports may have raised America's terms of trade enough to counterbalance (through a higher price of cotton in world markets) the deadweight loss from the tariff's discouragement of valuable imports. This issue will not be analyzed here.[2]

For the post–Civil War period as well, some have argued that this standard calculation is seriously off. Some have seen the coexistence of protectionist trade policy with America's successful nineteenth-century industrial revolution as demonstrating that protectionist policies can be a plus for a growing and industrializing economy, at least in the long run.

2. However, see Williamson (1964, 1974a); Pope (1972); Lee and Passell (1979); James (1981); Harley (1992); and Atack, Passell, and Lee (1994).

Such analysts claim that, in James Fallows' words, belief in free trade "fail[s] a test of history. . . . [Free trade principles] do not explain how the industrial old guard—first England, then America—rose to power. Indeed, those countries developed fastest when they paid least attention to today's . . . [orthodox free-trade] principles of economic growth."[3]

The argument for the beneficial effects of protection made by Fallows and others is the same argument noted and rejected in the case of the post–Civil War U.S. tariff by F. W. Taussig, or indeed the same "infant-industry" argument noted and grudgingly admitted by John Stuart Mill. Any who point to the coexistence of American protectionism with the industrial revolution in the United States are implicitly asserting that these benefits—from a greater degree of specialization in manufacturing induced by protection—are great and long lasting.[4]

Are they correct in general, over the entire span of American tariff history? That is too big a question. Instead, in the latter part of this chapter I analyze a similar but narrower question: Is it plausible to believe that the tariffs levied on manufacturing imports in the late nineteenth century induced enough benefits to economic growth to more than offset their economic cost?

In the first part of this chapter I provide a broad overview of tariffs and trade patterns in the century and a half before World War II; in the second part I take a closer look at the interaction of trade policy, industrial development, and living standards in the late nineteenth century. Did America's tariffs benefit the country, in terms of increased consumption or faster economic and real wage growth, in the generation after the Civil War?

The answer appears to be no. It is difficult to argue that America was a net gainer from the protectionist policies of the late nineteenth century. Moreover, the more stress one gives to the "external benefits" of investment, capital accumulation, the links between capital intensity and the

3. See Fallows (1994, pp. 193–94). Other arguments in the same tradition include Lazonick (1991); Amsden (1989); and McCraw (1986).

4. Taussig (1931, pp. 2–3):

> The essential point of the argument lies in the assumption that the causes which . . . render protection necessary, are not natural and permanent. . . . Suppose . . . the industry to be encouraged is the cotton manufacture. . . . There is no permanent cause why cotton goods should not be obtained at as low cost by making them at home. . . . But the cotton manufacture . . . is new; the machinery used is unknown and complicated, and requires skill and experience of a kind not attainable in other branches of production. The industry of the country runs by custom in other grooves. . . . If . . . communication of knowledge be slow, and enterprise . . . hesitating . . . the establishment of the cotton manufacture may be prevented [in the absence of tariff protection]. . . . Under such circumstances it may be wise to encourage the manufacture by duties on imported goods.

ability to use new technologies, and so forth, the worse the post–Civil War tariff looks. This tariff did accelerate the transfer of labor out of agriculture and into manufacturing. But it also retarded investment in America's capital stock by making domestic and, especially, foreign-made capital goods more expensive.

To argue that the tariff increased U.S. growth by boosting externalities to concentration in manufacturing, one has to hold the peculiar—and un-supported—belief that the U.S. nonagricultural sector, with its higher-labor, lower-capital-labor ratio generated by the tariff, was a better incubator of technology and total factor productivity (TFP) than the lower-labor but higher-capital-intensity sector that would have developed in the absence of the post–Civil War tariff.

Patterns of Trade and Protection before World War II

Patterns of Trade

Today imports and exports run 10 to 13 percent of national product. Between one in ten and one in eight dollars of economic activity in the United States is ultimately directed either toward imports or exports. Counting U.S. distributors and sellers of foreign-made products—for example, Americans who sell Hondas and Volvos, whose activities do not enter our trade accounts at all—one in four Americans today has a job that is closely linked to international trade.

Before World War II trade was a smaller proportion of U.S. total economic activity than it has been in recent years. As best we can reconstruct, trade took up about half as large a share of economic activity. Figures 8-1 and 8-2 depict this approximate picture of the evolution, at decade intervals, of the export and import share of national product from 1820 to 1930.

Estimates of how the trade share of national product evolved between 1800 and World War II are highly uncertain. Customs tariff collections form the basis for relatively good estimates of cross-border commodity flows. The numerator of estimates of trade share of national product is in relatively good shape. The problem is in the denominator—our estimates of national product themselves. Small errors in estimating pre-1900 growth compound to create large errors in estimating how important trade was in the American economy.[5]

5. See Berry (1978); Gallman (1960); Lipsey (1963).

Figure 8-1. *Exports as a Share of National Product, Selected Years,
1820–1930*[a]

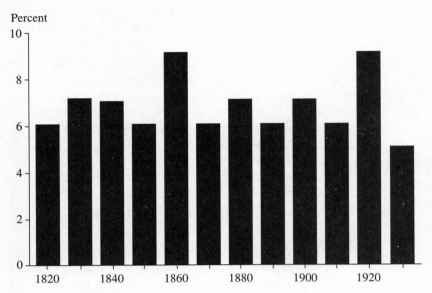

Source: U.S. Bureau of the Census, *Historical Statistics of the United States, 1789–1975* (GPO, 1979); author's
calculations based on Gallman (1960); Berry (1978).

a. All figures are approximate.

Nevertheless, before the Civil War, exports appear to have slowly increased
as a share of national product. They rose irregularly from approximately
6 percent of national product in 1820 to roughly 9 percent of national
product on the eve of the Civil War. The rise in exports as a share of national
product was in large part driven by cotton. Britain, the first industrial nation,
had an extraordinary hunger for cotton imports to feed its rapidly growing
textile industry—the "leading sector" of the first half of the nineteenth century.
Cotton exports accounted for more than 60 percent of U.S. exports in the 1850s.

The United States had land suitable for growing cotton, slaves who could
be forced to do the hard work to grow and pick it, and technology—from
cotton gins to scales and barrels to rivers, harbors, and ships—necessary to
turn cotton plants into the raw material needed by Britain's factories.

The Civil War and emancipation reduced the rate of growth of this trade.
After the Civil War, U.S. exports settled back to roughly 6 percent of
national product and maintained that pace until the boom in exports brought
on by World War I.

Figure 8-2. *Imports as a Share of National Product, Selected Years, 1820–1930*[a]

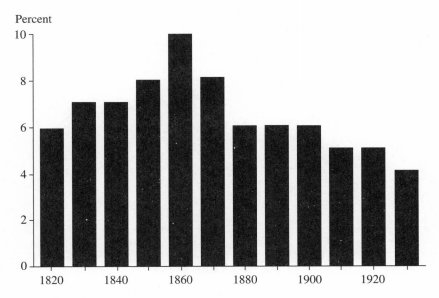

Percent

Source: U.S. Bureau of the Census, *Historical Statistics of the United States, 1789–1945* (GPO, 1949); Gallman (1960); Berry (1978).

a. All figures are approximate.

After the Civil War, other agricultural products replaced cotton as America's major export group. By 1901 agricultural exports excluding cotton were 25 percent of America's exports, whereas cotton exports were less than 20 percent. The food-growing West had replaced the South as America's major agricultural-product-exporting region. Imports roughly paced exports. In the first half of the nineteenth century, imports likely ran slightly ahead of exports, as the United States borrowed on net from Britain.

In the second half of the nineteenth century, interest and dividends paid on previous foreign investments came closer to offsetting new borrowing and investment from abroad. By the 1880s U.S. commodity exports exceeded commodity imports; by the 1890s, the United States was repaying its previous net borrowing from the industrial core of the world economy.[6] World War I brought heavy borrowing by the Allied powers of Britain and France from the United States, a large surplus of exports over imports, and the rapid transformation of the United States from a debtor to a creditor nation.

6. See Lipsey (1994).

Figure 8-3. *Nonfood Manufactures Share of Trade, 1820–1930*

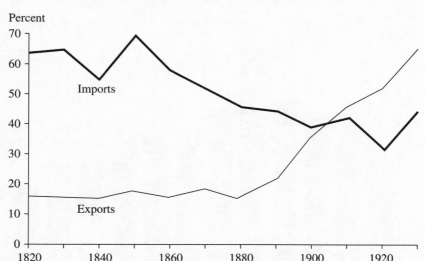

Source: U.S. Bureau of the Census, *Historical Statistics of the United States, 1789–1945* (GPO, 1949).

Figure 8-3 shows the relative shares of imports and exports made up of nonfood manufactures.[7] At the start of the nineteenth century, the United States had a pattern of trade that exactly fit that of a stylized periphery, agricultural economy. More than three out of every five import dollars paid for imports of manufactured goods, and slightly more than half of manufactures imports came from Britain. The early-nineteenth-century pattern of trade persisted late into the century. It was not until after the Civil War that the proportion of United States imports that were manufactured goods fell to less than half.

By contrast, less than one of every six American export dollars at the start of the nineteenth century was a manufactures export dollar. It was not until 1890 that the share of manufactured goods in U.S. exports was, for the first time, higher than 20 percent. After 1890, however, the share of manufactured goods in U.S. exports began a steep climb. By 1920, the share of manufacturing exports had risen to more than 50 percent of total exports.

7. Food-processing exports are omitted to sharpen the comparison; a high proportion of the value in processed foods, especially in the nineteenth century, was added in agriculture. America has always ranked relatively highly in exports of processed foods.

Figure 8-4. *Manufactures as a Share of Imports, Selected Years, 1820–1930*

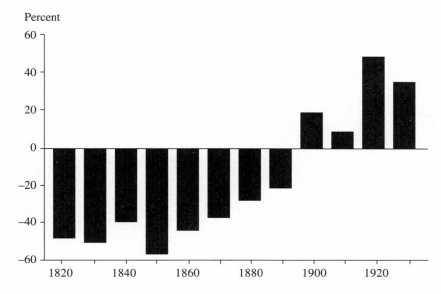

Source: U.S. Bureau of the Census, *Historical Statistics of the United States, 1789–1945* (GPO, 1949).

Figure 8-4 shows the balance of trade in manufactured goods, scaled by total imports. From 1820 until the Civil War, the U.S. deficit on manufactures was approximately half of total imports—an exchange of agricultural products for manufactured goods. After the Civil War the deficit in manufactures narrowed, at first slowly and then more rapidly. By 1900 there was a surplus in nonfood manufactures. In 1920 America's surplus on manufactured goods (measured as a share of total imports) was as large as America's habitual deficit had been a century before.

By the end of World War I, the United States had made the transition from a primary product-exporting, manufactures-importing economy to a manufactures-exporting, industrial economy. To the extent that pressures for nineteenth-century protectionism grew out of a habitual deficit in manufactures (and thus a view by manufacturing interests that free trade was not their friend), these pressures had vanished by the interwar period.

Patterns of Protection before the Civil War

Figure 8-5 shows the average tariff rate charged by the United States from 1800 to 1940: total tariff collections, divided by imports intended for domestic consumption. The average tariff rate was about 30 percent for

Figure 8-5. *Tariff Revenue as a Share of Total Imports, 1800–1940*

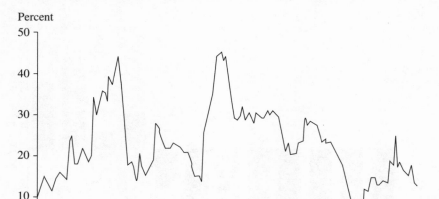

Source: U.S. Bureau of the Census, *Historical Statistics of the United States, 1789–1945* (GPO, 1949).

most of the nineteenth century. The average tariff rate was as high as 44 percent at the end of the 1820s—the so-called "Tariff of Abominations" that sparked one of the first in the series of sectional crises that led to the Civil War. The average tariff rate dipped below 20 percent for a few years around 1840 and a few years just before the Civil War.

These episodes aside, tariffs as a share of imports did not drop below 20 percent until 1910. They hovered around 10 percent for the interwar period. Even the infamous Smoot-Hawley tariff of 1930 merely raised total tariff collections as a share of imports to 20 percent, a level that in the nineteenth century would have been a low and not a high tariff.

After World War II, U.S. tariffs continued their decline. In not a single year after World War II were tariff collections as much as 10 percent of imports. With the phasing in of the Uruguay Round General Agreement on Tariffs and Trade (GATT) and the creation of the World Trade Organization (WTO), U.S. tariffs will be 3 percent of the value of imports or even less. The past generation has seen the rise of an alternative system of trade controls—for example, the quota regime of the Multi-Fiber Agreement (MFA), and the threat of antidumping suits serving as an incentive for the creation of voluntary export agreements. The quantitative, trade-restricting impact of this second layer of nontariff trade restrictions is hard to evaluate, but it is almost surely more important than the residual tariffs that remain today.

At the start of the nineteenth century, almost every single import was subject to some tariff; 96 percent of the value of imports were dutiable in 1821. The share of imports subject to tariff fluctuated between 50 and 96 percent before the Civil War, rising back up to the 90-plus percent range during the war, as the government's financial needs became overwhelming.

The post–Civil War period saw a slow decline in the share of imports subject to duty. The share of imports subject to tariffs dropped to roughly 50 percent by 1900 and even further to between 30 and 40 percent by the interwar period.

Note that the reduction in the share of imports subject to tariffs is in fact slightly faster than the reduction in tariff revenue as a share of the value of imports. There is no sign of any systematic fall before World War II in tariffs charged on those goods judged worth subjecting to tariff. The later nineteenth and early twentieth century saw more goods exempted from tariffs altogether, but also somewhat higher average rates of tariff charged on the remaining items.

Tariffs were at a relatively high level in 1820 (more than 40 percent of the value of imports that year), but this did not reflect any settled protectionist pressure. Instead, it was a combination of two factors: the War of 1812 and the central place of tariffs in federal finances.

The War of 1812 had left the U.S. government with what was then a staggering debt burden. Debt interest cost the governments of James Madison and James Monroe $7 million a year. This was more than three times the debt burden paid in George Washington's first term.

Combined with up to $3 million a year in veterans' compensation and an additional $7 million a year to support the enlarged, War of 1812–size military establishment, federal spending in 1820 was more than four times what it had been in Washington's first term.

Tariffs were also the federal government's only significant revenue source (see figure 8-6). Tariff revenues averaged 80 percent of federal revenue before the Civil War. The federal government could adjust to lower tariffs—it did so in the 1830s, cutting back on spending on internal improvements and shifting to other, internal revenue sources. But in the aftermath of the War of 1812, high tariffs were the only plausible way for the government to fund its military and pay off debt.

However, once tariffs had been raised to substantial levels because of the government's need for revenue, protected manufacturers soon noticed that by manipulating the tariff they could affect foreign competition. The first strong and explicit links between advocacy of protection and the encouragement of

Figure 8-6. *Tariff as a Share of Total Federal Revenue, Selected Years, 1820–1930*

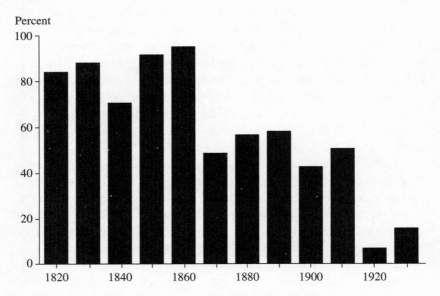

Percent

Source: U.S. Bureau of the Census, *Historical Statistics of the United States, 1789–1945* (GPO, 1949).

particular industries appeared in the United States in the late 1820s. The U.S. senators and congressional representatives from New England were not the first advocates of protection for the sake of industrial development; New England immediately after the War of 1812 was still more a mercantile than an industrial economy. The first advocates of protection for the sake of industry came from the middle states of Pennsylvania and New Jersey, where shipping interests were weaker and manufactures at least as strong.

However, New England manufacturers were not far behind. The woolen manufacturers of Boston in particular appear to have organized the first trade association, engaged in what was certainly one of the first formal lobbying efforts, and lodged the first unfair trade practice claims in 1826. Boston's woolen manufacturers claimed that British exporters were understating the value of their goods—thus evading a substantial part of the 33⅓ percent ad valorem tariff in effect.

The woolen manufacturers asked for a minimum valuation of 40 cents a yard on wool imports and for an imposed minimum valuation of $2.50 a yard on woolen goods worth more than 40 cents a yard. The effect of the woolen manufacturers' proposals would have been to keep (in the letter of the law) the 33⅓ percent ad valorem rate, but to charge an average tariff of approximately 80 percent on woolen-goods imports.

Explicit protectionism for industrial policy purposes won its first significant legislative victory in the passage of the 1828 "Tariff of Abominations."[8] But the high level of tariffs reached as a result of the 1828 act galvanized opponents; the tariff became a grievance of the South against the North. In 1833 consumer interests organized section by section reached a compromise that provided for gradual reduction of tariffs to a 20 percent rate, but that postponed realization of the 20 percent rate for a decade.

The 1840s saw a tariff increase proposed and enacted by a Whig congressional majority, then a Democratic rationalization of tariff rates in terms of efficiency. Tariffs increased roughly 23 percent on average. In 1857 a general tariff reduction was provoked by the federal budget's moving into structural surplus. Protectionist pressures were not brought to bear in opposition to the tariff reduction in 1857.

Patterns of Protection from the Civil War to the Great Depression

In 1860 the federal government spent $63.1 million—less than 2 percent of national product (see figure 8-7). In 1865 the federal government spent $1.30 billion—the first time the annual federal budget exceeded $1 billion, and the only time federal expenditures exceeded this amount until the United States entered World War I. Federal expenditures in 1865 amounted to about one-fifth of national product. After the Civil War, debt interest alone was as large a share of national product as all federal expenditures had been before the war.

The federal government financed the Civil War through every conceivable channel: creation of a national banking system, borrowing, income taxes, other internal revenues, and a large increase in tariffs. Measured as a share of imports, tariffs tripled as a result of the Civil War. The tariff structure was roughly even across broad groups of commodities (figure 8-8). Agricultural-product-based consumer goods faced the highest average tariffs of nearly 55 percent, but the average tariffs on other consumer goods and on capital goods were about 40 percent. A small break was given to industrial materials, with an average tariff of 30 percent or so ad valorem.

8. Passage of which John C. Calhoun later blamed on an inept and over-clever legislative strategy adopted by the Jacksonian Democrats. They sought to defeat the proposed tariff increase, but also to lay the blame for defeating the tariff on the supporters of John Quincy Adams. Thus southern Jacksonian Democrats voted against amendments to strip the "abominations" from the tariff. See Taussig (1931, pp. 88–102); Freehling (1990).

Figure 8-7. *Nineteenth-Century Federal Spending as a Share of National Product, 1800–1900*[a]

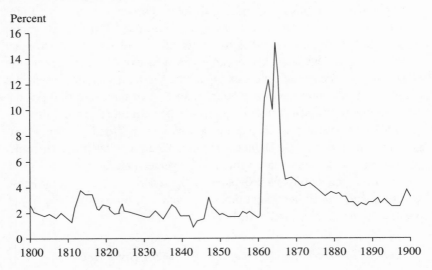

Percent

Source: U.S. Bureau of the Census, *Historical Statistics of the United States, 1789–1945* (GPO, 1949).

a. All figures are approximate.

More narrow tariff levels varied widely, from a low of 10 percent on imports of dyestuffs to a high of 252 percent on imported distilled liquors. But there is no discernible economic logic underlying the pattern.

For nearly twenty years after 1870, the tariff structure was more or less frozen in the form it had reached after the Civil War. Duties on pure-revenue goods such as tea and coffee were eliminated. Tariffs on some imports were lowered to satisfy consumer sentiment. Tariffs on other goods were raised, or goods were reclassified to fit into a higher-tariff category, in response to protectionist pressures.

There was some reduction in tariff rates immediately after the war. But tariffs were not returned to their pre-1861 level or even their average level circa 1840–60. For taxpayers, the reduction and elimination of the wartime income and excise tax machinery was a higher priority. For consumers, reductions in any tariffs were equally welcome. Industries that had grown comfortable behind the protectionist walls created by the more or less uniform tariff increases of the war lobbied for the preservation of their own duties and the reduction of others. The less a commodity was produced in the United States, the greater was the reduction in its tariff in the post–Civil War round of tariff reductions.

Figure 8-8. *Ad Valoren Tariff Rates, Four Sectors, 1870*

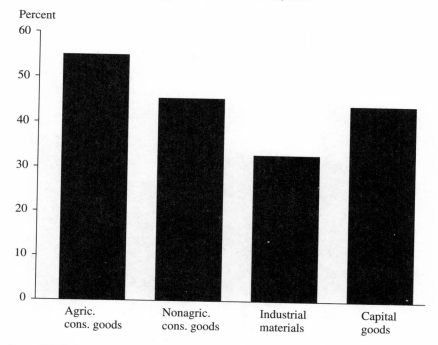

Percent

Source: U.S. Bureau of the Census, *Historical Statistics of the United States, 1789–1975* (GPO, 1979); U.S. Treasury; and author's calculations from Baack and Ray (1983), pp. 90–92.

The only major move toward across-the-board tariff reduction came in the late 1880s, and it ultimately proved ineffective (figure 8-9). President Grover Cleveland made tariff reduction—and Democratic championing of consumer interests out West—an important election issue. Subsequent Republican victories in the election of 1888 gave Republicans sufficient confidence to generate the first nonwar general tariff increase since the 1840s, the McKinley tariff of 1890.

The McKinley tariff was itself reversed when the elections of 1890 and 1892 gave the Democrats control of the Senate and the House, and the presidency as well. The reelected Cleveland sponsored a tariff reduction in 1894 that rolled back the 1890 increase and also cut duties by about one-fifth.

But the life span of the 1894 tariff reduction was even shorter than that of the 1890 tariff increase. The 1894 tariff reductions were reversed almost immediately, as the victory of William McKinley over William Jennings Bryan in 1896 carried the Republicans to legislative majorities as well.

Figure 8-9. *Ad Valorem Tariff Rates, 1910, and 1870–1910 Tariff Reduction,
Four Sectors*

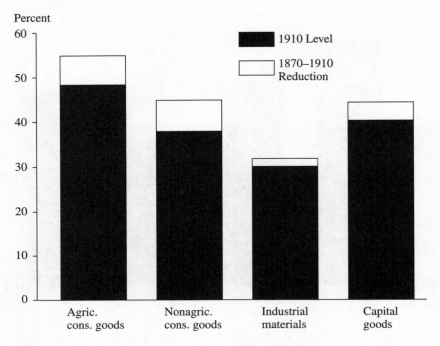

Source: U.S. Bureau of the Census, *Historical Statistics of the United States, 1789–1975* (GPO, 1979); U.S.
Treasury; and author's calculations from Baack and Ray (1983), pp. 90–92.

Tariffs as a share of imports fell by approximately one-third between
1898 and 1910, but not because of any legislative action. The cause was a
falloff in the relative amount of imports of heavily tariffed manufactures as
the United States became self-sufficient in more and more classes of industrial commodities. Around 1910, however, there was a significant break
in the strength of the pro-protection coalition that had kept tariffs at or near
their Civil War levels for more than a generation.

The Democratic Party began to run—and win elections—on a consistently pro-tariff reduction platform.

As is almost always the case, the links between good economic judgments and the terms of political discourse were extremely tenuous. The
Democrats blamed the tariff for the high cost of living and the slow annual
inflation rate of 1 to 3 percent that had taken hold since the 1890s.[9]

9. It is much easier to argue that the inflation was the result of a sudden increase
in the rate at which the world's monetary gold supply (the fundamental reserve of

Nevertheless, the number of Republicans in the House of Representatives fell from 219 in the sixty-first Congress of 1909–11, to 127 in the sixty-third Congress of 1913–15. The number of Republicans in the Senate fell from sixty in the sixty-first Congress to forty four in the sixty-third.

The tariff reductions of 1913 were themselves partially reversed a decade later, when agricultural and industrial producers demanded action to divert demand in their direction in the sharp post–World War I depression. But the tariff increase of 1922 did not restore the overall level of tariffs to its pre-1913 level, let alone the levels of 1900 or of 1880.

It took the Smoot-Hawley tariff of 1930 to boost the average level of protection above the pre-1913 level. This tariff itself was extremely short-lived; much of the increase passed in June 1930 was gone by the end of Roosevelt's first term.

Interpreting Pre–World War II Tariffs

One view, advanced by Taussig, is that the reduction of U.S. tariffs is a story of the interrupted triumph of economic rationality. In Taussig's narrative, tariffs start high in the aftermath of war because of the role of customs duties in federal finance; industrialists then seize on high tariffs for protectionist purposes. Eventually, however, Americans and their legislators see through the largely specious claims that protection is in the public interest, and tariffs fall. In Taussig's narrative the United States has gone through two such tariff cycles: one in the forty-five years after the War of 1812, and a second longer cycle—not complete as of Taussig's final edition—generated by the tariff increases of the Civil War.

A more cynical interpretation would be that told by Baack and Ray: the story of a shifting balance of power among different economic interest groups and a revenue-hungry federal government. It would also see two cycles, and it would see the same beginning to each one as Taussig's interpretation: a revenue-hungry government raises tariffs (both in the War of 1812 and the Civil War) to pay for its armies and navies; protected manufacturers then attempt to preserve the wartime tariff structure and warp it to their economic interest. Before the Civil War, Southern opinion leaders and legislators realized that their section had a stake in free trade. The South was a sufficiently powerful and (in large part because of its "peculiar institution") cohesive section that its legislators were able to put tariffs on a downward path. This ended the first protectionist cycle.

---

the international monetary system) grew. The rate of gold production had increased severalfold as a result of the construction of the South African gold mining industry.

The second protectionist cycle, in this interpretation, ended because those for whose sake protectionist barriers were constructed lost interest. The United States shifted from a manufactures-importing to a manufactures-exporting economy, and a high level of protection for manufactured goods became a less and less important politicoeconomic goal. This interpretation is essentially Taussig's in pessimistic guise. The standard economic arguments against protection were made, and eventually they were persuasive. It is difficult to untangle the degree to which their persuasiveness was established by their logical force, or by the balance of material interest in politically active pressure groups.

Protection and Nineteenth-Century Growth

But was this special-interest and war-debt-driven, late-nineteenth-century tariff in fact the "correct" policy for a rising, industrializing economy seeking to become a world power? Before the Civil War, the policy of protection to force the hothouse growth of an industrial sector was undermined by the strength and cohesion of Southern consumer interests. The Civil War eliminated the political power and cohesion of Southern pro–free trade slaveholders. And by World War I the United States was an industrialized economy, able to meet all comers in the struggle for the rents from ownership of the world's high-tech industries. It no longer needed a protectionist tariff. So to all appearances the post–Civil War protectionist policy worked.

But are the possible links from high tariffs to faster growth and industrial development large enough to carry the weight of this argument, as applied to the post–Civil War United States? Three channels are noted in the literature that call for "getting relative prices wrong" in order to assist industrial development. First is the role of trade policy in producing an economy oriented toward production and investment rather than "consumption." Second is the extent to which specialization in manufacturing shifts labor and capital toward high-value-added industries and activities. Third is the role of learning by doing and other externality-generating factors in giving production and employment in manufacturing a social rate of return in excess of its private rate of return.[10]

Consumption versus Production

One effect of high tariffs on imported goods is to bias spending patterns away from consumption of imported luxuries, and perhaps

10. Baack and Ray (1974, 1983).

toward investment. In an economy like the post–Civil War United States that imported 6 percent of national product, a 30 percent tariff on the average imported good would divert 1.8 percent of national product into the hands of the government.

A government that imposed such a tariff, used it to retire war debt more rapidly,[11] and succeeded by imposing the tariff in boosting the national savings and investment rate by half of this amount: 0.9 percentage points of national product per year. Such a policy could have a small but not insignificant effect on the rate of economic growth. The share of gross capital formation in American national product after the Civil War averaged 20 to 25 percent of national product. In a standard, neoclassical growth model, such a boost to annual gross savings and investment would in the long run raise the level of national product relative to the baseline growth path by 1 to 2 percent of national product.

However, it is far from clear that additional tariff revenue crowded in even half as much net investment in the United States. World capital markets were open in the second half of the nineteenth century.[12] The Civil War debt was retired relatively rapidly, but thereafter taxes were not lowered—Republican governments spent 1 to 2 percent of national product on pensions for Civil War veterans.[13]

Concentration in High-Value-Added Sectors

A second reason often advanced for why early specialization in manufacturing is beneficial is the claim that the manufacturing industry has a higher-than-average level of labor productivity, and the assertion that transferring workers from other, lower-productivity sectors to manufacturing boosts average productivity in the economy. Figure 8-10 gives some crude measures of relative raw labor productivity in different sectors in 1870, in the aftermath of the Civil War.

There are many reasons not to take such estimates of intersectoral productivity differences at face value. First, agriculture in 1870 was an extremely heterogeneous sector, made up of rich Northern farmers on

---

11. See Baack and Ray (1983, p. 83).

12. For studies of these factors in the context of American economic history, see Atack (1987); David (1975); Williamson (1972); Zevin (1971); Kim (1995); and especially Johnston (1990). For the more general literature on "increasing returns" broadly construed, see Romer (1986); Jaffe (1986); Bartelsman and others (1994); Arrow (1962); Murphy and others (1989); and Young (1928).

13. As in Johnston (1990).

Figure 8-10. *Raw Labor Productivity, Four Sectors, 1870*

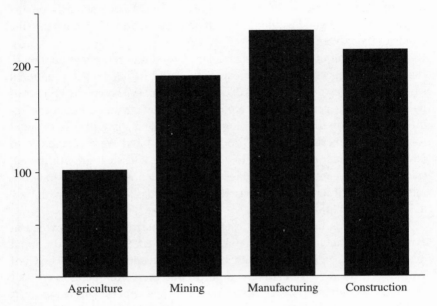

Source: U.S. Bureau of the Census, *Historical Statistics of the United States, 1789–1945* (GPO, 1949).

substantial ranges of good land with ample capital and tools and of poor Southern farmers on little land with next to no implements.

Second, the appearance of substantial differences in productivity across sectors may well be a reflection of the tariff, rather than a justification for it. To the extent that tariffs of more than 50 percent on British iron and steel products insulated Carnegie Steel from competition and made Andrew Carnegie rich, such tariffs could lead to large divergences in productivity. Carnegie was one of the few Americans licensed to use the Bessemer process in making steel, but this would be an argument for reducing the tariff, not increasing it.

Nevertheless, suppose we take the differentials in raw labor productivity at face value and assert that high post–Civil War tariffs averaging 50 percent on manufacturing imports aided the economy by allowing for the substitution of high-value manufacturing for low-value agricultural employment.

In the generation after the Civil War, imports of manufactured goods averaged 3 percent of national product. At an assumed import elasticity in the range of 0.5 to 2, between 0.7 and 3.0 percent more national product was produced in the manufacturing sector than if there had been no tariff. If the entire difference in raw productivity between agriculture and manufacturing were gained for each worker shifted into manufacturing as a result of the tariff, national product *might* have been on the order of 0.3 and 1.5 percent higher as a result of this effect.

The Tariff and Forgone Exports

Offsetting these possible benefits from a higher tariff are two certain costs. First, the tariff meant that the United States gave up the opportunity to export more high-value-added agricultural products to Europe to boost its national income. Suppose for simplicity's sake that the elasticity of demand for imports was one. Then a 30 percent tariff (a little lower than the average value over 1800–1940) would reduce the import share of national demand from a counterfactual level of 9 percent to the actual level of 7 percent of national product. The consumer and producer surplus foregone on each discouraged import would amount, on average, to 15 percent of the import's value.

The net result? A reduction in real TFP of 0.3 percent of national product as the United States was forced to shift economic activity away from its most efficient pattern of specialization in the world division of labor. More generally, a 30 percent tariff would generate a reduction of $0.3(e^2)$ percent in TFP, where e is the elasticity of demand for imports. There is little reason to think that such a reduction in real incomes would fall disproportionately on capital rather than on labor and so equalize the distribution of income and wealth. There is good reason to think that such a reduction in real incomes would transfer wealth from Western farmers to Eastern industrialists, making late-nineteenth-century America a more unequal society.[14]

Second, the tariff made a wide range of investment goods—from British machine tools and steam engines to steel rails to precision instruments—more expensive. For more than a generation after the end of the Civil War, British machinery and iron and steel exports remained competitive in much of the U.S. market. This implies that the roughly 50 percent tariffs imposed on imports of capital goods from abroad had an impact not only on the 1 or 2 percent of national product spent on imported goods for investment, but also on prices of domestically produced capital goods as well.

The Tariff and Forgone Investment

The impact of the tariff on accumulation of imported investment goods is straightforward. Because Americans chose to import them in spite of the

14. See Edelstein (1982).

tariff, they must have had a high economic value. The tariff meant that an American investor who spent £3 on British-investment goods received only £2 worth of goods in return. Thus the tariff diminished real investment in imported capital goods by about 1 percentage point of national product.

The effect of the tariff on the quantity of investment in domestically produced capital goods is harder to assess. In the post–Civil War generation, some 16 percent of national product on average was invested in domestically produced, nonresidential-construction capital goods. If each $1 of tariff imposed on a foreign-made capital good raised the cost of its domestic substitute by as little as 12.5 cents, then a 50 percent tariff on imported manufactures would diminish the share of national product devoted to investment in domestically produced capital goods by 1 percentage point of national product. If each $1 of tariff imposed on a foreign-made capital good raised the cost of its domestic substitute by 37.5 cents, then a 50 percent tariff on imported manufactures would diminish the share of national product devoted to investment in domestically produced capital goods by 3 percentage points of national product.

If this is indeed the plausible range, then the damaging effects of the tariff on investment were extremely important for nineteenth-century growth. In the long run, a reduction in the real investment share of national product of 2 to 4 percent carries with it a reduction in the capital output ratio of 10 to 20 percent—and a reduction in productivity and real wages of 5 percent or more.[15]

Such a loss is certainly as large as whatever offsetting effect the tariff might or might not have had in shifting the pattern of spending away from consumption by inducing savings, or in shifting employment into higher-value-added sectors.

Learning by Doing and "Increasing Returns"

A question remains: Doesn't this analysis ignore the dynamic, growth-increasing effects of investment and specialization in manufacturing to focus on the static, neoclassical, onetime effects? Would it not reverse

●

15. As Richard Sutch has pointed out, post–Civil War veterans' pensions were uniquely effective as a way of channeling government funds to Republican supporters and only Republican supporters. Urban immigrant voters for Democratic machines had not fought in the Civil War. Southerners had not fought in the Civil War on the right side. For analyses of Civil War debt retirement and its impact on growth, see Williamson (1974b); James (1978, 1984); James and Skinner (1977); Johnston (1990); Abramovitz and David (1973).

the verdict to consider a model in which investment, and specialization in manufacturing, had long-run, dynamic effects on the growth rate of TFP?

One line of thought—the line explored by Louis Johnston in reinvestigating analyses of the possible impact of Civil War debt repayment—is that, in a sense, the economy's "stock of industrial knowledge" is proportional to its stock of industrial capital.[16] Past net (not replacement) investments produce not only capital but knowledge—how to employ new production technologies, how to make machines run more efficiently, how to manage workers and businesses in an industrial environment. This knowledge cannot be kept the "private" property and resource of the firm that did the investing. Instead, it rapidly becomes available to all producers through inspection of their competitors' operations and the hiring away of their competitors' engineers.[17]

In this case, let us start from the standard, neoclassical production function

$$\Delta y = \alpha(\Delta n) + (1 - \alpha)(\Delta k) + \Delta a, \tag{8-1}$$

where Δy is the proportional change in total production, Δn is the proportional change in the economy's labor supply, Δk is the proportional change in the accumulated net capital stock, α is the share of national income earned by labor, and Δa is the proportional change in technological knowledge determined by some process of invention and innovation, unrelated to factor accumulation, elsewhere in society. But new growth models allow for feedback from factor accumulation to technological knowledge, and replace Δa with $\Delta a' + \mu \Delta k$. A portion $\Delta a'$ of advances in technological knowledge that truly is generated by factors outside the macroeconomy, and a portion $\mu \Delta k$ that is a byproduct of increases in the total net stock of accumulated capital. The aggregate production function is thus

$$\Delta y = \alpha(\Delta n) + (1 - \alpha)(\Delta k) + \Delta a' + \mu \Delta k, \tag{8-2}$$

$$\Delta y = \alpha(\Delta n) + (1 - \alpha + \mu)(\Delta k) + \Delta a'. \tag{8-3}$$

A given increment to the capital stock boosts production by more in new-growth models. A given investment not only increases the productivity of the investing firm, but adds to the stock of practical experience and social

16. See Williamson (1991).
17. For aggregate growth models fitted to nineteenth-century U.S. experience, see Abramovitz (1956); Abramovitz and David (1973).

knowledge about how to use modern machine technologies productively. Businesses, however, do not take into account the effect of their investment decisions on overall, economywide productivity. Because all their competitors rapidly gain access to the same technological knowledge as well, benefits of increased economywide productivity show up one for one in higher wages and have no effect on firm profits. But the economy as a whole exhibits increasing returns. Thus policies that boost savings, investment, and overall capital accumulation make a significant difference in faster productivity and economic growth, and higher standards of living. Could adopting this approach reverse the presumption that high late-nineteenth-century tariffs lowered output and retarded growth? The answer is no. The key problem is that the United States levied its heavy tariffs on those manufactured capital goods whose accumulation is the trigger for advances in knowledge and TFP.

To see this, close the model above with a simple capital accumulation equation. The proportional rate of growth of the capital stock Δk depends on the depreciation rate δ, on the economy's savings rate s, and on the price of capital goods, p^k, relative to the price of output in general

$$\Delta k = \left(\frac{s}{p^k} \frac{Y}{K} \right) - \delta \tag{8-4}$$

where capital Y and capital K are the levels of production and of the accumulated net capital stock, respectively. And, for simplicity, assume that labor force growth Δn and the exogenous component of productivity growth Δa (or $\Delta a'$) are constant. Consider three cases: the neoclassical model, in which TFP growth is unconnected with factor accumulation ($\mu = 0$); the particular specification used by Louis Johnston ($\mu = 0.05$), with the magnitude increasing returns estimated from his study of industry location in the nineteenth century; and a specification giving a stronger role to increasing returns ($\mu = 0.10$). The parameter values needed for the models made up of 8-1 and 8-4 or 8-3 and 8-4 to replicate growth over the post–Civil War generation, 1870–1910 in the baseline, high-tariff case are shown in table 8-1.

What is the effect of removing the tariff on this model? First, there is a onetime boost to TFP. With a counterfactual import share of gross domestic product (GDP) in the late nineteenth century of 8 percent, and with a 30 percent average tariff, the onetime boost to economywide TFP as a result of tariff elimination is 0.3 percent under an assumed unit elasticity of demand. Second, the tariff had artificially elevated the relative prices of industrial goods, including the relative price of capital goods. A higher price

Table 8-1. *Parameter Values, One-Sector Model*

	Parameter	Neoclassical model	*"Low-externality" model*	*"High-externality" model*
Δn	Annual labor-force growth[a]	2.7	2.7	2.7
s	Savings rate[a]	19.5	19.5	19.5
pk	Relative price of capital goods	1, 1.1, 1.2	1, 1.1, 1.2	1, 1.1, 1.2
δ	Annual depreciation[a]	3	3	3
α	Labor share of income[a]	68	68	68
Δa	Annual exogenous TFP growth[a]	1.13	0.87	0.64
μ	Productivity effect of investment	. . .	0.05	0.10

a. Values are given in percent.
. . . Not applicable.

of capital goods means that any given savings effort will generate less investment. Thus with a high tariff the rate of growth of the capital stock will be lower than with free trade, no matter what the original stock of capital. No matter where the economy starts, capital accumulation will be lower with a higher tariff—and so, over time, productivity will fall further behind. This will be the case because a lower-productivity economy will support a lower savings effort and also because the higher price of capital goods translates the lower savings effort into a still lower amount of net investment.

Table 8-2 shows the effect of tariff elimination in these three specifications for two cases: the "low-effect" case, in which removal of the tariff would have boosted net investment by only 2 percent of national product, and the "high-effect" case, in which removal of the tariff would have boosted net investment by 4 percent of national product. In the neoclassical, "no-externalities" model, removal of the tariff would have generated a substantial boost to economic growth; total national product in 1900 is 4.3 to 7.8 percent higher. But when analyzed in "new-growth" models— models that assume a link between investment, learning by doing, and the stock of social "technological knowledge" that boosts TFP—the late-nineteenth-century tariff imposed even higher costs on the U.S. economy. National product in 1900 was depressed by between 5.1 and 11.4 percent because of the late-nineteenth-century tariff. The mechanisms by which tariffs retard growth are the same. A high-tariff economy throws away some of the potential gains from the international division of labor. A high-tariff economy is a low-investment economy, and hence a slower-growth

Table 8-2. *Effect of Tariff on Economic Growth,*
One-Sector Model
Percent

	Boost to output over 30 years	Boost to annual growth
Neoclassical model		
Tariff elimination		
Low effect	4.3	0.14
High effect	7.8	0.25
Increasing returns		
Moderate case[a]		
Tariff elimination		
Low effect	5.1	0.16
High effect	9.4	0.30
High case[b]		
Tariff elimination		
Low effect	5.8	0.19
High effect	11.4	0.36

Source: Author's calculations.
a. 23.5 percent of TFP growth due to "externalities."
b. 46.5 percent of TFP growth due to "externalties."

economy. These effects are larger because the link between investment and growth is stronger as we move away from the simple, neoclassical specification.

Only if Eastern industrialists had a markedly higher propensity to save than Western farmers, or if Eastern workers responded to better opportunities in industry by investing especially heavily in their own educations (and we have no good reason to think that either of these was the case), would the standard, neoclassical growth analysis suggest that the late-nineteenth-century tariff might have boosted the growth of the American economy.[18]

Thus the particular structure of the late-nineteenth-century American tariff makes it hard to see how the fact that production is carried on in different sectors might reverse the one-sector model's conclusion that the tariff was bad for growth. Perhaps a tariff that focused on light manufactures or consumer goods and left investment goods duty-free might have been good for economic growth. But a tariff that lay heavily on capital goods needed for industrialization and accumulation was not.

18. In addition to Johnston (1990), see also James (1984).

Conclusions

The United States has been a free-trade country for a half century or even longer. Before the Great Depression, pressure for protection waxed and waned but was usually strong enough to maintain tariffs in the 30 to 50 percent ad valorem range on manufactured imports. Some—like Taussig —would argue that the dominance of protection in the United States before the Great Depression was the result of federal demands for revenue, coupled with industry demands for protection and an insufficient degree of economic literacy, and looked to education and rational debate to bring the country closer to free trade.

A second interpretation—one I favor—would argue that once industry has grown up inside a hothouse created by war-driven revenue tariffs, protection is all but inevitable until industry becomes sufficiently competitive to no longer value it highly. Under this interpretation, the United States outgrew its attachment to relatively high tariffs in the early twentieth century.

A third interpretation sees the coming of free trade as a horrible mistake, one that threatens to leave us defenseless against more ruthless practitioners in this century of the trade policy America used in the last century. But even on its own terms—a viewpoint that views growth, production, and national power as all, and consumption as nothing—it is hard to argue that America's protectionist impulses did its industrial development a favor in the nineteenth century. The benefits to early specialization and concentration in manufacturing are too small, and the costs to making the purchase of foreign-produced investment goods too great, to convincingly and quantitatively argue that America's nineteenth-century manufacturing tariffs were in any sense an aid to economic development.

The problem is that the dynamic effect of "new-growth theory" is a two-edged sword. It is hard to argue that the benefits of the tariff for growth had dynamic effects that greatly multiply their impact on national product without also implicitly arguing that the costs—a higher price of investment goods, and thus a reduced flow of investment and a slower pace of capital deepening—had dynamic effects that greatly multiplied their impact as well. Yes, the theorists of the new-growth theory have issued us a license to think of policies as possibly having effects orders of magnitude larger than in conventional neoclassical approaches to growth. However, destructive policies—like tariffs that diminish national product and make investment especially expensive—have their quantitative effects amplified as well.

It is therefore not simple or straightforward to point to the coexistence of a late-nineteenth-century tariff with America's industrial revolution, and to argue that the benefits of the late-nineteenth-century tariff in concentrating labor in industrial sectors where external economies and effects may have been important aided America's economic growth and standard of living. The first-order effect of the tariff was not to shift labor from agriculture to industry, but to make investment more expensive. There is no vision of industrial development that holds that the way to enhance it is to make investment difficult and expensive.

Comment by Barry Eichengreen

Peter Temin and I agreed on a division of labor in which he would concentrate on the period before 1860 and I would focus on the years since. In light of that agreement, I will start, perhaps to alarm of the organizers, with an event from the 1980s.

In 1986 the member states of the European Community agreed to the Single European Act (SEA). The SEA mandated the removal of barriers to intra-European trade and the creation of a single European market by the end of 1992. Commentators, both official and independent, set out to forecast the effects. In the best known of these studies, Baldwin assumed that the chill winds of intra-European competition would increase X efficiency and that the creation of an integrated market would allow European firms to more fully exploit economies of scale and scope.[19] The increase in productivity that resulted would, he argued, encourage capital formation. Using a "new-growth" model in which the returns to capital do not diminish sharply, Baldwin showed that the cumulative change in incomes could be enormous. He estimated that European incomes would rise substantially as a result of the SEA—as much as 10 percent within a decade.

De Long, playing devil's advocate, contemplates the possibility that trade protection rather than trade liberalization can be growth promoting and tests this hypothesis against late-nineteenth-century American historical experience. He describes a model in which tariffs enhance industrial efficiency by protecting sectors characterized by learning effects and economies of scale and scope. The resulting productivity gains stimulate capital formation and lead to unbounded growth.

Both Baldwin's and De Long's hypotheses are internally consistent. It is entirely within the capacity of theorists to construct models in which either

19. Baldwin (1989).

trade liberalization or trade protection can have growth-promoting effects. Progress on this issue therefore requires systematic empirical work. The variation provided by historical data is an obvious hunting ground for those wishing to undertake such research. For all these reasons, De Long's initiative is welcome.

De Long's first channel linking protection to growth we might call the aggregate-investment effect. The author provides back-of-the-envelope calculations suggesting that relatively little additional saving and investment were produced by the debt retirement financed by postbellum tariff revenues and that the impact on growth of this additional saving and investment was smaller still. This arithmetic is simply Harberger's iron law of iterated fractions; multiplying together several small fractions yields an even smaller fraction. Because the change in the savings ratio, the effect of savings on investment, and the effect of investment on growth are all fractions, the percentage change in the level of income is a still smaller fraction.

We have independent evidence on this effect courtesy of James.[20] He used postbellum time series to analyze the macroeconomic impact of debt retirement and found that the impact of fiscal surpluses and debt retirement on interest rates was small because interest rates in the United States were tied to those in the rest of the world (courtesy of the open, international capital markets of the late nineteenth century). Even had the impact on interest rates been large, the implications for capital formation would have remained small, given the modest interest elasticity of investment. The impact of the additional investment on growth would have been more limited still, given an incremental capital-output ratio significantly greater than unity. All this reinforces De Long's conclusion of the relative insignificance of the aggregate-investment channel.

A second potential connection of tariffs to growth is the allocative effect. De Long shows that average labor productivity differed dramatically across sectors of the economy in the second half of the nineteenth century, with output per worker in manufacturing double that in agriculture. One might imagine that significant income and productivity gains could have been reaped by a trade policy that shifted resources from agriculture to industry.

Faced with a free lunch of this magnitude, the economist's instinct is to question the accuracy of the data. Such a sizeable productivity gap implies very significant labor market imperfections, which some observers might find implausible. Here, fortunately, the historical literature provides us with

20. James (1984).

several independent bodies of evidence that speak to the plausibility of De Long's data. Jeffrey Williamson has documented the existence of comparable wage gaps in England in the first half of the nineteenth century, the country's period of rapid industrialization. David Weir and Pierre Sicsic have provided similar evidence for France at a somewhat later date. Wage gaps during industrialization are an empirical regularity, it would appear, not a figment of the data.

Does this mean that there would have been substantial productivity gains from reallocating resources from agriculture to manufacturing? De Long's bar graph encourages an answer in the affirmative. But if the marginal product of labor were diminishing, then the scope for productivity and income gains through intersectoral reallocation was limited. Williamson's simulations point to this conclusion, suggesting that although there existed scope for income gains from sectoral shift, their magnitude was small.

This need not be the case, however, if the sectors toward which resources shift are characterized by scale economies. This brings me to De Long's third channel: increasing returns internal or external to the firm. In the presence of increasing returns in manufacturing, a tariff policy that encouraged reallocation of resources in that direction could have significantly raised income and productivity growth. The question is whether increasing returns were in fact widespread. The conventional view is that they were not. For example, Jeremy Atack (1985) used census data to estimate scale economies at the firm level, finding little support for the hypothesis of increasing returns. This would seem to foreclose the operation of De Long's third channel.

Atack did not distinguish increasing returns internal and external to the firm, however, testing only for the former. The distinction is crucial, for if internal and external economies are correlated, not including the second in the econometric specification may obscure evidence of the first. Moreover, enterprise managers should have been able to exploit increasing returns internal to the firm without government intervention. However, external economies could have been reaped only with the aid of government intervention to coordinate the activities of the various enterprises concerned. In a second-best world where direct subsidies are not feasible, tariff protection may be justified on these grounds.

A comprehensive study of these questions for nineteenth-century America was done by Johnston.[21] Johnston used census data for the United States for 1860 and 1870. His formulation allowed for the existence of both

21. Johnston (1990).

internal and external economies. He found evidence of internal and external economies in lumber milling, flour milling, and certain textile subsectors. His results thus offer some justification for tariff protection of nineteenth-century American manufacturing, on the grounds that manufacturing sectors were the source of significant external economies.

It is worth emphasizing three limitations of Johnston's results. First, his evidence of external economies applies to only a subset of manufacturing industries. Second, these were not in fact the sectors most heavily protected by the postbellum tariff. Third and most important, the positive externalities identified by Johnston would not have continued to prevail indefinitely. There is good reason to think, in other words, that other sectors that grew up later would have become the predominant source of external effects. Certainly, no late-nineteenth-century industrial policymaker sensitive to the importance of scale economies and positive externalities would have wished to continue subsidizing the lumber and flour milling industries. By the 1870s the technological high ground was occupied not by the small-scale lumber mills, flour mills, and "manufactories" of the antebellum years, but by vertically integrated, multidivisional firms using continuous-process, high-speed-throughput, resource-intensive technologies to produce standardized, branded products. Chandler has shown that such firms, which arose first in the steel, chemical, meatpacking, and tobacco-processing industries, were the technological champions of the period.[22] They were integrated precisely to capture what would have otherwise been unappropriable external economies. Andrew Carnegie integrated vertically, for instance, combining in one enterprise of unprecedented size the mining of coal, the smelting of steel, the laying of steel rail, the production of sleeping cars, and the provision of passenger transportation services. This was done to capture the positive externalities generated by these activities for one another.

The implication for trade policy is direct. Because externalities could be internalized through vertical and horizontal integration, there was no justification for tariff protection on efficiency grounds. One might argue that Carnegie and his contemporaries required protection to build up the large, integrated enterprises needed to capture such externalities. But in fact, many of these meatpacking and cigarette-manufacturing firms faced only limited foreign competition.

I conclude that the historical record for the second half of the nineteenth century provides little support for the notion that tariff protection promoted

22. Chandler (1977).

growth. Positive externalities associated with manufacturing activities could be internalized by other means. Rather than enhancing the efficiency of resource allocation, tariff protection reduced it. And insofar as the vertically and horizontally integrated enterprises, whose creation allowed positive externalities to be captured, used natural resources and capital intensively rather than labor, measures promoting their expansion would have reduced real wages (and raised the return to natural resources and capital).[23] Postbellum U.S. history thus lends little support to the view that tariff protection improved the living standards of American workers.

Comment by Peter Temin

There are two aspects of this interesting chapter that set it apart from the other presentations at this conference. It is long run in nature, as opposed to the short-run focus of the other contributions. This is appropriate, of course, for an historical presentation. In addition, this chapter discusses the choice of trade policy, as opposed to taking the trade policy as given and inquiring about its effects.

I comment on both aspects, use long-run analysis in the spirit of De Long's new-growth-theory model, and then discuss the first of the two tariff waves that De Long describes. (His chapter 8 and the comment by the other discussant focus on the second wave.) De Long reminds us that the United States has been protectionist throughout most of its history, using tariffs both to protect industry and raise revenue for the federal government. He has provided an insightful capsule history of American tariff history and asked: Was the American economy helped or hurt by the tariff? The fate of American workers, De Long argues, followed the fate of the economy.

De Long concentrates on what he calls the second wave of protectionist tariffs. I will review the literature on the first wave from a slightly different point of view. Instead of extending De Long's calculations to the early nineteenth century, I want to pose the counterfactual of free trade for the early United States.

The literature begins with English visitors to the United States in the aftermath of London's 1851 Crystal Palace Exhibition. These visitors were amazed at the progress of American manufacturing in the face of a prosperous agriculture. They asked themselves how manufacturing could

23. Wright (1990).

be as productive as agriculture. They answered, "On account of the high price of labor, the whole energy of the people is directed to improving and inventing labor-saving machinery."[24]

Habakkuk suggested in 1962 that manufacturing in America existed only because of the labor-saving machinery.[25] If American industry raised the productivity of labor by increasing the quantity of machinery used per worker, then the rate of return on machinery should have gone down. Although wages would have been higher in Britain, the interest rate would have been lower. But, alas for clarity in simple models, it was not.[26]

Many authors have proposed ingenious ways out of this paradox. The most convincing answer is that a protective tariff allowed profitable investment in American industry even with the high American wage. The tariff raised American industrial prices, allowing industry to pay both high interest rates and high wages. High industrial wages drew labor from agriculture and allowed industry to exist.[27]

This can be seen clearly in the cotton textile industry, the largest single industry in the United States for the first two-thirds of the nineteenth century. American costs were substantially higher than British in the early years of the mechanized cotton industry. Only because the tariff created a protective home market could the American cotton industry thrive.[28]

Francis Lowell, the founder of the Boston Manufacturing Company, found himself in need of protection for his nascent cotton mill at the close of the War of 1812. Given the primitive state of American power-loom technology, the Boston Manufacturing Company was designed to weave a coarse, heavy cloth. Lowell therefore designed the relevant part of the Tariff of 1816 to protect this end of the cotton market.[29] Lowell's design was adopted by the woolen industry a decade later, as De Long describes.

The tariff had an important impact on American manufacturing. With the tariff, the American cotton textile producers could expand at the lower end of the market. Without it, Lancashire would have supplied the entire range of American consumption.[30] More generally, the tariff as a whole promoted industrial growth in the North. It enhanced the return to industrial capital

24. Great Britain (1854–55).
25. Habakkuk (1962).
26. Temin (1966, 1971).
27. Jones (1971); Temin (1991).
28. Harley (1992).
29. Temin (1988).
30. Bils (1984).

Table 8-3. *Composition of Argentinian and U.S.*
Exports, 1900[a]
Percent

	Argentina	United States
Wool	13	. . .
Cotton	. . .	18
Wheat	10	11
Meat	2	8
Petroleum	. . .	5
Machinery	. . .	5
Iron and steel	. . .	3

Source: Mitchell (1993, pp. 427–35, 498–512).
a. Averages are calculated from three-year averages, 1899–1901.
. . . Not available.

enough to offset the pull of agriculture. Many benefits of industrial expansion appear to have been externalities to the firms involved, making the tariff an appropriate policy instrument.[31]

Consider the counterfactual. What would have been the pattern of U.S. production in the absence of the antebellum tariff? If the foregoing reasoning is correct, industry would have grown more slowly in the United States. It would not have been absent, given the passage of time and transport costs.

In the absence of a model to predict what might have happened, I use an analogy. Argentina has a climate and fertile soil conducive to agriculture, like the United States. Argentina was among the richest countries in the late nineteenth century, based on agricultural exports. Disaggregated data are not available earlier, but table 8-3 shows part of the export composition of Argentina and the United States in 1900.

Both countries were big agricultural exporters, with substantial overlap of products. The United States also had industrial exports, as De Long has noted, but they were small. Differences between the two countries do not leap out of table 8-3.

Table 8-4 shows a decomposition of production in the two countries in 1900. The differences are clearer. Agriculture was almost twice as important for Argentina as for the United States; the other sectors, smaller. Without the tariff to encourage industry and provide resources for the federal government, perhaps the North would have lost the Civil War. If so, then it would not have been surprising if large parts of what is now the United States resembled Argentina at the turn of the century.

31. David (1970).

Table 8-4. *Composition of Argentinian and U.S. Production, 1900*
Percent

	Argentina	United States
Agriculture	33	17
Industry	16	22
Commerce and finance	20	31

Source: Mitchell (1993, pp. 775–78).

As De Long has noted elsewhere, Argentina failed to continue its successful development into the twentieth century.[32] If we think the difference between the United States and Argentina is simply religion or Yankee ingenuity, there is no problem with De Long's short-run analysis. But if we try to relate long-run development to economic factors, then the stimulus given to American manufacturing by what De Long calls the "first tariff wave" may have been important.

De Long argues that the increased price of machinery—caused by antebellum tariffs on iron as well as postbellum tariffs on steel—offset the effects noted here in the late nineteenth century. Without doing any calculations, I wonder if the infant-industry argument was more important in the antebellum economy. I do not refer to learning in any specific industry here, but—in keeping with the comparison to Argentina—to the generalized learning and change in cultural attitudes derived from having an abundance of resources in manufacturing and related urban occupations.

General Discussion

There was a lively discussion of whether the analysis in this chapter might have underestimated the positive role played by tariffs in promoting nineteenth-century U.S. industrialization. Dani Rodrik argued that the model leaves out a potentially important channel. A tariff on relatively capital-intensive manufacturing goods would have increased the return to capital and expanded manufacturing production, thereby increasing capital accumulation in the relatively capital-scarce United States. To make the point starkly, suppose that agriculture used no capital at all. Increasing the demand for capital (which would enhance industrialization) would be a

32. De Long (1992).

first-order effect from the tariff on manufactures, whereas inefficiencies due to the fact that the tariff imposes a tax on capital goods would clearly be second order.

Other participants focused on increasing returns and externalities. Adrian Wood suggested that the gains from learning by doing might not be fully captured in the chapter. Thus, the potential for protection to stimulate productivity growth may have been understated. However, Barry Eichengreen referenced literature concluding that although learning effects were quite important before 1860, they were considerably less so later on, which is the focus of this chapter. Eichengreen also argued that increasing returns post-1860 appear to have been primarily internal to the firm. Given that firms appear to have been able to borrow in international capital markets during this period, such externalities do not provide a rationale for protection. Robert Blecker returned to De Long's point that firms (such as Carnegie Steel) were able to capture external economies through vertical integration. He wondered whether the existence of the tariffs might have facilitated this integration, a channel that is not explored in the chapter.

Susan Collins noted that the issue of whether interventionist trade policy promotes growth (and if so, how) is one that arises in many contexts. For example, there is a long-standing debate about whether protection is part of the explanation for the high growth rates in South Korea and many other East Asian economies. Some participants expressed the view that, although difficult to measure, protection has at times played a positive role in other experiences.

Adrian Wood found the comparison between the United States and Argentina in Peter Temin's commentary potentially misleading. In particular, he stressed that significant differences in the two countries' average educational attainment, not differences in trade policy, may explain subsequent differences in industrial development.

Michael Piore raised a broader issue about drawing lessons from historical experience. He characterized the episode discussed in the chapter as focusing on how trade policy influenced U.S. development as it adjusted away from agriculture toward manufacturing. The United States is now on quite a different adjustment path. Although it is difficult to describe, features include a shift from manufacturing toward services and a new organizational structure that emphasizes flexibility, not vertical integration. He suggested that before we can do justice to the potential lessons from the historical episode, we must improve our understanding of how the adjustment paths differ.

Sharyn O'Halloran raised two points. First, she suggested that the near elimination of tariffs in 1913 may provide a natural experiment for examining the effects of protection on the development of U.S. manufacturing. Second, she noted that tariffs were maintained during the 1890s despite huge budget surpluses, making it difficult to argue that they were largely imposed to finance federal expenditures. However, one variable that she has found consistently important in explaining tariff policy is the party in power, with Republicans tending to raise tariffs and Democrats tending to lower them. These observations led her to advocate a fuller political-economy framework for explaining the observed cycles in protection than that presented in the chapter.

Finally, a number of participants were dissatisfied with the implicit linkage of workers' living standards to overall output growth of the economy. Robert Lawrence emphasized the need to focus more explicitly on additional measures of well-being. He pointed out that there may be a link from trade to average wages—indeed, this was a central theme of the conference discussion. Here, he would expect to see that average wage growth is primarily determined by productivity growth, not trade policy. However, the linkage might run in the opposite direction, with slow wage growth influencing trade policy. Further historical examination of both types of linkages would be interesting and informative.

References

Abramovitz, Moses. 1956. "Resource and Output Trends in the United States since 1870." *American Economic Review* 46 (May): 5–23.

Abramovitz, Moses, and Paul David. 1973. "Reinterpreting Economic Growth: Parables and Realities." *American Economic Review* 63 (May): 428–39.

Amsden, Alice. 1989. *Asia's Next Giant: South Korea and Late Industrialization.* Oxford University Press.

Arrow, Kenneth. 1962. "The Economic Implications of Learning by Doing." *Review of Economic Studies* 29 (June): 155–73.

Atack, Jeremy. 1985. *Estimation of Economies of Scale in Nineteenth-Century United States Manufacturing.* New York: Garland Press.

———. 1987. "Economies of Scale and Efficiency Gains in the Rise of the Factory in America, 1820–1900." In *Quantity and Quiddity: Essays in U.S. Economic History,* edited by Peter Kilby, 286–335. Wesleyan University Press.

Atack, Jeremy, Peter Passell, and Susan Lee. 1994. *A New Economic View of American History: From Colonial Times to 1940,* 2d ed. W. W. Norton.

Baack, Bennett D., and Edward John Ray. 1974. "Tariff Policy and Comparative Advantage in the Iron and Steel Industry: 1870–1929." *Explorations in Economic History* 11 (Fall): 3–23.

———. 1983. "The Political Economy of Tariff Policy: A Case Study of the United States." *Explorations in Economic History* 20 (January): 73–93.

Baldwin, Richard. 1959. "On the Growth Effect of 1992." Working Paper 319. National Bureau of Economic Research (September).

Baldwin, Richard. 1989. "The Growth Effects of 1992." *Economic Policy: A European Forum* 0 (October): 247–81.

Bartelsman, Eric J., Ricardo J. Caballero, and Richard K. Lyons. 1994. "Customer- and Supplier-Driven Externalities." *American Economic Review* 84 (September): 1075–84.

Berry, Thomas S. 1978. *Revised Annual Estimates of American Gross National Product: Preliminary Annual Estimates of Four Major Components of Demand, 1789–1889.* Richmond, Va.: Bostwick Press.

Bils, Mark. 1984. "Tariff Protection and Production in the Early U.S. Cotton Textile Industry." *Journal of Economic History* 44 (December): 1033–46.

Carter, Susan B., and Richard Sutch. 1996. "The Myth of the Industrial Scrap Heap: A Revisionist View of Turn-of-the-Century American Retirement." *Journal of Economic History* 56 (March): 5–38.

Chandler, Alfred D. Jr. 1977. *The Visible Hand: The Managerial Revolution in American Business.* Cambridge, Mass.: Belknap Press of Harvard University.

David, Paul A. 1970. "Learning by Doing and Tariff Protection: A Reconsideration of the Case of the Antebellum United States Cotton Textile Industry." *Journal of Economic History* 30 (September): 521–601.

————. 1975. "Learning by Doing and Tariff Protection: A Reconsideration of the Case of the Antebellum United States Cotton Textile Industry." In *Technical Choice, Innovation, and Economic Growth: Essays on America and British Experience in the Nineteenth Century,* edited by Paul A. David, 95–168. Cambridge University Press.

De Long, J. Bradford. (1997). "Productivity Growth and Machinery Investment: A Long-Run Look, 1870–1980." *Journal of Economic History* 52 (June): 307–24.

Edelstein, Michael. 1982. *Overseas Investment in the Age of High Imperialism: The United Kingdom, 1850–1914.* Columbia University Press.

Edwards, Richard C. 1970. "Economic Sophistication in Nineteenth-Century Congressional Tariff Debates." *Journal of Economic History* 30 (December): 802–38.

Fallows, James M. 1994. *Looking at the Sun: The Rise of the New East Asian Economic and Political System.* Pantheon Books.

Fishlow, Albert. 1965. *Railroads and the Transformation of the Antebellum Economy.* Harvard University Press.

Freehling, William W. 1990. *Road to Disunion: Secessionists at Bay: 1776–1854.* Oxford University Press.

Gallman, Robert E. 1960. "Commodity Ouptut, 1839–1899." In *Trends in the American Economy in the Nineteenth Century* (National Bureau of Economic Research Studies in Income and Wealth, vol. 24), edited by William N. Parker, 13–71. Princeton University Press.

Goldstein, Judith. 1993. *Ideas, Interests, and American Trade Policy.* Cornell University Press.

Great Britain. 1854–55. "Report of the Committee on the Machinery of the United States of America." *Parliamentary Papers* 50: 1–137.

Habakkuk, H. J. 1962. *American and British Technology in the Nineteenth Century: The Search for Labour-Saving Inventions.* Cambridge University Press.

Hansen, John M. 1990. "Taxation and the Political Economy of the Tariff." *International Organization* 44 (Autumn): 527–51.

Harley, C. Knick. 1992. "International Competitiveness of the Antebellum American Cotton Textile Industry." *Journal of Economic History* 52 (September): 559–84.

———. 1992. "The Antebellum American Tariff: Food Exports and Manufacturing." *Explorations in Economic History* 29 (October): 375–400.

Jaffe, Adam B. 1986. "Technological Opportunity and Spillovers of R&D: Evidence from Firms' Patents, Profits, and Market Value." *American Economic Review* 76 (December): 984–1001.

James, John A. 1978. *Money and Capital Markets in Postbellum America.* Princeton University Press.

———. 1981. "The Optimal Tariff in the Antebellum United States." *American Economic Review* 71 (September): 726–34.

———. 1984. "Public Debt-Management Policy and Nineteenth-Century American Economic Growth." *Explorations in Economic History* 21 (April): 192–217.

James, John A., and Jonathan S. Skinner. 1987. "Sources of Savings in the Nineteenth-Century United States." In *Quantity and Quiddity: Essays in U.S. Economic History,* edited by Peter Kilby, 255–85. Wesleyan University Press.

Johnston, Louis. 1990. "Endogenous Growth and the American Economy, 1840–1900." Ph.D. dissertation, University of California.

Jones, Ronald W. 1971. "A Three-Factor Model in Theory, Trade and History." In *Trade, Balance of Payments and Growth: Papers in International Economics in Honor of Charles P. Kindleberger,* edited by Jagdish N. Bhagwati and others, 3–21. Amsterdam: North-Holland.

Kaplan, Edward S., and Thomas W. Ryley. 1994. *Prelude to Trade Wars: American Tariff Policy, 1890–1922.* Westport, Conn.: Greenwood Press.

Kim, Sukkoo. 1995. "Regions, Resources, and Economic Geography: The Evolution of the U.S. Regional Economies, 1860–1987." Working Paper. Washington University, Department of Economics.

Lazonick, William. 1991. *Business Organization and the Myth of the Market Economy.* Cambridge University Press.

Lee, Susan Previant, and Peter Passell. 1979. *A New Economic View of American History.* W. W. Norton.

Lipsey, Robert E. 1963. *Price and Quantity Trends in the Foreign Trade of the United States.* Princeton University Press.

———. 1994. "U.S. Foreign Trade and the Balance of Payments, 1800–1913." Working Paper 4710. Cambridge, Mass.: National Bureau of Economic Research.

McCraw, Thomas K. 1986. "Mercantilism and the Market: Antecedents of American Industrial Policy." In *The Politics of Industrial Policy,* edited by Claude E. Barfield and William A. Schambra, 33–62. Washington: American Enterprise Institute.

Mitchell, B. R. 1993. *International Historical Statistics: The Americas, 1750–1988,* 2d ed. New York: Stockton Press.

Murphy, Kevin M., Andrei Shleifer, and Robert W. Vishny. 1989. "Industrialization and the Big Push." *Journal of Political Economy* 97 (October): 1003–26.

Pope, Clayne. 1972. "The Impact of the Antebellum Tariff on Income Distribution." *Explorations in Economic History* 9 (Summer): 375–421.

Romer, Paul M. 1986. "Increasing Returns and Long-Run Growth." *Journal of Political Economy* 94 (October): 1002–37.

Solow, Robert M. 1956. "A Contribution to the Theory of Economic Growth."
    Quarterly Journal of Economics 70 (February): 65–94.
Taussig, Frank W. 1931. *The Tariff History of the United States.* G. P. Putnam's
    Sons.
Temin, Peter. 1966. "Labor Scarcity and the Problem of American Industrial
    Efficiency in the 1850s." *Journal of Economic History* 26 (September): 277–98.
———. 1971. "Labor Scarcity in America." *Journal of Interdisciplinary History*
    (Winter): 251–64.
———. 1988. "Product Quality and Vertical Integration in the Early Cotton Textile
    Industry." *Journal of Economic History* 48 (December): 891–907.
———. 1991. "Free Land and Federalism: A Synoptic View of American
    Economic History." *Journal of Interdisciplinary History* 21 (Winter): 371–90.
U.S. Bureau of the Census. 1975. *Historical Statistics of the United States.* Govern-
    ment Printing Office.
Williamson, Jeffrey G. 1964. *American Growth and the Balance of Payments,
    1820–1913: A Study of the Long Swing.* University of North Carolina Press.
———. 1972. "Embodiment, Disembodiment, Learning by Doing, and Returns to
    Scale in Nineteenth-Century Cotton Textiles." *Journal of Economic History* 32:
    691–70.
———. 1974a. *Late Nineteenth-Century American Development: A General Equi-
    librium History: The Kuzets Memorial Lectures.* Cambridge University Press.
———. 1974b. "Watersheds and Turning Points: Conjectures on the Long-Term
    Impact of Civil War Financing." *Journal of Economic History* 34 (September):
    636–61.
———. 1991. *Inequality, Poverty, and History.* Cambridge, Mass.: Basil Black-
    well.
Wright, Gavin. 1990. "The Origins of American Industrial Success, 1879–1940."
    American Economic Review 80 (September): 651–68.
Young, Allyn. 1928. "Increasing Returns and Economic Progress." *Economic Jour-
    nal* 38 (December): 527–42.
Zevin, Robert B. 1971. "The Growth of Cotton Textile Production After 1815." In
    The Reinterpretation of American Economic History, edited by Robert W. Fogel
    and Stanley L. Engerman, 122–47. Harper and Row.

NINE

Trade Politics and
Labor Issues, 1953–95

I. M. Destler

IN THE EARLY decades of U.S. trade liberalization, organized labor was a consistent and reliable member of the free-trade coalition that found a comfortable home in the Democratic Party. Unions supported Cordell Hull and the Reciprocal Trade Agreements Act of 1934; the AFL-CIO backed John F. Kennedy and his Trade Expansion Act of 1962.

Nor was this stance limited to the United States. In a comprehensive cross-national comparison of foreign economic policies during the interwar period, Beth Simmons has shown that governments of the Left regularly backed policies of low tariffs (as well as depreciating exchange rates). This seems to have been related to their identification with consumer interests and their opposition to concentrated business power. In any case, it was governments of the Right that inclined toward protectionism,

I thank Mark Anderson, Steve Charnovitz, Susan Collins, Ellen Frost, Julius Katz, Sharyn O'Halloran, and J. David Richardson for their helpful critical comments, and William R. Cline for access to preliminary drafts of his Institute for International Economics book, *Trade and Income Distribution* (1997).

driven presumably by the sort of business lobbying that produced the Smoot-Hawley Act of 1930.[1]

This pattern continued, in the United States, from the Great Depression through the first two postwar decades. But there were signs of fundamental change that was to come. Raymond A. Bauer and his colleagues found the makings of "an amazing historical reversal of party stands" when they examined a Roper poll of 1953 that analyzed respondents with polar trade views. The poll indicated that "ultrafree traders" were strongly Republican, whereas "ultraprotectionists" were mostly Democrats. Prominent among the latter were "industrial workers who see a threat to their jobs."[2]

The reversal took decades to play out. Unions moved as economic pressures drove them, though sometimes with a lag time born of leaders' continuing attachment to free-trade ideology. Textile unions never favored liberal policies; the United Auto Workers (UAW) did not embrace protectionism until its calamitous job losses of 1979–82. But the major shift came in the late 1960s, after the Kennedy Round was completed but well before the Tokyo Round was authorized. AFL-CIO President George Meany became a vociferous critic of classical trade liberalism. By 1970, the AFL-CIO economic policy committee had declared "old 'free-trade' concepts and their 'protectionist' opposites increasingly irrelevant." What was needed were new policies emphasizing "an orderly expansion of world trade."[3] A particular labor target was the "export of jobs" by multinational corporations.

Why did labor's position change? The driving force was certainly the fierce foreign competition faced by members of the large industrial unions, particularly in steel and automobiles. Contributing to the speed and extent of the shift, however, was Washington's failure to develop effective policies for compensating the victims of trade expansion and facilitating their adjustment and movement into other jobs. I therefore begin this chapter with an exploration of the failure of U.S. trade adjustment policies. I then move to a review of labor's extensive efforts to fight trade liberalization, followed by a treatment of the Clinton administration's campaign to elevate the importance of labor standards in trade negotiations. The final sections address the possible political implications of the connection that some economists are finding between trade and income inequality in the United States.

1. Simmons (1994).
2. Bauer, de Sola Pool, and Dexter (1973, p. 91).
3. *New York Times,* February 22, 1970, as cited in Destler (1980, p. 135).

Trade Adjustment Assistance: The Rise and Fall of a Promising Idea

In 1953, David McDonald of the United Steelworkers Union made a proposal to the Randall Commission, which President Eisenhower had established to advise on future trade policy. The federal government, Mc-Donald argued, should offer direct aid to workers, firms, and communities hurt by imports.[4] The commission voted 16 to 1 against the proposal, but Democratic senators picked it up, among them John F. Kennedy of Massachusetts. Nine years later, the Kennedy administration included such a program in its draft Trade Expansion Act. It survived a close vote in the House Ways and Means Committee, and Trade Adjustment Assistance (TAA) became part of U.S. trade law. The program included weekly payments for qualifying trade-displaced workers and retraining programs to help them move to other jobs.

The idea underlying TAA was seen as radical by both proponents and critics. The classic analysis of the trade politics of this period called it "a proposal which, if adopted, could destroy the political basis of protectionism by giving the injured an alternative way out." On the other hand, two Republican members denounced its "mere insertion" in the Randall Commission report as indicating "a dangerous sentiment" in favor of such intervention.[5] Politically, however, TAA is better thought of as offering a middle course. It was particularly attractive to liberal Democrats who wanted to support open trade but needed something to offer organized labor as well. It was the sort of *good* government intervention that they wanted to believe in, something that could help distressed workers *and* make the economy more efficient by facilitating adjustment as well as trade.

For organized labor in the early 1960s, establishing TAA was key to maintaining a free-trade stance. Testifying in support of Kennedy's legislation before the Senate Committee on Finance, AFL-CIO President Meany declared: "There is no question whatever that adjustment assistance is essential to the success of trade expansion. And as we have said many times, it is indispensable to our support of the trade program as a whole."[6]

---

4. The discussion of TAA draws on Charnovitz (1986); Frank (1977); Hufbauer and Rosen (1986); Lawrence and Litan (1986); and my own previous work (Destler [1980, 1995]). Discussion here focuses on adjustment assistance to workers (directly relevant to this chapter), and not on assistance to firms and communities, which in any case proved less important.

5. Bauer, de Sola Pool, and Dexter (1973, p. 43).

6. Quoted in Charnowitz (1986, p. 158).

But though the 1962 law was a victory for TAA principle, its specific provisions made the assistance largely unavailable in practice. Section 302 restricted workers' eligibility severely; they had to demonstrate 1) serious injury (meaning loss of job) that was 2) caused by imports that 3) resulted from specific U.S. "concessions granted under [previous] trade agreements." Applying these criteria, the U.S. Tariff Commission rejected all worker petitions through fiscal year 1969, and less than 50,000 workers won benefits between then and 1974. By this time, the AFL-CIO had shifted its trade stance, and Meany was denouncing the program as "burial insurance."

When Congress took up Richard Nixon's trade expansion proposal in 1973, Democrats in particular were determined to reform TAA to make it a real alternative to protection. Though the administration was cool to the idea (Treasury Secretary George Shultz argued that trade-displaced workers should get no better benefits than any others who were casualties of economic change), Ways and Means reported out a proposal that relaxed the eligibility criteria and increased program benefits. With modest Senate changes, this was incorporated in the Trade Act of 1974. By this time, TAA could no longer bring labor to support the legislation, but labor did want changes to make the program more accessible. By enacting these changes, liberal Democrats could provide something for their labor constituents. These legislators found continuing attraction in a middle course between protectionism and the cruel logic of the market.

By 1975, TAA benefits were broadly available, and the program began to be employed on a wide scale. An early user of the enhanced authority was none other than President Gerald Ford. The Trade Act of 1974 had triggered an upsurge in "escape-clause" petitions from industries seeking trade protection, because it had also softened the criteria for obtaining such relief.[7] In nine cases during 1975 and 1976 the U.S. International Trade Commission (USITC) recommended that the president grant protection; in no less than five of these cases, Ford refused to impose import barriers but authorized "expedited adjustment assistance."[8] Like TAA's Democratic

---

7. The "escape clause," based on Article XIX of the General Agreement on Tariffs and Trade (GATT), authorizes temporary trade protection for industries hurt by imports. Under the 1962 law, however, petitioners had to establish that imports resulting from tariff concessions in prior U.S. trade negotiations were the "major cause" of economic injury. The 1974 act lowered the threshold to "substantial cause" and removed the requirement that the imports be the result of specific U.S. tariff concessions.

8. Destler (1986a, pp. 238–39).

sponsors, Ford found this remedy an attractive middle course, substantively and politically. So did his successor, Jimmy Carter. During the auto industry crisis of 1979–80, Carter resisted calls that he propose trade protection. But he turned on the TAA spigot. Program spending, which had been running around $200 million a year, shot up to $1.6 billion in fiscal year 1980.[9]

In its second decade, therefore, TAA was proving quite useful politically for liberal traders. It had helped build coalitions for major trade liberalizing legislation. It offered a nonprotectionist option for presidents reluctant to do nothing at all for trade-displaced workers. Finally, it served as a diluter of discontent among workers affected. Their first preference, of course, was to get their old jobs back, not higher unemployment compensation (UC) and opportunities for retraining. But the rewards from TAA surely softened their calls for trade protection.

Unfortunately, though TAA was now providing money to trade-displaced workers, it was not providing effective training. Steve Charnovitz catalogues the reasons: limited funding, delays, and other deficiencies in U.S. Department of Labor (DOL) implementation and enforcement of explicit statutory requirements. Thus, he concludes, "Despite their demand for counseling, training, and relocation assistance, most unemployed workers were not able to obtain these services. . . . Almost perversely, as the costs of [the direct payments to workers] went up, the amount DOL spent for adjustment went down. In FY 1980, DOL allocated less than half of what it had the year before."[10]

While labor's operating agencies were failing to implement the retraining side of the program, the department's policy evaluation shop had been studying the overall effort and its underlying rationale. The results were not reassuring. Labor-funded research offered "very little support for the notion that, in general, trade-displaced workers are very different from other displaced workers," thus undercutting the substantive rationale for a separate *trade* adjustment program. More seriously, the studies also offered little support for "the notion that TAA has encouraged much labor market adjustment."[11] In fact, the effect seems to have been perverse. Because its benefits were generous compared with standard UC and retraining opportunities were scarce, TAA encouraged trade-displaced auto workers to sit around and wait for their old jobs to reappear.

9. Aho and Bayard (1984, p. 184).
10. Charnovitz (1986, pp. 160, 161).
11. Aho and Bayard (1984, pp. 170–71).

The combination of burgeoning costs and questionable effectiveness made TAA an irresistible target when Ronald Reagan and his budget-cutting Office of Management and Budget (OMB) director, David Stockman, came to power in Washington. Notwithstanding its benefits for trade politics, the TAA Program was hard to defend against charges of both inequity (as between trade-displaced and otherwise-displaced workers) and ineffectiveness (in moving workers to new, competitive enterprises). Thus it was cut back severely in 1981. Benefits were limited to the level of regular unemployment insurance (UI) and paid only after UI eligibility was exhausted. Proponents fended off administration proposals to "zero out" TAA entirely, but it has limped along ever since. In 1991, the Bush administration promised an "adequately funded" worker adjustment program to help workers displaced by the North American Free Trade Agreement (NAFTA), and some new benefits were in fact provided. Clinton promised a broader labor adjustment program in his October 1992 speech offering conditional endorsement of NAFTA. But the administration put surprisingly little emphasis on worker adjustment programs in its NAFTA campaign.[12]

With the Republican capture of Congress in 1994, the political environment became even less favorable to government-interventionist solutions to market problems. As part of the drive to balance the federal budget in 1995, Republicans on Ways and Means initially voted to eliminate the TAA Program. They backed off at least temporarily when Democrats declared it a sine qua non for their support of further trade liberalization.[13] But no one believed that the program would have more than a minute impact on the real adjustment problems workers faced.[14] Its political contribution to trade liberalization was therefore limited as well, as indeed it had been since its curtailment in 1981.

The failure to develop effective trade adjustment programs reinforced the movement of labor unions to the protectionist camp.

12. On the Clinton promise and program, see Hufbauer and Schott (1993, pp. 32, 168–69).

13. "Ways and Means Recommends Super 301, GSP [Generalized System of Preferences] Be Extended in Budget Bill," *Inside U.S. Trade,* September 15, 1995, p. 1.

14. Jodie Allen summarized current U.S. DOL thinking about the (very modest) competence of government in providing effective worker retraining. Jodie T. Allen, "Why Retooling Workers Is No Quick Fix for Anxious America," *Washington Post,* January 22, 1995, p. C3. Louis Jacobson's chapter 11 in this book describes many of the reasons for this difficulty.

Labor and Trade Protectionism: Twenty-Five Years against the Tide

If we date labor's antitrade activism from the February 1970 economic policy committee report quoted earlier, it was twenty-five years old in 1995. These years brought few triumphs.

First came the proposed International Trade and Investment Act of 1971, better known as Burke-Hartke.[15] This legislation, introduced with strong labor backing, would have imposed thoroughgoing quantitative limits on imports and restraints on direct foreign investment (DFI) by U.S. firms. The bill raised the alarm among liberal traders, who feared that labor's shift might fuel a reversal of postwar U.S. trade policy. But legislatively it went nowhere. Instead, Congress moved in 1973 to consideration of the Nixon administration's proposal to authorize a new round of barrier-reducing negotiations.

In testimony before the House on that legislation, AFL-CIO representative I. W. Abel articulated labor's new protectionism: "The Congress must move quickly and decisively to slow the massive flood of imports into the U.S. market which are sweeping away jobs and industries in wholesale lots."[16] After two labor-backed amendments providing for broad quota protection failed in the House Ways and Means Committee, the AFL-CIO retreated to all-out opposition, branding the legislation "worse than no bill at all."[17] Its stand clearly affected members for whom labor was a prime constituency; northern Democrats, who supported the Trade Expansion Act of 1962, 141 to 7 in the key House vote, went against the Nixon trade bill 101 to 52 in December 1973. But Republicans shifted the other way. When the conference report was finally passed in December 1974, organized labor could claim no direct impact on its content, though it favored (and benefited from) the liberalization of TAA sponsored by House Democrats.

Organized labor's next big legislative push on trade came in 1982 and centered on automobiles. In the tradition of Walter Reuther, the UAW had been one of labor's last free-trade holdouts; Reuther's successor, Douglas Fraser, was giving qualified support to "the benefits of free trade" as late as 1979.[18] But beginning that year, the U.S. auto industry was devastated by

15. Its cosponsors were Senator Vance Hartke (D-Ind.) and Representative James A. Burke (D-Mass.).
16. U.S. House of Representatives (1973, pp. 1209–10).
17. Frank (1973, p. 1752).
18. Letter to Charles Vanik, reprinted in U.S. House of Reprsentatives (1979, pp. 655–58).

the second so-called oil shock, as a doubling of gasoline prices caused consumers to buy fuel-efficient, Japanese cars. When the Reagan recession brought on a further plunge in sales and more unemployment for UAW members, the union responded with "domestic content" legislation requiring that up to 90 percent of the value of cars sold on the U.S. market must originate within the country. The bill passed the House twice, in 1982 and 1983, with the backing of virtually all Democrats from the Northeast and the Midwest.

Actual belief in the wisdom of this remedy was scarce. Senate Trade Subcommittee Chairman John Danforth (R-Mo.), a champion of moderate auto protection, declared concerning the domestic content bill that "the overwhelming majority" of senators and representatives "view the domestic content legislation as a perfectly ridiculous piece of legislation."[19] No one expected the bill to become law, however, and it never even reached the Senate floor. It was a way for organized labor to show its power over "its" members, however, and it allowed these members to support the UAW with the comfort that they really were not making (bad) trade law.

In 1984, organized labor missed a big opportunity in the Senate to block or amend legislation that continued trade preferences (GSP) for developing nations and broadened fast-track, legislative approval provisions[20] to encompass bilateral free-trade agreements. These were included in legislation, developed late in the session, which pulled together several bills into what became the Trade and Tariff Act of 1984. GSP had long been a labor target, and the fast-track amendment would become the basis for negotiating NAFTA. Labor was actively engaged in the House, where it managed to link new protection for steel to a requirement that companies reinvest net cash flow in steel operations and allocate funds to worker retraining.[21] Labor also succeeded in getting trade preferences conditioned on adherence to internationally recognized labor standards. It lost, by a surprisingly wide 233:174 margin, on an amendment sponsored by Representative Richard Gephardt (D-Mo.) that would have eliminated trade preferences for

19. *Congressional Quarterly Almanac* (1983, p. 56).

20. These were provisions under which each house of Congress would vote expeditiously, without amendment, on legislation proposed by the president to implement trade agreements whose negotiation Congress had authorized.

21. Acting on an escape-clause case, President Ronald Reagan had ordered the negotiation of export-restraint agreements with the major nations selling steel to the U.S. market. The 1984 legislation provided backup enforcement authority to the administration in case these nations did not impose effective limits.

the three largest users: Korea, Taiwan, and Hong Kong.[22] On the Senate side, where four days of uncontrolled floor debate on the trade bill offered awesome procedural opportunities, organized labor failed to grasp them. According to several sources, labor representatives did not catch on to what was happening until near the end. Not a single labor proposal was among the fifty or so amendments the Senate considered.[23]

Union representatives, led by the AFL-CIO, had greater success in the long campaign that culminated in enactment of the Omnibus Trade and Competitiveness Act of 1988. This campaign responded to the unprecedented surge of imports fueled by the strong dollar of 1981–85, growing frustration over foreign barriers to U.S. exports, and congressional dissatisfaction with what leaders of both parties saw as a tepid response from the administration. Many Democrats also saw the trade issue as a major political opportunity. Labor worked with them in a broad coalition of interests seeking to "toughen" U.S. trade policy.

Their prime proposal was the Gephardt amendment penalizing nations that ran large trade surpluses with the United States. This passed the House twice, before being supplanted by the Super 301 proposal requiring the U.S. Trade Representative (USTR) to designate "priority foreign countries" chosen for the "number and pervasiveness" of their export-impeding "acts, policies, or practices." The coalition also worked, with some success, to strengthen the authority of the USTR and to reduce administration discretion *not* to act against foreign trade barriers. Organized labor won inclusion in the law of language designating "worker rights" as the fourteenth of sixteen "principal trade negotiating objectives" to be pursued in the multilateral Uruguay Round launched in 1986. One channel for labor influence during this period was the Labor-Industry Coalition for International Trade (LICIT), established in the early 1980s. LICIT lobbied unsuccessfully for a comprehensive U.S. policy to strengthen traded-goods industries, and somewhat more successfully to make the language of antidumping and countervailing duty laws more favorable to domestic petitioners.

Organized labor also won inclusion in the omnibus legislation of a nongermane provision requiring that U.S. workers be notified in advance of plant closings involving 100 or more workers. When this (and another) provision led to a Reagan veto, unions succeeded in having their proposal

---

22. Four years later, using the flexibility granted in the 1984 act, the Reagan administration ended preferences for these three nations, plus Singapore.

23. For a fuller description of this episode, see Destler (1995).

I. M. DESTLER

enacted as separate legislation. The Omnibus Trade and Competitiveness Act of 1988 was also resubmitted, and it became law as well. But though it contained—in diluted form—a number of provisions for which organized labor had pressed, it did not reverse the liberal course of U.S. trade policy. Indeed, it included few directly protectionist provisions and authorized U.S. participation in the most comprehensive negotiation yet undertaken to reduce barriers to international trade.[24]

In early 1991, the Bush administration notified Congress of its intention to negotiate NAFTA with Mexico and Canada. Labor emerged as a strong and vociferous opponent. The first congressional test was over the administration's request to extend the deadline for negotiations covered by the fast-track congressional approval provisions.[25] The AFL-CIO moved quickly in opposition and lined up early votes, particularly among liberal Democrats. To broaden support, Senate Finance Committee Chairman Lloyd Bentsen (D-Tex.) and House Ways and Means Chairman Dan Rostenkowski (D-Ill.) wrote the president seeking assurances concerning NAFTA's effect on jobs and worker rights (as well as the environment). So did House Majority Leader Gephardt. President Bush responded with assurances that imports from Mexico would cause no "mass dislocations" of workers, and he also promised (as noted earlier) "adjustment provisions," including services for those who lost their jobs.[26] These did not assuage labor, but they helped the administration win by 231:192 in the House and 59:36 in the Senate.

NAFTA was completed in August 1992 and signed that December. Speaking in October, presidential candidate Bill Clinton conditioned his support of the pact on negotiation of side agreements dealing with the environment, labor standards, and the threat of sudden import surges. The AFL-CIO withheld a formal position until the side agreements were completed in August 1993 (the slogan was "Not *this* NAFTA"), but worker opposition was deep and virulent. NAFTA became the most hotly debated American trade issue since the Smoot-Hawley Act of 1930. Independent presidential candidate Ross Perot made "jobs" the central issue with his forecast of "a giant sucking sound" pulling jobs across the border. But labor (supplemented by some environmentalists) generated the grassroots op-

24. For much more on the 1988 act, see Schwab (1994); Destler (1995, chapters 4 and 5; 1991, pp. 251–84).

25. The 1988 act had established a deadline of June 1991 for agreements to be completed, but provided for a two-year extension, on request of the administration, unless either house voted to block it. The administration needed the extension for NAFTA, and also to complete the multilateral Uruguay Round.

26. White House (1991, pp. 3, 5).

position. By September 1993, when President Clinton finally sprang into action, labor and its allies had lined up an impressive number of congressional opponents. Many inside and outside the labor movement believed that the unions would win this big trade battle, but the Clinton administration prevailed, with majority support from Republicans and the backing of a strong business coalition. Organized labor's hard-line opposition stance meant that, as on the Trade Act of 1974 and the domestic content proposal of the early 1980s, unions could not negotiate with the administration for policy concessions, as did representatives holding swing votes on behalf of producers of orange juice and sugar, for example.

Instead, in these as in earlier battles, organized labor pursued a strategy of taking a strong position, whipping its forces into line, and rebuffing initiatives for compromise. This approach seems to have been dictated in part by the difficulty in turning around an organization that relies on a coalition of localized organizations for its effectiveness. But the inflexibility made organized labor unable to use its leverage to win substantive concessions that would often have been available. Such an approach was perhaps appropriate in the days when organized labor was a rising political force—why settle for half a loaf today when you can hope for the full loaf tomorrow? But it made less tactical sense in the decades of labor's decline.[27]

The failure on NAFTA left AFL-CIO leaders and members embittered. Lacking the same local militancy on the Uruguay Round, they largely sat out that battle in 1994, even though the global agreement had greater potential impact on U.S. workers. Unions were chastised for their inaction by GATT adversary Ralph Nader, among others. And though there was never a systematic labor campaign to "punish" pro-NAFTA Democrats at the polls, reduced labor political enthusiasm in the November 1994 midterm election inadvertently punished all Democrats and organized labor as well.

Over the 1970–95 period, labor persistently opposed trade liberalizing initiatives sponsored by presidents of both political parties—with uneven political adroitness and limited substantive effect. Politically, the main impact of labor's trade protectionism was indirect: in curbing legislators who might otherwise have been pro-trade activists, and in encouraging an occasional aspiring leader like Gephardt to take a tough trade line. "Liberal" Democrats knew, from the 1970s onward, that they championed

---

27. In the case of NAFTA, the ferocity of grassroots opposition and the prospect of victory made compromise impractical. But this was not necessarily the case on other trade legislation like that of 1974 or 1984.

trade expansion at their political peril, so those with free-trade convictions *and* heavily organized labor constituencies found other issues on which to spend their entrepreneurial time. Similarly, the domestic consumer movement might have called for removal of trade barriers to bring lower prices and greater product choices. But it needed labor support for its broader agenda, so it stayed largely out of questions like sugar or textile quotas. One major national organization even backed the domestic content bill for autos, out of a declared "appreciat[ion for] all the work for consumer issues that the UAW has done over the years."[28]

But this was a specific political success for labor within a larger policy failure—failure to halt the general, market-opening direction of U.S. trade policy. After organized labor's political reversal, the United States inaugurated and completed the two most comprehensive GATT negotiations and embarked on regional trade liberalization in the hemisphere and beyond. Domestic opposition to organized labor's international negotiating agenda hardened as well, as revealed by the Clinton administration's efforts to bring issues involving foreign labor practices into the mainstream of future trade agreements.

The Clinton Administration and Fair Labor Standards

In its response to labor concerns during the NAFTA debate and in its efforts to repair its frayed labor connections thereafter, the Clinton administration signaled its desire to elevate the importance of labor standards in future trade negotiations. This raised the question of whether and to what extent the United States should link trade liberalization to enforcement of fair labor practices by our trading partners.

The contemporary issue of international worker rights grows out of two historical movements. One is the venerable tradition of workers in one nation "uniting" with those in another—from the Communist Manifesto, through the International Labor Organization (ILO), through the postwar International Confederation of Free Trade Unions, to the efforts of the AFL-CIO to promote union organization and basic worker rights overseas. The second is the equally venerable tradition of wage-based protectionism. In its pure form, this is the argument that it is "unfair" for American workers to compete with low-wage, foreign counterparts. But its logic can be (and

28. The executive director of the Consumer Federation of America, quoted in the *Wall Street Journal,* September 3, 1982. He admitted that "on the surface, this might appear to go against consumer interests." Destler (1986a, p. 194).

is) extended to comparative labor conditions, with foreign failures to enforce comparable laws on worker health and safety, child labor, the rights of unions to organize, and the like being viewed as unfair trade practices. The boundary between egregious practices that should be banned and work conditions endemic to poor countries is not easy to draw.

One manifestation of the concern with labor conditions, reflecting both traditions, is the conditioning of trade preferences (GSP) for developing countries on the labor practices of the beneficiaries. Specifically, in renewing and extending the GSP program, the Trade and Tariff Act of 1984 provided that the U.S. president is not to designate any country for GSP benefits "if such country has not taken or is not taking steps to afford internationally recognized worker rights to workers in the country." Such rights are defined as including "(A) the right of association; (B) the right to organize and bargain collectively; (C) a prohibition on the use of any form of forced or compulsory labor; (D) a minimum age for the employment of children; and (E) acceptable conditions of work with respect to minimum wages, hours of work, and occupational safety and health."[29]

In the years since, organized labor—which opposes GSP on principle—has pressed to have this provision applied to a range of countries, most notably Indonesia. Typically, the target has been laws obviously inconsistent with these criteria (such as Indonesia's requirement that unions have a substantial minimum size) or the failure of a nation to enforce the laws it has enacted.

The issue of Mexican labor practices was prominent in the 1991 debate over fast-track extension, and one of the side agreements that President Clinton negotiated dealt with worker standards and safety. It established a trinational commission on labor cooperation to monitor the enforcement of existing labor laws by national governments. Complaints about enforcement failures would be referred to the commission, which would seek voluntary compliance. Fines and trade sanctions could be imposed as a "last resort, and applicable only in cases involving workplace health and safety, minimum wage, and child labor."[30] These would be imposed only after elaborate dispute-settlement procedures were followed. Issues involving other trade laws could be the subject of intergovernmental discussions and expert reports, with

29. The president may waive this condition if he determines that designating such a country as a trade preference recipient "will be in the national economic interest of the United States and reports such determination to the Congress with his reasons therefor." (Language quoted here and in the text is from Section 502 of the Trade Act of 1974, as amended.)

30. Hufbauer and Schott (1993, p. 181).

the notable exception of disputes relating to the rights of labor organizations, which could only be discussed in ministerial-level consultations.

When he proposed the side agreement, Clinton had presumably hoped to ameliorate labor opposition to NAFTA and/or win the support of labor-oriented members of Congress. However, the administration failed to lobby these members during the critical months *before* the side agreement was reached. By August and September 1993, when Clinton launched his serious NAFTA campaign, labor had long since gone all out to defeat the agreement and had locked up the support of most labor legislators. Moreover, the AFL-CIO found the substance of the labor side agreement wanting, especially the limited access to trade sanctions. So the agreement made little contribution to Clinton's great November victory (in contrast to the side agreement on the environment, which brought endorsement of NAFTA by several mainstream environmental organizations).[31]

The Clinton White House, though euphoric about its NAFTA victory, was most unhappy about the breach with organized labor, a prime Democratic constituency. Trade policy was one possible means of healing the breach. In its post–Uruguay Round planning, the office of the USTR had made trade-related labor issues one of its three negotiating priorities. USTR Mickey Kantor began a public campaign in the early months of 1994 to make trade-labor issues part of the work program of the new World Trade Organization (WTO). He wanted to get a commitment to this included in the political declaration that trade ministers were preparing to issue on the April 15th signing of the Uruguay Round agreements at Marrakesh. He insisted that the goal was not protection against low-wage imports, seeking to distance himself from the French concept of "social dumping." Other countries were skeptical, particularly in the third world, and when the proposal encountered "overwhelming international opposition," the United States blocked approval of the draft ministerial statement.[32] In the end, Kantor won only a commitment that the WTO preparatory committee would take up the issue. But in the address he gave to the Marrakesh conference, Vice President Albert Gore signaled that the United States would continue to give the matter priority.

Kantor's next step was to include trade-related labor issues among those for which the administration sought advance negotiating authority from

31. Destler (1995, pp. 224–28). Labor officials were also unhappy with what they saw as a weak side agreement on import surges.

32. "U.S. Worker Rights Proposal Stalls Preparations for Marrakech," *Inside U.S. Trade* 12 (April 1, 1994), p. 1.

Congress as part of the Uruguay Round implementing legislation. Specifically, in June 1994 he unveiled draft language for extension of fast-track negotiating authority that included the following among its seven "principal trade negotiating objectives":

> (5) Labor Standards.—The principal negotiating objectives of the United States regarding internationally recognized labor standards are to—
>
> (A) promote respect for internationally recognized labor standards; and
>
> (B) ensure that the benefits of the trading system are available to all workers and that the denial of such standards is not a means for a country or its industries to gain competitive advantage in international trade.

Also included as a "principal negotiating objective" was "trade and the environment."[33]

The labor-environment emphasis won strong support from NAFTA opponent Dick Gephardt and NAFTA supporter Bill Richardson (D-N. Mex.), who were pushing to have worker and environmental protections included in the *text* of the proposed free-trade agreement with Chile, not just in side agreements like those of NAFTA. But the business reaction was vociferous and negative. Small- and medium-size companies saw labor and environmental talks as the road to yet more government regulation, and they backed a Republican counterproposal that would *prohibit* use of fast track for any agreement on labor/environment issues. Multinationals represented in the Business Roundtable took a more moderate position. But they were frustrated and angry and puzzled over USTR's lack of close consultation with them, particularly since their support was essential for any such proposal to win congressional approval. Republicans took a very hard line in response.[34]

Over the summer, Kantor retreated to a formulation that would not mention labor and environment as priority issues but would not absolutely rule them out. On this he won a shaky consensus from the House Ways and Means Committee. But the Senate Finance Committee had been resistant to including *any* follow-on, fast-track authority in the Uruguay Round bill, with Chairman Daniel Patrick Moynihan fearing that the controversy surrounding it would endanger final passage. To overcome this would have required strong support from Ways and Means Committee members as well as intense business lobbying. The battle over labor (and environmental) issues rendered this impossible. So "future fast track," one of the top administration priorities, was dropped from the draft legislation in Septem-

---

33. Reprinted in *Inside U.S. Trade* (special report), (June 21, 1992), p. S26.
34. This story is told in more detail in Destler (1995).

ber. The 103d Congress approved the Uruguay Round overwhelmingly, in a rare postelection session, but it left the guidelines for future trade negotiations to its successor.

By pressing the labor standards issue, Kantor was seeking to broaden the support base for liberal trade policy, or at least to soften labor opposition. He wanted to show that the trade negotiating process offered something for them. He was pursuing at least equally the Clinton administration's high-political goal of mending fences with labor and its congressional allies. Moreover, the statutory language he proposed, which was quoted above, was almost identical to that included without great controversy in the previous (1988) fast-track legislation. But perhaps because Kantor had highlighted it, or because conservatives feared he would actually pursue it seriously, or because these conservatives were growing in power, the proposal provoked a strong reaction from Republicans and business interests. This continued into the fall of 1995, reinforced by the Republican sweep of the midterm elections.

In the circumstances that prevailed, Kantor's initiative advanced neither trade liberalization in general nor negotiations on labor standards in particular. The effect of trying (loudly) to broaden trade's constituency on the left, at least in this manner, was to undercut it on the center-right and risk the bipartisanship that was a sine qua non for getting past agreements ratified and future negotiations authorized. Moreover, Kantor ended up setting back the cause of promoting international negotiations on labor standards issues. In September 1995, the House Ways and Means Committee voted out a proposal renewing fast-track negotiating authority for long-anticipated free-trade negotiations with Chile—part of the Bush-Clinton strategy to bind the Americas through reciprocally open markets. But the bill was drafted so as to rule out inclusion of labor and environmental issues in the agreement. The administration opposed it. The Senate Finance Committee seemed reluctant to consider any trade-negotiating matter. And with at least one eye to its labor and environmental constituencies, the administration was reluctant to yield or compromise. The result was a stalemate, with the issue effectively postponed until after the 1996 election.

Wage Stagnation and Unequal Income Distribution: Trade as the New Villain?

Ross Perot put the matter crudely: If U.S. workers must compete against Mexicans, then their wages will fall to the average of the two. As stated, the proposition was wrong on its face. U.S. workers' wages reflect their productivity, which is a product (in part) of the superior U.S. business environment and overall infrastructure. The U.S. economy dwarfs its southern neighbor, so whatever effect Mexican competition has on U.S. wages is likely to prove marginal. But the Perot argument put the matter on the trade political agenda, and the intellectual ease of rebutting his specific assertion should not blind anyone to its political power. Moreover, Perot could have been wrong about the magnitude of the impact but right about the direction. And if the country were not Mexico but, say, China, the magnitude might prove substantial.

Paralleling the rise of the "trade-versus-jobs" issue in the NAFTA context has been an outpouring of research by trade and labor economists on the connection between trade and income distribution.[35] This book includes important new work on this topic. The purpose of this chapter is not to critique this work but to explore its policy and political implications. The "trade-depresses-wages" argument gains plausibility from four considerations:

—Since 1970, the trade exposure of the U.S. economy has doubled, income inequality has grown, and wages have stagnated. (In the two previous decades, when trade was a much smaller share of gross domestic product [GDP], U.S. wages grew robustly and income inequality declined slightly.)

—Since 1970, trade has obviously been a wage-depressing force in certain circumstances, for certain highly visible groups—those who were auto workers in 1978, for example.

—Respectable (that is, Hecksher-Ohlin [HO], Stolper-Samuelson) trade theory sides with the commonsense view that trade expansion will reduce wages in a country where labor is relatively scarce, like the United States. (By contrast, the theory of comparative advantage, which clashes with common sense, refutes many of the standard trade protectionist arguments.)

—Although empirical tests have frequently not substantiated Hecksher-Ohlin, and current work on the trade-wages income-distribution connection in the United States yields divergent results, there are credible studies (including some in this book) that attribute a significant share (10 to 25 percent) of the recent growth in U.S. income inequality to the impact of international trade.[36]

35. One very useful summary and critique is Richardson (1995).
36. The question that economists (but not myself) are testing is whether a cause-effect relationship between trade and depressed wages that is theoretically predicted, and undeniably present in particular locations and sectors, is in fact consistent with what would be found looking at the U.S. economy as a whole, and using models that control for other variables.

Taking these four considerations together, there is the basis for a credible argument that trade is depressing U.S. wages, particularly for those with limited skills, and that further trade liberalization (particularly with populous countries like China and India) could depress them even more. Such an argument could, over time, attain an intellectual respectability that standard antitrade arguments have long lacked.

Income distribution has receded lately as a salient issue in American politics. The embattled middle class currently directs its ire not at the rich, but at the undeserving poor. But the economic squeeze facing the middle class is, by general agreement, one of the two main forces driving the current extraordinary level of discontent in the body politic of the United States today.[37] Many Americans think that something is deeply wrong— they are working harder and sliding backwards, and the promise of America is somehow not being fulfilled for themselves and their children. Such an environment fuels a search for causes or for something or someone to blame. Trade is now a candidate cause and a plausible villain.

The odds remain against this view becoming the dominant one, of course. Even if it were to become so, it is another substantial leap to the argument that trade protection offers a feasible and desirable cure. But support for *further trade liberalization* could erode seriously. Some Democrats, long torn between conscience and constituency on trade, might find themselves becoming protectionist out of conviction. The free-trade side would lose some of the intellectual and moral high ground. The long-standing consensus among the elite for free trade would weaken. The trade policy debate would grow ideologically polarized, like the current debate over taxes. This could make trade policy hostage to changes in party control of Washington, as it has not been since the 1930s.

It is not hard to spin out a disturbing scenario from the events and trends this chapter has treated. The nation gives up on efforts at positive adjustment, on programs to address the disruptive effects of economic change. Organized labor is still angry about trade and capable of mobilizing whenever an issue catches fire. U.S. income inequality deepens, and trade is plausibly established as one important cause. Negotiations on labor standards prove impractical, blocked by a combination of business opposition at home and resistance from trading partners abroad. This deepens the broad, popular sense that trade pits our workers "unfairly" against those of not just Mexico, but all of East Asia as well. The nongrowth of median incomes continues.

37. The other is rise of conflict across a range of behavioral and ethnic issues, summarized in the phrase "culture wars."

The increasingly volatile U.S. electorate swings over to a sharp focus on what is keeping the American worker down. The reader is invited to write the rest.

Four Possible Policy Responses

How should U.S. trade policy respond? There are at least four broad courses Americans could follow.

1. *Continue to negotiate trade liberalization, and leave adjustment to the market.* This would be close to recent U.S. policy, except that current token efforts to help trade-displaced workers would be abandoned. The fate of workers would be left entirely to the private market. Such an approach would be consistent with the strong, recent antigovernment trend in American politics, though not with the populist trend. Its substantive rationale would be that, over the long term, the welfare of Americans would best be served by economic growth and dynamism, which a laissez faire approach could best provide. Its political rationale would be that international interdependence was creating strong stakes in trade throughout the nation (particularly in the business community) and that these would suffice to win the inevitable trade-political battles as they had on NAFTA and the Uruguay Round.

2. *Continue to negotiate trade liberalization, but also pursue a comprehensive adjustment policy.* This would be a return to the aspirations of the early 1960s, the promise that won labor support for the Kennedy Round. Programmatically, it would call forth a broad effort to develop effective services for trade-displaced workers, upgrading their skills and connecting them to new work opportunities. This might be part of a broader economy-wide effort for those hurt by economic change, one including measures to make the U.S. economy more flexible and hence better able to absorb trade's losses and seize its gains. Its substantive rationale would be that a society that gains from trade has an obligation to use some of those gains to help those hurt by the process; government could develop practical, non-protectionist ways of making this principle work. Its political rationale would be to broaden liberal trade's political base, to reverse the tendency toward polarization on trade issues by offering something to those who lose out.

3. *Maintain current levels of trade liberalization, but stop seeking more.* Substantively, this would be based on a judgment that reversal of recent liberalization would be difficult and costly, but that removal of remaining

U.S. barriers would bring only limited further gains to the overall economy while exacerbating the negative impact of trade on wages and workers. Politically, it would reflect a view that bipartisan consensus in support of trade liberalization had eroded and would be difficult to restore, but also that the breadth of economic interests benefiting from existing international interdependence would act to prevent serious backsliding toward protection. This course could be pursued for a limited time, for a "cooling off" period, or on a more sustained basis.

4. *Reverse U.S. trade policy, moving toward selective or comprehensive protection.* Substantively, this would reflect a conclusion that the distributional impact of current levels of trade was unacceptable to us as a society and that at least *some* increases in trade protection could ameliorate the situation. Politically, it would represent a victory for anti-internationalist populism and much of the organized labor movement.

I did not aim in this chapter to provide a serious prescription, so my analysis will stop here, with the laying out of alternative courses as they appeared at the close of 1995. But the reader of this or of my previous work will not be surprised to learn that my personal preference is for option two. It would maintain the substantial economic (and global political) gains to the nation from international openness, while addressing serious problems of dislocation within American society. I would favor such a course even if studies were to refute any connection between trade and societywide income maldistribution. But the case becomes stronger to the degree that such a connection exists, or is believed to exist, in the economic life of the United States.

Comment by Jules Katz

It is a part of trade policy lore that organized labor was a supporter of trade liberalization after World War II and only began to turn against trade in the 1960s. Mac Destler reflects this view. He notes that organized labor supported the Trade Expansion Act of 1962. But a decade later, the AFL-CIO was a prime backer of the Burke-Hartke quota bill, which was the moral equivalent of Smoot-Hawley. What happened to cause this change?

For one thing, the change, I believe, was less dramatic than is currently recalled and that Destler suggests.

The traditional view of the older craft unions, which represented the American Federation of Labor part of the AFL-CIO, was much less supportive of a liberal trade policy than the industrial unions of the CIO. Destler does note that the textile unions were early protectionists. In fact, they were not early protectionists; they were *always* protectionists.

It is not just the textile unions, but also the Amalgamated Clothing Workers and the International Ladies Garment Workers Union. Indeed, they also fought the shift of production from New England to the South.

Support of organized labor for the 1962 act came at a price. To buy or build support, President Kennedy agreed at the same time to protect such industries as carpets and glass, lumber, oil, and, of course, textiles and apparel.

Those unions that had supported liberal trade began to fall off the wagon in the latter half of the 1960s as U.S. market shares for manufactures began to decline, both in terms of export markets and particularly in terms of the growth of imports. The principal reasons were, of course, the increasing globalization of production and declining U.S. competitiveness. Steel is an outstanding example of both the change in competitiveness and a change in support for trade.

By the late 1970s, about the only trade unions supporting trade liberalization were the longshoremen and the dockworkers.

My second comment deals with trade adjustment assistance, and I will not repeat some of the points that have been made. Destler notes that labor's attitude was not always consistent. Sometimes they sought TAA, but later it was characterized by George Meany as burial assistance.

I may be doing the AFL-CIO an injustice, but I do not recall that they were in the forefront of supporting the adjustment provisions of TAA, as opposed to the supplement to UI.

The issue that has been discussed here—whether to combine TAA with a broader economic program—is an old one and indeed has become a perennial issue. The first effort to combine the programs, I recall, was at the beginning of the second Johnson administration in 1964. I recall the opposition at the time of Stanley Ruttenberg, who was the assistant secretary for international labor affairs and a former AFL-CIO official. He argued that TAA was a cheap price to pay for a liberal trade policy. His viewpoint won the day.

In the 1980s, the broader economic adjustment program, known as the Economic Dislocation and Worker Adjustment Act (EDWAA), began to grow as TAA declined. Labor, for reasons that I am not clear on, was not happy about EDWAA as an alternative to TAA. The Bush administration strongly supported EDWAA over TAA, because it operated through block grants, stressed the link between training and job placement, and was showing results.

As part of the NAFTA package, the Bush administration proposed a substantial rise in EDWAA funding, but the administration ran out of time and the proposal was not legislated.

The Clinton administration offered a stopgap program of $90 million in connection with a NAFTA-TAA program, and I understand this may be extended for another year. But they have yet to present recommendations on a longer-term adjustment program. It may well be wrestling with the same issue of TAA versus a general adjustment program.

My next comment is directed toward the observation that, despite organized labor's efforts in opposition to trade liberalization, it has virtually nothing to show for it.

Organized labor, of course, has had an impact in the adoption of import restraints on a sectoral basis, such as those on textiles and apparel and the less permanent restraints on steel, autos, shoes, and a number of other smaller sectors. Organized labor can also claim some credit for the increasingly restrictive character of the Anti-Dumping Act, but, of course, these efforts were combined with those of management and industry.

The fact remains that, despite these small successes, organized labor has failed in its larger goal of holding back the tide of trade liberalization.

Why have they been ineffective? When you look at the power organized labor has had in Congress, especially in the past, one might have expected another result. The obvious answer is that, although they could count on strong core support from many members of Congress, particularly among Democrats, they lacked majority support. They could pass a bill through the House but not the Senate. Or, on some occasions, it was the other way around. They could get a bill through the Senate but not through the House. Sometimes they even got legislation passed through both houses and to the president's desk, but they could not get the signature of the president. Textile quota legislation, I believe, got to the president's desk three times but was vetoed each time. Despite the power of both the industry and organized labor, they could not muster the votes to sustain a veto.

Obviously, organized labor's political strength is somewhat less than what appears on the surface. Tom Foley, the former Speaker of the House, said with regard to NAFTA that on a secret ballot, NAFTA would have passed by a two-to-one margin.

Reflection on NAFTA and Uruguay Round votes may be instructive. There were enough votes to pass NAFTA, despite a determined campaign by organized labor, joined by that strange alliance of Ross Perot, Ralph Nader, and Pat Buchanan. The GATT vote was overwhelmingly favorable —again, despite the vigorous opposition of two of the three I think Perot had not wholly recovered from his encounter with the vice president.

Organized labor's opposition was somewhat more muted, but they were clearly against the GATT agreement. Why the GATT agreement fared so much better will be a matter for debate, but one possible explanation is that organized labor's threat to punish those who supported NAFTA proved to be an empty threat.

The salient fact is that organized labor could not control the outcome of these efforts any more than it could the other major decisions over the past several decades.

It is unfortunate that organized labor's energies and treasure have been wasted in an effort to arrest or, worse, to reverse what I think is an inexorable tide toward globalism, which is driving the move toward free and freer trade.

I do not have much to add to what Destler has said about the fair labor issue, except to highlight that the Clinton administration's pursuit of this matter has failed to achieve its apparent purpose, which is to obtain organized labor's support for NAFTA and for free trade generally. Instead, they seem to have irritated just about everybody. Organized labor was unhappy that that NAFTA side agreements didn't go far enough. They lacked the kind of enforcement provisions that organized labor demanded.

And, even then–Majority Leader Gephardt, who had pledged his support if Ambassador Kantor would get one more concession (namely an agreement to raise minimum prices in Mexico) reneged, even though Kantor got that concession.

On the other side, the effort to impose labor standards as a condition of trade agreements angered the business community and Republican members of Congress.

I think the most accurate summation on this matter was contained in draft language for the Statement of Administration Action to accompany the 1994 trade legislation. With respect to the proposed fast-track provisions, it said that there was no domestic or international consensus in support of the inclusion of labor standards in trade agreements. I think that says a lot.

Ironically, this issue of labor (and environmental) standards may represent the greatest threat to further trade liberalization in the near term. It blocked the extension of fast-track provisions in the last Congress, and we could see a further impasse if the Clinton administration adheres to its position of linking standards to trade sanctions. Republicans seem to be determined not only to not agree but also to absolutely prohibit the inclusion of labor standards and trade agreements.

Finally, Destler invites us to write the conclusion to his horror scenario, where all bad things happened and there is a new protectionist wave. I have never been good at predicting the future, but I believe the scenario he poses is improbable.

Despite the efforts to promote protectionism over the last several years, there has been much less of a groundswell of public support for protectionism. Even with the Uruguay Round scheduled after the election and much campaigning against the WTO, trade was not an issue in the campaign.

This may be another reason why, after the election, Congress voted overwhelmingly to support the WTO and the Uruguay Round agreement.

I do not share the pessimism over protectionism. We could face short-term setbacks. I have been encouraged by two noteworthy occurrences late in 1994. One was a remarkable statement by Senator Barbara Mikulski of Maryland, who said, in announcing her vote on the Uruguay Round, "All of my public life, I have been associated with planning to save jobs, and to save communities. Ordinarily, I am associated with the protectionist wing of the Democratic Party." Continuing, she said, "So there are those who might [ask] 'Why is Barbara Mikulski going to go GATT?' I am going to go GATT because I am absolutely convinced that the old ways are not working, that the world is changing, and that a new economy is about to be born. I don't want my own state of Maryland, or the United States of America, left behind. And I truly believe that the only way the United States will be able to continue as a world economic power is to go GATT."[38]

The second event was a story in the *Washington Post*. I think I heard a reference to the study earlier in this conference, but the story in the *Post* reported that a study was performed for the AFL-CIO.[39] The study found that an overwhelming majority of those polled preferred cooperative, labor-management committees over unions in their workplaces. Unions were not considered solutions to the problems facing workers in a rapidly changing world.

I confess that I am a confirmed optimist. I am therefore hopeful that organized labor will reassess the futility of its confrontational policies in opposition to trade liberalization and join in a cooperative effort to find constructive solutions to the legitimate concerns of workers.

Comment by Sharyn O'Halloran

This book explores the impact of recent U.S. trade policy on real wages, worker displacement, and the changing nature of the production process.

38. Barbara Mikulski, press conference. December 5, 1995.
39. Frank Swoboda, "Study: Unions Viewed as Obsolete." *Washington Post,* December 6, 1994, p. C3.

The central question addressed is whether or not trade expansion has contributed to the declining standard of living of the American worker. Regardless of whether trade is the culprit in this whodunit, it is certainly seen as a primary suspect. This comment investigates the mystery of the growing income disparity between skilled and unskilled workers from a different angle—the political economy of labor and trade—and asks why labor has been politically excluded from the benefits of trade expansion. Stated simply, if trade makes the pie bigger, why has labor not been able to secure a larger slice?

Toward this end, Mac Destler's chapter offers an excellent summary of organized labor's performance in the political arena over the last quarter-century. Destler argues that TAA originally provided the cement for a broad-based, free-trade coalition. Liberal Democrats who wanted to support free trade but needed something to offer their labor constituents had a way out. Republicans could promote the program as a way to expand free trade and at the same time make the economy more efficient by facilitating worker adjustment. TAA also supplied a nonprotectionist option for presidents reluctant to do nothing at all for trade-displaced workers. By diluting discontent among union members, TAA softened organized labor's demands for protection. Thus, TAA facilitated liberal trade by compensating those adversely affected by import competition.

By the mid-1970s, however, this coalition of labor and free traders began to unravel. On the one hand, labor took an increasingly activist antitrade stance as foreign competition increased, especially among members of the large industrial unions, such as in the steel and auto industries. On the other hand, successive administrations failed to develop effective policies for compensating the casualties of trade expansion. Destler cites evidence that the U.S. DOL never fully implemented the retraining side of TAA, whereas the Reagan administration cut back the level of direct TAA benefits to that of ordinary UI. Destler explores the results of this broken pact on the lackluster history of trade adjustment policies and characterizes labor's struggle against trade liberalization as more or less futile. He catalogs a number of instances in which labor's efforts to roll back the rising tide of imports merely led to their being excluded from the policymaking process entirely and failing to secure benefits for their constituents.

Destler's chapter concludes that the situation appears rather bleak for labor, as union leaders have lost battle after battle in the political trade wars. This is obviously a significant step down from the time when labor was quite influential in setting the trade agenda. Why has labor's influence fallen so precipitously? Is the answer a lack of political adroitness on the part of labor leaders, as Destler implies, or are there more structural issues at hand?

I argue that to understand labor's decline, one must begin with the basics of interest-group lobbying on issues where Congress delegates authority to the executive branch. In these issue areas, interest groups in general and labor unions in particular can influence the political process through two avenues: the legislative channel and/or the executive channel. In the legislative channel, groups pressure legislators for either specific benefits, such as sugar quotas, or to change the rules of the game—that is, the terms of delegation. But in the executive channel, emphasis is placed on influencing the president's trade agenda by building broad-based coalitions in support of labor issues.

Formerly, labor leaders could successfully use the legislative route alone, as organized labor wielded sufficient clout to block the implementation of unfavorable trade agreements. Organized labor's presence as part of a potential blocking coalition thus assured them a fair share of any newly generated benefits, or at least protection from any possible harm. But with labor's decline in numbers and influence, their ability to derail proposed legislation has declined as well, to the point where NAFTA passed despite vociferous union opposition. Organized labor has nonetheless chosen to continue working exclusively through the legislative channel, resisting opportunities to join in trade liberalizing coalitions at the executive level. The end result has been executive-negotiated trade agreements that do not fully address labor concerns, followed by organized labor's subsequent inability to block the enactment of these agreements in Congress. Because organized labor has lost political power and has rejected a strategy of compromise and coalition building, it has found itself excluded from much of the benefits of trade expansion.

A look at the history of labor and trade issues shows that at one time, organized labor was fairly successful in pursuing its trade policy goals, working mainly through the legislative track. The 1955 Reciprocal Trade Agreements Act extension, for instance, included a provision by which industries "vital to national security" could apply for exemption from tariff reductions. This clause was later invoked to protect the oil and coal industries, both strong Democratic constituencies. When the Johnson administration introduced a bill to repeal the American Selling Price (ASP) in 1967, Congress tacked on numerous protectionist import quotas, partly in response to Johnson's request for the repeal of ASP and partly in response to the tariff reductions enacted by the signing of the Kennedy Round agreement. These quotas included a range of items such as steel, oil, textiles, meat, dairy products, mink skins, strawberries, and baseball gloves. Johnson, in return, threatened to veto any quota bill passed by Congress. In the end, no quotas were enacted, and the ASP provision remained intact. In this way labor leaders could block policy initiatives they opposed and win protection for certain major industries threatened by import competition.

Recent legislative successes, however, have been fewer and farther between. In addition to labor's much-noted defeats on major trade agreements as discussed by Destler, a number of key industrial sectors have lost a good deal of their former clout. In 1989 the steel industry lobbied Congress to renew the voluntary restraint agreement on steel, which had expired. Union officials argued that steel manufacturers, battered by heavily subsidized competition from abroad, needed another five years of quotas to complete modernization. Although in the end Congress extended the president's authority to limit steel imports to 18.4 percent of the domestic market, the transition period was only for another 2½ years.[40]

Textile workers have fared even worse. In 1990 textile interests failed to enact legislation that would restrict imports (in the face of the third presidential veto in five years), falling ten votes short of an override in the House. In the 1993 NAFTA, despite strong textile opposition, all restrictions on textile trade were to be eliminated within ten years. And finally, GATT required that the Multi-Fiber Agreement (MFA) be phased out over ten years, although the textile industry did manage to obtain tariff reductions on textile and apparel imports significantly less than those required for other industrial goods.[41]

Why have we seen this decline in organized labor's influence over trade policy, and how does it relate to the two tracks of lobbying discussed here? Labor's lack of success can be traced to their use of a *Congress-only* strategy in an area now dominated by delegation of authority to the executive branch. Combined with organized labor's overall decline in membership, this has led to the recent string of unfavorable results. Although organized labor still has a good deal of influence over individual legislators, this influence is insufficient to swing major policy votes in their direction. Furthermore, organized labor's refusal at key moments to bargain with

40. *Congressional Quarterly Almanac* (1989, p. 144).
41. On the whole, U.S. textile and clothing tariffs were to be cut by about 12 percent, whereas tariffs on all other industrial goods were lowered by about 34 percent. See *Congressional Quarterly Almanac* (1993, p. 183).

executive-branch actors has resulted in major trade agreements that pay scant attention to labor concerns.

For the congressional side of the equation, consider legislative voting on three major trade issues in the 103d Congress: the 1993 extension of fast-track authority, NAFTA, and GATT. Organized labor opposed all three of these measures and lobbied hard against them, especially the 1993 extension and NAFTA. If labor has been completely ineffective in pursuing its legislative strategy, then neither labor campaign contributions nor the percentage of blue-collar workers in legislators' districts should have a significant impact on their voting decisions. More concretely, constituency and lobbying effects would not sway the decisions of many legislators when voting on these bills.

I empirically examine these hypotheses using probit analysis. Specifically, I estimate representatives' voting decisions on each bill as functions of the percentage of blue-collar workers in the member's district, and labor's campaign contributions as a share of total contributions. I do this while holding constant other variables, such as party, whether a member was on the Ways and Means Committee, and (for the GATT vote) if the member would be returning to office the following session.

What impact did labor have on voting decisions, and what would labor had to have done to defeat the bills? Answers to these questions are provided in the top two sections of table 9-1, which estimate the effect of changing the percentage of blue-collar and labor contributions on the probability that a member would have supported the three trade bills.[42] For instance, a 1 percent increase in blue-collar workers within a member's district would decrease the probability of that member voting for the 1993 fast-track extension by 1.35 percent.[43]

To translate these results into actual voting decisions, the table also shows that an across-the-board, 10 percent decrease in percentage of blue-collar and labor contributions would have lost an additional 44 votes for the

---

42. The probit estimates used in the analysis are:

93EXT = 1.80 − 4.04(BLUE COLLAR) + 0.47(PARTY) − 3.15(MONEY) + 0.32(WAYS & MEANS)

NAFTA = 0.75 − 1.01(BLUE COLLAR) + 0.21(PARTY) − 5.01(MONEY) + 0.40(WAYS & MEANS)

GATT = 1.32 − 2.39(BLUE COLLAR) − 0.25(PARTY) − 2.85(MONEY) + 0.70(WAYS & MEANS) + 0.61(LAME DUCK).

43. Apart from the impact of blue-collar workers on the NAFTA vote, these differences are all significantly different from zero at the 5 percent level.

Table 9-1. *Estimated Effects of Blue-Collar and Labor Money on the Probability of Voting for the 1993 Fast Track Extension, NAFTA, and GATT*
Percent, unless otherwise specified

	1993 extension	NAFTA	GATT
Blue collar			
Pr (yes) at mean	73.24	53.66	67.90
Pr (yes) at mean + 1 percent	71.89	53.25	67.04
Difference	−1.35	−0.04	−0.86
Labor			
Pr (yes) at mean	73.24	53.66	67.90
Pr (yes) at mean + 1 percent	72.20	51.66	66.87
Difference	−1.05	−1.99	−1.03
Number of votes lost by a 10 percent decrease in blue-collar and labor money	44	21	15
Additional blue collar needed per district to defeat bill	15.35	9.08	19.45

Data sources for table 9-1 and probit estimates provided in footnote 39:

1993 Extension—Vote on the 1993 Fast Track Extension, *1993 Congressional Quarterly Almanac* (Washington, D.C.: Congressional Quarterly);

NAFTA—Vote on final passage of NAFTA implementing legislation, *1993 Congressional Quarterly Almanac* (Washington, D.C.: Congressional Quarterly);

GATT—Vote on final passage of GATT implementing legislation, *1994 Congressional Quarterly Almanac* (Washington, D.C.: Congressional Quarterly);

Party—Coded 0 for Democrats and 1 for Republicans, Michael Barone and Grant Ujifusa, *1994 Almanac of American Politics* (Washington D.C.: National Journal);

Lame Duck—Coded 1 for those members who lost in the 1994 elections, 0 for others, Michael Barone and Grant Ujifusa, *1994 and 1996 Almanacs of Ameriican Politics* (Washington D.C.: National Journal);

Ways and Means—Coded 1 for members on the Ways and Means Committee, 0 for others, Michael Barone and Grant Ujifusa, *1994 Almanac of American Politics* (Washington D.C.: National Journal);

Blue Collar—Percent of district population employed in blue collar jobs, *1990 Census of Population and Housing: Population and Housing Characteristics of the 103[d] Congress;*

Labor Money—Contributions from labor-affiliated PACs in the 1992 election as a percent of total campaign receipts. Data provided by Janet M. Box-Steffensmeier, Laura W. Arnold, and Christopher J. W. Zorn, from "Strategic Position-Taking and the Timing of Voting Decisions in Congress: The Case of The North American Free Trade Agreement." Manuscript, Ohio State University, 1995.

1993 extension, 21 votes for NAFTA, and fifteen votes for GATT. In fact, for labor to have garnered the 218 votes necessary to defeat these measures would have required an additional blue-collar population ranging from 9.08 percent per district to defeat NAFTA, to an extra 19.4 percent per district to defeat GATT.[44]

44. These simulations were conducted using Excel's Goal Seek procedure. The percent of blue-collar workers was permitted to vary until the average expected vote was against the measure, holding all other variables at their predicted values.

These results suggest that organized labor *did* have a significant impact on legislators' voting decisions, both through campaign contributions and membership pressure. Yet this influence was insufficient to sway final outcomes toward the position held by labor leaders; all three bills passed despite labor's opposition. This statistical analysis provides a concrete assessment of the structural political difficulties organized labor faces in an increasingly service-oriented economy.

Given this record of mixed success in Congress, how has labor fared in the executive arena? Here I argue that decisionmaking procedures (like fast track) have enfranchised labor into the policymaking process.[45] But in the crucial moments when labor could have chosen to play the type of coalitional politics that characterize executive branch bargaining, they refused, preferring instead to retain a stance of implacable opposition to trade liberalization. It is clear that this strategy has not worked to organized labor's advantage, serving only to exclude it from the benefits of expanded trade.

Consider, for instance, Destler's recounting of the events directly following the passage of NAFTA. Concerned about labor's bitterness after the NAFTA fight, President Clinton and USTR Mickey Kantor reached out to labor leaders for input as the final touches were put on GATT, both in the rules for the newly formed WTO and in the domestic GATT implementation legislation. However, neither initiative met with success. In the WTO negotiations, attempts to appease labor were opposed strongly by third-world nations, and domestic labor concessions were voted down in the Senate. In the end, the Clinton administration had to retreat on both fronts, accepting weaker language that gave labor no guaranteed influence. Even on those occasions where the executive branch actively reached out to labor to try and form a coalition, the political realities of the situation therefore meant that appeasing labor would lose more support than it would gain.

What lessons can be drawn from this analysis? It is fair to say that although organized labor still has an impact on legislators' voting decisions, it simply no longer has the political resources (that is, money and votes) it once did, and it therefore can no longer block unfavorable trade legislation. Organized labor has proved to be unwilling or unable to build national

---

Similar results were obtained in determining the percentage of blue-collar workers that would have been necessary to achieve the 218 votes necessary to defeat the bills.

45. For an overview of fast-track procedures and their effect on policy outcomes, see O'Halloran (1994).

coalitions at the executive level to put labor issues on the trade agenda. This is partly because organized labor has been reluctant to compromise, but it has also been partly due to the political fact that catering to labor demands now means losing support elsewhere.

Having stated this, where is the room for mutual gains? What issues can serve both labor interests and a coalition in support of trade liberalization? Destler argues for a program of trade promotion combined with comprehensive adjustment assistance. He therefore proposes a return to the old-time coalition between labor and business in expansion of markets, while assuring that those injured will have the opportunity to get assistance. Unfortunately, Destler provides us with no concrete vision of how such a policy is to be implemented given current political realities.

There is a general sense that workers displaced by international trade are in some ways distinct from other workers who lose their jobs. The Randall Commission established in 1953 by President Eisenhower recognized the uniqueness of workers facing unemployment due to international trade. Unlike workers who are laid off because of a cyclical decline in business or because of an individual firm's lack of profitability, workers displaced by international trade represent a structural change in the economy. These are firms and industries that can no longer compete with foreign competition, and their workers need special assistance in retraining and job placement.

There is no doubt that unemployment assistance has been made available to trade-displaced workers. Nor is there any doubt that retraining has proven relatively ineffective. Although the causes are unclear—poor implementation, reluctance by workers, or lack of knowledge of available programs—the question is simply, what can be done?

To begin with, TAA is currently administered entirely by the U.S. DOL, which has little experience in the field of retraining. A more natural administrative structure is to split the TAA Program into two parts: a supplement to UI, as traditionally addressed by the U.S. DOL; and continuing education and vocational training programs implemented by the U.S. Department of Education.

What are the advantages of these structural changes? They allow each department to use its relative expertise. They also will provide the broad-based, bipartisan support that has been at the heart of postwar trade liberalization, which will be needed for the future expansion of trade. And finally, they will help ensure that U.S. businesses will have a labor force skilled and productive enough to take advantage of the opportunities that expanded trade affords.

Trade expansion and worker retraining necessarily go hand in hand. Whether one believes in any of the other possible effects of trade on lower wages, trade diversion, reduced health and safety standards, and the growing income gap between skilled and unskilled labor, the trade pie will only continue to grow if an increasingly productive work force gets its share of the rewards.

General Discussion

A number of participants expressed concern that the analysis both understated the extent of growing suspicion that trade adversely affects U.S. workers and took an overly narrow view of the ways in which this could influence trade policy. Michael Piore referred to personal conversations with a labor leader who described the "groundswell" against NAFTA as having been tremendous, forcing labor leaders into taking a more active stance. He also argued that the reason GATT did not become as politically contentious an issue as NAFTA was because of its complexity, not because workers' concerns about trade had dissipated.

J. David Richardson stressed that organized labor—a primary focus of the chapter—may not speak for the relevant worker in the context of how policy gets made. If that worker is taken to be the median wage earner, the critical point is that median wage earners have seen their income decline over the past fifteen years, in striking contrast to previous trends. Recent work in political economy that emphasizes the role of the median voter in determining policy outcomes may suggest significant policy implications from such a shift, with the politics of open trade recast in terms of the politics of elites versus the average worker. Thus, the effectiveness of organized labor may not be the key to determining whether (and if so, how) labor issues will influence trade policy down the road.

Susan Collins noted that the apparently growing uncertainty about job security could reinforce concerns about potentially adverse effects of trade, making this more likely to be an issue for the median voter than it has in the past. She referred to a 1992 paper by Fernandez and Rodrik that shows how uncertainty can lead to the defeat of a trade liberalization that would have been strongly supported ex post facto.

Susan Aaronson emphasized that many different types of workers believe their jobs are at risk from trade, including professionals as well as less-skilled workers. For example, American engineers may see themselves competing with engineers in Asia, many of whom have been trained at U.S. universities. She also noted that public opinion polls show an erosion in support for freer trade. However, Jules Katz expressed skepticism about inferences made from such polls, arguing that trade does not have a "serious audience among the general public" and that public opinion is hostage to the quantity and quality of media attention to trade issues.

Representatives from organized labor took issue with Destler's characterization of the objectives and the effectiveness of unions. Mark Anderson pointed out that the AFL-CIO did indeed achieve some of its key objectives both in the 1984 Trade Act and the Omnibus Trade and Competitiveness Act of 1988. In particular, the 1988 bill did reduce the discretion of the executive branch not to act in the face of trade policy problems through introduction of Super 301 and amendments to Section 301. Both he and Mark Beeman (of the UAW) disagreed with the characterization of organized labor as inflexible, and consistently supporting protection against trade liberalization.

References

Aho, C. Michael, and Thomas O. Bayard. 1984. "Costs and Benefits of Trade Adjustment Assistance." In *The Structure and Evolution of Recent U.S. Trade Policy,* edited by Robert Baldwin and Anne O. Krueger, 153–90. University of Chicago for National Bureau of Economic Research.

Bauer, Raymond A., Ithiel de Sola Pool, and Lewis A. Dexter. 1963. *American Business and Public Policy: The Politics of Foreign Trade.* New York: Atherton.

Charnovitz, Steve. 1986. "Worker Adjustment: The Missing Ingredient in Trade Policy." *California Management Review* 28 (Winter): 156–73.

Congressional Quarterly Almanac, 97th Congress, 2nd Session. 1982. Washington: Congressional Quarterly Press.

Congressional Quarterly Almanac, 101st Congress, 1st Session. 1989. Washington: Congressional Quarterly Press.

Congressional Quarterly Almanac, 103rd Congress, 1st Session. 1993. Washington: Congressional Quarterly Press.

Destler, I. M. 1980. *Making Foreign Economic Policy.* Brookings.

———. 1986a. *American Trade Politics: System Under Stress.* Institute for International Economics and Twentieth Century Fund.

———. 1986b. *Trade Adjustment in the American Political Environment.* Washington: Institute for International Economics.

———. 1991. "U.S. Trade Policymaking in the Eighties." In *Politics and Economics in the Eighties,* edited by Alberto Alesina and Geoffrey Carliner, 251–84. University of Chicago Press for National Bureau of Economic Research.

———. 1995. *American Trade Politics,* 3d ed. Washington: Institute for International Economics and Twentieth Century Fund.

Frank, Charles R., Jr. 1977. *Foreign Trade and Domestic Aid.* Brookings.

Frank, Richard S. 1973. "Trade Report: Administration's Reform Bill Threatened by Dispute over Relations with Russia." *National Journal* 5 (November 24): 1752.

Hufbauer, Gary Clyde, and Howard F. Rosen. 1986. *Trade Policy for Troubled Industries.* (Policy Analyses in International Economics no. 15.) Washington: Institute for International Economics.

Hufbauer, Gary Clyde, and Jeffrey J. Schott. 1993. *NAFTA: An Assessment,* rev. ed. Washington: Institute for International Economics.

Lawrence, Robert Z., and Robert E. Litan. 1986. *Saving Free Trade: A Pragmatic Approach.* Brookings.

O'Halloran, Sharyn. 1994. *Politics, Process and American Trade Policy.* University of Michigan Press.

Richardson, J. David. 1995. "Income Inequality and Trade: How to Think, What to Conclude." *Journal of Economic Perspectives* 9 (Summer): 33–56.

Schwab, Susan C. 1994. *Trade-Offs: Negotiating the Omnibus Trade and Competitiveness Act.* Harvard Business School Press.

Simmons, Beth A. 1994. *Who Adjusts? Domestic Sources of Foreign Economic Policy during the Interwar Years.* Princeton University Press.

U.S. House of Representatives. 1979. *Multilateral Trade Negotiations.* Hearings before the Subcommittee on Trade. Government Printing Office.

———. 1973. *Trade Reform Act of 1973.* Hearings before the House Committee on Ways and Means, 93 Cong. 1 sess. Government Printing Office.

White House. 1991. *Response of the Administration to Issues Raised in Connection with the Negotiation of a North American Free Trade Agreement.* Government Printing Office (May 1).

TEN

International Trade and Job Displacement in U.S. Manufacturing, 1979–1991

Lori G. Kletzer

THE DOMESTIC labor market consequences of expansions of international trade is an area of long-standing national concern. The United States has become an increasingly open economy over the past three decades. Between 1965 and 1993, imports as a share of real gross domestic product (GDP) rose from 5 to 13.2 percent, while the share of exports rose from 4.8 to 11.6 percent.[1] Over the latter half of this period (1979–93), employment in the manufacturing sector (the one most affected by trade) fell by 15 percent. Millions of workers have lost their jobs following plant closures, plant relocations, or large-scale reductions in operations. Many labor market participants and observers have linked the growth of international trade to the decline of manufacturing employment and the stagnation of real wages. As evidenced by

This research was supported by the Brookings Institution and the Social Sciences Division and the Academic Senate Committee on Research of the University of California, Santa Cruz. I am grateful to Jeannine Bailliu for her excellent research assistance, and to Henry S. Farber, Larry Mishel, Robert Bednarzik, Gregory Schoepfle, Susan Collins, Rob Fairlie, and Ken Kletzer for their comments and suggestions.

1. *Economic Report of the President* (February 1994, table B-22, p. 293).

the recent debate about the North American Free Trade Agreement (NAFTA), there is a clear public perception that "trade costs jobs."[2] As nations move on their current course of economic integration, there will be heated discussion about the domestic employment costs. Amidst calls for protection, it is increasingly important to understand the facts about trade and job loss.

In this chapter I examine the relationship between international merchandise trade and job displacement. As commonly defined, job displacement is an involuntary (from the worker's perspective) termination of employment based on the employer's operating decisions, and not on a worker's individual performance. Many job displacements occur through plant closings or the employer going out of business. Although there are now a number of studies on trade and employment (and wages), many motivated by an interest in the effects of trade on currently employed workers, there are virtually no studies of trade and displacement.[3] Most of the literature on trade and employment focuses on industry net employment changes. These net employment changes are a result of changes in the gross flows of new hires, recalls, quits, displacements, temporary layoffs, and retirements (accessions minus separations). My focus here on one of the gross flows, displacement, is motivated by the perspective that the amount of social and private adjustment to freer trade greatly depends on gross employment changes. It is precisely the job loss component of employment change that concerns workers, the general public, and policymakers. Job displacements are arguably the most policy-relevant component of gross separations. For example, the private welfare implications of an employment reduction undertaken through (voluntary) quits together with no replacement hiring are vastly different from the welfare implications of the same percentage employment reduction undertaken through displacements. These costs and concerns play an important role in the domestic political economy of free trade, as evidenced by the strong historical support for transfer programs such as Trade Adjustment Assistance (TAA).

This examination of trade and job displacement joins and complements recent work on trade, wages, and employment. The role of international trade in accounting for declining manufacturing employment (particularly

2. The notion that trade costs jobs has a long history in the labor movement. Organized labor's official position has alternated between strong calls for protection and quiet support for trade liberalization (support eased by the passage of workers adjustment-assistance legislation, including the recent NAFTA Transitional Adjustment Assistance Program). See Mitchell (1976) for a review and analysis of labor issues in international trade.

3. Exceptions are recent. See Haveman (1994); Addison and others (1995).

low-skill employment) and increasing income inequality between high-skill and low-skill workers is still debated. There are two excellent reviews of this extensive and diverse literature: one by Dickens, with a focus on trade and employment, and another by Belman and Lee, with a more general review of trade, wages, employment, and wage inequality.[4] Dickens assessed the literature up to the mid-1980s as reaching a common conclusion that import competition caused only a small fraction of employment losses. Most employment change was judged to result from changes in domestic demand, real wages, and productivity.[5] In their review of more recent studies, Belman and Lee reach a different assessment—that increased import competition negatively affects both employment and wages, with the employment effects several times larger than the wage effects.[6] It may be fair to conclude that the jury is still out with respect to whether trade has a large or small impact on the domestic labor market. However, virtually all studies conclude that increasing internationalization alone cannot explain the large changes in employment and relative wages that have occurred in the U.S. labor market since the late 1970s.

The relationship between international trade and job displacement is examined in two related parts. These two approaches together provide a framework for examining both the incidence and consequences of trade-related job displacement. In the first part of the chapter, I treat measures of trade influence and job displacement as industry characteristics and examine the cross-section and time series evidence for manufacturing industries. This approach basically asks, "Is the incidence of job displacement across industries related to trade?" There is considerable variation across industries in job displacement, and I attempt to control for industry characteristics not related to trade. As a caveat, I note that the analysis is empirical; no formal model of job loss (how firms implement a reduction in desired employment) is presented.

In the second part of my analysis, I turn to individual-level data to consider how the "trade" characteristics of the lost job are related to the consequences of job displacement. To isolate the impact of trade, it is

4. Dickens (1988); Belman and Lee (1996).
5. Grossman (1986, 1987) is widely cited on this point. A number of studies written after Dickens (1988) reach a similar conclusion. See Mann (1988); Krugman and Lawrence (1993); Lawrence and Slaughter (1993); Lawrence (1994). Berman, Bound, and Griliches (1994) conclude that trade plays a small role in increasing the relative employment of skilled workers.
6. See Borjas, Freeman, and Katz (1992); Freeman and Katz (1991); Leamer (1993, 1994); Murphy and Welch (1991); Revenga (1992); Sachs and Shatz (1994); Wood (1994).

important to control for individual characteristics. Import-competing industries such as apparel, textiles, and footwear employ many lesser-skilled,
low-wage, disadvantaged workers, making it important to try to separate
general labor market difficulties from difficulties related to trade. This part
of the analysis considers the question, "Are trade-displaced workers different
from other displaced workers?"[7] Answers to this question will be informative
about the social desirability of trade-displacement-assistance policies.

The empirical analysis is based on industry-level trade data for manufacturing industries over the 1979–91 period. This was a period of increased
trade flows and large swings in the value of the dollar, thus making it an
interesting time to study both trade flows and trade prices. This period was
also characterized by widespread permanent job loss, particularly in
manufacturing. Over the 1980s, knowledge about the consequences of job
displacement was greatly expanded by the availability of the Displaced
Worker Surveys (DWS), biennial supplements to the Current Population
Survey (CPS) first released in 1984. Almost every study of job displacement completed in the last ten years has noted, at least in passing, the likely
role of increased international competition in manufacturing job loss.[8]

Measuring Industry Trade Sensitivity

What is the best indicator of how changes in international trade affect
domestic labor? The trade and employment literature is divided on the
answer to this question, with some studies measuring trade changes and
increasing foreign competition as changes in import prices, and other studies
using changes in import share quantities. There is no unique "best" measure
in the sense that the choice of a proxy for an exogenous shock in the foreign
sector is model specific (more on this point below). Causality aside, there is
also a question in the literature about how to classify industries as "trade
sensitive" or "trade impacted." In this section I take a somewhat agnostic
approach and discuss the various measures available and how the measures
may (or may not) be related to changes in employment and job loss.

7. This part of the study is linked to an established tradition of examining the
worker characteristics of import-competing and exporting industries. Kruse (1988)
asked similar questions using the 1984 Displaced Worker Survey. Other papers
include Aho and Orr (1981); Schoepfle (1982); Bednarzik (1993). See Neumann
(1978); Corson and Nicholson (1981); and Decker and Corson (1995) for studies of
recipients of TAA.
8. There is now a sizable literature on the consequences of job displacement.
This literature is reviewed in Kletzer (1995).

Import penetration ratios (or import shares) provide an intuitively appealing way to categorize industries facing significant foreign competition. More generally, industries with a large (or rising) share of output (or supply) internationally traded are often labelled "trade sensitive" (or import/export sensitive) on the basis of calculated import (and export) penetration ratios. If the flow of imports reduces domestic employment, high-import-penetration-ratio industries are where that result is most likely to be found.[9] Using these measures of trade sensitivity, Freeman and Katz find that a 10 percent increase in imports reduces industry employment by 5 percent and industry wages by up to 0.64 percent.[10]

Causality does not necessarily follow from the intuitive appeal of a quantity-based categorization of industries. From a theoretical perspective, there is no simple causal link between the volume of trade and employment changes, because the rise in import share could indicate a number of foreign or domestic developments. A few examples may be illustrative. Take the case of perfect competition, increasing but different marginal costs of production for both domestic and foreign firms, with substitutability between domestic and foreign goods. Let foreign supply expand, perhaps from technological diffusion (or an export promotion scheme) that lowers foreign costs while domestic costs remain unchanged. This reduces the foreign-good price and imports rise. With constant demand, the rise in imports reduces price, domestic output, and domestic employment. With declining domestic output, import share also rises. How much import share rises depends on the elasticity of domestic supply. As domestic supply becomes more elastic, a given increase in imports produces a bigger reduction in domestic quantity (and presumably employment), and rising import share.

9. An import penetration ratio is calculated by dividing industry imports by the sum of industry output plus imports (the denominator is industry supply). An export penetration ratio is calculated by dividing industry exports by industry output. See Schoepfle (1982) for classifications in 1972–79 and Bednarzik (1993) for the period 1982–87. Davis, Haltiwanger, and Schuh (1994) find high rates of job destruction for plants in industries with very high import penetration ratios in 1972–88. Plants in the top quintile of industries ranked by import penetration ratios had average annual employment reductions of 2.8 percent.

10. Freeman and Katz (1991, table 8-2, p. 245). Borjas, Freeman, and Katz (1992) estimate the factor content (effective labor supply) of imports and exports as a way of estimating how trade affects the wages of U.S. workers. There are a number of studies of the effects of trade on the labor market through estimates of the factor (labor) content of imports. The direct and indirect labor content of trade is calculated by allocating imports and exports to input-output sectors and then using average output/employment ratios to derive employment requirements. See Aho and Orr (1980); U.S. International Trade Commission (1986).

When trade is measured as quantity flows, it is important also to consider (or control for) demand. In the perfectly competitive case, imports may also rise if domestic demand increases. Price moves accordingly, and if foreign supply is more elastic than domestic supply, import share will also rise because the increase in imports will exceed the increase in domestic output. Alternatively, if domestic supply is more elastic than foreign supply, the rise in imports will be accompanied by a decline in import share. Here, the use of quantities reveals an ambiguity. Rising imports and import share are associated with increased domestic employment and presumably less displacement, and rising imports may not be associated with rising import share. These two cases imply that over time, industry import shares will differ as a result of differences in supply elasticities as well as the varying competitiveness of domestic firms relative to foreign firms.

In a standard Heckscher-Ohlin (HO) model, industries face increasing import price competition when import prices fall—hence the appeal of using a price measure to examine whether job loss occurs when imports become more competitive. The link between import price competition and industry employment is fairly straightforward. If the price of an imported (substitutable) good falls, labor's marginal-revenue product falls. This drop in the derived demand for labor reduces employment (on an upward-sloping labor supply curve). Flexible wages dampen the fall in employment. If wages adjust fully to equate labor demand and labor supply (a competitive labor market), employment falls to desired levels through (employee-initiated) quits. How much wages and employment change will depend on supply and demand elasticities, but there will be no displacement. Only if prices fall enough that firms find it more profitable to shut down than to continue to operate will displacements occur (through plant closings).

In a market where wages differ from market clearing, the likely consequences of increasing import competition are a bit more complicated. In unionized labor markets, if current wages exceed opportunity wages, the presence of rents may leave room for wage concessions. These concessions may dampen employment loss.[11] Alternatively, senior union members may prefer to maintain wages (and their jobs), with layoffs reducing the employment of junior workers.[12] In a limited number of cases, unions may even push for higher wages as labor demand falls, with an "endgame" bargaining strategy that tries to get as much for the union as possible before the industry disappears. If wages diverge from market clearing for efficiency

11. Although direct evidence is difficult to find, there is a common belief that workers are limited in their ability to offer wage decreases.

12. Unionized firms most often operate with inverse-seniority layoff rules. These rules are also common in the nonunion sector; see Abraham and Medoff (1984).

wage reasons, firms may be reluctant to impose wage reductions if they anticipate negative productivity consequences.

Studies using import price measures reach conflicting conclusions. Grossman examined nine manufacturing industries over the 1969–79 period and found a significant effect of declining import prices on employment in only one.[13] In a separate study of the steel industry, Grossman concluded that most of the employment reduction in 1976–83 was due to the appreciation of the dollar and not increasing international competition.[14] Revenga shows that for a sample of manufacturing industries in 1977–87, changes in import prices have a sizable effect on employment and a smaller yet significant effect on wages.[15] She concludes that most of the adjustment in an industry to an adverse trade shock occurs through employment. With somewhat inflexible wages (consistent with her finding that the elasticity of industry wages with respect to import prices is smaller than the employment elasticity), these employment reductions must be occurring through involuntary separations (unless industry quits are high).

There are at least two reasons to think that price, conceivably the preferred measure, is not completely informative about the effect of changes in trade policy or foreign supply. The first is that during the study period some industries had quota protection (apparel, footwear, radio, and television). Import price changes will not necessarily reflect these quantity restraints. More important, these quota restraints imply that market share (import share) is likely to be a determinant of foreign and domestic supply.

The second difficulty with price alone is more fundamental. Using a monopolistically competitive dominant/fringe model, Mann shows how market share is likely to be a determinant of both foreign and domestic supply.[16] First, quantity is a key variable in monopolistic competition with heterogeneous outputs.[17] Second, she notes that in a three-factor, Cobb-Douglas production function with no restrictions on returns to scale and with capital fixed in the short run, increasing returns to scale are an important determinant of price. In her empirical analysis, Mann finds that foreign competition (measured as both import prices and import share) plays a small role in determining employment relative to the role played by domestic demand and prices.[18]

13. Grossman (1987).
14. Grossman (1986).
15. Revenga (1992).
16. Mann (1988).
17. See Spence (1976).
18. For footwear (leather and rubber) and radio and TV, Mann does find that competition in both import price and import share is important for employment determination.

Trade, Employment, and Displacement:
An Empirical Relationship

In this section I develop a simple empirical framework for examining the relationship between international trade, changes in employment, and job displacement. The discussion of trade and employment change is similar to Revenga's study.[19] A model of labor turnover is used to relate employment change to displacement.

To simplify the analysis, assume wages adjust to equate labor supply and labor demand. Using first differences, the demand for labor in industry i in year t (N_{it}) can be written

$$dln\ N_{it} = \beta_1 dln\ W_{it} + \beta_2 dln\ X^1_{it} + \beta_3 dln\ X^2_{it} + v_{1it}, \tag{10-1}$$

where W_{it} is the industry wage, X^1_{it} is a vector of trade-related factors (discussed in more detail below) that shift labor demand for industry i in year t, X^2_{it} is a vector of non-trade-related factors, and v_{1it} is the error term. Also in first differences, labor supply can be written as

$$dln\ N_{it} = \alpha_1 dln\ W_{it} + \alpha_2 dln\ H_{it} + v_{2it}, \tag{10-2}$$

where H_{it} is a vector of factors that shift labor supply and v_{2it} is an error term. Labor market clearing implies

$$dln\ N_{it} = \gamma_1 \beta_2 dln\ X^1_{it} + \gamma_2 \alpha_2 dln\ H_{it} + \gamma_3 \beta_3 dln\ X^2_{it} + \varepsilon_{it}, \text{ and} \tag{10-3}$$

$$dln\ W_{it} = \lambda_1 \beta_2 dln\ X^1_{it} + \lambda_2 \alpha_{2d} ln\ H_{it} + \lambda_3 \beta_3 dln\ X^2_{it} + u_{it}. \tag{10-4}$$

Equation 10-3 is a basic reduced-form equation for net changes in employment. This relationship must be modified and narrowed to focus on displacement, which is just one of the gross flow components of net employment change. A simple model of turnover is helpful. Firms implement net employment reductions through the use of displacements and unreplaced attritions. Attritions are separations due to quits, discharges (for cause), retirements, and deaths. Attritions that are not replaced by employers are called unreplaced attritions.[20] For an industry, net employment change in year t can be written as

$$DIS + ATT = -\delta N, \tag{10-5}$$

where DIS is displacements and ATT is unreplaced attritions (Quits + Discharges) minus Accessions.[21] This change in employment can be expressed as a proportion of total employment:

19. Revenga (1992).
20. The term, "unreplaced attritions," appears in Brechling (1978).
21. Accessions are new hires and rehires.

$$DIS/N_{t-1} = \text{Displacement Rate} = -(N_t - N_{t-1})/N_{t-1} - ATT/N_{t-1} \tag{10-6}$$

Relying on the approximation of the rate of change of employment, $(N_t - N_{t-1})/N_{t-1}$, to the change in log employment, $(\ln N_t - \ln N_{t-1})$, for small changes, equation 10-6 is approximately equal to

$$\text{Displacement Rate}_t = - \text{ dln } N_t - ATT \text{ Rate}, \tag{10-7}$$

where ATT Rate $= ATT/N_{t-1}$.

Equations 10-3 and 10-7 can be combined to yield a reduced-form equation for industry displacement:

$$\text{Displacement Rate}_{it} = \gamma_1\beta_2\text{dln } X^1_{it} + \gamma_2\alpha_{2d}\text{ln } H_{it} + \gamma_3\beta_3\text{dln } X^2_{it} \tag{10-8}$$
$$+ \gamma_4ATT \text{ Rate}_t + (\varepsilon_{t} + \eta_t),$$

where η_t captures unobservable factors related to displacement.

A key difficulty with this specification is that it attempts to isolate just one of the endogenous turnover flows that together constitute net employment change. In the context of a turnover model, it is inappropriate to include quits, discharges, and accessions (summed here as ATT Rate) as independent variables in a displacement relationship. Quits are likely to be influenced by conditions within the industry.[22] Reducing (or eliminating) replacement hiring, influencing quits, and implementing displacements are all measures under the firm's control as ways of changing employment levels in response to changes in the international trade environment. Firms and industries are likely to differ in their use of the various components of turnover to implement desired changes in employment.[23]

For the purposes of this chapter, a practical way of recognizing differential turnover by industry is to include industry fixed effects in the displacement rate specification. Separate industry constants will capture industry-specific differences in the rate of displacement that result from industry differences in turnover, and more generally, other interindustry differences in displacement.

The elements of the vector X^1 need be specified. As I discussed in the previous section, there are two alternatives. The first, using relative import prices, yields

22. Brechling (1978) presents a model of turnover with endogenous quits. In that model, quits rise and fall with industry employment growth and the state of the overall economy. In depressed industries, workers are much less likely to quit; therefore, "normal" attrition cannot be counted on to reduce employment.

23. The likely interdependence of the various components of turnover indicate the desirability of a more complete model of turnover in response to changing labor demand. Such a model is beyond the scope of this chapter.

Displacement Rate$_{it}$ = $\delta_1$dln P^m_{it} + γ_i + e^1_{it},   (10-9)

where P^m_{it} is the domestic price (\$) of the import good (relative to the aggregate price level).[24] The elements of X^2 and ATT Rate are subsumed in the industry fixed effect γ_i, δ_1 is a coefficient to be estimated, and e^1_{it} is the error term.

An alternative specification uses import (and export) share. The discussion in the previous section suggests that import share be used along with controls for domestic demand. Studies have shown that changes in domestic sales and the overall level of domestic economic activity have significant effects on industry employment.[25] One option, following Freeman and Katz, is to decompose total sales into its component parts: the domestic market (Domestic = Sales − Exports + Imports); exports; and import share.[26] A first-order approximation gives

dSales = $w_1$dln (domestic) + $w_2$dln exports − w_3d(import share), (10-10)

where w_1 = (sales − exports)/sales, w_2 = exports/sales, and w_3 = domestic/sales. The weights adjust changes in the three components for the difference in the absolute magnitude of sales generated by the domestic side as compared to the trade side.[27] The following equation relates changes in sales to displacement:

Displacement Rate = δ_{2w1}dln (domestic) + δ_{3w2}dln (exports)   (10-11)
$\quad\quad\quad\quad\quad\quad + \delta_{4w3}$d(importshare) + $\Pi_{i + e}2_{it}$,

where the δ's are coefficients to be estimated, Π_i is the industry fixed effect, and e^2_{it} is the error term.[28]

24. The aggregate price level is measured as the aggregate Producer Price Index (PPI).
25. See Mann (1988); Freeman and Katz (1991).
26. Freeman and Katz (1991).
27. This decomposition of sales is explained in detail by Freeman and Katz (1991).
28. Equations 10-9 and 10-11 will be estimated by ordinary least squares (OLS). In Revenga's (1992) estimation of the elasticity of net industry employment change to changes in import prices, she discusses the potential correlation of the import price variable with the components of the disturbance term. Several factors may induce this correlation, such as unmeasured, worldwide shocks to material costs or unobserved and unmeasured taste or demand shifts in the United States that influence import prices due to the size of the U.S. market. With this correlation, OLS parameter estimates will be biased and inconsistent. Revenga uses an instrumental-variables procedure to obtain consistent estimates of the import price elasticity, and she shows that the OLS estimates appear downwardly biased. A similar case could be made here when industry displacement is the dependent variable. Correlations between import price and the error term for displacement may be weaker than in the net employment change model however, because displacement is just one of the components of net employment change.

Data: Measuring International Trade and Job Displacement

The task of constructing a data set with industry trade measures and individual displacement information presents a number of challenges. Data are available on imports, exports, and total shipments starting in 1958 for four-digit Standard Industrial Classification (SIC) manufacturing industries. Coverage into the late 1980s is problematic because of changes in the SIC system in 1987 that changed the scope of many four-digit industries. The new industry definitions changed the allocation of imported and exported goods across industries. Post-1987 trade flow data, using 1987 SIC codes, cannot be compared with early 1980s trade data that used 1972 SIC codes.[29]

Import and export price indices are available for many four-digit SIC manufacturing industries starting in 1983–84, with coverage of some industries available from 1978. The price measure is a fixed-weight Laspeyres index with a 1985 base period. Relative import and export prices are obtained by deflating by the PPI as a proxy for the aggregate price level.

Combining trade measures with displacement information at the industry level requires considerable aggregation. Individual information on job loss is available from the biennial DWSs. In these household surveys, industries are classified according to the Census of Population Industrial Classification (CIC) system, and the most detailed level is three digit. Therefore the SIC-based trade data must be aggregated up to a three-digit CIC level to conform to the industries for which displacement information is available. As a consequence, the industry trade effects studied here may be different from other recent work on trade, wages, and employment where no individual information is used and industries are defined on a more disaggregated basis.

Aggregating the import, export, and shipments data up from the four-digit SIC level yields fifty-eight, three-digit CIC industries, covering the period 1975–85. Aggregation is more "costly" for the price data. Price

29. The appendix to this chapter contains more information on the trade flow data. The National Bureau of Economic Research (NBER) Trade and Immigration data set is the source of the import, export, and total shipments data used to calculate import and export shares and domestic demand. That file contains trade data for the period 1958–85. Import and export data for 1986–87 are available from the Department of Commerce (1987 shipments data are not available). In that data release, the Department of Commerce warns that data are not consistent with earlier department trade releases (which are the source of the NBER files). This means that an NBER-based trade data set cannot be extended with the Department of Commerce data, as the two are inconsistent.

index coverage is not complete for all manufacturing industries, so that not all four-digit SIC industries within a three-digit CIC industry have information available for constructing an aggregate CIC industry price index. I calculated a three-digit CIC index if approximately 40 percent or more of the underlying four-digit industry price indices were available. I adopted this decision rule recognizing that inaccuracies may be introduced by calculating an aggregate index from only a subset of constituent four-digit industries. This rule produced a sample of 24 three-digit CIC industries with an import price index for some part of the period 1978–91, and a total of 213 industry and year observations. More details are available in the appendix to this chapter.

Identifying Displaced Workers

I draw my sample of displaced workers from the DWSs of 1984, 1986, 1988, 1990, and 1992. The DWSs were administered as supplements to the January CPS. In each survey, adults (aged twenty years and older) in the regular, monthly CPS were asked if they had lost a job in the preceding five-year period due to "a plant closing, an employer going out of business, a layoff from which he/she was not recalled, or other similar reasons." If the answer was yes, a series of questions followed concerning the old job and period of joblessness.[30]

A common understanding of displacement is that it occurs without personal prejudice; terminations are related to the operating decisions of the employer and are independent of individual job performance. In the DWSs, this definition can be implemented by drawing the sample of displaced from individuals who respond that their job loss was due to the reasons noted above. Other causes of job loss, such as quits or firings, are not considered displacements.[31] This operational definition is not without ambiguity. The displacements are "job" displacements, in the sense that an individual displaced from a job and rehired into a different job with the same employer is considered displaced.[32]

The job loss measured in the DWSs is permanent. These job losses, though a small fraction of total job loss and of total turnover and employ-

---

30. My sample construction and measures of incidence follow the discussion in Farber (1993). There is a sizable literature of DWS-based studies of the consequences of job displacement. Examples include Podgursky and Swaim (1987); Kletzer (1989); Topel (1990); Gibbons and Katz (1991); Farber (1993).

31. Individuals may also respond that their job loss was due to the end of a seasonal job or the failure of a self-employed business. These individuals are not considered displaced.

32. The survey instrument provides no information that would allow these workers to be removed from the displaced sample.

ment change, may well account for much unemployment and individual suffering.[33] At the same time, some of the distinctions may be too narrow or arbitrary. The distinction between quits and displacements is muddied by the ability of employers to reduce employment by reducing or failing to raise wages. Wage changes may induce some workers to quit (and not be in the sample), whereas others opt to stay with the firm (and are displaced and enter the sample).[34] This distinction means that the displaced worker sample will underestimate the amount of job change "caused" by trade. If the workers who stay on with the firm until displacement are those who face the worst labor market outcomes of all those at risk of displacement, then the displaced sample will be potentially nonrandom and will overstate the costs of job loss. Without data on quits, these questions cannot be answered.[35]

The analysis sample is limited to workers displaced from manufacturing industries who were ages twenty to sixty-four at the time of displacement. Because the information is retrospectively gathered, it has potential recall error. Problems of recall are compounded by the overlapping coverage of years of displacement by surveys, with some years covered in two or three surveys.[36] This bias is believed to be significant.[37] As Topel and Farber show, it is likely that the surveys seriously underestimate job loss that occurred long before the survey date because of inaccuracies in recall as well as question design.[38] This makes it desirable to have nonoverlapping recall periods (that is, each year of displacement drawn from only one survey).

A solution to recall bias that is easy to implement in this context was advanced by Farber.[39] He restricted his sample to displacements occurring

33. Permanent job losers account for a rising share of unemployment; see Medoff (1992).

34. Recent work by Jacobson, LaLonde, and Sullivan (1993) shows that wages fall for displaced workers before they are displaced.

35. I do not distinguish between layoffs without recall and plant closings. See Gibbons and Katz (1991) for a discussion of whether workers displaced by layoff are less able than workers displaced by plant closings (because employers have some discretion over whom to lay off while the plant remains open, and presumably plant closings involve all workers).

36. The 1984 DWS covered the period 1979–83; the 1986 survey, 1981–85; the 1988 survey, 1983–87; the 1990 survey, 1985–89; and the 1992 survey, 1987–91. Displacements that occurred during the survey month (January) were also counted, but it is common to omit these workers.

37. Events far back in the past may be less likely to be remembered. On the other hand, with time, events that result in serious economic and psychological costs may be more likely to be remembered. See Akerlof and Yellen (1985) for a discussion of research on recall bias.

38. If more than one job was lost, information is gathered only for the job held longest. See Topel (1990); Farber (1993).

39. Farber (1993).

in the two-year period preceding each survey. This makes recall periods shorter and eliminates overlapping-year coverage. I follow the spirit of his construction by restricting the analysis sample to displacements occurring in the two-year period in the middle of each survey's time coverage. From the 1984 survey, I drew individuals displaced during 1981–82; from the 1986 survery, 1983–84; from the 1988 survey, 1985–86; from the 1990 survey, 1987–88; and from the 1992 survey, 1989–90. This sampling framework differs somewhat from Farber, whose two years preceding the survey date design drew 1982–83 from the 1984 survey. Interest in the consequences of displacement guided my choice of years drawn. By starting three years before the survey date, I have a sample with "enough" time to become reemployed, at the cost of including workers who reported displacements three years in the past. Because the trade flows data currently end in 1985, I drew a larger sample from the 1984 survey by also including workers displaced during 1979–80. Although recall for these workers may be questionable, I included them to get the displacement data and the trade flows data to overlap as much as possible in years covered. Unless the early displacements are included, the two time series analyses overlap only for 1981–85.

Job Loss and Trade by Industry: A First Look at the Data

To study the link between an industry's trade indicators (import and export share and prices) and industry job loss, I calculated industry displacement rates by dividing the number of workers displaced from a three-digit CIC industry in a year by the number of workers employed in that industry in that year. The annual industry employment numbers were calculated from merged CPS Outgoing Rotation Group data files, and are a proxy for industry workers at risk of displacement.[40] Figure 10-1 plots an annual manufacturing displacement rate for 1979–91. This aggregate displacement rate is the ratio of the number of workers who report a manufacturing displacement in a year divided by the number of individuals employed in manufacturing in the same year. In 1979, 2.7 percent of manufacturing workers were displaced; the rate rose to slightly less than 7 percent in 1982. It then fell steadily down to 2.4 percent in 1988, rising again in the late

40. All cell counts were weighted using the CPS final weights. A proper measure of workers at risk of displacement (the denominator of the displacement rate) requires interviewing workers at two points in time to ascertain jobs held and jobs lost. The DWS only asks displaced workers about the job lost; for non-displaced workers, there is no retrospective information about jobs not lost.

Figure 10-1. *Annual Displacement Rate for Manufacturing, 1979–91*

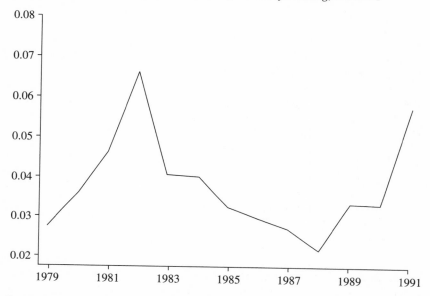

Sources: Current Population Survey; and merged OGRG files.

1980s, to 5.7 percent in 1991. Displacements follow a business cycle pattern, reaching a peak during the 1981–82 recession and then falling continuously throughout the recovery. Displacement rates rose again during the early 1990s recession.

Univariate classifications are a useful way to examine the link between displacement and international trade at the industry level. As a first step, I stay within the tradition of using import and export shares to classify industries as "trade sensitive." Mean import share for the industries in the sample was 8.2 percent in 1975–85, ranging from 0.07 percent to 67.2 percent.[41] If industries with average import penetration ratios of 15 percent or higher in 1975–85 are considered "import sensitive," the table below shows that displacement rates were high for some of these industries in 1979–86 (the mean industry displacement rate was 5.1 percent), although there was considerable variation and some industries had quite low displacement rates.[42]

41. Author's calculations based on data from NBER Trade and Immigration data set (see appendix).
42. Schoepfle (1982) adopted a similar definition of "import sensitive." Bednarzik (1993) uses a 30 percent import penetration ratio cutoff.

Import-sensitive industry (CIC)	Displacement rate
Knitting mills (132)	0.029
Apparel and accessories (151)	0.051
Tires and inner tubes (210)	0.046
Footwear, except rubber/plastic (221)	0.094
Pottery and related products (261)	0.100
Blast furnaces, steelworks (270)	0.078
Other primary metal products (280)	0.039
Metalworking machinery (320)	0.045
Computers (322)	0.027
Radio, TV, and communication equipment (341)	0.031
Electrical machinery (342)	0.045
Motor vehicles (351)	0.044
Cycles and miscellaneous transport (370)	0.047
Scientific instruments (371)	0.026
Toys and sporting goods (390)	0.072
Miscellaneous manufacturing (391)	0.042

As I discussed, one difficulty with this simple import share classification is that it ignores the role of domestic demand. If domestic demand increases and foreign supply increases faster than domestic supply, then import share will rise without a reduction in employment or a rise in displacement. In fact, the industries on this list with low displacements rates and high import share were those with strong domestic demand in 1975–85.

This method of classifying industries as import sensitive cannot address the question of whether *changes* in imports are associated with job loss— that is, does an increase in import share lead to job displacement? Changes in import and export penetration ratios and changes in domestic demand are examined in tables 10-1 to 10-3. These three tables report classifications of industries by changes in import share, export share, and domestic demand, respectively, over the period 1975–85, and for each industry, report an average displacement rate for 1979–86.[43] For each of the three quantity measures, industries were classified by their quantity change quartile, from highest to

43. The analysis sample does not include all three-digit CIC industries. Some industries were excluded due to incomplete time series information on displacement, employment, or trade flows. The displacement numbers may be "noisy." There are a few industry/year observations where the reported number of displaced in a year equals zero. It seems unlikely that the actual number displaced would truly be zero. Recall error and sampling may account for some of this, as well as errors in the recording of industry. Some "smoothing" of the industry displacement series is an attractive alternative, although one would be more confident if there was another source of displacement information to serve as a check.

lowest. For example, table 10-1 reports a categorization of industries by their median import share change quartile (from highest to lowest) and, for each industry, its mean displacement rate. There is substantial variation in changes in import and export share and domestic demand across industries. This classification offers a simple perspective on the question of whether industries facing import share increases had high average displacement rates.

The average displacement rates reported in the last row of table 10-1 do not appear to rise systematically with increasing industry import share. High-displacement-rate industries are somewhat evenly spread across the table by import share. Industries with the highest displacement rates, such as footwear (CIC 221), wood buildings and mobile homes (CIC 232), and railroad locomotives (CIC 361) faced medium to low changes in imports. A number of industries with large positive changes in import share had low displacement rates over the period, including paperboard containers and boxes (CIC 162), aircraft and parts (CIC 352), and photographic equipment (CIC 380).

The strength of the dollar over the latter half of the 1975–85 period is a concern when considering the link between increases in export share and job displacement. The average annual change in export share was 8.6 percent, with a range of 0.04 percent to 60.5 percent. Table 10-2 classifies industries by average changes in export penetration ratios. Given the level of industry aggregation, it is not surprising that some industries have both large positive increases in import share and large positive increases in export share. As in table 10-1, high-displacement-rate industries are somewhat evenly spread across the table by changes in export share. Based on quartile average displacement rates, there is little suggestion that displacement falls as export share increases.

Table 10-3 reports an industry classification based on average annual changes in domestic demand. In this table we see that strong growth in domestic demand was associated with lower rates of displacement over the study period. High-average-displacement-rate industries are clustered in the lowest domestic demand change quartile. These industries include wood buildings and mobile homes (CIC 232), with an average displacement rate of 0.118; iron and steel foundries (CIC 271), 0.069; fabricated structural metal products (CIC 282), 0.061; construction and material handling machines (CIC 312), 0.080; and railroad locomotives and equipment (CIC 361), 0.140.

Figures 10-2 and 10-3 are scatterplots of annual industry displacement rates and percent changes from the previous year, in import penetration ratios (figure 10-2) and in relative import prices (figure 10-3). Each plot contains a regression line for the simple regression of the displacement rate on the chosen trade indicator. Turning first to figure 10-2 for 1979–85, there are

Table 10-1. *CIC Industries Classified by Median Annual Change in Import Penetration Ratio, 1975–85, with Mean Annual Displacement Rate for 1979–86*

Highest import change (≥ 0.115)	High import change (0.078–0.115)	Medium import change (0.040–0.078)	Low import change (< 0.040)
Miscellaneous fabricated textiles (152) 0.044	Canned, frozen fruits and vegetables (102) 0.034	Dairy products (101) 0.046	Meat products (100) 0.041
Miscellaneous paper and pulp products (161) 0.035	Bakery products (111) 0.022	Grain mill products (110) 0.033	Sugar and confectionery (112) 0.063
Paperboard containers and boxes (162) 0.021	Knitting mills (132) 0.029	Yarn, thread, fabric mills (142) 0.046	Beverages (120) 0.014
Newspaper publishing and printing (171) 0.033	Apparel and accessories (151) 0.051	Drugs (181) 0.018	Miscellaneous food preparations (121) 0.036
Plastics and synthetics (180) 0.032	Industrial and miscellaneous chemicals (192) 0.028	Tires and inner tubes (210) 0.046	Carpets and rugs (141) 0.061
Soaps and cosmetics (182) 0.036	Miscellaneous plastics (212) 0.040	Other rubber products (211) 0.037	Pulp, paper, paperboard (160) 0.017
Paints, varnishes, related products (190) 0.042	Leather products, except footwear (222) 0.074	Footwear, except rubber and plastic (221) 0.094	Printing, publishing (172) 0.028
Furniture and fixtures (242) 0.043	Glass and glass products (250) 0.045	Sawmills and millwork (231) 0.051	Petroleum refining (200) 0.030
Cement, concrete, gypsum (251) 0.053	Miscellaneous nonmetallic mineral and stone (262) 0.043	Wood buildings and mobile homes (232) 0.118	Logging (230) 0.044

Industry	Rate	Industry	Rate	Industry	Rate	Industry	Rate
Iron and steel foundries (271)	0.069	Other primary metal (280)	0.039	Miscellaneous wood products (241)	0.041	Screw machine products (290)	0.038
Miscellaneous fabricated metals (300)	0.043	Cutlery, hand tools (281)	0.032	Pottery and related products (261)	0.100	Ordnance (292)	0.043
Construction and material handling machines (312)	0.080	Fabricated structural metal products (282)	0.061	Blast furnaces and steelworks (270)	0.078	Engines and turbines (310)	0.047
Household appliances (340)	0.049	Metal forgings and stampings (291)	0.048	Primary aluminum (272)	0.034	Farm machinery and equipment (311)	0.079
Aircraft and parts (352)	0.019	Metalworking machinery (320)	0.045	Office and accounting machines (321)	0.031	Radio, TV, and communication equipment (341)	0.031
Ship- and boatbuilding (360)	0.053	Computers and related equipment (322)	0.027	Machinery, except electrical (331)	0.050	Railroad locomotives and equipment (361)	0.140
Photographic equipment (380)	0.029	Electrical machinery, equipment (342)	0.045	Motor vehicles and equipment (351)	0.044	Guided missiles and parts (362)	0.033
Miscellaneous manufacturing (391)	0.042	Scientific and controlling instruments (371)	0.026	Cycles and miscellaneous transportation equipment (370)	0.047	Medical, dental, optical instruments (372)	0.033
		Toys and sporting goods (390)	0.072				
Mean displacement rate for import change quartile	0.042		0.042		0.053		0.046

Sources: Author's calculations from sample of industries drawn from the NBER Trade and Immigration data set; and the Displaced Worker Survey.

Table 10-2. *CIC Industries Classified by Median Annual Change in Export Penetration Ratio, 1975–85, with Mean Annual Displacement Rate for 1979–86*

Highest export change (≥ 0.017)	High export change (+0.017 – −0.021)	Medium export change (−0.021 – −0.044)	Low export change (< −0.044)
Meat products (100) 0.041	Dairy products (101) 0.046	Canned, frozen fruits and vegetables (102) 0.036	Knitting mills (132) 0.029
Bakery products (111) 0.022	Grain mill products (110) 0.033	Miscellaneous paper and pulp products (161) 0.035	Carpets and rugs (141) 0.061
Sugar and confectionary (112) 0.063	Beverages (120) 0.014	Printing, publishing (172) 0.028	Yarn, thread, fabric mills (142) 0.046
Paperboard containers and boxes (162) 0.021	Miscellaneous food preparations (121) 0.036	Other rubber products (211) 0.037	Miscellaneous fabricated textiles (152) 0.044
Newspaper publishing (171) 0.033	Apparel and accessories (151) 0.051	Miscellaneous plastics (212) 0.040	Pulp, paper products (160) 0.017
Plastics and synthetics (180) 0.032	Drugs (181) 0.018	Miscellaneous wood products (241) 0.041	Tires and inner tubes (210) 0.046
Soaps and cosmetics (182) 0.036	Paints, varnishes, related products (190) 0.042	Primary aluminum (272) 0.034	Sawmills and millwork (231) 0.051
Industrial and miscellaneous chemicals (192) 0.028	Petroleum refining (200) 0.030	Other primary metal (280) 0.039	Wood buildings and mobile homes (232) 0.118
Footwear, except rubber and plastic (221) 0.094	Logging (230) 0.044	Cutlery, hand tools (281) 0.032	Cement, concrete, gypsum (251) 0.055

Column 1	Column 2	Column 3	Column 4
Leather products, except footwear (222) 0.074	Glass and glass products (250) 0.045	Fabricated structural metal products (282) 0.061	Blast furnaces and steelworks (270) 0.078
Furniture and fixtures (242) 0.043	Misc. nonmetallic mineral and stone (262) 0.043	Engines and turbines (310) 0.047	Iron and steel foundries (271) 0.069
Pottery and related products (261) 0.100	Metal forgings and stampings (291) 0.048	Metalworking machinery (320) 0.045	Screw machine products (290) 0.038
Ship- and boatbuilding (360) 0.053	Farm machinery and equipment (311) 0.079	Machinery, except electrical (331) 0.050	Ordnance (292) 0.043
Railroad locomotives and equipment (361) 0.140	Construction and material handling machines (312) 0.080	Radio, TV, and communication equipment (341) 0.031	Misc. fabricated metals (300) 0.043
Cycles and miscellaneous transportation equipment (370) 0.047	Computers and related equipment (322) 0.027	Motor vehicles and equipment (351) 0.044	Office and accounting machines (321) 0.031
Toys and sporting goods (390) 0.072	Household appliances (340) 0.049	Scientific and controlling instruments (371) 0.026	Aircraft and parts (352) 0.019
	Electrical machinery, equipment (342) 0.045	Medical, dental, optical instruments (372) 0.033	Guided missiles and parts (362) 0.033
0.056	0.043	Mean displacement rate for export change quartile 0.038	0.048

Sources: Author's calculations from sample of industries drawn from the NBER Trade and Immigration data set; and the Displaced Worker Survey.

Table 10-3. *CIC Industries Classified by Median Annual Change in Domestic Demand, 1975–85, with Mean Annual Displacement Rate for 1979–86*

Highest domestic demand change (≥ 0.098)	High domestic demand change (0.086–0.098)	Medium domestic demand change (0.064–0.086)	Low domestic demand change (< 0.064)
Miscellaneous paper and pulp (161) 0.035	Carpets and rugs (141) 0.061	Canned, frozen fruits and vegetables (102) 0.036	Meat products (100) 0.041
Newspaper publishing and printing (171) 0.033	Apparel and accessories (151) 0.051	Bakery products (111) 0.022	Dairy products (101) 0.046
Printing, publishing (172) 0.028	Miscellaneous fabricated textiles (152) 0.044	Beverages (120) 0.014	Grain mill products (110) 0.033
Plastics and synthetics (180) 0.032	Pulp, paper, paperboard (160) 0.017	Yarn, thread, fabric mills (142) 0.046	Sugar and confectionary (112) 0.063
Drugs (181) 0.018	Paperboard containers and boxes (162) 0.021	Soaps and cosmetics (182) 0.036	Miscellaneous food preparations (121) 0.036
Miscellaneous plastics (212) 0.040	Industrial and miscellaneous chemicals (192) 0.028	Paints, varnishes, related products (190) 0.042	Knitting mills (132) 0.029
Pottery and related products (261) 0.100	Footwear, except rubber and plastic (221) 0.094	Tires and inner tubes (210) 0.046	Petroleum refining (200) 0.030
Ordnance (292) 0.043	Logging (230) 0.044	Other rubber products (211) 0.037	Sawmills and millwork (231) 0.051
Computers and related equipment (322) 0.027	Miscellaneous nonmetallic mineral and stone (262) 0.043	Leather products, except footwear (222) 0.074	Wood buildings and mobile homes (232) 0.118
Radio, TV, and communication equipment (341) 0.031	Blast furnaces and steelworks (270) 0.078	Miscellaneous wood products (241) 0.041	Glass and glass products (250) 0.045

Motor vehicles and equipment (351) 0.044	Primary aluminum (272) 0.044	Furniture and fixtures (242) 0.043	Cement, concrete, gypsum (251) 0.053
Aircraft and parts (352) 0.019	Other primary metal (280) 0.039	Screw machinery products (290) 0.038	Iron and steel foundries (271) 0.069
Guided missiles and parts (362) 0.033	Cutlery, hand tools (281) 0.032	Metal forgings and stampings (291) 0.048	Fabricated structural metal (282) 0.061
Scientific and controlling instruments (371) 0.026	Engines and turbines (310) 0.047	Miscellaneous fabricated metals (300) 0.043	Farm machinery and equipment (311) 0.079
Medical, dental, and optical instruments (372) 0.033	Metalworking machinery (320) 0.045	Household appliances (340) 0.049	Construction and material handling machines (312) 0.080
Photographic equipment (380) 0.029	Office and accounting machines (321) 0.031		Railroad locomotives and equipment (361) 0.140
Miscellaneous manufacturing (391) 0.042	Machinery, except electrical (331) 0.050		Cycles and miscellaneous transportation equipment (370) 0.047
	Electrical machinery, equipment (342) 0.045		
	Ship- and boatbuilding (360) 0.053		
	Toys and sporting goods (390) 0.072		

Mean displacement rate for domestic demand change quartile

0.036	0.043	0.041	0.060

Sources: Author's calculations from sample of industries drawn from the NBER Trade and Immigration data set; and the Displaced Worker Survey.

Figure 10-2. *Industry Displacement Rate and Change in Import Share, 1979–85*

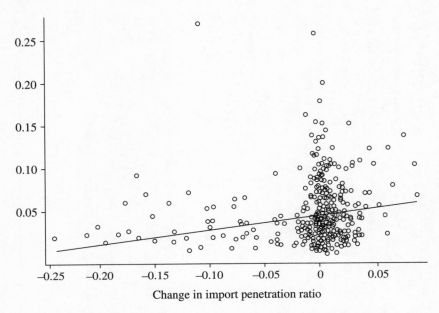

Change in import penetration ratio

Source: Author's calculations from sample drawn from NBER Trade and Immigration dataset and the Displaced Worker Surveys.

Figure 10-3. *Industry Displacement Rate and Change in Relative Import Price, 1981–91*

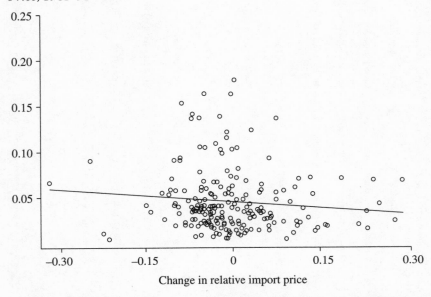

Change in relative import price

Source: Author's calculations from sample drawn from NBER Trade and Immigration dataset and the Displaced Worker Surveys.

a number of industry and year observations where import share changes little and displacement is high. At the same time, there are enough industries where positive (negative) changes in import share are associated with a high (low) displacement rate so that the regression line has a positive slope (with *t*-statistic of 1.761 for the estimated slope coefficient).[44] A few traditionally trade-sensitive industries, such as footwear and apparel, are important in determining the slope of the regression line.

Figure 10-3 presents the plot of industry displacement rate against the percent change in relative import price. The price coverage is far less comprehensive than the trade flow coverage (only twenty-four three-digit CIC industries are included), and the period of coverage is 1981–91. There are a cluster of industry observations where an increase in import prices (a reduction in import competition) is associated with lower displacement rates. The regression line has a negative slope, with a *t*-statistic of –1.520.[45] There are also a number of industry observations with high displacement rates and little change in relative import prices.

Remarks on the Simple Evidence on Trade and Displacement

A few observations stand out from these descriptive figures and tables. Considerable variation in job displacement exists both within and across industries. There are a sizable number of industry observations where displacement is high in the absence of exposure to increasing foreign competition. To this end, controls for industry-specific effects will be used in the next section. Second, the perception that trade displaces domestic jobs has some basis in fact. There are some industries, many identified in the past as import sensitive, where high rates of displacement are found along with increases in import penetration ratios and/or decreases in relative import prices.

Multivariate Analysis of the Cross-Industry Evidence on Trade and Jobs

Table 10-4 reports OLS and weighted least squares (WLS) estimates of a simple specification relating annual industry displacement rates to two

---

44. The estimated regression, with standard errors in parentheses, is:

   Displacement rate = 0.0460 + 0.1722 (% Δ import penetration ratio).
   (0.0017) (0.0978)

45. The estimated regression, with standard errors in parentheses, is:

   Displacement rate = 0.0458 – 0.0418 (% Δ relative import price).
   (0.0023) (0.0275)

Table 10-4. *Industry Displacement Rates, Import Penetration Rates, and Import Price*[a]

	(1)	(2)	(3)	(4)
Estimation technique	OLS	WLS	OLS	WLS
Dependent variable	Displacement rate	Displacement rate	Displacement rate	Displacement rate
Panel A				
Log change relative to import price index	−0.0489 (0.0246)	−0.0489 (0.0206)	−0.0328 (0.0286)	−0.0328 (0.0242)
Log change GDP	−1.8917 (0.6436)	−1.8917 (0.7866)	−1.8226 (0.7492)	−1.8226 (1.2094)
Industry effects	Yes	Yes	No	No
R^2	0.799	0.799	0.027	0.027
N	213	213	213	213
Panel B				
Weighted log change in import share	0.0081 (0.0080)	0.0081 (0.0078)	0.0162 (0.0091)	0.0162 (0.0117)
Weighted log change in exports	−0.1833 (0.0566)	−0.1833 (0.0469)	−0.1965 (0.0608)	−0.1964 (0.0511)
Weighted log change in domestic demand	−0.0708 (0.0174)	−0.0708 (0.0193)	−0.1038 (0.0188)	−0.1038 (0.0241)
Industry effects	Yes	Yes	No	No
R^2	0.789	0.789	0.099	0.099
N	401	401	401	401

Sources: Author's calculations from the NBER Trade and Immigration data set; U.S. Bureau of Labor Statistics U.S. Import and Export Price Indices; and the DWS.

a. Standard errors are shown in parentheses.

industry trade indicators.[46] Panel A reports estimates from a specification using changes in relative import price indices. Industry-specific characteristics, such as differential quits and accessions, and changes in technology that may be related to industry displacement are captured by the industry fixed effects in columns 1 and 2. There is some evidence that as relative import prices fall and imports become more competitive, displacement rises. The coefficient on the log change in relative import price is negative and statistically significant. The sensitivity of displacement rates to the business cycle is captured by the log change in GDP,

46. With a displacement rate as the dependent variable, error terms are potentially heteroscedastic.

with the estimated coefficient showing the countercyclical nature of displacement.[47]

Panel B of table 10-4 reports estimates from a specification of trade flows and domestic demand. Despite the increasing openness of the U.S. economy, the domestic market still represents the vast majority of demand for almost all industries.[48] Import and export share and domestic demand changes are weighted, using 1985 values, to adjust for the difference in the magnitude of sales generated domestically. Displacement rates are lower with increases in export share and domestic demand. Increases in import share are positively correlated with industry displacement rate although the coefficient is imprecisely estimated (P value = 0.305 in the column 2 estimate).

Columns 3 and 4 report estimates from specifications without industry fixed effects. Overall, the coefficient estimates are modestly sensitive to the inclusion of the industry-specific constants. However, industry-specific effects do account for a substantial amount of the variation in displacement rates. Further work will attempt to measure this interindustry variation more directly, using proxies for technological change, changes in capital stock, changes in investment, and perhaps unionization. Industry-level protectionist policies, such as tariff and nontariff barriers (NTBs), may be important industry characteristics for this time period.[49]

Who Are the Workers Displaced from "Import-Sensitive" Industries?

Although this analysis does not settle the debate about trade and displacement, a natural next question is whether workers displaced from import-sensitive industries face different (or worse) postdisplacement outcomes than workers displaced from manufacturing industries less influenced by trade.[50] To distinguish a set of import-sensitive industries, I use

47. The log change in GDP also captures some of the time variation in displacement rates.

48. The highest average export share in the analysis sample is 0.38.

49. See Gaston and Trefler (1994) for an analysis of the effects of trade protection policies on industry wages.

50. This is not a new question. The Bureau of International Labor Affairs (ILAB) of the U.S. Department of Labor (DOL) sponsored a number of empirical studies of trade-affected workers in the 1970s and early 1980s. An alternative comparison, not implemented here, is to compare workers displaced from trade-sensitive industries to workers displaced from all other, including nonmanufacturing, industries.

the common measure of a high import penetration ratio. My choice of this measure is for descriptive purposes only, and it is not meant to convey causality.

Table 10-5 presents summary statistics of worker characteristics by displacement industry. Industries are classified according to their average import penetration ratio for 1975–85, with workers displaced during 1979–86. High-import industries are those with import penetration ratios above 20 percent, medium-import industries those with import penetration ratios between 10 and 20 percent, and low-import industries those with penetration ratios less than 10 percent. Workers in high-import-share industries are younger, less educated, less tenured, and more likely to be female than workers in medium- and low-import-share industries. These characteristics are commonly found for import-sensitive industries.[51] Average predisplacement, real weekly earnings are significantly lower in high-import industries, and a smaller proportion of high-import displaced workers had health insurance on their old jobs than was the case for workers displaced from less-import-sensitive industries. There is no difference in fraction displaced from full-time employment.

Turning to the consequences of displacement, the lower part of table 10-5 lists survey date labor-force status and mean change in real weekly earnings. Reemployment proportions are significantly lower for workers displaced from high-import industries, and a larger share of these workers were not in the labor force at the time of the survey.[52] The log changes in earnings are sizable, and there is no significant difference in mean earnings changes by industry import sensitivity.

Table 10-6 reports coefficient estimates from a logit estimation of the probability of survey date employment.[53] The trade sensitivity of an industry is measured by its mean import or export penetration rate in 1975–85. With just mean import share as a regressor, column 1 shows that reemployment probability falls as import share rises. Column 2 uses mean export share along with mean import share and controlling for level of imports, larger export share is associated with a higher probability of reemployment. Columns 3, 4, and 5 add the individual characteristics of educational attainment, age, job tenure, and race, and account for time since displacement. The addition of these characteristics slightly changes the

51. See Aho and Orr (1980, and 1981).
52. Differences in survey date labor market status by industry import sensitivity are significant at $\alpha = 0.05$.
53. Employment is defined as either full-time or part-time employment.

Table 10-5. *Worker Characteristics by Displacement Industry, 1979–86*[a]

	High import share (>20 percent)	Medium import share (10–20 percent)	Low import share (<10 percent)
Proportion female	0.615	0.435	0.319
Proportion nonwhite	0.127	0.151	0.148
Age at displacement			
20–30 years	0.449	0.407	0.444
31–40 years	0.288	0.291	0.274
41–50 years	0.166	0.155	0.142
51+ years	0.096	0.146	0.139
Education			
Less than high school	0.121	0.076	0.083
High school	0.671	0.625	0.633
Some college	0.156	0.174	0.165
College degree	0.044	0.086	0.075
Post-B.A.	0.008	0.039	0.044
Previous job tenure			
<3 years	0.551	0.520	0.557
4–6 years	0.226	0.159	0.168
7–10 years	0.123	0.131	0.110
11–15 years	0.055	0.086	0.071
16–20 years	0.013	0.038	0.039
21+ years	0.031	0.065	0.054
Employed full-time on previous job	0.948	0.965	0.954
Mean real weekly earnings on previous job	$291.52 (179.88)	$405.58 (246.24)	$390.33 (203.37)
Health insurance on previous job	0.682	0.791	0.758
N	328,029	1,893,348	3,458,894
Labor-force status			
Employed	0.596	0.665	0.685
Unemployed	0.069	0.070	0.079
Not in labor force	0.335	0.265	0.236
Mean log change in real weekly earnings	−0.403 (1.286)	−0.386 (1.126)	−0.378 (1.148)

Source: Author's calculations from the DWS.

a. Observations are weighted by final sampling weights. Reported nominal earnings are deflated using the Personal Consumption Expenditures deflator (1987 U.S. dollars).

Table 10-6. *Logit Estimates of the Probability of Survey Date Employment: Effect of Import Penetration, Export Share, and Worker Characteristics*[a]

Variable	(1)	(2)	(3)	(4)	(5)	(6)
Import penetration	−0.8540	−0.9404	−0.7994	−0.8194	−0.9292	−0.2439
ratio	(0.5000)	(0.4992)	(0.5120)	(0.5123)	(0.5161)	(0.5275)
Export share		1.2006	0.7128	0.7613	0.6991	0.3068
		(0.4818)	(0.4946)	(0.4956)	(0.4978)	(0.5034)
Education						
High school			0.2215	0.2239	0.2178	0.2427
			(0.1331)	(0.1332)	(0.1341)	(0.1355)
Some college			0.5203	0.5264	0.5223	0.5029
			(0.1574)	(0.1575)	(0.1586)	(0.1602)
B.A. degree			1.1861	1.1925	1.1857	1.1295
			(0.2041)	(0.2042)	(0.2053)	(0.2067)
Post-B.A.			1.1519	1.1561	1.1451	1.0893
			(0.2645)	(0.2646)	(0.2658)	(0.2674)
Age at displacement						
20–30 years			0.6578	0.6535	0.7041	0.6330
			(0.1236)	(0.1237)	(0.1247)	(0.1262)
31–40 years			0.9110	0.9149	0.9646	0.9335
			(0.1239)	(0.1240)	(0.1252)	(0.1264)
41–50 years			0.8141	0.8093	0.8547	0.8597
			(0.1345)	(0.1346)	(0.1356)	(0.1371)
Job tenure at displacement						
0–3 years			0.1902	0.1016	0.1190	0.2767
			(0.1151)	(0.1152)	(0.1161)	(0.1191)
4–6 years			0.3619	0.3587	0.3872	0.5240
			(0.1354)	(0.1355)	(0.1364)	(0.1389)
7–10 years			0.1363	0.1322	0.1481	0.2734
			(0.1432)	(0.1433)	(0.1443)	(0.1470)
Years since displacement				0.678	0.0710	0.0772
				(0.403)	(0.0406)	(0.0410)
Nonwhite					−0.7084	−0.6616
					(0.1064)	(0.1075)
Female						−0.6016
						(0.0792)
Constant	0.7309	0.6370	−0.4562	−0.6143	−0.5609	−0.4569
	(0.0568)	(0.0676)	(0.1585)	(0.1844)	(0.1858)	(0.1881)
Log likelihood	−2190.50	−2187.34	−2109.93	−2107.91	−2086.12	−2057.22

Source: Author's calculations from the 1984–86 DWS.

a. Asymptotic standard errors in parentheses. Base group in last column is white men older than fifty (at the time of displacement), with less than twelve years of education and previous job tenure exceeding ten years. Sample size is 3,414.

negative coefficient on imports, with a somewhat larger change for the estimated coefficient on export share. As expected, the correlation between education and reemployment is strongly positive. Older workers (ages fifty-one and over) are less likely to be reemployed than younger workers, and reemployment probability falls with job tenure. Nonwhites are considerably less likely to be reemployed following displacement (15 percentage points).[54] The probability of survey date employment increases with time since displacement (1.5 percentage points for each year since displacement).

Column 6 shows that the negative correlation between this measure of trade sensitivity and reemployment is largely the result of import-competing industries employing large numbers of women. With the addition of the dummy variable for female workers, the estimated coefficient on import share falls considerably. Women and nonwhites are approximately equally unlikely to be reemployed (about 14 percent). Comparing estimates in column 6 with the other estimates shows that it is the correlation between female employment share and trade sensitivity that is important for understanding the simple finding that "trade-displaced" workers are less likely to be reemployed.

Briefly, the determinants of the log change in real weekly earnings for the reemployed are examined in table 10-7.[55] As is typical for earnings change regressions, only a small fraction of the variance is explained by the regressors. Earnings changes are not significantly related to the trade sensitivity of the predisplacement industry. Earnings losses rise with previous job tenure and are smaller for more educated workers. Full-time or part-time status before and after displacement plays an important role in postdisplacement earnings changes. Workers reemployed in part-time jobs have significantly larger earnings losses than workers reemployed full-time. Because these differences in hours worked are due to both labor supply and labor demand influences, they are difficult to interpret.[56]

54. The derivative of the probability in the logit model is $\beta P(1 - P)$. The sample average value of P for the period 1979–86 is 0.654.

55. An important weakness of the DWS is the lack of a control group. The proper measure of earnings loss is not the comparison between pre- and postdisplacement earnings; rather, it is the difference in earnings between observationally similar displaced and not-displaced workers. Future research will include the construction of a control group of not displaced from the CPS. See Ruhm (1991) and Jacobson, LaLonde, and Sullivan (1993) for two different displaced worker studies using control groups.

56. The inclusion of these variables also complicates interpretation of the estimated coefficient on female workers. A comparison of columns 3 and 4 indicates that there is also an important correlation between educational attainment and hours worked.

Table 10-7. *OLS Estimates of Log Change in Real Weekly Earnings for Reemployed Displaced Workers, 1979–86*[a]

Variable	(1)	(2)	(3)	(4)
Import penetration ratio	−0.0562 (0.1639)	0.0540 (0.1615)	0.0663 (0.1638)	0.0996 (0.1550)
Export share	−0.0727 (0.1480)	−0.1608 (0.1463)	−0.1720 (0.1477)	−0.1712 (0.1398)
Education				
High school		0.0581 (0.0459)	0.0585 (0.0459)	0.0012 (0.0437)
Some college		0.1214 (0.0513)	0.1207 (0.0514)	0.0392 (0.0490)
B.A. degree		0.1922 (0.0575)	0.1916 (0.0575)	0.0867 (0.0549)
Post-B.A.		0.2053 (0.0690)	0.2041 (0.0691)	0.1105 (0.0657)
Job tenure at displacement				
0–3 years		0.2412 (0.0331)	0.2434 (0.0334)	0.2248 (0.0316)
4–6 years		0.1748 (0.0396)	0.1772 (0.0397)	0.1695 (0.0376)
7–10 years		0.0748 (0.0439)	0.0768 (0.0441)	0.0692 (0.0417)
Nonwhite			−0.0128 (0.0367)	0.0107 (0.0349)
Female			−0.0130 (0.0246)	0.0044 (0.0238)
Previous job part-time				0.6015 (0.0742)
Current job part-time				−0.3911 (0.0304)
Both jobs part-time				0.2147 (0.1154)
Years since displacement				−0.0118 (0.0117)
Constant	−0.1478 (0.0217)	−0.4075 (0.0519)	−0.4037 (0.0523)	−0.2638 (0.0575)
Adjusted R^2	−0.0008	0.039	0.039	0.139

Source: Author's calculations from the 1984–88 DWS.

a. The base group in the last column is white men with less than twelve years of education, previous job tenure exceeding ten years, whose previous jobs were full-time. Nominal earnings are deflated by the Personal Consumption Expenditures deflator (1987 U.S. dollars). Standard errors in parentheses. Sample size is 2,107.

Conclusion

In this chapter I have investigated the relationship between international trade and job displacement for a sample of manufacturing industries over the period 1979–91. Although the results are perhaps best viewed as preliminary, they are broadly consistent with the perception that imports displace some domestic jobs. This broad consistency appears to be a result of a reasonably strong positive relationship between increases in import share and job displacement for industries long identified as import sensitive—industries such as apparel, footwear, and textiles. Aside from these industries, the relationship between increasing foreign competition and permanent job loss appears much less systematic. What is unknown is whether the trade versus job loss relationship might be stronger within more narrowly defined industries. The displacement data do not allow further industry detail.[57]

Across industries, increasing foreign competition accounts for a small share of job displacement. There are high rates of job loss for industries with little trade. This conclusion would be highlighted if the analysis sample included trade and service industries, where rates of job loss are high while the services produced are mostly nontradables. These industries cannot be included in the analysis sample to date, as there is little time series information on trade outside of manufacturing.

There is an important limitation to this analysis. Displacement is just one of the flows that contribute to net changes in employment. It is likely that firms use all the components of turnover (quits and new and replacement hiring, as well as displacement) to move actual employment toward its desired level as foreign competition changes. It may be difficult for the data to isolate one flow in the absence of the others.

Results from the individual-level analysis may contribute to the "displaced versus disadvantaged" debate about the appropriate "targets" of adjustment assistance programs. Although workers displaced from high-import-share industries are less likely to be reemployed, their lower reemployment probabilities are accounted for by individual characteristics such as education, age, race, and (in particular) gender. Trade-displaced workers may have more difficult labor market adjustments, but the source of the difficulty is their otherwise disadvantaged characteristics, not the characteristics of their displacement industry.[58]

I conclude with a comment about the likely direction of future research. An important element in the relationship between increasing globalization and job displacement may be the geographic concentration of trade-sensitive industry employment. By major industrial sector, mining is the most concentrated geographically, followed by agriculture. Perhaps surprisingly, manufacturing is justly slightly less concentrated than agriculture. High-export-penetration-ratio industries tend to be in the West (Pacific region),

---

57. For related studies using establishment- and plant-level data, see Davis, Haltiwanger, and Schuh (1994); Bernard and Jensen (1995).
58. See Kruse (1988, 1991) for more on this point.

whereas high-import-penetration-ratio industries are concentrated in the Mid-Atlantic and New England regions.[59] These concentrations imply that a downturn in a highly concentrated, import-sensitive industry can adversely affect the local economy and make individual adjustments to permanent job loss more difficult. Although import- and export-sensitive industries have both job losses and job gains, these general characteristics imply that trade-related job losses occur in separate labor markets from trade-related job gains. Previous research on job displacement reveals the importance of local labor markets.[60] Measures of industry geographic concentration offer a way to further understand how local labor markets are influenced by trade flows and changes in trade policy.

Appendix

Import and Export Penetration Rates

The NBER Trade and Immigration data set contains information on imports, exports, and the value of shipments by four-digit 1972 SIC industry from 1958 to 1985. The basic classification system for imports and exports is by commodity type (using the Tariff Schedule of the U.S. Annotated (TSUSA). A concordance between TSUSA and SIC categories allows the development of an industry-based trade data set. The NBER data file is described in detail in Abowd (1991).

Import Prices

Import price data are available by four-digit SIC industry in *U.S. Import and Export Price Indices,* published by the U.S. Bureau of Labor Statistics. This variable is a quarterly, fixed-weight, Laspeyres price index based on a 1985 import market basket. These indices are described in more detail in U.S. Bureau of Labor Statistics (1992). They are based on a survey of actual transactions prices, and to the degree possible, they reflect c.i.f (cost, insurance, and freight) prices. Robert Z. Lawrence provided me with annual average tabulations for a collection of two-, three-, and four-digit SIC industries for the period 1980–91, and the NBER trade data were used to aggregate up to three-digit CIC. When aggregation was needed, the SIC indices were weighted by their relative shares in total imports. Quarterly

---

59. See Shelburne and Bednarzik (1993). See Krugman (1991) for a more general discussion of industry geographical concentration.
60. See Carrington (1993).

U.S. Bureau of Labor Statistics data (available on-line from the BLS via ftp) were used to extend the Lawrence data back to 1978 for as many three-digit CIC industries as possible.

Industry Employment

Data on industry employment used to construct the industry displacement rates were obtained from the merged 1979–91 CPS Outgoing Rotation Group files.

Comment by Henry Farber

Lori Kletzer has carried out an interesting analysis of the relationship between international trade and the extent and consequences of job loss. This is an important and difficult problem. I will comment briefly on the theoretical framework and then more extensively on the empirical analysis.

The theoretical framework is based on a standard supply-demand equilibrium model. Equilibrium employment and wages are derived as a function of demand and supply factors, including trade-related factors. Simple first-differencing yields employment change as a function of changes in the demand and supply factors, including changes in the trade-related factors. A difficulty with this approach is job displacement (job loss due to layoff), rather than employment change, is the focus of the analysis. Kletzer notes that displacement is only one component of the gross flows that make up net employment change, the others being quits, accessions (new hires and rehires), and firing for cause. There are at least two reasons why displacement is likely to understate any effect of international trade on employment. Workers might quit in anticipation of being laid off, and these workers will not be counted as displaced. There is also a background level of worker attrition due to factors such as geographic relocation for family reasons or retirement. Firms may adjust employment in response to demand shifts at least in part by adjusting the rate at which they replace workers who leave voluntarily. For example, it is common for firms that want to reduce the size of their work force by a moderate amount to do so through attrition.

Nevertheless, Kletzer is correct in stating the job loss component of employment change is of considerable concern to policymakers and the public. Though the analysis of displacement cannot answer the question of how trade affects employment, Kletzer therefore performs a valuable service with her analysis of job loss.

The empirical analysis has two parts. The first part uses data aggregated to the industry level to examine the relationship between the incidence of displacement and measures of international trade. The second part of the analysis uses individual-level data from the DWSs to investigate the extent to which postdisplacement employment and earnings are related to international trade.

Table 10-1 presents industry-level displacement rates for four categories of industry defined by the extent of change in import penetration ratio. It is clear that there is no systematic relationship here. The industries with larger increases in their import penetration ratio do not have displacement rates systematically different from those of other industries. Table 10-2 carries out the analogous exercise for change in the export penetration ratio; again, there is no systematic relationship with displacement rates. Table 10-3 examines the relationship between change in domestic demand and displacement rates. Not surprisingly, there is a strong relationship; industries with large increases in domestic demand have lower displacement rates, on average. Despite Kletzer's assessment that "the perception that trade displaces domestic jobs has some basis in fact," this preliminary analysis shows little evidence of a systematic relationship between international trade and job loss.

Next, Kletzer carries out a multivariate analysis of the relationship between job loss and international trade using industry-level data. This analysis uses changes in four criteria: an import price index, the import penetration ratio, the export penetration ratio, and domestic demand as measures of international trade. Only the latter two show a significant relationship with job loss at the industry level as measured by the DWSs. Basically, increases in either exports or domestic demand yield less job loss. This is not surprising; both are direct products of domestic production and employment.

In my view, the most interesting part of the analysis relates to the characteristics of displaced workers and the consequences of displacement. The tabulations in table 10-5 make it clear that workers in high-import-share industries are less skilled (younger, less educated, with lower earnings) and more likely to be female than workers in low- and medium-import-share industries. Essentially, our less-skilled workers are competing for jobs with similar workers in other countries.

The simple tabulations in table 10-5 also show that the postdisplacement employment probabilities of displaced workers is related to import share, with workers displaced from jobs in high-import-share industries having significantly lower reemployment probabilities. This may be because these workers are relatively less skilled. Kletzer presents a multivariate logit analysis of postdisplacement reemployment probabilities in table 10-6 designed to get at this issue. The results are quite striking. The negative relationship between postdisplacement employment probabilities and the import penetration ratio is not due to the relatively low skill level of displaced workers. In fact, the relationship seems entirely because a much higher fraction of workers displaced from high-import-share industries are female and that females have a significantly lower probability for postdisplacement reemployment. This is not explored further by Kletzer. However, part of the explanation is that females are more likely than males to withdraw from the labor force after displacement from the work force. This is only partially offset by the fact that males are more likely than females to be unemployed after displacement.

The chapter concludes with a brief analysis of the relationship between the change in real weekly earnings of displaced workers. Kletzer finds no relationship between the import penetration ratio and the change in earnings. She concludes that this is partly because the data do not permit precise control of hours.

There is a potential problem of interpretation with the analysis of both reemployment probabilities and earnings change. Kletzer interprets the difference in outcomes between industries with high and low import-penetration ratios as the effect of being "trade displaced." But, as Kletzer makes clear in her earlier analysis, it is *changes* in international trade that could lead to job loss. The level of imports ought not lead to job loss, and workers who lose jobs in industries with high import penetration are not necessarily trade displaced. It is more likely that workers who lose jobs in industries with rising import penetration are trade displaced. It would therefore have been more relevant to consider the effect of changes in the import penetration ratio on outcomes.

Overall, we learn that job loss at the industry level is related to changes in domestic production and in exports in the expected directions. There is a weaker relationship between job loss and changes in imports. These are interesting patterns, but, as Kletzer notes, they do not make a strong case for large effects of international trade on job loss. What does seem clear is that job loss is inversely related to changes in domestic production and, presumably, changes in domestic employment. Thus the link between domestic employment and international trade would seem to be the key to understanding how international trade affects the labor market.

Comment by Lawrence Mishel

This chapter deserves high marks for attempting to plough new ground. Lori Kletzer clearly labels the analysis "preliminary," so it is possible that more will be learned and these remarks can be taken as suggestions for further work.

Kletzer examines the relationship between trade sensitivity and rising import penetration on industry displacement rates and on displaced workers' reemployment experiences. The topic is thus a subset of how trade affects employment levels and the employment structure (the distribution of jobs across industries). This is because the employment impact of trade is also the result of net changes in employment accommodated by changes in new hires and voluntary attrition. Consequently, this research, though interesting, is only tangentially related to the larger questions of trade's impact on living standards and inequality. The strength of the research is the light it can shed on the extent of the short-term and medium-term adjustment costs that accompany increased trade.

Before reviewing the findings, it is worthwhile to reflect on several data questions. The first is conceptual and relates to whether the sample should be limited to manufacturing workers. When asking the question, "Are trade-displaced workers different from other displaced workers?" it is understandable to want to select industries for which trade measures are available. Nevertheless, even if trade-displaced manufacturing workers have similar displacement experiences to other manufacturing workers, it is still possible that trade-displaced workers have more adverse experiences relative to workers displaced from service industries or the average displaced worker. Much of the effect of trade on wages is based on differences between manufacturing and other sectors and not on any within-manufacturing impact (import and export jobs have similar characteristics). The analysis therefore needs to examine the degree to which manufacturing workers have more adverse displacement experiences.

Two technical data issues concern me. First is the use of the retrospective data for 1979 and 1980 (years four and five from the 1984 DWSs). Because it is acknowledged that these data have serious recall-bias problems, it is worth excluding these years to see whether the results are sensitive to their inclusion. Second, the use of the middle two years of the five-year retrospective seems reasonable for examining reemployment experiences. However, it would be better to use a sample of the first two years when constructing displacement rates.

The first set of results comes from the multivariate analysis of changes in imports and exports on industry displacement rates (table 10-4). We learn that trends in domestic sales, exports, and imports explain little of the variation in displacement rates, but that industry fixed effects explain a great deal. Imports are associated with greater displacement, but the relationship does not achieve statistical significance when industry-specific effects are included.

These results raise an issue of interpretation. Is there really a question whether industry displacements are greater when import penetration grows, if growth in demand and other factors are held constant? That is, is there any dispute about whether imports displace domestic jobs in import-competing industries? If the empirical work finds that imports displace workers, then it seems it proves the obvious. If the results are otherwise, then it might call into question whether there is a proper set of controls or other measurement problems. In fact, if rising import penetration is not accompanied by displacement, then all of the adjustment is absorbed by attrition, or increased trade does not generate any reallocation of employment (and therefore no gains in allocative efficiency).

I suspect that in this instance the import variable does not adequately capture the structural shifts toward greater import competition. One reason is that it is specified as a percent change in import share. A 50 percent increase from 2 percent import penetration (a rise of 1 percentage point) is treated as equivalent to a 50 percent increase from 20 percent import penetration (a rise of 10 percentage points). Also, the change in import penetration is measured over one year, too short a time to reflect structural shifts. In addition, the use of a linear specification of import share imposes an overly strict test, asking whether a marginal growth in imports raises displacement rates. A less imposing specification would be to use a step function reflecting a small, moderate, or large growth in import penetration. Note that age, tenure, and education are all specified in a similar manner in the other estimations, and that import penetration is treated qualitatively in the descriptive tables.

The final results focus on the relationship between import sensitivity and worker displacement outcomes. The analysis switches from an examination of the effect of *growing* import penetration on displacement to one examining whether higher *levels* of import penetration (the average over the period) are associated with different displacement outcomes. As such, it is not clear to me that the analysis examines whether workers displaced from the growth of import penetration fare differently from other workers displaced from manufacturing. As a result, I would like to see imports specified in the reemployment and earnings loss equations in the same manner as I proposed for the industry displacement estimations—a step function reflecting long- or medium-term growth in import share.

The chapter finds that workers displaced from import-sensitive industries (that is, those with greater import penetration rates) have a lower chance of reemployment. When a gender control is added, however, the coefficient on imports becomes statistically insignificant. Kletzer interprets this trade sensitivity as unrelated to reemployment problems—rather, that trade-sensitive industries employ workers (that is, women) who have reemployment difficulties. I suspect the relationship between trade sensitivity and reemployment is driven by the high propensity women displaced from the apparel and textile industries have toward withdrawing from the labor force. An appropriate interpretation of these findings might be that workers displaced from trade-sensitive industries do have more negative reemployment prospects, primarily because of the types of workers that tend to be employed in trade-sensitive industries. Does this not follow from the usual analysis of what types of industries are likely to be affected by imports (requiring low-skilled workers, and so on)?

My last suggestion is that it would be worth examining the displacement experience of women separately from men and examining non-college-educated workers separately from those with college degrees.

The Wage Inequality Literature

Let me turn to some general comments about the wage inequality literature and the evaluation of trade's impact on living standards.

There is an unspoken assumption that the forces causing wage inequality (either trade, technology, and perhaps even weakened labor market institutions) are somehow associated with "progress" or are at least leading to an overall growth in living standards. In fact, after examining trends in productivity or investment, one is hard put to find a superior performance in the 1980s or 1990s than in the 1970s (nonfarm, business-sector productivity was roughly 1.0 percent in each period). It may be that the post-1979 period is "all pain, no gain." If so, then the efficiency benefits of a range of laissez faire policies—deregulation, expanded openness to trade, erosion of the social safety net, weakened unions and minimum-wage protections, and privatization—must be small. One could argue that productivity would have collapsed further in the absence of these policies. But I am not sure why recent circumstances were more adverse than the 1970s, an era beset by a deep recession and several energy and food supply shocks. It may be that the productivity boost is not captured in our statistics, but I have not seen any credible analysis showing that *aggregate* productivity is measured more poorly for recent years than for earlier ones.

In addition, there is the presumption that we have been shifting employment toward more-skilled work, as seen in the relative growth of college graduate and white-collar (or nonproduction) employment. This framework suggests that what we need to explain is why skilled employment is rising even though the relative price of skill is also rising. One gets quite a different feel, however, after examining the share of workers earning low, middle, and high wages, especially men. As table 10-8 shows, the work force did shift toward higher-education groups over the 1973–93 period. However, since 1979 there has been a sizable shift from middle-wage to low-wage employment among men. At the same time, there was no significant growth in the number of high earners. There has also been an erosion of middle-wage earners among women since 1979, but the shift has been to both high- and low-wage employment. Perhaps the question (especially for men) is why there is an erosion of middle-wage earners and an increase in low-wage earners despite the increases in education and white-collar work.

This is another way of saying that we need to be careful to distinguish between shifts in education premiums and shifts in wage inequality. Rising education premiums explain only half the growth of wage inequality in the 1979–89 period and, according to Burtless, only about one-third of the growth of wage inequality in the 1969–93 period.[61] This means that one must explain the growth of within-group wage inequality (among workers with similar education and experience) to explain the overall growth in wage inequality.

It is also important to be careful in the rhetoric used to describe the dynamics of wage inequality. The usual description—"the wages of the more educated/skilled workers being bid up relative to the wages of less educated/skilled workers due to [pick your choice of factor]"—is both misleading and uninformative. It is misleading on two counts. This description leaves the impression that skilled, educated workers are faring well, when they are not—the real wages of "college-only" or white-collar workers, especially men, have been stagnant or falling since about 1987. The ninetieth-percentile male wage has been essentially flat since 1979. This group is only doing well in *relative* terms.

61. Burtless (1995).

Table 10-8. *Educational Upgrading and Changes in Wage Structure, 1973–93*
Percent

	Share of employment				Percentage point change		
	1973	1979	1989	1993	1973–79	1979–89	1989–93
Education[a]							
Men							
Less than high school	30.6	22.4	15.9	n.a.	–8.2	–6.5	n.a.
High school	38.1	38.6	38.7	n.a.	0.5	0.1	n.a.
Some college	15.6	18.7	21.0	n.a.	3.1	2.3	n.a.
College	8.9	11.5	14.2	n.a.	2.6	2.7	n.a.
More than college	4.5	6.1	7.8	n.a.	1.6	1.7	n.a.
Women							
Less than high school	25.4	17.2	11.2	n.a.	–8.2	–5.0	n.a.
High school	47.2	46.8	42.7	n.a.	–0.6	–4.1	n.a.
Some college	14.5	19.6	23.9	n.a.	5.1	4.3	n.a.
College	8.8	10.4	13.9	n.a.	1.6	3.5	n.a.
More than college	2.3	3.5	5.8	n.a.	1.2	2.3	n.a.
					Annualized		
Percentile wage range[b]							
Men							
1–20	18.9	20.0	26.1	33.6	0.18	0.60	1.51
21–50	34.6	30.0	30.0	28.3	–0.78	0.00	–0.34
51–75	26.1	25.8	20.9	17.9	–0.06	–0.48	–0.61
76–90	11.7	15.0	13.2	10.4	0.54	–0.17	–0.56
91–100	8.6	9.3	9.8	9.7	0.11	0.05	–0.00
Women							
1–20	23.3	20.6	25.6	27.9	–0.46	0.50	0.46
21–50	28.1	29.4	17.3	20.3	0.22	–1.21	0.60
51–75	26.7	25.1	22.6	20.3	–0.27	–0.25	–0.47
76–90	14.4	14.9	16.1	13.7	0.09	0.12	–0.48
91–100	7.5	10.0	18.3	17.7	0.42	0.83	–0.11

Source: Mishel and Bernstein (1994, tables 3.10, 3.19).

n.a. Not available.

a. Excludes those with seventeen years of schooling.

b. Wage ranges are defined relative to 1979 wage distribution. For men, the wage ranges (in 1989 U.S. dollars) correspond to: $1.00–$6.98, $6.98–$11.06, $11.06–$15.08, $15.08–$20.11, and $20.11–$100.00. For women, the wage ranges (in 1989 dollars) correspond to: $1.00–$5.03, $5.03–$6.74, $6.74–$9.22, $9.22–$12.32, and $12.32–$100.00.

It is also misleading to put the "unskilled" label on groups comprising 80 percent (for example, production or nonsupervisory workers) or 75 percent (non-college-educated workers) of the work force, especially those with two-year college degrees or skills based on long apprenticeships. Unfortunately, "unskilled" frequently gets translated in the media as the losers being uneducated, miseducated, or poorly educated. This terminology is especially misleading, because the public believes that less than one-fourth of the work force is "unskilled" (based on my nonrandom sampling of audiences and classes over the last few years). Finally, the empirical work that uses a broad category for "unskilled" workers is also uninformative; the usual suspects (trade, technology, unions, and so on) affect the various subgroups differently.

Trade and Wage Inequality

The consensus estimate of the impact of trade and globalization on wage inequality has been rising in recent years and now falls in the 10 to 25 percent range (that is, the share of the rise in overall wage inequality explained by "trade"). However, there is little analytical discipline in the choice of adjectives used to describe this impact. Is it small, modest, or large? One could argue that if trade explains 20 percent of the growth of wage inequality, then it explains as much as any other identifiable factor. Or one could say that trade explains only a "small part of the problem/ phenomenon." Let me strongly suggest that analysts be clear about what yardstick they are applying when they attribute an adjective to the role of any factor. Let me also suggest some yardsticks. If trade explains 10 to 25 percent of the 15 percentage point change in the male 90/50 wage differential over the 1979–93 period, then trade can be said to have cost the median male a 1.5 to 3.75 percent wage loss (note that the 90-percentile wage was flat over this time period). Is this small or large?

There are several possible comparisons. One would be to compare the loss to the benefits of expanded trade, which would have to be estimated for various income classes or "skill" groups. Unfortunately, there are no studies available that quantify benefits from expanded trade by income group.

Another yardstick could be to judge losses from trade relative to the benefits of various policies that economists highly recommend, such as the General Agreement on Tariffs and Trade (GATT) and deficit reduction. With this yardstick, the losses from trade would seem large.

Unanswered Questions

The topic of whether trade (or other factors) has altered the income split between labor and capital has been prematurely tabled. The basis for believing that there is no profit versus wages story is that national income shares reveal no shift in the 1980s. This analysis is too simple and shallow for several reasons. First, in contrast with most topics in economics, there is no comparison of actual outcomes relative to what one might expect given a *model* of what drives factor income shares. This means we need to look at the current period relative to earlier periods, and we should examine variables that affect income shares.

Several factors suggest that, other things being equal, capital's share should have declined. One is that the capital-to-output ratio has fallen rapidly since the early 1980s. Computations of capital income relative to assets, rather than total income, show that the return to capital has achieved near-record highs in the 1990s.[62] The Organization for Economic Cooperation and Development (OECD) finds the same trends for the United States and for most other advanced countries.[63] There has also been a strong advance in the quality of labor (that is, human capital) that should have led to upward pressure on labor's share. That is, as the ratio of human capital to output rises, there is a tendency for labor's share to expand.

Another factor is the growth of the government and nonprofit share of national income, which grew by 2.3 percentage points of national income from 1979 to 1993 but fell 1.0 percentage points from 1973 to 1979.[64] Because the government and nonprofit sector has labor income but no capital income, this trend makes shares of national income a misleading indicator of private sector trends. The bias is to understate the growth of labor's share in the 1970s and overstate it in the 1980s.

Finally, it is curious that much of the analysis of trade and technology trends has focused on manufacturing, but the discussion of factor shares focuses on national income. It is noteworthy that labor's share of income in manufacturing fell rapidly in the 1980s and early 1990s, and that the return to capital in manufacturing has risen strongly. My conclusion is that there is evidence that capital is benefiting from the structural changes since 1979, and it is worthy to inquire why.

A second area of needed research is on the role of capital mobility and trade flows in weakening the general bargaining power of workers. The

62. See Baker (1996); Poterba and Samwick (1995).
63. OECD (1995a).
64. Mishel and Bernstein (1994, p. 50).

issue is how prevalent are threats, implicit or explicit, to move production offshore in collective bargaining and in the wage expectations of nonunion workers. Likewise, how much does the message, "we have to keep labor costs down to maintain or improve our competitiveness with our import or export competition," play a role in wage determination?

A third area that might be explored is to contrast European and North American outcomes because of their varied experiences with trade with low-wage countries. Specifically, low-wage-country import penetration in manufacturing nearly doubled in North America in the 1980s, whereas in Europe and Japan the level of penetration was less and did not increase.[65]

The assumption that trade pressures on wages only arise from imports from low-wage countries should also be reexamined. The tough labor negotiations at Boeing and Caterpillar suggest that an export orientation can increase the need to curtail labor costs and constrain prices (certainly a benefit of trade). Moreover, increased global competition can put pressure on wages whenever an import can potentially displace production and jobs, which is true of imports from both low-wage and high-wage countries.

General Discussion

Steven Davis related the results in this chapter to his recent work (with John Haltiwanger) on employment using plant-level data at the four-digit industry level. These data provide a longer time period (1972–88) and avoid the problem of recall bias. It is worth noting that they suggest a job destruction rate two to three times as large as the displacement rates that come from CPS data. Their analysis finds high rates of job creation and job destruction everywhere and little evidence of any difference among trade-exposed industries. The exception is the highest quintile of import penetration ratios, including textiles and apparel. However, job turnover is strongly inversely related to the wage level. Once wages are controlled for, even this result disappears, leaving no relationship between trade exposure and job displacement.

Davis expressed the view that it is interesting to examine the relationship of job displacement to the level of international openness as well as to changes in openness over time. He noted that, theoretically, a greater level of openness could lead to more or to less employment volatility, because

65. OECD (1995b).

openness helps to insulate producers from disturbances in domestic demand. This ambiguity makes it a good empirical question. Finally, he argued that neither the import penetration (quantity) nor the import price indicators are satisfactory measures of trade exposure. In particular, relative import price changes need not reflect a purely foreign disturbance—they may reflect changes in technology in both the United States and abroad. He advocated construction of more direct measures of openness, such as indicators based on measures of transport costs.

Marina Whitman raised the point that difficult welfare issues are implicit in the discussion of this chapter as well as others in this book. She, like many participants, believed that there are typically real costs to adjustment, such as the kind of job displacement studied in Lori Kletzer's chapter. Such an adjustment process can also bring about longer-run gains—for instance, through more rational allocation of resources. However, we do not have an adequate framework for assessing the net effects of these adjustments. Other participants also recognized this as an important area meriting more study.

Adrian Wood was struck by the differences in findings for males versus females. Kletzer's chapter found that female concentration explained most of the finding that workers displaced from high-import-penetration sectors fared poorly. Wood found this puzzling, given Richard Freeman's chapter 3, which found that women had been doing better than men (in terms of wages). He suggested that part of the explanation for the puzzle might be that women who are displaced appear to be relatively easily reabsorbed—in other parts of manufacturing and also in the service sector. In this context, he also cautioned against interpreting an industry as a labor market.

Some comments focused on the role of business cycles. James Tybout noted that the measure of import penetration used will tend to rise during recessions, because domestic output (which is in the denominator) will fall. Marina Whitman wondered whether including year dummies would capture the systematic variations in displacements and quits over the business cycle. Catherine Mann suggested that this issue is important; the appropriate policy response to a finding that associates foreign competition with particularly severe job displacement may be quite different, depending on whether the linkage reflects cyclical or secular trends.

Mann also noted that those sectors that have high import penetration and have experienced high displacement (apparel/textiles and footwear) are also sectors that are heavily protected. Thus, if one were to conclude that trade were a problem in terms of causing employment volatility, trade protection cannot be the answer.

Edward Leamer stressed the importance of distinguishing between short- and long-run developments. Although apparel and textiles is in long-term decline, other industries such as transportation equipment, are experiencing increased volatility and uncertainty as a result of increased exposure to foreign shocks. He interpreted the regressions that omitted industry fixed effects as primarily capturing longer-run industry trends, and regressions that include industry fixed effects as being dominated by the shorter-term effects.

Finally, Woodhead questioned Kletzer's characterization of the AFL-CIO as being strongly protectionist. He also reiterated the dissatisfaction, previously expressed by Robert Blecker and others, about how well our measures capture actual differences in worker skills.

References

Abowd, John M. 1991. "The NBER Immigration, Trade, and Labor Markets Data Files." In *Immigration, Trade, and the Labor Market,* edited by John M. Abowd and Richard B. Freeman, 407–22. University of Chicago Press.

Abraham, Katharine G., and James L. Medoff. 1984. "Length of Service and Layoffs in Union and Nonunion Work Groups." *Industrial and Labor Relations Review* 38 (October): 87–97.

Addison, John T., Douglas A. Fox, and Christopher J. Ruhm. 1995. "Trade and Displacement in Manufacturing." *Monthly Labor Review* 118 (April): 58–67.

Aho, C. Michael, and James A. Orr. 1980. "Demographic and Occupational Characteristics of Workers in Trade-Sensitive Industries." Economic Discussion Paper 2. U.S. Department of Labor, Bureau of International Labor Affairs (April).

———. 1981. "Trade-Sensitive Employment: Who Are the Affected Workers?" *Monthly Labor Review* 104 (February): 29–35.

Akerlof, George A., and Janet L. Yellen. 1985. "Unemployment through the Filter of Memory." *Quarterly Journal of Economics* 100 (August): 747–73.

Baker, Dean. 1996. "Trends in Corporate Profitability: Getting More for Less." Economic Policy Institute (February).

Bednarzik, Robert W. 1993. "An Analysis of U.S. Industries Sensitive to Foreign Trade, 1982–87." *Monthly Labor Review* 116 (February): 15–31.

Belman, Dale, and Thea M. Lee. 1996. "International Trade and the Performance of U.S. Labor Markets." In *U.S. Trade Policy and Global Growth: New Directions in the International Economy,* edited by Robert A. Blecker. M. E. Sharpe.

Berman, Eli, John Bound, and Zvi Griliches. 1994. "Changes in the Demand for Skilled Labor within U.S. Manufacturing: Evidence from the Annual Survey of Manufactures." *Quarterly Journal of Economics* 109 (May): 367–97.

Bernard, Andrew B., and J. Bradford Jensen. 1995. "Exporters, Jobs, and Wages in U.S. Manufacturing: 1976–1987." *Brookings Papers on Economic Activity: Microeconomics* 67–112.

Borjas, George J., Richard B. Freeman, and Lawrence F. Katz. 1992. "On the Labor Market Effects of Immigration and Trade." In *Immigration and the Work Force:*

Economic Consequences for the United States and Source Areas, edited by George J. Borjas and Richard B. Freeman, 213–44. University of Chicago Press.

Brechling, Frank. 1978. "A Time Series Analysis of Labor Turnover." In *The Impact of International Trade and Investment on Employment: A Conference on the Department of Labor Research Results,* edited by William G. Dewald and others, 67–86. U.S. Department of Labor, U.S. Bureau of International Labor Affairs.

Burtless, Gary. 1995. "Widening U.S. Income Inequality and the Growth in World Trade." Paper presented at Tokyo Club meeting in Dresden, Germany. Brookings.

Carrington, William J. 1993. "Wage Losses for Displaced Workers: Is It Really the Firm that Matters?" *Journal of Human Resources* 28 (Summer): 435–62.

Corson, Walter, and Walter Nicholson. 1981. "Trade Adjustment Assistance for Workers: Results of a Survey of Recipients under the Trade Act of 1974." In *Research in Labor Economics,* vol. 4, edited by Ronald Ehrenberg, 417–69. Greenwich, Conn.: JAI Press.

Davis, Steven J., John C. Haltiwanger, and Scott Schuh. 1994. *Gross Job Flows.* U.S. Department of Commerce. U.S. Bureau of the Census, Center for Economic Studies.

Decker, Paul T., and Walter Corson. 1995. "International Trade and Worker Displacement: Evaluation of the Trade Adjustment Assistance Program." *Industrial and Labor Relations Review* 4B (July): 758–74.

Dickens, William T. 1988. "The Effects of Trade on Employment: Techniques and Evidence." In *The Dynamics of Trade and Employment,* edited by Laura D'Andrea Tyson, William T. Dickens, and John Zysman, 41–85. Cambridge, Mass.: Ballinger.

Farber, Henry S. 1993. "The Incidence and Costs of Job Loss: 1982–91." *Brookings Papers on Economic Activity: Microeconomics: 1,* 73–119.

Freeman, Richard B., and Lawrence F. Katz. 1991. "Industrial Wage and Employment Determination in an Open Economy." In *Immigration, Trade, and the Labor Market,* edited by John M. Abowd and Richard B. Freeman, 235–60. University of Chicago Press.

Gaston, Noel, and Daniel Trefler. 1994. "Protection, Trade, and Wages: Evidence from U.S. Manufacturing." *Industrial and Labor Relations Review* 47 (July): 574–93.

Gibbons, Robert, and Lawrence F. Katz. 1991. "Layoffs and Lemons." *Journal of Labor Economics* 9 (October): 351–80.

Grossman, Gene M. 1986. "Imports as a Cause of Injury: The Case of the U.S. Steel Industry." *Journal of International Economics* 20 (May): 201–23.

———. 1987. "The Employment and Wage Effects of Import Competition in the United States." *Journal of International Economic Integration* 2 (Spring): 1–23.

Haveman, Jon D. 1994. "The Influence of Changing Trade Patterns on Displacements of Labor." Purdue University, Krannert School of Management.

Jacobson, Louis, Robert LaLonde, and Daniel Sullivan. 1993. *The Costs of Worker Dislocation.* Kalamazoo, Mich.: W. E. Upjohn Institute for Employment Research.

Kletzer, Lori G. 1989. "Returns to Seniority after Permanent Job Loss." *American Economic Review* 79 (June): 536–43.

———. 1995. "What Have We Learned about Job Displacement?" Working Paper 333. University of California, Santa Cruz, Department of Economics (October).

Krugman, Paul R. 1991. *Geography and Trade.* MIT Press.

Krugman, Paul R., and Robert Z. Lawrence. 1993. "Trade, Jobs, and Wages." Working Paper 4478. Cambridge, Mass.: National Bureau of Economic Research (September).

Kruse, Douglas L. 1988. "International Trade and the Labor Market Experience of Displaced Workers." *Industrial and Labor Relations Review* 41 (April): 402–17.

———. 1991. "Displaced versus Disadvantaged Workers." In *Job Displacement: Consequences and Implications for Policy,* edited by John T. Addison, 279–96. Wayne State University Press.

Lawrence, Robert Z. 1994. "Trade, Multinationals, and Labor." Working Paper 4836. Cambridge, Mass.: National Bureau of Economic Research (August).

Lawrence, Robert Z., and Matthew J. Slaughter. 1993. "International Trade and American Wages in the 1980s: Giant Sucking Sound or Small Hiccup?" *Brookings Papers on Economic Activity: Microeconomics* 2:161–210.

Leamer, Edward E. 1993. "Wage Effects of a U.S.-Mexican Free Trade Agreement." In *The Mexico-U.S. Free Trade Agreement,* edited by Peter M. Garber, 57–125. MIT Press.

———. 1994. "Trade, Wages and Revolving-Door Ideas." Working Paper 4716. Cambridge, Mass.: National Bureau of Economic Research (April).

Mann, Catherine L. 1988. "The Effect of Foreign Competition in Prices and Quantities on the Employment in Import-Sensitive U.S. Industries." *International Trade Journal* 2 (Summer): 409–44.

Medoff, James. 1992. "The New Employment." Harvard University Department of Economics paper for the Joint Economic Committee.

Mitchell, Daniel J. B. 1976. *Labor Issues of American International Trade and Investment.* Johns Hopkins University Press.

Mishel, Lawrence R., and Jared Bernstein. 1994. *The State of Working America 1994–95.* Economic Policy Institute Series. Armonk, N.Y.: M.E. Sharpe.

Murphy, Kevin M., and Finis Welch. 1991. "The Role of International Trade in Wage Differentials." In *Workers and Their Wages: Changing Patterns in the United States,* edited by Marvin H. Kosters, 39–69. Washington: American Enterprise Institute.

Neumann, George R. 1978. "The Labor Market Adjustments of Trade-Displaced Workers: The Evidence from the Trade Adjustment Assistance Program." In *Research in Labor Economics,* vol. 2, edited by Ronald G. Ehrenberg, 353–81. Greenwich, Conn.: JAI Press.

Organization for Economic Cooperation and Development. 1995a. *OECD Economic Outlook.* No. 57. Paris: Organization for Economic Cooperation and Development (June).

Organization for Economic Cooperation and Development. 1995b. *Linkages: OECD and Major Developing Economies.* Paris: Organization for Economic Cooperation and Development.

Podgursky, Michael, and Paul Swaim. 1987. "Job Displacement and Earnings Loss: Evidence from the Displaced Worker Survey." *Industrial and Labor Relations Review* 41 (October): 17–29.

Poterba, James M., and Andrew A. Samwick. 1995. "Stock Ownership Patterns, Stock Market Fluctuations, and Consumption." *Brookings Papers on Economic Activity* 2: 295–357.

Revenga, Ana L. 1992. "Exporting Jobs? The Impact of Import Competition on Employment and Wages in U.S. Manufacturing." *Quarterly Journal of Economics* 107 (February): 255–84.

Ruhm, Christopher J. 1991. "Are Workers Permanently Scarred by Job Displacements?" *American Economic Review* 81 (March): 319–24.

Sachs, Jeffrey D., and Howard J. Shatz. 1994. "Trade and Jobs in U.S. Manufacturing." *Brookings Papers on Economic Activity* 1: 1–69.

Schoepfle, Gregory K. 1982. "Imports and Domestic Employment: Identifying Affected Industries." *Monthly Labor Review* 105 (August): 13–26.

Shelburne, Robert C., and Robert W. Bednarzik. 1993. "Geographic Concentration of Trade-Sensitive Employment." *Monthly Labor Review* 116 (June): 3–13.

Spence, Michael. 1976. "Product Selection, Fixed Costs, and Monopolistic Competition." *Review of Economic Studies* 43 (June): 217–35.

Topel, Robert. 1990. "Specific Capital and Unemployment: Measuring the Costs and Consequences of Job Loss." *Carnegie-Rochester Conference Series on Public Policy* 33 (Autumn): 181–214.

U.S. Bureau of Labor Statistics. 1992. *BLS Handbook of Methods for Surveys and Studies.* Bulletin 2414.

U.S. International Trade Commission. 1986. *U.S. Trade-Related Employment: 1978–84.* Report on investigation 332–217 under section 332 of the Tariff Act of 1980.

Wood, Adrian. 1994. *North-South Trade, Employment and Inequality: Changing Fortunes in a Skill-Driven World.* Oxford, England: Clarendon Press.

ELEVEN

Compensation Programs

Louis Jacobson

THIS CHAPTER describes the range of policy instruments that can be used to aid trade-affected workers, the effectiveness of those instruments, and the appropriate timing for their use. Because compensation programs can substantially reduce the costs borne by workers, they can be important tools for reducing opposition to trade-liberalizing agreements.

Clearly, the more effective are the compensation programs, the more likely they are to reduce the negative effects of trade liberalization and improve the chances such actions are taken. Knowing which policy instruments are most effective allows policymakers to maximize the value of any given amount spent on aid and to minimize the cost of compensation designed to win over enough votes to gain passage of trade legislation.

Another use for knowledge about the cost-effectiveness of compensation programs is to estimate whether on balance trade legislation is beneficial. Even if the net costs imposed on workers by a trade bill were far lower than the net gains, the cost of distributing the compensation could be so great that the net cost of the legislation would be greater than its benefits.

Why have compensation programs not been an effective vehicle for gaining wider acceptance of expanding and even maintaining free trade? One central problem is accurately apportioning harm across each factor that contributes to an earnings loss. It often is difficult to persuade individuals that the compensation they would receive is at least equal to the costs they are likely to bear as a result of a government action or policy. Most often those hurt by trade legislation along with other market factors feel they are entitled to full compensation. This greatly raises the cost of compensatory programs, requiring narrowly focused programs like Trade Adjustment Assistance (TAA) to offset losses due to international competition rather than losses stemming from congressional action to change trade rules. A second problem is that workers show little interest in paying for insurance that would reduce costs imposed from any source. As a result, there has been little political support for expanding broader programs such as those in the Reemployment Act (REA) of 1994. Questions to be addressed include:

—What forms of compensation have the greatest effect, per dollar spent, on reducing the costs borne by workers?

—How can compensation be most effectively targeted on those hurt?

—Under what conditions can focused programs be replaced by general programs?

This chapter does not address issues that can only be resolved in the political arena, such as:

—What level of protection should be offered trade-affected workers?

—Who should pay for the aid?

—Should workers affected by trade be treated differently from workers hurt by other sources?

These issues cannot be resolved on the basis of objective evidence because there are no widely accepted principles for judging trade-affected workers worthy of compensation and other groups unworthy.

The strongest justification for compensation is that society took something belonging to a group in order to make society as a whole better off. For example, society pays "fair market value" to take the physical property of home owners to build a freeway under eminent domain laws. Compensation need not be paid when impersonal market forces hurt certain individuals, nor is there a legally enforceable "property right" to the benefits of import protection. Compensation is not a legal necessity when Congress hurts some individuals by changing trade rules.

Perhaps the next strongest justification for compensation is that restitution should be made when a policy change benefits high-income groups at the expense of low-income groups. Auto, steel, and petrochemical workers have been hurt by trade but are among the highest paid U.S. manufacturing workers, and their high salaries have made it difficult to justify providing assistance to those workers.

A related problem in establishing a moral imperative to compensate trade-affected workers is that a number of factors contribute to a firm's reduction in labor demand. It is hard to make the case that *only* those who are trade-affected merit special consideration. Indeed, arguments in favor of protecting all members of "needy" groups usually are more persuasive than those in favor of aiding only certain segments of such populations.

In practice, notions of fairness *and* self-interest in securing the benefits from trade liberalization combine to make narrowly focused compensation programs politically attractive. In contrast, noncategorical programs tend to be so expensive society is unwilling to bear those costs. A key issue is why individuals adversely threatened by trade and other factors appear to lack the willingness to pay for actuarially fair insurance.

To understand why it would be difficult to fully offset losses of those hurt by trade (even if society accepted that goal), I devote the next section to describing a "typical" instance of costly job loss. Particular attention is given to the three years before job loss, when long layoffs followed by recall are common. This difficulty in predicting when a layoff is permanent makes it hard for workers to accept adjustment services and even harder for service providers to narrowly target aid.

The remainder of the chapter reviews the evidence on the effectiveness of alternative means to aid dislocated workers. Two major conclusions are reached. The first is that for most dislocated workers, job search assistance (JSA) is more effective in boosting earnings than classroom training. The second is that there is no inexpensive way to substantially reduce the large losses of high-tenure, dislocated workers.

The juxtaposition of high costs of dislocation (as much as $80,000 per worker), with great difficulty in narrowly targeting benefits, makes it difficult to even please some of the people hurt by import competition some of the time.[1] As a result, most policy analyses have concluded that society would best be served by a comprehensive program of earnings *insurance*. The sticking point in implementing such a policy is that neither society at large nor members of the risk pool potentially affected by costly job loss appear willing to pay for such insurance.

Defining the Problem

How can society minimize the harmful effects on some individuals or groups of structural economic changes that make our nation as a whole

1. Jacobson, LaLonde, and Sullivan (1993b, p. 137).

better off? It is widely recognized that a government action, such as reducing trade barriers, should be judged good only if the winners' gains are great enough to fully compensate the losers' losses. But there is no consensus that compensation should be paid to ensure that some individuals are made better off and no one is made worse off. Indeed, only rarely does society even attempt to compensate those who lose out.

A key impediment to implementing compensation programs is that transaction costs associated with doing so are likely to be many times larger than the costs imposed on those adversely affected by change. Compensation programs such as TAA attempt to provide aid to individuals who are most clearly harmed by trade, not just by the removal of trade restrictions, and to target benefits on those with the largest losses—those who lose their jobs and subsequently experience long spells of unemployment. Broadening protection to those hurt by import competition, not just increased competition stemming from government actions to liberalize trade, such as reducing tariffs and quotas, avoids having to make complex assessments of the reason loss occurs. Compensating only for large losses avoids making small payments to a huge number of individuals. Moreover, general protection against small losses has been established through public programs such as unemployment insurance (UI) and through individual and collective work contracts that include compensation provisions such as severance pay and early retirement.

When the adverse effects are considerably greater than can be handled by existing protection and are largely unanticipated, it is reasonable to assess the need for additional public and private protection. The enormous drops in employment in the early 1980s concentrated in manufacturing centers such as Pittsburgh and Detroit are a good example of large, unanticipated, adverse events that raise questions about the adequacy of the assistance offered displaced workers. The substantial dislocations that have occurred in other regions, other industries, and more prosperous times suggest that the threat of job loss has not materially diminished.

Dislocation

Figure 11-1 shows the actual average earnings reductions of Pennsylvania workers with six or more years of tenure who lost jobs due to plant closures and mass layoffs between 1980 and 1986.[2] The modal worker in

2. Jacobson, LaLonde, and Sullivan (1993a).

Figure 11-1. *Overall Earnings Losses of Displaced Workers by Time Relative to Separation*

Thousands of 1987 U.S.$ (quarterly)

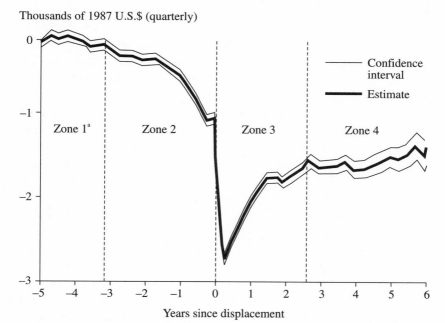

Years since displacement

Source: Jacobson, Lalonde, and Sullivan (1993c, p. 10).

a. See text, following page, for definition of zones.

the study was a thirty-seven-year-old male high school graduate, from western Pennsylvania, earning $25,000 a year, who worked in the steel industry and was displaced in 1982. The estimated reductions are based on comparisons covering earnings from 1974 through 1986 using an unusually large sample of high-tenure workers—6,435 who lost their jobs and 13,704 who kept theirs.[3] About 18 percent of the 1.5 million U.S. workers displaced each year have job tenure of more than five years.

The present discounted value of lost earnings averaged $80,000. The same pattern is observed when losses are computed for workers in different

3. These figures are largely taken from Jacobson, LaLonde, and Sullivan (1993b, table 5.1, pp. 87–88). The modal displacement year for primary metal (steel-)workers was 1982, which is derived from unpublished tabulations. The modal worker is a high school graduate; this is inferred from Dislocated Worker Survey (DWS) reports that describe the education of high-tenure, manufacturing workers.

age, sex, and industrial groups using workers in the same industry as the comparison group.[4] The earnings losses fall into four time-dependent zones:

1. From labor force entrance to about three years before job loss: when earnings of those who left jobs and those who stayed are identical.

2. The three years preceding dislocation: when earnings show a substantial dip amounting to about 12 percent of the total loss. Most of these losses are due to prolonged periods of layoff followed by recall.

3. The two and a half years immediately following dislocation: when earnings show a sharp drop followed by a substantial recovery. About 13 percent of the earnings loss occurs during this period. About half the loss is due to unemployment and half due to earnings reductions at new jobs.

4. From two and a half years after dislocation to retirement: when there is little, if any, additional recovery. Earnings permanently remain roughly 25 percent below those of similar workers who were not affected by a plant closing or mass layoff. About 75 percent of the total loss occurs after new permanent jobs are found. Almost all of the loss is due to reductions in wage rates rather than reduced employment.[5]

Two key policy-relevant conclusions follow from the above evidence: postdislocation earnings of many high-tenure workers never come close to those of workers who stay in their jobs. Before permanent job loss, there often is an extended period of long-duration layoffs followed by recall. The persistence of large postdislocation earnings reduction suggests that present compensation programs do not come close to offsetting those losses. Indeed, almost all of the public and private programs are primarily aimed at

4. When compared with the average person who stayed on the job, displaced steelworkers showed much larger than average losses, and displaced workers in the business and financial service sectors showed much smaller than average losses. Jacobson, LaLonde, and Sullivan (1993b, table 6.2, pp. 128–29). This is because workers who *stayed* in the steel industry experienced considerably below-average earnings growth, whereas workers who stayed in the business and financial service sector experienced considerably above-average growth. These results are consistent both with decreases in union/nonunion wage differentials and increases in college/noncollege differentials. Also, we regard our $80,000 estimate as conservative. We only included workers in our sample who were employed at some point in each year following job loss, and eliminated from our sample workers who were age fifty or older in 1980.

5. Our data included quarterly earnings (wages times hours) and weeks of unemployment, but did not include hourly wage rates. We found that there were no differences in weeks of unemployment between leavers and stayers in the period beginning two and a half years after displacement, but there could be differences in holding part-time jobs and working overtime.

Figure 11-2. *Earnings Losses and Losses in Total Income, Including Unemployment Insurance and Trade Adjustment Assistance Benefits*

Thousands of 1987 U.S.$ (quarterly)

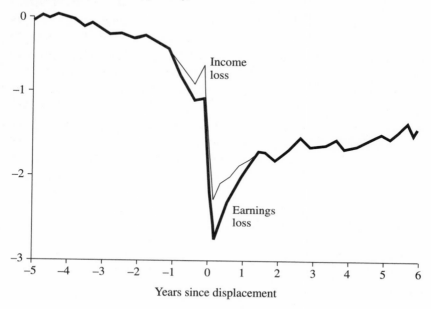

Years since displacement

Source: Jacobson, Lalonde, and Sullivan (1993c, figure 3, p. 14).

shortening the period between job loss and acquisition of a new permanent job (zone 3), and providing transfer payments to offset some of the lost earnings in that period and the preceding period where layoffs ended with recall (zone 2).

Figure 11-2 describes the extent to which these transfers offset earnings losses. Given the size of the losses, high-tenure workers would hardly be expected to face the prospect of dislocation with equanimity. Thus it is not at all surprising that opposition to trade liberalization is strongest in areas such as St. Louis, where job loss among well-paid, high-tenure workers is most likely. It is significant that evidence of large, permanent losses suggests a great deal more needs to be done if the goal of dislocation policy is to increase acceptance among those who might lose their jobs regarding changes in trade and technology that would improve U.S. competitiveness.

This conclusion may be old news to policymakers in Washington and to voters in areas affected by widespread mass layoffs. Nevertheless, there has been relatively little discussion of specific policy responses that could effectively reduce long-term losses. The policy implications of the widespread temporary layoffs that proceed permanent separations are even less widely recognized. They are of great importance, however, in designing policies aimed at reducing the time between worker dislocation and acquisition of a new permanent job. One major implication is that a history of long layoffs followed by recall makes it difficult for high-tenure workers to recognize when job loss is permanent. They are therefore likely to substantially delay searching for new jobs. Moreover, potential employers are reluctant to hire workers whom they believe are likely to accept recall by their former employer, and this adds to workers' difficulties in obtaining new jobs. A second implication is that providing benefits to all laid-off workers, even those who have been unemployed for long periods, diverts a lot of resources to workers who are ultimately recalled and who experience relatively small, long-term losses. Difficulty in effectively targeting aid greatly raises the cost of such programs.

Policy Options in Each Zone

What should be the objectives of policy at different stages of adjustment to structural change? What is the appropriate role of government and the private sector in attaining these goals?

Before Long Layoffs Occur

Figure 11-1 makes it clear that dislocation of high-tenure workers rarely occurs without some indication that workers' jobs might be in jeopardy. Although interpreting the signals often is difficult, usually the necessity for some employment adjustment can be inferred at least two years before actual job loss. Even a two-year warning, however, is rarely sufficient to prevent employment declines.

ATTRITION AND INCREASED PRODUCTIVITY.   Avoiding layoffs altogether would minimize the costs borne by workers. With rare exceptions, retirements and quitting plus buyouts such as early retirement packages, are much more common than net employment reductions within narrowly defined industrial groups. It might appear that downsizing could thus be accomplished without mass layoffs.

A major advance in the analysis of labor turnover, development of comprehensive longitudinal data on individual firms, shows that attrition can absorb some but not nearly all of most net employment declines. The key problem is that there is enormous variation in the net employment change of individual production units. Closings and mass layoffs are often narrowly concentrated in certain plants and areas and cannot possibly be accommodated by attrition. Even in growing, stable industries, some individual units close or have major declines that are balanced by start-ups of new units and expansions. These gross flows are many times larger than the net employment change. The result is a considerable amount of dislocation, even in industries with stable employment. Dislocation is much above average in growing industries where only a small fraction of the many new firms created survive even as long as four years.[6]

These conclusions are strongly reinforced by evidence from the DWSs conducted every other year since 1982 as part of the March Current Population Survey (CPS). The DWSs consistently show that the number of dislocations varies only slightly over the business cycle. Although dislocation is common in many economic sectors, the concentration of high-tenure workers is highest in durable manufacturing. Since that industry also is cyclically sensitive and dislocated high-tenure workers usually bear large costs, firm-level employment reductions that impose the greatest cost on workers occur most often during general economic downturns. But strong regional contractions have occurred in a variety of industries since 1979. Particularly costly job loss has been reasonably widespread and has resulted from competition from new and expanding domestic firms as much as from external factors.

There are opportunities, however, to improve the competitiveness of individual firms that would lead to less job loss. Some small and medium-size firms lag behind others in assimilating efficiency-improving changes, and many face capital constraints that make it difficult to rapidly adopt innovations. There have been attempts (most notably in the auto and aerospace industries) among major firms to work with independent suppliers to improve their performance. These industrial groups have strived to develop clear specifications for product design, quality, and delivery and to create detailed plans for revamping management and production techniques to meet those specifications. These efforts appear to be successful in helping the suppliers remain in business, although some of the gains from outsourcing have come at the expense of workers in the major firms.

6. Interplant transfers based on seniority could substantially reduce the number of high-tenure workers displaced. Offers of transfers often are made to high-skill workers, but relatively rarely to production workers. Distressed firms usually lack the resources to pay the direct relocation and retraining costs, or the indirect disruption costs. However, restructuring of strong firms, such as the breakup of AT&T, sometimes includes extensive offers of transfers and retraining.

Federal, state, and local governments have attempted to complement such industry-based efforts. In particular, several state programs, such as the Michigan Modernization Service, have been modeled after the U.S. Agricultural Extension Service to assist smaller firms, and the Small Business Administration (SBA) makes below-market loans to such firms. The scope of the governmental programs is small and their effectiveness questionable. In the absence of rigorous evaluations, it is difficult to separate the contribution of industry actions from those of government, determine whether the success of some firms comes at the expense of others, and assess whether those firms that would be most successful anyway were also most adept at taking advantage of government aid.

A related approach is for a large, multiplant firm to work with state and local governments to boost productivity at existing units to forestall movement of operations elsewhere or disproportionate investment in labor-saving equipment. Paul Gerhart has written an outstanding book, *Saving Plants and Jobs,* that systematically compares successful to unsuccessful attempts for struggling companies to save existing operations.[7] He reaches four conclusions: someone in the plant must recognize that there is a problem long before layoffs occur; local management and workers must both be persuaded that the operations will be cut back; major investments in plant and equipment must take place; and worker concessions are valuable only in conjunction with new investment. These conclusions are consistent with econometric analyses, such as that by Marie Howland, of the degree to which underlying economic factors can explain decisions to close plants.[8] These analyses strongly suggest that production at branch plants of major firms is often sacrificed in favor of maintaining employment at the headquarters site.

Widespread attempts have been made to sensitize workers and union leaders to the dangers of ignoring investment decisions that jeopardize job security and focusing instead on wage levels. The U.S. Department of Labor (DOL) and the National Governors Association have been particularly active in promoting efficiency-enhancing actions designed to avoid displacement. Much of their effort has been geared to adopting the approach of the Canadian Adjustment Service: government provides honest brokers to work with labor/management committees on both forestalling layoffs and dealing with them if they occur. Similarly, major unions such as the United Auto Workers (UAW) and Communication Workers of America have been

7. Gerhart (1987).
8. Howland (1988).

actively working with management to maintain employment and boost productivity. These actions have had some success, and continued emphasis on educating management and labor about "best practices" is warranted. But it is likely that such efforts will only slightly complement the strong incentives already created by the invisible hand of competition.

ENCOURAGING RETRAINING. Competitive forces are likely to continue to cause employment to contract in manufacturing and other industries, much as we have seen dramatic reductions in agricultural employment accompanied by increasing output. Attrition and renewal of existing plants cannot be expected to come close to eliminating costly dislocations. As a result, it also is important to help workers prepare for job loss. In many cases the same forethought and human-capital enhancing measures that an effective management team would implement to improve its competitive position would also assist workers in finding new jobs, should that become necessary. In particular, assessing worker skills and assisting them to use community or firm resources to improve their competence appears to be mutually advantageous. Sometimes employers' fears of losing workers makes them reluctant to help workers improve their human capital and consider alternative careers. At least for blue-collar and clerical workers, such programs probably increase allegiance to their current firm.

Like other measures to boost firm productivity, introduction of programs to build human capital depends on management competence. There is insufficient information to judge whether a firm fails to implement educational programs because it does not recognize their value or because their value is lower than other uses of that firm's resources. In addition, most human-resource investment is focused on the best-educated, most-skilled, and therefore most adaptable workers. It is unclear how much effort is required to get relatively untrained workers to participate in skill-building programs. Many workers who would benefit from improving their literacy and math skills appear resistant to take advantage of any but the most carefully crafted programs. Similarly, many workers appear to be unwilling to participate in more-advanced classroom training programs; they may not want to give up the time needed to study, or they lack the prerequisites to gain much from these programs. This is true of even the best-crafted and most generous programs, such as the Ford/UAW and GM/UAW programs.

The bottom line is that the achievements of human-capital enhancing programs are similar to those of programs to avoid layoffs. There have been some notable successes, and continued emphasis on educating management and labor about "best practices" is warranted. But it is likely that such efforts will only slightly complement the strong incentives workers already have to improve their skills. Because of the difficulty in enforcement and in reaching less-well-educated workers, there is little support for introducing a version of the requirement French firms have to devote 1.7 percent of their payroll to worker training.[9]

Long, Temporary Layoffs and Possible Job Loss

When a firm or industry begins the economic downturn that ultimately leads to substantial downsizing, it usually is too late to save the weakest plants. However, clear evidence of impending, permanent employment reductions can increase worker responsiveness to getting retrained. At this point workers need income replacement programs and help in assessing whether job loss will be permanent.

SHORT-TERM INCOME REPLACEMENT. For most dislocated workers the "regular" unemployment compensation (UC) program mandated by the Social Security Act of 1935 provides a substantial income cushion for jobless spells shorter than six months. Under UC, states have considerable discretion in setting up their programs. As a result, state weekly maximums show considerable variation. Today states such as Michigan, with high maximums, pay up to about $300 a week; states like Indiana, with low maximums, only pay up to about $220 a week. Since high-tenure workers tend to have high earnings, these maximums largely determine their benefit levels. Most workers are eligible to receive twenty-six times their weekly benefit amount over a benefit year of fifty-two weeks.[10] UC is fully funded by an experience-rated payroll tax that attempts to match each firm's payments to the benefits its workers received over the preceding three to five years. Experience rating is not perfect. The percentage of payments not covered by taxes paid by firms from which workers leave varies over the

9. Barnow, Chasanov, and Pande (1990).

10. U.S. DOL (1997). More precisely, the weekly benefit amount (WBA) typically is set at 1/25th of "high-quarter" earnings—earnings in the quarter with the most earnings in the "base period." The base period is the earliest four of the last five quarters following filing of an initial claim. The WBA applies throughout the "benefit year," the following fifty-two weeks, and the maximum benefit amount (MBA) typically is set at twenty-six times the WBA. Benefits can be exhausted either because the entitlement is used up or the benefit year expires. After the benefit year ends, claimants who are or become unemployed must requalify based on a new base period. During long periods of repetitive unemployment, the WBA often falls in successive benefit years as unemployment reduces high-quarter earnings of each new base period. A good review of how UI works can be found in Woodbury and Rubin (1997).

business cycle and across states. In 1988 and 1989, 34 percent of all UI benefit payments to workers were not charged to individual employers. In the recessionary year of 1992, however, 44 percent of benefit payments were not charged to individual employers.[11] In most states, as a result, high-unemployment firms (particularly those in the construction industry) receive substantial subsidies from low-unemployment firms.

For relatively short periods of unemployment, say thirteen out of fifty-two weeks, the combination of UI benefits and reductions in family expenditures is sufficient to avoid substantial financial hardships. As periods of unemployment lengthen, it becomes progressively more difficult to meet obligations such as mortgage payments and tuition expenditures. The most serious financial consequences occur at the point UC benefits are exhausted, after six months of unemployment. But long periods of intermittent unemployment followed by recall are troublesome even if workers never exhaust their UC benefits. Such episodes are common before permanent job loss, and they deplete savings and reduce entitlements when job loss occurs.

In prosperous times only about 28 percent of UI claimants exhaust their UC benefits. Because the duration of unemployment is bimodal, with those who have not exhausted benefits usually collecting less than eight weeks' worth, those who have run out of benefits collect about 45 percent of all benefits. In recessions the average duration of unemployment increases by more than 50 percent, to about eighteen weeks, but a disproportionate cause of the shift is increases in unusually long spells of unemployment that often lead to UC exhaustion.[12] To ease the financial distress of long-term unemployed workers, separate programs have been implemented during each recession since 1974 to extend the duration of UI payments. To increase the countercyclical effect of the spending and avoid depleting the state UI trust funds, these increases are largely financed with federal funds.

There is a permanent second-tier program, extended benefits (EB), that is funded equally by state and federal revenue. The EB program extends benefits by thirteen weeks based on the level, or changes in level, of state unemployment rates. In 1981 changes in the triggers made it difficult for the program to "trigger on." As a result, during the last two recessions temporary third-tier programs were the main source of extended benefits. Third-tier programs are fully federally funded, tailored to meet the needs of particular downturns, and have to be renewed periodically. The most recent

11. Advisory Council on Unemployment Compensation (1995, table 6-5, pp. 83–84).

12. U.S. DOL (1994, p. 208).

program under the Emergency Unemployment Compensation (EUC) Act more than doubled the total duration of benefits that could be received by unemployed workers in states with exceptionally high unemployment, but the need to renew the program four times caused considerable uncertainty about the availability of benefits.

TAA is another special, federal program that currently extends the duration of UI payments, but only for trade-impacted workers. Since 1981 TAA has guaranteed 52 weeks of full UI payments at the same weekly rate as UC over a 104-week period to certified workers who enter a training program within 16 weeks of becoming unemployed, or who receive a waiver stating that training is unnecessary or unavailable. Workers still in training after receiving fifty-two weeks of benefits qualify for an additional twenty-six weeks of benefits. TAA is paid only after all other forms of UI are exhausted, and administered by state employment security agencies (SESAs) that also run the state federal UI system. Thus, while EUC was in place from 1991 through 1994, TAA expenditures were unusually low.[13]

To be certified eligible a worker must file a petition with the U.S. DOL demonstrating that imports that directly compete with the plant's output have increased absolutely and that those imports contributed significantly to major employment declines in the plant. Only workers in the manufacturing and mining industries have qualified for TAA.

One of the major criticisms of TAA is that it only covers those who are harmed by direct imports. For example, workers in auto assembly plants usually are covered, but workers supplying parts to those plants usually are not. Tertiary declines among service firms dependent on the purchases of manufacturing workers, such as restaurants and retail stores, also are not covered. The recently enacted North American Free Trade Agreement (NAFTA)–bridge TAA Program lifted some restrictions, particularly granting automatic certification to workers in plants that relocate abroad, whether or not the other tests are met.

There is overwhelming evidence that extended benefit programs are well targeted on workers with exceptionally large earnings losses. Figure 11-3 shows that among high-tenure workers in Pennsylvania who lost their jobs, those who exhausted UI had by far the largest long-term earnings losses, whereas those who changed jobs without receiving any UI had remarkably

13. For a basic description of the TAA Program, see Jacobson (1993a, chapter 2, pp. 4–6) U.S. House of Representatives (1994, section 9, pp. 311–23).

Figure 11-3. *Earnings Losses for Workers Not Collecting and Collecting Unemployment Insurance*

Thousands of 1987 U.S.$ (quarterly)

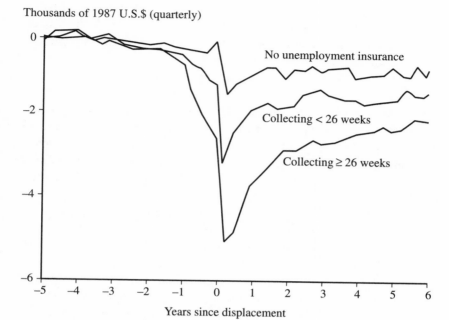

Years since displacement

Source: Jacobson, Lalonde, and Sullivan (1993c, figure 4, p. 14).

small long-term losses.[14] Unpublished tabulations showed that about 15 percent of the high-tenured, Pennsylvania workers who changed jobs did not collect UI, while 25 percent exhausted UI benefits.

It is equally clear that a high percentage of those who exhaust UI benefits lose jobs. A study of manufacturing claimants in Pennsylvania showed that about 60 percent of claimants receiving less than fifteen weeks of benefits were recalled. About 40 percent of those who had not used up all UI but, received fifteen or more weeks of benefits, were recalled, and less than 20 percent of those who had exhausted UI were recalled.[15] But recall rates were considerably higher for high-tenure workers in trade-impacted industries.[16] A related study showed that from 1974 to 1981 about 60 percent of TAA-certified workers in Pennsylvania who collected UC benefits exhausted

14. Jacobson, LaLonde, and Sullivan (1993c, p. 14).
15. Jacobson (1993b, table 6.2, p. 5).
16. Jacobson (1993c, table 6.1, p. 4).

those benefits, but only about 25 percent lost their jobs in that period. About 60 percent of Pennsylvania TAA recipients were in the steel industry and most of the rest were in apparel.[17] Nationwide, however, most 1981 TAA recipients were autoworkers in the midwest. Exhaustion of UC benefits also was widespread among those workers, and job loss rates were even lower.

During the severe 1981 recession, TAA payments were being made at the rate of $1.9 billion a year, an amount equal to about 10 percent of all UI payments. At the time it was widely believed that auto employment would rebound and was not a precursor to massive, permanent layoffs. Moreover, auto (and steel) workers were exceptionally well paid and received generous Supplemental Unemployment Benefits (SUB) payments.[18] In a period of huge, federal budget cuts, TAA was therefore an easy target. Before the 1981 revisions, TAA weekly payments were set at 70 percent of past earnings, up to a maximum of the average weekly wage in manufacturing, or about $650 (in 1994 dollars). In contrast, UC paid about 50 percent of past earnings up to a maximum, which rarely exceeded $300 (in 1994 dollars). There was strong sentiment to eliminate the program entirely. Instead, TAA weekly payments were reduced to those of UC benefits, and qualifying requirements were modified to greatly restrict eligibility. As a result, payments tumbled from $1,440 million in 1981 to $103 million in 1982.[19]

The irony is that about half of the steelworkers who received TAA and one-third of the autoworkers ultimately lost their jobs. A key problem was that downsizing did not peak in steel until 1982 and had only begun in the auto industry at the time of the TAA cuts. Clearly, there was a lack of recognition that widespread temporary layoffs begin years before substantial job loss occurs. After 1984 the certification process was liberalized, but enormous damage had been done. Not only did the cuts in benefits and certifications severely reduce the compensation available to trade-affected workers, but the cuts were also widely regarded as reneging on promises to provide some measure of protection to workers in exchange for maintaining support for trade liberalization. These actions heavily colored attitudes that led to strong opposition to NAFTA and other measures to reduce trade restrictions.

17. Jacobson (1994, table 4, p. 236).
18. A key cause of the lack of sympathy for autoworkers was that SUB paid the difference between governmental UI and 95 percent of straight-time weekly pay. As a result high-seniority autoworkers opted to be laid off first rather than last.
19. U.S. House of Representatives (1994, table 9-3, p. 317).

A more subtle, and perhaps more important, irony is that the strong correlation between UI exhaustion and long-term earnings reductions following reemployment has largely been ignored. A central question is why has there be so little interest in shifting UC to cover long-term unemployment more effectively, even if that means reducing payments covering short-term unemployment. This is precisely the approach taken with respect to TAA, and indisputably this dramatically shifted the targeting of available funds to workers with the largest losses.

One possible explanation is that efficiency concerns inhibit extending UC payments. It is possible that extending the duration of UC would waste resources by increasing the length of temporary layoffs, reduce overall competitiveness, and slow the pace of productivity-enhancing structural change. Studies of the behavior of firms facing different UC tax systems suggest that unemployment would be about 2.5 or more percentage points higher in the United States if we had no experience rating, and conversely would drop by about 1.2 percentage points if we had perfect experience rating.[20] Firms' reactions to non-experience-rated TAA and third-tier programs reinforce the view that firms quickly take advantage of opportunities to pay their unemployed workers with someone else's funds by increasing the incidence and duration of layoffs.[21] Analogous theoretical and empirical studies (by Martin Feldstein and others in the 1970s) of the incentives created from not taxing UI payments led to making such payments taxable.[22]

Further, firms that downsize or close rarely have built up sufficient trust funds to pay the UI benefits of their former workers. Given the way experience rating adjusts future payments to "recapture" previous pay-

20. Studies by Topel (1985) and Card and Levine (1994) suggest that moving to complete experience rating would reduced temporary layoffs by roughly 60 percent, which would reduce the unemployment rate by about 1.2 percentage points. The effect of removing experience rating entirely is more difficult to estimate, but undoubtedly would be much larger than the effect of making experience rating more complete. A reasonable estimate is two to three times greater, or between 2.5 and 3.6 percentage points.

21. The second renewal of the EUC program allowed workers the unprecedented option of either establishing a new, first-tier claim or collecting EUC based on an earlier claim. Unpublished interviews I conducted revealed that a major impetus to reverse this provision came from knowledge that major employers and their unions were urging unemployed workers to opt for the non-experience-rated EUC benefits and had timed layoffs to take advantage of this unusual option.

22. Feldstein (1978).

ments, it is most unlikely that firms permanently reducing payrolls will cover those costs. The UC payroll tax is based on a fixed base that today is usually $7,000 per worker, and a variable rate based on the ratio of current payroll to benefits paid out, usually over the preceding three-year period.[23] As the payroll of a firm declines, the amount of taxes paid declines as well. The decline is more than proportional because declining payroll also reduces the tax rate. Thus to build up trust funds in advance of layoffs it would be necessary to reduce UC expenditures for short-term unemployment or (shudder) increase tax rates. A third option is to finance an increase in benefit duration from general revenue, as is currently done for TAA and third-tier UI programs. Such a plan probably would reduce opposition from healthy firms to extending benefits but would boost incentives for weak firms to increase the duration of layoffs.

Perhaps the most attractive option in today's political environment is to leave the tax system unchanged but reduce payments to short-term unemployed workers. One widely discussed means to do that is to have claimants wait two weeks following the start of each unemployment spell. At present, most states have claimants serve a single waiting week at the start of their benefit year. Another alternative that would be more efficient, but perhaps difficult to implement politically, is to make experience rating more perfect by raising the maximum tax rate and lowering the minimum tax rate.

Despite the attractiveness to policy analysts of increasing the potential duration of UI payments, it is clear that workers and their representatives have little interest in improving coverage of low-probability, costly, long spells of unemployment by reducing protection for reasonably predictable, less costly, short spells. It therefore appears that workers value the income-smoothing benefits of the UI system far more than its insurance aspects.

Given the dramatic increase in costly job loss, one might conclude that workers are myopic or have difficulty solving probability problems. For example, it appears people are prone to underinsure themselves against low-probability, high-cost events such as auto accidents, fires, floods, and earthquakes. The problem is sufficiently widespread that purchasing auto and fire insurance has been made mandatory, even though only in rare instances would car or home owners be better off declaring personal bankruptcy to escape debt rather than paying the modest cost of actuarially fair insurance. Whether educating workers to recognize more clearly the trade-off between income smoothing and insurance would change their

23. U.S. DOL (1997).

views is unknown. But there is little question that workers' unwillingness to pay for additional insurance is a major impediment to dealing more effectively with the problem of long-term unemployment.

ADVANCE NOTICE AND UI PROFILING. Job loss imposes huge losses on many high-tenure workers. Long periods of temporary layoff often precede job loss, but a substantial number of workers subjected to long temporary layoffs do not lose their jobs. It follows that waiting for recall is entirely rational; most high-tenure workers would be much better off staying with their original firms than leaving. For example, steelworkers who stayed in steel suffered losses of about 15 percent relative to the average worker, but workers dislocated from the steel industry had losses of about 50 percent on average.[24]

Uncertainty about recall substantially slows the recovery of those who lose their jobs. For example, unemployment following a plant closing is much shorter than that following a mass layoff among otherwise identical workers. The need to find work quickly to avoid major financial distress is particularly great because UI in the United States covers a relatively short period, and much of the benefit could be exhausted by the time it becomes obvious job loss is permanent. To make matters worse, it is possible that the financial and psychological stress associated with long periods of unemployment make it difficult for workers to search effectively for new jobs when that becomes necessary. Employers may discriminate against long-term unemployed individuals unless they perform volunteer work or obtain training while they are out of work.

It would therefore be highly desirable for workers to know as quickly as possible that job loss is permanent. Workers would be heavily damaged if firms withheld critical information needed to guide decisions. But it is not at all clear that firms routinely conceal potentially valuable information about the permanence (or duration) of layoffs. To a large extent the length and permanency of layoffs depend on fluctuations in demand that are inherently difficult to predict. Moreover, the weakest firms in a given industry are likely to be particularly bad at making such predictions.

This is not to say that firms always share highly relevant information with their workers. Undoubtedly there are situations where multiplant firms delay announcing well-laid plans to curtail production at a given facility in order to forestall local opposition or to mislead competitors. In some cases, unions fail even to ask whether such plans exist; but in the worst cases, management conceals plans even when asked. Probably the most effective

24. Jacobson, LaLonde, and Sullivan (1993b, table 6.2, p. 128).

means to deal with the asymmetry in information between management and labor is to establish a harmonious labor relations climate. There is plenty of evidence that treating workers humanely improves profitability and vice versa.

Although management and labor in some firms hit hard by structural change made a real effort to improve labor relations, in other firms labor relations became even more adversarial. In the early 1980s charges of failure to bargain in good faith grew as confidence in the fairness of the National Labor Relations Board (NLRB) plummeted. As a result a major effort was launched by organized labor to mandate advance notice. The Worker Adjustment and Retraining Notification (WARN) Act, which took effect on February 4, 1989, requires firms with 100 or more employees to give sixty days' notice of layoffs of fifty or more employees if such layoffs are likely to last six months or more. Firms that fail to give advance notice are liable to pay each affected worker up to sixty days' worth of wages and fringe benefits.

Studies of advance notice suggest that mandatory notice has limited effect on the incidence of formal advance warnings,[25] and advance notice has at best a modest positive effect, primarily by helping a few workers avoid unemployment entirely. There is little evidence that advance notice helps workers once they begin to collect UI. In addition, firms giving advance notice do not appear to be hurt by premature defections of personnel. Finally, advance notice assists government agencies to rapidly register workers for UI and provide information about other forms of assistance.

The effects of advance notice are modest for three key reasons. Mass layoffs are much more common than closures, and there is nothing preventing firms from giving false positives—that is, warning of a layoff and then not laying workers off, or laying them off for less than six months. Workers also have incentives to stay with firms up to the point of layoff because firms often increase overtime in order to stockpile output as a closing approaches. Firms sometimes offer bonuses for staying until the closure occurs, and those who leave early and change jobs risk losing their UI entitlements if they later find those jobs unsuitable and quit to find other work. It also appears that highly skilled workers benefit the most from advance notice, but skilled workers also tend to have the easiest time finding new jobs when no such notice is given.

In the final analysis it is important for workers and firms to work together to improve productivity and share information. But it is unclear

25. Ehrenberg and Jakubson (1988); Addison and Portugal (1987); Ruhm (1992).

that government mandates for advance notice can do much more than eliminate the worst practices (where management conceals definitive information of considerable value) and increase awareness of best practices (sharing relevant information with workers).

An alternative approach to helping workers judge the duration and permanency of layoffs is for the UI system to predict each claimant's duration of unemployment and likelihood of recall to work. (Since recall probabilities decline with length of unemployment, the choice of dependent variable makes little difference.) The U.S. Unemployment Insurance Service (USUIS) has championed the development of a system that would determine which claimants were likely to lose jobs or be unemployed for substantial periods by the fifth week of an unemployment spell. It would also quickly provide adjustment services to claimants who could benefit from those services. One possible rationale behind the system is closely related to figure 11-3, which shows the correlation between long periods of unemployment and large permanent losses. The view is that by helping workers to search more quickly for work, these workers would suffer smaller losses in both the long and short term.

A more obvious rationale is that helping workers quickly find work would dramatically reduce UI payouts and increase the short-run incomes of claimants, since the pay at new jobs is likely to be higher than UI payments. The U.S. DOL tested this concept in the exceptionally informative New Jersey demonstration (NJD) project. The results of this random-assignment experiment suggested that it was possible to select claimants who would benefit from readjustment services, substantially reduce the duration of unemployment for this group, and reduce UI payments.

The primary intent of the experiment was to determine the merits of alternative services. Little attention was paid to assessing the accuracy or value of the information provided by the screening equation alone. Claimant predictions were not compared with those of the screening equations, nor was the extent to which claimants modified their behavior when the screening equation differed from their own beliefs. Nevertheless, the UI system could have improved job search outcomes simply by increasing the information available to claimants. This could have been done by pooling the information gained from interviewing many claimants from the same firm or by receiving more accurate information from the firm itself. In particular, firms may be willing to share information with the UI system when they believe it will reduce UI payments by helping workers find new jobs more quickly or by helping the UI system monitor job search. The UI system is obligated to deny UI benefits to workers who violate the job search requirements, which includes requiring long-term, unemployed workers to accept relatively low-wage jobs outside of their usual professions.

Largely on the basis of the success of the NJD and support by service providers, a new program is being implemented in every state to profile UI claimants within the first few weeks of layoffs to determine their expected duration of unemployment, and to refer to supportive services claimants who are likely to remain unemployed for a long period and are unlikely to be recalled.[26]

There is considerable evidence that the duration of unemployment can be reduced without adversely affecting subsequent earnings. Methods include selectively calling UI claimants in for interviews; reviewing their job search plans and actions; requiring certain claimants to participate in reemployment programs; and denying benefits to claimants who do not report for the interview, mandatory services, or otherwise fail to search for work.

Several studies have examined work-test enforcement.[27] The UI work test requires that claimants be available for work (actively searching for work); be able to work (not ill, carrying for dependents, or on vacation); and have not refused suitable work (job offers in their field at pay reasonably close to former levels). The penalty for failing the weekly able-and-available conditions is a loss of benefits for that week but no loss of entitlement. The penalty for failing the refusal condition is an indefinite denial—that is, the claimant is barred from receiving any additional benefits during the current unemployment spell. To reestablish eligibility in future unemployment spells, the claimant must return to work for a certain period or earn a particular amount.

One of the few studies of work-test denials showed that only indefinite denials lead to substantial savings of UI payments, and the tests are effective in isolating claimants who are not seriously looking for work.[28] There

26. The profiling system was authorized in the second renewal of the EUC as a *budget-neutral* means to pay for the EB program. (The EUC program also was financed by retaining a 0.2 percent payroll tax scheduled for elimination.) Although UI savings were substantial, they were not sufficient to more than pay for the services. Technically, the profiling *with* mandatory referral to services was considered budget neutral, based on more than covering the additional cost of profiling with UI savings and *shifting* resources in existing service programs from non-claimants to claimants, rather than expanding services.

27. These studies include analyses of special demonstration projects in New Jersey (Corson and others [1989]), South Carolina (Corson and Nicholson [1985]), and Washington (Johnson and Klepinger [1991]), as well as normal operations in states such as Arizona (Jacobson and Schwarz-Miller [1981]).

28. Jacobson and Schwarz-Miller (1981).

also is evidence that work-test stringency has a strong indirect effect of deterring individuals who are unlikely to comply with the job search requirements from filing claims for UI. States that stringently enforce the work-test requirement tend to have substantially shorter periods of covered unemployment, holding other factors constant.[29]

There also is evidence on the effectiveness of denying benefits to claimants who fail to come in for required interviews or participate in mandatory assistance programs. The Charleston Work-Search random-assignment demonstration called in certain claimants for screening interviews and, as needed, assignment to mandatory services.[30] Unlike the NJD, however, claimants who failed to report for interviews or services were told in advance that they would receive indefinite denials of UI benefits unless they could adequately explain these failures.

The evaluation showed that failure to report was much greater in Charleston than in New Jersey (about 25 percent versus 10 percent) and the probability of denial for lack of compliance much higher. The Charleston program led to substantial reductions in UI payments. However, the entire effect was associated with the denial of benefits. There were virtually no reductions in payments following completion of the mandatory week of half-day job search workshops. As in other cases, it appears that denials did not prevent individuals who were ready to accept reasonable jobs from continuing to collect benefits. Rather, it appeared to screen out individuals who had a marginal attachment to the labor force or little need for UI payments. The higher threat of denial itself was also a major reason that many more claimants failed to report in the Charleston demo than in the New Jersey one.

In summary, the evidence suggests that an array of UI office activities can reduce claimants' duration of unemployment, reduce expenditures on transfers, and, in most cases, raise claimant income.

When Layoffs Become Permanent

Although it is unclear whether advance warning and profiling substantially improve the timing and accuracy of information possessed by

29. Cross-state variability in work-test stringency has diminished following the 1981–82 recession, when many states' UI trust funds became insolvent and the federal government, for the first time, instituted interest charges on loans and placed surtaxes on states with large debts. To reduce UI outlays, states more strictly enforced the work test, as well as reduced entitlements and tightened qualifying requirements.

30. Corson and Nicholson (1985).

workers about inherently uncertain events, it appears that those steps help government more effectively target services. It is significant that providing income support, monitoring job search, and offering supportive services are appropriate for long-term unemployed workers even if they are recalled to work. However, it is obvious that long-term unemployed individuals who are not recalled suffer the largest long-term earnings losses. As a result, there is a premium on helping workers who lose their jobs to find relatively high-paying new ones.

What types of adjustment assistance are most effective in aiding dislocated workers? The central choice is between different forms of JSA and forms of retraining. Duane Leigh provides an excellent summary in *Does Training Work for Displaced Workers?* of the four major studies that were completed in the 1980s that directly compare the effectiveness of JSA and classroom training.[31] Two of the studies were based on random-assignment experiments, the other two on the use of comparison groups.

The two well-conceived, random-assignment experiments that were designed to test the merits of JSA versus retraining are the federally funded NJD, and the state-funded Texas Worker Assistance Demonstration (WAD).[32] As noted above, the NJD was designed as much to reduce UI payments as to assist dislocated workers to quickly find new jobs.[33] At its heart, then, was testing the effect of rapidly screening claimants and assigning them to supportive services. The NJD selected more than 11,000 claimants who were found to be in need of adjustment services and tested the merits of three options: JSA alone; JSA combined with training or relocation assistance; and JSA combined with a cash bonus for quickly finding work.[34]

The result of central importance is that only about 15 percent of those offered training took it, and during the short follow-up period this training had no discernable positive effect. (Virtually no one took the relocation assistance.) The treatment effects for the JSA alone and JSA with training were therefore nearly identical. The cost of training, however, was about $3,200 per participant, compared with about $500 per person for JSA. JSA consisted of orientation, testing, a job search workshop, a resource center,

31. Leigh (1990).
32. Corson and others (1989); Anderson and others (1990); Bloom and Kulik (1986); Bloom (1990).
33. The sources used in this section include Leigh (1990); Bloom (1990); Corson and others (1985, 1989); Kulik and others (1984).
34. Leigh (1990, pp. 18, 37).

an assessment/counseling interview, and job referral. These treatments reduced unemployment by half a week on average, saving about $85 in UI payments, and increasing earnings by about $500.[35]

The average effect of JSA accompanied by a bonus was about twice that of JSA alone. But the bonus was much more expensive than JSA. The initial bonus was set at half the remaining UI entitlement; it was awarded if a worker took a job within two weeks of becoming eligible for the bonus and held that job at least four weeks. As the return to work was delayed, the bonus was reduced 10 percent a week until it reached zero, eleven weeks after the initial date of eligibility. Those who filed for the bonus collected about $800 each.

The Texas WAD also directly compared JSA alone with JSA followed by training. The services were provided as part of the ordinary operations of Title III programs in Houston and El Paso under the Job Training Partnership Act (JTPA). In contrast, the NJD was a special one-shot demonstration conducted by the state agency that runs the UI and Employment Service (ES) system. WAD used the normal intake procedures of JTPA Title III programs, not the procedures to rapidly refer claimants used in the NJD.

About 1,200 dislocated workers participated in WAD in Houston and El Paso.[36] For an average participant the program increased earnings by about $800 and reduced UI payments by about $170.[37] Virtually all the benefits accrued in the first year after leaving treatment as a result of participants finding work more quickly. Unlike the NJD, the take-up rate for training was substantial, but at least in the one-year follow-up period, there was no advantage to taking training. The difference in cost, however, was large. JSA cost about $1,531 per person, compared with $4,991 for JSA plus training. For male workers in Houston where it was possible to measure the incremental effect of training, it appeared to take longer for trainees to find work, but these participants may have had higher earnings when employed. The returns to training might have proven greater had the study included a longer follow-up period.

Two additional studies directly compared the returns to JSA and training. Neither the study of the Downriver Community Conference Economic Readjustment Program in Michigan nor the study of the Buffalo (N.Y.) Displaced Worker Project used a pure experimental design.[38] But the Buf-

35. Leigh (1990, pp. 42, 45).
36. Leigh (1990, p. 18).
37. Leigh (1990, p. 21).
38. Kulik and others (1984); Corson and others (1985). The studies of the Downriver and Buffalo programs also determined that on-the-job-training (OJT) was reasonably effective in reducing unemployment, but considerably more expen-

falo study produced reasonably clear-cut results, particularly for a group of workers who, because of capacity constraints, were randomly selected to be offered services. The program lasted a year starting in October 1982 and served about 300 workers. As might be expected for a program in Buffalo, the target group were mostly steel and auto workers with high tenure and high pay. Most important, a majority of participants had been unemployed for about a year before being offered assistance, and only about 16 percent of those offered services accepted those offers. The evaluators attempted to model the determinants of participation to reduce selection bias.

The overall conclusion was that JSA raised earnings by about $134 per week, which was roughly the same as the $122 increase for those receiving classroom training. Even with the assistance, however, the weekly earnings of about one-third of the target group were more than 50 percent below predisplacement levels. Classroom training raised the probability of some employment by 47 percentage points, while JSA raised the probability by 33 percentage points. As a result, employment rates were about twice as high for targets than for members of the comparison group. Finally, the cost of JSA was only $851 per person compared with $3,282 for classroom training.[39]

A second group, comprising 300 program participants, was also studied, but the comparison methodology was less robust.[40] That group had lower predisplacement earnings and less tenure, and its members were only unemployed about eight weeks at enrollment and were considerably more likely to accept assistance. About 28 percent of offers of aid were accepted. The evaluators concluded that classroom training was about as effective for the second group as the first, but JSA had little effect.

The final study of the quartet is an evaluation of the Downriver Program designed to help displaced auto workers who lost jobs near Detroit in 1980

---

sive than JSA. OJT usually offers to pay firms a portion of new hires' salaries for a short period, usually three to six months, and sometimes also pays for work-based training. The presumption is that workers who do well during OJT will be kept on as permanent employees. The most controversial aspects of OJT are the extent to which firms would hire dislocated workers in the absence of the OJT subsides, and the closely related issue of the extent to which training is needed for targets to be employed. Thus, a key reservation about the utility of OJT is that it reduces the effectiveness of JSA and classroom training by making firms reluctant to hire program targets without the subsidy. The U.S. DOL has discouraged JTPA Title III programs from using OJT, because of these reservations as well as the high costs of monitoring the suitability of the training component and whether workers are appropriately retained.

39. Leigh (1990, p. 29).
40. Leigh (1990, p. 18).

and 1981.[41] The overall results are positive but vary depending on the comparison group used. The effect on weekly earnings ranges from about $33 a week to about $122 a week.[42] There are no precise breakdowns for JSA and classroom training because the evaluators note that training did not significantly improve performance over JSA alone. Yet the cost of training was more than twice that of JSA. As Duane Leigh concludes:

> The Buffalo, WAD, and NJD projects are unanimous in indicating that JSA services strongly affect in the intended direction a variety of labor market outcomes including earnings, placement, and employment rates, and amount of UI benefits. Given the relatively low cost of JSA, much of the evidence suggests that JSA services are cost effective. For the other employment services, evidence across all four demonstrations indicates that classroom training fails to have a sizable incremental effect on earnings and employment above that of JSA only. It certainly does not appear to be the case that the additional effect of classroom training is large enough to compensate for its higher cost. The authors of the major evaluations are plainly troubled by these unexpectedly weak results for classroom training, and they offer a number of caveats for their findings.[43]

Leigh also cites a key conclusion from the report by Corson and others on the dislocated worker demonstration projects that included Buffalo and five other sites where only process evaluations were conducted: "The key lessons learned are that (1) many displaced workers will not be able to adapt to classroom training, and (2) that despite attempts to base course selection on labor market data, many successful program graduates might not be able to locate training-related jobs."[44]

Reviews of the four dislocated worker studies by Duane Leigh and others played a major role in overcoming the strongly held conventional wisdom that classroom training was far more effective in boosting long-term earnings than JSA. Today the prevailing view is that inexpensive JSA should be the first line of defense in aiding dislocated workers, and, by and large, expensive retraining should be turned to only after JSA has failed. But the conventional wisdom was held so strongly that it took about six years (and several additional studies, discussed below) to reverse long-held views. Despite having most of the above information available, the Economic Dislocation and Worker Adjustment Act (EDWAA) of 1988

41. Kulik and others (1984).
42. Leigh (1990, p. 18).
43. Leigh (1988, p. 29; 1990, pp. 47–48).
44. Leigh (1990, p. 107).

modified JTPA to require that half of all Title III funds be spent on training.[45]

One reason the conventional wisdom about the effectiveness of training was not more quickly overcome by these studies is that the studies left open the possibility that longer-lasting training, accompanied by income support, with longer follow-up would show more favorable results.[46] The EDWAA amendments were specifically aimed at prompting program operators to spend more resources on each person, even if fewer people were served, in the hope that the results would be more favorable. In addition, there was an emphasis on reaching dislocated workers far closer to the point of job loss, when they would be more amenable to enter training and had used up only a small fraction of their UI entitlements.

It is worth noting that there were no large-scale evaluations of JTPA Title III programs following EDWAA's inception. Instead, the key study that sapped much of the remaining support for classroom training as the primary means to aid dislocated workers was a major twelve-state study funded by DOL comparing the operations of the TAA Program before and after training became mandatory for most recipients in 1988. Although training vouchers were available to TAA recipients from the program's inception, they were rarely used until November 1981, when emphasis on training was substantially increased, and considerably more funds were allocated to pay for vouchers.[47] In 1988, at the same time EDWAA strongly increased the

45. Unlike JTPA Title II programs for economically disadvantaged people, which are run exclusively by about 640 Private Industry Councils (PICs), JTPA Title III programs are run, at the discretion of each governor, by PICs, substate organizations, at the state level, or some combination of the three alternatives. In particular, it is common to have state-level, rapid-response teams deal with major plant closings and mass layoffs.

46. In the interventions examined, reducing UI expenditures was given at least as much emphasis as reducing the duration of unemployment and long-term losses. In addition, training rarely lasted more than six months, and the programs provided income support above that of UI only in cases of unusual need. Perhaps of greatest importance, the follow-up periods of the studies might have been too short to capture the full benefits of training. For example, male trainees in the Houston WAD took longer to find work, but they appeared to have had higher earnings when employed. Thus, the returns to training may have proven greater had the study included a longer follow-up period.

47. As noted earlier, TAA benefits were paid only after other forms of UI were exhausted and provided for a total of fifty-two weekly payments over a two-year period, plus an additional twenty-six weeks of benefits to workers in training. From 1974 through 1981, TAA provided weekly benefits equal to 70 percent of prior weekly earnings up to 100 percent of the average wage in manufacturing. From November 1981 to the present, the weekly benefit amount was reduced to that of regular UC. This made the transfer payments into a form of UI extended benefits.

emphasis on training in Title III JTPA programs, new legislation also dramatically heightened the emphasis on TAA training. It did so by requiring TAA recipients to enter a training program or receive a waiver stating that training was not needed or unavailable by the sixteenth week of unemployment covered by TAA. Most important, there were no federal standards for granting waivers or requiring that training be particularly rigorous, and no limit on the per-person size of the voucher. As a result of these changes, spending on TAA training went from less than 5 percent of all costs from 1974 to 1981, to about 30 percent from 1982 to 1988, to more than 50 percent after 1988.[48]

The twelve-state study concluded that the training vouchers accompanied by stipends had no statistically significant effect on earnings. However, Bob Lalonde's review of this study noted that the point estimates showed a positive effect of about $294 per quarter, but the size of the sample was too small to produce statistically significant results.[49] My own review suggested that the large variance surrounding the point estimates was due to the broad differences in the scope and rigor of the training received. In particular, it was difficult to determine which workers were taking the minimum amount of training needed to qualify for the stipends and which were substantially upgrading their skills. Unfortunately, the underlying data set did not provide the information needed to distinguish key differences in the training received, such as cost or hours of training received.

Also, the analysis failed to note the significance of other evidence. Before the 1988 changes in TAA, about 25 percent of TAA recipients received training vouchers; but those who received the vouchers did so close to the end of the fifty-two weeks of regular TAA and then proceeded to exhaust the twenty-six-week extension offered trainees. In addition, after the 1988 changes the incidence of voucher receipt rose to about 70 percent, but few trainees received any of the twenty-six weeks of additional benefits offered to those who exhausted regular TAA. The average number of payments to trainees went from seventy-two weeks before 1988 to fifty-four weeks after. This suggests that making training mandatory had the desired effect of increasing participation, but even when offered "free" training supported by vouchers, few individuals elected to continue in programs for more than a year.

Finally, the TAA study did not capture the complex pattern of layoffs followed by recalls that most TAA recipients probably experienced. For

48. Jacobson (1993b, chapter 9, p. 9).
49. LaLonde (1995, p. 162).

example, my analysis of workers certified eligible for TAA in Missouri in 1985 and 1986 showed that 43.6 percent of those who exhausted UC (and received at least one TAA payment) did not lose jobs, and the majority of displacements occurred toward the end of the two-year certification period.[50] This is further evidence of the enormous difficulty workers face in predicting the incidence and timing of job loss and that governments confront in targeting adjustment services when they are most needed. TAA-certified workers probably know they are likely to exhaust UC benefits but are uncertain about whether they will lose jobs. As a result, they have stronger incentives to make sure that they are eligible for extended UI payments than to use vouchers to prepare for new jobs.

In summary, these are the key conclusions from the TAA analyses:

—A majority of trade-affected workers exhaust UC benefits.

—TAA provides a substantial financial cushion that would not otherwise be available.

—Large training vouchers accompanied by stipends did little to reduce the huge permanent reductions in earnings of job leavers, even if they sometimes had a positive effect on earnings.

—Many trade-affected workers did not lose jobs, and displacements often occurred toward the end of their entitlement period. Uncertainty over the permanence of layoffs may have substantially reduced the effectiveness of the training vouchers.

—Encouraging the rapid use of training vouchers reduced rather than increased the total length of unemployment of TAA recipients, suggesting that recipients strongly preferred taking available jobs to continuing in training.

—Although the cost of the training vouchers was about equal to the savings in TAA payments per trainee, the large increase in vouchers greatly increased the cost of the program, suggesting that targeting of vouchers could be greatly improved.

One crucial caveat in the TAA analyses is that the effectiveness of the training vouchers was adversely affected by the requirement to take training to qualify for the cash payments. Another concern was the lack of resources and administrative rules to ensure trainees were appropriately screened and referred. As a result many trainees may have failed to build skills that could realistically lead to high-paying jobs. In addition, little attention was paid to the possible incentive effects of TAA in prolonging layoffs.

50. Jacobson (1993b, chapter 9, p. 10).

A study that Maureen Cropper and I conducted of TAA before 1981 strongly suggested that firms reacted to the incentives inherent in TAA by substantially prolonging layoffs.[51] But much of that effect may have been because, during the period studied, TAA offered much higher WBAs before UI benefits were used up. This evidence is consistent with that of many other studies on the effects of increasing WBAs. In contrast, relatively little is known about how changes in the duration of payments affect unemployment. Preliminary results from a study Steve Woodbury and I are conducting using Pennsylvania and Missouri data suggest that the disincentive effects of TAA for those who leave jobs are small but could be substantial for those who stay in jobs. That is, firms lengthen layoffs when TAA is available. They do this because they do not bear the cost of these transfers, but obtain the benefits in terms of reducing the likelihood workers will take other jobs and not return when recalled.

The last study discussed in this subsection draws inferences about the importance of screening potential trainees, and the returns on differences in duration, intensity, and subject matter. This study examines the returns from a program that offered free tuition at the Community College of Allegheny County (CCAC) from 1983 through 1985 to every unemployed resident of Allegheny County (metropolitan Pittsburgh). It is significant that the Dislocated Worker Employment and Training Program (DWETP) that Bob LaLonde, Dan Sullivan, and I studied was widely advertised and required applicants to be screened to make sure that they enrolled in a program that matched their skills and interests.[52] Besides the regular courses at this large, multicampus college, special courses in career development and coping with unemployment were established by the college. About 12,000 out of 150,000 eligible people applied to the program. After screening, about 8,600 individuals signed up for at least one class.

We were able to examine how returns varied with the length of attendance, grades, and rigor of the major, because we had access to exceptionally detailed transcript data as well as UI administrative wage records covering quarterly earnings for about thirty-six quarters both before and after enrollment. Our significant findings included:

—Attendance at CCAC boosted earnings by about 12 percent per year of full-time attendance. This is roughly the return measured for attendance at two- and four-year colleges for traditional students, not dislocated workers.

51. Cropper and Jacobson (1983).
52. Jacobson, LaLonde, and Sullivan (1994).

Figure 11-4. *Earnings of Male DWETP*[a] *Participants, 1974–92*[b]

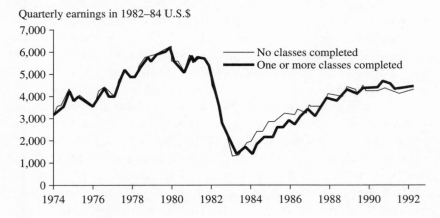

Quarterly earnings in 1982–84 U.S.$

No classes completed
One or more classes completed

Source: Jacobson, LaLonde, and Sullivan (1994, figure 1).

a. DWETP = dislocated Worker Employment and Training Program.

b. Program enrollment began in August 1983. Observations are for males with earnings in each two calendar years from 1978 to 1991 (except 1982–83) and three or more years' tenure when displaced from any firm. Sample sizes: no classes, 1,081; classes, 1,740.

—Despite the high returns, students rarely remained at CCAC for more than one year. The net returns of remaining for long periods were low because, as shown in figure 11-4, individuals who left DWETP without completing a single class showed substantial earnings gains. Indeed, there was evidence that those who did best at CCAC also would have done best without additional schooling.

—Almost all of the positive effect accrued to workers who got high grades in rigorous technical courses requiring some math and science background. The importance of taking "hard" courses is illustrated in figure 11-5.

—The gains from schooling did not come close to eliminating the large permanent losses of the workers.

Our conclusions were remarkably similar to those of the studies reviewed by Duane Leigh and highly consistent with the results of the TAA studies. For the majority of DWETP participants, the returns from quickly returning to work were about the same as the returns from attending school full time. Although many students excelled at their studies, many others did not adapt well to returning to school. The key new results are that the choice of curriculum was of paramount importance (there was a high return only on programs requiring excellence in math and science). Long-term follow-

Figure 11-5. *Returns from Female and Male Participants in DWETP Based on Completed "Hard" and "Easy" Classes*[a]

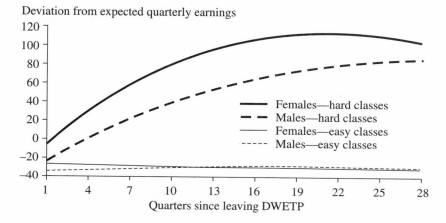

Deviation from expected quarterly earnings

Females—hard classes
Males—hard classes
Females—easy classes
Males—easy classes

Quarters since leaving DWETP

Source: Jacobson, Lalonde, and Sullivan (1994, figure 11).

a. Controlled for number of DWETP classes, former industry, noncredit courses, degrees, and grade point average.

up is a prerequisite to accurate measurement of the benefits of training (positive returns were obvious only about four years after entrance to CCAC).

The bottom line is that training can be of substantial value to some dislocated workers, but policymakers appear to underrate the ability of most workers to acquire substantially more human-capital–enhancing knowledge on the job rather than in the classroom. As suggested by the direct comparisons between JSA and retraining, the high forgone earnings associated with continued attendance at a community college, not the low return from continued schooling (or absence of stipends), are what makes full-time attendance of only marginal value even for able, nontraditional students. In fact, the more successful the assisted and unassisted job search in finding jobs that lead to substantial growth, the lower the net return from training.

The obvious policy implications of this study are that training should be used sparingly. In general, potential trainees should be carefully screened to make sure that they will do well, and just as carefully counseled concerning the expected returns from various course selections. More speculatively, the use of vouchers as in DWETP and TAA has three major advantages over contracting for training, as was commonly done under the Comprehensive

Employment and Training Act (CETA) of 1973 and under JTPA Title III. Vouchers offer access to the widest possible range of programs. In addition, by competing for grades with other students, dislocated workers have a more valuable credential to demonstrate their worth to employers and can better assess for themselves the value of continuing with school. Finally, because the per-course cost of voucher training is one-third to one-half that of Title III programs, workers can afford to take longer and more rigorous programs and can also explore a range of subject areas. It is worth noting that improved screening, counseling, and use of vouchers are key benefits of establishing honest brokers and one-stop career centers—all of which were strongly advocated by the Clinton administration in the REA of 1994.[53]

I have long been interested in why the negative evidence on retraining is so difficult to accept. I suspect that the aura of the GI Bill is the primary source of the belief that retraining is a panacea. There are excellent studies of the Korean and Vietnam War versions of the GI Bill that clearly indicate not only that the returns were high, but also that participants tended to be ten to twenty years younger than dislocated workers, and therefore rarely had been well established at high-wage jobs. Perhaps most important of all, contrary to the conventional wisdom, individuals who gained the most from the GI Bill already had considerable college experience. It therefore appears that the GI Bill was most effective in aiding those people whose education was interrupted, not those who sacrificed solid careers by entering the military. Also, unlike TAA vouchers, the GI Bill reduced payments for less-than-full-time attendance. Finally, it is likely that the GI Bill was more effective in eliminating financial market imperfections in past decades than it is today, when the cost of postsecondary education has been greatly reduced by easy access to low-cost community colleges and increases in federal assistance.

Despite current interest in a GI bill for all workers, the need for a "new" training program with generous vouchers and stipends (like TAA) is far from obvious. The well-funded "old" program of Pell grants and federal

53. Although the REA was not passed, it reflected the administration's review of what needs to be done to improve dislocated worker programs. The REA advocated more balance between JSA and training, but still earmarked half its funds to training supported by transfer payments. The administration and its supporters' strong defense of the REA's retraining as a "magic bullet" having a much higher return than JSA suggests just how difficult it is to completely overturn an established paradigm, even one with little empirical support. A more supportable defense for retraining is that JSA invariably will fail to help some workers locate work, and these individuals need skill enhancement to complement JSA.

loans appears to provide adequate access to retraining. Although federal aid technically is need based, from 1988 through 1992 provisions of the Higher Education Act made it easy for dislocated workers to qualify for Pell grants. They eliminated most asset tests and required schools to consider current income, rather than income in the preceding year. About 75,000 dislocated workers a year qualified for Pell grants, slightly more than those receiving JTPA-sponsored training. About 10 percent of the grants were used to support training at four-year colleges and 30 percent at proprietary schools.[54] Both these types of schooling are considerably more expensive and more intensive than that usually sponsored under JTPA.

Restoring the special provisions for dislocated workers that lapsed when the Higher Education Act was reauthorized in 1992 should sufficiently remove financial constraints to allow dislocated workers who have special promise to attend school, but discourage those individuals who would be better off working from needlessly prolonging unemployment. Also, use of vouchers might improve course selection and rigor as well as permit government-sponsored honest brokers to avoid conflicts of interest by fully separating the tasks of screening and referral from the provision of services.

Perhaps the strongest argument in favor of limiting grants through means testing is that workers who are likely to benefit the most from retraining will probably do better than average even without training. In terms of improving equity, it would make even more sense to extend transfer payments to all low-income dislocated workers, not just those who enter training programs.[55]

JOB SEARCH ASSISTANCE. JSA has several key advantages over retraining:

—JSA is effective in reducing time out of work. In contrast, training usually lengthens unemployment, and a key cost of training is foregone earnings.

—JSA is inexpensive, costing from one-third to one-tenth less than training. As a result, government programs relying on JSA can serve three

54. Jacobson (1993a).
55. Requiring recipients of long-lasting UI or TAA to enter training is similar to requiring welfare recipients to perform volunteer work or enter training as a condition of receiving benefits. In both cases, the value may be greater to those who want recipients to "do something" in exchange for taxpayer "largess," than those receiving mandatory services. Although getting unemployed individuals out of their homes may have substantial value, it probably is the case that the "something" could be more broadly defined to include inexpensive job search clubs rather than expensive training, and the choice of "treatment" could be based on an assessment of individual needs and projected benefits from program participation.

to ten times as many people as training programs with the same amount of funds and with no loss of effectiveness.

—JSA is far more flexible than retraining, since it does not depend on the ability of adults who have been out of school for decades to excel in a classroom setting or do well at math and science.

—JSA also does not require that job openings match a narrow set of skills. A major problem with retraining is that poor course selection can leave even strong performers without training-related new jobs.

The one explanation for the success of JSA already discussed was that workers acquire substantial amounts of productivity-enhancing knowledge on the job as well as in school. More specifically, dislocated workers who quickly return to work can impress employers enough to gain promotions with or without formal training, learn about job openings that better match their skills, and have the funds to enter training programs that complement the requirements of current jobs or jobs obtainable with added skills.

Three additional explanations are also highly relevant. The first is that dislocated workers seeking new jobs are likely to be good at certain occupations and not so good at others. Finding just the right slot makes an enormous difference. Second, the job search skills of high-tenure workers are likely to be rusty. Although many workers find good jobs on their own, many others can benefit from instruction on how to search for work more effectively. Also, experts in matching available openings to the skills of job seekers often can make better matches than can workers and firms acting by themselves. Just as real estate brokers play a crucial role in the housing market, job developers and placement specialists can play a crucial role in the job market.[56]

Table 11-1 uses information from the analysis of dislocated workers in Pennsylvania to illustrate how important finding a job in the same sector is to the future earnings of workers who lost jobs.[57] For high-tenure, displaced manufacturing workers, remaining in manufacturing cuts long-term earnings losses in half. Five years after dislocation, the earnings of workers

---

56. As in the housing market, both "buyers" and "sellers" could gain from the use of labor market intermediaries. Thus, it is possible that firms gain from the effects of JSA on reducing the duration of job search because their vacancies are more quickly filled. What little evidence there is on this issue, however, suggests that JSA has a much stronger effect on "leveling the playing field" for workers who lack good information about available jobs. Thus, most of the gains to those placed come at the expense of very small losses spread across a large number of job seekers.

57. Jacobson, LaLonde, and Sullivan (1993c, table 4, p. 13).

Table 11-1. *Earnings Losses of Displaced Workers by Sector of New Job*

	First year after separation		Fifth year after separation	
	Loss[a]	Percent[b]	Loss[a]	Percent[b]
Manufacturing workers				
Same SIC[c]	6,700	27.5	4,020	16.5
	(212)	(0.1)	(281)	(0.1)
Same sector	8,188	33.6	4,702	19.3
	(186)	(0.1)	(258)	(0.1)
Different sector	12,538	51.5	9,280	37.8
	(168)	(0.1)	(239)	(0.1)
Nonmanufacturing workers				
Same SIC	5,214	21.0	5,098	20.5
	(276)	(0.1)	(416)	(0.2)
Same sector	8,288	33.4	6,510	26.2
	(243)	(0.1)	(305)	(0.1)
Different sector	10,436	42.0	7,791	31.4
	(549)	(0.2)	(694)	(0.3)

Source: Jacobson, LaLonde, and Sullivan (1993c, table 4, p. 13).

a. In 1987 U.S. dollars.

b. Loss as a percentage of 1979 earnings.

c. SIC = Standard Industrial Classification. Standard errors in parentheses.

leaving manufacturing are $9,280 (37.8 percent) below that of similar, nondisplaced workers. In contrast, the earnings of workers finding new manufacturing jobs in the same two-digit industry code are $4,020 (16.5 percent) below that of similar nondisplaced workers. Losses of those in nonmanufacturing jobs are $5,098 (20.5 percent), whereas losses of those leaving jobs are $7,791 (31.4 percent). The advantages of remaining in the service sector are not quite as great as of remaining in manufacturing, but remaining in the same two-digit industry code is far more important in the service sector than in manufacturing. Although the evidence in table 11-1 is not conclusive, it certainly provides a plausible mechanism by which JSA can be highly effective. Moreover, a key factor making some short-term retraining effective is probably that it provides skills that help workers find new jobs in their former economic sectors.

In addition to the studies already discussed that directly compare JSA with training, there are several highly informative studies of the effectiveness of the U.S. ES.[58] The ES rarely provides a full range of JSA services

58. These studies include Johnson, Dickinson, and West (1985); General Accounting Office (GAO) (1989); Jacobson (1994); Katz and Jacobson (1994). The

similar to those provided by JTPA Title III programs. The ES serves about 22 million registrants each year at a per capita cost of $75. In contrast, Title III serves about 150,000 participants at a per capita cost of about $1,700. Because the ES has limited resources, the primary service it provides is as a low-cost, public labor exchange. For the most part firms voluntarily list openings and job seekers examine the openings to find suitable slots with limited help from ES staffers. By law the ES is open to any job seeker, but registration is mandatory for many UI claimants and some welfare recipients.

Given its meager resources, the ES primarily places workers at jobs that require little screening and pay relatively low wages. Nevertheless, the two major studies of the ES's ability to aid UI claimants showed that it is highly cost effective in reducing the duration of unemployment and does not place registrants in dead-end jobs. The only nationally representative study estimated that the benefit-cost ratio of state ESs was 1.6, based on highly conservative assumptions.[59] A more detailed study of the ES in Pennsylvania suggested that the ES was a key source of jobs for claimants who had exhausted UI benefits.[60]

Paradoxically, both studies indicated that claimants who found jobs on their own returned to work quicker and at higher wages than those who were placed by the ES. But when access to job openings as well as personal and work history characteristics were taken into account, the ES was found to be highly effective in helping precisely those workers who were likely to have the most difficulty finding work on their own. Helping individuals who need it the most is a hallmark of a successful government program. But complex statistical controls usually are required to show that such programs are effective. As a result, it is difficult for many policymakers to accept this type of evidence.

To make matters worse, simple JTPA measures of effectiveness that are both unreliable and unfair to the ES have been accepted as accurate. As a result, Congress and the U.S. DOL have far more generously funded JTPA programs at the expense of the ES. The prime comparison that places the ES in a poor light is that between the ES placement rate (the number of individuals who took jobs to which they were referred by the ES) and the JTPA-entered employment rate (the number of participants who find jobs by any means, even through use of the ES).

---

discussion in this section is largely taken from Jacobson (1995), which summarizes these and related studies.

59. Johnson, Dickinson, and West (1985).

60. Katz and Jacobson (1994).

Finding convincing and accurate performance measures in the absence of random, assignment experiments, however, has proven difficult. For example, the procedures used to control for the selectivity bias in the ES study conducted by Johnson and others, which was completed in the early 1980s, leave considerable room for debate over the precise point estimates. That is why conservative assumptions were used in estimating the net return.

The ES study conducted by Arnold Katz and me used a more robust evaluation scheme based on comparing claimants placed by the ES to claimants referred but not placed, as well as claimants who were not referred. It used hazard functions to compare the subsequent duration of unemployment for claimants who had already been unemployed for a given number of weeks.[61] This technique also has the advantage of describing how the effectiveness of placements varies over time. The analysis showed that the ES makes by far the greatest difference after claimants have exhausted UI benefits. This makes sense because the best jobs are usually filled by recommendations from friends and relatives, responses to want ads, and applications at work sites. It generally takes months for claimants to exhaust their own resources for finding jobs and turn to the ES for help. Also, many dislocated workers can only find jobs paying little more than UI benefits. It makes sense to many of those individuals to defer taking those jobs until their UI benefits are close to being used up.

My study of the Washington State Claimant Placement Program (CPP) further illustrates how the optimal timing of services depends on whether the goal is to maximize the social return in terms of reducing UI payments or minimize the earnings losses of dislocated workers.[62] Washington (and several other states) used their own funds to reduce UI payments by enhancing ES services to claimants based on the success of the NJD. Washington state was unusual because it required that CPP be evaluated.

Table 11-2 displays the key results from the CPP evaluation. Columns 1 and 2 show that the number of weeks of benefits saved by each referral and placement declines sharply as the number of weeks claimed increases. Column 3 shows that the decline is likely to occur simply because the number of remaining payments falls sharply. It would therefore seem that providing services quickly would maximize the number of UI payments saved. Columns 4 and 5 show, however, that claimants' willingness to

61. Katz and Jacobson (1994).
62. Jacobson (1993c).

Table 11-2. *Shift in Unemployment Insurance and Referral Status as a Claim Progresses in Washington State, 1983–91*
Percent, unless otherwise specified

Claim period (weeks)	Mean number of weeks saved for		Mean remaining number of payments (3)	Probability a referral leads to a placement (4)	Probability of being referred (5)	Claimants remaining at period end (%) (6)
	Referrals not leading to placement (1)	Placements (2)				
0–4	0.98[a]	2.49[a]	12.1	8.3	1.2	78
	(0.32)[b]	(1.13)	(8.7)			
5–9	0.66[a]	1.48[a]	8.8	10.7	2.0	75
	(0.24)	(0.73)	(7.8)			
10–14	0.34	0.66	6.4	12.9	2.8	59
	(0.18)	(0.49)	(6.3)			
15–19	0.19	0.30	3.7	13.6	3.2	38
	(0.13)	(0.34)	(5.1)			
20–24	0.25[a]	0.70[a]	1.6	14.6	4.2	22
	(0.10)	(0.25)	(3.7)			
25–30	0.14[a]	0.26[a]	0.0	18.3	5.4	0
	(0.06)	(0.13)	(1.9)			

Source: Jacobson (1993c).
a. Result significantly different from zero at 5 percent confidence level.
b. Standard deviation is shown in parentheses.

accept referrals and accept jobs to which they are referred increases substantially as the duration of unemployment lengthens. This strongly suggests that, from the claimants' point of view, ES placement services become more and more valuable as the duration of unemployment increases. It also suggests that the greater UI savings of early placement must be balanced against the lower probability of making a placement.

Finally, column 6 shows that the number of claimants left in the pool of unemployed declines sharply with length of time collecting benefits. Thus, despite low placement probabilities, the majority of placements are made to claimants with relatively short collection durations. The total UI saving is determined by multiplying the number of claimants referred in each category times the saving in weeks of each referral times the average UI payment, and then adding the analogous calculation for placements. The study determined that the total savings equaled about $17 million, while the cost of the program was about $15 million. The program therefore more than paid for itself in UI savings alone. Additional preliminary results suggest that, just as in the Pennsylvania ES study, the Washington ES saves the most weeks of UI compensated and uncompensated unemployment by helping long-term unemployed workers.

A key conclusion of the ES analyses is that focusing aid on dislocated workers who have been unemployed for a substantial period rather than on those who are recently unemployed would dramatically improve equity by saving months of unemployment for workers who have exhausted UI benefits. Acting on this finding would move in precisely the opposite direction from state-funded programs such as CPP, as well as the new policy to profile and immediately refer dislocated claimants to supportive services. However, the two approaches may both have merit. Profiling is aimed at helping dislocated workers and reducing the cost of transfer payments. The initial services include assistance on how to search effectively for work on one's own, screening to determine if retraining is appropriate, and counseling on what services are available to help claimants cope better with the stress of dislocation and avoid becoming so discouraged that they give up trying to find work.[63]

The above studies strongly support the view that JSA is more effective than training for most dislocated workers. However, there are no studies that directly compare different types of JSA analogous to the DWETP study of classroom training. As a result, we know little about the relative merits of alternative JSA strategies, such as helping workers develop better search plans, teaching them to search more effectively, providing resource centers and job search clubs, and directly placing them at jobs (having brokers match workers with job openings) with and without job development (having agents search for especially suitable job openings for clients).

However, the effectiveness of various ES administrative practices has been studied by the GAO, the investigative arm of the U.S. Congress.[64] The GAO studies are based on detailed surveys of overall ES operations for every state and one-third of the 1,700 local ES offices. The main conclusions for these studies are that ES offices show wide variation in performance and cost, holding client and economic conditions constant. Placements at the most efficient offices cost about $150 each; placements at the least efficient offices are three to four times more expensive.

63. In resolving how to best balance gains in reducing UI payments against gains in offsetting earnings losses a key question to ask is: who is paying for the services? Since the Washington state program was financed by a payroll tax, employers felt that they paid for the program, and therefore, were entitled to receive most of the gains. Even if, as is likely, the incidence of payroll taxes is on consumers, consumers too would best be served by reducing the cost of the UI system, *unless* they strongly valued the insurance aspect of the services.

64. GAO (1989).

The most efficient offices maintain close contact with the employer community, use performance-measurement systems that reward excellence, are not colocated with the UI office, and serve primarily rural populations.

Earnings Subsidies

Except in rare instances government-provided adjustment services cannot prevent a substantial fraction of high-tenure dislocated workers from suffering large losses, as about 75 percent of the total earnings losses following dislocation accrue after a permanent new job is found.

In the final analysis, therefore, it appears that the primary deficit in public policy responses to job dislocation is the inability to offset these large, permanent losses. Although it is not true that the only thing dislocated workers have to fear is fear itself, it probably is true that uncertainty associated with precisely who may lose jobs due to structural change makes many more individuals fear change than would actually be hurt. This exaggerated fear has made it difficult to implement policies such as trade liberalization that make the economy better off as a whole at the cost of imposing large losses on a limited group of individuals.

The technically correct solution for limiting the harm from costly, low-probability events is to insure those who are potentially adversely affected against the risk. There simply is no getting around the fact that retraining may be highly effective in some instances but cannot be expected to come close to fully offsetting long-term earnings losses. JSA can be effective in improving the match between worker skills and employer needs. But there appears to be no panacea that can restore the lost firm- or industry-specific human capital that makes workers much more valuable to their current employers than any other potential ones.

Policymakers who want to substantially reduce fears of job loss are faced with a Hobson's choice—no choice at all. Income transfers are the only means to guarantee that no worker will suffer earnings losses greater than a set amount. There are several options to providing such transfers, however. The most efficient income transfer system is earnings insurance that pays a fraction of the difference between actual earnings and an earnings target. For example, a plan that Bob LaLonde, Dan Sullivan, and I discuss in our monograph would pay 40 percent of previous earnings to dislocated workers who earned 30 percent or less of predislocation earnings and reduce the payment by four-sevenths of a dollar for each dollar earned above 30 percent.[65] According to this design, the payment would decline

65. Jacobson, LaLonde, and Sullivan (1993a).

from 40 percent of predislocation earnings to zero as postdisplacement earnings rose from 30 percent to 100 percent of their predisplacement levels. In effect, this plan would set a floor on losses of 70 percent. Because most workers would earn at least 50 percent of previous earnings, the effective floor would be about 85 percent of predislocation earnings.

Key elements of this design are that most of the funds would go to workers with the largest losses, and workers would have strong incentives to earn as much as they can. In contrast, a plan that would pay 100 percent of the difference between actual earnings and predislocation earnings would eliminate incentives for most recipients to work at all and pay relatively large amounts to workers with small losses.

The earnings insurance concept has been widely accepted as a means to aid the working poor. The earned income tax credit (EITC), which was greatly expanded by President Clinton, employs the same conceptual framework. With respect to dislocated workers, the REA proposed offering earnings insurance to workers over age fifty. Also, a TAA earnings insurance demonstration was funded that would have reduced the TAA payment by fifty cents for each dollar earned to cover "partial" unemployment. States currently reduce weekly UI payments by one dollar for each dollar earned above a relatively low disregard of about $75. (Pennsylvania has an exceptionally generous disregard that is set at 40 percent of the WBA, and thus reaches a maximum of about $130.) The experiment could not be implemented, however, because EUC drastically reduced TAA payments. Finally, from 1974 through 1991 TAA included a form of earnings insurance. My analysis suggested that most TAA recipients who exhausted TAA took jobs that paid less than the TAA payment; therefore, they could have substantially increased their income by taking the same jobs months earlier and using the subsidy.[66] The earnings insurance was little used, however, possibly because its existence was not well known or because TAA recipients only realized late in their entitlement periods that they would not be recalled.

The key problem with implementing earnings insurance is its high cost. For example, the plan described in my monograph would cost about $9 billion per year.[67] A program lasting only two years after job loss, however,

66. Jacobson (1994).
67. We assume that the average loss would be 80 percent of predislocation earnings averaging $19,200, making the average payment $2,700; the distribution of losses and earnings would be symmetric about the mean; and about 350,000 dislocated high-tenure workers a year would be eligible for the subsidy that would last until retirement.

would "only" cost about $1 billion. This is only about 5 percent of the cost of UI in recessionary years and an even smaller fraction of gains from removing trade restrictions. Middle-of-the-road estimates of the gains from NAFTA suggest that ratification would raise gross domestic product (GDP) by about 1 percent a year, or roughly $60 billion.

Even if society at large cannot be persuaded to pay for earnings insurance to improve equity or to reduce opposition to beneficial change, it might be reasonable for those potentially hurt by job loss to pay for this insurance. Earlier I discussed shifting UI toward compensating long-term losses at the expense of reducing coverage for short-term losses. The earnings insurance idea is a logical extension of that concept. Like changing UI, the binding constraint on effectively reducing fears of long-term losses largely depends on whether workers understand the value of the insurance aspects of such transfer programs and would be willing to bear the costs. In the present political climate it appears that there is little interest in sacrificing current income for substantially higher future returns, let alone insurance against possible calamities.

Summary

Table 11-3 summarizes the goals of policies aimed at assisting dislocated workers during each of four time-dependent stages in the dislocation process, and the potential means to reach those goals. The above analysis has isolated four reasonably clear-cut *primary* policy goals:

—preventing costly dislocation years before firms need to temporarily lay off workers for extended periods;

—offsetting the cost of unemployment with transfer payments starting about three years before permanent layoffs when temporary layoffs are common and ending about two years after permanent layoff;

—reducing the time it takes dislocated workers to find new permanent jobs; and

—offsetting the large, permanent earnings reductions associated with the loss of firm- or industry-specific human capital.

Table 11-4 lists the programs that are in place to reach these goals. The existing social safety net for dislocated workers can do the following:

—complement actions by firms and workers to maintain their competitive positions;

—offset losses due to unemployment lasting less than six months per year through the UI system; and

Table 11-3. *Policy Goals and Means to Reduce Worker Losses at Various Stages in the Adjustment Process*

Zone 1: Prior to three years before job loss[a]

Goal 1: Increase competitive position of the firm to avoid layoffs

Means: Develop plans to shift product lines, enhance physical capital and effectiveness of human capital, improve labor-management cooperation

Goal 2: Increase workers' skills making them more adaptable at their present job and it easier to quickly find new, high-paying jobs

Means: Encourage attendance at literacy and vocational education programs

Zone 2: Three years before job loss to point where recall appears most unlikely[b]

Goal 1: Offset earnings losses

Means: Public and private unemployment insurance (UI), work-sharing arrangements

Goal 2: Provide early warning to workers of firm's intentions to lay off workers

Means: Establish good labor-management relations, mandate early warning

Goal 3: Encourage workers to build skills and contacts facilitating moving to new, high-paying jobs

Means: Provide relevant courses at the workplace, educate workers about opportunities at community colleges and proprietary schools

Zone 3: Point where recall appears unlikely to acquisition of a new job[c]

Goal 1: Offset earnings losses

Means: Public and private UI, wage insurance

Goal 2: Help workers develop long-run financial plans and ways to cope with psychological effects of job loss

Means: Public and private counseling services

Goal 3: Assist workers' job search

Means: Public and private instruction on how to effectively search for jobs, job search clubs, direct-placement services, tax credits to firms hiring target groups

Goal 4: Help workers develop new skills to assists in finding new, high-paying jobs

Means: Assess workers' suitability for retraining; educate workers about retraining opportunities; provide direct-training services, vouchers (grants), and loans

Zone 4: From acquisition of new permanent job to retirement[d]

Goal 1: Substantially reduce long-term earnings reductions

Means: Earnings subsidies, severance agreements, retraining, pension guarantees

---

a. Earnings of "stayers" and "leavers" are identical.

b. Workers experience long-lasting layoffs usually followed by recall.

c. Workers experience substantial unemployment and actively search for work.

d. Workers' earnings have fallen about 25 percent relative to what they would have earned without job loss.

Table 11-4. *Major Programs Aiding Dislocated Workers*

State employment security agencies (SESAs)

UI system provides income support for as long as six months a year during
prosperous times and for a year or more during major recessions[a]

Employment Service (ES) maintains a public labor exchange and works closely
with the UI system to monitor job search[b]

State-funded programs to supplement services provides by the ES

Trade Adjustment Assistance (TAA) Program provides income support for an
additional six months after other forms of UI are exhausted, and training
vouchers paying as much as $10,000 for each of two years[c]

Requirement for the UI and ES systems to work together to profile claimants for
likelihood of long periods of unemployment and mandatory referrals to
appropriate services.[d]

State and local programs under the Job Training Partnership Act (JTPA) of 1981

Private Industry Council (PIC) programs funded under JTPA Title III provide
assessment, testing, counseling, and referral to job search assistance (JSA) and
training services

College-run programs under the Higher Education Act of 1972

Pell Grants and Stafford Loans provide need-based financial assistance for
postsecondary education

Legally mandated program

Worker Adjustment and Retraining Notification (WARN) Act requires firms with
over 100 workers to give at least sixty days advanced notice of layoffs likely to
last more than six months

---

a. Created by the Social Security Act of 1935.
b. Created by the Wagner-Peyser Act of 1932.
c. Originated with the Trade Act of 1974.
d. Authorized under the Emergency Unemployment Compensation (EUC) Act amendments of 1993.

—assist dislocated workers to find new jobs through JTPA, ES, and community college programs plus UI profiling.

However, it cannot offset large permanent reductions in earnings.

The analysis has suggested that government's ability to forestall plant closing is limited, because it is natural in all industries for some firms to prosper while others decline. Nevertheless, at least on the margin, government action can improve the information available to workers and firms to make the range of options to forestall declines more obvious. This will help labor and management to work to their mutual benefit to raise productivity and reduce the risk of layoffs.

Government plays a much larger role in providing transfer payments, JSA, retraining, and warning that permanent layoffs are likely to occur.

Indeed, the joint actions of workers and firms in these arenas tend to complement government actions, not the other way around. The most positive aspect of this social safety net is that existing programs are reasonably effective in offsetting short-term losses due to unemployment (zone 2 of figure 11-1) and reducing the period between job loss and finding a new permanent job (zone 3). There is some question, however, whether the programs to assist the return to work are sufficiently well integrated to provide appropriate services at the right time. In particular, the strong interest in saving UI funds may have focused attention on short-term unemployment to the detriment of UI exhaustees and long-term un-employed workers—groups that need help the most. Studies suggest that programs focused on the beginning of periods of unemployment primarily assist workers who would not be unemployed for long periods anyway. Although funding those programs is warranted because their cost is less than the UI savings they generate, providing additional assistance to long-term unemployed individuals can reduce unemployment following UI exhaustion by three or more months per person helped. In contrast, programs targeted to short-term unemployed people reduce unemployment (and UI payments) by less than two weeks per person helped.

One-stop career centers advocated in the REA could substantially improve the delivery of services to dislocated workers by overcoming the major declines in funding for ES services and improving the balance between inexpensive JSA and expensive retraining. The key elements of ideal, one-stop career centers include the following:

—initial intake for UI payments;

—initial assessment to determine the need for government aid and suitability of alternative services;

—provision of low-cost JSA;

—referral to other service providers for JSA and retraining; and

—monitoring job searches to determine when and what types of additional services are needed.

Several SESAs have systems that come reasonably close to the ideal, and many states are developing such systems. Most states with effective programs have a single administrator responsible for the UI, ES, and JTPA programs. A major constraint is that referrals are usually to JTPA programs. Most SESAs currently do not provide information about Pell Grants and federal loans. Among U.S. DOL programs, only TAA provides vouchers allowing a wide choice of supportive services; but training is mandatory under TAA, and little screening and referral aid is provided. Expanding use of voluntary vouchers and providing thorough assessment and referral services have considerable merit. Moves in that direction are being seriously considered and would likely resolve the key structural problem with JTPA Title III—that the same organization is responsible for assessment, provision of services, and evaluation of results. The current system reduces the choices available to clients and sometimes precludes competition for grades against other job seekers. But perhaps of greatest importance, it prevents JTPA staff from serving as honest brokers, fostering competition based on the quality and suitability of the services provided.

Although brokers need to be honest (that is, to give advice they believe is in each client's best interest), they also need to be well informed. The key element missing from current and proposed programs providing JSA and retraining is development of sufficient information to know the optimal type and timing of assistance. Performance measures that accurately reflect the value added of the treatments are not currently used but are crucially important to giving honest brokers the information they need to do their job. The basic measurement tools and data, however, are available to provide much more reliable feedback.[68] What has been lacking so far is the will to implement a first-rate system. The cornerstone of any system is use of a comparison group to determine the baseline outcome in the absence of government aid for workers with a given set of personal and work history characteristics in a particular labor market. Of course, just giving the baseline information to dislocated workers might dramatically improve their job search. For example, knowing the size of the earnings reductions at initial jobs and the growth path of earnings obtained by similar workers in their own local area might reduce some workers' reluctance to take relatively low-paying jobs.

Constructive attention is directed to shortening the duration of un-employment of dislocated workers, but little consideration is being given to dealing with the greatest unmet need—more effectively offsetting large, permanent losses. As noted earlier, uncompensated losses are so large and sufficiently widespread that they pose a major impediment to taking actions such as trade liberalization that benefit society at the expense of a relatively small group of individuals. Moreover, fear is greatly multiplied, because it is hard to know which workers actually will be affected adversely by change. Even though the benefits of offsetting large losses would be great,

---

68. Ideally, service providers would follow Gary Burtless's suggestion of ran-domly assigning a small number of qualified applicants to a control group that would be followed up using the same procedures as participants. Despite major improvements in econometric methods for using comparison groups, random assignment designs still provide the most accurate performance measures.

the high cost of any effective solution may make implementation infeasible. There are three possible ways to reduce long-term losses: retraining, JSA, and transfers.

The retraining option is attractive to politicians. Completing four years of college substantially raises earnings, and the GI Bill was effective in offsetting the effects of having education and civilian work disrupted by military service. However, there is strong evidence that retraining is only of value to a small segment of the dislocated workers with large losses. The take-up rate for training programs is low, and many individuals who start programs are unable to adapt to a classroom setting. Of greatest importance is the evidence from a special community college program in Pittsburgh, which suggests that only workers able to do well at rigorous technical courses showed large gains. Moreover, even successful programs require substantial sacrifices of current income. The foregone income greatly reduces the net gain. This evidence suggests that crucial components of a retraining program are ensuring training is appropriate through careful screening and counseling, limiting losses of foregone earnings by combining training with work either before or after job loss, or starting training as close to the point of job loss as possible.

At first glance, JSA may seem to be even less likely to offset large losses than training. As I have noted, JSA could make a substantial difference by helping workers find job slots that provide opportunities to substantially boost human capital over time. There is powerful evidence that for most workers, quickly taking available jobs even if they offer low pay provides considerably more earnings-enhancing learning than they would receive from attending classes. That evidence comes from a variety of sources, including analysis of JSA and training supported by the UI system, funded under JTPA, paid for with TAA vouchers, and made available at no cost at the CCAC. In addition, it is possible that long-term unemployment debilitates the ability to effectively search for work and is viewed so negatively by employers that it becomes difficult for long-term unemployed workers to find work. Thus substantially shortening unemployment by helping workers set reasonable expectations and search more effectively could have a big payoff. Although we do not have definitive measures of the "scarring" effect of prolonged unemployment, we have even less reason to believe that classroom training can overcome problems stemming from a lack of marketable skills.

The bottom line, however, is that even with major improvements, neither JSA nor retraining can fully restore the losses resulting in breaking the ties that bind long-term workers to particular firms. The technically correct solution to dramatically reducing the expected dislocation losses, therefore, is providing cash payments. One key component is lengthening the potential duration of UI for all claimants, not just those covered by TAA or those unemployed during recessions. Virtually every study of worker dislocation shows that there is a strong positive correlation between the initial duration of unemployment and long-term earnings losses, and most long-term, unemployed individuals end up exhausting all forms of UI, including TAA. As a result, lengthening the potential duration of benefits is justified on equity grounds.

Finding a way to pay for the extension in the current political climate could be difficult. But it would seem that workers should, if necessary, be willing to trade off reductions in compensation for short periods of unemployment for greater protection against protracted spells. Despite the logic of this trade-off, workers appear to value the income-smoothing aspects of UI more highly than the insurance aspects.[69] Potential efficiency problems stemming from the disincentive effects of extending UI could be minimized by modifying UI partial-benefit formulas to eliminate the currently prevalent 100 percent tax rates on earnings, requiring participation in job search workshops, and more assiduously enforcing the work test.

The same principles that support restructuring UI to provide more "insurance" against devastating losses and less "income smoothing" during relatively short, temporary layoffs support providing long-lasting compensation after workers are reemployed. It appears that the only means to place an effective floor on the size of the loss experienced by dislocated workers is to provide some type of earnings insurance. In a few industries, firms offer guaranteed lifetime employment. Early retirement programs and various forms of buyouts are more widely available. But there is no comprehensive program of protection against the large earnings reductions associated with job loss. Probably the most cost-effective means to substantially reduce those losses is to provide earnings insurance that pays a portion of the difference between actual and predislocation earnings. The

69. A key reason that the UI/ES system effectively provides compensation for *temporary* layoffs is that in cyclical declines firms no more want to lose the services of experienced workers than those workers want to leave. In sharp contrast, during structural declines firms have no recourse but to *permanently* lay off workers. The primary value to firms of ensuring against job loss is in lowering any compensating wage differential associated with the risk of dislocation. That differential solely depends on workers recognizing the potential harm of job loss. Thus, it is the asymmetry in interests between workers and firms during downsizing that places the onus for creating job loss insurance on workers.

cost of such a program—about $9 billion per year—may be prohibitively high in today's political climate. Even a more limited program lasting two years might add about $1 billion a year to the cost of the UI program. That amount, however, is less than 5 percent of UI outlays during typical recessions. The prospects for implementing a longer-lasting insurance program would be considerably improved if workers did not appear to undervalue the benefits of an insurance policy that would basically guarantee that earnings would not fall more than 15 percent below current levels.

There recently have been major advances in our understanding of how best to assist dislocated workers in rapidly finding new jobs and offsetting earnings losses due to unemployment. Additional cost-effective improvements in the delivery of services that are highly feasible include:

—more widely adopting the idea of using honest brokers in conjunction with one-stop career centers;

—relying more heavily on low-cost JSA;

—providing more counseling and assessment to make sure training is worthwhile;

—using vouchers for training to maximize choice and separate provision of services from referral and evaluation;

—continuing to track job search for dislocated workers to provide services when they are likely to be most needed and most effective; and

—extending the duration of UI payments and allowing UI to be used as earnings insurance to reduce work disincentives and offset earnings losses over a two-year period.

But in the final analysis, accurate measurement of the effectiveness of the treatments delivered would do the most to improve short-term aid to dislocated workers. Both the JTPA and UI/ES system currently collect detailed information about each service given every participant, but appropriate comparisons have not been made with readily available comparison groups. A uniform system to accurately measure program effects would have two exceedingly important benefits. It would be possible to far better isolate what does and does not work for different individuals in various settings. In addition, a better understanding of the conceptual issues in measuring performance could dramatically improve decisionmaking. Different measures are currently used to assess various programs, most notably the much more rigorous placement rate that is applied to the ES, versus the entered-employment rate used for JTPA.

Without clear measures of the value added by treatments, program operators lack the information they need to help those individuals they can help the most, choose the best treatments and deliver them at just the right time, and ensure that sufficient resources are devoted to aiding long-term unemployed workers—those individuals who have the largest losses.

Comment by Gary Burtless

Louis Jacobson has written a discursive—and shrewd—survey of research on worker displacement and policy remedies for displacement. His survey is filled with information that is useful to policymakers. On the whole, his policy conclusions are sound. I will focus on the policy prescriptions with which I disagree.

Before turning to Jacobson's substantive conclusions, it may be helpful to describe two elements missing from the chapter. First, it contains little information about other nations' policies to help workers displaced as a result of international trade. The analysis focuses exclusively on policies in the United States, though other countries have tried a variety of alternative approaches. Some of these alternatives have been conspicuously less successful than the ones tried in the United States. Have any been more successful?

Second, the chapter contains a detailed examination of policies aimed at helping workers who are harmed by trade, primarily as a result of temporary or permanent job loss. A chapter in Wood's book on North-South trade contains a more general treatment of the same range of issues.[70] It examines the theoretical underpinnings of basic policies aimed at helping *all* workers affected by trade developments, including those who hold on to their jobs (inside or outside the traded-goods sector) but who suffer a loss in hourly earnings. Wood's outstanding discussion should be read as a supplement to the narrower discussion of this chapter.

Rather than examine each of the claims advanced in Jacobson's chapter, I want to concentrate on a few central questions. What should be the goals of policies that help workers affected by trade? Does it make sense to focus policy on trade-affected, displaced workers? Or should public policy provide aid to displaced workers more generally? What policy tools can help achieve this goal?

In his discussion of policy goals, Jacobson offers readers a sketch of four crucial "zones" that precede or follow actual displacement. He then briefly

70. Wood (1994).

summarizes the goals that he thinks are sensible for each zone. Zone 1 is the period that ends three years *before* job loss actually occurs; zone 2 ends at the point of job loss; zone 3 ends when the displaced worker has found a new job; and zone 4 covers the remainder of the worker's career.

Jacobson makes wonderful recommendations about what firms and governments should try to accomplish during zone 1. They should innovate, be prepared, and otherwise follow the wise counsel found in the Boy Scout *Handbook.* But this is not really trade policy, nor is it worker adjustment policy. It is sensible business practice. Jacobson suggests that the best *preventive* policy to avoid the costs of worker displacement is to boost worker productivity *before* layoffs are needed. This cannot be true in the aggregate, because rapid productivity improvement will rob workers in *some* companies of job opportunities, even if the productivity gains help the nation *as a whole* avoid loss of market share in trade-affected industries.

The main problem in zone 2 is that neither workers nor firms can be certain whether they are in zone 2. Displacement may never occur. A firm and its workers may be experiencing temporary problems associated with low demand, possibly originating in trade. It will be unknown whether those problems are severe enough or long-lasting enough to result in per- manent job loss. The problems may result in temporary job loss. What policies are needed to deal with such job loss? I see no strong reason to do anything different from what we currently do. A sound unemployment insurance system—one that is optimally financed and contains good reemployment incentives—is the best protection we can offer to trade- affectedworkers on temporary layoff. Of course, a good insurance system is also the best protection we can offer to workers affected by *any* temporary drop in demand. The current financing of UI and the present structure of benefits could be modified to improve efficiency and income protection. But these improvements would be desirable whether or not temporary layoffs occur as a result of international trade.

Jacobson's suggestions for policy in zone 2 represent sound ideas for a closed economy, for companies that face stable demand, and even for firms facing *growing* demand. They are sensible goals for policy and business practice *whether or not employment can be interrupted as a result of international trade.* Readers will have difficulty finding fault with Jacobson's ideas about policy in zone 2. But the ideas would be good ones whether or not a country is engaged in international trade.

In zones 3 and 4 the discussion is much more interesting. These are also areas where most of the discussion in the chapter is concentrated. A worker has become permanently displaced. He or she is unlikely to be recalled to the same job. What should our policy goal be? Jacobson suggests several possible goals:

—offset earnings losses until the worker becomes reemployed;

—help workers develop financial plans and cope with the trauma of job loss;

—help workers find new jobs as quickly as possible;

—in some circumstances, help displaced workers learn new skills that will assist them in finding jobs and boosting future earnings; and

—replace a portion of earnings loss after displaced workers are reemployed.

The first three of these goals seem to me defensible under any plausible theory of public welfare. Jacobson offers sensible guidance on how these objectives can be achieved, based on the best recent evidence from good policy evaluations. I have no quarrel with his summary of this evidence.

In the remainder of this comment, I focus on the goal of reducing short- and long-term earnings reductions while workers are unemployed and after they are reemployed. This goal is best viewed from the perspective of optimal insurance. Baily, in a pair of articles published in the 1970s, was the first economist to look at UC in this way.[71]

How much insurance is sensible? Who should pay for it? What is the best way to combine cash insurance payments with tests of a worker's commitment to be reemployed? What is the most effective method of combining cash insurance payments with services that help workers become reemployed? What is the optimal combination of earnings *replacement* (for periods when a worker is unemployed) and earnings *supplementation* (for periods after a worker has become reemployed)? Does the optimal insurance package depend on whether displacement occurs as a result of international trade?

The most basic question is, "How much insurance should we offer?" UC systems have two basic features that determine their generosity. The best known is the benefit replacement rate, usually expressed as the ratio of weekly benefits to weekly earnings on the lost job. The other determinant of generosity is the duration of benefits. Low-wage and moderately paid U.S. workers face a replacement rate of about 50 percent and can usually collect unemployment benefits for up to six months. In comparison with other industrialized countries, the United States offers moderately low replacement rates and unusually short benefit durations. This implies that the contribution rate to pay for benefits is low. The insurance protection is poor, but the bill is small.

Can the system be improved to help workers who are displaced by trade? Jacobson thinks benefits should be offered for longer than six months. This extension could be financed by asking unemployed workers to wait longer

71. Baily (1977, 1978).

before they receive their first check. The proposal is a good one but is likely to be unpopular. Both workers and firms appreciate the short-term earnings protection that is offered when there is a short waiting period for benefits.

An analogy from health insurance might be helpful. Many insurance plans do not cover the cost of annual medical checkups. This exclusion is extremely unpopular and widely ridiculed in the popular press. It is thought to discourage people from obtaining useful preventive care. Yet from the point of view of optimal insurance, it represents a sensible exclusion. The goal of insurance is to protect people against huge bills that are unaffordable, not small, routine bills that they face every year. Publicly provided UI should offer workers good protection against catastrophic losses, such as long-term unemployment arising from displacement. Few economists see much justification for publicly insuring workers against small and predicable losses, such as seasonal unemployment or brief layoffs. In an optimal compensation system, short-term UI would be fully financed by the firm that causes the unemployment. Long-term UI protection would be financed with a more general tax on workers or employers, one that is not tied to firm-specific experience of unemployment.

I agree with Jacobson that optimal UI should last longer than compensation typically available in the United States. I would add that benefits should fall over the course of the unemployment spell. Payments should decline, in my view, at the point that general taxpayers—rather than the displacing firm—become responsible for financing the benefits. I also see a strong justification for limiting benefits to a fixed duration tied to the state of the labor market. Benefits should last longer when the prevailing unemployment rate is high, because job finding in those circumstances is harder. Benefits should be limited to some fixed period, however, whether the unemployment rate is high or low.

Unfortunately, UI has undesirable side effects. Without good monitoring, people who are not really looking for work will continue to receive benefits for a long time. Jobless workers will postpone accepting a new job, or they will look less intensively for jobs than they would if they had no insurance protection. For that reason, I agree with Jacobson that it makes sense to supplement UI with earnings insurance.[72] Experienced workers who lose their jobs should be offered temporary earnings supplementation to cushion the blow of permanent job loss. This insurance should offset a percentage of the earnings loss they sustain on their new jobs. If their gross earnings drop 30 percent, for

72. In fact, with my colleagues Martin Neil Baily and Robert E. Litan, I made a specific proposal in 1993. See Baily, Burtless, and Litan (1993).

example, the temporary earnings insurance could replace one-half of that loss, or 15 percent of their earnings on their past job.

I think this kind of insurance would be valuable to workers. It could have desirable incentive effects if the benefits ended at some fixed date that is linked to a layoff date. For example, workers might be eligible to receive earnings insurance payments for a period that ends exactly twenty-four months after they are laid off. If workers delay finding a job for one year, they will effectively lose the right to collect earnings insurance for that year. Unlike UC, which prolongs spells of insured unemployment, earnings insurance should spur workers to seek jobs more intensively and accept job offers more quickly than they do without any insurance.

Whether the country offers UI or earnings insurance (or both), the insurance protection should be limited in duration. Jacobson seems to make the case that insurance benefits should continue for a long time. He believes an important goal of policy is to offset the huge earnings losses sustained by displaced workers, especially in the period after they become reemployed.

If Jacobson's goal is interpreted to mean that a high percentage of earnings losses should be offset by the *unsubsidized wages* earned by the workers themselves, it is easy to agree with him. If his goal is interpreted to mean that publicly provided cash insurance should offset most of the displacement losses, I strongly disagree. Some workers earn wages much higher than their transferable skills would justify in another industry. Workers with the good fortune to be in a steel plant or on an auto assembly line may earn 70 percent more than they could earn in another industry. If these workers are displaced, they will clearly have a hard time matching the earnings they enjoyed on their predisplacement jobs. Generous, long-term unemployment and earnings insurance would clearly have value to these workers.

In contrast, other workers hold jobs in which they are paid a wage equal to the wage they can earn on other jobs. These workers are often paid below-average or average wages. Long-term-unemployment and earnings insurance programs are less valuable to these workers. When they are displaced, they can easily find jobs that pay them as much as they earned on their former jobs. Most financing schemes for unemployment or earnings insurance will exact contributions from workers earning below-average or average wages to finance insurance protection that is most valuable for workers who have the good fortune to hold jobs at much higher wages than they could earn anywhere else. The luck of the labor market has given many of these high-wage workers a windfall. They earn an above-average wage, which, as a result of economic displacement, may come to an end. I do not think it makes sense to offer displaced workers in this situation a public insurance plan that allows them to enjoy this income advantage for the rest of their careers. For a worker who has been lucky in obtaining an exceptionally high-paying job, the insurance scheme Jacobson prefers is a little like promising lottery winners they will be insured against ever losing the lottery again. A more equitable scheme would offer time-limited UC and time-limited earnings insurance to *temporarily* cushion the blow of job displacement.

The goal of public policy is not to fully replace the earnings losses sustained when workers are displaced. If this goal were attained, it would eliminate the incentive for workers to adjust appropriately to changing labor market conditions.

Is there any justification for limiting protection to workers whose displacement has occurred as a result of trade? I cannot think of a single equity or efficiency reason that trade-affected workers deserve better protection than workers who lose their jobs as a result of other changes in the economy. I am not a purist, however. If extra protection is needed for *political* reasons to advance the cause of good trade policy, I would favor extra protection. At the same time, I would also favor such protection if it improved the odds Congress will adopt good environmental or defense policy.

One question remains: have special protection programs, such as TAA, actually advanced the cause of good trade policy? I have yet to see persuasive evidence on this question.

Comment by J. David Richardson

I enjoyed coming back to a literature that I contributed to fifteen years ago. Lou Jacobson appeared in this literature then as prominently as now, but, apart from that, much has changed. His chapter is a treasure trove of new information from surveys of displaced U.S. workers and a synthesis of the many rigorous evaluations of government programs aimed at alleviating labor displacement.

I have two categories of remarks. The first is a summary of the highlights as I saw them along with a few dark corners that I wish Jacobson had illumined. The second is a brief reconsideration of the choice between narrow, categorical, trade-linked policies and broad policies to cope with structural dislocation of all kinds. Jacobson pays lip service to the categorical programs in his introduction, and ignores them thereafter. But he admits that his preferred structural programs are not supported in either the private market for insurance or the political market for government programs. I think it is worth considering cheaper, more-targeted alternatives.

Here are Jacobson's highlights. The one with the gloomiest clarity, around which the others orbit, is the growing consensus on the profile of U.S. worker displacement. There is the expected spell of unemployment and temporarily foregone earnings. But it is not the dominant source of earnings loss. There is an important predisplacement period for seasoned workers—three years of furloughs, reduced time, and other warning tremors—that actually accounts for about $10,000 of the typical $80,000 cost of displacement to the worker (in present, discounted-value, 1987 dollars). There is also an important lifetime effect. Relative to otherwise comparable, seasoned workers who were not displaced, the typical displaced worker loses $60,000 (of the $80,000 total) because of less remunerative job opportunities over the duration of his or her time in the labor force.

Other highlights include Jacobson's deft summaries of the growing statistical evidence: that workers on average have a hard-to-rationalize preference for short-term income smoothing relative to avoidance of catastrophic income loss; that OJT is far more effective, dollar for dollar, than classroom training; that government job search support is therefore also far more cost effective (three to ten times as much) than such training; and that displaced workers who have to switch industries incur earnings losses one and one-half to two times larger than those who move to other jobs within an industry, even when the switch is from a services to a manufacturing industry.

These last two highlights, however, leave certain issues obscured. The data Jacobson provides on costs and benefits (reduced displacement and enhanced earnings) of training and JSA make *both* apparently fail the usual cost-benefit tests, unlike U.S. and Washington state ES programs discussed later in the chapter. Jacobson's strong endorsement of job search over classroom training loses its punch if I am right in thinking it means merely that the former is the lesser of the two evils—significantly less cost ineffective. And Jacobson's discussion of the extra earnings losses of industry "migrants" obscures the issues surrounding industry-specific (and job-specific) rents—payments for experience and skills that have no value anywhere else in the economy (that is, no "social value"). Should any society commit to compensate foregone rents on the same terms as it compensates involuntary unemployment, which clearly does have social as well as personal costs? I do not think so. Jacobson pays almost no attention to these distinctions. But if we trust his figures, up to half of the $80,000 estimate of average earnings loss is rents. An even larger share of the losses of those hurt severely is rents, those toward whom Jacobson wants to increase attention in his preferred programs. Not only do such rents have no social value, but in many cases they also have slender roots in equity reasoning. They are often the result of mere happenstance, not merit—the luck of a worker's finding him- or herself in an industry with skills or equipment so specialized that the work earns a (lucky, not merited) share of the ensuing surplus.

There were other dark corners where I would have wished for a little more light. First, there is remarkably little material on the economics of insurance markets. That literature has grown deep roots and broad foliage at almost the same rate as the literature evaluating training and other labor programs. It is extremely relevant to some of Lou's preferred programs, but concepts such as copayment, lump-sum settlements (buyouts), moral hazard, and adverse selection never appear. Second, there is too little information on variations in the typical profile of displacement for the seasoned worker. Jacobson gives an elegant discussion of the mean profile, complete with cogent graphics. But he gives us no information on inter-action or conditioned profiles. For example, did people who moved geographically after displacement have different profiles? Those in multiple-earner families? Those who received advance notice? Those who were reemployed within the same *firm,* not just the same industry? Did workers who had tamer predisplacement tremors have better postdisplacement profiles? Or perhaps the opposite, because of the hard-to-ignore signals that tremors send?

Most important for this book would have been more illumination on the debate between universal and categorical approaches. Categorical programs are admittedly not in fashion today. There was no Uruguay Round attention to them and only a grudging NAFTA program. But the outlook for sweeping earnings insurance programs is equally grim in Washington and the private markets. Though Washington is taking the first steps toward rationalizing the chaos of myriad training programs, efforts so far amount to little more than good intentions.

Why have we abandoned categorical programs as if there is strong evidence that they really failed? I do not read the record of TAA in the United States that way. Where did the perceptions of others come from? From design flaws in TAA that Jacobson does discuss, such as ill-crafted training contingencies or lack of experience rating for TAA? Perhaps. But if the problem is design, then it is wrong to blame the categorical character of the programs.

Many of Jacobson's policy recommendations fit categorical as well as universal programs. For example, in the spirit of his enthusiasm for UI profiling, why not TAA profiling? Why not have government do studies of environments that are most likely to lead to TAA petitions and be readier than they would be otherwise to respond to the petitions? Why not make the TAA Program even more narrowly targeted by restoring the link it had in its early years to explicit, societywide policy change—negotiated concessions on border barriers or those setting limits to foreign investment? Why no mention of one of the most comprehensive and savvy recent blueprints for a categorical, trade-linked program—that of Robert Z. Lawrence and Robert E. Litan in their 1986 Brookings book, *Saving Free Trade: A Pragmatic Approach*?

Jacobson's brief answers to these questions, from early in his chapter, are that categorical programs require judgments that are more complex than universal programs, and that there is no evidence that trade-displaced workers are any different from other displaced workers. I disagree with him on the first point; there is no difference in the amount of complexity, just differing types of complexity. But I think he is wrong on the second point. Lori Kletzer's chapter in this book shows the evidence for difference, as do several papers by Jon Haveman of Purdue University, all based on the special Displaced Worker Surveys (DWSs) that have been carried out since 1979. Kletzer shows how workers displaced from import-sensitive industries have particularly inauspicious personal characteristics for labor market adjustment. Haveman shows how for pairs of workers with comparable personal characteristics, those displaced from industries with strong price pressures from abroad have on average ten weeks more unemployment in their first spell and 5 to 9 percent lower earnings recovery.

My own inclination toward categorical programs is more sympathetic. Such programs can be justified in many ways. Early work on TAA left many intriguing but unexplained regularities. For example, I found evidence that workers certified for TAA had an admittedly sharper short-term adjustment than other comparable workers, but briefer and less frequent subsequent spells of unemployment. If this is the case, then perhaps trade-displaced workers have relatively more need of programs aimed at short-term transition. Jacobson's suspicion for workers in general is the opposite—a relative need for programs aimed at those injured for long periods.

I think it is worth reopening the debate on these broad questions of public choice. Jacobson's chapter is an excellent starting point, but I am looking forward to his next paper as well.

General Discussion

There was some discussion about how to interpret the apparent public preference for insurance schemes that smooth income over schemes that insure against catastrophic risk that arises in the context of both UI and health insurance. In particular, Peter Temin wondered whether the conventional economists' view that consumers fail to understand the relevant probabilities is correct or whether it is the economists who are failing to understand something about the relevant market. Temin also noted that the proper parallel with health insurance would be earnings insurance, not UI.

Adrian Wood thought that the chapter did not adequately draw on the lessons to be learned from experiences with adjustment assistance programs in Europe. He noted that studies comparing countries find that those nations with long durations of unemployment benefits tend to have high proportions of long-term unemployed among their unemployed populations. Although the causation could go in either direction, he believed that these experiences could inform a debate about whether to extend the duration of unemployment benefits in the United States. However, Howard Rosen noted that "underevaluation" of European programs makes it difficult to learn from them.

At the same time, Rosen argued that we should be cautious in interpreting the extensive evaluations that have been done on programs in the United States. Programs that actually get implemented are often quite different from what was initially designed and lack the funding to operate as intended. Therefore, evaluations of actual programs may not be helpful in assessing the initial design.

Rosen also pointed out that the existing system of UI can work perversely, given the significant differences in economic performance across regions. A major objective of adjustment assistance is to help displaced workers become reemployed, which may involved relocation. However, states in distress may be the least able to assist in such relocations.

Robert Lawrence suggested two proposals (discussed in more detail in the book he wrote with Robert Litan). First, he suggested a mechanism to enable communities to ensure their tax bases. This would help to offset the difficulties communities face in facilitating adjustment when they find themselves in a downward spiral. A copayment or other means would be required to minimize the problems of communities lowering tax rates or collection efficiency.

Second, Lawrence raised the option of more extensive use of EITCs. Although this discussion has focused on displaced workers, there are also large numbers of workers who do not lose their jobs but suffer significant earnings reductions that could be related to technological change and globalization. Given his view that labor market flexibility facilitates adjustment to these changes, EITCs could retain flexibility while providing a mechanism for supplementing incomes. However, issues on the appropriate design of such a policy would need to be worked out.

Lawrence was struck by the apparent predictability of the four zones associated with job displacement that are laid out in the chapter. However, he raised the possibility that the finding of a zone 2 (the two-and-a-half-year period preceding job loss in which prolonged layoffs contribute to substantial declines in earnings) may simply be picking up the fact that the 1982 recession was preceded by the 1980 recession.

Steve Charnovitz suggested that the politics of the debate over the role of general versus categorical assistance programs would change dramatically if the devolution of the federal government's role in training and other programs proceeds. Indeed, he thought that if all assistance was financed through block grants to states, there was a sense in which any program for dislocated workers could be called a categorical program. He advocated additional analysis of the implications of these developments.

References

Addison, John T., and Pedro Portugal. 1987. "The Effect of Advance Notification of Plant Closings on Unemployment." *Industrial and Labor Relations Review* 41 (October): 3–16.

Advisory Council on Unemployment Compensation. 1995. *Unemployment Insurance in the United States: Benefits, Financing and Coverage.* Washington.

Anderson, Patricia, Walter Corson, and Paul Decker. 1990. *The New Jersey Unemployment Insurance Reemployment Demonstration Project, Follow-Up Report.* Princeton, N.J.: Mathematica Policy Research, Inc.

Baily, Martin Neil. 1977. "Unemployment Insurance as Insurance for Workers." *Industrial and Labor Relations Review* 30 (July): 495–504.

———. 1978. "Some Aspects of Optimal Unemployment Insurance." *Journal of Public Economics* 10 (December): 379–402.

Baily, Martin Neil, Gary Burtless, and Robert E. Litan. 1993. *Growth with Equity: Economic Policymaking for the Next Century*. Brookings.

Barnow, Burt F., Amy B. Chasanov, and Abhay Pande. 1990. "Financial Incentives for Employer-Provided Worker Training: A Review of Relevant Experience in the U.S. and Abroad." Policy Memorandum. Washington: Urban Institute (April 2).

Bloom, Howard S. 1990. *Back to Work: Testing Reemployment Services for Displaced Workers*. Monograph. Kalamazoo, MI: W. E. Upjohn Institute for Employment Research.

Bloom, Howard S., and Jane Kulik. 1986. *Evaluation of the Worker Adjustment Demonstration: Final Report.* (Report to the Employment and Training Administration, U.S. Department of Labor.) Cambridge, Mass.: ABT Associates.

Card, David, and Phillip Levine. 1994. "Unemployment Insurance Taxes and the Cyclical and Seasonal Properties of Unemployment." *Journal of Public Economics* 53 (January): 1–29.

Corson, Walter, and Walter Nicholson. 1985. "Evaluation of the Charleston Claimant Placement and Work Test Demonstration." Unemployment Insurance Occasional Paper 85-2. Employment and Training Administration, U.S. Department of Labor. Government Printing Office.

Corson, Walter, Sharon Long, and Rebecca Maynard. 1985. *An Impact Evaluation of the Buffalo Dislocated Worker Demonstration Program.* Princeton, N.J.: Mathematica Policy Research (March 12).

Corson, Walter, and others. 1989. "The New Jersey Unemployment Insurance Reemployment Demonstration Project." Unemployment Insurance Occasional Paper 89-3. U.S. Department of Labor. Government Printing Office.

Cropper, Maureen L., and Louis S. Jacobson. 1983. "The Earnings and Compensation of Workers Receiving Trade Adjustment Assistance." Unpublished report to the Office of the Assistance Secretary for Policy, Evaluation, and Research, U.S. Department of Labor (July).

Ehrenberg, Ronald, and George Jakubson. 1988. *Advance Notice Provisions in Plant-Closing Legislation.* Kalamazoo, Mich.: W. E. Upjohn Institute for Employment Research.

Feldstein, Martin. 1978. "The Effect of Unemployment Insurance on Temporary Layoff Unemployment." *American Economic Review* 68 (May, *Papers and Proceedings, 1977*): 834–46.

General Accounting Office. 1989. *Employment Service: Variation in Local Office Performance*. GAO/HRD-89–116BR. Government Printing Office (August 31).

Gerhart, Paul F. 1987. *Saving Plants and Jobs: Union-Management Negotiations in the Context of Threatened Plant Closing*. Kalamazoo, Mich.: W. E. Upjohn Institute for Employment Research.

Howland, Marie. 1988. *Plant Closings and Worker Displacement: The Regional Issues*. Kalamazoo, Mich.: W. E. Upjohn Institute for Employment Research.

Jacobson, Louis S. 1993a. *Dislocated Workers, Post-Secondary Schooling Costs, and Sources of Funds to Cover Costs*. (Report to the Office of Workplace-Based Learning, U.S. Department of Labor.) Rockville, Md.: Westat, Inc. (April 29).

————. 1993b. *Making Workers Feel Secure: Trade Adjustment Assistance in an Uncertain World.* Monograph. Kalamazoo, Mich.: W. E. Upjohn Institute for Employment Research.

————. 1993c. *Measuring the Performance of the Claimant Placement Program (CPP) and the Employment Service (ES) in Aiding Unemployment Insurance (UI) Claimants.* (Report to the Washington State Employment Security Department.) Rockville, Md.: Westat, Inc. (June 18).

————. 1994. "The Ability of Trade Adjustment Assistance's Wage-Subsidy and Generous Benefits to Offset Dislocated Workers' Earnings Losses." (Report to the Unemployment Insurance Office, U.S. Department of Labor.) Rockville, Md.: Westat, Inc. (October 11).

————. 1995. "The Effectiveness of the U.S. Employment Service." In *Advisory Council on Unemployment Compensation: Background Papers,* vol. II. 1996–403–281:40538. Government Printing Office (July).

Jacobson, Louis S., Robert J. LaLonde, and Daniel G. Sullivan. 1993a. *The Costs of Worker Dislocation.* Kalamazoo, Mich.: W. E. Upjohn Institute for Employment Research.

————. 1993b. "Earnings Losses of Displaced Workers." *American Economic Review* 83 (September): 685–709.

————. 1993c. "Long-Term Earnings Losses of High-Seniority Displaced Workers." *Economic Perspectives* 17 (November–December): 2–20.

————. 1994. *The Returns from Classroom Training for Displaced Workers.* (Report to the Office of Workplace-Based Learning, U.S. Department of Labor.) Rockville, Md.: Westat, Inc. (October).

Jacobson, Louis, and Ann Schwarz-Miller. 1981. *The Effect of UI Administrative Screening on Job Search.* (Report CRC 451 to the Office of the Assistant Secretary for Policy, Evaluation, and Research, U.S. Department of Labor.) Alexandria, Va.: Public Research Institute of the Center for Naval Analyses.

Johnson, Terry R., Katherine P. Dickinson, and Richard W. West. 1985. "An Evaluation of the Impact of ES Referrals on Applicant Earnings." *Journal of Human Resources* 20 (Winter): 117–37.

Johnson, Terry R., and Daniel H. Klepinger. 1991. "Evaluation of the Impacts of the Washington Alternative Work Search Experiment." (Report to the W. E. Upjohn Institute for Employment Research.) Seattle, Wash.: Battelle Human Affairs Research Centers.

Katz, Arnold, and Louis Jacobson. 1994. *Job Search, Employment, Earnings, and the Employment Service: Comparison of the Experience of Unemployment Insurance Beneficiaries in Pennsylvania, 1979–87.* (Report to the W. E. Upjohn Institute for Employment Research (Fall)).

Kulik, Jane, D. Alton Smith, and Ernst W. Stromsdorfer. 1984. *The Downriver Community Conference Economic Readjustment Program: Final Evaluation Report.* Cambridge, Mass.: Abt Associates (May 18).

LaLonde, Robert J. 1995. "The Promise of Public Sector–Sponsored Training Programs." *Journal of Economic Perspectives* 9 (Spring): 149–68.

Leigh, Duane E. 1988. *Does Training Work for Displaced Workers? A Survey of Existing Evidence.* (Report to the International Labor Affairs Bureau, U.S. Department of Labor.)

————. 1990. *Does Training Work for Displaced Workers? A Survey of Existing Evidence.* Kalamazoo, Mich.: W. E. Upjohn Institute for Employment Research.

Ruhm, Christopher J. 1992. "Advance Notice and Postdisplacement Joblessness." *Journal of Labor Economics* 10 (January): 1–32.

Topel, Robert. 1985. "Unemployment and Unemployment Insurance." In *Research in Labor Economics,* edited by Ronald Ehrenberg, 91–135. Greenwich, Conn.: JAI Press.

U.S. Department of Labor, Employment and Training Administration. 1994. *Unemployment Insurance Financial Data, Employment and Training Handbook.* Series No. 394.

U.S. Department of Labor, Unemployment Insurance Service. 1997. *Significant Provisions of State Unemployment Insurance Laws.* Government Printing Office (January 5).

U.S. House of Representatives, Committee on Ways and Means. 1994. *Overview of Entitlement Programs—1994 Green Book.* Government Printing Office.

Wood, Adrian. (1994). *North-South Trade, Employment and Inequality: Changing Fortunes in a Skill-Driven World.* Oxford, England: Clarendon Press.

Woodbury, Stephen A., and Murray A. Rubin. 1997. "The Durationn of Benefits." In *Unemployment in the United States: Analysis of Policy Issues,* edited by Christopher J. O'Leary and Stephen A. Wandner, 211–93. Kalamazoo, Mich.: Upjohn Institute.

Conference Participants

Jagdish Bhagwati, School of International and Public Affairs, Columbia University

Barry Bluestone, John W. McCormick Institute of Public Policy, University of Massachusetts, Boston

Gary Burtless, Brookings Institution

William R. Cline, Institute for International Economics

Susan M. Collins, Brookings Institution

Steven J. Davis, Graduate School of Business, University of Chicago

J. Bradford De Long, Department of Economics, University of California, Berkeley

I. M. Destler, School of Public Affairs, University of Maryland

William T. Dickens, Brookings Institution

Barry Eichengreen, Department of Economics, University of California, Berkeley

Henry Farber, Princeton University

Robert C. Feenstra, Department of Economics, University of California, Davis

Richard B. Freeman, National Bureau of Economic Research

Gene M. Grossman, Woodrow Wilson School, Princeton University

Louis Jacobson, WESTAT

Ronald W. Jones, Department of Economics, University of Rochester

Jules L. Katz, Hills & Company

Lori G. Kletzer, Department of Economics, University of California, Santa Cruz

Robert Z. Lawrence, Kennedy School of Government, Harvard University

Edward E. Leamer, Anderson Graduate School of Management, University of California, Los Angeles

Lawrence Mishel, Economic Policy Institute

Claudio E. Montenegro, Poverty Reduction and Economic Management Network, the World Bank

Sharyn O'Halloran, Kennedy School of Government, Harvard University

Michael J. Piore, Department of Economics, Massachusetts Institute of Technology

Ana L. Revenga, the World Bank

J. David Richardson, Institute for International Economics

Dani Rodrik, Department of International and Public Affairs, Columbia University

Jeffrey D. Sachs, Department of Economics, Harvard University

Howard J. Shatz, Harvard University

Peter Temin, Department of Economics, Massachusetts Institute of Technology

James R. Tybout, Department of Economics, Georgetown University

Marina Whitman, Institute of Public Policy, University of Michigan

Adrian Wood, Institute of Development Studies, University of Sussex

Index

541